A Missiology of the Road

American Society of Missiology Monograph Series

Series Editor, James R. Krabill

THE ASM MONOGRAPH SERIES provides a forum for publishing quality dissertations and studies in the field of missiology. Collaborating with Pickwick Publications—a division of Wipf and Stock Publishers of Eugene, Oregon—the American Society of Missiology selects high quality dissertations and other monographic studies that offer research materials in mission studies for scholars, mission and church leaders, and the academic community at large. The ASM seeks scholarly work for publication in the Series that throws light on issues confronting Christian world mission in its cultural, social, historical, biblical, and theological dimensions.

Missiology is an academic field that brings together scholars whose pro-fessional training ranges from doctoral-level preparation in areas such as scripture, history and sociology of religions, anthropology, theology, international relations, interreligious interchange, mission history, inculturation, and church law. The American Society of Missiology, which sponsors this series, is an ecumenical body drawing members from Independent and Ecumenical Protestant, Catholic, Orthodox, and other traditions. Members of the ASM are united by their commitment to reflect on and do scholarly work relating to both mission history and the present-day mission of the church. The ASM Monograph Series aims to publish works of exceptional merit on specialized topics, with particular attention given to work by younger scholars, the dissemination and publication of which is difficult under the economic pressures of standard publishing models.

Persons seeking information about the ASM or the guidelines for having their dissertations considered for publication in the ASM Monograph Series should consult the Society's website—www.asmweb.org.

RECENTLY PUBLISHED IN THE ASM MONOGRAPH SERIES

Jonathan S. Barnes, *Power and Partnership: A History of the Protestant Mission Movement*

Gregg A. Okesson, *Re-Imaging Modernity: A Contextualized Theological Study of Power and Humanity within Akamba Christianity in Kenya*

vanThanh Nguyen, *Peter and Cornelius: A Story of Conversion and Mission*

Jukka A. Kääriäinen, *Mission Shaped by Promise: Lutheran Missiology Confronts the Challenge of Religious Pluralism*

Ethan Christofferson, *Negotiating Identity: Exploring Tensions between Being Hakka and Being Christian in Northwestern Taiwan*

David P. Leong, *Street Signs: Toward a Missional Theology of Urban Cultural Engagement*

Shawn B. Redford, *Missiological Hermeneutics: Biblical Interpretation for the Global Church*

A Missiology of the Road

Early Perspectives in David Bosch's Theology of Mission and Evangelism

J. KEVIN LIVINGSTON

◥PICKWICK *Publications* · Eugene, Oregon

A MISSIOLOGY OF THE ROAD
Early Perspectives in David Bosch's Theology of Mission and Evangelism

Copyright © 2013 J. Kevin Livingston. All rights reserved. Except for brief quotations in critical publications or reviews, no part of this book may be reproduced in any manner without prior written permission from the publisher. Write: Permissions, Wipf and Stock Publishers, 199 W. 8th Ave., Suite 3, Eugene, OR 97401.

Pickwick Publications
An Imprint of Wipf and Stock Publishers
199 W. 8th Ave., Suite 3
Eugene, OR 97401

www.wipfandstock.com

ISBN 13: 978-71-61097-387-8

Cataloguing-in-Publication data:

Livingston, J. Kevin.

    A missiology of the road : early perspectives in David Bosch's theology of mission and evangelism / J. Kevin Livingston.

    xvi + 402 pp. ; 23 cm. Includes bibliographical references.

    ISBN 13: 978-71-61097-387-8

    1. Bosch, David Jacobus. 2. Missions—Theory. 3. Evangelistic Work—Philosophy. I. Title. II. Series.

BV2063 B6493 L45 2013

Manufactured in the U.S.A.

For my patient wife Irene
and our dear children Sarah, David, and John Wesley

Contents

Acknowledgments | ix
Abbreviations | x
Introduction | xiii

Part One: David Bosch in Context

1. Apartheid and Afrikaner Identity | 3
2. Bosch's Theological Pilgrimage: A Biographical Sketch | 42

Part Two: Bosch's Theology of Mission and Evangelism

3. Theology, Mission, and Missiology: Bosch's Theological Method | 61
4. The Historical and Theological Context of Mission: Major Motifs in Bosch's Thought | 87
5. The Biblical Foundation for Mission | 152
6. Mission, Evangelism, and Church Growth | 210

Part Three: Crucial Theological Dimensions for a Missionary Church

Introduction: The Missionary Nature of the Church as the Theological Horizon for Bosch's Missiology | 253

7. The Eschatological Dimension of the Missionary Church: The Church as Witness to the Kingdom of God | 256
8. The Ecclesial Dimension of the Missionary Church: The Church as God's "Alternative Community" | 292
9. The Soteriological Dimension of the Missionary Church: The Church as a Sign and Agent of God's Reconciliation | 325
10. Epilogue | 360

Bibliography | 365
Names Index | 391
Scripture Index | 395
Subject Index | 399

Acknowledgments

THIS BOOK HAS BEEN a long time in coming, and there are many people to thank for having contributed to its emergence.

I am deeply grateful to the Faculty of Divinity of the University of Aberdeen for providing me with the opportunity to live and study in Scotland. I was especially fortunate in having Prof. James Torrance and Dr. Chris Wigglesworth as co-supervisors of my research. Their advice, counsel, and friendship were a great source of encouragement to me. Tribute must also be paid to Prof. Andrew Walls and the Centre for the Study of Christianity in the Non-Western World for their invaluable assistance in helping me procure missiological materials from every corner of the earth. A huge debt of thanks is owed to Prof. David Bosch and his wife Annemie for their gracious hospitality during my visits to South Africa, and to the many other South Africans, black and white, who made my visits so memorable.

Special thanks also go to fellow Aberdeen postgraduates Dr. Conrad Gempf, Lecturer in New Testament at London Theological Seminary and Dr. Tim Palmer, Professor of Systematic Theology at the Theological College of Northern Nigeria, for strategic assistance. I am grateful to my colleagues at Tyndale Seminary in Toronto for their prayers and encouragement.

Finally I mention my wife, Irene. I would have abandoned this project long ago had it not been for her encouragement. The support she has given and the sacrifices she has made are beyond telling. Only she knows the debt of gratitude I owe her.

Kevin Livingston
Pentecost, 2012

Abbreviations

JOURNALS

AEN	Africa Enterprise News
AHR	American Historical Review
CC	Christian Century
CT	Christianity Today
EcuNews	EcuNews: Bulletin of the South African Council of Churches
EMM	Evangelisches Missions Magazin
ER	Ecumenical Review
EvRT	Evangelical Review of Theology
EvT	Evangelische Theologie
Exchange	Exchange: Bulletin of Third World Christian Literature
ExpT	Expository Times
IAMSN	International Association for Mission Studies Newsletter
IBMR	International Bulletin of Missionary Research
IMR	Indian Missiological Review
IRM	International Review of Mission
JAS	Journal of African Studies
JBL	Journal of Biblical Literature
JCS	Journal of Church and State
JMAS	Journal of Modern African Studies
JRA	Journal of Religion in Africa
JTSA	Journal of Theology for Southern Africa
Miss	Missionalia
MF	Mission Focus

Miss Stud	Mission Studies
Missiology	Missiology: An International Review
NGTT	Nederduitse Gereformeerde Teologiese Tydskrif
NTS	New Testament Studies
OBMR	Occassional Bulletin of Missionary Research
OBMRL	Occassional Bulletin from the Missionary Research Library
RESNE	Reformed Ecumenical Synod News Exchange
RJ	Reformed Journal
RHP	Revue d'Histoire et de Philosophie religieuse
RvEx	Review and Expositor
SJRS	The Scottish Journal of Religious Studies
TE	Theologia Evangelica
ThFB	Theological Fraternity Bulletin
TT	Theology Today
Trans	Transformation
ZM	Zeitschrift für Mission
ZMR	Zeitschrift für Missionswissenschaft und Religionswisseschaft

BOSCH'S MAJOR WRITINGS

Church 301	Bosch, *Church and Mission MSR 301*
Heidenmission	Bosch, *Die Heidenmission in der Zukunftsschau Jesu*
Missiology 101	Bosch, *Introduction to Missiology MSR 101*
TCAC	Bosch, *The Church as the Alternative Community*
Theology 201	Bosch, *Theology of Mission MSR 201*
Witness	Bosch, *Witness to the World*

OTHER ABBREVIATIONS

AC	Alternative Community
CRESR	Consultation on the Relationship between Evangelism and Social Responsibility
CWME	Commission on World Mission and Evangelism
DRC	Dutch Reformed Church

Abbreviations

GK	Gereformeerde Kerk ("Dopper Kerk")
GNB	Good News Bible (Today's English Version)
IMC	International Missionary Council
LCWE	Lausanne Committee for World Evangelization
NEB	New English Bible
NGK	Nederduitse Gereformeerde Kerk (White)
NGKA	Nederduitse Gereformeerde Kerk in Afrika (Black)
NGSK	Nederduitse Gereformeerde Sendingkerk (Coloured)
NHK	Nederduitsch Hervormde Kerk
NIV	New International Version
NT	New Testament
OT	Old Testament
PACLA	Pan African Christian Leadership Assembly
RCA	Reformed Church in Africa (Indian)
RES	Reformed Ecumenical Synod
SACLA	South African Christian Leadership Assembly
SACME	South African Congress on Mission and Evangelism
UNISA	University of South Africa
WARC	World Alliance of Reformed Churches
WCC	World Council of Churches

Introduction

THIS BOOK IS A slightly revised version of my doctoral thesis on South African missiologist David Bosch, completed at the University of Aberdeen under the tutelage of James B. Torrance and Andrew Walls in 1990. It describes the theology of mission and evangelism in the writings of David Bosch as it developed up to 1989 (just prior to the publication of his historic *Transforming Mission*), and evaluates his contribution to the church in South Africa and beyond. When originally written, it was the first systematic study of Bosch's theology of mission and evangelism, and is now the first such study to be published in North America.

I had two original motives in studying Bosch's theology of mission and evangelism during my years in Aberdeen. First, David Bosch was indisputably one of the foremost mission theologians of the twentieth century. His writings ran the gamut of missiological concerns. His involvement as an active participant within the South African church struggle against apartheid as well as the global conciliar and evangelical mission movements was extensive. His contribution to the academic study of missiology in his many writings as well as through such organizations as the Southern African Missiological Society and the International Association for Mission Studies has been widely acknowledged. These were reasons enough to justify an exposition and analysis of his thought.

I was also motivated to explore Bosch's missiological thought because it provided an "entry point" into the global missiological discussion. His perspective brought greater clarity to many of the contentious issues facing the mission of the church in our era, and moved the debate forward in a constructive manner. Furthermore, Bosch's missiological "style"—living as he did in creative tension, a bridge builder between races, church denominations, and conflicting political and theological perspectives—gave me a trustworthy model of how missiology was to be "done." His work was marked by biblical fidelity, ecumenical breadth, theological sensitivity, historical awareness, and social relevance.

Yet so much has changed in the intervening years since the writing of my original doctoral thesis, most notably South Africa's emergence from a white-dominated apartheid state into a multiracial democracy. Why then should an academic work

Introduction

rooted in realities now more than twenty years old be published at all? Let me answer in two ways.

First, David Bosch's influence has only grown since his untimely and tragic death in 1992. Shortly after the completion of my thesis, Bosch published his magisterial *Transforming Mission*, a work that has now been translated and published in eleven languages and has become the most widely used missiological textbook in the world, what Lesslie Newbigin once called a *Summa Missiologica*. In the years since, a variety of significant studies have emerged that continue to assess Bosch's theological legacy and build on his insights.

Particularly noteworthy book-length contributions include two appraisals of Bosch written by South African colleagues and friends;[1] a retrospective evaluation of Bosch's work by a distinguished international panel of senior missiologists;[2] a doctoral dissertation on Bosch's theology of contextualization from a Finnish missiologist;[3] a reading guide and "commentary" for *Transforming Mission* from one of Bosch's former students;[4] a study undertaken at the Gregorian University in Rome analyzing Bosch's "ecumenical paradigm" from the perspective of a Vietnamese Roman Catholic theologian serving the church in Norway;[5] and a fascinating reading of Bosch through the lens of the suffering church of Christ in Ethiopia.[6] Significant shorter analyses of Bosch's life and legacy include my own contribution in the *IBMR* "Legacy" series,[7] as well as essays by Andrew Walls,[8] Timothy Yates,[9] Willem Saayman,[10] and most recently, Darrell Guder and Martin Reppenhagen's insightful exploration of Bosch's ongoing influence in the revised twentieth-anniversary edition of *Transforming Mission*.[11]

What makes the present work unique is its exposition and analysis of Bosch's missiological perspective in light of his distinctive role in the South African church's struggle against apartheid. For those who have become acquainted with Bosch only through his magnum opus, this book can function as a kind of "prequel" to *Transforming Mission*, illuminating the earlier legacy of Bosch's life and thought and

---

1. Kritzinger and Saayman, *Mission in Creative Tension*; Kritzinger and Saayman, *David J. Bosch: Prophetic Integrity, Cruciform Praxis*.

2. Saayman and Kritzinger, *Mision in Bold Humility: David Bosch's Work Considered*.

3. Ahonen, *Transformation Through Compassionate Mission: David Bosch's Theology of Contextualization*.

4. Nussbaum, *A Readers Guide to Transforming Mission*.

5. Pham, *Towards an Ecumenical Paradigm for Christian Mission: David Bosch's Missionary Vision*.

6. Bekele, *The In-Between People: A Reading of David Bosch through the Lens of Mission History and Contemporary Challenges in Ethiopia*.

7. Livingston, "Legacy," 26–32.

8. Walls, "Missiologist of the Road," 273–78.

9. Yates, "David Bosch: South African Context, Universal Missiology," 72–78.

10. Saayman, "Personal Reflections," 214–28.

11. Bosch, "The Continuing Transformation of Mission," in *Transforming Mission* (2011), 533–55.

contributing to a deeper appreciation of the integrity and the wholeness of Bosch's praxis in the South African context.

Another purpose of this present work is to show Bosch's stellar influence on the contemporary missional church movement. Beginning in the mid-1980s, there emerged from the writings of Lesslie Newbigin, Darrell Guder, George Hunsberger and a legion of others a new way of conceiving the church and its witness to the world, particularly the church in North America and Western Europe. Again, what is less well known is the substantial contribution Bosch made to this conversation. Bosch was speaking and writing about fundamental missional church themes before the word "missional" had even been coined. This becomes apparent in the third part of this book, where we analyze how Bosch conceived the essentially missionary nature of the church through the lens of three *loci* of dogmatic theology, from the perspectives of eschatology, ecclesiology, and soteriology. Bosch had only begun to turn his attention to the missional church discussion at the time of his death with the posthumous publication of his *Believing in the Future: Toward a Missiology of Western Culture*. But the topics developed in this brief work were grounded in theological themes he had been addressing for years, stretching back four decades to his doctoral studies in Basel under Oscar Cullmann and Karl Barth. Bosch was a vital forerunner to and early prophet of the missional church conversation.

Three "horizons" shaped Bosch's understanding of the missionary task. These horizons are the historical and ideological context from which Bosch emerged, the biblical foundations for mission that Bosch developed, and the theological structure of mission that informs and gives coherence to missionary practice. Throughout the present work, we will analyze these three horizons, showing how each functioned as an integral part of Bosch's approach.

The structure of the argument unfolds as follows: Part One examines the historical and theological context out of which Bosch emerged. Bosch's Afrikaner identity is probed, with special reference to the relationship between the Dutch Reformed Church and the ideology of apartheid. We then survey Bosch's theological pilgrimage, and outline the breadth of his activities as a missiologist and ecumenical personality.

Part Two expounds Bosch's theology of mission and evangelism. First, we explore Bosch's theological method and his understanding of missiology as a theological discipline. Then we review Bosch's analysis of the tensions inherent within the missionary situation of the late twentieth century by means of three models: *mission in crisis; evangelical-ecumenical;* and *First World-Third World*. In each model, Bosch attempted to discover a way forward, moving beyond intractable polarizations in mission theology and practice. Next we analyze Bosch's understanding of the biblical foundation for mission, including his critique of traditional approaches, as well as his understanding of the meaning and relationship of evangelism, mission, and church growth.

In Part Three, we seek to give a creative interpretation of the structure of Bosch's thought from the perspective of the missionary nature of the church. Three doctrines

Introduction

provide a framework for our analysis of Bosch's theology of mission: eschatology, ecclesiology, and soteriology. In the eschatological dimension of her existence, the church is *the kingdom community*. She is called to act as a witness to and instrument of the eschatological reign of God. Here we explore the creative tension between the kingdom, church, and world, and evaluate the centrality of the kingdom of God for the church's missionary practice. In the ecclesiological dimension of her existence, the church is *the alternative community*. She is set apart from the world and called to discipleship. She is set apart, however, precisely *for the sake of the world*, in order to exemplify to the world the radical implications of life in Christ's new community. In the soteriological dimension of her existence, the church is *the reconciled and reconciling community*. She serves as a sign and agent of God's reconciliation, embodying in her life and actions the love of God in Christ. She strives to live out the unity and mission to which Christ calls her. We shall argue that in each dimension of the church's existence, Bosch linked his missiological reflection with practical, concrete involvement in the social and ecclesial struggles in South Africa and elsewhere. These commitments by Bosch are not as well known and thus merit the focus this study has given them.

The scope of this book is limited in two important ways. First, it is limited to Bosch's life and writings up until 1989, just prior to the publication of his *Transforming Mission*. For later analyses of Bosch, readers are directed to the works mentioned earlier, particularly Ahonen's *Transformation Through Compassionate Mission* and Guder and Reppenhagen's concise summary of Bosch's continuing legacy over the last two decades. The present work is also limited to the main themes of Bosch's theology of mission. It is not an exhaustive review of his entire theological agenda. Such subjects as the relationship of mission and culture, the theology and practice of mission down through church history, the Christian theology of religions, and the communication of the gospel to African traditional religions (all subjects that Bosch addressed at considerable length) are only be touched upon here. Instead, our goal is to provide an overall perspective on Bosch's life and thought, concentrating on his understanding of mission and evangelism, and asking how he worked out these concepts in practice in the tumultuous world of apartheid South Africa. We thus make no claim to speak a final word on Bosch's contribution to the theology of mission and evangelism but instead seek to provide a faithful witness to Bosch's legacy as a "missiologist of the road" who integrated his theology and practice in a faithful, contextually relevant way within his beloved South Africa as well as the global church.

Part One

David Bosch in Context

1

Apartheid and Afrikaner Identity

THE LIFE AND WITNESS of David Jacobus Bosch represented a systematic and creative theological response to the missionary and evangelistic challenges facing the Christian church in the latter half of the twentieth century. In the chapters that follow we will explore this response, but first it is necessary to outline the forces that shaped Bosch's personal and theological pilgrimage. These elements provide the larger "context" through which Bosch's missiological perspective can be understood and analyzed.

It is never a simple task to grasp the contours of human identity. In an essay on the life of Beyers Naudé, Charles Villa-Vicencio has noted that "it is a risky business to delve into the dark recesses of the human psyche or the social maze of character formation, in order to explain a life . . ."[1] While we make no claim of being able to *explain* a life as complex as Bosch's, it is vital to highlight those components that fundamentally molded his mind and character.

David Bosch was a fascinating blend of four worlds. First he was an Afrikaner, indelibly marked by the white South African experience. Second, Bosch was an academic theologian, trained in the classic European tradition. His extensive missiological writings, wide in range and systematic in scope, bear witness to his continental training. Third, Bosch was a missionary. Again and again in his writings one senses a cross-cultural sensitivity and a pastoral concern borne from years of missionary service. Finally, Bosch was an ecumenically minded churchman with a passionate concern for reconciliation between churches, races and theological camps. This blend of four identities (Afrikaner, academic, missionary, churchman) makes any analysis of Bosch's thought a complex affair. In this chapter we will first consider the Afrikaner legacy Bosch inherited. Although we are not concerned to give a comprehensive account of Afrikaner history, it provides the fundamental historical context within

1. Villa-Vicencio, "A Life of Resistance and Hope," 4.

Part One: David Bosch in Context

which Bosch's theology of mission was forged. We will then review the relationship of the Dutch Reformed Church to the ideology of apartheid that reigned in South Africa from 1948 to 1994. Almost all of apartheid's stalwart defenders emerged from this tradition, as did many of apartheid's severest critics—including David Bosch.

THE AFRIKANER HERITAGE AND THE IDEOLOGY OF APARTHEID

Apartheid and Ideology: An Introduction

Particularly since Bishop Desmond Tutu received the 1984 Nobel Peace Prize, the struggle against the South African government's system of apartheid received renewed attention and widespread condemnation, leading to its collapse with the release of Nelson Mandela in 1990 and four years later, South Africa's first truly democratic general election. But for forty-six years, South Africa's rigid system of racial separation and white political and economic dominance made it the pariah of the international community. To the outside observer, the South African situation was a blatant example of white racism, pure and simple.

The ironic factor was that many white South Africans not only accepted and endorsed the apartheid system, but also claimed a Christian basis for doing so. "Separate development" was not only been a pragmatic policy for white self-preservation; it was seen as a God-ordained means to preserve the Afrikaner people and "Christian civilization" in southern Africa. Writing at the height of the church struggle against apartheid, South African theologian Allan Boesak wrote:

> Apartheid is unique. But its uniqueness does not lie in the inherent violence of the system, or in the inevitable brutality without which the system cannot survive, or in the dehumanization and the contempt for black personhood, or even in the tragic alienations and the incredible costs in terms of human dignity and human relationships. No, the uniqueness of apartheid lies in the fact that this system claims to be *based on Christian principles*. It is justified on the basis of the gospel of Jesus Christ . . . Apartheid was born out of the Reformed tradition; it is, in a very real sense, the brainchild of the Dutch Reformed churches. It is Reformed Christians who have split the church on the basis of race and color, and who now claim that racially divided churches are a true Reformed understanding of the nature of the Christian church.
>
> It is Reformed Christians who have spent years working out the details of apartheid, as a church policy and as a political policy. It is Reformed Christians who have presented this policy to the Afrikaner as the only possible solution, as an expression of the will of God for South Africa, and as being in accord with the gospel and the Reformed tradition. It is Reformed Christians

who have created Afrikaner nationalism, equating the Reformed tradition and Afrikaner ideals with the ideals of the Kingdom of God.[2]

Most Afrikaners denied any racist motives in their desire to keep races separate. The outrage of the international community against the apartheid system was matched by the contempt and moral indignation that most Afrikaners felt toward outsiders who did not understand the peculiar dynamics of the South African situation.

The facts of apartheid have been well documented.[3] At the time of apartheid's collapse in the early 1990s, there were approximately 31 million inhabitants of South Africa. Some 22.7 million of these were black Africans, divided into sixteen major language groups. The next largest population group were the whites, with some 4.5 million. Although the whites hailed from numerous European backgrounds, they were divided into two distinct subgroups: those whose first language was Afrikaans (60%) and those whose mother tongue was English (40%). The third largest group was classified as "Coloured." This racially mixed group constituted nearly 2.8 million persons. They were the offspring of unions between the early Dutch settlers and slaves or indigenous peoples. The fourth group was made up of those of Indian descent, some 870,000 persons.[4]

Through a comprehensive set of laws, the apartheid structure maintained white supremacy since 1948 when the pro-apartheid Nationalist Party came to power. Apartheid divided the population into the aforementioned groups. Under apartheid, people's whole lives were determined by their racial classification, established at birth. This classification decided what kind of schools and hospitals they could use. It governed where they had to live. It determined what careers would be open (or closed) to them, which university they could attend, which parks they might visit, in which restaurants they could eat.

At the heart of the Afrikaner vision of apartheid (literally "apart-ness") was the belief that different racial and ethnic groups had a right to separate self-determination. The ideologues of apartheid argued that every *volk* (people) has an inherent right to preserve their separate identity, embodied in separate political and social structures. The government, therefore, established ten "homelands" for black Africans, based on the model of separate development, with each *volk*, in theory, controlling its own affairs.

2. Boesak, *Black and Reformed*, 85–86.

3. For good introductions to the political and social structure of apartheid, see Omond, *The Apartheid Handbook* and *This is Apartheid*. The population statistics that follow are from Omond, *The Apartheid Handbook*, 19.

4. In South Africa, racial terminology is a confusingly complex subject. Under apartheid, there were four main population groups ("white," "black," "Coloured," and "Indian"). As Omond notes, this ethnic categorization "reflects the political attitudes and position in society of the user." The term "Black" is often used by the majority of South Africans as a generic term, describing all of those who are on the "receiving end" of apartheid, whether black, Coloured, or Indian. In this way, "black" takes on a sociopolitical meaning rather than an ethnic one. See Omond, *The Apartheid Handbook*, 20. In this thesis, we shall follow this usage of the word "black," except when referring to sources that use the South African government's terminology.

Yet apartheid was much more than a staunch policy of enforced segregation between the races. The tragic disparities between black and white revealed the fundamental inequality and injustice of apartheid. Although whites composed only 15% of the population, they had been allocated 84% of the available land, leaving the majority black population with a mere 16%.[5] Blacks had a much higher infant mortality rate, directly attributable to the lack of adequate health care and proper nutrition.[6] In 1982–83, the South African government spent 1,385 Rand for the education of every white student, but only 593 Rand for every Coloured student and a mere 115 Rand for every black student.[7] These statistical disparities could be repeated for nearly every facet of life. To most observers, apartheid policies were ultimately based on racism and a concern to maintain white privileges. But many Western critics make a major blunder when they simply assume that all white supporters of apartheid were *consciously* racist. Most Afrikaners vehemently denied that the policy of separate development, as they defined it, was necessarily racist.[8]

What can explain the apparent inability of so many sincere white South Africans to see the patently racist nature of apartheid? The answer is to be found in the role that *ideology* plays in the formation of corporate political and social life. The term "ideology" has numerous definitions, both neutral and pejorative.[9] Here, however, it is used to signify, in the words of Peter Berger, any system of thought that "serves to legitimate a particular social institution."[10] An ideology explains, justifies and sanctifies a certain way of behaving and acting; it provides a coherent worldview for a vested interest in society. Berger gives the following illustration:

> Let us assume that in a primitive society some needed foodstuff can be obtained only by traveling to where it grows through treacherous, shark-infested waters. Twice every year the men of the tribe set out in their precious canoes to get this food. Now, let us assume that the religious beliefs of this society contain an article of faith that says that every man who fails to go on this voyage will lose his virility, except for the priests, whose virility is sustained by their daily sacrifices to the gods. This belief provides the motivation for those who expose themselves to the dangerous journey and simultaneously a legitimation for the priests who regularly stay at home. Needless to add, we suspect

---

5. *South African Hansard*, February 26, 1985, Col. 292 as quoted in Omond, *The Apartheid Handbook*, 34.

6. The Johannesburg *Star* reported (January 21, 1985) the findings of the National Medical and Dental Council: the infant mortality rate was 100.2 per 1000 live births for blacks and 20.1 for whites. Malnutrition was said to be the cause of death of 55% of the black children who die under the age of five. See Omond, *The Apartheid Handbook*, 73.

7. See Omond, *The Apartheid Handbook*, 77–81.

8. Stamoolis, "Church and State in South Africa," 19.

9. Leatt et al., *Contending Ideologies in South Africa*, viii–x. Cf. De Gruchy, *The Church Struggle in South Africa*, 209–17.

10. Berger, *Introduction to Sociology*, 129.

in this example that it was the priests who cooked up the theory in the first place. In other words, we will assume that we have here a priestly ideology.[11]

This amusing example makes a serious point. An ideology serves a vested interest in society. It also interprets (and easily distorts) reality, in order to provide a plausible explanation and justification for the actions of the vested interest. Finally, perfectly sincere, rational persons believe an ideology. In their minds, the ideology they propound is completely plausible; they are not intentionally lying or deceiving in order to justify their beliefs.[12] Thus an ideology *serves* a vested interest in society; it *explains* reality, making the worldview that the ideology offers a plausible one; and it *justifies* the ideologist in pursuing his or her present course of action.

Using these three traits as a guide, it seems clear there was an ideology at work in South Africa. In the rest of this section, we will highlight how, through a variety of historical, theological, and cultural forces, the ideology of apartheid developed. This will provide a deeper context for understanding the cultural heritage of David Bosch. It will also help to explain why so many Afrikaners, in the face of massive opposition at home and abroad, stubbornly clung to apartheid right up to its bitter end.

The Historical Origins of Afrikanerdom

Christianity arrived in southern Africa, as in so many other places, in tandem with the commercial and colonial expansion of a European power.[13] The earliest permanent settlers came from Holland under the auspices of the Dutch East India Company. In 1652 they organized the Cape Town settlement and proceeded to clash with the indigenous inhabitants of the region. Other European groups soon arrived to expand the settlement, most notably French Huguenots (1668) and later, Germans. Almost all the pioneers were Protestant, and but for the German Lutherans, all were Reformed. The established church in the colony was the Dutch Reformed Church, controlled from afar by the Classis of Amsterdam.

For some 150 years, colonists went further inland, pressing into the interior of South Africa. Most settlers became *Boers* (farmers) and adopted a rural, agricultural lifestyle. As was common in their day, they made extensive use of African slaves, whom they considered to be naturally inferior to whites. Sporadic efforts were made by certain Pietist groups to evangelize the indigenous peoples, but these efforts were rarely successful. The evangelical ethos and the gospel of universal grace that the pietists proclaimed collided with the Calvinistic orthodoxy of the Dutch church.[14]

---

11. Ibid., 129–30.

12. Ibid., 131.

13. The definitive work on the history of South Africa is Wilson and Thompson, *The Oxford History of South Africa*. For the historical origins of the church in South Africa, see De Gruchy, *The Church Struggle*, 1–52.

14. De Gruchy, *The Church Struggle*, 2. He notes "the first European missionary sent specifically to

By the beginning of the nineteenth century, the Boers faced three crises. First, as the Boer settlers moved further east, the Xhosa people, who fought to protect their land from white encroachment, abruptly stopped their progress. Second, in 1806 the British government gained control of the Cape region with colonial plans of its own. British settlers and missionaries began to pour in, threatening the Boer way of life with a foreign language, alien values, and "liberal" tendencies. Especially aggravating to the Boers was the British concern to "Christianize the heathen." Most Afrikaners resented the non-Calvinistic Methodist and Anglican missionaries and their evangelistic endeavors.[15] In 1828 the British administration further aggravated the Afrikaner Cape community by enacting "Ordinance Fifty" which established the principle of legal equality for all free persons irrespective of color or race.[16]

The final crisis came in 1834 when the British government abolished slavery throughout the lands under its control. This abolition threatened the Afrikaners in two ways. First, it was an economic disaster for many of the frontier farmers. Although the slave population was relatively small in South Africa, slaves represented the major capital investment of many small farmers. Arrangements for compensation were intended, but due to various political factors most Afrikaner slave owners received no compensation at all.[17] Second, the abolition of slavery was a serious social threat to Afrikaner society. To put a slave on an equal footing with a white person was an intolerable burden for most Boers.

For many Boer farmers, the combined pressures of Xhosa warriors and British meddlers drove them further inland. Between 1835 and 1838, some 10,000 Voortrekkers ventured into what is now known as Natal, and later into the Orange Free State and the Transvaal.[18] An Afrikaner woman, Anna Steenkamp, spoke for many who undertook the Great Trek when she declared: "It is not [the slaves'] freedom that drove us to such lengths, as their being placed on an equal footing with Christians, contrary to the laws of God and the natural distinction of race and religion, so that

---

minister to the indigenous population at the Cape was not Dutch Reformed but a Moravian, George Schmidt." Not only were Schmidt's teachings and practice a threat to the Dutch church's authority, they were also seen "as a threat to the social life of the settler community to which the church ministered" (ibid.).

15. De Gruchy points out that Boer objections to Christian missions among the "heathen" were often not theological in nature. Charles Brownlee of the London Missionary Society noted that the Afrikaners opposed Christian missions because, in the words of one Afrikaner he spoke with, "Christian heathen are not such good servants as the wild heathen" (ibid.). Both the Dutch and English settlers alike resented the missionaries "because the missionaries not only evangelized the indigenous peoples, but took their side in the struggle for justice, rights and land . . . Whatever the faults of the missionaries . . . it is true to say that the church's struggle against racism and injustice in South Africa only really begins in earnest with their witness in the nineteenth century" (ibid., 13).

16. Ibid., 18.

17. Hexham, *The Irony of Apartheid*, 9.

18. Ibid., 9–10. For further details see Ransford, *The Great Trek*.

it was intolerable for any decent Christian to bow beneath such a yoke; wherefore we withdrew in order to preserve our doctrines in purity."[19]

It should be noted that the vast majority of Afrikaners did not participate in the trek. In fact, the 1837 Synod of the DRC denounced the trek and forbade their ministers from participating in it. So as the trekkers journeyed across the borders of the Cape Province, they left the jurisdiction of both the British and the DRC. But who were these trekkers? John de Gruchy describes them as a people

> . . . in search of a new land where they could build a republic of their own. They were devout men and women; avid readers of the family Bible, and able marksmen as well. But they went without the blessing of their church . . . [The Trekkers] went ahead led by devout laymen, and [were] sometimes ministered to by preachers of other traditions, but without the DRC clergy. The theological interpreters of the events that were to shape Afrikaner tradition indelibly were not trained by Dutch or Scottish faculties of Calvinist theology, but by their own experience and their reading of the sacred book. As they journeyed, the pages came alive with meaning and relevance. The exodus of the people of Israel and their testing in the wilderness were happening again. Any obstacle along the way to the promised land had to be overcome, by sheer grit and by the gun. Any doubt of divine providence was not only unthinkable, but blasphemy, a harbinger of disaster. The church at the Cape was no longer relevant, but the saga of Israel in the holy book was.[20]

Special mention should be made of the Battle of Blood River (December 16, 1838). On that day during the Great Trek, over 10,000 Zulu warriors met a party of almost 400 Boer pioneers and their Coloured servants. The Trekkers formed their wagons into a defensive circle, a *laager*. Using guns and cannons, they mowed down the Zulus, who were armed only with spears. Although some three thousand Zulus were killed the Afrikaners sustained only three injuries and no deaths.[21] In the collective psyche of the Trekkers, it was a miraculous event. They saw their victory as a direct intervention of God in which he established a new covenant between himself and the Afrikaner people. God would grant protection, freedom, and future prosperity to the Afrikaners as long as they remained faithful to their covenant with him. The Trekkers eventually founded two independent Boer republics (the Orange Free State and the Transvaal Republic) in which they could pursue their rural way of life free from outside interference.

---

19. De Gruchy, *The Church Struggle*, 19.

20. Ibid., 20.

21. Hexham, *The Irony of Apartheid*, 10. It should be noted that the battle was not as decisive in crushing the Zulus as Afrikaner historians have often portrayed it. In 1879, the same Zulu nation handed the British Army its worst defeat since the Crimean War at the Battle of Isandlwana (1879), when some 1,600 men were lost. See Wilson and Thompson, *The Oxford History of South Africa*, 2:264.

Part One: David Bosch in Context

Meanwhile in the Cape, where the majority of Afrikaners still resided, the advent of British rule made it difficult to obtain clergy from Holland. Without a seminary of their own, the Boers asked for Scottish Presbyterian clergy to fill the gap. Their Reformed theology was acceptable to the Calvinist Boers, and their British citizenship was acceptable to the governors of the Cape. These Scottish preachers were to have a profound effect on the DRC, especially in the person of Andrew Murray Jr., an Aberdeen University graduate. His pietism and zeal for Christian missions profoundly shaped the ethos of much of the present-day DRC. By the mid-nineteenth century, the DRC began to express concern for blacks, both for mission work to be done among them, and for better treatment of blacks at the hands of their fellow Afrikaners. These attitudes further soured the relationship between the Trekkers and the Cape DRC. Although some of the Trekkers wanted to remain members of the DRC, they resented its growing evangelical and pietistic tendencies. This ultimately led to a formal split among Afrikaner Reformed people.

By 1859, two separate new Afrikaner churches had been born in the independent Boer republics, the *Nederduitse Hervormde Kerk* (NHK) and the *Gereformeerde Kerk* (the so-called "Dopper Kerk"). Both were self-consciously Calvinistic, anti-British, and traditional in racial matters. It is within the Dopper Kerk that numerous scholars have located the specific roots of the ideology of apartheid and Christian Nationalism.[22]

---

22. I am aware this is a debatable point. Many scholars in the past have attributed the ideological roots of apartheid to the Calvinism of the early white Cape settlers. This is the so-called "Calvinist" or "Puritan paradigm," first propounded by non-Afrikaner David Livingstone (see Du Toit, "No Chosen People"), and popularized by such works as W. A. de Klerk's *The Puritans in Africa*. While there is no doubt that Calvinism has played a decisive role in Afrikaner history, there is less agreement as to whether Calvinism alone can be blamed for the emergence of apartheid. In his volume *Die Evolusie van 'n Volksteologie*, A. J. Botha has analyzed various contemporary theories concerning the origins of apartheid, including apartheid as a manifestation of "civil religion" (T. D. Moodie); as a "dogmatic racialist ideology" (S. Ritner); as a peculiar outgrowth of a severely modified version of Calvinism found in the Dopper-Kerk (I. Hexham); and the above-mentioned "Puritan Paradigm" (W. A. de Klerk). Other scholars view the ideological basis of apartheid in such disparate sources as fascism, chauvinism, the Marxist class struggle, and Western colonialism. (See Adam and Giliomee, *The Rise and Crisis of Afrikaner Power*, 16–60. Most recently Leonard Thompson, a leading historian of South Africa, has emphasized the role of political myth in the creation of the apartheid ideology. See his *The Political Mythology of Apartheid*.

While I acknowledge fundamental agreement with numerous of the above-mentioned theories—particularly the work of Thompson—I find Hexham's approach most persuasive, and shall emphasize his line of thought in this thesis. Hexham believes that "Afrikaner Nationalism and its mythology of apartheid developed as a popular movement in the years immediately following the Second Anglo-Boer War which ended in 1902. *Afrikaner Nationalism and the mythology of apartheid were not at all the inevitable theo-political development of the Calvinist tradition. They were, rather, innovations created by the Dopper community which saw itself as a persecuted group.* Seeking redress from the effects of British imperialism, this community of about ten percent of all Afrikaners, contributed to the development of Afrikaner Nationalism and created the system of apartheid . . ." (my emphasis). See Hexham, *The Irony of Apartheid*, 1.

The Ideological Roots of Apartheid

Poor but proud, the Doppers were a relatively small religious group within the Afrikaner community. The Doppers emerged as a result of theological schism in Holland. Their theological foundation lay in the Dutch neo-Calvinist revival of Abraham Kuyper.[23] They disdained the evangelical emphasis upon personal devotion and a conversion experience as "anti-Calvinist mysticism." True Dopper piety consisted in orthodox beliefs and high ethical standards. The believer was to trust in the promises of God to sanctify him, not an emotional experience.[24]

In contrast to the individualism of the Arminians and the evangelical pietism within the DRC, the Dopper Kerk emphasized the solidarity of the covenanted community.[25] The Dopper vision of Afrikaners as a separate, covenanted people "reflected their own social reality in which the Dopper Community lived as a religious group apart from other Afrikaners."[26] The way in which this small group of Afrikaners laid the foundation for apartheid will be outlined shortly but mention should first be made of a crucial event that helped spawn Afrikaner nationalism and its emphasis on separate development: the discovery of gold and diamonds within the borders of the Boer republics.

The Boer republics were rich in gold and diamonds, and the discovery of the potential wealth led to tremendous pressure from British imperial interests for their annexation. The Boers, however, did not give in without a prolonged and costly struggle. It took two wars for the British to gain control of the Boer republics. The second war, the Anglo-Boer War of 1899–1902, left a legacy of bitterness and hatred that remains to this day. The Boers fought a guerilla war against the British, and the British responded with a "scorched earth" policy in an attempt to deprive the Boer fighters of their food supply. Particularly cruel was the British Army's tactic of putting Boer women and children in "concentration camps,"[27] punishing those whose husbands and fathers were fighting by withholding adequate food rations. During the period

---

23. For more about the Doppers, see LaGrand, "Those Double-Jointed Doppers," 3–5. It is of interest to note that Kuyper's revival affected American Calvinism as well. Rather than affiliate with the Reformed Church in America, the neo-Calvinists formed a new denomination, the more strongly confessional Christian Reformed Church.

24. Hexham, *The Irony of Apartheid*, 95–96.

25. In Hexham's characterization, these groups "aimed at leading people, especially children of believers, to Christ through means of an individual "conversion experience," instead of trusting God to honor His promises to the community of believers. Following the Methodists these evangelical groups placed their faith not in the power and promises of God but in their ability to effect conversions. This theology was thoroughly Arminian and opposed to the very essence of Calvinism. Theology and history were ignored by holiness movements which placed their entire emphasis on present experience at the expense of the lessons God had taught the Christian community throughout its history . . . as a result the individual's spiritual well being replaced that of the community of believers" (ibid., 97).

26. Ibid., 53.

27. The now infamous term has its origins here. For a graphic description of the camps and their tragic aftermath, see Patterson, *The Last Trek*, 33–36.

Part One: David Bosch in Context

of the war, it is estimated that only 3,000 Boer men died in combat, but some 26,000 women and children (in addition to many black servants) died of starvation, disease, and exposure to the elements at the hands of the British army.[28]

Defeated on the battlefield, the Boers were then subjected to a humiliating plan of Anglicization under the leadership of Lord Milner, the British Governor. Milner held the Boers in contempt as an ignorant, uneducated, and backward people.[29] The colonial administration tried to indoctrinate the youth to see "the greatness of the English Imperial idea" through the imposition of a compulsory English-language school system. In essence, "the school was to be a political tool to cement the bonds of the Empire."[30] But Milner's plan failed miserably. Far from "converting" the Boer populace, the Anglicization plan had the opposite effect; Afrikaner nationalism grew more determined than ever.

To understand the growth of Afrikaner nationalism, one cannot overestimate the importance of two factors: the Afrikaans language movement and the Dutch neo-Calvinist revival led by Abraham Kuyper. The Dopper community played a crucial role as advocate for both.[31]

First, to preserve their unique and separate identity as Afrikaners, the Doppers emphasized the development of their own language (Afrikaans) to set themselves apart from the English. Beginning around 1875, the Afrikaans language movement spread across the Afrikaner community, creating a new written language from a spoken dialect of Dutch that had developed over the centuries among the Boer settlers.[32] Following the war, the use of Afrikaans became linked with the Afrikaner concept of national self-identity.[33]

Special mention should be made of Totius (Jakob Daniël du Toit), the most famous Afrikaans poet. Totius, who took a doctorate at the neo-Calvinist Free University of Amsterdam, was at once a minister, professor of theology, politician, and poet. More than any other author he captured the passionate grief of his people after the war. Through his poetry (especially his *By Die Monument*, written in memory of the women and children who died in the camps) he "articulated [the Afrikaner people's] suffering and gave meaning to the events of their recent past through the myth of

---

28. See Hexham, *The Irony of Apartheid*, 18–19; and De Gruchy, *The Church Struggle*, 24–26.

29. Hexham, *The Irony of Apartheid*, 15.

30. Ibid., 20.

31. David Bosch also noted two other factors that contributed to the unique shape of Afrikaner nationalism: evangelical pietism (which encouraged a complacent attitude towards sociopolitical matters) and neo-Fichtean romantic nationalism (which elevated the concept of "nation" to a semi-sacred status). See Bosch, "The Roots and Fruits of Afrikaner Civil Religion," 14–35.

32. Afrikaans is "a mixture of High Dutch, Malay, a few tribal words, and new idioms emerging from the rugged life of the Boers . . ." (Hope and Young, *The South African Churches in a Revolutionary Situation*, 28).

33. For a detailed analysis of the link between the Afrikaans language movement and Afrikaner nationalism, see Hexham, *The Irony of Apartheid*, 123–46.

the divine destiny of the Afrikaner people."³⁴ In Totius' poetry all the basic themes of Afrikaner nationalism appear: a rock-solid faith in God, an overwhelming sense of God's providence, the shaping of a distinct Afrikaner people who have a divine mission and destiny, and an identification of the Afrikaner people with the biblical people of Israel. His poetry "popularized the myth of apartheid in such a way that ordinary people could identify with what he said."³⁵

The second crucial factor related to the creation of Afrikaner nationalism was the Dutch neo-Calvinist revival, under the leadership of Abraham Kuyper (1837–1920), the extraordinarily gifted politician, journalist, theologian, and statesman. He wrote both popular and scholarly works on Calvinism, politics and culture. He founded the Free University of Amsterdam. He served as Holland's Prime Minister (1901–5). The central thrust of Kuyper's thought was that Calvinism was an all-embracing philosophy, a "life-system." God is sovereign over every sphere of life: church and state, education and family, politics and art. Every dimension of life exists under the common grace of God, and has its own unique "sovereignty." Because the various spheres exist under God's common grace, rooted in the creation order itself, Kuyper discerned a theoretical basis for "Christian Nationalism," a Christian ordering of society and culture.³⁶

Kuyper sought to reform the Dutch nation by recalling it to its Calvinistic foundation, and away from the temptations of rationalism and liberalism. This sentiment was first expressed in a slogan by the neo-Calvinist politician Groen van Prinsterer, who declared "in isolation lies our strength." According to Bosch, this slogan was intended "as a rallying cry for the small, scattered forces of authentic Calvinism to unite and spread their message throughout the Dutch nation. In other words, it was

---

34. Ibid., 33.

35. Ibid., 46. Bosch draws similar conclusions: "In the burgeoning civil religion of the post-war period the young Afrikaans language was utilized to foster Afrikaner sentiments. Poets had an enormous influence. In 'Vergewe en vergeet' ('Forgive and Forget'), Totius (J. D. du Toit) compared the Afrikaner with a small thorn tree, which had been trampled down by a large ox wagon, symbolizing Britain. The tree slowly stood up again and healed its wounds with the ointment of its own resin. In another poem Totius selected the hardy and resilient *besembos*, a semi-desert weed, as a symbol of the Afrikaner people. The *besembos* flourishes where most stronger plants would die. Even if you burn it down, it just sprouts forth anew and flourishes as before. Poems became a lens through which Afrikaners were looking upon their past. They conveyed to generations of Afrikaners the notion that they are there to stay. Afrikaners are irrevocably part and parcel of the soil of Africa, of the veld and the mountains and the rivers. No earthly force would ever succeed in subduing them, let alone routing them" (Bosch, "Afrikaner Civil Religion and the Current South African Crisis," 25).

36. For an exposition of this approach, see Kuyper's classic work *Lectures on Calvinism*, especially the chapter "Calvinism as a Life-System." John de Gruchy points out how Kuyper's theology blunted the historic Calvinistic stress on the prophetic role of the church in society. His division of church and state into separate spheres under God resembles the Lutheran "two kingdoms" concept, in which the church *as church* restricts itself to its "spiritual tasks" while the state involves itself in the "secular" realm, guided by individual Christians who possess a political vocation. In this scheme, the church's sociopolitical impact is severely crippled, and is far removed from Calvin's dynamic understanding of the church's relation to the state. See De Gruchy, *The Church Struggle*, 90.

isolation for the sake of mission. It aimed at winning the Dutch people back to original Calvinism."[37]

Another key ingredient in the Kuyperian neo-Calvinist program was the creation of a social apartheid system. Catholics, secular liberals and Reformed Christians all developed their own schools, newspapers, trade unions, political parties, and even their own shops. This system was intended to accommodate and preserve each community within the Dutch state, but it achieved that goal at the cost of a rigidly segmented Dutch society.[38]

It takes little imagination to see how attractive the Dutch neo-Calvinist program appeared to many Afrikaners. Their aim was the creation of a Calvinist society along the lines of the Dutch model. Kuyperian neo-Calvinist thought gave Afrikaners the tools they needed to resist the theological Arminianism and the cultural liberalism of their English colonial rulers. It also provided them with concrete models of a distinctly Christian political party, schools, and social institutions. It seemed uniquely fitted to serve the needs of the Afrikaner nation.[39] Since the Dopper *Gereformeerde Kerk* was intimately related to Kuyper's Dutch church (the *Christelijke Gereformeerde Kerken*), the Doppers naturally took the lead in advocating Dutch neo-Calvinist thought throughout the Afrikaner community after the Anglo-Boer War.

Afrikaners such as J. D. du Toit and W. J. Postma were among the key pioneers in adapting Kuyperian principles to the South African situation. In the process, they significantly modified what they received from their Dutch neo-Calvinist cousins. They wanted to "speak to their specific situation as an embattled people struggling to define and protect [their] identity."[40] Through the use of the developing Afrikaans press, they lobbied passionately among Afrikaans-speaking whites for a thorough program of "Christian Nationalism" based on the Dutch model. This program entailed a strict separation from foreigners (i.e., British) and blacks for the protection of the Afrikaner *volk;* the creation of Afrikaans-language schools that would instill Christian National principles into Afrikaner youth; and the founding of a Christian Nationalist political party. These proposals were frequently couched in biblical terms, reminding the people of the parallels between the Afrikaner nation and Israel. As early as 1881, du Toit maintained that "with the exception of Israel, as the specifically chosen people of the Lord, God's hand has never been more visible in the history of any people on earth than amongst us in connection with the Transvaal events."[41]

---

37. Bosch, "The Roots and Fruits of Afrikaner Civil Religion," 26.

38. Hexham, *The Irony of Apartheid*, 116. It should be noted that the Kuyperian vision of social divisions was based on *theological* divisions (Catholic, Protestant, secularist) and not on racial or ethnic grounds.

39. Ibid., 115.

40. Bosch, "The Roots and Fruits of Afrikaner Civil Religion," 29.

41. As cited in ibid., 28.

In the hand of the Afrikaner neo-Calvinists, van Prinsterer's slogan "In isolation lies out strength" came to refer not simply to Reformed Christians of whatever race, but specifically to the Afrikaner people. The slogan was transformed from isolation for the sake of mission, into isolation *for the sake of survival*.[42] Calvinism had become inextricably linked with Afrikaner nationalism; the vision of apartheid had become the source of Afrikaner nationalist ideology.[43]

By 1914 the Dopper ideology of apartheid "had been accepted by the [Nationalist] Party and Dutch neo-Calvinist theories provided the intellectual legitimation for its program."[44] At the same time, more ministers of the DRC began to study at the Free University. While there they imbibed Christian Nationalist principles. In time, this modified the evangelical and pietist tenor of the DRC, aligning it squarely within the streams of neo-Calvinism and Afrikaner nationalism.[45]

Slowly but surely, Afrikaner nationalist thought increased its influence over the white population of South Africa. Particularly crucial was the decade of the 1930s, which witnessed the emergence of the National Party under the leadership of D. F. Malan, a former DRC minister turned politician. The party's original *raison d'etre* was not anti-black racism (although this no doubt existed) but the desire to help and uplift the Afrikaner *volk* from the depression of the 1930s.[46] Other significant events of the 1930s that increased Afrikaner nationalist political aspirations included the centennial reenactment of the Great Trek, the increasing use of Afrikaans as an official language equal to English, and an intense intellectual ferment on the part of Afrikaner academics (especially sociologists and theologians) to develop ideological and theological justifications for the theory of apartheid.[47] All these elements melded together to create a "resentful nationalism," reacting against English condescension and the *swart gevaar* (black threat).[48]

The Implementation of Apartheid

In 1948 the National Party came to power. They immediately passed three legislative foundations of apartheid, the Race Classification Act, the Group Areas Act, and the Mixed Marriages Act. While it is true that the Nationalists did not introduce segregation and apartheid to South Africa, they transformed what had been "an *ad*

42. Ibid., 27.
43. Hexham, *The Irony of Apartheid*, 187.
44. Ibid.
45. Ibid.
46. Omond comments that "by the 1930's a total of 300,000 Afrikaners–17.5 per cent–were living in penury, many of them in the cities, displaced from their farms. In this period were launched campaigns for self-help for the 'poor whites' which eventually led to the growth of a large Afrikaner industrial and commercial empire" (*The Apartheid Handbook*, 13).
47. Ibid.
48. De Klerk, *The Puritans in Africa*, 98.

hoc traditional way of life into a closed ideological system that claimed theological justification."[49] From that day right up to apartheid's collapse, the Nationalists remained faithful to their forefathers' vision by enacting and enforcing a complex web of apartheid legislation. They pushed the logic of the apartheid ideology into all realms of life (in true Kuyperian fashion). Perhaps the supreme tragic irony of the apartheid system is that its original target was the imperialism of the British government, yet it was black Africans who suffered for British sins![50]

Through the 1950s, the political and civil rights of the black and Coloured communities were further eroded, as the Nationalists abolished the limited voting rights the two groups had preserved. By 1959, the grand strategy of apartheid became clear with the enactment of the Bantu Self-Government Act, which laid the foundations for the "independent" homelands.[51] There were critics of the new dispensation, of course. In parliament some opposition members attacked the apartheid legislation. Nonviolent black protests and boycotts were channeled through the African National Congress and the Pan-Africanist Congress, culminating in the writing (in 1955) of "The Freedom Charter," a visionary document outlining the dream of an interracial South Africa. But the end result of protest was arrests, detentions and the banning of individuals. The Sharpeville massacre of 1960 (in which sixty-nine people were shot dead during a peaceful, anti-pass law demonstration) ended the first stage of protest against apartheid. A state of emergency was declared, the ANC and PAC were banned, and thousands of people were detained without trial. At this point the ANC and PAC went underground, resolving that the days of nonviolent protest were over.[52]

The 1960s witnessed the beginning of a long campaign against apartheid by churches, foreign governments and other bodies. Most notable among these was the Christian Institute, founded in 1963 and directed by Dr. Beyers Naudé. The irony remained however that the National Party actually *increased* its number of seats in the Parliament after every election from 1948 to 1966.[53] In the late 1960s and early 1970s the Black Consciousness movement emerged as the major challenge to the status quo, led by Steve Biko and other black nationalists.

By 1976, Black Consciousness had made a strong impact on black youth, instilling pride in black languages and cultures. Black students began to protest against the mandatory use of Afrikaans in their schools, a protest that culminated in the Soweto uprising that began on June 16, 1976.[54] Again, trouble spread throughout the country

---

49. De Gruchy, "The Relation Between the State and Some of the Churches in South Africa," 445.

50. De Gruchy notes that "British imperialism has a great deal to answer for; it helped spawn a nationalism whose racial policies have become as hideous to the world at large as the war Britain waged against the Afrikaners" (*The Church Struggle*, 26–27, 212). Also see Thompson, *The Political Mythology of Apartheid*, 239.

51. Omond, *The Apartheid Handbook*, 14–15.

52. Ibid., 17.

53. Wilson and Thompson, *The Oxford History of South Africa*, 2:423.

54. Language has been a potent political symbol in South Africa. What other nation has erected a

and hundreds of blacks were killed in the ensuing weeks. Many fled South Africa to join ANC guerillas, believing that change was possible only through armed struggle. By the autumn of 1977, Steve Biko was dead (dying under suspicious circumstances while in detention) and the Christian Institute and its leaders were banned.

In the early 1980s, hints of some reform in the apartheid system emerged in National Party policy as it tried to do away with some of the more offensive elements of apartheid legislation. The National Party was no longer the bastion of classical Afrikaner religio-political thinking. Beginning in the mid-1970s, it began to take a somewhat more pragmatic line,[55] de-emphasizing Afrikaner nationalism.[56] In the waning days of apartheid, the emergence of two ultra right-wing parties (the *Herstigte Nasionale* Party and the Conservative Party) and the neo-fascist *Afrikanerweerstandbeweging* (Afrikaner Resistance Movement) represented both the fragmentation of Afrikanerdom and the continuing appeal of the ideology of apartheid to many South African whites.

By 1985 State President P. W. Botha said that Afrikaners had "crossed the Rubicon"; the old policies were being modified or scrapped altogether. Indeed, David Bosch noted that "1985 has seen more fundamental political reform in South Africa than the total preceding period."[57] In 1985, however, a new, unprecedented level of violence emerged, changing the scene fundamentally and permanently. "Violence of both kinds—structural *and* revolutionary—is no longer sporadic; it has become endemic. In the black community those who are regarded as collaborators with the

---

monument to their national language, as the Afrikaners have near Cape Town? In an ironic similarity, de Klerk notes the similarities between Black Consciousness and Afrikaner Nationalism: both originated in "the human urge to be oneself and to live in accordance with one's essential nature, as a free intelligence with a particular idiom" (*The Puritans of Africa*, 98).

55. This did not mean, however, that the National Party had abandoned the apartheid system. Bosch noted in 1986 that "for all its growing pragmatism, the National Party finds it cannot break out of the ideological straight-jacket it donned generations ago. So the realities of present-day South Africa lead the main body of Afrikaners to a curious mixture of ideological motivations and pragmatic considerations. In the final analysis, however, the forces that moulded the Afrikaner and Afrikaner civil religion continue to determine Afrikaner attitudes and prevent them from embracing a new paradigm" (Bosch, "Afrikaner Civil Religion and the Current South African Crisis," 29).

56. This shift away from Afrikaner nationalism had a more sinister side. Although the old religio-political rhetoric was giving way to secular and pragmatic considerations, numerous observers posited that the Republic of South Africa was taking on many of the characteristics of a Latin American style "National Security State." Evidence for this includes vastly expanding military and intelligence budgets; increasing state censorship over news and other forms of communication; massive evidence that torture was being routinely used by the South African security forces; and the heightening rhetoric about the threat of atheistic communism. The state was facing a "total onslaught," and thus the state had to develop a "total strategy" to fight a "total war." In such a situation, the highest aim of the state is not the welfare of its people but merely *survival*. See Prior, ed., *Catholics in Apartheid Society*; and Villa-Vicencio, "The Covenant Restructured," 13–16.

57. David Bosch, "Afrikaner Civil Religion and the Current South African Crisis," 29. Specifically, Bosch noted the restoration of citizenship to blacks, the scrapping of the Influx Control Act and its passbook system, and abolition of the Mixed Marriages Act. These piecemeal efforts were guaranteed to fail, however, since blacks did not perceive these as part of a comprehensive strategy to dismantle the entire apartheid system.

system are no longer just ostracized; they are executed."[58] In the white community there seemed to be a hardening of attitudes as well. An opinion poll in the autumn of 1985 revealed that two-thirds of all white South Africans believed that South Africa would *never* have a black majority government.[59]

How odd this all now sounds in light of the transformation of South Africa into a multiracial democracy. What enabled a peaceful settlement between the conflicting interests of South Africa rather than an apocalyptic bloodbath, as so many predicted? Arguably it was, at least in part, a change in Afrikaner self-understanding. But before we document that change, let us examine two aspects of Afrikaner self-understanding that profoundly shaped their worldview and their adoption of the ideology of apartheid.

Threat, Providence and the Afrikaner Identity

In this rapid survey of the long and difficult history of South Africa, two themes run like interwoven threads through the soul of the Afrikaner people: *threat* and *providence*. The emergence of the Afrikaner nation and the ideology of apartheid that it created must be understood in light of the constant interplay between these two historical forces.

The first key concept that profoundly shaped the Afrikaner identity has been the notion of being a *threatened* people. Afrikaners continually perceived themselves to be a small, vulnerable people, always on the brink of destruction from outside forces.[60] The threat came from a variety of sources: from Zulu warriors to meddling colonial administrators, from marauding British soldiers to radical black "agitators." The common thread that linked these disparate groups together was the implied threat they presented to the stability and continuity of the Afrikaner culture. In the graphic words of one black South African, the Afrikaners have had "an image of themselves as survivors of a catastrophe and as an embattled people . . . Boer nationalism is continuing its vigil. There is African nationalism lurking in the shadow out there . . . The dread of extinction—body, language and all—keeps scratching and breathing at the door out there like a pack of bloodthirsty wolves."[61]

If this description is accurate, it helps explain why the preservation of a separate identity for the Afrikaner people (through such elements as language, education,

58. Ibid.

59. Ibid. Bosch sees the main body of Afrikaners developing a "Masada complex"; if pushed far enough, they will "fight literally to the bitter end."

60. "From their earliest days the Afrikaner people have felt themselves threatened, from inside their borders and from without, to a degree few other nations or groups have experienced or believed" (Wilson and Thompson, *The Oxford History of South Africa*, 2:365). Or as a professor from the Free University of Amsterdam has put it, "The history of the white Afrikaners has always been one of fundamental threat to their people" (Goudzwaard, *Idols of Our Time*, 40).

61. Mphahlele, "South Africa: Two Communities and the Struggle for a Birthright," as cited in Bosch, "Racism and Revolution: Response of the Churches in South Africa," 17.

religion, and politics) became such an all-encompassing goal of their existence throughout the twentieth century. It also explains why South African whites could maintain a defensive *laager* mentality when fundamental change in the apartheid system was demanded. They were deeply afraid of the future, captivated by their own turbulent past.[62] They had become prisoners of their own history.[63]

The Afrikaner self-understanding was also nourished by a sense of *divine purpose* in the events of their nation's history; they perceived the providential hand of God behind the historical events of the Afrikaner people. This view of history has not been unique to Afrikaners, of course. The Christian doctrine of God's providence over the affairs of humankind is solidly rooted in Christian thought, especially in the Reformed tradition. What made the Afrikaners' faith in the sovereignty of God more conspicuous was their belief in an Afrikaner "manifest destiny" in southern Africa, and their self-conscious identification of the Afrikaner *volk* with the ancient people of Israel.

From their earliest beginnings, Afrikaner nationalists were convinced that God himself had ordained the presence and prosperity of Afrikanerdom in southern Africa. The proof of such a "manifest destiny" was seen, so the nationalists said, in the Afrikaners' own miraculous history, as God delivered and protected them. In the words of the first National Party Prime Minister, D. F. Malan: "The last hundred years have witnessed a miracle behind which must lie a divine plan . . . Afrikanerdom is not the work of men but the creation of God."[64]

From the Trekkers and Totius to Andreis Treurnicht, Afrikaner leaders buttressed their arguments of manifest destiny by linking Old Testament motifs such as "exodus," "liberation," "wilderness," "promised land," and faithfulness to a "national covenant" with the history of the *Afrikaner* nation.[65] In the context of their history, it is entirely understandable that the Afrikaners responded by creating a "civil religion." As John de Gruchy noted:

> A defeated people need an interpretation of their history, a mythos, which can enable them to discover significance in what happened to them. The continuity of the Afrikaner demanded such a world-view which would provide coherence to their shattered hopes. Such a mythos was not difficult to construct, especially for a people with such a strong belief in providence and an existential awareness of the plight of ancient Israel as it sought liberation from the Egyptian yoke. So it is not surprising that Afrikaner history, like that of other nations, took on a sacred character. God's providential action became

---

62. The Afrikaners "carried into the twentieth century attitudes that served their survival in the colonialist nineteenth century, but ultimately can only destroy the *volk* in the future. Preoccupied with preserving their identity and obsessed by fear of the *swart gevaar* ("Black danger"), they seem bent on fulfilling the conditions that will justify their worst fears" (Hope and Young, *The South African Churches in a Revolutionary Situation*, 3).

63 Bosch, "Prisoners of History or Prisoners of Hope?," 14–18.

64. As cited by Bosch, "Racism and Revolution: Response of the Churches in South Africa," 16.

65. See De Klerk, *The Puritans in Africa*, 213–22.

Part One: David Bosch in Context

grounded in the Afrikaners' historical experience, creating a sense of "manifest destiny" for the Boer nation.[66]

This providential understanding of history performed a valuable function of sustaining Afrikaners during times of crisis, but it also had deeply negative effects.[67] First, the history of the Afrikaner nation *(volk)* became elevated to a quasi-sacred level. The historical experience of the nation became a vehicle of God's revelation and salvation.[68] Second, with this ethnically specific understanding of God's providence, the Afrikaner people (as an ethnic group) became a special, holy people. On the basis of their unique covenant with God, they were called to live separated lives from other ethnic groups—even if those groups were fellow Christians! Third, government policies (including apartheid) had the tendency to take on a divine character, since the Afrikaner political order has been ordained of God. To radically question the sociopolitical status quo was to question the will of God, as plainly revealed in the orders of creation.[69] To sum up, the doctrine of providence had become permanently chained to Afrikaner history, and served to legitimate the current order.[70] The aims of God had become identified with the aims of the Afrikaner people, and the people's with those of God.[71] In light of these twin themes of threat and providence, it becomes more comprehensible how and why Afrikaner intellectuals developed the ideology of apartheid and its concomitant social and political philosophy of "Christian Nationalism." Christian Nationalism gave Afrikaners

---

66. De Gruchy, *The Church Struggle*, 30. An example of this "manifest destiny" mindset, linking politics and religion into a powerful framework of ideological nationalism, is found in the words of Dr. H. F. Verwoerd, the sociologist and one-time South African Prime Minister, who said: "We shall keep on fighting for the survival of the White man at the southern tip of Africa and the religion which has been given to him to spread here" (Hope and Young, *The South African Churches in a Revolutionary Situation*, 34).

67. Ibid., 201–2.

68. Theologian F. J. M. Potgieter of the Divinity Faculty at Stellenbosch University once declared: "God saved the Afrikaner people at Blood River and allowed them to carry on to where they are today." The old Nationalist Party-inspired Constitution of the Republic of South Africa affirmed it was "Almighty God" who "controls the destinies of nations and the history of peoples, who gathered our forebears together from many lands and who gave them this their own, who has guided from generation to generation; who has wondrously delivered them from the dangers that beset them." Both citations are from Wilson and Thompson, *The Oxford History of South Africa*, 2:371.

69. De Gruchy perceptively observes that "in such a distorted view of providence the orders of creation stand in the way of the purposes of redemption. Thus, we can see that belief in providence can become, as G. C. Berkouwer remarks, 'a piously disguised form of self-justification'. In the New Testament, providence has been transformed by the incarnation, God's radical inbreaking into history to fulfill his purposes of redemption. Thus [God's] purposes are not read in creation alone, they are discerned in Jesus Christ, his death and resurrection, and the fulfillment of all things in him. The Almighty who is worshipped is the Father of our Lord Jesus Christ. Thus, our history, our nation, and our politics do not automatically have God's blessing because they exist, or because we believe in him, but only if they conform to his will in Christ. Karl Barth has reminded us that the separation of providence from Christology always leads to a false belief in our own history . . ." (*The Church Struggle*, 202).

70. On the ideological abuse of the doctrine of providence (and of theology in general), see Villa-Vicencio, "Where Faith and Ideology Meet," 78–85.

71. Wilson and Thompson, *Oxford History of South Africa*, 2:371.

a theoretical justification for what they had long practiced, namely an opportunity to live separately from other peoples in order to promote a distinctly *Afrikaner* way of life. It was thus the mother of the apartheid system.[72]

Christian Nationalism fused elements of religious belief and nationalist sentiment into a powerful ideology.[73] It provided a credible explanation of the Afrikaner past and gave Afrikaners a coherent and positive understanding of their historical experience as a people. It justified their present, providing them with plausible reasons for preserving an apartheid-based political system. It served to guide their understanding of the future, giving Afrikaners, until recently, a compelling eschatological vision of "a theocratic utopia of order where every tribe and person has his rightful place in the economy of God and the republic."[74] It is precisely at this point—at the level of the ideological justification of apartheid—that it becomes necessary to explore the heritage of the Dutch Reformed Church, for it is from this church that the strongest moral and theological justifications for apartheid developed, and from this church as well that some of apartheid's strongest critics emerged.

THE DUTCH REFORMED CHURCH AND APARTHEID

Introducing the DRC

Religion has long been a crucial force in South Africa. David Bosch states that "above all, the Afrikaner is a religious animal."[75] This has been no less true of the black community. A large majority of the population (both black and white) continues to identify themselves as Christian.[76] They are divided into a bewildering array of different denominations, including (1) the three white Afrikaans Reformed Churches, along with the DRC's quasi-separate "daughter" churches, black, Coloured, and Asian—now known as the Uniting Reformed Church in Southern Africa, the Dutch Reformed Church in Africa, and the Reformed Church in Africa, respectively; (2) the "English-speaking churches," including the Methodists, Anglicans, Presbyterians, Congregationalists, and Lutherans;[77] (3) the Roman Catholic Church; (4) the

---

72. We must emphasize that cultural and historical forces in the Afrikaner experience, and not simply a pre-designed theoretical system, played the major role in the creation of apartheid. Christian Nationalism, as a *theological* movement, is a prime example of "contextual theology" gone awry. Cultural and historical forces rewrote theology to suit the prejudices and pre-understandings of the people, rather than challenge them. See De Gruchy, "The South African Theological Debate," 90.

73. For more on the intimate link between religious belief and nationalism, see Smart, "Christianity and Nationalism," 37–50.

74. De Gruchy, *The Church Struggle*, 200.

75. Hope and Young, *The South African Churches in a Revolutionary Situation*, 16.

76. Bosch, "Racism and Revolution," 13.

77. Although known collectively as the "English-speaking churches," this is a misnomer. While all of these churches (except the Lutherans) have their roots in Great Britain, most members are black persons whose mother tongue is not English. See Hope and Young, *The South African Churches in a*

Conservative Evangelical churches; and (5) the nearly 3,000 separate African Independent churches.[78]

For the purposes of this chapter, we will limit our attention to the first of Bosch's church types, the Dutch Reformed "family," and particularly to what in Bosch's lifetime was the all-white *Nederduitse Gereformeerde Kerk* (Dutch Reformed Church, or DRC). We focus on the DRC because it has been the largest of the white Reformed churches, playing a decisive role in the development (and the demise) of apartheid, and also because it is from the DRC that Bosch emerged, and in which he remained throughout his lifetime as an ordained minister, missionary, and missiologist.

The significance of the DRC cannot be overestimated, due to its size and influence among the Afrikaner people. The DRC, which extends into almost every town and village, has not only been South Africa's largest Christian denomination. It was described by Bosch in 1979 as "the key institution in sustaining and developing the Afrikaans language and culture . . . [leading] to a closeness of relationships between church, language, culture, and people that would be difficult to equal anywhere else. To be a true Afrikaner (*ware Afrikaner*) means to speak Afrikaans, to belong to one of the Dutch Reformed churches, and to support the National Party. When one of these three elements is missing in any specific individual, he or she can hardly claim to be a *true* Afrikaner."[79]

Here Bosch highlights a crucial element in the ideology of Christian Nationalism: church and state functioned as one in the defense of the Afrikaner *volk*. In order to support the continued existence and strength of the Afrikaner nation against perceived external and internal threats, Church, Party, and Nation maintained a united front. In a very real sense, the Dutch Reformed Church was the National Party at prayer.[80]

With a few notable exceptions, the DRC gave firm, unwavering support to the Nationalist Party's policy of separate development up until 1986. In what follows, we will summarize three contextual factors that shaped the DRC's *volksteologie*,[81] discuss

---

Revolutionary Situation, 45.

78. We follow Bosch's typology of church traditions here. Bosch, "Racism and Revolution," 13–14.

79. Ibid., 13.

80. Wilson and Thompson, *The Oxford History of South Africa*, 2:372–73. The author cites Beyers Naudé's claim that the DRC and the National Party were linked in "a spiritual alliance . . . The salvation of the [Afrikaner] people is not . . . synonymous with the policy of apartheid, with the politics of the National Party, with the self-maintenance of the Afrikaner amidst the 'dangers' which 'threaten' his identity, the white colour of his skin, his language, his culture, his economy, his political predominance; and the selfless service which the N.G.K. owes the people is not a slavish subservience to a sectionalist, party political, white Afrikaner ideal . . . In the present political situation in South Africa it [the DRC] has only one meaning: it is the bulwark of a particular political party. It is the servant of a foreign master" (ibid., 372).

81. Botha's work *Die Evolusie van 'n Volksteologie* should be noted here. He highlights three factors that influenced the DRC to develop a *volksteologie* (a theology in the service of Afrikaner interests). These included: *Kuyperian neo-Calvinism* (which served as a theological response to both theological liberalism and Andrew Murray-style evangelical pietism); *German missiology* (which influenced South African mission strategy with regard to the policy of establishing ethnically-segregated denominations); and *the long struggle for Afrikaner cultural identity and political power* (embodied clearly in the

the DRC's theological defense of apartheid, and survey some of apartheid's most strident critics, particularly from *within* the DRC.

The Development of Separate "Mission" Churches

The first factor that helped forge the DRC's stance toward apartheid was the way it developed separate "mission churches," based on a particular missiological theory of church planting. This story has been told in much detail elsewhere.[82] We shall briefly review the fateful steps that led to this historical development, and the way in which it provided the DRC with a theological legitimation for the practice of apartheid.

Many of the early white settlers were undoubtedly prejudiced against the indigenous population of southern Africa. "Non-whites" were enslaved, discriminated against and segregated from whites on a wide scale. In theory, however, all baptized and confirmed Christians, irrespective of race, had the right to worship together. Classic Reformed theology taught that Christian baptism rendered all distinctions based upon race or class void. This equality before God was to be visibly embodied in the Lord's Supper.[83] Early nineteenth-century DRC records confirm that whites and "non-whites" worshipped and communicated *together* in many churches, although acts of racial discrimination continued to occur on a wide scale.[84]

As early as 1829, church authorities took a firm stand against discrimination at Holy Communion on the basis of color. Some white members of the Somerset West congregation objected to a "coloured" member of the church receiving the Lord's Supper with the white membership, urging that a separate communion be arranged for him. A bitter debate within the church ensued, pitting the elders against the *dominie*. The elders desired to exclude "persons of color" from communion with "born Christians" (whites). The issue was taken to the Presbytery of Cape Town on April 29, 1829, which ruled against the elders. The Presbytery advised "that it is compulsory, according to the teaching of Scripture and the spirit of Christianity, to admit such persons [non-whites] simultaneously with born Christians to the communion table."[85] Those who continued to oppose this ruling were to be disciplined according to church law.[86]

---

emergence of the Broederbond and the National Party). In this section, I will give particular attention to the latter two factors. For more on the historical and theological development of the apartheid ideology in the DRC, see De Gruchy, "The South African Theological Debate," 88–92; and the various essays in De Gruchy and Villa-Vicencio, *Apartheid is a Heresy*.

82. See De Gruchy, *The Church Struggle*; Hinchcliff, *The Church in South Africa*; and Van der Merwe, *The Development of Missionary Attitudes in the Dutch Reformed Church in South Africa*.

83. De Gruchy, *The Church Struggle*, 7.

84. Loff, "The History of a Heresy," 20. Loff notes, however, that discriminatory practices emerged early on. Blacks and "Coloureds" were to form "separate congregations where possible, otherwise a separate section of the church for black people, usually at the back of the church, sometimes under the balcony and sometimes on the balcony" (ibid., 19).

85. Bosch, "Nothing But a Heresy," 31.

86. Loff, "The History of a Heresy," 20.

An 1834 Synod reinforced this judgment, maintaining that Holy Communion was to be administered "simultaneously to all members without distinction of colour or origin." This was "an unshakable principle based on the infallible Word of God."[87]

Social pressures and ingrained racial prejudice proved stronger than the theological convictions of the Presbytery and Synod declarations, however, as more black converts sought to affiliate with the DRC. Many DRC churches resisted or ignored the decisions and refused to allow blacks the privilege of worshipping with them.[88] By 1857, another Synod granted a reprieve to those whites who desired to worship separately from blacks. The Synod declared that it was "desirable and in accordance with Scripture that our converts from paganism be received and incorporated into existing congregations, wherever possible; however, where this practice, because of the weakness of some, constitutes an obstacle to the advancement of Christ's cause among pagans, congregations formed or still to be formed from converts from paganism should be given the opportunity to enjoy their Christian privileges in a separate place of worship."[89]

These fateful words from the 1857 Synod opened the door to the DRC's eventual legitimation of apartheid, although Bosch notes that the Synod qualified this separation in three ways.[90] First, the scriptural norm was that all were to worship together, with converts being incorporated into existing congregations. Second, congregations could be organized on an ethnic basis, but there is no mention of establishing separate, ethnic *denominations*. Third, the decision was seen "as a concession to the 'weakness' of White brothers who did not have the moral strength to accept the presence of Coloreds and Africans."[91]

By 1881, the temporary expedient of separate, ethnic congregations became the permanent norm. In a striking change from the 1857 Synod position, the Commission for Inland Missions of the DRC recommended that the Coloured members of the DRC be organized into a separate denomination, the *Nederduitse Gereformeerde Sendingkerk* (Dutch Reformed Mission Church or NGSK).[92] The Commission did not consult Coloured church leaders about the change; they decided on the change after consulting with the white DRC missionaries.[93]

---

87. As cited in De Gruchy, *The Church Struggle*, 7–8.

88. The veteran anti-apartheid DRC theologian B. B. Keet has pointed out the tragically racist nature of this approach when he asked: "Why could the Coloured Christian not have come into his own inside the Church of the Europeans? The answer is obvious: It is because the white man was not prepared to give him the opportunity" (cited in De Gruchy, *The Church Struggle*, 9).

89. Bosch, "Nothing But a Heresy," 32. For the original Dutch text of the 1857 Synod see ibid., 37–38.

90. Ibid., 32.

91. Hope and Young, *The South African Churches in a Revolutionary Situation*, 18.

92. In a similar fashion, the DRC later formed separate Reformed churches for blacks (the *Nederduitse Gereformeerde Kerk in Afrika* or NGKA, in 1951) and for Indians (the Reformed Church in Africa or RCA, in 1968).

93. Botha, "Belhar—A Century-Old Protest," in Cloete and Smit, *A Moment of Truth*, 67.

The Influence of German Missiology

The mention of DRC missionaries brings us to a neglected dimension in the historical emergence of apartheid: the influential role of German missiological thought.[94] The Germans, with a characteristically Protestant emphasis on the preaching of the Word in the vernacular of the people, propagated the missiological theory of separate "national" churches for every ethno-linguistic "nation."

In nineteenth-century German mission theory there existed a longstanding debate over the proper aim of mission.[95] Among Pietists such as von Zinzendorf, the aim of Christian mission was *Einzelbekehrung*, the conversion of individuals. For other German missions, particularly those from the Lutheran tradition, the aim of mission was *Volkschristianisierung*, the Christianization of a people as an ethnic or national unit. These two aims of mission came together in the thought of Gustav Warneck, the great pioneer of modern missiology.

Warneck, and the generation of German missiologists that followed him, emphasized the foundational role of culture and race as the decisive factor in the planting and development of younger churches.[96] This was grounded in Warneck's exegesis of Matthew 28:19-20, the so-called Great Commission, where Jesus commands his followers to make disciples of all nations. Warneck translated "nations" (*ta ethne*) as *Völker* in the ethnological and sociological sense; peoples as ethnic units.[97] Thus the Great Commission, in Warneck's understanding, offered a clear rationale for the foundation of autonomous, ethnic churches on the mission field.

Bosch observes that this missionary strategy of developing separate, racially determined churches squared well with the strongly Protestant emphasis on reading and hearing the Word of God in one's own language. This ecclesiological emphasis on the proclamation of the Word in the vernacular naturally tended to divide churches along racial/ethnic lines, since language is a fundamental dimension of ethnicity.[98]

Allied with this notion of the fundamental significance of the *Volk* in German missiological thought was a parallel development in German political thought of the day. The concept of *Volk* was deeply influenced by Romanticism, which stressed the immutability and permanence of the nation; the *Volk* was thus transformed into an order of creation.[99]

---

94. For an excellent survey of the impact of German missiological theory and practice on the ideology of apartheid, see Gensichen, "Mission and Ideology in South Africa," 86-97.

95. Hoekendijk, *Kirche und Volk in der deutschen Missionswissenschaft*, 44-110. Cf. Bosch and Verryn, *Church and Mission MSR 301*, 93-97.

96. We are referring here to missiologists like Bruno Gutmann and Christian Keysser. See Bosch, "Nothing But a Heresy," 26.

97. Warneck, *Evangelische Missionslehre*, vol. 3:1:247-51.

98. Bosch, "Nothing But a Heresy," 24-25.

99. Bosch, "Racism and Revolution," 15.

Part One: David Bosch in Context

DRC missionaries quickly seized upon Warneck's ideas and applied them to the South African context.[100] The Pietist wing of the DRC, with their zeal for missionary outreach, supported Warneck's approach because it provided an efficient, speedy way to evangelize the black population along linguistic and ethnic lines. The neo-Calvinist Kuyperian wing of the DRC also supported the Warneck position, but for different reasons. Warneck's theological concept of "nation" as an immutable order of creation matched well with the neo-Calvinists' concern to preserve the separate identity of the Afrikaner nation. They could thus actively evangelize the heathen and promote separate development simultaneously! By 1932, DRC missiologist Johannes du Plessis published the first Afrikaans missiological textbook, which was essentially a simplified restatement of Warneck's *Evangelische Missionslehre*.[101] This guaranteed that German *"Volkstheologie"* would continue to shape DRC mission policy well into the twentieth century.[102]

The link between the DRC's post-1881 mission policy and the development of the apartheid ideology appears to be strong. The DRC itself served as a pioneering and exemplary model for the policies of separate development.[103] It also provided the moral justification and the structural basis for apartheid. Dr. Frans Geldenhuys, former chief executive officer of the DRC, noted in 1980 "the NGK developed a missionary policy in . . . which it presented the Gospel to various population groups in their own language. This caused the establishment of autonomous churches for all the groups, which in turn acted as a model for the present government policy of separate development."[104]

---

100. In fairness, it should be remembered that this missionary strategy was not peculiar to the DRC. As Brown notes: "Various missionary societies and Churches from Europe, amongst them the Church of Scotland, working in South Africa, followed the idea of a separate Christian community (and churches) [for each ethnic group]. Also, the International Missionary Council endorsed this approach when it met at Tambaram in 1938" (Brown, *A Historical Profile of the Nederduitse Gereformeerde Kerk (Dutch Reformed Church) in South Africa*, 32). This approach is far from dead! The "Church Growth" movement has utilized many similar concepts, although it is by no means identical with the German missiological approach mentioned here. See chapter 6.

101. Du Plessis, *Wie Sal Gaan? Die Sending in Teorie en Praktyk*. For further information on du Plessis, see Bosch's "Johannes du Pessis as Sendingkundige," 66–76.

102. Bosch comments that "Dutch Reformed missiological thinking in South Africa has been more directly influenced by German Lutheranism than by Calvinism in the Netherlands." See his "Racism and Revolution," 16.

103. See du Toit, "Missionaries, Anthropologists, and the Policies of the Dutch Reformed Church, 617–32.

104. Serfontein, *Apartheid, Change and the NG Kerk*, 64. Serfontein also quotes Dr. E. P. J. Kleynhans, as saying: "It is not the NGK which is following the government: it is the other way round. We were the first with a policy of separate development which began in the 1850s when separate church structures were provided for each separate racial group to enable them to listen to the Word of God among their own people and in their own language." Serfontein comments that the "honour" for being first with the concept of apartheid thus belongs not to the National Party, but to the DRC (ibid., 64–65). For a full discussion of this from a *verligte* Afrikaner viewpoint, see Geldenhuys, *In die Stroomversnellings*, 27–77.

As we have argued previously, the ideology of apartheid began to emerge just after the turn of the twentieth century. The Dopper Kerk, and then the mainstream DRC, increasingly identified itself as the *volkskerk*, the church of the Afrikaner people. By 1915, at a meeting of the Federal Council of the Dutch Reformed Synods, Dr. D. F. Malan (later to be Prime Minister) submitted a motion, which explicitly confirmed this *volkskerk* mindset. It maintained "our church has received from God a special calling in respect of the Afrikaner people, with which it is so intimately connected. It should therefore also be regarded as [the church's] duty to be national itself, to watch over our peculiar national interests and to teach our people to detect the hand of God in its history and genesis; it should also keep alive in the Afrikaner people the awareness of its national calling and destiny."[105]

By 1948, when Dr. Malan and his National Party came into power, the DRC had developed an elaborate theological justification of apartheid, rooted in her own historical experience of missionary outreach, with an emphasis on separate ethnic churches for each *volk*.

The Broederbond

The third key ingredient that helped forge the DRC's stance toward apartheid was its close relationship with the Afrikaner *Broederbond*.[106] The *Broederbond* began in 1918 as a service organization to marginalized Afrikaners, helping them face the confusing demands of urban (Anglo-Saxon dominated) life.[107] It later developed into the vanguard of Afrikaner political and cultural aspirations. The *Broederbond* became a fraternity of zealously committed Christian Nationalists, what Wilkens and Strydom labeled "the Super-Afrikaners."[108] In the words of P. J. Meyer, a one-time chairman of the *Broederbond:* "The main purpose of this cultural movement was to purify Afrikaans nationalism of all elements by which it could destroy itself and to build it on a Christian-Protestant basis, with (as yardstick) the legal principles of the Holy Writ, the guidelines of our Christian national tradition and the demands of the time in which we live, in all spheres of life to full independence and maturity."[109]

---

105. As cited in Bosch, "The Fragmentation of Afrikanerdom and the Afrikaner Churches," 66.

106. On the Broederbond, see Wilson and Thompson, *The Oxford History of South Africa*, 2:395–402; and Serfontein, *The Brotherhood of Power*. The word "Broederbond" is the Afrikaans word for "fraternal society."

107. Hope and Young, *The South African Churches in a Revolutionary Situation*, 30.

108. Wilkins and Strydom, *The Super-Afrikaners*. It should be noted that, like the National Party, the Broederbond underwent a split in 1982–83 over whether to endorse the 1983 tri-cameral political dispensation. Carel Boshof, DRC *predikant* and at that time chairman of the Broederbond, resigned in protest and founded an alternative organization, the *Afrikaner Volkswag*. See Thompson, *The Political Mythology of Apartheid*, 228.

109. Wilson and Thompson, *The Oxford History of South Africa*, 2:395.

The Broederbond represented the Afrikaner elite. Members included most Nationalist Party politicians (and every Nationalist Prime Minister and State President between 1948 to 1994), as well as leaders in all other walks of life: church, education, media, police, government services, and farming communities.[110] It linked leaders "from Parliament to church councils and local village committees in the smallest centres."[111] The aims of the Broederbond were fourfold: to maintain a separate white Afrikaner volk, to guarantee Afrikaner political domination in South Africa, to seek the subtle "Afrikanerization" of the English segment of the population, and to maintain a white South African nation "built on the rock of the Afrikaner volk with the Broederbond the hard core of that volk."[112]

The Broederbond's influence was particularly strong within the Afrikaans Reformed Churches. In 1977, it was estimated that 7% of all Broederbond members were clergymen (848 persons).[113] According to Serfontein, this meant that nearly half of all DRC ministers were Broederbonders. As late as 1982, eleven of the twelve members of the DRC "cabinet," the *Breë Moderatuur*, were Broederbonders. So were the moderators of seven of the DRC's synods, as well as the editor of *Die Kerkbode*, the official DRC periodical. So were many of the teaching staff at the three DRC theological schools.[114]

Serfontein documented numerous cases of improper *Broederbond* interference in the internal affairs of the DRC.[115] Through the years, it stifled dissent by threatening and cajoling anti-Broederbond DRC rebels.[116] It functioned as a secret "church within a church," deciding in advance the positions to be adopted at upcoming Synod meetings. It challenged the integrity of the Gospel itself, by putting loyalty to the Afrikaner cause on a par with loyalty to Christ.

Clearly, the Broederbond's influence was strong within the apartheid-era DRC, serving as a major force for preserving solidarity between the DRC, the National Party and the Afrikaner people and as a foil to Afrikaners like David Bosch who refused to conform to the apartheid paradigm. We now turn from the Broederbond back to the DRC itself, where the ideals of the Broederbond became embodied in the ecclesiastical realm.

110. Hope and Young, *The South African Churches in a Revolutionary Situation*, 30.

111. Serfontein, *Apartheid, Change and the NG Kerk*, 87.

112. Ibid., 88.

113. Ibid., 91.

114. Ibid., 93.

115. See "Broederbond and Church," in Serfontein, *Apartheid, Change and the NG Kerk*, 87–108.

116. Professor Ben Marais, a veteran anti-apartheid theologian and former Dean of the Faculty of Theology at the University of Pretoria, commented on the stifling influence of the Broederbond within the DRC: "In the last 25 years our church has been pushing out and shunting on the sidelines, all those who think independently and who, with regards to church policy, take a standpoint which does not tally with the traditional line. The result is that three-quarters of our really able men are sitting on the fringes, either at UNISA, or elsewhere, while your church leader is the man who totally conforms to the old historical pattern. That is why our church is today experiencing a leadership crisis and finds itself in the theological wilderness" (Serfontein, *Apartheid, Change and the NG Kerk*, 100).

The Theological Justification of Apartheid

As we have seen, the ideology of apartheid did not develop in a vacuum. Behind it lay centuries of historical experience. This historical experience of the Afrikaner people (as interpreted by Afrikaner writers) provided the framework or "pre-understanding" within which later Afrikaner intellectuals constructed the apartheid ideology. Afrikaner leaders from all walks of life (politicians, poets, teachers, theologians, sociologists, historians) were marshaled to serve Afrikanerdom by helping to formulate a comprehensive, cohesive theory of apartheid.

The DRC, as an integral part of the Afrikaner *volk*, took her place in this process. According to Bosch, five characteristics defined the self-undertanding of the DRC in the apartheid era.[117] They included: (1) a firm conviction of a "manifest destiny" in southern Africa; (2) a mystical identification with the people of Israel; (3) a sense of "missionary calling" to other "less privileged" races, both to evangelize and uplift the blacks and to defend "white Christian civilization"; (4) a strong desire to maintain the racial and cultural purity of the Afrikaner people, in order to fulfill their destiny and calling; and (5) a positivistic attitude to the law, which regards present sociopolitical conditions as inevitable, as willed by God. These five characteristics, formed in the crucible of the DRC's own historical experience, help explain the DRC's defense and support of apartheid.

On an official level, the DRC produced numerous documents defending the theory and practice of "separate development." Up to the 1986 Synod, the most authoritative policy statement was *Human Relations and the South African Scene in the Light of Scripture*.[118] In this document the DRC set out to investigate the teaching of the Bible with regard to racial matters, and develop policy guidelines for the DRC with regard to its mission in South Africa. It purported to analyze the whole question of racial relations on the basis of the Scriptures, which were to be "interpreted in their own context and in the context of the entire history of salvation."[119] Throughout the rest of the document, however, the authors depart from their avowed method and betray an unacknowledged "hidden agenda." They elevated the idea of the *diversity of peoples* into a biblical *principium*, ignoring the relatively minor place the biblical authors give to this concept in the history of salvation.[120]

---

117. Bosch, "Racism and Revolution," 16–17.

118. Edited by the Executive Council (*Breë Moderatuur*) of the DRC and published in 1976, and hereafter referred to as *Human Relations*. Critiques of the document abound. See especially Bax, *A Different Gospel: A Critique of the Theology Behind Apartheid*; and his "A Different Gospel;" Johanson, "Race, Mission and Ecumenism: Reflections on the Landman Report," 60–67; and Villa-Vicencio, *The Theology of Apartheid*.

119. *Human Relations*, 11.

120. Durand, "Bible and Race: the Problem of Hermeneutics," 4–5. Durand's admirable critique looks behind the content of the documents to see whose *interests* are served by them.

Contrary to popular misconceptions, the authors of *Human Relations* did not teach white racial superiority, nor did they simplistically use proof texts to demonstrate apartheid from the Bible. They built their case gradually, arguing that if the Scriptures acknowledged that ethnic and national diversity were consistent with God's created order, then a case could be made for such individuation within both the political and ecclesiastical spheres of life.[121] Durand summarized the approach thus: "The document presupposes that, if [the] positive valuation of the diversity of peoples can be vindicated as a biblical principle, the conclusion can be drawn that the policy of separate development is acceptable from a Christian point of view."[122] After working through the biblical data the report drew just such a conclusion: "From the fact that the existence of a diversity of peoples is acceptable as a relative, but nevertheless real, premise, one may infer that the New Testament allows for the possibility that a given country may decide to regulate its inter-people relationships on the basis of separate development—considering its own peculiar circumstances, with due respect for the basic norms which the Bible prescribes for the regulation of social relations and after careful consideration of all possible solutions offered."[123]

From this point on in the report, the "possibility" that the New Testament allowed apartheid moved from being a relative premise to a foundational principle.[124] Examples abound. "A political system," said the document, "based on the autogenous or separate development of various population groups can be *justified* from the Bible . . ."[125] Although the New Testament teaches the unity of the church under Christ, "the existence of separate Dutch Reformed Church affiliations for the various population groups is recognized as *being in accordance with* the plurality of church affiliations described in the Bible."[126] Interracial marriage was prohibited, since it "would eventually destroy the *God-given diversity and identity* [of peoples]."[127] Thus in the

---

121. Hope and Young point out that "traditional DRC theologians maintain that the Scriptures teach the essential unity of humankind and the fundamental equality of all peoples–and also that ethnic diversity is in accordance with the will of God. The ultimate restoration of the unity of humankind, which has been shaken because of human sin, will occur only at the final coming of the Kingdom of God. Meanwhile, however, in the words of one synodal document, 'The church must exert itself to give concrete substance to the blessings of the gospel in the life and social structure of a people.' The role of the DRC thus becomes that of insisting that separate development be implemented in a just manner." Hope and Young, *The South African Churches in a Revolutionary Situation*, 47. One wonders, however, whether such egalitarian principles truly reflected the opinions of the average DRC member.

122. Ibid., 7.

123. *Human Relations*, 32.

124. Durand, "Bible and Race: The Problem of Hermeneutics," 7.

125. *Human Relations*, 71 (my emphasis).

126. Ibid., 82 (my emphasis).

127. Ibid., 99 (my emphasis). Referring to this section of *Human Relations*, Durand notes that "the idea of a 'God-given diversity and identity' is elevated to the sphere of being an unassailable and unchangeable principle of enduring division between peoples . . . Substantial differences in religion, social structure and cultural pattern might be overcome in the course of time, but substantial biological differences are permanent. The document arrives at a kind of biological order of creation or order of

spheres of state, church and family life, the "relative premise" of ethnic diversity was turned into an *imperative*, serving to divide peoples.[128]

This concern to preserve national identity at all costs was perhaps most insidious when it came to the issue of church membership. The report made clear that one's "national identity is the key element in the believer's religious experience."[129]

> Just as members of a certain people or nation may *in principle* not be prevented from becoming members of another people or nation, so members of one "national" church may not be forbidden to become members of another "national" church. In other words, *in principle* there is no exclusive national church . . . even if we should uphold the importance of national identity for the preaching of the gospel and for experiencing the communion of the saints . . .
>
> If, however, such a transfer of membership should disturb the order and peace of both church and people (peoples or sections of people) to such an extent that the kingdom of God is no longer served, that the fellowship of believers and their ability to serve should suffer and the nation or nations concerned should find it difficult or impossible to give full expression to their national identity—in these circumstances a temporary arrangement against the transfer of membership cannot be condemned since it would enhance the well-being of the churches concerned.[130]

The authors thus acknowledged that an exclusively "national" church was, in principle, biblically unjustifiable. But they proceeded to argue (in language remarkably similar to the 1857 Synod) against allowing members of other races to join the DRC. The irony of this practice of ecclesiastical apartheid was that this "temporary arrangement against transfer of members" has lasted many decades!

At the root of *Human Relations*, indeed of all pre-1986 official DRC teaching on racial matters, was the inviolable principle of Afrikaner national identity. As Stamoolis characterizes it, Afrikaners could not conceive of a situation where their national identity could be superseded or set aside.[131] Their very identity as Afrikaners had been linked to the concept of being separate from other racial groups, and to think otherwise would have been to contemplate national suicide.[132] John de Gruchy captured the DRC's apartheid-era predicament thus: "We are face to face with the dilemma of the DRC. It does not claim to be a *volkskerk* like the NHK [Nederduitse Hervormde Kerk] but it finds itself pushed in that direction time and again . . . The survival of Afrikaner

---

providence" (Durand, "Bible and Race: The Problem of Hermeneutics," 8).

128. Ibid. It should be noted that at the 1983 General Synod of the DRC, the attitude toward interracial marriage was relaxed. Synod admitted that the legislative acts which forbade interracial marriage contradicted the Scriptures (Omond, *The Apartheid Handbook*, 191).

129. Stamoolis, "Church and State in South Africa," 18.

130. *Human Relations*, 47.

131. Stamoolis, "Church and State in South Africa," 19.

132. Ibid.

identity and power seems to play such a determinative role. At all costs, the concept of separate development must not be surrendered—which means that its theological basis must be affirmed—for the future of the Afrikaner people is regarded as tied up with the success or failure of this policy."[133]

Not all Afrikaners adopted this line of thinking, of course. There were a significant (albeit numerically small) group of DRC dissenters who, in various ways, refused to remain silent in the face of apartheid. It is to this group of individuals that we now turn.

Critics of Apartheid and the Isolation of the DRC[134]

During the 1950s, three distinct positions emerged vis à vis apartheid within the Afrikaner *Federale Sendingraad* (Federal Mission Council).[135] Some believed that racial separation was a necessary, scriptural mandate; others attacked it as unscriptural; still others felt it was not the ideal, but pragmatically necessary in the South African situation.[136] To a large extent, these divisions typified the three "wings" of the white Reformed community throughout the apartheid era.

During the 1950s two veteran Afrikaner theologians spoke out sharply against the National Party policies: Professors B. B. Keet of Stellenbosch and Ben Marais of Pretoria.[137] As early as 1952, Marais raised the essential dilemma of white South Africa: how ". . . to maintain ourselves, but not to do it in such a way that the non-whites and their aspirations will be the victims of our selfishness and self-interest."[138]

By 1960, the Sharpeville massacre and the subsequent state of emergency riveted the attention of the world on South Africa. In response, the World Council of Churches held the now famous Cottesloe Consultation.[139] At the time the DRC and NHK were members of the WCC and they sent representatives to the Consultation. After long hours of discussion the delegates hammered out a statement setting forth Christian principles related to race relations and the unity of the church. The

---

133. De Gruchy, *The Church Struggle*, 76.

134. For reasons of space, we cannot deal with the anti-apartheid protests and actions that emerged from the Roman Catholic, "English-speaking," and African Independent Churches. For details, see De Gruchy, *The Church Struggle*, 85–147; Hope and Young, *The South African Churches in a Revolutionary Situation*, 63–219; Mosala, "African Independent Churches,"103–11; Prior, *Catholics in Apartheid Society*; and Villa-Vicencio, "An All-Pervading Heresy," 59–74.

135. This council, founded in 1942, was established to coordinate the mission policies of the various Dutch Reformed Synods. For a history of the Federal Mission Council, with special reference to DRC racial policies, see Strassberger, *Ecumenism in South Africa 1936–1960*, 181–245.

136. Hope and Young, *The South African Churches in a Revolutionary Situation*, 48.

137. For more on their pioneering work, see Durand, "Afrikaner Piety and Dissent," 39–51; and Saayman, "Rebels and Prophets," 52–60.

138. From Marais's book *Colour: Unsolved Problem of the West*, as cited in De Gruchy, *The Church Struggle*, 83.

139. The story of the Consultation is contained in the WCC's *Mission in South Africa*.

Consultation affirmed that all racial discrimination was unjust. Among its conclusions were the following:

> 1. We recognise that all racial groups who permanently inhabit our country are a part of our total population, and we regard them as indigenous. Members of all these groups have an equal right to make their contribution towards the enrichment of the life of their country and to share in the ensuing responsibilities, rewards and privileges . . .
>
> 6. No-one who believes in Jesus Christ may be excluded from any Church on the ground of his colour or race. The spiritual unity among all men who are in Christ must find visible expression in acts of common worship and witness, and in fellowship and consultation on matters of common concern . . .
>
> 10. There are no Scriptural grounds for the prohibition of mixed marriages . . .
>
> 11. We call attention once again to the disintegrating effects of migrant labour on African life. No stable society is possible unless the cardinal importance of family life is recognised, and, from the Christian standpoint, it is imperative that the integrity of the family be safeguarded . . .
>
> 13. The present system of job reservation must give way to a more equitable system of labour which safeguards the interests of all concerned . . .
>
> 15. It is our conviction that the right to own land wherever he is domiciled, and to participate in the government of his country, is part of the dignity of the adult man, and for this reason a policy which permanently denies to Non-white people the right of collaboration in the government of the country of which they are citizens cannot be justified.
>
> 16. It is our conviction that there can be no objection in principle to the direct representation of Coloured people in Parliament.[140]

These far-reaching conclusions made the Cottesloe Consultation a landmark in the churches' response to apartheid. However they were deemed far too "liberal" for both the government and the conservative elements within the DRC. As a result, the DRC later repudiated its own theologians and denounced the Cottesloe Statement. Shortly thereafter, the DRC and NHK withdrew from the World Council of Churches and began to tread the path of ecumenical isolation.[141]

One of the DRC delegates who refused to retract his endorsement of the Cottesloe Statement was Dr. Beyers Naudé, who was destined to play a major role in the campaign against apartheid.[142] With twenty other Dutch Reformed ministers, this

---

140. Ibid, 30–32.

141. For an insightful overview of the Cottesloe Consultation and its aftermath, see Strassberger, *Ecumenism in South Africa 1936–1960*, 218–37.

142. For a brief survey of the achievement of both Dr. Naudé and the Christian Institute, see Villa-Vicencio, "A Life of Resistance and Hope," 3–13; " and De Gruchy, "A Short History of the Christian Institute," 14–26.

former Broederbonder founded the Christian Institute of Southern Africa in 1963.[143] Its goal was "to enable members of all races of the Afrikaans and other churches to share together in bearing witness to the unity of the church and the lordship of Christ over society."[144] The Institute carried out its mandate by forming Bible study groups across South Africa, issuing study guides, and publishing the periodical *Pro Veritate*. All these endeavors sought to challenge Christians in South Africa to take seriously God's call for social justice and reconciliation between races and churches. Along with the South African Council of Churches (SACC), the Christian Institute gave leadership to the churches' struggle against apartheid throughout the 1960s and 1970s. Of particular note during this time was the release in 1968 of the SACC's "Message to the People of South Africa" (the first church document to label apartheid a heresy and false gospel)[145] and the joint SACC-Christian Institute-sponsored Study Project on Christianity in Apartheid Society (Spro-cas).[146]

By the early 1970s, the Christian Institute came under growing criticism from the government. In 1970 the World Council of Churches organized its Programme to Combat Racism and the South African government became acidly critical of the WCC. As was to be expected, all South African groups with WCC connections (e.g., the SACC and the Christian Institute) were immediately suspect. At the same time the Institute increasingly identified itself with the newly emerging Black Consciousness Movement.[147] Both of these new factors increased the government's hostility toward the Institute. By 1976 when the Soweto riots burst onto the scene and violence flared throughout the country, the government decided to crack down on numerous anti-apartheid groups, including the Institute. On October 19, 1977 the Institute was banned, as were Dr. Naudé and some of its other leaders. On the same day, eighteen other organizations were banned.[148] Thus ended a remarkable story of one response to apartheid.

143. Naudé, who at the time was moderator of the influential Transvaal Synod of the DRC, was forced to resign his moderatorship and give up his DRC clerical status. See Villa-Vicencio, "A Life of Resistance and Hope," 10.

144. De Gruchy, *The Church Struggle*, 104.

145. For the text of the Message, see *Apartheid is a Heresy*, 154–59. De Gruchy comments elsewhere "the Message attempted to show how apartheid and separate development are contrary to the gospel of Christ. Taking as its starting-point the conviction that, in Christ, God has reconciled the world to himself and therefore made reconciliation between people both possible and essential to the Christian faith, the Message proceeded to draw out the implications of this atoning work of Christ in terms of South African society . . . [A]partheid and separate development attacked the church at its center; they denied the work of Christ . . . The task of the church was to demonstrate the reality of this reconciling work of God in its own life." See his *The Church Struggle*, 119–20.

146. The Spro-cas project sought "to work out in detail the implications of the [1968] *Message* for our national life" through the creation of six commissions. Each commission was charged to analyze a specific area of South African life (economics, education, law, politics, society, and the church), and envision the practical implications of a non-racial, non-apartheid South Africa. See Randall, *Apartheid and the Church*, 1–2.

147. For example, by 1972 Steve Biko, the Black Consciousness student leader, was editing the Spro-cas-sponsored publication *Black Viewpoint*.

148. The full story of the Christian Institute, see Walshe, *Church Versus State in South Africa: The*

Since 1977, however, numerous other expressions of dissent within and beyond the Dutch Reformed community emerged. We briefly note the following:[149]

The Koinonia Declaration (1977). This statement emerged from a group of young, theologically conservative, Dopper Kerk Calvinists based in Johannesburg and Potchefstroom. In it, they challenged the state to live up to the lofty ideals of justice to which the state frequently appealed. In strong terms it condemned numerous government policies, including the security laws and the Immorality Act, and asked for equal political and economic opportunities for all racial groups. The statement further maintained that Calvinist doctrine did not justify the apartheid system.[150]

The South African Christian Leadership Assembly (1979). This unique ecumenical assembly, which received its impetus from Michael Cassidy and the Africa Enterprise mission agency, and was chaired by David Bosch, gathered together 5,000 persons from all races and churches with the purpose of "discovering what it means to be faithful and effective witnesses to Jesus Christ as Lord in South Africa today." Major speakers included Cassidy and Bosch, as well as Orlando Costas, Ron Sider, Manas Buthelezi, Hendrikus Berkhof, and John Howard Yoder. Although it issued no formal statement, its very *existence* served as a witness against apartheid, since all apartheid legislation was suspended for the duration of the SACLA gathering.[151]

The Witness of the Eight (1980). Eight *verligte*[152] DRC theologians caused a stir when they criticized the DRC (and by implication, the National Party) for its "apparent powerlessness . . . to carry out its divine calling of reconciliation on a meaningful and credible basis in a situation of increasing tension and polarization between the various population groups in our country." They further urged that the DRC strive for "a form of church unity in which the oneness of believers adhering to the same confession can take visible form." Although the "Witness" spoke from within the apartheid framework and its criticisms were somewhat vague and veiled, the eight *verligtes* caused a furor among the *verkrampte* wing of the DRC.[153]

Case of the Christian Institute; and the International Commission of Jurists, *The Trial of Beyers Naudé*.

149. For a lengthy analysis of dissent *within* the DRC up to 1982, see Serfontein, *Apartheid, Change and the NG Kerk*, 135–204. We should note that the following expressions of dissent were by no means uniform; some appear to be an appeal to make the apartheid system more humane (i.e., the Koinonia Declaration and the 1980 Witness Statement); others were a direct challenge to the basic foundations of apartheid itself (i.e., the 1982 Open Letter and the 1985 Kairos Document).

150. Hope and Young, *The South African Churches in a Revolutionary Situation*, 173. For the text of the declaration, see "The Koinonia Declaration," 58–64. While the declaration was anything but radical, the fact that it emerged from *within* Afrikanerdom was of some significance.

151. For the major speeches and some theological responses to SACLA, see the December 1979 edition of the *Journal of Theology for Southern Africa*.

152. The Afrikaans words *verlig* ("progressive") and *verkramp* ("conservative") have been used to mean two different political factions *within the National Party framework*. The *verligte* were those who are considered more liberal and tolerant, favoring the abandonment of the so-called petty apartheid legislation. The *verkrampte* were the hard-line "true believers," who resist attempts to moderate the apartheid system.

153. For the text of the "Witness," see Serfontein, *Apartheid, Change and the NG Kerk*, 270. For a discussion of its effect in the DRC, see ibid., 153–57.

Storm-kompas (1981). Three DRC theologians edited *Storm-kompas* [Storm compass], a compendium of twelve essays and responses that attempted to guide the DRC through the "storm" it was enduring. The twenty-four contributors varied in their sociopolitical perspectives. Some were more outspoken Afrikaner dissidents including David Bosch, Nico Smith, and Jaap Durand. Others represented the more cautious *verligte* approach, e.g., Johan Heyns, Malan Nel, and Pierre Roussouw. At the end of the book, the editors compiled forty-four propositions reflecting the main points of the essays. In particular, they urged the DRC to repudiate the domination of the *Broederbond* over the DRC, called for the unification of the four Dutch Reformed "sister" churches (DRC, NGKA, NGSK, and RCA), and rejected political apartheid as unjust by the standards of the gospel.[154]

Die Ope Brief (1982). On June 8, 1982, an *Ope Brief* [Open Letter] was published in the DRC periodical *Die Kerkbode*. Veteran anti-apartheid journalist Hennie Serfontein hailed the letter, signed by 123 white ministers within the DRC, as "the most important development in the Afrikaans Churches in more than 20 years."[155] The letter contained "a fundamental, total condemnation of the apartheid system."[156] It pled for the DRC to establish "visible unity" with its black sister Reformed churches. The uniqueness of the Open Letter was not in its message; its crucial significance lay in the fact that two decades after Dr. Naudé was forced to leave the DRC, 123 DRC ministers were taking the same road as Keet and Naudé. The Open Letter was the largest single protest ever to emerge from within the ranks of the DRC clergy.[157]

"Apartheid is a Heresy:" The Ottawa Meeting of the World Alliance of Reformed Churches (1982). A momentous step was taken in August 1982 when the WARC declared apartheid sinful and its theological and moral justification a heresy. This declaration placed the debate over apartheid squarely into the theological realm. Supporting apartheid was no longer merely a political debate; it was a *status confessionis*, a matter of confessional integrity.[158] As Allan Boesak declared: "In South Africa . . . apartheid is not just a political ideology. Its very existence as a political policy has depended and still depends on the theological justification of certain member churches of the WARC. For Reformed Christians, this situation should constitute a *status confessionis*. This means that churches should recognize that apartheid is a heresy, contrary to the Gospel and inconsistent with the Reformed tradition, and consequently reject

---

154. Smith, Geldenhuys, Meiring, *Storm-kompas*. For an English translation of the forty-four statements, see Serfontein, *Apartheid, Change and the NG Kerk*, 271–74; for a discussion of its effects, see 172–75.

155. Serfontein, *Apartheid, Change and the NG Kerk*, 182.

156. Ibid.

157. See Bosch, König, and Nicol, *Perspektief op die Ope Brief*. For a discussion of its significance see Serfontein, *Apartheid, Change and the NG Kerk*, 182–89.

158. It should be noted that it was the Lutheran World Federation that first declared apartheid to be a *status confessionis* issue in 1977. See De Gruchy, "Towards a Confessing Church," 88.

it as such."¹⁵⁹ Besides issuing its "Racism and South Africa" Statement, the WARC suspended the membership of the DRC and the NHK, and elected Boesak (an NGSK minister) as its new President.¹⁶⁰

The Belhar Confession (1982). Soon after the WARC's decision, the "Coloured" NGSK distanced itself further from the DRC by adopting a new confession of faith. Like the WARC statement, the Belhar Confession grounded its criticism of apartheid in the doctrine of the work of Christ. His work of reconciliation was the sole and complete ground for reconciliation between persons and for the visible unity of the church. Any doctrine that absolutized natural diversity and the separation of people to the extent that the visible unity of Christ's church is broken was rejected as "ideology and false doctrine."¹⁶¹

The Chicago Meeting of the Reformed Ecumenical Synod (1984). This body, representing some 5.5 million members of various conservative Calvinist denominations, met for ten days in Chicago and voted to condemn South Africa's racial policies in strong terms. It defined apartheid as "an ideology that is contrary to holy Scripture" and declared "any teaching of the church that would defend this theological defence of apartheid must be regarded as heresy." It condemned any effort to bar Christians from the Lord's Table solely on the basis of race and instructed the DRC and the smaller GKSA ("Dopper Kerk"), both member churches of the Reformed Ecumenical Synod, to "re-evaluate its position [on apartheid] in light of the biblical norms of love and justice."¹⁶² Following the vote, the DRC executive committee (the *Breë Moderatuur*) voted to provisionally suspend its membership in the RES, thereby isolating itself even further from contact with other Christians.¹⁶³

National Initiative for Reconciliation (1985).¹⁶⁴ In August and September, 1985 two meetings were held under the auspices of Africa Enterprise. Originally the meetings were called to set up regional follow-up meetings to the 1979 SACLA conference. Events overtook the planning process, however, when the South African government in August 1985 declared a State of Emergency. Numerous would-be participants were detained in prison, while others were unable to get to Pietermaritzburg for the August meeting. From September 10 to 12, a larger gathering of 400 Christian leaders met in

159. These words, originally spoken by Boesak at the WARC's Ottawa Assembly, are found in his essay, "He Made Us All, But . . .," 8.

160. See Section II:4 of the WARC's statement "Racism and South Africa," as cited in ibid., 171–72.

161. For the text of the Confession, along with nine explanatory essays on the theological significance and practical consequences of the document, see Cloete et al., *A Moment of Truth: The Confession of the Dutch Reformed Mission Church*.

162. Information about the RES meeting, including all quotations, is taken from an Ecumenical Press Service news release, as cited in *Southern Africa: The Continuing Crisis*, 59–60.

163. Bosch, "The Fragmentation of Afrikanerdom and the Afrikaner Churches," 73.

164. The following information, including citations, is taken from "Initiative for Reconciliation in South Africa," 1–8. The full text of the "Statement of Affirmation," as well as a description of the origins and significance of NIR, is found in Lee, *Guard Her Children: Hope for South Africa Today*, 188–95, 199–202, 244–46.

a context of escalating violence, with South African Defence Forces in the townships and thousands in detention. The group was diverse; forty-eight denominations were represented, with a spectrum that went from White Dutch Reformed, evangelical, and charismatic groups on the one hand to Black liberation theologians on the other. Such leaders as Bishop Tutu, David Bosch, Bonganjalo Goba, Archbishop Dennis Hurley, and Michael Cassidy addressed the gathering. Time was given to share information about what was actually happening in South Africa (particularly the townships), and to pray together concerning the church's response to the deteriorating situation. Cassidy then proposed a "National Initiative for Reconciliation" (NIR) movement, in which interracial teams would be sent into local churches around the country in an attempt to foster dialogue at the local level between Christians of the various racial and language groups. The goal was that such efforts would begin the slow process of repentance and reconciliation needed in South Africa.[165] The meeting also produced a "Statement of Affirmation" which, among other things, called a one-day work boycott, so that Christians could "give the day to repentance, mourning and prayer for those sinful aspects of our national life which have led us to the present crisis." What made the meeting significant was that it sought "to foster dialogue and co-operation between incredibly diverse and even opposing groups of Christians."[166]

The Kairos Document (1985). At nearly the same time as the NIR meeting, some 150 Black and White theologians and pastors were producing the Kairos document. Meeting in Soweto in the midst of unprecedented violence and unrest, the assembled Christian leaders were urgently seeking to discern the will of God in the face of increasing violence and anarchy. They also sought to give moral guidance to Christians (including many of their own parishioners) who were involved in the struggle against apartheid. In stark, uncompromising terms, it condemned both "state theology" and "church theology" as hopelessly inadequate to deal with the South African crisis. The South African government was denounced as "irreformable," "the enemy of the people;" it had "lost all legitimacy." In apocalyptic terms it declared that God's *kairos* had arrived for South Africa, a moment of truth, filled with danger and opportunity. Since God sides with the oppressed, the church cannot be a neutral "third force" standing between oppressors and oppressed. Rather, the church was called, in the name of God the liberator, to participate in the struggle for the liberation of South Africa. In a particularly controversial section, the document emphasizes that God's forgiveness depends on prior repentance. As the document forcefully states: "Reconciliation, forgiveness and negotiations will become our Christian duty in South Africa only when the apartheid regime shows signs of genuine repentance."[167]

---

165. The NIR teams, and the regional follow-up meetings, had been planned long before the state of emergency had been declared. The subsequent declaration simply added urgency to these tasks.

166. Bosch, "The Christian Church in a Revolutionary Situation," 14.

167. *The Kairos Document*, 12. For a sympathetic yet critical response, see Oestreicher, "Assessing the Signs," 49. Oestreicher criticizes the document's one-sidedness, noting: "Their [the defenders of the status quo] liberation–as Desmond Tutu never fails to stress–is the greatest challenge of all. Because

Evangelical Witness in South Africa (1986).[168] Following on the heels of the NIR and Kairos, yet another statement emerged. This time 132 "Concerned Evangelicals" from Soweto and the Pretoria-Witwatersrand-Vaal area released a document after nine months of meetings. The *Witness* critiqued the deficiencies of evangelical theology and practice in light of the crisis in the South African townships. In tone the statement resembled the Kairos document, although it was produced by, and aimed specifically at, those blacks and whites that identified themselves as "evangelicals." It criticized evangelicalism for its social conservatism and theological dualism, for its tacit support of the current sociopolitical order in South Africa, for its inadequate social ethic, for the mixed and worldly motives of many white evangelical evangelists and missionary groups who enter into the black community, and for its neglect of the radical demands of the gospel of Christ. It is significant to note that numerous Black church leaders, including Frank Chikane, who later became General Secretary of the South African Council of Churches, and Caesar Molebatsi, a black evangelical leader, signed both *Kairos* and *Evangelical Witness*.

Dutch Reformed Church Synod (1986).[169] This synodical meeting of the DRC (October 14–25, 1986) provided some (albeit ambiguous) evidence that the DRC leadership and laity were finally beginning to officially move away from its previous pro-apartheid stance. In a new study document *Kerke en Samelewing (Church and Society)* the DRC declared that its earlier theological rationales for the enforced segregation of different races were an error that should be rejected. It also affirmed, at least in principle, that non-whites could now join DRC congregations as members.[170]

---

they are human and no less God's children they are in no sense expendable. To fight apartheid is to fight against them in one sense, for them in another" (ibid.). For a similar critique, see Torrance, "The Kairos Debate: Listening to Its Challenge," 42–45.

168. The text of the was published as *Evangelical Witness in South Africa: Evangelicals Critique Their Own Theology and Practice* and reprinted in the World Council of Churches' *Monthly Letter on Evangelism*. See Concerned Evangelicals, *Evangelical Witness in South Africa*.

169. For two strikingly different evaluations of the meeting from the Reformed world, see Villa-Vicencio, "Report from a Safe Synod," 9–12; and Schrotenboer, "Turning the Tide?," 10–11, 31–32.

170. Schrotenboer cites references from the *Kerk en Samelewing* report and summarizes the most significant aspects of the synod document as follows:

The church's former defense of apartheid was wrong; this error must be rejected: "The Dutch Reformed Church is convinced that apartheid as a political and social system by which human dignity is adversely affected, and whereby one particular group is detrimentally suppressed by another, cannot be accepted as a Christian-ethical principle because it contravenes the very essence of neighbourly love and righteousness and inevitably that of human dignity of all involved (par. 307).

The NG Kerk will resume contacts with the South African Council of Churches and the Reformed Churches in the Netherlands and will continue in its membership in the Reformed Ecumenical Synod. It will consider with the NG Mission Church the implications of the Belhar Confession.

The doors, the membership, and the Communion Table are open to all of like faith regardless of race. This leaves no room for local option, and any church that does not open its doors, membership, and communion table is in violation of [the Synod]. See Schrotenboer, "Turning the Tide," 11.

Part One: David Bosch in Context

It elected Johan Heyns, a *verligte* pastor and theological disciple of Karl Barth, as its new moderator.[171]

On the other hand, the synod continued its commitment to separate educational establishments for the various races. It retained the concept that South Africa was not a single nation, but a land of many "ethnic minorities," one of the crucial concepts underpinning then-current government policies. In his critique of the Synod, Johannes Adonis of the NGSK noted that "It is not only a question of an open church, it is a question of becoming one church," and the Synod made no move toward the structural unification of the various ethnic churches of the Dutch Reformed family (DRC, NGSK, NGKA, RCA).[172] At the very least, the 1986 Synod declarations represented a significant departure from the DRC's past, although one could argue the Synod's actions were simply a *mirror* of the South African government's similar policy shifts with regard to sociopolitical issues.[173] Critics noted that nowhere did the 1986 Synod address the landmark 1982 WARC declaration that apartheid was not merely an "error" but a heresy.

The DRC's Legacy of Unevangelical Conservatism

Events that followed within the DRC closely mirrored the landmark changes that occurred in South Africa, beginning with President F. W. de Klerk's unbanning of the ANC and other opposing political parties on Feb. 2, 1990 and subsequent release of Nelson Mandela nine days later after twenty-seven years in prison. Later that year the DRC Synod meeting in Bloemfontein promulgated a revision of the 1986 *Kerke en Samelewing* report, declaring and acknowledging its personal guilt and responsibility for the political, social, economic and structural injustices inherent in South African society. This was a remarkable turnabout from almost a century of theological justifications for apartheid in church and society.

Yet for many decades the DRC stood resolute in its adherence to the policies of separate development at both the ecclesiastical and sociopolitical levels. It betrayed a spirit of stubborn individualism, acting as if it could "go it alone," oblivious to the wider Christian community.[174] A painful example of this spirit occurred before the 1979 SACLA Conference, whose stated objective was to "[examine] together what

---

171. For a fascinating and generally sympathetic portrait of Heyns, see Neuhaus, *Dispensations*, 27–30.

172. See "Church is Easing Apartheid Stand," *New York Times*, October 26, 1986.

173. This belief that the church frequently *mirrors* society at large was strengthened by the 1987 split within the DRC. A small but influential splinter group of conservative Afrikaners, decrying the perceived liberal tendencies within the DRC, formed a rival Afrikaans Reformed Church. The denomination vowed to uphold the principles of rigid apartheid and a whites-only membership policy. This ecclesiastical split simply completed the chain of divisions within Afrikanerdom; from National Party to Broederbond to DRC, the once-solidly united Afrikaner community had now become decidedly fragmented. See Turner, "Afrikaner Church Needs 'Critical Solidarity,'" 645–46.

174. Bosch, "The Fragmentation of Afrikanerdom," 72. Also see Bosch's "You Can't Go It Alone!," 3.

it means to be faithful witnesses of Christ as Lord in South Africa today." When the invitation was received by the Northern Transvaal *Moderamen* of the DRC, it urged all local church councils to refrain from participating in the event. What reason did they advance for rejecting the call to participate? The group stated: "We, as Church, need not discover what it means to be faithful and effective witnesses of Jesus in South Africa. We daily study God's Word and know what it is."[175]

This self-sufficient attitude expressed by the *Moderamen* was a clear example of what Karl Barth once labeled "unevangelical conservatism." As De Gruchy points out:

> Whereas for Barth the danger of theological liberalism was that of undermining the historical continuity of the faith, the danger of theological conservatism was that of denying the need for the living Word of God to speak afresh to the Church in every situation. The Church comes to regard itself as the custodian of the truth, and believing that the content of the Gospel is securely held, it passes it on from one generation to the next. In the process it assumes that doing this involves faithfulness to the Gospel. In fact, says Barth, "In these circumstances it is not the Gospel which gives to the community the faith . . . on the contrary, it is the community which imposes on the Gospel its own faith, mode of thought and outlook."[176]

It was this "unevangelical conservatism" that kept the DRC from responding more creatively to its growing chorus of its critics during the apartheid era. With this historical background in mind, we now turn to investigate the life and career of David Bosch, surveying the development of his thought and highlighting the formative influences upon his life. We will show how he grew far beyond the narrow "unevangelical conservatism" of his Afrikaner Nationalist past, and observe how the crossing of numerous ethnic, geographic, and ideological frontiers profoundly influenced his own life.

---

175. Bosch, "The Fragmentation of Afrikanerdom," 72.

176. De Gruchy, "Toward a Confessing Church," 89. De Gruchy's citation from Barth is taken from Barth's *Church Dogmatics* IV/3, 818.

2

Bosch's Theological Pilgrimage
A Biographical Sketch

PROFILE OF THE YOUNG BOSCH[1]

DAVID JACOBUS BOSCH WAS born into an Afrikaner home on December 13, 1929, near the town of Kuruman in the Cape Province of South Africa.[2] Both his parents were "very simple rural folk," as were the overwhelming majority of Afrikaner families around him. His father worked a small farm. At the age of six, as a result of the severe 1933–34 drought, Bosch's family moved to the Western Transvaal, in the district of Schweizer-Reneke, where his father began maize farming, plowing the fields with oxen and donkeys. His father was an elder in the Dutch Reformed Church, and the family attended church when they were able.[3] Bosch began his schooling there.

Bosch described his own childhood as a very typical one. During the first fifteen years of his life, he rarely heard a word of English outside the classroom and knew very few English-speaking people.[4] From his earliest childhood, he began receiving a "Christian Nationalist" education. Bosch stated how

---

1. Most of the biographical data that follows is taken from a personal interview of Bosch by the author on September 8, 1986, hereafter cited as "Interview." For a sympathetic sketch of Bosch's life and work, see Saayman's "David J. Bosch: A Tribute to the Man," 6–10; "Some Personal Reflections," 214–28; and especially Kritzinger and Saayman, *Prophetic Integrity, Cruciform Praxis*.

2. It is of historical interest to note that Bosch's birthplace (Kuruman) was where Robert Moffat, the famed Scottish pioneer missionary, labored. Latourette, A *History of the Expansion of Christianity*, 5:345.

3. Bosch recalled that with no mechanized transport, getting to church was a time-consuming affair. They went to church by wagon or buggy approximately once a month. Because of the distance involved, they would journey all day Saturday to get to the meeting place, and would depart for home immediately after the Sunday service. Apart from this, the family maintained the typical Dutch Reformed devotional tradition of daily family Bible reading and Psalm singing. "Interview."

4. Ibid. Cf. Bosch, "Prisoners of History or Prisoners of Hope?," 14.

> . . . at a very early stage already our minds were influenced by teachers and other cultural and political leaders to see the English as perpetrators of all kinds of evil and as oppressors of the Afrikaner. We read poems of Totius and Jan Celliers, we read *Een eeuw van onrecht*—a century of injustice—and we were convinced beyond a shadow of doubt that no people were a patch on the English when it comes to arrogance, self-righteousness and brutal oppression of others. After all, my own mother could tell stories about the concentration camp to which she was taken at the age of eight.[5]

If the English were the "enemy" to the young Bosch, blacks were essentially non-persons. The typical Afrikaner attitude toward blacks was not overt hostility but benign neglect. Blacks were hewers of wood and drawers of water, "a part of the scenery but hardly a part of the human community . . . They belonged to the category of 'farm implements' rather than to the category 'fellow-human beings.'"[6]

The depth to which the dehumanization of blacks could go is illustrated in Bosch's own life. He recalled how he and his friends were once shocked to hear that some of the local Anglican and Roman Catholic priests actually shook hands with blacks! No self-respecting Afrikaner would have considered shaking hands with a black man; that would have "been a sign of full acceptance into the human community."[7]

After secondary school, Bosch went to Pretoria with the intention of training as a teacher. In May 1948, the pro-apartheid National Party was swept into power during his first year at the Teachers Training College. All the students there were solidly behind the National Party. "It was to us like a dream come true when the Nationalist Party won that victory. [We had] no reservations whatsoever."[8] Typical of the early period of Bosch's life is a Nationalist speech he delivered, in which he forcefully reminded his hearers of the providential deliverance of the Afrikaner *volk* and urged his fellows to solidarity and endurance in the continual struggle to develop a Christian Nationalist civilization. He concluded with a pointed admonition:

> . . . Ek besweer u by die heilige nagedagtenis van u voorouers, ek besweer u by u eie siele, bowe alles besweer ek u by die lewende God, om saam met Naboth aan elkeen wat u wil verlei van die regte spoor, beslis te antwoord: "Mag die Here my daarvoor bewaar, dat ek die erfenis van my vaders aan u sou gee!"
> Laat Jong Suid-Afrika sy nasionale erfenis bewaar, laat hy sy geloofsbelydenis onderteken, nie met sy naam nie, maar met sy lewe, en dan het ons niks te vrees vir die toekoms nie!
> "Daar's 'n nasie te lei,
> daar's 'n stryd te stry,
> daar's werk!

5. Bosch, "Prisoners of History or Prisoners of Hope?," 14–15.
6. Ibid., 15.
7. Ibid.
8. "Interview."

Part One: David Bosch in Context

> Daar's nie na guns of eer te kyk,
> daar's nie na links of regs te wyk,
> daar's net te swyg en aan te stryk.
> Komaan!"[9]

At university, Bosch became involved with the Student Christian Association (SCA), an ecumenical youth movement linked to the World Student Christian Federation. Following his first year at school Bosch participated in a SCA-sponsored summer evangelistic campaign at a lakeside tourist camp. There Bosch became convinced that God was calling him into the Christian ministry.[10]

Following the summer camp Bosch did a curious thing. Upon returning to his parents' farm he organized a Sunday service for the black laborers. A large crowd of black workers gathered. What happened next can only be described as a "conversion" of sorts.

> As I arrived, trembling, at the place of meeting, everybody came forward to shake hands with me! It was one of the most difficult moments in my life. When they saw my hesitation, they assured me that it was quite alright, that, in fact, it was normal for Christians to shake hands with one another! Only then did I discover that many of them were Christians: Methodists, Anglicans, members of the African Independent Churches, and so on. Previously I only thought of them as pagans and, at best, semi-savages.
>
> Looking back now to that day, thirty years ago, I guess I can say that that was the beginning of a turning-point in my life. Not that, from then on, I accepted Blacks fully as human beings. Far from it. But something began to stir in me that day, and all I can say is, that by the grace of God, it has been

---

9. I charge you by the holy memory of your ancestors, I charge you by your own souls, most of all I charge you by the living God, that together with Naboth, you should answer thus to each and every one who would try to mislead you: "The Lord forbid that I should give you the inheritance of my fathers!"
Let young South Africa preserve her national heritage. Let us affirm this confession of faith, not only in name, but with our lives, and then we have nothing to fear in the future!
"There's a nation to lead,
There's a battle to fight,
There's work!
Neither caring for the favor of people,
Nor withdrawing to the left or the right,
Only keep silent and march onward.
Come along!"
See Bosch, "Ons Geskiedenis in Gevaar" [Our history under threat], 14 (my translation).

10. Bosch commented that from the age of ten, he had desired to be a pastor, but at the time this had seemed far too lofty a goal. As a youth he struggled with an inferiority complex. But at the camp, he again sensed a call into the Christian ministry. As Bosch put it: "At camp during those two weeks, although I cannot pinpoint a time, I knew that I could do it [be a pastor]. I knew now that I had the intellectual capacity to make the grade. By then I had shed some of the inferiority feelings I think I had as a child. And then surely it was a spiritual experience . . . It was not a conversion experience . . . I only knew that when I went away from there I knew I had to change my plans." He also notes that this was a call, as far as he knew, to the white Dutch Reformed Church pastorate, not to mission. "Being a pastor in the DRC was as far as my horizon went. I had little understanding of a missionary calling" ("Interview").

growing ever since. Gradually, year by year, my horizons widened and I began to see people who were different from me with new eyes, always more and more clearly. I began to discover the simple, self-evident fact, that the things we have in common are more than the things which divide us.[11]

Within this short account, we observe two themes that will emerge frequently in our study of Bosch: a commitment to communicate the gospel to others and an ecumenical openness to those of other races and ecclesial traditions.

EARLY THEOLOGICAL ORIENTATION

When Bosch returned to university after that summer he changed to the pre-divinity course in languages. He went on to take two degrees from Pretoria: the M.A. in languages (Afrikaans, Dutch, German)[12] and the B.D. in theological studies. During that time Bosch sensed a further calling into mission work.[13] He also began to have some doubts about the adequacy of the apartheid system. "In the early 50's," Bosch recalls, "there were already signs that upset some of us, particularly . . . the removal of the Coloureds from the common voters roll. It was one of the first shocks; the honeymoon was over with the new National Party government."[14] This was a clear sign to Bosch and other theological students that something was wrong. By his final year in the B.D. program, when Bosch was chairman of the SCA branch at Pretoria, he was asked to go to the University of Witwatersrand to discuss the moral legitimacy of an apartheid government. When pressed to defend apartheid, Bosch realized that he could not. "I went to my vice-chairman and discussed it with him and said 'I can't defend it any more . . . That [invitation] forced me to make a decision, and break with the paradigm.'"[15]

11. Bosch, "Prisoners of History or Prisoners of Hope?," 15. In the interview, Bosch added: "I still can't quite understand today why I did that, because there was no preparation for it in my own background. I felt I had to do something about the state of affairs among the black people and so I organized services on a Sunday afternoon . . . The important thing that stuck was that I discovered that many of them were in fact Christians, and then all of a sudden, there was a different relationship. I had never known them as anything but farm-laborers, and now all of a sudden, even those who were not confessing Christians, were now put into a new context and into a different relationship with me. And I kept on doing that for another year or two when I went on holidays from school until my father sold the farm."

12. Bosch wrote a "Proefskrif" (master's thesis) in 1954 at the University of Pretoria, entitled 'Die Probleem van tyd in die epiek, aan die hand van 'Joernaal van Jorik.'" A copy of the thesis can be found at the University of South Africa Library.

13. After reading a book on DRC missionary work in Nyasaland (Malawi), Bosch recounted, "I just knew then that I had to go into 'black' work, either in Nigeria or Malawi . . . I never looked back after that. I knew that it was going to be mission work" ("Interview").

14. Ibid.

15. Ibid. Bosch elaborated on his feelings about this as a young Afrikaner. "As students, we discussed it [the political and moral inadequacies of apartheid], but *very tentatively*, because none of us dared to say it out loud and clear that we had broken with apartheid. It sounded like treason, like turning our backs upon our own people. The Afrikaner is like the German and very different from the Englishman and the American. The Afrikaner is a herd animal, and the Afrikaner follows a leader. They rally around a cause, around a person. The typical British individualness, of having a point of view irrespective of

Part One: David Bosch in Context

During his theological studies Professor E. P. Groenewald, the Professor of New Testament, particularly influenced him. Groenewald was a peculiar mix, in that he was the first person to work out a "scriptural foundation" for apartheid in 1947, but he was also a champion of the ecumenical movement, and a staunch defender of DRC participation in the fledgling World Council of Churches. Groenewald also introduced Bosch to the writings of Oscar Cullmann, particularly his *Christus und die Zeit*, a book that was to have a profound influence on his theological perspective. During his divinity studies Bosch also became acquainted with other DRC pastors and students, including Dr. Beyers Naudé, Dr. Ben Marais, Nico Smith, Willie Jonkers, and Johann Heyns.[16]

Before commencing missionary work, Bosch journeyed to the University of Basel for doctoral studies in New Testament under Oscar Cullmann.[17] Cullmann influenced Bosch deeply.[18] It is no accident that Bosch's thesis linked together two prominent themes within Cullmann's thought: mission and eschatology. These themes have dominated Bosch's career ever since.[19] Bosch graduated *magna cum laude* in 1956 after submitting a dissertation entitled *"Die Heidenmission in der Zukunftsschau Jesu."*[20]

---

whatever other people think, was totally absent. This has to do with our history of being pushed back. We always had to close ranks, and this is what we always did and that created safety. And to this day, it is one of the reasons why very few Afrikaners who today think the way I think can break out of the grip of the group ... [Afrikaners] constantly have to go back and be re-assured that they belong ... I won't use the word 'suffer,' but sometimes one *longs* to belong. One wants to have a place to feel at home, etc. and now you're neither this nor that" ("Interview").

16. Bosch, "The Fragmentation of Afrikanerdom and the Afrikaner Churches," 68. In the course of time, each man would come to renounce apartheid and the DRC's support of it. Cf. "Interview."

17. Bosch majored in New Testament with Cullmann as his principal supervisor, minoring in Systematic Theology under Karl Barth and Missiology under Johannes Dürr. Bosch chose Basel over the Free University of Amsterdam and Tübingen primarily because of his desire to study under Cullmann ("Interview").

18. Reviewing Bosch's doctoral thesis, Ludwig Wiedenmann actually labeled Bosch a "*Cullmannschüler.*" See Wiedenmann's *Mission und Eschatologie*, 126. Bosch himself admitted that Cullmann's eschatological distinction between the "now" and the "not yet" of the kingdom of God is one of the few theological insights that have remained absolutely constant in his thinking, although he acknowledged he had moved beyond the sharp Cullmannian distinctions between "salvation-history" and "world history" ("Interview").

19. For a full discussion of the eschatological dimension of Bosch's missiology, including the influence of Oscar Cullmann, see chapter 7.

20. Subsequently published under the same title in Zürich by Zwingli Verlag, 1959. The thesis can be summarized as follows: In *Die Heidenmission*, Bosch sought to address the question of the attitude of Jesus towards the Gentiles. Was mission to the Gentiles a central part of Jesus' earthly ministry, or was it a product of the early church's reflections on the universalistic implications of Jesus' teachings? Bosch tried to take a middle ground in the debate. He was convinced that "a positive attitude of the historical Jesus towards the Gentile mission was basic to a scriptural foundation of mission" [a position Bosch no longer maintains, see chapter 5 of this book] and Bosch's thesis attempted to show just such an attitude in the ministry and teaching of Jesus.

Although Jesus confined his activity to Israel during his lifetime, he envisaged a future inclusion of the Gentiles. In his earthly ministry, Jesus sought to call Israel to repentance and decision. Jesus commanded his followers to undertake a universal mission only *after* his death and his resurrection. Mission was now a possibility, thanks to his resurrection and the sending of the Spirit to empower his disciples.

While at Basel Bosch also came under the influence of Karl Barth, whose theological perspective has significantly influenced twentieth-century missiology. Although his thesis shows a familiarity with Barth's line of thought,[21] Barth's main impact on Bosch's thought was to emerge only later, in Bosch's more systematic attempts at a theological foundation for mission.

While at Basel, Bosch distanced himself further from the Nationalist Party and the politics of apartheid, although as yet he had no alternative "paradigm" to substitute in its place. He began to feel isolated from the Afrikaner mainstream. "By the time I arrived [in Switzerland]," Bosch recounted," I had little doubt about the fact that apartheid was immoral and unacceptable. If I say I had by that time broken with the paradigm, one must take that with a grain of salt, because I had not replaced it with another paradigm. It was still very haltingly true of myself. In my early days as a student, my viewpoint was inarticulate, but it *was* a shift out of the *laager*."[22]

During that time, Bosch also visited Willie Jonkers, a classmate from Pretoria studying at the Free University of Amsterdam under G. C. Berkouwer. Jonkers had completely broken from the apartheid paradigm and the Nationalist Party. Bosch recalls that the two days he spent with Jonkers helped him tremendously, because he finally met a fellow Afrikaner who could speak articulately to the apartheid issue and say why it was wrong. Jonkers thus played an important part in Bosch's development.[23]

MISSIONARY SERVICE (1957–1972)

In 1957 Bosch returned to South Africa to begin work as a DRC missionary among the Xhosa people in the Transkei. For nine years Bosch labored as a missionary pastor in Madwaleni. His work consisted of village evangelism and church-planting in a large, remote area. The country was rugged and accessible only by horse. Although those years had their disappointments, Bosch recalls, "These were our best years, absolutely wonderful."[24] Of the many lessons learned in his years of missionary service, two seem to have been of special significance for Bosch.

These events were clear eschatological signs that the "new age" had come, that God's *kairos* had arrived, that the time to "make disciples of all nations" had begun.

As Bosch summarized it: "Heidenmission ist erst möglich, nachdem Jesus durch seinen Bussruf das israelitische Volk in die Entscheidung gestalt hat, nachdem er für die 'Vielen' gestorben und auferweckt ist, und nachdem er seinen Heiligen Geist als 'Missionar' in die Völkerwelt gesandt hat" ["A mission to the Gentiles is not possible till *after* Jesus, by his call to repentance, has brought the Israelite people to a decision, *after* he has died for the 'many' and been raised from the dead, and *after* he has sent his Holy Spirit as 'missionary' into the world at large"] (my translation and emphasis). See Bosch, *Die Heidenmission*, 194.

21. Particularly Barth's exegetical work on Matt 28: 16–20. See Bosch, *Die Heidenmission*, 187, 189.
22. "Interview."
23. Ibid.
24. Ibid.

First, although Bosch acknowledged that he continued to hold deeply paternalistic attitudes toward black people, he believed that his missionary experience taught him to *trust* people, particularly his African Christian coworkers.[25] Second, his missionary experience helped him integrate theory and practice. By day, Bosch would be out among the people, learning from and visiting with them. By night, he would study, particularly in the areas of anthropology and religion, trying to integrate his experience in the Transkei with the scholarly insights of various anthropologists, theologians and missiologists. Through that study, his early theological convictions began to change considerably. Bosch identified this time as the decisive decade in his theological development. "I started with a very conservative theological framework and only moved to a wider approach towards the end of the 1960's."[26]

Although Bosch did not feel his missionary work at Madwaleni was finished, a severe back injury rendered him incapable of continuing with the rugged style of work (on horseback) that the job required. In 1967 Bosch was asked to serve as Senior Lecturer in Church History and Missiology at the DRC's Theological School in Decoligny, Transkei, training black pastors and evangelists. Bosch enjoyed teaching, but the limited scope of the work (four teachers, twenty students) impelled Bosch to seek other avenues of ministry beyond the little theological college.

Bosch became involved in the work of the Transkei Council of Churches, serving as its first president. This work provided much ecumenical contact with a variety of church traditions, particularly Roman Catholics and Anglicans. Bosch commented that "in the sixties . . . the Transkei was the only place in the Dutch Reformed Church setup where there were practical, structural, working relationships with people from other denominations. There was no other place where you had any practical expression of ecumenical contact."[27]

---

25. Bosch recounted a humorous anecdote of asking a black colleague to crank-start a water pump motor. Try as he could, Bosch's African coworker could not get the motor started when Bosch was present in the motor-room. Finally the man asked if he could attempt to start the engine without Bosch being present with him. Bosch was skeptical that the man could start the motor but he reluctantly agreed. Moments later, Bosch heard the sound of the engine puffing away. "How did you do it?" Bosch asked. "You could never do it when I was there!" And his African friend answered, "That was precisely the problem!" Bosch recalled that the African man was saying, in effect, "Your presence intimidated me, and the moment I was on my own and I knew that I had to do it because you are not there to do it for me, then I did it." "That was one of the most important lessons I had to learn," Bosch concluded. "It taught me that you have to trust people, and when you trust them, they can do the job" ("Interview").

26. Personal letter to the author, December 12, 1985. Elsewhere, Bosch has commented that: "I have come to the conclusion that the major changes in my theological thinking took place during the previous decade (the 'sixties), and not to the same extent during the 'seventies. Perhaps, for me, the 'seventies were, rather, a decade of clarification and consolidation of a theological position that had already developed reasonably clear contours before that time. After all, not many people change their views very radically once they have turned forty!" See his "How My Mind has Changed: Mission and the Alternative Community," 6.

27. "Interview."

Bosch's Theological Pilgrimage

That work was particularly significant for many of Bosch's DRC mission colleagues, most of whom had not been overseas and had grown up in an exclusively DRC setting.

A second avenue for self-expression that Bosch developed during his Decoligny years was writing, almost exclusively in the area of missiology. During that period Bosch published his doctoral thesis, wrote three short books,[28] and authored numerous articles. He also edited five books for the fledgling South African Missiological Society.[29] Bosch's written work from the period reflect two dominant themes: the missionary practice of the DRC, particularly the relationship of the "mother church" to the "daughter churches," and studies related to the biblical theology of mission. Most of them are in Afrikaans.

Bosch's two early Afrikaans books provide evidence of an emerging, wider theological framework, exemplifying both a broadening missiological approach and a departure from traditional Afrikaner sociopolitical perspectives. We will now outline their main arguments in order to understand some emerging themes in Bosch's early thought.

The first of the two booklets was *Jesus, Die Lydende Messias, En Ons Sendingmotief* [Jesus, the Suffering Messiah, and Our Missionary Motive].[30] This Afrikaans' publication was based largely on the fruit of Bosch's doctoral research. In it he applied his studies to the South African situation. Bosch argued: "Dit het algaande duidelik geworddat daar 'n enge verband bestaan tussen die via dolorosa van die Messias van Israel en die via missionis na die heidenvolke."[31] The mission of Jesus can be understood only in terms of the suffering servant of the Lord who, like a grain of wheat, must die in order to bear fruit. Jesus' encounters with the Gentiles exemplified this ethos of servanthood, as did the early church. It is with the same mindset of costly servanthood that the modern church must understand its motive for mission as well.[32]

The significance of his argument becomes apparent only when we consider the historical context in which they were written. The booklet appeared at an important crossroads in DRC missions policy. The Tomlinson Commission report, published in

---

28. Besides the two books mentioned in the text below, Bosch privately published a missionary training manual, *Julle sal My Getuies Wees* [You Shall Be My Witnesses], in 1967.

29. The books edited by Bosch were *Sendingwetenskap vandag: 'n terreinverkenning* [Missiology Today: A Survey] (1968); *Sodat hulle kan verstraan: Kommunikasie as sendingprobleem in Afrika* [So That They May Understand: Communication as a Missionary Problem in Africa] (1969); *Church and Culture Change in Africa* (1971); *Gemeeteopbou in Afrika* [Building Up the Church in Africa] (1972); and *Ampsbediening in Afrika* [The Ministry in Africa] (1972).

30. Published as the third volume in the *Kerk en Wêreld* series.

31. "It cannot be doubted that a strong bond exists between the *via dolorosa* of the Messiah of Israel and the *via missionis* to the Gentiles" (Bosch, *Jesus, Die Lydende Messias*, 32; my translation).

32. See Saayman, "David J. Bosch: A Tribute to the Man," 7. Bosch contrasts this with three other (improper) motives for mission. Some have been motivated on humanitarian grounds to help the *"arme heidene"* (poor heathen), filled with patronizing attitudes of cultural superiority. Others have been motivated by the goal of establishing the kingdom of God on earth, in optimistic, liberal fashion. Still others went out with a colonialistic urge, seeking to realize the political ambitions of their own nations. See *Jesus, Die Lydende Messias*, 34–35.

1955, had uncovered statistical evidence of a large number of unevangelized blacks within South Africa. That prompted DRC mission enthusiasts to promote an expanded evangelistic outreach among them.[33] Bosch, however, discerned non-theological factors at work among some of the proponents. Numerous DRC missiologists and politicians linked the evangelization of blacks to the unfolding government policies of separate development and Afrikaner solidarity. Missionary work was therefore (unconsciously?) coupled to the defense of the *volk* and the preservation of a white-dominated South Africa.[34] Bosch warned against such mixed motives in strong terms.

> Wat is die uiteindelike doel van die sending wat so gemotiveer word? Is dit behoud van 'n blanke volk in Suid-Afrika—of is dit die stigting van 'n kerk van Christus wat sy wederkoms tegemoetgaan? Is dit diens aan Suid-Afrika—of diens aan God? Is dit gehoorsaamheid aan die stem van sentiment en eie bloed—of gehoorsaamheid aan die laaste bevel van Christus? Anders gestel: Het ons dit by hierdie sendingmotivering te doen met 'n skaap in wolfslere—of is dit dalk 'n wolf in skaapsklere?[35]

Any missionary enthusiasm must be tempered with the realization that mission in Christ's way is *the way of the cross, the way of costly servanthood toward others*. Anything less was simply religious propaganda and prone to ideological manipulation.[36]

The second booklet that exemplified Bosch's broadening missiological approach was *Sending in Meervoud* [Mission in the Plural], coauthored with his medical missionary colleague, G. Jansen.[37] It was written to clarify the theological relationship between proclamation and social service in the church's missionary outreach.

In the history of Christian missions, medical work has nearly always accompanied the proclamation of the gospel. In most instances, however, the medical missions were an afterthought, *theologically* speaking; they had not been adequately integrated (at the theological level) with the traditional missionary tasks of

---

33. Saayman, "David Bosch: A Tribute to the Man," 7.

34. Bosch exposed these tendencies by citing the writings of M. D. C. de Wet Nel, an Afrikaner ideologue. De Wet Nel maintained that "Sendingwerk is die enigste weg waarlangs ons ons toekoms as blanke volk kan verseker . . . Elke seun en dogter wat Suid-Afrika liefhet, moet hulleself, in een of ander vorm, tot aktiewse sendingaksie inspan, want sendingwerk is nie alleen Godswerk nie, dis ook volkswerk." *[Mission work is the only way whereby we can insure our future as a white nation. . . . Each son and daughter who loves South Africa, must themselves, in one or another form, actively contribute to the missionary effort, because mission work is not only God's work; it is also work for the nation]* (my translation and emphasis). See Bosch, *Jesus, die Lydende Messias*, 36–37.

35. "What is the end goal of mission with such a motivation? Is it to maintain the white people in South Africa—or is it the foundation of the church of Christ . . . ? Is it to serve South Africa—or to serve God? Is it to hear together the sentimental voice of our own blood—or to hear together the last command of Christ? Have we, by this missionary motive, created a sheep in wolf's clothes—or is it perhaps a wolf in sheep's clothes?" (ibid., 36–37; my translation).

36. Ibid., 37.

37. Published as the fifth volume in the *Kerk en Wêreld* series.

proclamation and church planting.[38] Although the scope and quality of medical missions grew dramatically, they continued to be labeled "auxiliary services" by most mission agencies, an indication that they were regarded as being of secondary importance.[39] By the early 1960s, increasing costs and the rise of national health services in many traditional "mission fields" forced the Christian community to rethink the theological basis of medical mission work. Should Christian medical work continue to be considered an "auxiliary service" or did it deserve to be considered as an aspect of mission *in its own right?* In light of the ever-increasing costs and questions, should Christian medical mission continue at all? At bottom was a theological debate concerning the nature of Christian mission. Bosch and Jansen's book was a part of the re-thinking process within the DRC.

In South Africa as elsewhere, there was a rapidly growing network of missionary hospitals and schools. Yet these institutions were still considered *hulpdienste* ("auxiliary services").[40] Bosch sought to address this concern in an essay entitled "Sending Deur Woord en Daad" [Mission through Word and Deed]. He argued that it is unbiblical to subordinate deed under word, *diakonia* under *kerugma*. While Bosch did not confuse the two concepts, he refused to divide them either.[41] In the life of Jesus and the early church, service and proclamation were complementary to each other. Both remain indispensable aspects of the gospel of Christ.[42]

For Bosch, the theological basis for medical missions is rooted in the compassion of God. The Scriptures reveal a God who acts with compassionate love toward his creation, particularly through the healing ministry of Jesus. In the New Testament the term used almost without exception for these works of love is *diakonia*. Inasmuch as medical missions express God's compassion through diaconal works of healing, they remain an essential task of the church.[43] In addition, medical missions function as a sign of God's kingdom. They point beyond themselves, giving witness to the reality of the complete healing God intends for the world. The ultimate purpose of medical missions, then, is not simply to alleviate human need. As signs of the Lordship of God over all life they have an essential *witness-bearing* function.[44] It

---

38. Kritzinger et al., *You Will Be My Witnesses*, 70.

39. Saayman notes that in South Africa, medical missions frequently had the function of enticing an otherwise reluctant people into hearing the proclamation of the Word, which was considered to be the primary goal. See Saayman, "David J. Bosch: A Tribute to the Man," 7.

40. Bosch and Jansen, *Sending in Meervoud*, 20–22.

41. It should be noted that Bosch had not completely resolved the issue of the *primacy* of evangelism within the mission of the church. Although he argued that subsuming one concept under the other is unbiblical, he still referred to proclamation *(kerugma)* as *"the primus inter pares"* (ibid., 10–14).

42. Ibid., 10–19. Twice in his essay Bosch cites with approval the famous dictum of the 1952 Willingen Missionary Conference of the I.M.C.: "This witness is given by proclamation, fellowship and service."

43. Ibid., 12–13, 38–40. See also Bosch, "Die diens van die genesing in sendingperspektief," 156.

44. Kritzinger et al., *You Will Be My Witnesses*, 71.

is precisely at this point that Christian medical service finds its missiological foundation and significance.[45]

In these early writings we note that Bosch raised themes that were to remain central to his thought. We also note that by this time Bosch had begun to raise the ire of his fellow Afrikaners, by publicly questioning some of the government's policies and criticizing the DRC's support of apartheid.

Inevitably, these departures from Afrikaner "orthodoxy" isolated Bosch from the mainstream of Afrikanerdom and the DRC. He was no longer a *"ware Afrikaner,"* a true Afrikaner, and began to pay a price for his stand.[46] Despite Bosch's outstanding academic credentials, he was reportedly refused a position on the DRC theological faculty at the University of Pretoria. The appointment went instead to fellow classmate Carel Boshoff, a member of the Broederbond, even though Boshoff did not have a doctoral degree.[47] Instead, in 1972 Bosch accepted the invitation to become Professor of Missiology at the University of South Africa in Pretoria. Bosch and his wife did so, however, with some trepidation. As he described it, they "moved back to Pretoria, very afraid of Afrikaners, very afraid of white people. We were returning home, in a sense, but returning *very different* from what we were when we had left [Pretoria] in the early 1950's."[48] With his appointment, a new phase in Bosch's career began, to which we now turn.

PROFESSOR OF MISSIOLOGY (1972–1992)

The University of South Africa (UNISA) was unique among academic institutions in apartheid-era South Africa. It was a fully interracial university with staff from all ethnic groups, and whose student body extended throughout southern Africa because coursework was done by extension. UNISA was also unique because of its theology faculty, described as "a bastion of those theologians rejected and discarded by the Broederbond [dominated] NGK establishment,"[49] and as a "faculty-in-exile

---

45. Bosch cites Hendrik Kraemer approvingly at this point: "... a missionary should live by the ardent desire that all men will surrender to Christ as the Lord of their lives. Whosoever does not stress that, does not sufficiently consider the passionate prophetic and apostolic spirit of the Gospel. The core of the Christian revelation is that Jesus Christ is the sole legitimate Lord of all human lives.....[Therefore] ... all activities of the Christian church . . . only get their right missionary foundation and perspective if they belong as intrinsically to the category of witness as preaching or evangelization" (Bosch and Jansen, *Sending in Meervoud*, 25, citing Hendrik Kraemer, *The Christian Message in a Non-Christian World*).

46. For an in-depth socio-psychological study of the roots, formative influences, and current attitudes of more than a score of "dissident Afrikaners," including Bosch, see Louw-Potgeiter, "The Social Identity of Dissident Afrikaners."

47. Serfontein, *Apartheid, Change and the NG Kerk*, 101.

48. "Interview."

49. Serfontein, *The Brotherhood of Power*, 174.

for anti-apartheid, anti-Broederbond NGK theologians."[50] Bosch's move to UNISA placed him, officially at least, on the periphery of the DRC.

During his time at the university, Bosch distinguished himself as an author and administrator. Bosch published more than a dozen books and booklets,[51] numerous book-length study guides,[52] and a host of journal articles and edited works. As a "systematic missiologist," his writings covered a broad range of missiological themes. They can be grouped into the following categories: (1) biblical and theological foundations for mission; (2) the mission and unity of the church; (3) the theology of evangelism and its relationship to justice, service and social transformation; (4) issues in African and Black theology, particularly the problem of evil and the nature of God; (5) the communication of the gospel, particularly in the African context; (6) mission and theological education; (7) missionary practice and spirituality; (8) the ecumenical/evangelical debate in mission; (9) the meaning of mission in the polarized and violent South African context; (10) the academic discipline of missiology; (11) the theology of religions; and (12) the theology of liberation.

One key ingredient contributing to Bosch's academic stature as a missiologist was his facility in languages. He is conversant in many languages, including Afrikaans, English, German, Dutch, French, and Xhosa. His linguistic abilities enabled Bosch to play a role as a "bridge builder" between the theological and cultural gulf that frequently divides Continental, Anglo-Saxon and African missiologies.

Besides Bosch's prolific work as a teacher and author, he was also an active academic administrator and editor. As a practicing missiologist, Bosch helped found the Southern African Missiological Society (SAMS), a multiracial and ecumenical fraternity of mission scholars, serving as its General Secretary from its formation in 1968 until his death.[53] A major aspect of the work of the SAMS is the production of *Missionalia*, the Society's missiological journal. From its inception in 1973, Bosch served as its editor. As the dean of the Faculty of Theology at UNISA, Bosch also served as editor of the Faculty's journal *Theologia Evangelica*.

---

50. Serfontein, *Apartheid, Change and the NG Kerk*, 193.

51. Besides the aforementioned *Die Heidenmission in der Zukunftsschau Jesu*; *Jesus, die lydende Messias, en ons Sendingmotief*; *Julle sal My Getuies Wees*; and *Sending in Meervoud*; see also *Het Evangelie in Afrikaans Gewaad*; *A Spirituality of the Road*; *Witness to the World*; *The Church as Alternative Community*; *The Lord's Prayer: Paradigm for a Christian Lifestyle*; *Transforming Mission*; and posthumously, *Believing in the Future*.

52. These are part of a series of publications for UNISA's massive extension education program, including *Introduction to Missiology MSR 101*; *Theology of Mission MSR 201*; *Church and Mission MSR 301*; and *Theology of Religions MSR 303*.

53. Saayman has commented: "In the fragmented South African society and churches, the value of the SAMS as a rallying point and forum for the honest exchange of views, cannot easily be overestimated. It is certainly no exaggeration to suggest that the personal integrity of David Bosch has a lot to do with the credibility of the SAMS itself" ("David J. Bosch: A Tribute to the Man," 8).

Part One: David Bosch in Context

BOSCH THE ECUMENICAL CHURCHMAN

It would be inadequate, however, to understand Bosch only through the lens of his academic career. He was also a committed churchman and ecumenist, seeking to contribute to the life and health of the church both in South Africa and globally. Within the multidenominational context of UNISA, Bosch devoted his theological energies to three separate but interrelated issues, three prominent missiological frontiers:[54] probing the meaning and communication of the gospel in Africa today; developing new models to overcome the "evangelical"/"ecumenical" polarization in Protestant missiology; and forging a theological and practical response to apartheid, addressing both the South African state and the Christian community. These three concerns form the basis for most of his pre-*Transforming Mission* writing and serve to integrate his theology around the central question: *What is the meaning of authentic Christian witness in our day?* We will frequently return to these themes as we probe Bosch's theology of mission and evangelism. We introduce them here in summary form.

Probing the Meaning and Communication of the Gospel in Africa

Since the early 1970s, Bosch contributed to the multi-faceted issue of communicating the gospel in Africa. He addressed issues related to both "African Theology" and "Black Theology." According to Saayman, Bosch was widely appreciated for his perceptive and sympathetic approach to African theology, especially the complex issue of communicating the gospel in the context of African traditional religions.[55]

Bosch also wrote an in-depth study of the communication process in Africa, *Het Evangelie in Afrikaans Gewaad* [The Gospel in African Robes] which analyzed the communication of the gospel in relation to the African understanding of God and the problem of evil in African society.[56]

---

54. For a summary of the development of his own theological thought between 1972–82, see Bosch's article "How My Mind Has Changed," 6–10.

55. Saayman has commented on Bosch's contribution to the Umpumulo Missiological Institute's 1972 "Relevant theology for Africa" Consultation: "At this consultation there was a strong undercurrent of black/white tension on the question whether white theologians could contribute in any way to such a relevant theology. Yet when problems arose in the discussions about the concept of *God*, the assembled theologians and pastors asked David Bosch to read an unscheduled paper on 'God through African eyes' in an attempt to gain greater clarity." See Saayman, "David J. Bosch: A Tribute to the Man," 7. Bosch's paper was later published as "God through African Eyes." Also see Verstraelen, "Africa in David Bosch's Missiology," 8–39.

56. Bosch, "Missionary Theology in Africa," 122. The chapters in *Het Evangelie in Afrikaans Gewaad* were "Op weg naar een theologia Africana" [Towards an African theology]; "God in Afrika: Gevolgtrekkingen voor de verkondiging" [God in Africa: Implications for the Kerygma]; "Een missionair dilemma in Afrika: Het probleem van het kwaad" [A Missionary Problem in Africa: The Problem of Evil]; and "Stromingen in de Zuidafrikaanse Zwarte Theologie" [Currents and Crosscurrents in South African Black Theology]. All but the first essay was republished in English translation.

Another dimension of the gospel in Africa was the rise of Black Theology as it emerged in North America and South Africa. As early as 1972, Bosch showed an awareness and critical appreciation of the movement, interacting with such leaders as Steve Biko, Manas Buthelezi, James Cone, and others. It is significant that his essay "Currents and Crosscurrents in South African Black Theology" was one of the few white contributions included in Cone and Wilmore's standard work on Black Theology.[57]

Bosch also made an impact on the church in Africa through his contributions at regional and continental Christian gatherings. Particularly significant was his impassioned address on the "Renewal of Christian Community in Africa Today" at the 1976 Pan African Christian Leadership Assembly (PACLA) in Nairobi.[58] Bosch spoke of the need for the church to be an "alternative community," embodying within its own life the values of God's kingdom and thus serving as an agent of reconciliation and a sign of hope for the world. Bosch appealed to the cross as the model for the life of the church in Africa. In the cross, God's model of costly reconciliation was demonstrated, and serves as a challenge for believers to walk in its way. Of all Bosch's public addresses, this message has been the most widely disseminated.

Overcoming the "Evangelical"/"Ecumenical" Debate in Mission

The second missiological frontier to which Bosch devoted himself was the divide in modern Protestant missiology between the so-called evangelicals and ecumenicals. His major work *Witness to the World* was, in large part, an attempt to describe this controversy and propose a way forward.[59] Three particular elements of Bosch's work deserve special mention.

First, Bosch was an *active participant* in both movements. In the 1970s Bosch attended a variety of conferences, including the South African Congress on Mission and Evangelism (Durban, 1973);[60] the International Congress on World Evangelization (Lausanne, 1974); the Pan African Christian Leadership Assembly (Nairobi, 1976); and the South African Christian Leadership Assembly (Pretoria, 1979).

In 1980, Bosch was the only South African to attend both of the major world conferences on Christian mission: the WCC's Conference on Mission and Evangelism at Melbourne, as well as the LCWE's Consultation on World Evangelization at Pattaya,

57. For Bosch's evaluation of Black Theology, see chapter 4.

58. For the text of Bosch's address, see Bosch, "Renewal of Christian Community in Africa Today," 92–102.

59. Bosch commented: "In 1978, when I was writing *Witness to the World*, the evangelical/ecumenical issue was uppermost in my mind . . . In my case, it was existential. I had this struggle going on in my own theological mind and my own existential heart. It wasn't simply an attempt to balance the two. I was looking for a way forward, beyond both of them" ("Interview").

60. The South African Council of Churches and African Enterprise, an evangelical mission agency, jointly sponsored this unique gathering, at which both Billy Graham and the WCC's Hans-Ruedi Weber spoke. Bosch addressed the gathering on the subject of "Evangelism and Special Needs." For the text of his address see Cassidy, ed., *I Will Heal Their Land*, 207–12.

Thailand. Bosch played a major role in four other world-level gatherings in the 1980s. In June 1982, Bosch was a main speaker at the Grand Rapids Consultation on the Relationship between Evangelism and Social Responsibility (CRESR), co-sponsored by the LCWE and the World Evangelical Fellowship.[61] In June 1983, the World Evangelical Fellowship sponsored Wheaton '83, an international conference on the nature and mission of the church. Bosch was involved in the Consultation on the Church's Response to Human Need, and was on the drafting committee for the Consultation's influential "Transformation" statement.[62] In March 1987 Bosch was a participant in a WCC Consultation on Evangelism in Stuttgart, where he served on the drafting committee for the Consultation's statement on evangelism.[63] In 1989, Bosch served as a Section leader at the WCC's Conference on World Mission and Evangelism in San Antonio, Texas.

Second, Bosch *described the historical and theological roots* of the ecumenical/evangelical division. We will discuss his analysis of the controversy, with particular reference to his critique of the 1980 Melbourne and Pattaya meetings, in chapter 3.

Finally, Bosch attempted to *develop a way beyond* the evangelical/ecumenical controversy. Bosch believed that both sides had been impoverished by ignoring the concerns of the other. As a result, both failed to develop a truly adequate theology of mission for our era. Bosch gave particular attention to the development of more adequate concepts of "mission" and "evangelism." The two concepts, while closely related to one another in God's salvific intention for the world, should not be confused or identified—as they often are in both evangelical and ecumenical circles. We will deal extensively with these issues in chapter 6.

Developing a Christian Response to the South African Conflict

Bosch also devoted his energies to the South African dilemma and the challenge it represented to the integrity of the Gospel and the mission of the church. He was a critic of the apartheid system for many years, and worked for change in the pro-apartheid stance of the South African government and of the DRC. Bosch's critique focused on exposing the *ideological* nature of apartheid, and the Afrikaner "civil religion" in which it is embedded.[64] The heart of matter, according to Bosch, was that the Afrikaner

---

61. Bosch delivered the paper "Perspectives on Evangelism and Social Responsibility," which was later published as "In Search of a New Evangelical Understanding," 63–83. See also his and Chris Sugden's article "From Partnership to Marriage," 26–27.

62. Bosch delivered the paper "Evangelism and Social Transformation," 43–55. For the final text of the statement "Transformation: The Church in Response to Human Need" (which Bosch helped draft) see *Trans* 1/1 (January 1984) 23–28.

63. See the "Statement of the Stuttgart Consultation on Evangelism" in the WCC/CWME's *A Monthly Letter on Evangelism*.

64. See the following works of Bosch: "Prisoners of History or Prisoners of Hope?," 14–18; "Racism and Revolution: Response of the Churches in South Africa," 13–20; "Die religiösen Wurzeln der gegenwärtigen Polarisation zwischen Schwarz und Weiss in Südafrika," 98–105; "The Roots and Fruits

people are prisoners of their own history, afraid of the future. The ideological nature of apartheid had seemingly blinded most Afrikaners to any future besides the one held out by the South African government. Yet in this desperate situation, Christians had to remain hopeful, for it was not "fate" that controlled the destiny of South Africa, but the Lord of history.[65]

In his critique of apartheid, Bosch also emphasized the cruciality of ecclesiology. Tragically, the DRC served as a bulwark of the status quo rather than the vanguard of change. A truly biblical understanding of the church, Bosch argued, demanded that it be both an agent of judgment and of reconciliation within every society. Drawing on elements within Reformed and Anabaptist ecclesiologies, Bosch argued for a concept of the church as an "alternative community," believing that this concept provided a model or paradigm by which South African Christians could transform their society. It is precisely as Christians work for the renewal and unity of the church, and live out the implications of their faith in the world, that they most effectively challenge the values and standards of the society around them. The church is not to copy the world's agendas or strategies; instead it must furnish an alternative vision of reality, of life in the kingdom of God. The concrete political and evangelistic implications of the church as "alternative community" will be explored in chapter 8.

The concept of the church as "alternative community" is grounded on the reconciling work of Christ. On the cross, Jesus reconciled the world to God, and broke down all barriers that divide humankind. Thus all differences among persons (racial, economic, linguistic, cultural, religious), while still real, have been *relativized* in Christ. It is thus wrong, even heretical, to divide the one church of Jesus Christ by ascribing "an unduly high value to racial and cultural distinctiveness."[66] This would raise the value of one's *national* identity above one's identity *in Christ*. Yet this is exactly what the white Reformed churches of South Africa had done and, as such, they have been perpetrating what Bosch called "nothing but a heresy."[67] Instead of polarizing the society by highlighting racial, ethnic, social, or economic distinctions, the mission of the church is to be an agent of reconciliation and a witness to the unity won for the world in Christ. We will further explore the implications of Christ's reconciliation for the unity and mission of the church in chapter 9.

Apart from his writings, Bosch was actively involved in the struggle against apartheid in other ways. Bosch was a major impetus behind the 1979 SACLA gathering, serving as chairman of the executive committee and delivering four plenary addresses. He was also a leading proponent of the 1982 *Ope Brief* [Open Letter], which

---

of Afrikaner Civil Religion," 14–35; "The Fragmentation of Afrikanerdom and the Afrikaner Churches," 61–73; "Afrikaner Civil Religion and the Current South African Crisis," 23–30; "The Afrikaner and South Africa," 203–16; "The Christian Church in a Revolutionary Situation."

65. Bosch, "Afrikaner Civil Religion and the Current South African Crisis," 29–30.

66. Bosch, "Mission and the Alternative Community," 9.

67. These were the stinging words Bosch used to describe his own DRC at the 1982 Pretoria Theological Conference. See Serfontein, *Apartheid, Change and the NG Kerk*, 176–81.

publicly condemned apartheid and urged the DRC to pursue visible unity with its black "sister" churches. As an editor of *Perspektief op die Ope Brief*, he was involved in the discussion of the Open Letter's significance. Since its launch in 1985, Bosch was involved in African Enterprise's National Initiative for Reconciliation and in 1988 became its National Chairman. In the late 1980s Bosch participated with a variety non-governmental organizations that were seeking a non-military resolution to the growing struggle between the apartheid regime and various internal and external liberation movements, including the National Convention Movement, the Five Freedoms Forum, and the Movement Towards Democracy, attempting to facilitate the transformation of South Africa.[68]

Perhaps the most telling evidence of Bosch's concern for the future of South Africa was his refusal to leave. In 1985 and again in 1987 Bosch was offered the prestigious Chair of Mission and Ecumenics at Princeton Theological Seminary. Bosch made the difficult decision to refuse the offer, believing that he could not leave South Africa during such a dangerous and historic time in her history.[69]

We have seen some of the complexities of Bosch's Afrikaner heritage, and have been introduced to Bosch's life story. We have discussed his professional and academic achievements, and highlighted three central aspects of his recent work: the meaning and communication of the gospel in Africa; overcoming the missiological division between evangelicals and ecumenicals; and developing an appropriate Christian response to the troubled South African situation. We now turn to analyze Bosch's theological method in order to gain insight into the theoretical foundations of his missiological approach.

---

68. Kritzinger and Saayman, *Prophetic Integrity, Cruciform Praxis*, 92–96.
69. Personal correspondence with the author, February 24, 1986.

Part Two

Bosch's Theology of Mission and Evangelism

3

Theology, Mission, and Missiology
Bosch's Theological Method

HAVING REVIEWED BOSCH'S LIFE and work, we now turn to consider some basic presuppositions that undergirded his theology of mission. In this section we will not attempt an exhaustive analysis of Bosch's theological method; instead we seek rather to provide a concise summary of Bosch's approach to the missiological task. We will analyze Bosch's conception of the relation of theology and mission, and probe his understanding of the nature and function of missiology at both the academic and ecclesial levels.

THEOLOGICAL REFLECTION AND THE CHURCH'S PRAXIS

In his landmark essay "The Missionary Obligation of Theology," Herbert Jackson lamented that "mission" and "theology" appeared to be mutually exclusive categories in the life of the church.[1] In Jackson's understanding, Christianity emerged as an *event*— a dramatic revelation of a God who entered human history in the person of Jesus of Nazareth. The heart of the Christian gospel revolves around historical events of his life death and resurrection. Mission, Jackson argued, was essentially an active witness to the historical event of God's self-revelation in Christ. Yet along with the "event-character" of Christianity, Jackson posited a "theologizing trait." Human beings have always inquired about the *meaning* of this revelation. Christians through the ages have reflected upon and "theologized" about the nature of God and his purposes for the world. Yet these two important dimensions of the Christian faith have often seemed to be mutually exclusive in the history of the church.[2]

---

1. Jackson, "Missionary Obligation," 1–6.
2. As Jackson put it: "These two 'facts'—the event-character of Christianity and the theologizing trait

Part Two: Bosch's Theology of Mission and Evangelism

Jackson went on to argue that during those generations when Christianity was "event" oriented—and winning people to the Christian faith—the era was characterized by a lack of formal, theological output. When, on the other hand, the church spent its energies systematizing and "theologizing," it was marked by an absence of missionary activity. He concluded that practical mission work and theological reflection appeared mutually incompatible. He urged, however, that new understandings of theology and mission be formulated so that the apparent incompatibility could be resolved.

In his writings David Bosch attempted to provide such a reformulation in order that the dynamic categories of theology and mission, theory and practice, might be brought together in a creative tension. Against Jackson, Bosch maintained that "theology" has *always* been present in the words and actions of the church in mission. Theology, according to Bosch, concerns "the basic presuppositions and underlying principles that give direction to our ecclesiastical activities."[3] We limit the nature of theology unduly if we consider it valid only when it has taken on the systematic form of creeds, dogmatic treatises and conciliar statements. Theology does not become theology only when it is theoretical, verbal, and systematic.[4] In the Bible and much of today's "Third World" theology is primarily oral rather than written. It emerges through hymn, parable, celebration, dance, and story. "Anyone who denies that one can practice proper theology in such categories," Bosch argued, "will have to prove that the Bible is not a theological book."[5]

This perspective is helpful when we consider that the missionary enterprise, due to its "event-character," has frequently been accused of neglecting to engage in theological reflection on its task, methods and theoretical foundations. While this charge is undoubtedly valid in many cases, Bosch nevertheless emphasized that "behind every missionary enterprise in the various periods of missionary revival there was indeed theological reflection, albeit not always formally articulated. Theology was, therefore, decidedly not absent. No mission is possible without theology."[6]

---

of religious man—are both essential . . . intrinsic to the work of God and the being of man. Yet through nearly two millennia, the two 'facts' have remained parallel but largely isolated aspects of our faith. More tragically . . . whenever and wherever the 'event' quality has been dynamic there has invariably been mission; whenever and wherever the paramount concern has been with theology, or dogma, mission has been little in evidence or at best has been carried forward by a small group within the Church . . ." (ibid., 1–2).

3. Bosch, *Witness*, 24.

4. Bosch elaborates on this point: "Something does not become theology only when it has been neatly systematized. Thus Paul's letters do not become theology only after certain 'truths' have been distilled from them and systematized . . . they are theology *to begin with*. In the same way the gospel according to Matthew is theology *to begin with*—it does not become so only when some modern theologian has written some book entitled 'The Kingdom of Heaven According to Matthew.' In the same way any modern-day sermon or action of the church is theology—even if not necessarily *sound theology!*" (Bosch, *Theology of Mission 201*, 13).

5. Ibid., 12; cf. Bosch, "Salvation Tomorrow *and* Today," 20–21.

6. Bosch, *Witness*, 24.

The reverse, however, *is* possible. All too frequently in the church's history there has been "theology" without mission. Church history abounds with eras during which the church, due to internal or external pressures, seemed incapable of reaching beyond its immediate frontier. Neglecting its relationship to the world, the church's energies were consumed instead with ecclesiastical self-analysis and doctrinal refinement.[7] Bosch questioned whether much of this can be called *genuine* theology. "Authentic theology, after all, does not develop where the church is preoccupied with herself or where she is desperately erecting defensive barricades on her own soil. What we then get is not theology but rather orthodoxy. Salvation becomes a treasure the church has at her magnanimous disposal, the gospel self-evidently a possession of the church, the Kingdom of God an institution, and new life in Christ a good habit."[8] Instead Bosch believed that authentic theology develops where the church lives "in a dialectical relationship with the world . . . where the Church is engaged in mission, in the widest sense of the word. Internal renewal of the Church and missionary awakening belong together."[9]

Indeed, Bosch affirmed that authentic theology cannot arise except through missionary practice.[10] He maintained (with Martin Kähler) that mission is "the mother of theology," for it is precisely at the point where faith meets unbelief that the most dynamic theological reflection takes place.[11] Bosch called not simply for a new theological definition of *mission*, but also for a redefinition of theology itself. Authentic theology will always be "missionary theology" in the sense that reflection on God and his purposes can only be accomplished as God's people are involved in the world through concrete acts of service and witness.[12]

Positively speaking, Bosch posited that theology and mission stand together in a relationship of dynamic, *creative tension*. Each needs to take the other seriously.

7. For example, Bosch highlights the post-Reformation era of "Protestant scholasticism" as an example of the dominance of the "theologizing trait." Theology became focused on the church itself, "especially on the past and on correct doctrine . . . In Lutheran orthodoxy in particular, mission disappeared completely beyond the horizon of Church and theology" (*Witness*, 123–24).

8. Ibid., 25. Elsewhere, Bosch has commented that when the missionary dimension was neglected, theology inevitably became a "luxury of the world-dominating Church." Following the eight great Ecumenical Councils, theological development was perceived to have finished. The "Christendom" mentality took over. By the late Middle Ages, theology had "positioned itself outside or above the conflicts of this world and increasingly defined itself as a metaphysical science of speculation, with philosophy as its only 'outside' partner, in the process forfeiting completely the missionary thrust that had given it birth." See Bosch, "An Emerging Paradigm for Mission," 492.

9. Bosch, *Witness*, 25. Walbert Bühlmann, the noted Roman Catholic missiologist, has made a similar observation. See his *The Coming of the Third Church*, 8.

10. That theology and mission can become mutually estranged from one another is a constant danger. At times, those engaged in theological reflection reject any practical application of their work, "almost as a matter of principle." Similarly, those doing practical activities have at times refused "to be guided by theological reflection" (Bosch, *Witness*, 22).

11. Ibid., 24. Bosch elaborates on this concept frequently in his writings. See esp. *Witness*, 137–39; "Systematic Theology and Mission," 165–89; and "Missionary Theology in Africa," 106–7. In this regard, also see Allmen, "The Birth of Theology," 37–55.

12. Bosch, "An Emerging Paradigm for Mission," 492–95.

Part Two: Bosch's Theology of Mission and Evangelism

This was precisely the approach of the apostle Paul. He integrated his extensive missionary activities with intense theological reflection. Paul's theology decisively influenced his practice; conversely, the way he responded to practical matters had a clear bearing on his theology.[13]

Bosch summarized the dynamic relationship between the church's theologizing and the church's missionary practice in the form of four guidelines.[14] First, theology is a science of the church, and should be done *in solidarity with the church*. Its main task is to "explore the nature and content of the gospel," asking whether the church's present attitudes and practices faithfully reflect the gospel or not. This first guideline implies that theology can never be "denominational" in its orientation, but only in allegiance to the whole church of Jesus Christ. The church's only critical criterion of judgment is the gospel itself, and not any denominational principle. It also implies that theology cannot be practiced from a "safe" or "objective" location, in isolation from the Christian community.[15]

Second, theology is *a critical science*, and should ask the church whether, in its words and deeds, it is living up to its calling as the church of Jesus Christ. Despite the fact that the church's future, like its past, is likely to be filled with failures, "theology nevertheless persists in challenging the Church to become what, in Christ, she already is, and to cease being what she reflects in practice."

Third, theology is *a hazardous enterprise*. Theology, including its premises as well as its conclusions, is not above making grave mistakes. It is pre-eminently a human task, prone to failure and error. The theologian, along with the rest of the church, knows only in part (1 Cor 13:12). Thus theology is always an imperfect approximation of the truth, and the theologian should be humble in his or her pronouncements.[16]

---

13. Bosch, *Witness*, 24. In *Theology 201*, 13–14, Bosch provides some concrete illustrations of the notion that practical missionary involvement influences one's theology. Bosch cites the example of Paul, who discovered the depth and meaning of the gospel *only as he crossed frontiers* from the Jew to the Gentile. "When the Spirit sent Paul to the Greeks, it was not only to evangelize them; it was also to make it possible for Paul himself to see the real heart of his message. Does not the same apply to today's missionary? Is it not true that the Spirit reveals to us many new things through the mediation of Christians in other cultures and contexts?"

14. The following guidelines are taken from Bosch, *Witness*, 22–23 and Bosch, *Theology 201*, 10–11. All quotations that follow are found in *Witness*.

15. Elsewhere, Bosch expands on this by urging that theology not only be grounded in the life of the church, but that it be a theology of the *laity*, and not simply a "guild theology," limited to professional theologians. He comments: "Theology is born not only when scholars systematize their thinking, but wherever the believer engages in his or her 'secular' calling. The Bible can only be read and understood within the community of the faithful, 'together with all God's people' (Eph. 3:18). This missionary theology is beginning to manifest itself today in several ways: the development of base Christian communities, the renewal movement in its diverse forms and hundreds of other ways" (Bosch, "An Emerging Paradigm," 493).

16. Bosch emphasized this dimension in his lecture "God through African Eyes," given at the 1972 Mapumulo Consultation on a "Relevant Theology for Africa." Bosch stated: "I . . . stand here as your fellow-Christian believing that God has encountered you and me, and who now together with you attempts to stammer out something of what this encounter ought to mean to us all, blacks and whites.

Fourth, theology is not a *substitute* for the ministry of the church, but should act as a *corrective* to it. Theology alone cannot arouse faith or vision or hope or zeal; this is solely the task of the Lord of the church. Rather, theology's proper role is to give greater clarity, raise up examples from history, refine the church's methods and serve as a corrective to one-sided or inadequate views.

CHANGING UNDERSTANDINGS OF MISSION

"Mission" in Common Usage

We have already used the term "mission" although we have not yet defined what Bosch means by it. As Bosch frequently pointed out, this is a part of the problem in much contemporary theology! Many persons and groups use the word but with radically different understandings of its meaning. Bosch pointed out that mission, in its broadest sense, is a general religious concept denoting "when a religious community (of any religion) becomes conscious of its unique role and somehow tries to persuade others to share its convictions."[17] In this sense "mission" is not limited to Christianity (it is found in Islam and Buddhism) or even to religions (non-religious ideologies such as Socialism or Marxism have a missionary dimension to their existence).

In its more common usage, however, "mission" refers to *Christian* mission, the church's proclamation of the gospel of Christ and the expansion of the church among non-Christians.[18] The term mission is derived from the Latin *missio* (send), and was originally used in dogmatic theology to describe the action of the triune God: the Father sent the Son; the Father and Son sent the Holy Spirit. By the sixteenth century the Jesuits were using the term in their commissioning service. From that time until now, "mission" has described that action of the church in which certain persons are sent out to proclaim the gospel.[19]

This definition, however, does not adequately convey the meaning of mission. In reality, Bosch acknowledged that our image or definition of mission is profoundly conditioned by whether we have been the "object" or the "subject" of the church's missionary endeavors. The average churchgoer in the West perceives himself or herself to be the subject of mission, part of the church that is doing "missionary work." Bosch cited a tongue-in-cheek answer to the question: What is mission?

> It's spreading-the-gospel-of-Jesus-Christ-overseas. It's the projector in the church hall breaking down in the middle of the slides brought by the lady from

---

In all this we ultimately remain, all of us, but fools who rush in where angels fear to tread. However, we have no choice but to do just that: to try to say in human words what this encounter means, thus trying to spell out the consequences of this our belief, however inadequate and sometimes even almost sacrilegious it may happen to be or to appear" (Bosch, "God through African Eyes," 11–12).

17. Bosch, *Introduction to Missiology MSR 101*, 1.
18. Ibid., 2.
19. Bosch, "Missiology," 1st ed., 160.

Part Two: Bosch's Theology of Mission and Evangelism

> darkest Peru who belongs to one of the 81 missionary societies. It's the steaming jungle and the insects and the hard work and the faith, slogging on in that alien land where, fancy, women don't even have the vote. It's super-spirituality and missionary Sundays and people you've never seen before talking about people you're never going to meet. It's hymns about Greenland and thoughts about perishing heathen. It's demands for money and demands for prayer. It's generalities and success stories and an attaché case of mission literature set out on a trestle table by the door.[20]

While humorous and stereotypical, this description of mission is too uncomfortably close to the truth to merit much laughter; it closely resembles the reality in many churches in the West. The description becomes even more incredible if we reverse the roles and consider mission from the other side: from the perspective of those who have been the "objects" of Western mission. How would a non-Western person describe the meaning of mission? Bosch gave a very different picture:

> For such a person—the "product" of the missionary labour of one of the hundreds of missionary societies—mission is often synonymous with paternalism, white superiority, and an absence of sensitivity. For him "mission" is the crude preaching of whites who, with no proper appreciation either of the language or of the culture of the indigenous people, blithely assume that the "Christian World" has all the answers to life's questions, while people in other lands live in gross darkness. The man of Africa or Asia is thus also continually regarded as the "object" of mission. So he sees mission as part and parcel of Western domination, a relic of the colonial era. The missionary is [in the words of E. Nacpil] "the apostle of affluence, not sacrifice; cultural superiority, not Christian humility; technological efficiency, not human identification; white supremacy, not human liberation and community."[21]

How did the church get to this point, with such radically differing perceptions of the meaning and value of mission? In the following pages we will briefly summarize Bosch's understanding of the historical legacy of modern missions, and describe how the modern discipline of missiology developed during this era.

Church, Mission, and the Roots of Missiology[22]

Throughout the history of the church, men and women have witnessed to Jesus Christ by word and deed, participating in God's mission. In the early centuries of the church the apologists and fathers proclaimed the faith, while far to the north, the Celtic

---

20. Beale, "Mission Is my Calling," 19, as cited by Bosch, "Missiology," 2nd ed., 230.
21. Bosch, "Missiology," 2nd ed., 230–31.
22. For Bosch's full historical and theological analysis of the frequently tenuous relationship between church and mission, see Bosch and Verryn, *Church and Mission MSR 301*, esp. 1–171.

missions evangelized large parts of northern Europe. By the Middle Ages, however, the church had largely turned inward. It chose not to evangelize but to make a military crusade against Muslims. Even so, numerous monastic orders, exemplified by such men as Raymond Lull, kept the concern for a mission beyond Christendom alive, seeking to bring Muslims to faith in Christ through acts of love and service rather than through the sword. By the Reformation, with the era of discovery and Western colonialism dawning, we note the extensive activities of the Roman Catholic Jesuits as well as various Anabaptist groups. Both groups, in quite different ways, took the gospel to those who had not heard it. There were, however, early voices within Protestantism urging a similar concern, such as Justinian Welz, J. Heurnius, and Gisbertus Voetius, but not until the advent of the Pietist and Moravian movements did mission become firmly established within European Protestantism. In Britain we recall the rise of William Carey and the Wesley brothers whose influence upon the Christian missionary endeavor was immense. In America the faith of John Eliot and Jonathan Edwards, as two prime examples, gave a new impetus for believing that God desired the evangelization of the whole earth. Then came the "Great Century of Missions" (to use the terminology of K. S. Latourette) when a host of names emerged: Robert Moffat, Adoniram Judson, J. Hudson Taylor, Henry Martyn, David Livingstone, Henry Venn, Thomas Coke, to name only a few.

In the nineteenth century, as newly formed missionary societies began sending out more workers, the discipline of missiology was born. A few far-sighted individuals won a place for the academic study of mission in the theological curriculum.[23] Lectureships in "missions" were established at Princeton Theological Seminary (1830) and the University of Erlangen (1864). The first chair of missiology was established at the University of Edinburgh in 1867, filled by the famed Scottish missionary Alexander Duff.[24] Pride of place, though, must be given to the German theologian Gustav Warneck of Halle (1834–1910). It was Warneck more than any other individual who first developed a comprehensive *science* of mission. His influence lasted well into the twentieth century, particularly in Germany.[25]

Bosch maintained that Protestant missiology thus emerged from a fascinating hybrid of pietist and reformed circles, typified supremely in the person of William Carey. "In a certain sense Carey, a Calvinistic Baptist, combined the pietism of Halle and Herrnhut with the Reformed theology of Geneva—a combination that typifies nearly all Protestant mission. After Carey it was especially from the pietistic circles in

---

23. Bosch qualifies this, however. "We must, of course, bear in mind that, while the teaching of Missiology as a fully-fledged theological subject goes back only to 1836, its *field* is hoary with age. From the hour of its birth the Christian church engaged in missionary work as a matter of course, without stopping to enquire why it was doing so or whether its methods were correct"("Missiology," 3rd ed., 283).

24. Duff was officially the Professor of "Evangelistic Theology" (ibid., 263).

25. Bosch, "Missiology," 1st ed., 161; Bosch, *Witness*, 137.

Part Two: Bosch's Theology of Mission and Evangelism

Germany and the Reformed-Presbyterian churches in Scotland and America that the stimulus came for a systematic study of Missiology."[26]

With the dawn of the twentieth century, a general air of optimism prevailed among the leaders of the Western missionary movement. Such confidence was epitomized in the proceedings of the 1910 World Missionary Conference held in Edinburgh, and perhaps supremely in the person of John R. Mott, the ecumenical pioneer, and the Student Volunteer Movement's stirring call for "the evangelization of the world in this generation." Indeed there were strong grounds for believing that this would be "the Christian century," with a steady advance of the church across all human barriers.[27] The advance was grounded in a clear understanding of the *goals* of mission, shared by Roman Catholics and Protestants. Traditional aims of mission centered on the conversion of individuals and the establishment of the church in every nation.

Traditional Concepts of Mission become Problematic

As the twentieth century progressed, however, Bosch noted that two factors made the traditional understanding of mission increasingly problematic.[28] First was the *continuing link between the missionary movement and Western colonialism.* As Bosch commented: "it was more than a coincidence that the beginning of the modern missionary movement (i.e., the movement since the sixteenth century) coincided with the start of Western colonial expansion into the American, Asia, and Africa."[29] For many years, this historical legacy of Christian mission posed no real problem for Western Christians. Neither Protestants nor Catholics saw any contradiction between missions and colonial rule, between "commerce and Christianity."[30] Thus at the heart of Western mission—and of Western missiology—there has been an historical alliance between the Christian mission and Western colonialism that has ". . . cast a shadow over *all* missionary endeavour originating in the West."[31]

---

26. Bosch, "Missiology," 160–61.

27. Stephen Neill maintained this optimism was not simply a reflection of the *zeitgeist*; there were solid reasons for their confident expectation that God would continue to expand his church. See Neill, *Salvation Tomorrow*, 1–12.

28. Bosch admits that these are but two of the many factors that have challenged the traditional understanding of mission. For a detailed analysis of the entire historical legacy, see Bosch, *Witness*, chaps. 10–17. Cf. Bosch, "Missiology," 3rd ed., 265–69, 284 n. 4.

29. Bosch, "Missiology," 3rd ed., 265.

30. Indeed as late as 1909, Bosch cites an example of the German Ministry of Education instructing the Roman Catholic theology faculty at Münster to study the relationship between missions and the German colonies. This ultimately led to the establishment of a chair of Missiology (occupied by Joseph Schmidlin, the pioneer Catholic missiologist) "with the express purpose of studying 'mission in the German protectorates'" (ibid., 266).

31. Ibid. See also Neill, *Colonialism and Christian Missions*, 11–12. Cf. Bosch, "The Question of Mission Today," 7–8.

Bosch allowed that this judgment may be unduly harsh, for there have been many examples of missionaries who served as a force for liberation and human rights rather than colonialism and oppression (e.g., Bartolomé de Las Casas). Yet the Western missionary movement has not been able to escape the shadow of ambiguity in which it finds itself. Even in our own day, Bosch painfully noted, there are "innumerable examples of Western paternalism and attitudes of superiority, of which the Western church and its representatives remain blissfully unaware, though the 'products' of mission (the members of young churches) are all too conscious of them."[32]

A second problematic factor in the traditional Western approach to missions was the anomaly that *missions came into being and developed outside of institutional church structures*. The Reformation era was a time of internal reform and self-analysis among both Catholics and Protestants. Neither group regarded "mission" as an essential dimension of their identity. Instead, the true nature and function of the church was defined by what happened within it, i.e., preaching, sacraments, and discipline. To Reformation-era theologians, the church was seen as "the place where things *are done* (passive!), not a community actively engaged in doing something."[33] The result, then, was that when Western Christians began missionary work, the institutional churches and official structures frowned upon their activity. As Bosch put it, "mission became the concern of *missionary societies*, not of the Church itself."[34]

With significant exceptions, this model dominated the missionary movement throughout the nineteenth century and well into the twentieth, with profound effects upon the emerging discipline of missiology. Since mission was linked to parachurch organizations and not the institutional church, missiology entered the theological curriculum as a "step-sister." Bosch summarized the tension as follows: "When eventually [missiology] was accorded a place in theological institutions, it was not because of theological considerations, but due to the pressure exerted by the missionary societies, or (in the U.S.A.) at the instigation of students, or in certain circumstances as a consequence of government intervention. Broadly speaking, neither the Churches

---

32. Bosch, "Missiology," 3rd ed., 266.

33. Ibid., 267. Bishop Newbigin's comments are appropriate here. "The period in which our thinking about the church received its main features was the period in which Christianity had practically ceased to be a missionary religion . . . The congregation was not a staging post for world mission but a gathering place for the faithful of a town or village. The ministry was not understood in terms of leadership in mission but in terms of guardianship of those already in the fold. Theology was not concerned so much to state the Gospel in terms of non-Christian cultures, as with the mutual struggle of rival interpretations of the Gospel. Church history was taught not as the story of missionary advance in successive encounters of the Gospel with different forms of human culture and society, but rather as the story of the doctrinal and other conflicts within the life of the Church. To put it in one sentence, the Church had become the religious department of European society rather than the task force selected and appointed for a world mission" (Newbigin, *Honest Religion for Secular Man*, 103–4).

34. Bosch, "Missiology," 3rd ed., 267.

Part Two: Bosch's Theology of Mission and Evangelism

nor the theological schools welcomed the gate-crasher. Mission was merely an ancillary to the Church, and missiology would be no more than that in the theological curriculum!"[35]

The missionary movement thus faced two major challenges by the early twentieth century: how could mission rid itself of the legacy of colonialism, with its excess baggage of cultural imperialism and paternalism? And how could church and mission become more integrated, bringing mission to the center of the church's life? Some urged that missions, as traditionally understood, be discarded.[36] Others, unaware of the changes occurring in their midst, saw no crisis and felt missions could continue with business as usual. Bosch maintained that both of these approaches were wrong. At bottom, these approaches misunderstood both *the true goal of mission* and *the essentially missionary nature of the church*.

Bosch described the traditional missionary aim as either the conversion of individuals (the "saving of souls") or the establishment of churches.[37] While not denying the essential validity of these enterprises,[38] Bosch argued that both fall short as a description of the *full purpose* of the church's mission. Conversion and church-planting frequently became ends in themselves. All too often the concern for religious conversion implied that the main task of mission was simply "to prepare people for the hereafter," ignoring their contemporary needs. All too often the concern for church planting was a thinly disguised attempt at ecclesiastical propaganda, promoting the growth of a particular denomination or theological tradition as an end in itself.[39]

Kähler, Barth, and a New Understanding of the Church

Bosch argued that a fundamental theological reorientation took place that redefined both the nature of the church and the content of its mission, beginning with the writings

---

35. Ibid., 268. In an earlier essay, Bosch notes how missiology has "acquired citizenship" among the theological sciences, yet is often merely *tolerated*. "It has . . . gained admission to the 'forecourt of the Gentiles,' but the 'holy place' of theology often remains closed to it" (Bosch,"Missiology," 1st ed., 159).

36. Examples of this radical reappraisal of the role of missions would be the writings of Ernst Troeltsch, who urged that the goal of mission be reconceptualized in terms of imparting the spiritual and cultural values of Western civilization to the less developed lands; and the 1932 Laymen's Foreign Missions Enquiry report "Re-Thinking Missions," which urged a more relativistic approach to Christianity. See Bosch, *Witness*, 132–37, 161–64.

37. Protestants and Catholics alike were divided over which of the two goals took priority. Among Roman Catholics, Bosch contrasts the approaches of the Münster and Louvain "schools." "The Münster school laid stress on evangelization, the Louvain school on the establishing of the Church" (Bosch, Missiology," 2nd ed., 235).

38. Bosch admits: ". . . there is merit in each of these traditional aims of mission. Rightly understood, both are essential. Unless in our missionary activity we lead people to a saving encounter with the living Christ, and unless those who have had this encounter are incorporated into a worshipping community, we shall fall sadly short of our calling" (Bosch,"Missiology," 3rd ed., 271–72).

39. Ibid., 272.

Theology, Mission, and Missiology

of Martin Kähler, Abraham Kuyper, and particularly Karl Barth.[40] Kähler and Kuyper rooted the mission of the church solidly in theology (in the doctrines of the atonement and the Trinity, respectively). Kähler was the first theologian to place the mission of the church at the very center of his theological thinking, declaring (in 1908) that "die Mission wurde zur Mutter der Theologie . . ."[41] The church was called to servanthood rather than self-assertion, to the proclamation of the gospel rather than confessional or cultural propaganda, to the way of the cross rather than the way of success and cultural superiority.[42] Kähler's theology of mission signaled the end of one theological era and the beginning of another. It remained the task of a critical admirer of Kähler, Karl Barth, to work out the full theological implications of the concept that the church's very being and existence was grounded in its mission to the world.

Karl Barth decisively influenced twentieth-century understandings of church and mission. Bosch cites an example from Barth's *Church Dogmatics* that summarizes this new understanding: "As an apostolic Church the Church can never in any respect be an end in itself, but, following the existence of the apostles, it exists only as it exercises the ministry of a herald . . . Its mission is not additional to its being. It is, as it is sent and active in its mission. It builds up itself for the sake of its mission and in relation to it."[43]

Barth developed an ecclesiology that moved away from the static, institutional categories of post-Reformation thought. The church was called to be the *servant of the world*. The church was also called to understand its own existence in dynamic, missional categories. Barth expounded these concepts throughout volume IV of the *Church Dogmatics* by highlighting three interconnected dimensions of the church's existence. Under the Holy Spirit, the church as Christian community is gathered (IV:1 §62), built up (IV:2 §67) and sent out into the world (IV:3 §72). The special contribution of Barth, according to Bosch, is the recognition that these three modes of the church's existence must never be isolated from one another; the church's being, edification and mission are "inextricably interwoven."[44]

This new understanding of mission as belonging to the essential nature of the church (which Kähler pioneered and Barth spelled out) had profound effects in both Protestant and Roman Catholic circles. For Protestants, the new understanding served as a call to seek a deeper integration of church and mission at both the theological and organizational levels. Perhaps most significantly, we can see the 1961 integration between the WCC and the International Missionary Council as the ultimate fruit of this new approach. If the church is not in mission, then it ceases to be the church. But

---

40. For a full review of these developments, see Bosch's survey "Kaleidoskoop," 13–27, which deals with the relationship between mission, theology, and church; see also Bosch, *Witness*, 159–95.

41. Kähler, *Schriften zu Christologie und Mission*, 190. For his evaluation of Kähler, see Bosch, "Systematic Theology and Mission," 165–89; and Bosch, *Witness*, 137–39.

42. Bosch, "Systematic Theology and Mission," 183, 187.

43. Bosch, "Missiology," 3rd ed., 273. Cf. Barth, *Church Dogmatics* IV:1 724–25.

44. Bosch, "Missiology," 3rd ed., 273.

Part Two: Bosch's Theology of Mission and Evangelism

likewise if missions are not somehow related to the church, then they cease to be truly missionary.[45] For Roman Catholics, the new understanding of the church dramatically affected the Second Vatican Council (1962–65). Bosch notes that in the documents of Vatican II, the church is no longer simply a static, self-centered institution, the "dispenser of salvation." It is rather the mystical body of Christ, God's pilgrim people in the world, a "kind of sacrament" of God's presence in the world. "She is thus described essentially as not in relationship to herself, but to God and the world."[46]

New Understandings of Mission

For Bosch, the new view of the church led to new understandings of the meaning of Christian mission. Although the conversion of individuals and the establishment of worshipping communities remain essential aspects of "mission," they do not exhaust the full meaning of the word. Mission concerns all those aspects of the church's life where it crosses frontiers toward the world.[47] Bosch affirmed the definition of mission given at the 1963 Mexico City CWME Conference; it is "the common witness of the whole church, bringing the whole gospel to the whole world."[48]

Building on the work of Bengt Sundkler, Bosch defined mission as *the crossing of frontiers*. "Mission has to do with the crossing of frontiers. It describes the total task which God has set the Church for the salvation of the world. It is the task of the Church in movement, the Church that lives for others, the Church that is not only concerned about herself, [the Church] that turns herself 'inside out' (Hoekendijk), towards the world."[49]

Mission was thus understood by Bosch more broadly than in the traditional approach. God is involved, through his church, with the whole world. Mission is "the church-crossing-frontiers, witnessing to the Kingdom of God."[50] What are some of the frontiers that the church should cross in its witness to the world? "These frontiers may

---

45. Cf. Bosch, "Missiology," 2nd ed., 236.

46. Bosch, *Witness*, 183–85, Bosch, "Missiology," 3rd ed., 273.

47. Bosch, *Witness*, 17.

48. Ibid. Cf. Orchard, *Witness in Six Continents*, 173.

49. Bosch, *Witness*, 17. The theme of mission as "the crossing of frontiers" has been a popular missiological approach. D. T. Niles, in his *Upon the Earth*, 159, highlighted the "frontier-crossing" nature of mission, and particularly that the *deepest* frontier was not geographical boundaries, but rather the line between faith and unbelief. Orchard, in his *Out of Every Nation*, 97–105, developed the concept more fully. This approach was also at the heart of Sundkler's thought. For a full overview of the subject, see Beyerhaus and Hallencreutz, *The Church Crossing Frontiers*, esp. Beyerhaus' article "The Ministry of Crossing Frontiers," 36–54. Evangelical missiology, particularly in North America, has witnessed a revival of interest in the "frontiers" concept, albeit with some significant differences from the above-mentioned understanding through work of missiologist Ralph Winter. See Starling, *Seeds of Promise*, 45–123.

50. Bosch, "Theologies of Mission," [1]. We used the unpublished manuscript version of this essay, and so pagination for this source does not correspond with the published version. Page numbers from the unpublished version will be in brackets.

Theology, Mission, and Missiology

be ethnic, cultural, geographical, religious, ideological or social. Mission takes place where the Church, in her total involvement with the world and the comprehensiveness of her message, bears her testimony in word and deed in the form of a servant, with reference to unbelief, exploitation, discrimination and violence, but also with reference to salvation, healing, liberation, reconciliation and righteousness."[51]

We note here that the church's mission is modeled after the form of God's mission, e.g., "in word and deed" and "in the form of a servant." Mission is *incarnational*, modeled after God's own involvement in the world, which was supremely manifested in Jesus Christ, the servant of the Lord.

Mission is primarily the *missio Dei*, God's work of salvation for the sake of the world. And yet mission also properly involves the church if, as Barth maintained, the Christian community is essentially missionary in its being and nature.[52] The church is an instrument of God's mission as it witnesses to the King and his kingdom. The church crosses frontiers in the name of the compassionate Father, in the manner of Jesus the servant, and in the power and hope of the Spirit.[53] In this way Bosch grounded mission in a number of key theological motifs, including the doctrines of the Trinity, Christology, soteriology, ecclesiology, and eschatology.[54] It will be the burden of the latter part of this book to unpack some of the implications contained in these comprehensive statements.

MISSIOLOGY AS A THEOLOGICAL DISCIPLINE[55]

The Nature and Scope of Missiology

If mission is "the church crossing frontiers," then missiology, according to Bosch, is theological reflection on the church crossing frontiers, on the nature and activities of "frontier-crossing."[56] A comparison with some other definitions of missiology would be helpful here. Johannes Verkuyl defined missiology as "the study of the salvation activities of the Father, Son and Holy Spirit throughout the world geared towards bringing the kingdom of God into existence."[57] Three factors stand out in Verkuyl's analysis: mission is grounded in the *missio Dei*, God's mission; the scope of mission includes everything that is "salvation-oriented," everything that is a manifestation of

---

51. Bosch, *Witness*, 18.
52. Bosch, "Missiology," 3rd ed., 278.
53. Bosch, *Witness*, 239–48.
54. These doctrines inform the theological structure of Bosch's missiological agenda. See chapters 7–9.
55. Besides the aforementioned sources, Bosch has dealt with this subject in his "Theological Education in Missionary Perspective," 13–34; and republished in slightly modified form as "Missions in Theological Education" xv–xli.
56. Bosch, "Missionary Theology in Africa," 107.
57. Verkuyl, *Contemporary Missiology*, 5.

Part Two: Bosch's Theology of Mission and Evangelism

God's kingdom; and the church's task is to join with God in communicating the total gospel through word and deed to all humankind.[58]

Orlando Costas defined missiology as "a theology of the crossroads." It is "a critical reflection at the point where cultures, ideologies, religious traditions, and social, economic, and political systems confront each other, and where the gospel seeks to cross the frontier of unbelief."[59] In this statement Costas emphasizes the contextual nature of theology, and the frontier-crossing dimension inherent to the gospel and the Christian mission. He goes on to emphasize that missiology, if it is to have any credibility, demands not only reflection but action. It demands "a commitment to a more effective engagement in mission."[60]

Verkuyl, Costas, and Bosch all defined missiology in broad rather than traditional, narrow categories. Like Verkuyl, Bosch grounded his missiology on a trinitarian perspective and acknowledges that the breadth of mission is as wide as God's salvific purposes. Like Costas, Bosch emphasized the multidimensional nature of Christian mission, as the church acts in crossing a variety of frontiers with the gospel.

Based on these convictions, Bosch also clarified what missiology is *not*. First, missiology is not limited to the study of the life and growth of the church in the so-called Third World, in what used to be termed "the mission field." The frontiers of mission, as recent missiological thought has emphasized, are on *all six continents*.[61] In every land the churches find themselves in "missionary situations."

Second, all theology is *not* missiology. A problem arose as a result of the new understanding of church and mission. If the church's nature is essentially missionary, some argue, then does it not follow that all that the church does is mission, and that all theology is essentially missiology? Bosch drew attention to the fact that in ecumenical circles in particular, there has been a radical broadening of the concept of mission.[62] In response to this approach Bosch recalled Bishop Stephen Neill's famous quip that "when everything is mission, then nothing is mission." In other words, if mission is defined so broadly as to include everything the church does and thinks, then "mission"

---

58. Ibid., 4–5.

59. Costas, *Christ Outside the Gate*, xiv. See also his *Theology of the Crossroads*, 9ff., 325ff.

60. Costas, *Christ Outside the Gate*, xiv.

61. Bosch, "Missiological Developments in South Africa," 12. This was one of the primary emphases at the 1963 Mexico City meeting of the CWME.

62. Bosch states that "The escalation in the use of the concept 'mission' has indeed had an inflationary effect, for 'mission' has now become the flag under which practically every ecclesiastical (and sometimes every generally human) activity is sailing . . . This development reached its apex at the Fourth Assembly of the WCC (Uppsala, 1968) where practically everything was brought under the umbrella-term 'mission'—health and welfare projects, youth projects, activities of political interest groups, projects for economic and social development, constructive applications of violence, combating racism, the introduction of the inhabitants of the Third World to the possibilities of the twentieth century, and the defence of human rights. Small wonder that Donald McGavran, in an open letter, criticised the Uppsala assembly for allowing mission to develop into 'any good activity at home or abroad which anyone declares to be the will of God'" (Bosch, *Witness*, 11).

Theology, Mission, and Missiology

as a distinct theological concept is lost. In like manner, Bosch commented that "when all theology is missiology, then nothing is missiology."[63]

How then do we distinguish between "missiology" and "theology"? What are the criteria that determine the *scope* of mission and missiology? Bosch here made use of the distinction that Hans-Werner Gensichen made between "dimension" and "intention."[64] Summarizing Gensichen's position, Bosch commented: "Everything the Church is and does . . . must have a missionary *dimension*, but not everything has a missionary *intention*. To put it differently: the Church's entire nature is missionary but she is not, in all her activities, explicitly aimed at the world. The Church must in all circumstances be 'missionary', but she is not in every moment 'missionising.'"[65]

Bosch thus posited a dynamic, creative tension between the missionary dimension and the missionary intention of the church's existence. In this schema, the missionary *dimension* is primary. In order for the church to become involved with the world in an intentional way, the church must be authentically "missionary" in its inner workings and at the local level. As it lives out its essential calling to kindness, unity, love of neighbor and brother, obedience, joy, and good works, it is already proclaiming good news to those outside of the fellowship.[66] It can be authentically "missionary" by its very existence, "before she has crossed any frontiers to the world . . ."[67]

All too often, however, the church lamely attempts to become involved in missionary activities even though *it lacks this missionary dimension within its own life!* When this happens, Bosch reasoned, when it "creates a colossal mission-machinery without itself being missionary," the results are disastrous. "The Church transmits its own ghetto-mentality to the people it 'reaches.' It gets caught up, not in *mission*, but in *propaganda*, reproducing copies of itself."[68]

In a similar manner, Gensichen's "dimension"-"intention" categories help us to understand the nature and scope of *missiology itself*.[69] In one sense, missiology is *dimensional*; it pervades the other disciplines of theology by calling them to see the inherently missionary implications of their subjects. Missiology warns theology not to become isolated and parochial by forgetting the church's relationship to the world. Missiology reminds theology that its true calling is to be theology *for mission*.[70]

In another sense, however, missiology is *intentional*; it reflects upon a unique concern that no other theological discipline examines: the church's calling to move

---

63. Bosch, "Missiological Developments in South Africa," 11.

64. Gensichen, *Glaube für die Welt*, esp. 80–96, 168–86. The distinction was first made, as far as I can find, by Newbigin in his *One Body, One Gospel, One World*, 21.

65. Bosch, *Witness*, 199–200. Cf. Bosch, "Missiology," 3rd ed., 276.

66. Bosch, *Witness*, 200.

67. Ibid.

68. Bosch, "Missiology," 3rd ed., 277. This is precisely the argument of Martin Kähler.

69. Bosch, "Missiological Developments in South Africa," 12.

70. Bosch, "Missiology," 3rd ed., 278.

beyond herself and take the gospel into all the world. The science of mission is "the theology-of-the-Church-crossing-frontiers . . . More than any other discipline it must remain flexible so that it can face up to the demands resulting from the crossing of every fresh boundaries."[71]

Understood in this light, the scope of missiology is simultaneously very wide yet very narrow. For Bosch, missiology's range is remarkably comprehensive. "It must . . . be familiar with and answerable to the various dominant theologies—of hope, of liberation, of revolution, the theology of the cross, the theology of reason, black theology and the like . . . And all the time it must take account also of geographic, anthropological, religious, political, social, and economic factors."[72]

Yet missiology's task is also narrow. It continually strives to describe and evaluate all these aspects of the church's life and thought with a single question in mind: how does this relate to the church's task of crossing frontiers into all the world with the gospel? This question keeps the *intentional* aspect of missiology in focus.

The Elements of Missiology

Missiology studies the church in its frontier-crossing dimension, and develops guidelines for the church's life as a missionary instrument of God. For practical reasons, however, the discipline of missiology must also be subdivided into various elements of study and research. In an early essay, Bosch classified the study of mission as follows.[73]

A. Encounter between mission and theology—the foundation of mission

B. Encounter between church and mission—the place of mission

C. Encounter between mission and the "mission field"—approach in mission

D. Encounter between mission and the world—the scope of mission

We can also discern Bosch's approach to the classification of the major elements of missiology by analyzing the titles of the missiological courses offered at UNISA during his tenure there. As Dean of the Faculty of Theology, Bosch had the opportunity to shape the missiological curriculum of the institution. Elements in the study of missiology at UNISA included: introduction to missiology; the theology of mission; church and mission; the theology of religions; The communication of the gospel; mission in context; missionary methods; the church in the Third World; the gospel in an industrial society.[74]

---

71. Bosch, "Missiology," 2nd ed., 240.
72. Ibid., 239–40.
73. See Bosch, "Kaleideskoop," 13–44.
74. As found in the *University of South Africa 1987 Calendar*, 26–28.

A third, more comprehensive scheme of missiological categorization can be found in *Missionalia* when Bosch served as its editor. Since 1973, *Missionalia* has provided abstracts of relevant missiological literature using the following categorization:[75]

The World

1. Bibliography and the Study of Mission
2. Christian and World Surveys
3. History and Theology of Mission
   (Mission in the Bible; History of Missions; Theology of Mission; Black Theology; Charismatic movement; Christian social responsibility; Church and mission; Church and state: Church and nationalism; The congregation in mission; Contextualisation; Conversion; Ecumenism and mission; Hermeneutics; Inculturation; Liberation Theology;; Third World theologies; The younger churches)
4. Religion, religions and dialogue
   (Religion in general; Christianity and other faiths; African traditional religions; Buddhism; Confucianism; Hinduism; Islam; Japanese religions; Judaism; Marxism; New religious movements; Primal religions)
5. Environment, society and development
   (Structures of society, revolution, peace; Art, architecture, music; Colonialism and mission; Development; Industry, urbanisation, technology; Marriage and family; The poor; Race; Women in church and society)
6. Forms of ministry and witness
   (Basic Christian communities; Catechesis; Communication and culture; Diakonia; Evangelism and Church growth; Health, medicine, healing ministry; Homiletics; Inter-church relationships; Laity; Linguistics, translation, use of Scripture; Literature, literacy; Mass media; Ministry; The missionary; Missionary agencies; Pastoralia; Spirituality; Theological education; Urban ministry; Worship, liturgy, prayer and sacraments; Youth work)

Africa

1. Africa in general
2. Africa: Christian theology
3. African Independent Churches

---

75. The categorization adopted by *Missionalia* followed the same general pattern as that set by the "Bibliography on World Mission" formerly in the *International Review of Mission*, organized by Professor Andrew Walls of the Centre for the Study of Christianity in the Non-Western World, New College, University of Edinburgh. There are some significant differences between the two, however.

4. There follows a list the nations of Africa

   [The categorization continues in similar fashion for every continent.]

A few observations should be made at this point. First, it is obvious from such an exhaustive list that missiology's scope is incredibly wide. It is also significant that nearly all of the elements of missiology cited in the list above presuppose some practical and theoretical training in *other disciplines*. The missiologist is, in nearly every aspect of his work, reliant upon other subjects of theology, including biblical studies, systematic and practical theology, and church history. But the missiologist must also have expertise in a few *non-theological* disciplines.[76] Such cognate disciplines of missiology would include communications, religious studies, anthropology, sociology, history, economics, etc. The list is extensive.

With this wide variety of subject matter, the individual missiologist must of necessity become a specialist, focusing on certain specific areas. Although Bosch's writings covered a broad spectrum of missiological topics, an analysis of Bosch's bibliography shows that the major focus of his work has been the *theology of mission*. For this reason, we will take a deeper look at this "subdivision" of missiology, highlighting Bosch's understanding of its role and functions within missiology as a whole.

The Theology of Mission

What is the "theology of mission"? As noted above, it is one subdivision of the more comprehensive discipline of missiology, and it is to this subject that Bosch devoted much of his professional work.

Bosch maintained that "every missionary activity has a theological basis, however implicit and inarticulate it is."[77] The goal of the theology of mission is to make explicit what the church believes and does in relation to the world. Bosch defined the theology of mission as follows: "Theology concerns itself with reflection on the nature of the gospel, and the theology of mission with the question of the way in which the Church spreads this gospel. Putting it differently: the theology of mission concerns itself with the relationship between God and the world in light of the gospel."[78]

The theology of mission deals with three intertwined subjects: the *foundation*, *motive*, and *aim* of mission. It asks fundamental questions, such as: What is mission? Why do we do mission work? How has the church through the centuries understood its responsibility towards the world? What do we hope to achieve in the world as a result of missionary involvement? Are we concerned only with saving souls, or do we also seek to change social structures? What is the relationship between mission and

---

76. This is the burden of Kirk, *Theology and the Third World Church*, 59.
77. Bosch, *Witness*, 25.
78. Ibid., 10.

evangelism?[79] All these questions can be reduced them to one: "What does it mean to be the church of Christ in relation to the world of today?" This is the essential question with which Bosch grappled, most significantly in his *Witness to the World* and of course in his capstone work *Transforming Mission*.

The theology of mission has been defined by Gerald Anderson as the study of ". . . the basic presuppositions and underlying principles which determine, from the standpoint of the Christian faith, the motives, message, methods, strategy and goals of the Christian world mission."[80] The theology of mission is therefore not concerned with the *how* of mission, of missionary methods and practice; this belongs elsewhere.[81] Responding to Anderson's definition, Bosch maintained that the theology of mission concerns "the 'basic presuppositions and underlying principles'—in other words that which *underlies* missionary praxis rather than missionary praxis per se. However it is concerned with presuppositions and principles 'which *determine* . . .' This implies that these principles and presuppositions have an impact on missionary praxis, colouring it and influencing it."[82]

Within the theology of mission there are two distinct subdivisions: the biblical foundation for mission, and the theology of mission proper. Bosch noted that some people find this distinction problematic. In effect they say that *only* a biblical foundation for mission is needed: "We have only to read what the Bible says, and act accordingly. In other words: in a book on Missiology we do need a chapter on the biblical foundations of mission . . . but *not* one on 'theologies of mission.'"[83]

This is shortsighted, according to Bosch. Even after we determine what the Bible says about a certain topic, the need exists to *contextualize* our mission, to "translate Scriptural teaching into the realities of our time."[84] The theology of mission includes

---

79. The aforementioned questions are found in ibid., ix–x; and Bosch, "Theologies of Mission," [1–2].

80. Anderson, "Theology of Mission," 594.

81. Bosch, *Witness*, 21.

82. Bosch, *Theology 201*, 9–10.

83. Bosch, "Theologies of Mission," [2].

84. Ibid. Bosch elaborated on the inadequacy of this "Bible alone" approach with four points. See ibid., 3–6. First, the Old Testament provides us with only limited guidelines for the church's mission today. Its focus is on one people, the Jews. Mission is perceived primarily in centripetal terms. Second, mission, understood as the call for God's people to witness to the kingdom of God beyond the church's boundaries, is more prominent in the New Testament. And yet the "New Testament writings span a short period of time, portraying only the earliest stages of the mission, and written by and to a few in a fairly homogeneous socio-political context." Third, when the church-in-mission moves into another culture or sociopolitical context, it cannot appeal to the New Testament in a direct and simple way. "It has to interpret that message for its own time and context." We too must do this by developing our own "theologies," in dialogue with the Scriptures. We must seek to creatively appropriate the message of the Bible in our own very different social context. Fourth, we see evidence of this "contextualizing" process *in the Bible itself*. In the New Testament we see not one but different, complementary theologies of mission that exist side by side. They stand in tension, but do not fundamentally conflict. We must not seek to "straightjacket" the witness of the Bible with a single, monochromatic approach to its view of mission. Rather we must see that "each author described the Christ event in such a way that it would make sense to *his* audience and *his* community . . ." The gospel of Christ is thus like "a multi-faceted prism and each

both the tasks of biblical foundation and theological "translation," of exegesis and contextualization. Taken together, these twin tasks constitute the fundamental ground and justification for the church's missionary methods and practices.

The Place of Missiology in the Theological Encyclopedia

Within the history of theological education missiology is a newcomer to the field, with no clear place in the traditional theological encyclopedia; this is still true in the contemporary theological arena.[85] Lutheran missiologist James Scherer has surveyed the place of missiology in the theological curriculum. He notes three major objections to including missiology in the theological encyclopedia. Some regard missiology as an interloper, since it is not one of the classical theological disciplines. Others see missiology as an anachronism since the great era of Western missionary expansion is now past history rather than present reality. Still others view it as superfluous, since its concerns should be covered by the other disciplines.[86]

Bosch gave little credence to the first two positions. The first is simply an *argumentum ad antiquitam*, and carries little weight. The second objection, that mission is an anachronism, mistakenly equates "mission" with "Western mission." As we have seen, this is illegitimate, because mission now spans six continents. Mission is the task of the entire global church, not simply the preoccupation of the church in the First World.

Bosch was sympathetic to the last objection, however. Ideally at least, missiology should disappear, if the other theological disciplines could *see mission as a vital dimension of their work*. Bosch gives the following example: "In concrete terms we could argue thus: the moment the church has crossed the frontier and reached a given group—say the Kikuyu of Kenya—the development of religious belief becomes the object of study of *systematic theologians*; the church's ministry becomes the focus of *practical theologians*; the study of social and other problems (e.g., polygamy) becomes a matter for *ethicists*, and so on. In terms of this argument the *missiologist* would cease to exist."[87]

Yet Bosch went on to point out that this rarely happens. Most theologians continue to occupy themselves with Western theology, Western methods, and Western problems, with the result that the missiologist is, for all practical purposes, the only person to take an active *theological* interest in the two-thirds of the world that most

---

author revealed to his readers that 'colour' that made most sense to them . . . As we reflect today on our own theologies of mission, we too should—like the New Testament authors—attempt to recapture the spirit and ethos of Jesus and the early church and interpret those for and in our own context." See ibid., 6.

85. Bosch noted that "In Eberhard Jüngel's division of theological disciplines, for example, the subject matter of 'the theological science of the Word of God' is divided into the following traditional categories: Biblical Studies and Exegesis—the *text;* Church History—the *tradition;* Systematic Theology—the *truth;* and Practical Theology—the *event*." In this categorization, Bosch comments, Jüngel leaves no place for missiology. "The best it can hope for is recognition as a sub-section of one of the classic disciplines or as a supplement to it" (Bosch, "Missiology," 3rd ed., 263).

86. Scherer, "Missions in Theological Education," 143–53. Cf. Bosch, "Missiology," 2nd ed., 231.

87. Bosch, *Missiology 101*, 7–8.

Western theologians ignore. Missiology thus has what Bosch called an "emergency" function, an *expedient* right to exist. It exists even *after* the frontiers have been crossed because the other theological disciplines usually fail to show any theological interest in the non-Western world.[88] The missiologist is frequently the only person who tackles such "hot issues" as the relationship of Christian faith to other faiths, poverty and wealth, race relations, secularization, and the role of cultures and ideologies. The missiologist undertakes such interests not because he or she has the "exclusive prerogative to do so, but simply because his colleagues seldom seem willing to take over."[89]

Bosch argued, however, that missiology also has a *fundamental* right to exist as a legitimate branch of theology. If missiology is characterized by the study of the church's crossing of frontiers, then missiology must continue to exist, because new frontiers are always emerging. Missiology does not stand, strictly speaking; rather it *moves*. It moves between those frontiers that divide Christians from non-Christians, the First World from the Third World, the "younger churches" from the "older churches," the universal church and the local congregation.[90] Missiology is unique and irreplaceable.

> Because of its frontier position it raises issues for other theological disciplines, reminding them of dimensions that are easily overlooked, points out that the Bible can be read in more than one way, questions many of the clichés of Western theology. In this way missiology renders theological service to the universality of the church. It does not confine itself to a few isolated themes, nor does it concern itself solely with the training of "missionaries." In a very special sense it is the theological "port of trans-shipment" to facilitate traffic between (predominantly) Third World churches and their situation, and traditional Western and ecumenical theology.[91]

If missiology has a permanent right to exist, then where should it "fit" in the theological curriculum? Bosch highlighted four different solutions.[92] Some theorists, particularly in Britain, regard missiology as an element that should permeate all theological subjects. Bosch labeled this the "total integration" approach. The goal is to bring mission into the other disciplines, and thus into the church's life and minis-

---

88. Bosch, "Missiological Developments in South Africa," 12–13.

89. Bosch, "Missiology," 2nd ed., 240.

90. Bosch, *Missiology 101*, 8. Bosch approvingly cited Ivan Illich in this regard: "Missiology is the science about the Church in her becoming; the Church in her borderline situations; the Church as a surprise and puzzle; the Church in her growth; the Church when her historical appearance is so new that she has to strain herself to recognize her past in the mirror of her present; the Church where she is pregnant of new revelations for a people in which she dawns . . . Missiology studies the growth of the Church into new peoples, the birth of the Church beyond its social boundaries; beyond the linguistic barriers within which she feels at home; beyond the poetical images in which she taught her children . . . Missiology therefore is the study of the Church as surprise . . ." See Illich, *Mission and Midwifery* as cited in Bosch, *Missiology 101*, 8.

91. Bosch, *Missiology 101*, 8–9.

92. For more details about the following alternatives, see Bosch, "Missiology," 2nd ed., 237–38; and "Missiology," 3rd ed., 270–71.

try. But for integration to be effective, theologians must have both the time and the inclination to learn about mission and make the necessary "links" with their own fields. This happens all too infrequently.

A second alternative has been to replace missiology with a new subject, e.g., ecumenics, Third World theology, world religions, world Christianity. Bosch noted this to be a growing trend, particularly in schools related to denominations that are members of the WCC.[93] Yet Bosch thought this trend was unfortunate. Although each of the disciplines mentioned above embody certain aspects of missiology, the fundamental and unique concern of missiology—the concern to cross frontiers with the whole gospel—is usually lost in the process.

A third alternative is to make missiology a branch of another discipline, a subdivision. This is a common alternative, particularly in the U.S. and among numerous Catholic groups. Many theologians (including Schliermacher, Kuyper, Bavinck, and Rahner) have placed the concerns of missiology under the umbrella of practical theology. Others have urged that missiology come under the wing of church history. Many of the foremost American missiologists (K. S. Latourette, R. P. Beaver, R. Winter) follow this tradition. Bosch objected that this too is an unsatisfactory alternative, because missiology is "unjustifiably constricted" if it is regarded as simply a branch of another discipline. Its unique perspective flows over the boundaries of the other subjects.

A final alternative for missiology is total independence. This alternative was adopted particularly in Germany and northern European lands. Out of this "Teutonic" tradition, large tomes have been written advocating missiology as a separate discipline.[94] Bosch found a danger in this approach as well: missiology can be "banished to the periphery" and isolated, precisely because someone else is teaching it. As Bosch characterized it: "[Missiology] can so easily be regarded simply as a department of foreign affairs, with the result that the missionary dimension of the other theological subjects is neglected, even excluded, on the grounds that—praise be!—there is now someone responsible for this special field . . . But what actually happens is that mission is eventually written off again—a reality *alongside* the Church, *alongside* theology, a perennial *addendum*, and not just in the activities of the theologians, but in the hearts and minds of believers as well."[95] Furthermore, Bosch argued, this absolute academic independence forces the missiologist to become his own (frequently amateurish) exegete, ethicist, historian and systematic theologian, since his colleagues are not concerned with the missionary dimensions of their particular subjects.[96]

93. Bosch, "Missiology," 3rd ed., 264.

94. We note Bosch's comment in the preface to *Witness* that general and systematic introductions to missiology appear to be a continental European rather than an Anglo-Saxon phenomenon. Of the major introductions to missiology in English, most are translations, including Bavinck's *Introduction to the Science of Missions*; Sundkler's *The World of Mission*; and Verkuyl's *Contemporary Missiology*; and of course, Bosch's own *Witness to the World*. Bosch, *Witness*, ix.

95. Bosch, "Missiology," 2nd ed., 237.

96. Bosch, "Missiology," 3rd ed., 269.

Theology, Mission, and Missiology

For Bosch, none of these alternatives were satisfactory. Missiology's place in the theological encyclopedia is, in reality, a *combination* of these approaches. Returning to Gensichen's concept of "dimension" and "intention," Bosch urged that missiology be perceived as a complementary discipline, the "handmaid" of theology.

First, it must serve as a *complementary* theological discipline, bringing the dimension of mission into every aspect of theology.[97] The missiologist must acknowledge that missiology is dependent upon the other theological subjects; it serves as "a *synoptic* subject in the theological curriculum, a *catalyst*."[98] But the missiologist must also serve as an apologist to his or her fellow theologians, making them aware of the number and variety of frontiers to be crossed.[99] Therefore the missiologist should be in continual dialogue with his or her colleagues in other disciplines.[100] Only then can missiology become "a necessary dimension for theology as a whole, accompanying the other subjects in their task."[101]

Second, missiology must serve as an *independent* theological discipline, calling the church to be faithful to its calling as an instrument of God's mission.[102] Missiology has a particular calling to work out the practical implications of the church's task of crossing frontiers. It must "supply concreteness to the missionary dimension with reference to the present-day situation of the Church."[103] Bosch clarified some of missiology's *intentional* tasks as follows:

> The specific sphere to which Missiology ought to give attention includes the whole expanse of cross-cultural communication, along with the evaluation of non-Christian and pseudo-Christian religions and ideologies; the approach of Western, post-Christian secular man; the contextualizing of the Gospel in those countries and cultures it has only recently reached; the relationship between the older and younger churches; and so on . . .[104]

Missiology therefore must take into account both the missionary dimension and the missionary intention; it must be both a *complementary* yet *independent* science. Only then can it be of use to God, the church, and the world. Bosch endorsed Scherer's evaluation of its role. "Its presence among other disciplines will be dialogical and attentive,

---

97. We note that Johannes Verkuyl and Manfred Linz endorsed this viewpoint of missiology as a "*komplementar-Wissenschaft.*" See J. Verkuyl, *Contemporary Missiology*, 9.

98. Bosch, "Missiological Developments in South Africa," 12.

99. Ibid.

100. For a detailed evaluation of the way Bosch sees missiology addressing the various theological disciplines (biblical studies, church history, systematic theology, practical theology, ecumenics and religious studies) see Bosch, "Missiology," 3rd ed., 278–81. Cf. J. Verkuyl, *Contemporary Missiology*, 9–11.

101. Bosch, "Missiology," 2nd ed., 238.

102. Bosch's approach in this regard is similar to O. G. Myklebust, who has urged missiology to retain its independence, and not forfeit its unique contribution by being assimilated into one of the other theological disciplines. See Myklebust, "Integration or Interdependence."

103. Bosch, "Missiology," 3rd ed., 281.

104. Ibid., 282.

Part Two: Bosch's Theology of Mission and Evangelism

provocative and responsive. It will assist and support sister disciplines as well as the Church . . . It should strive to be the most charismatic of all disciplines, at once confident of its own validity and urgency, but flexible and humble enough to learn from all."[105]

Doing Missiology: Functions, Benefits and Qualifications

Bosch drew attention to the two functions of missiology. Missiology has a *descriptive* function. It describes what the church has been doing. It attempts to give a scientific description and analysis of the missionary activity of the church in the past and in the present.[106] Here the cognate disciplines of historical analysis, religious studies, anthropology, and sociology come to the fore. Only when missiology begins to understand and describe the church as it was and as it is can it go on to speak normatively about the church's future.

The second function of missiology—the *normative, critical* function—offers norms and guidelines for the church's future actions; how its activities *should* be conducted.[107] Missiology seeks to "give a lead to the Church concerning the fulfillment of its missionary task. It can only do this by setting out a scripturally based concept of the definitions, goals, and method of mission."[108] This normative, critical function of missiology is essential lest the church become either *irrelevant* to the situation in which it lives, or *disobedient* to the Lord who calls it to mission in his world.[109] This critical function is also painful, for it exposes the weaknesses and failures of the church. Missiology, Bosch concluded, "has a critical function. In theology it works like yeast. It creates unrest, a movement among dry bones. It articulates mission as the conscience of the Church, for it is perpetually asking questions, uncovering, delving deeper—and irritating! It investigates the church, and pronounces it guilty. No groups of people can ever cosset God's mission or boast to having carried it out. Mission is dynamite, and if we do not handle it properly, it will explode in our faces."[110]

Besides these clear functions of missiology, Bosch noted at least two benefits to missiological study. First, it not only gives students a better understanding of the situation of others; it provides them with a new perspective on *their own situation*.[111] Missiology thus bears fruit in the student's own church and culture. Bosch remarked that this had been his own experience and the experience of many others. "Time and again it happens that ministers working in the monocultural, Western context testify that they have profited enormously by their study of this subject . . . In one way or

---

105. Scherer, "Missions in Theological Education," as cited in Bosch, "Missiology," 2nd ed., 238.
106. Bosch, *Missiology 101*, 6; and Bosch, "Missiology," 2nd ed., 239.
107. Bosch, *Missiology 101*, 6.
108. Bosch, "Missiology," 2nd ed., 239.
109. Bosch, *Witness*, 3; Bosch, *Theology 201*, 2.
110. Bosch, "Missiology," 3rd ed., 278.
111. Ibid., 283.

another this study leads them to discover the other in themselves and themselves in the other. They become aware of points of contact they had never before imagined between their own situation and that of people in another world."[112]

Second, Bosch reminded the student of what Martin Kähler long ago maintained: that a detailed study of the missionary situation would shed light upon our understanding of the Scriptures. Kähler maintained that "when we study the New Testament in the light of events on the present-day mission fields we may discover that many obscure portions of the New Testament become much more intelligible . . ."[113] Certain aspects of Scripture (beliefs, practices) that seem culturally distant from modern readers come alive when studied in light of the contemporary missiological issues, particularly in places where the church has only recently been established.[114]

Besides highlighting the functions and benefits of missiological study, Bosch also *qualified* the study of missiology with two caveats. First, it should be remembered that the primary purpose in studying missiology is not to learn how to preach better, but to learn how to *listen* better.[115] Bosch recounted hearing of a minister who revealed, upon retiring after forty-five years as a pastor: "I am proud to say that in all these years I have never once had occasion to change a viewpoint." Bosch concluded that such a man is to be pitied. "By refusing to be influenced by any other view he has deprived himself. In a very literal sense he has learnt nothing, because he was unable to listen . . ."[116] Listening does not, of course, exclude preaching or witnessing. In fact, the person who has "listened carefully and is affected by what he has heard will feel compelled to tell to others what he has heard." That person will witness and preach in a new way.[117]

Second, Bosch reminded his colleagues that missiology cannot awaken and motivate the church to mission, for this is the sole task of the Lord of the church. Missiology simply acts as a corrective, servant and teacher.

> [Missiology] is there to serve the Church, to assist it in gaining greater clarity concerning missionary goals and motives; it may cite the Church's own history as an example; it may help those involved in mission to compare strategies and methods; it may act as a corrective to the Church's own caprices and partialities. But to motivate and activate the Church is outside its province . . . It is the Lord of the Church, not theology, who bestows faith and vision, zeal and

---

112. Ibid., 282–83.

113. Bosch, "Systematic Theology and Mission," 184–85.

114. What, for example, do baptism and the Lord's Supper mean? Kähler urged theologians to ask the missionaries and young converts this question, for they will frequently have a fresh insight into its meaning. "Don't try to decide whether something is an essential feature of Christianity and the church, unless you have ascertained what meaning that feature has in areas where the church has recently been planted . . ." (ibid., 186–87).

115. Bosch, *Missiology 101*, 76.

116. Ibid.

117. Ibid., 11–12.

perseverance. Theology cannot supply the Church with the ammunition or the resources that will enable the believer to dispense with faith in God or that will lessen the hazard of the Church's activities. Theology may—must—speak to the Church's conscience, but it may never become the substitute for decisions and acts of faith.[118]

---

118. Bosch, "Missiology," 3rd ed., 283.

4

The Historical and Theological Context of Mission

Major Motifs in Bosch's Thought

IN ORDER TO COMPREHEND Bosch's views on mission and evangelism we need to understand the *interpretive framework* with which he operated. In the previous chapter we spelled out some of Bosch's fundamental *methodological* and *theological* assumptions. In this chapter, we shall continue this task, but with a slightly different focus. We shall now highlight Bosch's evaluation of the *contemporary historical* dynamics of mission. It is our task in this chapter to clarify the foundational motifs in Bosch's thought that informed his evaluation of Christian mission.

Prior to the publication of *Transforming Mission*, when Bosch used the model of paradigm theory to explore Christian understandings of mission over the last two millennia, Bosch analyzed the contemporary missionary situation by means of three motifs or models: a) *mission in crisis*; b) *evangelical and ecumenical*; c) *First World and Two-Thirds World*.[1] These motifs represent dominant recurring themes in his writing and help explain the "mental grid" through which he discusses the missiological data.

At the outset we note that the motifs used by Bosch were *conflictive*, depicting profound theological and ideological tensions; yet in Bosch's use of these analytical models, he was not bound by them. Bosch understood his work as an exercise in

---

1. A fourth major motif, *Black and White*, was used frequently by Bosch and particularly relevant to South African theology. We shall attempt to develop this motif throughout the latter chapters of this book. Perhaps surprisingly, given his traditional Dutch Reformed heritage, the motif of *Catholic and Protestant* did not seem to be a particularly important one for him. Not that Bosch's neglected Catholic missiology (cf. Bosch, *Witness*, 112–23; 182–86). It appeared, however, that he subsumed this division into the three major motifs mentioned above. He frequently commented that contemporary Roman Catholic missiology manifests the same splits and tensions as modern Protestant missiology, thus relegating the Protestant/Catholic tension to a secondary level. See Bosch, *Witness*, 29.

"bridge-building," analyzing the tensions within each motif *creatively* in order to reconcile the opposing perspectives. He endeavored to move beyond the polarizations in mission that he observed in his lifetime. Bosch spoke his own mind of course. He believed the conflicts described in the motifs were both real and substantial, and was sharply critical of those who did not recognize the reality of these divisions. Yet the tone of Bosch's writing was generally pastoral and not argumentative, urging that the debate go on, but also that those involved in the debate listen deeply to one other, exercising self-criticism and rejecting facile stereotypes of the other.[2]

THE MOTIF OF "CRISIS"

The first way Bosch portrayed the shape of the Christian mission in the late twentieth century was the motif of *crisis*. The church, particularly in the West, has been in the midst of a profound identity crisis, uncertain as to what her mission should be. Bosch alluded to numerous representative works that typified the crisis with their graphic titles.[3] Bosch attributed the crisis to a fundamental change in Western Christian self-understanding. In broad terms, Bosch argued that after the first three centuries of the church's life, the "Constantinian period" arose which lasted from the fourth century until the twentieth century.

The advent of the Constantinian era had profound effects on the church, including the following characteristics.[4] The church went from being a small, disparaged community to a large and influential institution. It went from being a persecuted sect to being a persecutor of sects and dissidents. Church and state became increasingly intertwined, so that throne and altar were frequently linked. Church membership

---

2. As an excellent example of Bosch's "style" of creative reconciliation of strongly differing points of view, see his "Dissension among Christians: How Do We Handle Contentious Issues?" In this article, Bosch commented that: "Over against such apodicticism I would like to posit the possibility of a different style and attitude: that of tolerance. Tolerance does *not* suggest papering over our difficulties, fogging out conflicts and freezing over confrontations. Neither does it suggest a disposition of relativism. It suggests, rather, a real and continuing recognition of the right to have differences, and effort to listen and to learn, and a willingness not to dodge the issues but—and this is important—*to stay with my 'opponent' to the end*, in forthright and fraternal confrontation . . . What I plead for, then, does not imply softness or surrender, but, rather, resolute confrontation of one another in a spirit of mutual acceptance. The Christian community is the one place where adversaries can coexist facing one another openly and still find it possible to gather around the same table. But we can only do that if we do not take our stand on positions defined once and for all, but are willing to move forward, in faith, to a common goal" (Bosch, "Dissension among Christians," 8).

3. Bosch mentioned such titles as *Revolution in Missions* (W. C. Lamott), *Missions in a Time of Testing* (R. K. Orchard), *Missions at the Crossroads* (T. S. Soltau), *The End of an Era* (E. Kendall), *The Eye of the Storm* (D. A. McGavran), *The Battle for World Evangelism* (A. Johnston), *The Church and its Mission: A Shattering Critique from the Third World* (O. Costas); *Was heisst heute Mission?* (K. Bockmühl). These titles, Bosch noted, "reflect something of the extent and the gravity of the present crisis." See Bosch, "Missiology," 3rd ed., 269. To this list, we could add many other works, including *Shaken Foundations: Theological Foundations for Mission* (P. Beyerhaus); *The Missions on Trial* (W. Bühlmann); *Roots of the Great Debate in Mission* (R. Hedlund); *What Next in Mission?* (P. Hopkins); and *Crises of Belief* (S. Neill).

4. See Bosch, *Witness*, 4.

became a formal affair, and attention shifted away from preoccupation with the imminent coming of Christ. The gifts of the Spirit were downplayed and ecclesiastical offices became institutionalized. The church became wealthy, resulting in the watering down of the ethical demands of the gospel. Finally, Christian doctrine and practice became increasingly fixed in rigid molds. Bosch maintained that the church, by and large, retained this "Constantinian" mindset until this century. Christianity and the churches in the West were in positions of decisive dominance and power, and their style of mission reflected this.

But by the last decades of the twentieth century, Bosch maintained, old-style Constantinianism was dead in most of the world.[5] The Christian churches had lost their preferential positions in their respective cultures, and with this loss came a crisis over the very nature and meaning of the Christian faith and mission. The delegates to the Edinburgh 1910 Missionary Conference were confident and optimistic about the future progress of Christian faith and human history. But by mid-century, this confidence had waned dramatically. As Bosch put it: "It required two world wars to make Christianity aware that not only mission but the church herself was experiencing a period of crisis unprecedented in her history."[6]

Bosch offered five reasons for why he believes there is a crisis in mission. Taken together, they represent an end to the "Constantinian era" of the Christian church and its mission.[7]

First, there had been a change in the *power structure*. Bosch drew upon the work of Eugene Nida to show how humankind had shifted from perceiving itself at the bottom of the pyramid of power to being at the top position of power.[8] In the Middle Ages, God was seen as supreme over all other powers. The feudal structure embodied a hierarchical view of the world: God-church-kings-nobles-people. Power emanated from the top down, and people were recipients, the "objects" of history, the "pawns" of both the church and the state. This, in essence, was the epitome of the Constantinian worldview. Beginning with the age of the Enlightenment, but particularly with the advent of the modern scientific world, all phenomena (physical, social, mental) began to be explained without reference to God.[9] With the emphasis upon natural laws, and particularly evolution, humanity no longer had to look "up" to God or church or

---

5. Bosch later qualified this judgment somewhat, pointing out that although in the West the dismantling of Constantinianism began as long ago as the Renaissance, "there are even to this day regions and communities where for all practical purposes the population still thinks and acts in Constantinian categories," including South Africa, and, within Islam, such nations as Iran (Bosch, *Witness*, 4. Cf. Bosch, *Missiology 101*, 46; and *Theology 201*, 3).

6. Bosch, *Witness*, 3.

7. These five reasons are drawn from Bosch, *Witness*, 3–9.

8. Bosch, *Missiology 101*, 46–48. Bosch was drawing upon the analysis of Eugene Nida in his *Religion Across Cultures*, 48–57.

9. In this regard, one recalls the famous reply of Laplace when some objected that he had neglected to include God in his system: "I had no need of that hypothesis." See Newbigin, *Foolishness to the Greeks*, 65.

Part Two: Bosch's Theology of Mission and Evangelism

king. Humans found the legitimizing source of power within themselves, collectively or individually (explaining the rise of such ideologies as Marxism and Nationalism). Thanks to modern science, humankind could look "down" upon the natural world. Man had truly become the measure of all things, and occupied the supreme place in the hierarchy of power. From the perspective of this secular Enlightenment view of humanity and nature, the very concept of mission, or of theism itself, is called into question. God (and mission) becomes irrelevant to the modern Western worldview.

A second condition that led to the crisis in Christian mission was the changed *political situation*. In the sixteenth century, Christianity was almost exclusively a European affair. With the advent of Vasco de Gama and the era of European exploration and colonialism also came the expansion of the church into the non-Western world. There was a clear and irrefutable linkage between Western colonialism and Christian mission. Gradually, however, the era of Western dominance has been receding and this has had a strong impact upon the church and her mission. As Bosch explained, "the end of the dominance of the 'Christian West' has brought, as an inevitable consequence, far-reaching changes in the way the religion of the West is regarded in the erstwhile colonial territories. In some former colonies missionaries from the West are no longer welcome."[10]

Mission and Western colonialism were being seen, fairly or unfairly, as part and parcel with one another. If the one had run its course, critics of mission ask, had not the other as well?

A third factor in the crisis in mission in the modern era is the massive change in the *church's center of gravity*.[11] Thanks to the missionary enterprise of the churches over the last centuries, the Christian faith has now become a truly worldwide religion. "Younger churches" exist in practically every nation on earth. In contrast to this bright picture, the church in the West continues to decline numerically at an alarming rate. While the churches of Africa, Asia and Latin America are rapidly growing, the European (and to a lesser extent North American) churches of old Christendom are steadily declining.

With this shift in the center of the church from the West to the Third World, one-way missionary traffic is no longer acceptable. Some of the younger churches, Bosch noted, had begun to refuse to accept certain forms of assistance from the Western churches, "because such help is regarded as indefensible paternalism and enslavement."[12] This new and perplexing situation raises many questions for both the older and younger churches, which have long operated in certain traditional patterns.

Fourth, the present crisis in mission is prompted by a *new evaluation of the place of non-Christian religions*. In the long history of the modern missionary movement,

---

10. Bosch, *Witness*, 5.

11. See Bosch, "An Emerging Paradigm for Mission," 485–87, for some statistics which confirm this trend.

12. Bosch, *Witness*, 5.

most Christians had no doubt that the Christian religion was the only true faith, and that in the end it would eventually triumph over its rivals. One has only to read the nineteenth and early twentieth-century missionary literature to discern this spirit of extreme optimism, in which the whole world would be "Christianized" and all the non-Christian religions would steadily crumble with the advance of Christianity.[13] Yet Bosch notes that in the current era, one rarely finds this style of Christian triumphalism any more, apart from some segments of the evangelical and fundamentalist branches of the church. The other world faiths are a permanent part of the religious landscape. There is evidence that the so-called "higher religions" are not declining, but holding their own, and indeed, in some cases, growing at a much faster rate than Christianity. The Christian mission has had strong success among people from backgrounds of primal religions. Islam, Hinduism, and Buddhism, however, have yielded comparatively few converts. Christianity, as a percentage of world population, has actually *declined*.[14]

Besides the statistical data, two other factors have contributed to the changing perceptions of other religions. First, in many circles there has arisen a deep questioning of traditional Christian teaching regarding the salvation of non-Christians. Is salvation found only in the fold of the church and are those outside of it lost? How can this be true if Christianity is actually shrinking slightly as a world faith? Some Roman Catholic and Protestant theologians have therefore called for a serious reevaluation of the traditional Christian theology of religions. Bosch mentions such theologians as Hans Küng, Karl Rahner, and William Cantwell Smith in this regard. Second, Bosch noted there has also been a renaissance of missionary consciousness among some of the other world religions. Islam, Hinduism, and many new religious movements are currently engaging in active missionary work in the West, a situation that would have been unimaginable to the confident young Warneck in 1909.

Fifth, many modern Christians, particularly in the West, exhibit a *deep uncertainty as to what mission really is, and what its goal ought to be.* The combined pressure of the tour aforementioned factors has "given rise to the question whether Christian mission work still makes sense and, if it does, what form it should take in today's world."[15]

13. Bosch noted the title of Johannes Warneck's 1909 book *The Living Christ and Dying Heathenism* as an example of the spirit of the age. He also cited one Lars Dahle, who in 1900 confidently predicted that, based on the growth rate of Christianity in the nineteenth century, the entire world would be Christian by the year 1990! (ibid., 6).

14. See ibid., where Bosch notes that in 1900, some 36% of the world's population belonged to the Christian faith, but by 1973 that percentage had fallen to 26%. But David Barrett, in his monumental *World Christian Encyclopedia*, takes a less pessimistic perspective. According to his data, Christianity, as a percentage of world population, has declined only slightly in this century (1900–34.4%; 1970–33.7%; 1980–32.8%; 2000–32.3% (estimated). In light of the massive population explosion, Christianity must grow aggressively even to stay even. See David Barrett, *World Christian Encyclopedia*, 6 (Global Table 4, 'Global Adherents of All Religions').

15. Bosch, *Witness*, 8. Bosch cited evidence of this uncertainty in the remarks of three of the twentieth century's senior missionary statesmen. The famed general secretary of the Church Missionary Society, Max Warren, lamented that there was a "terrible failure of nerve about missionary enterprise

Part Two: Bosch's Theology of Mission and Evangelism

The situation of mission in the contemporary age is changing, complex, and urgent. Echoing the words of Emilio Castro, Bosch noted "an era is at its end, and a new one [is] in the process of being born. We do not yet know what the new era will be like, neither what our role and responsibility will be."[16] Most Christians are unable, as yet, to see the radical implications of the new era into which we have irrevocably passed. For many in the church, especially in the West, this state of affairs has prompted a profound uncertainty about the future of Christianity.

Bosch injected a note of encouragement here, however. The crisis being experienced by Christians today should not paralyze them into inactivity or cause them to lose heart. Christians must open their eyes outward, particularly upon the growing church in the Two-Thirds World, and recognize that "the twentieth century is a watershed of possibly greater importance than any other in the history of the Church since its inception . . ."[17] "Missions" have been a historically conditioned phenomenon, and we are now entering into a new era. But what should be the response of God's church this new situation?

> First, we may regard the Christian mission as a time-bound phenomenon, eulogize it for what it did accomplish and bury it. Secondly, we can do everything in our power to revivify missions as they were, in the process trying to convince ourselves and others that all the historical conditions still obtain, although we may formulate some of them more carefully. Thirdly, we may accept that missions as we have known them since the time of the Jesuits and William Carey belong to an era irrevocably past, yet without burying or revivifying them in their traditional form. Rather, we may accept that *by the grace of God missions did indeed make a unique contribution to the world and for the Kingdom, and then set out to define what genuine mission means today.*[18]

Bosch affirmed that the third option is the only responsible choice available to the church.

It is also important to recognize that the church's mission to the world has *always* been a bone of contention, and that crisis, however grave, is the *normal* situation for the church to be in. What was abnormal in the church's history was that for so long she seemed to endure in a crisis-free existence. In the twentieth century, the church had returned "back to normal," in order to truly *be the church once again.*[19] Bosch

---

in many circles today." Bishop Stephen Neill confessed a similar deep concern. And Samuel Moffett, longtime missionary to Korea and now Professor of Mission and Ecumenics at Princeton Theological Seminary stated: "In my father's day coming home was a kind of triumph. The missionary was the hero. Today he is an anti-hero. Even in Christian churches I am eyed askance as a throw back to a more primitive era" (ibid).

16. Bosch, "Evangelism and Mission: The Contemporary Debate," 5. Castro used similar terminology at the 1973 Bangkok Assembly of the CWME.

17. Bosch, "An Emerging Paradigm for Mission," 487–88.

18. Ibid., 488 (my emphasis).

19. Bosch commented: ". . . the Church's missionary enterprise [is] something that, because of its

The Historical and Theological Context of Mission

endorsed the perspective of Kosuke Koyama, who noted that crisis is not the end of opportunity but its beginning. Crisis is the place where *danger* and *promise* meet.[20] The contemporary church cannot be content to ignore the present crisis in mission; rather it is called to participate with God creatively in discerning "the signs of the times" by considering what faithfulness to Jesus Christ means for today.[21] Under the sovereign, creative Spirit of God, the whole church stands in constant need of clarifying its relationship to the world.

It is from within this overall framework of *mission in crisis* that Bosch moved on to develop two further understandings of the contemporary world mission situation. We turn now to the evangelical/ecumenical motif.

THE EVANGELICAL/ECUMENICAL MOTIF

Far and away the most significant motif in Bosch's missiological thought prior to *Transforming Mission* was the evangelical/ecumenical tension. That this tension existed and that it profoundly shaped the missiological discussion in the latter half of the twentieth century is recognized by nearly all missiologists.[22] We shall focus on Bosch's own understanding and critique of the two movements,[23] particularly as manifested

---

very nature and being, will always be in dispute. It was an anomaly that there was a time when mission was not disputed . . . The practical missionary endeavours of the Church always remain, under all circumstances, ambivalent. Mission is never something self-evident, and nowhere—neither in the practice of mission nor in even our best theological reflection on mission—does it succeed in removing all confusions, misunderstandings, enigmas and temptations" (Bosch, *Witness*, 10).

20. "An Emerging Paradigm for Mission," 508. Bosch is citing Koyama's *No Handle on the Cross*, 4.

21. Bosch, *Witness*, 9.

22. A voluminous literature on the subject has emerged. Among the most significant works which make use of these categories, see Bassham, *Mission Theology: 1948–1975*; Beyerhaus, *Missions: Which Way?* and *Shaken Foundations*; Berkhof "Berlin versus Geneva," 80–86; Castro, "Ecumenism and Evangelicalism: Where are We?," 8–17; and "Evangelical and Ecumenical," 17–22; Glasser and McGavran, *Contemporary Theologies of Mission*; Hedland, *Roots of the Great Debate in Mission*; Wolfgang Hering, *Das Missionsverständnis in der ökumenisch-evangelikalen Auseinandersetzung*; Hoekstra, *The World Council of Churches and the Demise of Evangelism*; Horner, *Protestant Crosscurrents in Mission*; McGavran, ed., *The Conciliar-Evangelical Debate*; Goodall, "'Evangelicals' and the WCC-IMC," 210–15; Johnston, *World Evangelism and the Word of God* and *The Battle for World Evangelism*; Kramm, *Analyse und Bewährung theologischer Modelle zur Begründung der Mission*; Saayman, "Integration, Polarisation and Justification," 78–84; Stott, *Christian Mission in the Modern World*; Stowe, *Ecumenicity and Evangelism*.

23. Bosch repeatedly returned to this *leitmotif*. The following works by Bosch are particularly useful: "Ecumenical Deadlock or Prophetic Opportunity?," 7–10, 18; "Possibilities and Limitations of Ecumenical Action in South Africa," 20–24; "Crosscurrents in Modern Mission," 54–84; *Witness*, 28–40, 159–229; *Theology 201*, 125–95; "Behind Melbourne and Pattaya," 21–33; "The Melbourne Conference: Between Guilt and Hope," 512–18; *De Achtergrond van Melbourne en Pattaya*; "In Search of Mission: Reflections on 'Melbourne' and 'Pattaya,'" 3–18; "Melbourne and Pattaya: The Left Foot and Right Foot of the Church?"; "Creatieve spanning tussen oecumenisch en evangelisch"; "Evangelism and Mission: The Contemporary Debate"; "An Emerging Paradigm for Mission," 485–510; "Theologies of Mission," 41–55; and "'Ecumenicals' and 'Evangelicals': A Growing Relationship?," 458–72.

Part Two: Bosch's Theology of Mission and Evangelism

in the two contrasting World Mission Conferences in 1980 in Melbourne, Australia and Pattaya, Thailand.

Defining the Evangelical/Ecumenical Motif

From his earliest writings on Christian mission, Bosch revealed an awareness of the issues of theological conflict between the evangelical and ecumenical missionary movements. It is only after 1970, however, that he began to use the terms "evangelical" and "ecumenical," and only after the 1974 Lausanne Congress and the 1975 Nairobi Assembly that the motif appeared as the predominant factor in his analysis of missionary theology.[24]

Bosch recognized that both "ecumenical" and "evangelical" are imprecise terms. A number of churches use the term "evangelical" as a synonym for "Protestant."[25] But Bosch, like many others, used the term "evangelical" in the sociological sense. "Evangelical" is used, particularly in the English-speaking world, to define that inter-confessional, international stream within Protestantism that has its roots in both the Protestant Reformation and in the subsequent renewal movements of continental Pietism and Anglo-American Puritanism. Despite the large variety of groups who define themselves as "evangelicals,"[26] most commentators point to three predominant characteristics that link evangelicals together and identify evangelicalism as a distinct theological movement. Evangelicals are "those Protestants who stress the personal experience of conversion, the high authority of the Bible, and the mandate to evangelize others."[27]

In light of their zeal to proclaim the Gospel to all persons, it should come as no surprise that "evangelicals" have become a diverse, dynamic and powerful force within the Christian world mission. Although most evangelical mission agencies are related to the Lausanne Committee for World Evangelization (LCWE), a significant minority of evangelicals are involved in the mission structures of the WCC and its member churches.

With regard to their theology of mission,[28] evangelicals have tended to understand mission as the proclamation of the gospel (in the more restricted, verbal sense)

---

24. For example, see the completely different approach taken in relation to the dynamics of mission theology between his 1972 essay "The Question of Mission Today," and his 1976 essay "Crosscurrents in Modern Mission." The former makes no mention of an "evangelical/ecumenical" debate, whereas in the latter the debate provides the organizing principle of the entire article.

25. For example, in the Lutheran tradition and also in all Protestant traditions in Latin America, where the preferred term is "evangélico," due to the pejorative understanding of the word "Protestant" in Roman Catholic Latin America.

26. Bosch endorsed Peter Beyerhaus' analysis of evangelicalism's diversity. Beyerhaus distinguishes at least six "branches" within the larger evangelical movement; 1) mainline evangelicals, 2) separatist fundamentalists, 3) confessional evangelicals, 4) pentecostals and charismatics, 5) radical evangelicals, and 6) ecumenical evangelicals. See Bosch, *Witness*, 30.

27. See Costas, *Theology of the Crossroads*, 40–41.

28. What follows is a summary derived from Bosch's "Ecumenical Deadlock or Prophetic

and the "planting" of the church in every culture. The motive for mission is found in the Great Commission (Matt 28:16–20) that, as part of the infallible Word of God is to be received and obeyed. This command has functioned as the sufficient theological basis for world mission, although other bases and motives have also played their part. Evangelical mission emphasizes the eternal lostness of humankind due to its own sin, and the necessity of a personal confession of faith in Christ as the divine Savior and Lord. The church's mission is conceived in essentially "spiritual" terms, and world evangelization is her primary task. Social service is a significant but secondary aspect of the Christian mission. The world is perceived to be evil and hostile to the message of the gospel. The non-Christian religions are viewed in negative terms as well, as shields by which people hide from the true God of the Christian faith.

Since the 1974 Lausanne Congress, however, there has been much ferment on the question of whether the pursuit of social justice is a legitimate aspect of Christian mission. Due to the mediating influence of such men as John Stott and Ron Sider, many evangelicals have broadened their understanding of mission to include both evangelism *and* social service/action. For many other evangelicals, however, the pursuit of social justice is still not a legitimate aspect of the church's mission. It is at best, secondary, and at worst, a distraction from the first priority of the church: evangelization and church planting. The persistence of this negative attitude towards social involvement is due, in large part, to the dominance of premillenialist and dispensationalist eschatologies among evangelicals, with their profoundly pessimistic views of the future. Sin, salvation, and the Christian life and mission are still viewed predominantly in individualistic terms. Structurally, this has meant that evangelical mission agencies (with some notable exceptions), have tended to be free associations of individual Christians rather than official, church-related "mission boards." These evangelical "faith missions" have traditionally undertaken quite specific and specialized functions (e.g., student evangelism, church planting, literature work, relief and development assistance). In the past these "missions" have frequently cooperated only with like-minded evangelical agencies, although this too has begun to change.

The ecumenical movement has its roots in a number of diverse streams. It was born out of a common quest for Christian unity among various Protestant churches and movements, most notably the nineteenth-century missionary movement. This link between mission and unity has been at the heart of the ecumenical vision. Indeed the ecumenical pioneer W. A. Visser 't Hooft defined the word "ecumenical" as "that which concerns the unity and the worldwide mission of the Church of Jesus Christ."[29] In the classic wording of the 1951 Rolle Statement, the word "ecumenical" was used "to describe everything that relates to the whole task of the whole Church to bring the Gospel to the whole world. It therefore covers equally the missionary movement

---

Opportunity?," 9–10; *Witness*, 31–35; "Melbourne and Pattaya: the Left Foot and the Right Foot of the Church?," 11; and "Theologies of Mission," [12–21].

29. See Visser 't Hooft, "The Word 'Ecumenical'—Its History and Use," 735.

and the movement towards unity . . . Both the International Missionary Council and the World Council of Churches are thus properly to be described as organs of the Ecumenical Movement."[30]

From its outset the ecumenical movement has been theologically broader and more inclusive than evangelicalism.[31] It has included within itself numerous (and frequently conflicting) theological tendencies. Structurally at the center of the ecumenical movement is the World Council of Churches and its member denominations and national church councils. Following the 1961 integration of the International Missionary Council (IMC) into the WCC, the missionary dimension of the ecumenical movement has existed in the Commission on World Mission and Evangelism (CWME), whose constitutional aim is "to assist the Christian community in the proclamation of the gospel of Jesus Christ, by word and deed, to the whole world to the end that all may believe in him and be saved."[32]

With regard to the ecumenical movement's theology of mission,[33] Bosch discerned a clear shift of focus. From the first World Missionary Conference in Edinburgh (1910) until Tambaram (1938), the focus was on mission understood as *evangelism*. From Tambaram until New Delhi (1961), the focus was on the *church*. Indeed, Bosch noted that "one of major reasons for the integration of the IMC and the WCC at New Delhi was that mission should be seen as pre-eminently an ecclesiastical enterprise."[34] But from New Delhi until the 1980s, the ecumenical movement had evolved to view the *world* rather than the church as the primary focus of God's concern, under the influence of such theologians as Hans Hoekendijk, Paul Lehmann, and Richard Shaull.[35]

With this shift of focus, ecumenical mission theology increasingly became concerned with such issues as development, justice and liberation. Ecumenical theology sees mission in holistic terms, and reflects the desire to overcome the perceived dualism in the evangelical viewpoint.[36] No longer are there Christian "sending" countries and pagan "receiving" countries, but a world mission with "witness in six continents" in the words of the Mexico City slogan. Mission is defined as "witness" in all its forms, accomplished through proclamation, dialogue, silent presence, service, prophetic criticism, and social action. The goal of mission in the ecumenical literature has been described in equally broad terms, variously as humanization, *shalom*, evangelization, development, and liberation. Likewise the concept of salvation has to do with every

30. As cited in Bassham, *Mission Theology*, 32.

31. Castro, "Ecumenism and Evangelicalism: Where are We?," 15.

32. Paton, *Breaking Barriers*, 390.

33. What follows summarizes Bosch's characterization of ecumenical missiology as developed in "Ecumenical Deadlock or Prophetic Opportunity?," 8–9; *Witness*, 31–35; and "Theologies of Mission," [12–21].

34. Bosch, "Melbourne and Pattaya: The Left Foot and the Right Foot of the Church?," 4.

35. Bosch adopted this threefold typology of the changes in the focus of ecumenical mission theology from the work of Gort, *Your Kingdom Come. World Missionary Conference: Melbourne, May 1980*, 1ff.

36. Bosch, *Witness*, 35.

The Historical and Theological Context of Mission

aspect of human life that hinders humankind from attaining a true, human existence; salvation therefore impinges on the current day concerns for peace, justice, and human community as well as the traditional concern for eternal life with God after death.

As mentioned above, a crucial characteristic of ecumenical mission in the contemporary era has been its desire to be open to the world. The world provides the primary frame of reference and, in a sense, sets the church's agenda, because God is actively speaking through the world to the church. For many ecumenical Christians, the world and not the church is the crucial arena of God's activity. God speaks through world-historical events, human experience, and non-Christian faiths and ideologies as well as through the Holy Scriptures and the Christian community. Hence the church's first task is not to speak but to listen. The church seeks to interpret what God is saying through "the signs of the times" in the events of the modern, secular world. As the church discerns what God is saying through his actions in the world (the *missio Dei*), she must continually structure herself to be an instrument of his mission, entering into "partnership with God in history." To paraphrase the titles of two famous ecumenical mission studies, she must be a church for others, a church for the world. In a similar fashion, many ecumenical Christians affirm various theologies of liberation. These Christians discern an eschatological "hand of God" in the various national movements for the liberation of the poor and oppressed. This concern for the poor and marginalized, and the demand for a radical sociopolitical response, has resulted in a very strong (and controversial) ecumenical commitment to social justice and human liberation on the part of the various ecumenical mission agencies. In the ecumenical missionary movement, therefore, the frontier between the church and the world, between salvation history and world history, has become increasingly vague. This extends particularly to the work of God in other religious traditions, where many ecumenical Christians would posit that God is already savingly involved.

To its critics, ecumenical mission theology has secularized and politicized the gospel, and downplayed the fundamental aspects of mission, which are to reconcile men and women to God by the proclamation of the gospel, and gather them into believing communities. In some ecumenical statements, so the critics say, salvation has almost been identified with sociopolitical liberation from capitalism. The quest for a new political and economic order has replaced the original ecumenical vision of "the evangelization of the world in this generation." Proclaiming the gospel has given way to dialogue with other faiths, whose aim is not the conversion of the nations to Christ but a partnership among the world religions to fight global human problems. Pioneer mission to convert the unreached billions to Christ has been downplayed due to a latent tendency in ecumenical thought towards universalism.

Ecumenicals, on the other hand, would reject much of this criticism, pointing out more diversity than evangelicals acknowledge. They would agree that "evangelization is the test of our ecumenical vocation," but would argue that the nature and context of evangelization is much more complex than evangelicals realize.[37] The gospel of Jesus Christ, ecumenicals answer, is *inherently* related to the struggle for justice. Any evangelistic strategy that neglects this dimension is a scandal to God and humanity. Many ecumenicals view evangelical mission agencies as anachronisms, intent on restoring an outworn, nineteenth-century style of imperialistic, crusading mission with little regard for national churches. What is needed today, they argue, is not a greater emphasis on "reaching the unreached," but upon greater faithfulness to the gospel where the church already exists. Only as the church's life and witness becomes authentic and credible to the world will it ever gain the right to be heard.

Qualifying and Justifying the Use of Evangelical/Ecumenical Motif

Bosch qualified his use of the ecumenical/evangelical motif in three ways. First, he acknowledged the ambiguity of terminology. Bosch admitted that it was patently unfair to categorize persons into neat, absolutely opposing camps. "The inadequacy of our terminology emerges . . . from the fact that we cannot declare all 'evangelicals' to be unecumenical or all 'ecumenicals' to be unevangelical."[38] Second, Bosch acknowledged that within both the evangelical and ecumenical movements, there existed an incredible diversity of theological perspectives; there is no monolithic "evangelical" or "ecumenical" position or spokesperson speaking *ex cathedra* for either movement.[39] Third, Bosch has acknowledged that his categorizations were perhaps "oversimplified," "overstated,"[40] and "extreme."[41] He urged his readers not to be ". . . too perturbed if you find that you are not quite at home in either of the two positions presented here—in fact, this is to

---

37. This was the theme of the World Council of Churches General Secretary Philip Potter's 1974 speech to the Roman Catholic Synod of Bishops in Rome. See his "Evangelization in the Modern World." The phrase was later cited in the WCC's landmark 1982 statement "Mission and Evangelism: An Ecumenical Affirmation."

38. Bosch, *Witness*, 29. Elsewhere, Bosch echoed the words of Paul Rees on the inadequacy of the terminology. "If men such as Lesslie Newbigin and John V. Taylor and James Scherer and John Gatu and Douglas Webster and Pierce Beaver and Eugene Smith and John Coventry Smith are impliedly non-evangelical because they are actively ecumenical, then words have ceased to be decent carriers of important meanings." Bosch goes on to add many other names, including Stephen Neill, Max Warren, Georg Vicedom, Johannes Verkuyl, Gerald Anderson, Bengt Sundkler, Hans-Werner Gensichen, and Mortimer Arias. See Bosch, "Crosscurrents in Modern Mission," 79; and *Witness*, 29.

39. Bosch, "Behind Melbourne and Pattaya," 22. Bosch further cautioned that "We should be careful with the terms "ecumenical" and "evangelical," however, and not, in a simplistic way, describe the ecumenical movement as being only interested in people's this-worldly aspirations, and the evangelical movement as concerning itself only with the salvation of souls. The picture is far more complex than that. At best, the two designations may be used to indicate two main *types*. There are, as a matter of fact, many variations of ecumenicals and evangelicals; there are, indeed evangelical ecumenicals and ecumenical evangelicals!" ("Theologies of Mission," [14]).

40. Bosch, "Evangelism and Mission: The Contemporary Debate," 13.

41. Bosch, *Theology 201*, 19–20.

be expected and hoped for! What is portrayed here is not two people, but two extreme viewpoints. Nobody will conform to either category all the way."[42]

Bearing these qualifications in mind, Bosch nevertheless believed it is possible, indeed necessary to use the terms "evangelical" and "ecumenical" as "distinguishable categories."[43] Many of the crucial debates in mission theology in the latter half of the twentieth century, Bosch maintained, arose from these two different worldwide constituencies of Christians, who had very different missiological agendas, priorities, and understandings.[44] Whatever one feels about the inadequacy of the terminology, Bosch reminded his readers that "the two terms are being used almost universally and . . . we can hardly ignore them."[45] Beyond this pragmatic argument, Bosch also justified his use of the motif on the ground that it provides the missiologist with a very useful "scale" or "model" by which to understand "the full spectrum of contemporary interpretations of the missionary task."[46] Thus Bosch clearly delineated the proper use of the ecumenical/evangelical motif: it is to function as an interpretive *model* of the realities of the contemporary Christian mission rather than as an exhaustive and exact representation of that reality. Like a parable, the model functions as a helpful conceptual tool that provides a true, albeit partial perspective on the underlying reality.

In his earlier works, Bosch sometimes presented somewhat extreme, even stereotypical descriptions of the ecumenical/evangelical polarization. In one article written after the WCC's 1968 Uppsala Assembly, Bosch labeled the ecumenicals "horizontalists" and the evangelicals "verticalists."[47] Bosch qualified his critique as an "oversimplification" and "inadequate," but the basic motif of immense polarization remained.[48]

Since that time, however, Bosch perceived a significant lessening in the ecumenical/evangelical polarization, and his rhetoric concerning the motif had likewise become more restrained and qualified. By 1976, following Lausanne and Nairobi, Bosch posited a growing convergence between the ecumenical and evangelical positions.[49] Yet in later writings Bosch qualified his own evaluation as overly optimistic. In different ways, both movements had become entrenched again into more polarized

---

42. Ibid.

43. Bosch, "Behind Melbourne and Pattaya," 22.

44. Bosch, "Evangelism and Mission: The Contemporary Debate," 5.

45. Bosch, *Witness*, 29.

46. Ibid., 28.

47. The ecumenical "horizontalists" lacked any sense of eschatological tension in their theology and who seemed quite optimistic about the perfectibility of humanity and social structures. Their concern was with the world rather than the church and evidenced almost no interest in conversion or the growth of the church. Likewise the evangelical "verticalists" were otherworldly pietists with an exclusive emphasis upon mission as verbal proclamation. Due to their understanding of the kingdom as an entirely future-oriented category, they viewed the present world in starkly pessimistic terms and eschewed all forms of social action. See Bosch, "Possibilities and Limitations of Ecumenical Action in South Africa," 22.

48. Ibid.

49. See Bosch, "Crosscurrents in Modern Mission," 79–84; *Witness*, 194–95.

positions.[50] Throughout his writings, Bosch continued to use the ecumenical/evangelical motif as the primary theoretical model by which he analyzes the theology of mission.[51] The motif was a constantly recurring theme in Bosch's thought.

Melbourne and Pattaya: The Historical Setting

As noted above, an in-depth historical and theological review of the evangelical/ecumenical debate is unnecessary; comparative studies of the movements are legion. Bosch himself surveyed the historical origins of the two movements, placing the theological roots of the modern evangelical/ecumenical debate as far back as the eighteenth century.[52] For our purposes, however, we shall focus on Bosch's evaluation of the two movements, as they were manifested in the two contrasting World Mission Conferences at Melbourne and Pattaya in 1980. Although these two conferences provide us with only a small "snapshot" of the larger debate, they provide us with concrete manifestations of the differing (complementary?) visions of Christian mission in the contemporary world. Bosch's evaluation was particularly valuable because he was one of a handful of missiologists to attend *both* conferences.[53]

The Commission on World Mission and Evangelism of the WCC sponsored the Melbourne conference. It was a direct descendant of previous ecumenical mission conferences, stretching back to the landmark Edinburgh gathering in 1910. Its theme was taken from the Lord's Prayer: "Your Kingdom Come." At Melbourne, most delegates were official church representatives, particularly from the mission agencies related to the WCC member churches.[54] In terms of the structure of the conference, the meeting worked in four "sections" which were devoted to specific theological themes. The sections ("Good News to the Poor," "The Kingdom of God and Human Struggles," "The Church Witnesses to the Kingdom," and "The Crucified and Risen Christ Challenges Human Power") addressed the missionary implications of each theme in light of contemporary realities in the world.

---

50. See Bosch, "In Search of Mission," 18.

51. Bosch admitted that "much of *Witness to the World* presupposes and addresses the ecumenical/evangelical controversy. In fact, the attempt to move beyond this controversy may be a *leitmotiv* of the book" ("Some Random Thoughts," 3–4). As recently as 1987, Bosch reaffirmed (with the necessary reservations) the use of the evangelical/ecumenical model as a proper paradigm by which to study the dynamics of contemporary mission theology. See "Theologies of Mission," [15].

52. Bosch, *Witness*, 28. For the full survey of the ways in which the theology of Christian mission has been perceived down by the church through the ages, see ibid., 86–195, esp. chapters 14–17; and Bosch, *Transforming Mission*.

53. Also valuable are essays by others who attended both conferences, including Costas, "A Prayer and a Question, 135–61; Scott, "The Significance of Pattaya," 57–76, and "The Fullness of Mission," 42–56; Stockwell, "What Really Did Happen at Melbourne?," 532–37, and his unpublished paper "What Did I Hear at . . . 'How Shall They Hear?'" Also see the entire January 1981 issue of *Missiology*, which was devoted to the two conferences.

54. Melbourne also contained a large contingent of "evangelicals" of all persuasions, serving both as delegates and as advisors.

The Pattaya conference was sponsored by the Lausanne Committee for World Evangelization, a coalition of evangelical mission agencies and leaders formed after the Lausanne Congress of 1974. It also stood in a direct line with the 1966 Wheaton and Berlin congresses.[55] Its theme "How Shall They Hear?" was taken from the Pauline question in Romans 10:14. At Pattaya, most of the attendees were not representatives of churches, but leaders of missionary agencies (mostly non-denominational) who were *invited* by the Lausanne Committee leadership. In terms of the structure of the conference, the major work was done in seventeen "mini-consultations" focusing concentrated attention on evangelistic strategies to "reach" specific "people groups" (e.g., "Reaching Muslims," "Reaching Buddhists," "Reaching Nominal Protestants," "Reaching the Urban Poor"). The goal of these consultations was to develop more effective strategies for world evangelization, e.g., the proclamation of the gospel so that people would be moved to repent and accept Jesus Christ as their Savior and Lord.

Melbourne and Pattaya: Issues of Theological Conflict

In order to clarify his criticisms of the two conferences (and the larger theological movements they represent), Bosch developed a comparative table, contrasting Melbourne and Pattaya.[56]

Melbourne	Pattaya
Showed a preference for the "Jesus of the Gospels	Showed a preference for the language of Paul's epistles
Began with "man's disorder"	Began with "God's design"
Stresses unity (at the expense of truth?)	Stressed truth (at the expense of unity?)
Believed that God is revealed also through contemporary experience	Believed that God is revealed only through Jesus Christ, Scripture and the church
Emphasized the deed (orthopraxis)	Emphasized the word (orthodoxy)
Regarded social involvement as part and parcel (or all?) of the Christian mission	Regarded social involvement as separate from mission, or as a result of conversion

---

55. Bosch made the interesting observation that these conferences, as well as the work of the World Evangelical Fellowship, are manifestations of an emerging "evangelical oecumene." Evangelicals, despite their general mistrust of the WCC's style of ecumenism, have nevertheless found it necessary to develop an ecumenical movement of their own, albeit on a much more limited and functional basis ("Crosscurrents in Modern Mission," 71).

56. See the following analyses by Bosch: "Melbourne and Pattaya: The Left Foot and the Right Foot of the Church?," 1–3; "In Search of Mission," 5–6; "Evangelism and Mission: The Contemporary Debate," 5–13; and "Evangelism," *Mission Focus* 1981), 65–66. The following table is taken from the latter article.

Part Two: Bosch's Theology of Mission and Evangelism

Judged societal ethics to be of prime importance.	Judged personal ethics to be of prime importance.
Viewed sin as having a corporate dimension.	Viewed sin as exclusively individual.
Tended to equate mission with humanization or social change.	Tended to equate mission with a call to conversion or church planting.
Viewed proclamation as *rendering support* to fellowship and service.	Viewed proclamation as primary; it *gives birth* to fellowship and service.
Emphasized liberation.	Emphasized justification and redemption.
Heard the cry of the poor and oppressed.	Heard the cry of the lost.
Considered man from the perspective of Creation.	Considered man from the perspective of the Fall.
Judged humanity positively.	Judged humanity negatively.
Denied the existence of clear boundaries between the church and the world.	Affirmed the existence of clear boundaries between the church and the world.
Regarded the world as the main arena of God's activity	Regarded the church as the main arena of God's activity
Underscored the church's credibility.	Underscored the church's opportunities.
Was concerned about witnessing where the church *is*.	Was concerned about witnessing where the church *is not*.
Divided the world into rich and poor, oppressor and oppressed.	Divided the world into "people groups."
Revealed a proclivity towards Socialism.	Revealed a proclivity towards capitalism.
Highlighted Jesus' human nature.	Highlighted Jesus' divine nature.
Focused attention on the universality of Christ.	Focused attention on the uniqueness of Christ.

Bosch qualified the use of this comparative chart by cautioning the reader that the two positions have been deliberately simplified "for the sake of clarity."[57] Significantly however, Bosch maintained that the Melbourne-Pattaya, ecumenical/evangeli-

---

57. Bosch commented: "Fortunately we do not always encounter the two approaches in pure form. I have here, simply for the sake of clarity, deliberately over-simplified the two positions. I have, in effect, compared the ultra-ecumenical position with the ultra-evangelical. I have treated them as two distinct and distinguishable types. So I may, here and there, have overstated my case. And yet, even where we do not get the respective positions in pure form, much of what they stand for can be clearly recognised in what I have said so far" ("Evangelism and Mission: The Contemporary Debate," 13).

cal typology was also a helpful tool in analyzing the South African scene. He believed the conflicts revealed in the typology bore a remarkable resemblance to the polarized theological positions of Christians in South Africa. Bosch maintained that Melbourne expressed views typical of those held by many Black South African Christians; and that Pattaya expressed views typical of those held by most White South African Christians. "If there is even a grain of truth in this contention," he urged, "it behooves us to look very carefully at the two conferences and at what they are saying to us."[58]

Bosch discerned at least eight areas where Melbourne and Pattaya exhibited serious theological conflict.

Terminology

The two conferences tended to use different *vocabularies*, so that frequently they used different words to describe the same concept, and conversely, they often intended different meanings even when they used the same terminology.[59] He pointed out how the latter became apparent particularly with regard to Melbourne and Pattaya's understanding of such basic concepts as "mission" and "evangelism."

Melbourne followed the recent ecumenical pattern of treating "mission" and "evangelism" as broad, virtually synonymous terms.[60] Ever since the 1952 Willingen conference, Bosch notes, the meaning of "mission" and "evangelism" have been broadened to signify the church's witness for Christ in the world.[61] During the 1960s, "mission" in the ecumenical jargon became practically synonymous with the church's participation in programs for social transformation. But since the 1973 Bangkok meeting, Bosch discerned a subtle shift to define "mission" in somewhat wider and "evangelism" in somewhat narrower terms, although ecumenical usage of the terms remains broad and imprecise.[62]

Melbourne was criticized by some for defining mission and evangelism too *broadly*, so that the specifically evangelistic aspect of the church's life in the world was slighted. Since Melbourne was not a meeting of the whole WCC but of its Commission on Mission and Evangelism, one would expect that all the sections at the

---

58. Bosch, "Evangelism: An Holistic Approach," 43–44. Elsewhere Bosch reaffirmed this idea. He gave a report on the two conferences at the 1981 Congress of the South African Missiological Society with the following preliminary remarks: ". . . the theme of our own Congress [ecclesiology] and the tension that we find right here among us and in the South African ecclesiastical scene at large is not unlike the global theological tensions dramatised by the two world missionary conferences. It may therefore help us to look at the global picture and, perhaps, deduce from that some guidelines for our own situation. This may provide us with a very necessary perspective in the often heated debate on our divergent local theologies" ("In Search of Mission," 3).

59. Bosch, "Behind Melbourne and Pattaya," 24.

60. Bosch, *Theology 201*, 173.

61. Bosch, "Behind Melbourne and Pattaya," 24.

62. Ibid.

Part Two: Bosch's Theology of Mission and Evangelism

conference would have dealt with themes explicitly related to mission and evangelism. Bosch noted that some complained that

> . . . only one of the four sections dealt with a specifically missionary theme: Section III, "The Church Witnesses to the Kingdom". However, the organisers of Melbourne defended the inclusion of the other three themes in a *missionary* conference . . . They contended that the socio-political realities in which millions of people (non-Christian and Christian) live—realities such as global poverty, oppression and exploitation, and manifestations of human power (military, financial, ideological and political)—all have a profound influence on the Church's missionary task in the world.[63]

Evangelicals have tended to be more precise in their definitions. Like the ecumenicals, they have used the terms "mission" and "evangelism" as synonymous, equivalent terms. But they have understood the words in a narrower fashion, connoting only the persuasive, verbal *proclamation* of the gospel.[64] Bosch noted that ever since the Lausanne Congress, evangelicals such as John Stott and Arthur Glasser had tried to broaden the definition of mission to include a social dimension to the church's witness in the world, but this has resulted in a dispute with those evangelicals who favor the narrower viewpoint of mission and evangelism as synonymous with verbal proclamation.[65]

At Pattaya, Bosch thought this narrower viewpoint won out, despite the concerns of many participants. "Pattaya reverted to [the] pre-Lausanne position."[66] Mission and evangelism were equated, but with a narrow meaning.[67] In fact, Bosch reported

---

63. Bosch, "Evangelism: An Holistic Approach," 45.

64. Bosch cited two examples of the narrower evangelical understanding of evangelism, taken from the 1966 Berlin and 1974 Lausanne meetings. Berlin defined evangelism as "the *proclamation* of the Gospel of the crucified and risen Christ . . . with the purpose of *persuading* condemned and lost sinners to put their trust in God by receiving and accepting Christ as Savior through the power of the Holy Spirit and to serve Christ as Lord in every calling of life and in the fellowship of his Church, looking toward the day of his coming in glory." Likewise Lausanne defined evangelism as "the *proclamation* of the historical, biblical Christ as Saviour and Lord, with a view to *persuading* people to come to him personally and be reconciled to God" ("Behind Melbourne and Pattaya," 25; my emphasis).

65. Bosch, "Behind Melbourne and Pattaya". Prominent among those who urge this viewpoint are Peter Beyerhaus and Arthur Johnston. Johnston's post-Lausanne book *The Battle for World Evangelism* is, in essence, a spirited attack upon Stott's position and a defense of the proposition that the mission of the church must be understood as consisting only of the verbal proclamation of the gospel.

66. Bosch, "Behind Melbourne and Pattaya," 25.

67. Bosch commented how Pattaya was criticized, even internally, for defining mission and evangelism too *narrowly* and thus "reneging" on the broader vision of mission envisioned by the 1974 Lausanne Covenant. Bosch noted "Pattaya had a passionate concern for reaching people who are eternally lost, and would not allow anything or any body to divert attention to other issues. Evangelism, narrowly defined as persuading people to accept Christ, was given priority. The primacy of evangelism was upheld, as it was in the Lausanne Covenant, but unlike the Lausanne Covenant, which emphasised sociopolitical involvement as an equally indispensable calling of Christians. Pattaya appeared to soft-pedal the latter. A 'Statement of Concerns' which was circulated privately at Pattaya challenged the Conference leadership on this point and alleged that it had in fact retreated from the Lausanne position where it had been

that many at Pattaya were reticent to use to term "mission" at all; they preferred the dynamic, active, goal-oriented term "evangelization." "Evangelization" suggests movement, reaching out to others. In Bosch's view, this was precisely the underlying vision of mission at Pattaya: "the Church as a body in action, moving into the world and *reaching* people outside of it."[68]

Theological Presuppositions

Bosch contends that Melbourne and Pattaya presupposed very different theological starting points in their evaluation of humankind. Melbourne, he contended, started from a more "anthropological" perspective, while Pattaya was, at least on the surface, more "theological," concerned more with God's design than the human situation.[69] Bosch explained that ecumenicals tend to see humanity from the perspective of *Creation*, and emphasize the essential goodness of humankind. They emphasize the humanity of Jesus, who as "the man for others" reveals to us our true humanity. In this scheme, sin is viewed primarily in structural rather than personal terms, and is found not so much in individuals as in an unjust social order. Evangelicals, on the other hand, tend to see humanity from the perspective of the *Fall*. From this perspective, humankind stands under the judgment of God due to every individual's sinful nature and behavior. Every person is lost, "dead in his sins," and stands in need of redemption and of a divine Savior.[70] Where is the origin of these contrasting points of departure? Bosch contended they sprang from different hermeneutical approaches.

Hermeneutical Approach; Appeal to and Use of the Bible

Both Melbourne and Pattaya, being Christian conferences, attempted to ground their theological reflection in specific biblical passages. Melbourne emphasized the "Jesus language" and "kingdom language" of the gospels, and used Scripture primarily in ethical categories, while Pattaya preferred the more "theological" language of Paul, appealing primarily to doctrinal and soteriological categories of thought.[71] Bosch

---

affirmed that 'the message of salvation implies also a message of judgment upon every form of alienation, oppression, and discrimination, and we should not be afraid to denounce evil and injustice wherever they exist' (*Lausanne Covenant*, para. 5). For all practical purposes, however, the Pattaya conference leadership ignored the 'Statement of Concerns'" (Bosch, "Evangelism: An Holistic Approach," 45–46).

68. Bosch, *Theology 201*, 173 (my emphasis). As evidence of this interpretation, Bosch noted how the structure of Pattaya focused on the fact that "each of the 17 mini-consultations at Pattaya was concerned with 'reaching' Buddhists, Marxists, etc . . . Pattaya—and the LCWE generally—moreover tended to avoid the word 'mission' because the organizers felt that it was too general and catholic: evangelization, by contrast, is a specific, circumscribed, goal-oriented activity" (ibid.).

69. Bosch, "Evangelism and Mission: The Contemporary Debate," 6.

70. Bosch, "Behind Melbourne and Pattaya," 23.

71. Bosch, "Evangelism and Mission: The Contemporary Debate," 6. Bosch credits Waldron Scott with this observation. See Bosch, "Behind Melbourne and Pattaya," 4.

believed that even in the selection and use of the chosen theme texts, contrasting theological agendas emerged. Melbourne emphasized the imperative dimension of the Lord's Prayer; we are called to *make* the kingdom come, to *do* something to inaugurate the kingdom. The emphasis, therefore, was upon ethical achievement, and the overriding feeling at Melbourne was *guilt*. Pattaya, on the other hand, emphasized the word ("How shall they *hear*?"). Pattaya had Bible expositions rather than Bible studies. It emphasized listening to God through the proclamation of the gospel, and accepting his word. "Pattaya," wrote Bosch, "was confident that if only the word were to be communicated faithfully and intelligibly, people would become Christians and consequently, change their environments."[72]

Beyond the differing biblical sources of the conference themes, Bosch discerned a deeper issue which Melbourne and Pattaya broached: what is the *locus* of God's revelation? Scripture alone or human experience as well? "Pattaya," Bosch argued, "declared that God reveals Himself only in Scripture and through Jesus Christ," but in contrast "Melbourne believed that God reveals Himself also through contemporary experience."[73] Bosch acknowledged these contrasting ways of *appealing to* and *using* Scripture are an example of the larger hermeneutical debate between evangelicals and ecumenicals, namely the deductive and inductive approaches to interpreting the Bible.[74]

Eschatology and a Theological Evaluation of the "World"

One clear example of the way in which these differing hermeneutical starting points affected the theologies of Melbourne and Pattaya was their strongly contrasting evaluations of the relationship between God, the church and the world. Bosch argued that most evangelicals have, since the early twentieth century at least, reduced eschatology to a hope for an exclusively futuristic, other-worldly kingdom. The eschatological concept of the kingdom of God has been neglected, and has had almost nothing to do with God's purposes for the world *in history*. Apart from a rather feeble doctrine of providence, evangelicals have said very little about the world as an arena of God's redemptive activity. Rather, the world has been perceived as essentially evil, unchangeable, and therefore irredeemable. This eschatological fatalism has contributed to a general neglect among evangelicals of any serious grappling with issues of social

---

72. Bosch, "Evangelism and Mission: The Contemporary Debate," 7.

73. Ibid. The ecumenical use of Scripture differs from evangelical usage. Bosch cited the example of the 1966 Geneva Church and Society Conference, which stated that "Holy Scripture, *together with* Christian history, contemporary Christian experience and the insight of the social sciences and other secular disciplines, *inform* the situation, and that the Christian, in light of all this is called to be obedient to *his understanding* of God's will in *his particular situation*" (Bosch, "Behind Melbourne and Pattaya," 23; emphasis original). At Melbourne, Bosch maintained that three of the four section reports embodied this hermeneutic.

74. For more on this, see chapter 4. Cf. Bosch, *Witness*, 38, 43–45. Orlando Costas, in his review of Melbourne and Pattaya, came to similar conclusions. See his *Christ Outside the Gate*, 138.

The Historical and Theological Context of Mission

justice.[75] Evangelicals have traditionally drawn a sharp boundary line between the church and the world. At Pattaya, Bosch argued, this continued to be the case. Evangelicals perceive the church as being exclusively *over against* the world, and mission is therefore defined as winning people from the world into the church. The key word at Pattaya's various mini-consultations was "reach," like a lifeboat rescuing the perishing. The church was regarded as "the main arena of God's activity . . . a divine agency, God's supernatural instrument for saving people from the world."[76]

Ecumenicals, on the other hand, have not been as interested in drawing strong boundary lines between the church and the world, due to their different eschatological emphasis. Bosch frequently observed that beginning with the differing understandings of the *missio Dei* concept that emerged at Willingen, but particularly since the 1961 New Delhi Assembly (when the IMC was integrated into the WCC), the ecumenicals have placed the world rather than the church at the center of God's salvific activities. This emphasis, building on the work of Hoekendijk and others, has given positive emphasis to what God was doing in *this* world, in the here and now. Whereas Cullmann and Barth emphasized the priority of "salvation history" and the church, Hoekendijk wanted to show the indissoluble link between the church and the world, between world history and salvation history. If the focus of God's work, the *missio Dei*, was upon *this* world and its agonies, then the focus of the church's mission should be changed to emphasize the goals of humanization, human rights, struggling against racism and injustice. In some circles, the traditional missionary aims of conversion and church-planting were downgraded to a secondary if not illegitimate status. Particularly since the mid-seventies, there had been a swing away from the more extreme elements of this line of thought, but there remains in ecumenical thought a certain vagueness about the transcendent, future dimension of the kingdom of God. In ecumenical eschatology, mission, indeed God himself, has become primarily "this-worldly" in orientation.[77] At Melbourne, Bosch argued, the world was main arena of God's activity. The church, far from being God's supernatural instrument, was rather part of the problem.[78]

The Church

Another example of the way in which these differing hermeneutical starting points affected the theologies of Melbourne and Pattaya was their strongly contrasting ecclesiologies. Both Melbourne and Pattaya concerned themselves with the church, but their evaluations of its nature, mission, and unity differed sharply. Whereas Melbourne

---

75. Bosch, "Behind Melbourne and Pattaya," 28–30.
76. See Bosch, "Evangelism and Mission: The Contemporary Debate," 11–12.
77. Bosch, "Behind Melbourne and Pattaya," 28–30. Bosch singled out the contribution of Ernst Käsemann as indicative of this trend at Melbourne (ibid., 29).
78. Bosch, "Evangelism and Mission: The Contemporary Debate," 11–12.

emphasized the church's *credibility* (or lack thereof), Pattaya emphasized the church's evangelistic *opportunities*.

After Tambaram 1938, ecumenical missiology (under the combined influence of Karl Barth and Hendrik Kraemer) placed the church at the center of God's purposes for the world. The church was "the divinely appointed agent for spreading the gospel." It was an order of *redemption* rather than creation, and could never identify itself completely with any human program, structure, or ideology.[79] But this view changed dramatically in the 1960s. As Bosch characterized it: "Whereas Willingen 1952 still hesitated to express itself on God's work outside the Church, Mexico City 1963 had no difficulty in doing so; instead it grappled with defining the relationship between God's work inside and outside the Church. The preparatory documents for Uppsala 1968 went one step further, and Hoekendijk claimed, 'In no respect can the Church regard itself either as the subject of the Mission or as its sole (and exclusive) institutionalized form.'"[80]

In the influential 1967 WCC report *The Church for Others*, Bosch noted how "evangelism as a call to join a church was summarily dismissed as 'a form of proselytism' and conversion redefined as a movement not away from, but towards the world."[81] By the time of subsequent conferences at Bangkok 1973 and Nairobi 1975, these positions were significantly qualified. But there can be little doubt that Melbourne followed the general ecumenical trend since New Delhi of replacing the *church* with the *world* as the central focus of God's saving involvement with his creation.

At Melbourne, the church was viewed as a thoroughly ambivalent body, and frequently perceived as an *obstacle* to the transmission of the gospel. It was no longer a spiritual community that was above human conflicts; it was simply another institution which functioned as part and parcel of an unjust social order.[82] According to Bosch, Melbourne portrayed the church as failing miserably, often serving as a sign of the anti-kingdom rather than the kingdom.[83] Rather than serving as the agent and goal of

---

79. Bosch, "Behind Melbourne and Pattaya," 30.

80. Bosch, "Melbourne and Pattaya: The Left Foot . . . ?," 4–5. The Hoekendijk quote is taken from Thomas Weiser, *Planning for Mission*, 44.

81. Bosch, "Melbourne and Pattaya: The Left Foot . . . ?," 5. Bosch's citation is taken from *The Church for Others*, 75.

82. Bosch, "In Search of Mission," 6–7.

83. Bosch, "Evangelism and Mission: The Contemporary Debate," 8. Elsewhere, Bosch noted examples of this trend of being severely critical of the institutional church. "In the Report of Section 1, mention is made of churches '[which] are indifferent to the situations of the poor—or, far worse—actively allied with those forces which have made them poor.' The Report also refers to the missionary enterprise of the churches [which]. . . has been financed with the fruits of exploitation, conducted in league with oppressive forces and [which has] failed to join in the struggle of the poor and oppressed against injustice. This did not go unchallenged, however. Emilio Castro, the able and sympathetic director of CWME, intervened when this paragraph was put to the plenary. There was a difference, he said, between repentance and masochism, and what we had just heard smacked of the latter rather than the former. In spite of his objection, however, the paragraph in question was passed virtually unaltered. The mood of the conference led it to castigate particularly Western churches and society" (Bosch, "In Search of Mission," 7). Bosch's reference is to para. 18 of section 1 of the Melbourne report, found in *Your Kingdom Come*, 176–77.

mission, the church, particularly in the West, was now viewed as an embarrassment and as a sign of guilt rather than hope.[84]

For Bosch, this tension was a paradigm of the entire Melbourne conference.[85] In his essay "The Melbourne Conference: Between Guilt and Hope," Bosch compared the work of Section 1 ("Good News to the Poor") with the work of Section 3 ("The Church Witnesses to the Kingdom"), and found a deep division *within* the Melbourne documents and participants: was the church a sign of guilt or of hope in the world today? Bosch posed the tension as follows: "I do not suggest that the one saw the Church purely in the perspective of guilt and the other entirely in the perspective of hope, yet something of this characterization may indeed be applicable. It would also be true to say that there is more than just a grain of truth in the contention that Section I looked at reality from the perspective of *creation*, of the Church's *prophetic* calling and of *ethics*, whereas the perspective of Section III tended to be that of the doctrine of *redemption*, of the Church's *evangelistic* calling, and of *theology*."[86]

Bosch noted that sections 2 and 4 were similar to section 1. They criticized the church relentlessly, especially the church in the capitalist West. They emphasized the desperate plight of the human situation and the malaise of the churches in the face of the massive oppressions and injustices that daily afflicts the poor of the earth. In light of this apocalyptic situation, many of the delegates (particularly some Latin Americans) urged a radical realignment in the church's mission: she must align herself unreservedly to the poor, and become a force for the political and economic liberation of the oppressed masses. Apart from this new commitment to liberation, the church would simply be perceived as being on the side of the oppressors.

Although most delegates from socialist and Marxist nations were conspicuously silent about criticizing situations of injustice within their own lands, Bosch rejoiced that speakers from the capitalistic West could be so forthrightly self-critical. The recognition for self-criticism is a mark of maturity. Yet Bosch lamented that "in the midst of their merciless flagellation of themselves, their churches and societies there [were] so few signs of *hope*. In Melbourne . . . the burden of guilt was increased, people were smothered by it, while the joy of forgiveness and renewal somehow went by the board. It was a case of law without the gospel, judgment without compassion, works without grace."[87]

Section 3, however, breathed a very different air. Its hermeneutical approach was more explicitly theological than contextual. Its attitude towards the empirical church was basically positive, although not triumphalist. This can be explained in part because Section 3 attracted the participation of many evangelicals and Orthodox

---

84. This was an observation made by Halina Bortnowska, Polish Roman Catholic social worker, "The Church—Sign of the Kingdom," 145–56. Cf. Bosch, "In Search of Mission," 7.

85. Bosch, "The Melbourne Conference: Between Guilt and Hope," 512.

86. Ibid., 512–13.

87. Bosch, *Theology 201*, 149–50. Cf. Bosch, "The Melbourne Conference: Between Guilt and Hope," 516–17.

Part Two: Bosch's Theology of Mission and Evangelism

at Melbourne.[88] In Bosch's evaluation, the theology of Section 3 was traditional, in the sense of being in line with the classic ecclesiological emphasis of Tambaram and Willingen. He also noted that Section 3, in some aspects of its theology, resembled the Roman Catholic documents on mission *Ad Gentes* (1965) and *Evangelii Nuntiandi* (1975).[89] The church, although not identical to the kingdom, does serve as a *witness* to the kingdom, and herein she finds her identity. The Section, Bosch noted, gave "proclamation" a crucial role. "[Proclamation] is described as 'distinct and indispensable'; it concerns a story that 'has to be told', for the Church's life can never fully reveal God's love, holiness and power. It is, furthermore, with reference to Mark 1:15, defined as the *announcement* that the Kingdom is at hand, as a *challenge* to repent, and as an *invitation* to believe."[90]

With regard to the church's credibility, Bosch affirmed that Section 3 held out the church as a sign of hope.

> It would, I believe, be true to say that in the report of Section III, in spite of the clear admission of the guilt and failures of the Church—or rather, precisely *because of* this admission!—the Church is upheld as a sign of hope. People are invited to join the Church, to support it, to help it become what it already is, in Christ. The document offers no cheap grace, no easy solutions. In fact, the five searching questions at the end, which take up the themes of the five sub-sections of the document, cannot help creating in the heart of the serious reader a haunting awareness of the fact that his best efforts have been inadequate. Still, the overall tenor of the report is one of *hope*.[91]

While Bosch acknowledged that there were severe tensions at the conference between those who favored the ecclesiological approach of Section 3 and those who preferred the approach of the other sections,[92] there is little doubt in which direction Bosch's sympathies lay. Section 3 embodied many of the main themes in Bosch's

---

88. Glasser, "Melbourne 1980," 5.

89. Bosch, "The Melbourne Conference: Between Guilt and Hope," 513. If it is true that Bosch's own position is extremely similar to the approach of section 3, then this admission is significant, for it shows that Bosch perceives *himself* as standing in continuity with the Tambaram/Willingen tradition as opposed to the newer "world-centered" ecumenical theologies of the sixties.

90. Ibid. Beyond this, the document emphasizes such central missiological issues as conversion, the new birth, the reality and ideal of true Christian community, the need for the church to be a healing community, the need for a common witness to people of other faiths, and the missionary implications of the eucharist.

91. Ibid., 514. The five concluding questions from the document are as follows, as found in *Your Kingdom Come*, 206–7. "1. Do we know Jesus Christ in such a way that we can speak convincingly of him? 2. Is our congregation reaching out and truly welcoming all those in need, and all those who seek? 3. Are we expressing the Spirit's ministry of healing for those with broken hearts, disturbed minds and sick bodies? 4. Are we sharing with all Christians the deep concern in our neighbourhood and nation for better ways of living? 5. As we receive the Eucharist, God's all for us, are we giving our all to him and his needy children?"

92. See Bosch, "The Melbourne Conference: Between Guilt and Hope," 514.

thought.⁹³ Bosch's central critique of Melbourne was that the conference was captivated by a sense of *guilt* with regard to the church and her mission, which manifested itself in two unfortunate errors.

First, Melbourne's ecclesiology was too one-sidedly activistic and legalistic. Bosch acknowledged that the church must indeed seek *credibility* before the world, and it must repent of its complicity with the powers of oppression.⁹⁴ And yet Melbourne, in its passionate and unquestionably Christian concern for the liberation of poor and oppressed peoples, all too often stressed only the activistic, imperative dimension of the kingdom's coming, that we are called to *make* the kingdom come.⁹⁵ At Melbourne, Bosch confessed, "we were relentlessly goaded into action; this merely intensified the guilt, frustration and despair. If the demand to repent does not go hand in hand with the free offer of forgiveness and new life, we have law without gospel, judgment without mercy and works without grace. We then become so preoccupied with the miserable quality of the earthenware vessels that we are blinded to the treasure they contain."⁹⁶

A second error that Melbourne made was its presumption that the church can and must assume responsibility for every problem in the world. While sympathizing with Melbourne's zeal to strive with all available energies to present the whole gospel to the world, Bosch believed the church cannot do everything.

---

93. The following are some specific examples of the "Boschian" character of the introduction to Section 3.
    1. The section's claim that the *empirical* church witnesses to the kingdom, which is "a frightening claim but a wonderful reality";
    2. The confession that "we have no proprietary rights on the kingdom, no claim for reserved seats at the great banquet";
    3. The emphasis and peculiar translation of 2 Cor 5:17 in para. 4;
    4. The use, in para. 6, of Gensichen's "tests" of an authentically evangelizing community;
    5. The emphasis on "frontiers" and "pilgrimage" language, of the church "on the way";
    6. The emphasis, in para. 10, of the twofold nature of conversion as turning from *and* to; and the emphasis upon the church as *paroikia* ("emergency dwelling").

Interestingly, Bosch included the text of the introduction to section 3 *in full* in his UNISA Study Guide, *Theology 201*, on 142–47. For the official text of section 3, see *Your Kingdom Come*, 193–207.

94. Bosch, "Melbourne and Pattaya, the Left . . . ?," 5.

95. Ibid. Bosch notes that Jerald Gort, in his analysis of Melbourne, maintained that the conference theme "Your Kingdom Come" has three dimensions. The *indicative*, where we confess that the kingdom has already come; the *subjunctive*, where we pray for its coming in fullness; and the *imperative*, where we are called to make it come. Bosch adds: "In Melbourne, the emphasis was on the third; the other two were largely ignored. The delicate tension between the indicative, subjunctive and imperative were somehow lost" (ibid.).

96. Bosch, "Melbourne and Pattaya, the Left . . . ?," 5. Bosch commented that he was in total agreement with Melbourne's focus upon the materially poor, the exploited and the oppressed. If God hears the cry of his people, then we in the church must hear and respond as well. But he urged that this response made to God and his gospel should not be grounded in the fact that we have been goaded and scourged into action. We should respond to God not on the basis of his wrath but his love. "It is not the wrath but the love of Christ that leaves us no choice (cf. II Cor. 5:14). It is the Good News, and not the Law, that will crush our hearts." See Bosch, "The Melbourne Conference: Between Guilt and Hope," 518.

Part Two: Bosch's Theology of Mission and Evangelism

> We have indeed to do everything in our power—no, everything in God's power—to present a gospel that is Good news for the whole of man and for all of society. And yet, *we cannot do everything.* There comes a point where we have to say that, not as an excuse or a sign of resignation but as a humble confession of our weakness and of our faith in God. Halina Bortnowska put it in the following words: *"There are wrongs that cannot be repaired by human means."* We can say this only with tears in our eyes, but unless we can say it, we will be spiritually crushed and paralysed by our sense of guilt . . .[97]

Perhaps because of Melbourne's intense emphasis upon the *credibility* of the church, Bosch argued, Melbourne failed to emphasize the "frontier-crossing" nature of the church's witness. Bosch endorsed Waldron Scott's critical appraisal of Melbourne, who noted that Melbourne manifested a strong concern to witness to the kingdom where the church *is*. But should the focus of a mission conference also be concerned about witnessing to the kingdom where the church is *not*? According to Scott's evaluation, Melbourne took almost no notice of the many places and cultures where the church is either nonexistent or a tiny minority, surely a disturbing omission at a world missionary conference.[98]

The Pattaya conference took exactly the opposite approach from Melbourne, in that it evidenced less concern for the church's credibility and wanted instead to exploit the church's missionary *opportunities*.[99] It identified those places and peoples where no church exists (known as "hidden peoples" or "unreached peoples"), and attempted to devise effective strategies to reach such groups with the gospel. Bosch cited numerous evangelical leaders at Pattaya, including "radical evangelical" leader Vinay Samuel of India, who criticized the WCC for its smallness of vision and lack of faith; Melbourne appeared to have lost the ability to believe in the evangelization of the world.[100] Likewise, the evangelical understanding of the church's essential nature contrasted sharply from the ecumenical understanding. Whereas at Melbourne a variety of images of the church were present, at Pattaya the narrower model of the church as *herald* predominated.[101]

The heart of the church's mission at Pattaya was the desire to see men and women converted to Jesus Christ as Lord and Savior. Bosch found great merit with this approach, and affirmed that on this point, the evangelical approach was deeper than what he found at Melbourne.

---

97. Bosch, "Melbourne and Pattaya, the Left . . . ?," 5.

98. Bosch cites Scott's comments on Melbourne in *Theology 201*, 174.

99. Bosch also quoted Scott as noting that "The whole approach at Melbourne was, 'We've lost our credibility; we've got nothing to say to the world.' but what about the limitless opportunities among people who are *open* to the Gospel?" (Bosch, "In Search of Mission," 7).

100. Ibid.

101. Ibid.

> [The] evangelical recognition that we need new men if we are to hope for a new world and that, in order to become such new men, people have to experience a personal and life-giving encounter with the risen Christ. The root of the world's problems is spiritual and has to be recognized as such. Repentance and faith are decisive steps in accepting what God offers in Christ. It is inadequate to understand the Gospel in terms of social and political liberation. To dispense with the centrality of repentance, redemption and faith is to divest the Gospel of its central significance.[102]

In light of this distinctive characteristic of evangelical thought, Bosch commended Pattaya's mini-consultation on the urban poor in particular. The consultation on the urban poor was "able to present a more distinctively Christian response than had been possible for the corresponding section at Melbourne."[103]

On the debit side, however, Bosch criticized Pattaya for having a "high" view of mission but a "low" functional view of the church. He was not alone in recognizing this deficiency in evangelical theology. He acknowledged what Howard Snyder (a Methodist missiologist who has devoted himself to problems of evangelical ecclesiology) admitted at Lausanne; that there is "a fundamental theological problem which evangelicals have yet to deal with adequately . . . the problem of the church."[104]

This dichotomy between church and mission manifested itself in a number of ways at Pattaya.[105] Pattaya (unlike Melbourne) was organized by the Lausanne Committee, which is a loose coalition of independent evangelical missionary agencies. No official church representatives were on the Lausanne Committee, nor were they present at Pattaya, except as observers.[106] In its very organizational structure then, Pattaya embodied the idea that the mission agency is more important than the church.[107]

Symptomatic of the priority of "mission" over "church" in evangelical thinking was the reaction to an overture from the more churchly World Evangelical Fellowship for the LCWE to merge with it. It was proposed that the LCWE become the

---

102. Bosch, "Melbourne and Pattaya: The Left . . . ?," 11.

103. Ibid.

104. Ibid. Bosch is citing Snyder's article in René Padilla's symposium on the Lausanne Covenant, *The New Face of Evangelicalism*, 131, 138.

105. The following observations on evangelical ecclesiology are taken from Bosch's "Behind Melbourne and Pattaya," 31; "In Search of Mission," 7; and "Melbourne and Pattaya," 10–12.

106. Whereas Bosch saw this lack of official church representation at Pattaya as a weakness of evangelical mission, Melbourne served as a reminder of the other side of the coin, exhibiting a weakness of ecumenical mission. At Melbourne, most participants were national church leaders and ecclesiastical bureaucrats; there was very little participation from those who were actually serving as cross-cultural missionaries in either Western or Third World missionary societies. See Glasser, "Melbourne 1980," 774.

107. Indeed, Bosch believed there is still a strong tendency among evangelicals in Third World contexts to elevate missionary agencies to a higher prominence than the local indigenous church. In the eyes of both the Christians and non-Christians, the mission is more important. According to Bosch, this was nothing short of ecclesiastical colonialism. Bosch noted that numerous Third World Christian leaders attending Pattaya lamented this situation, as they did at Lausanne 1974 and Berlin 1966, but to little avail. See Bosch, "Behind Melbourne and Pattaya," 31; and "In Search of Mission," 7.

WEF's commission on mission. Most Third World representatives at Pattaya favored the merger, but most North American mission leaders did not, fearing a merger with the WEF would dilute the specifically missionary focus of the LCWE. The overture was turned down as "premature," to the disappointment of many Third World leaders.[108] It seemed clear that the difficult theological and structural issues related to the relationship of church and mission remains one of the great unresolved issues on the evangelical agenda.

Another evidence of Pattaya's "low" ecclesiology, according to Bosch, was the dominance of concern for the *numerical* growth of the church. This is undoubtedly the result of the growing influence of the church growth movement within evangelicalism. We shall reserve Bosch's critique of the church growth movement for a later chapter; at present it is enough to point out that Bosch was extremely critical of certain aspects of the movement's theology, especially the homogeneous unit principle.

A final evidence of Pattaya's deficient ecclesiology, according to Bosch, was its concept of *church unity*.[109] Although both conferences spoke about the unity of the church, and stressed its importance, the two movements meant very different things. Ecumenicals emphasize visible, structural unity and (despite the evangelical contention that ecumenicals lack concern for "doctrine"), invest much theological work in resolving major doctrinal differences. Evangelicals, however, stress spiritual and doctrinal unity, but not *visible* unity. Bosch contended that evangelical church unity, like evangelical ecclesiology in general, tends to be based on *pragmatic* rather than theological grounds ("for the sake of sharing resources, mutual encouragement, joint planning, etc."). But this vision of unity, according to Bosch, was very different from the full, biblical understanding of the oneness of the church.

Bosch also commented that evangelicalism's conception of church unity tends toward *exclusivism*. In its crudest form, evangelical exclusivism maintains "true Christians are those, and only those, who agree with evangelicals." This exclusivism, according to Bosch, reared its head more than once at Pattaya. Some participants felt that Roman Catholics could not be authentic Christians, and there was a tendency among some to regard not only nominal Catholics but *all* Catholics as legitimate objects of evangelization. The same would probably have been said about Orthodox Christians, and even many mainline Protestants.

In summary, Bosch criticized both evangelical and ecumenical missiology for failing to develop a truly biblical ecclesiology for our day. "The pervasive despair about the Church in some WCC circles is no more justifiable than is the overweening confidence in the ranks of the LCWE."[110]

---

108. Stockwell, "What Did I Hear at . . . 'How Shall They Hear?,'" 8.

109. For what follows, see Bosch, "Behind Melbourne and Pattaya," 31–32; and "Melbourne and Pattaya: Left . . . ?," 12.

110. Bosch, "In Search of Mission," 8.

Salvation and the Social Dimension of the Gospel

Perhaps in no other area has the contrast between evangelicals and ecumenicals been more pronounced than in their differing attitudes toward salvation and social concern. Bosch rightly recognized the existence of a diversity of opinions on the subject, among both evangelicals and ecumenicals. No simple stereotypes adequately explain such a complex picture. Broadly speaking, however, Bosch believed that Melbourne and Pattaya illustrated two differing understandings of the meaning and extent of salvation, and two contrasting attitudes towards the necessity of social involvement as an authentic aspect of the Christian mission.

Bosch pointed out that the evangelical Christians have not always been hesitant in affirming a strong social dimension to the Christian faith. Their involvement in social reform movements, particularly in the nineteenth century, was extensive and varied.[111] But with the Fundamentalist-Modernist controversy of the early twentieth century, there emerged the so-called "Great Reversal"; evangelicals became inward-looking and opposed to involvement in movements for social change.[112] Only in the latter half of this century, particularly since Lausanne, has evangelicalism again begun to reflect deeply about the relationship of evangelism and social responsibility.[113]

Most of the participants at Pattaya, according to Bosch, affirmed that social involvement was an important but *separate* and *secondary* Christian concern, to be distinguished from the church's evangelistic mission, which is primary. The church's mission was viewed essentially in "spiritual" terms. Humanity was evaluated from the theological perspective of the Fall; people were lost, guilty, estranged from God, and stood primarily in need of repentance, justification and redemption rather than sociopolitical liberation.[114]

---

111. See Bosch, "Theologies of Mission," [3–5].

112. See Bosch's "In Search of a New Evangelical Understanding," 68–71 for an detailed analysis of this trend.

113. Bosch highlighted the varying main viewpoints which have typified the evangelical attitude to social involvement in the twentieth century. At its most extreme, a few evangelicals have viewed social involvement as a *betrayal of the gospel*, "gospel" being understood in completely dualistic, "spiritual" terms. Other evangelicals have viewed social involvement as *a means to an end*; it is the bait to bring people to conversion to Christ, the forerunner of "real mission," understood solely as evangelistic proclamation. Numerous evangelicals have seen social involvement as simply *an optional extra*; alright for some but not a necessary priority of the church in mission. Many evangelicals, finally, have viewed social involvement as *the "fruit" of personal redemption*. Personal redemption, the "seed," is primary, while social concern, the "fruit" is secondary. The assumption has been that if people were truly converted, they would, as a matter of course, become socially concerned. Only through redeemed individuals can nations and governments become more godly and just in their dealings with people. A fifth viewpoint among evangelicals holds that both evangelism and social concern are equally authentic dimensions of Christian mission, although between these two "mandates," evangelism retains a certain position of primacy. A final viewpoint among a minority of evangelicals is that, while evangelism and social action can be distinguished as distinct aspects of the total mission of the church, they are indivisibly, inseparably linked together. Evangelism and social concern are both intrinsically related to the gospel itself (Bosch, *Witness*, 203). Cf. Adeyemo, "A Critical Evaluation of Contemporary Perspectives," 41–61.

114. Bosch, "Evangelism and Mission," 10–11.

Part Two: Bosch's Theology of Mission and Evangelism

Bosch affirmed the essential validity of the evangelical concern to analyze humankind from the perspective of the Fall. Pattaya, he said, was to be commended for affirming that "Man is first and foremost a sinner in need of redemption."[115] From this starting point, four sound theological implications followed.[116] First, Pattaya affirmed that all persons were sinners, and thus stood in equal need of God's grace. Second, Pattaya made a clear distinction between the church and the world.[117] Third, Pattaya recognized that the root of the world's problems are spiritual, and that it is inadequate to define the Gospel solely in terms of any political or social programme. It affirmed the absolute necessity of a personal, life-changing encounter with the risen Christ. Fourth, Pattaya acknowledged that God alone, not humans, would usher in his kingdom.

Despite these helpful affirmations, however, Bosch remained deeply dissatisfied with the evangelical approach to Christian social responsibility. Despite the praiseworthy efforts of many evangelical relief and development agencies such as World Vision and TEAR Fund, Bosch believed that evangelical social involvement had not yet been integrated, in a proper theological manner, into the evangelical worldview.[118] In particular, Bosch faulted evangelicals at three points.

First, Bosch criticized evangelicals' *"micro-ethical" understanding of the Christian faith*. Many evangelicals act as if their Christian ethical obedience is limited to their personal and domestic lives, and to interpersonal attitudes.[119] Linked to this is evangelicalism's profound pessimism about humankind's ability to change the broader structures of society. The world order is seen to be fundamentally irredeemable. Little true change can be wrought in this world except in the souls of men and women, and this should be the church's priority.[120] This approach, with its limited ethical framework and its despair of any fundamental reformation of society, was typified at Pattaya in the discussions concerning the Cambodian refugees. Bosch noted that although there was much mention made of their plight, and although there was encouraging news of how many hundreds of Cambodians had turned to Christ in the refugee camps, he was troubled by much of what he heard.

---

115. Bosch, "In Search of Mission," 11.

116. The following principles are found in ibid.

117. "Pattaya knew that the Church was the community of believers, granted the forgiveness of sins, living in communion with the Triune God, and sent to serve the world in solidarity with all mankind and to proclaim the message of God's love" (ibid.).

118. Bosch, *Witness*, 203.

119. As an example of this, Bosch cited Peter Wagner's definition of how an evangelical is identified. According to Wagner, an evangelical is identified by "a code of life which includes certain positive behaviour traits such as daily Bible reading and prayer, grace before meals, and regular church attendance, as well as certain negative traits such as total abstinence from or extremely moderate use of tobacco, alcoholic beverages and profanity in speech." Bosch pointed out that all of these traits are "micro-ethical" in scope; none challenge any evils beyond the interpersonal level (Bosch, "Melbourne and Pattaya, Left . . . ?," 12).

120. Ibid., 13.

First, there seemed to have been no uneasiness about the possible motivation for these conversions from among what amounted to captive audiences in camps with a powerful presence of Christian relief organisations which might hold the key to the future life of the refugees. Secondly, several people, speakers included, came to within a hair's breadth of praising God for the disaster that had befallen the Kampucheans, as this had made them aware of their need of Christ. Thirdly, Pattaya's understanding of social involvement was basically conceived along the lines of rescue operations after a disaster has struck, but was little concerned about the *causes* of the disaster. To quote from a "Statement of Concerns" that was circulated privately at Pattaya, "We have a working group on 'Reaching Refugees', but none on those that are largely responsible for the refugee situation around the world: politicians, armed forces, freedom fighters, national oligarchies, and the controllers of international economic power."[121]

Bosch believed that these attitudes spring from a deeper source; evangelicals also tend to *deny the intrinsic relation of social involvement to the gospel itself*, with serious consequences. Some, such as John Stott, argued that in the church's mission both evangelism and social action are authentic "mandates." The majority at Pattaya, however, viewed social involvement is a *separate* and *secondary* concern, to be distinguished from the church's evangelistic mission, which is primary. Evangelism is the seed and social involvement is the fruit.[122] To Bosch this approach was completely untenable. He argued that it is fundamentally dualistic, in that it divides the gospel, indeed reality itself, into "public" and "private" realms, into "spiritual" and "physical" spheres. Inevitably, this mindset of "non-interference" in the public and social realms leads to an unhealthy quietism in which the church abandons her responsibility to announce the whole gospel in word and deed. This approach also manifests a strong tendency to give theological legitimacy to the current sociopolitical order, however corrupt or oppressive the government might be, so long as it allows for freedom to preach the gospel verbally.[123]

121. Bosch, "In Search of Mission," 12–13.
122. Bosch, "Melbourne and Pattaya: The Left Foot . . . ?," 13.
123. Bosch commented: "I cannot possibly subscribe to such a view. To regard social involvement as the mere fruit of the Gospel is to divorce faith from public life, to espouse an atomistic view of reality, and to succumb to the insidious influence of Greek dualistic thought. This leaves a free field open to all the demons of power-politics and creates political helplessness in the face of societal injustices. Once we subscribe to the principle of non-interference we irrevocably drift towards allowing our thinking and living to be shaped by the views and values of the surrounding society (Rom. 12:2!). From there it is but one step towards finding theological justification for the dominant social order, particularly if that society allows evangelism to continue unhampered" (Bosch, "In Search of Mission," 13).
Bosch illustrated the harmful consequences of this narrow, dualistic understanding of the relationship of evangelism and social justice by recounting the following incident. At Pattaya, a South African Black commented that the evangelical/ecumenical debate was meaningless to him, because both evangelicals and ecumenicals alike oppressed Blacks in South Africa. In a subsequent interview with the press in South Africa, Bosch affirmed the essential validity of this observation. Later, Bosch received a telephone call from a leader in a large evangelical organization in South Africa who complained bitterly about Bosch's comments, expressing concern that these kinds of statements would endanger his

Part Two: Bosch's Theology of Mission and Evangelism

Bosch's final criticism of Pattaya's social outlook is that *it fell prey to the ethos of capitalism and Western values.* Bosch noted that evangelicals regularly chastise the WCC for a supposedly Socialist or Marxist bias. Yet, Bosch asked, does not the Lausanne Committee and evangelicalism as a whole have an equal bias towards capitalism? At Pattaya, Marxism was regarded as un-Christian, as evidenced by the consultation on "Christian witness to Marxists." But why was there no similar consultation on reaching capitalists?[124] Bosch criticized Pattaya's evangelicals for allowing the values of the affluent, materialistic West to shape the church's missionary thinking, to the point where many Christians seem genuinely incapable of critically evaluating the ideology of capitalism. "How else," Bosch asked, "can we explain the ethos of consumer research and promotional methods at Pattaya, the subtle—and frequently not so subtle—approval of Western values, the emphasis on strategies, methods and solutions?"[125]

Not all the mini-consultations downplayed the social dimension of the gospel, however. In particular, Bosch cited the consultations on reaching Marxists and the urban poor as exceptions to this trend.[126] The dominant attitude at Pattaya, though, was the superiority of evangelism over social responsibility, grounded in a dualistic understanding of the nature of the gospel.

The Melbourne Conference perceived the relation of mission and social involvement in a very different light. Most participants at Melbourne viewed social concern as an inherent dimension of the gospel, and an essential (and in some cases predominant) aspect of Christian mission. Melbourne argued that social, economic and political forces profoundly influence the lives of persons and societies. The church, therefore, has no alternative but to address these forces in the name of Christ. When the church fails to do this, she betrays her Lord. Mission at Melbourne, therefore, primarily meant the liberation of the poor and oppressed, the freeing of the exploited, the feeding of the hungry. Bosch argued that Melbourne evaluated humanity from the perspective of the doctrine of Creation, and focused most attention upon humanity's physical *needs* rather than its *guilt* before God.[127]

---

organization's chances of obtaining visas to enter other countries, hindering the work of evangelism there. Bosch concluded: "He appeared to be completely unconcerned about the possibility that the Black South African might have been right in what he said. Evangelism is so high a priority that it should be allowed to continue unhampered, regardless . . ." (ibid., 13–14).

124. Bosch, "Melbourne and Pattaya, the Left . . . ?," 14.

125. Bosch, "In Search of Mission," 14. Others have made a similar critique of Pattaya. Eugene Stockwell, in his "diary" of Pattaya, noted similar concerns. Commenting on the papers of Peter Wagner of Fuller Seminary and Ed Dayton of World Vision, he notes: "Strategy is the big thing at COWE, how to reach the unreached. At this point, apart from Osei-Mensah, I cannot help but be impressed by the strong U.S. impact here: Ford as chairman, David Howard as organizer of COWE, Peter Wagner, Ed Dayton, several references to Ralph Winter, and so on. The sociological-technical analysis, the basis for strategy, is very U.S., very Western. Not that we in ecumenical circles are free of it, but I do find it a bit much. Later, I discover that some Third World peoples here share some of my reservations" (Stockwell, "What Did I Hear at . . . "How Shall They Hear?," 2).

126. Bosch, "In Search of Mission," 15.

127. Bosch, "Evangelism and Mission," 10.

Bosch strongly affirmed the ecumenical emphasis on the social dimension of the gospel. Indeed, this concern is *the* distinctive characteristic of the ecumenical movement, in Bosch's opinion,[128] and it served as a needed corrective to the dualistic evangelical position.[129] In particular, he drew attention to five praiseworthy aspects of the ecumenical emphasis on the social dimension of the Christian faith.[130] Bosch affirmed that:

1. Social involvement is an inherent dimension of the gospel itself, not something superimposed on it from outside. There can therefore be no dualistic, absolute distinction between the personal and the social, between the spiritual and the physical.

2. Salvation and the kingdom of God are not only future but also *present* realities. Salvation is for *today* as well as tomorrow, as the 1973 Bangkok Conference stated. In Christ's advent, the kingdom *has* come. In light of the affirmation of 2 Corinthians 5:17, Bosch affirmed "something of this new world, of this new order, should be made manifest in the societies in which we live. God's will is to be done *on earth* as in heaven."

3. It is right and proper that Christians be involved in all the various movements that seek to preserve and enhance human life, particularly the human rights movement.

4. Sin must be understood to have a corporate, social dimension within institutions and structures, as well as a personal dimension within the lives of individuals. These collective sins, which cannot be traced to identifiable individuals, are "woven into the very fabric of society." In the words of Jacques Ellul, "What is characteristic of this type of sin is that no one commits it, but it is still committed."[131]

5. The plight of the poor and oppressed must be a central concern for the Christian church and its mission. Melbourne's bias towards the poor was entirely legitimate, and highlighted the theological truth that "it was not so much that the poor needed the Church as that the Church needed the poor if it wished to be true to its Lord—a Church *of* the poor rather than a Church *for* the poor." Bosch acknowledged that the church had not yet begun to emulate her Lord in taking seriously the plight of the poor.[132]

---

128. "The most distinctive characteristic of the ecumenical movement is the attention it pays to the social dimension of the Christian message. This has been the case at least since the Jerusalem Conference of 1928, though it is only since the beginning of the 1960's that this emphasis has become dominant" (Bosch, "Melbourne and Pattaya: The Left . . . ?," 5). Also see Bosch, *Witness*, 213–14.

129. Bosch, *Witness*, 212.

130. See Bosch, "Melbourne and Pattaya: The Left . . . ?," 6–7; and "In Search of Mission," 8–9 for an expansion upon these five points. All quotations come from these sources.

131. Ellul, *The Meaning of the City*, as cited in Bosch, "Melbourne and Pattaya: The Left . . . ?," 6.

132. After commenting upon the increasing economic disparity between rich and poor, Bosch asked of Christians: "Can there be any doubt that we are at least partially responsible for the present (and

Part Two: Bosch's Theology of Mission and Evangelism

Bosch wholeheartedly applauds these ecumenical emphases, yet he remained sharply critical of certain tendencies in ecumenical social thought that manifested themselves at Melbourne.

First, Bosch criticized Melbourne for *not grounding their present sociopolitical activities in a proper theological framework*.[133] While affirming the need for Christians to be involved in the transformation of their societies to more fully conform to the standards of the kingdom of God, Bosch cautions ecumenicals against the heresy of Pelagianism, in which humans think themselves capable of achieving salvation and the kingdom by their own powers. "Salvation," Bosch wrote, "has indeed to be effected today, but unless our salvation is grounded in the yesterday of God's normative revelation in Christ crucified and risen, and unless it stretches out towards the tomorrow of our ultimate salvation, we are engaged in the futile effort of building God's kingdom with our own hands. We cannot separate the message of the present kingdom from the past and future work and person of the King, for that would signify a degradation of the gospel as being nothing more than a derivative of the world of human experience."[134]

Any Christian social ethic must be grounded in the doctrine of reconciliation in order to preserve the needed eschatological tension in their historical projects and programs.[135]

Second, ecumenicals have frequently *trivialized the radical nature of sin*.[136] Bosch noted an increasing tendency in ecumenical documents to maintain that sin manifests itself only in certain persons and groups or almost exclusively within the institutional structures of society. This approach portrays some people as being essentially good; they are *only* victims of sin (the "sinned-against") but not sinners themselves. For

---

future) discrepancies? When the people asked John the Baptist, 'What are we to do?', he replied 'The man with two shirts must share with him who has none, and anyone who has food must do the same' (Luke 3:11). If the Church had taken that challenge seriously, or the challenges of the Sermon on the Mount, would the world not have been different today? But we have defused those challenges and referred to them as examples of 'interim ethics'. In doing so, we have been able to continue undisturbed" (Bosch, "The Melbourne Conference: Between Guilt and Hope," 517).

133. Bosch, "Melbourne and Pattaya: The Left . . . ?," 7; "In Search of Mission," 9.

134. Bosch, "Melbourne and Pattaya: The Left . . . ?," 7.

135. Interestingly, Emilio Castro acknowledges the same concern in an essay written just after Pattaya. He writes: "Some persons have pointed out that [Melbourne's] concentration on the incarnational kenosis of Christ did not pay enough attention to the atonement dimension of his death on the cross and of his resurrection. *While several passages from the documents of Melbourne make reference to the once-forever event of Jesus Christ, it is clear that much more effort should be made to relate the reality of the forgiveness of sins through the atoning death of Jesus Christ to our participation in the historical struggles of today.* By experience we know of the tremendous power that is generated by the assurance that God in Jesus Christ reconciled the world with himself, liberating us from all our pretensions and releasing us for historical actions in the ambiguities of daily history. This theological task remains before us" ("Reflection after Melbourne," in *Your Kingdom Come*, 227; emphasis his).

136. Bosch, "Melbourne and Pattaya: The Left . . . ?," 7; and "In Search of Mission," 9.

The Historical and Theological Context of Mission

Bosch, this approach was dangerous and fruitless, because it neglected to recognize the presence of sinful tendencies in the lives of *all* persons and societies.[137]

Third, ecumenicals at Melbourne ran the risk of *uncritically beatifying the poor*.[138] While Bosch found no fault in Melbourne's strong emphasis upon the poor,[139] he felt the conference tended to speak of the poor as if they were the God's chosen people — citizens of the kingdom—*solely* because of their material poverty. It tended to elevate the materially poor to a theological category. The discussions (particularly in section 1—Good News to the Poor) also tended to polarize people unhelpfully into exclusive categories: the "materially poor" versus the "poor in spirit," the "sinned-against" versus the "sinners." The existence of poverty was attributed, *without qualification*, to the exploitation of some by others. The conference resisted all attempts to maintain that the poor might in any way be partly responsible for their poverty, due to ignorance or lack of initiative.[140] Bosch praised the contributions of Kosuke Koyama and Raymond Fung who brought a greater balance in their analyses of God's relationship to the poor than did some other plenary speakers and participants.[141]

Finally, and most importantly for Bosch, Melbourne's approach to social involvement tended to *blur the lines of distinction between the church and the world*.[142] As we have already noted above, Bosch believed the ecumenical movement, since the 1960s, has shown an increasing tendency to center its attention on the world. The church was in danger of becoming redundant, a human institution with no *unique* ministry or calling in the world. Bosch summarized the dilemma:

> If—as happened at Uppsala 1968—mission is defined almost exclusively in terms of participation in secular programs of urban renewal, the civil rights movement, the "constructive use of violence, community development, etc., it is legitimate to ask whether we need a *Church* to do all this. This question is indeed being asked in some ecumenical and even Roman Catholic circles. Johannes B. Metz, who argues along these lines, avers with perfect logic, "The abstract distinction between Church and world is, in the final analysis,

---

137. The tendency to see sin exclusively in institutions or in *some* individuals "obscures the hard reality of man's inveterate drive to self-seeking and corruption" (Bosch, "In Search of Mission," 9).

138. Ibid.

139. Bosch commented: "There can be little doubt that the 1980's will be marked by growing economic imbalance and that the Church will *have* to take heed of this. Melbourne at least attempted to do so. True, there are people who are upset by the conference's tendency to pay more attention to material, rather than spiritual, poverty. However, it is fairly certain that those who are upset are themselves *not* materially poor" (ibid., 10).

140. Bosch, *Theology 201*, 151–52. For a similar critique of Melbourne's understanding of the poor, see Gort, *Your Kingdom Come*, 15–17.

141. Bosch, "In Search of Mission," 9–10; and also his "The Melbourne Conference: Between Guilt and Hope," 516–18. Koyama's contribution on this point is found in his lecture "The Crucified Christ Challenges Human Power," in *Your Kingdom Come*, 167.

142. Bosch, "Melbourne and Pattaya: The Left . . . ?," 8–10; and "In Search of Mission," 9–11.

meaningless." The Church's earlier ghetto existence in isolation has here given way to an almost unqualified absorption by the world.[143]

This ecumenical tendency to "secularize" the church's mission and make the church a redundant entity was, for Bosch, a fatal mistake. When the church loses its *distinct* identity as the unique, messianic community, as the vehicle of God's salvific purposes in history, a curious reversal takes place. When salvation-history begins to lose its unique character, then *world history* begins to take on messianic and salvation-historical attributes!

In this new mindset, the kingdom of God becomes equated with a particular political ideology, and one political system is deemed to be authentically "Christian." In this new theology of history, certain political and historical events assume the status of *revelation*; God is seen directly at work within certain political and revolutionary events. Bosch believes this approach lies at the heart of many (though not all) of the current theologies of liberation, and it was a dominant feature at Melbourne.

Many at Melbourne, particularly some Latin Americans, propounded that God was at work

> only in events which [bore] a particular stamp, namely, that of Socialism . . . Just as a century ago, God was seen at work in the movement of Western imperialistic expansion and colonization, he is today seen at work in the socialist movement. Biblical concepts such as "redemption" and "community" are being replaced respectively by "liberation" and "solidarity." This was evident at Melbourne . . . Julia Esquivel, for instance, saw in the victory of the people of Nicaragua a "glorious experience of the Resurrection"; Israel en route from Egyptian slavery "may for us today mean Zimbabwe, El Salvador, Nicaragua or Guatemala.[144]

Numerous problems resulted from this new, world-centered "theology of history" approach. First, biblical categories were blurred or equated with contemporary categories of thought (i.e., liberation, oppression, poverty, or justice), resulting in an *uncritical identification of the Christ of the gospels with any so-called liberation struggle.* Bosch declared this to be a hermeneutically defective approach that did little justice to the relativities and failures inherent within *all* historical events, including struggles for justice and liberation.[145]

Second, this approach, as applied at Melbourne, was *in danger of being highly selective in its criticisms.* Just as Pattaya seemed incapable of uttering any prophetic judgment against capitalism, so Melbourne seemed incapable of condemning any

---

143. Bosch, "Melbourne and Pattaya: The Left . . . ?," 8. The Metz citation is from his *Kirche im Prozess der Aufklärung*, 82 (Bosch's translation).

144. Bosch, "Melbourne and Pattaya: The Left . . . ?," 8.

145. Bosch, "In Search of Mission," 10.

of the Socialist nations whose records on human rights were equally blemished.[146] Melbourne condemned specific social injustices in Australia, South Korea, El Salvador, Guatemala, and South Africa, and deeply criticized the United States and other capitalist nations for its duplicity in the oppression of the Third World. But no mention was made of the plight of the millions of refugees in Southeast Asia, victims of a genocidal Marxist regime in Cambodia. With some degree of sarcasm, Bosch concluded that "some victims of oppression are apparently experiencing tremendous difficulties in receiving any attention, probably because they are not being oppressed by the 'right' people."[147]

At its root, Bosch thinks this theological absolutization of the socialist (or capitalist) political program stems from a *false understanding of the true nature of the kingdom of God*. The kingdom of God in the Scriptures is a *critical* category. The kingdom "always remains beyond any human achievement or blueprint. There is no economic or social system that does not need improvement when looked at from the perspective of the Kingdom."[148] Although Melbourne was not naively infatuated with Marxism, some participants did seem to believe that the socialist utopian vision of a classless society was an accurate model of the kingdom of God on earth.[149]

Both Melbourne and Pattaya reflected deep convictions about Christian social responsibility in a needy world. But in Bosch's view, the polarization remained serious. He captured the essential tension by averring to a debate between John Stott and Emilio Castro that took place at Pattaya. The evangelicals rightly ask the WCC whether it weeps for the *lost*, but ecumenicals pose a proper counter-question to evangelicals: do they weep for the *poor*?[150]

---

146. By the last day of the conference, after numerous attempts at mentioning situations of oppression in Marxist and Third World nations had been quashed, Bosch submitted a resolution which confessed the WCC's failure to be as prophetic as she ought to be, and affirmed Christian solidarity with those who, despite their situations not being specifically mentioned at Melbourne, were also victims of suffering. After some acrimonious debate as to whether to condemn the Russian invasion of Afghanistan, Bosch's motion was carried by a large majority. His resolution played a crucial mediating role at Melbourne, and made up for some of Melbourne's embarrassing "silences" over victims of suffering in socialist nations. Indeed, Bosch had several representatives from Marxist countries subsequently thank him for offering the resolution, because the motion meant that their plight had been tacitly acknowledged by a representative WCC gathering. For more on this story, see Costas, *Christ Outside the Gate*, 146–47; and Bosch, "In Search of Mission," 15–16. See *Your Kingdom Come*, 251 for the text of the resolution.

147. Bosch, "Melbourne and Pattaya: The Left . . . ?," 9. Bosch commented that as long as this apparent one-sidedness prevails, the credibility of the WCC will remain in serious doubt. A Burmese Christian at Melbourne, U Kyaw Than, is reported to have remarked that "we have been more charitable to Socialist than to Capitalist countries." Bosch also explained that "representatives from Western countries often ruthlessly castigated their own societies whereas those from Marxist countries (particularly Russia) used the opportunity to extol the virtues of theirs" (Bosch, "In Search of Mission," 11).

148. Bosch, "Melbourne and Pattaya: The Left . . . ?," 9.

149. Ibid.

150. Bosch, "Behind Melbourne and Pattaya," 33. Both Emilio Castro and Waldron Scott have subsequently made the observation that there is fruitful ground for working together in these concerns, since the vast majority of the "unreached" also happen to be among the poor peoples of the earth! See Castro, "Ecumenism and Evangelicalism: Where are We?," 16; and Scott, "The Fullness of Mission," 44.

Part Two: Bosch's Theology of Mission and Evangelism

Christian Faith and Other Faiths

Neither Melbourne nor Pattaya explicitly addressed the issue of a Christian theology of religions. But there is a deep underlying contrast between the ecumenical and evangelical evaluation of the salvific significance of other religions, which played their part in the proceedings of the conferences.

The evangelical movement, according to Bosch, has never developed a consistent "theology of religions," apart from the need to learn about other faiths in order to more effectively convert them to Christian faith. Evangelicals stand clear in their convictions that Christ is the *unique* Son of God, the only way to the Father, and that people outside the Christian faith stand eternally lost. It is this basic concern that prompts evangelicals to go into all the world preaching the gospel.[151]

Ecumenicals, on the other hand, focus primary attention on Christ's *universality*. According to Bosch, ecumenical leaders (at least since New Delhi) have de-emphasized or denied the "lostness" of humanity, and have given a fairly positive evaluation of the salvific value of non-Christian faiths.[152] Bosch discerned a theological pattern in the ecumenical movement's zeal to be open to the world. In the "secular world" of sociopolitical realities, the church's task is to discern what God is doing in history and then become involved in various secular movements for social justice, acknowledging that God is already at work to liberate people. Similarly, in the "religious world" of non-Christian faiths and ideologies, the church's task is to discern what God is doing and saying within the other faith traditions (thus the emphasis on *dialogue*), and then work with them in addressing issues of common concern. The church, according to this view, should not be primarily concerned with the question of whether adherents of non-Christian religions are "lost," but rather about vital concerns which affect *all* persons; issues such as racism, injustice and poverty.[153]

---

151. Bosch, "Behind Melbourne and Pattaya," 32; and Bosch, "Evangelism and Mission: The Contemporary Debate," 12–13. Elsewhere Bosch commented that many evangelicals accept *a priori* "that all non-Christian religions are nothing but idol worship and therefore do not merit any serious theological consideration. If evangelicals study Hinduism, Islam, etc., the sole purpose is to know their 'enemy' better so as to be more effective in winning adherents of those religions over to the Christian faith" (Bosch, "Theologies of Mission," [20]).

152. Bosch, "Evangelism and Mission: The Contemporary Debate," 12.

153. Bosch spelled out his understanding of this approach, popular in ecumenical circles, as follows: "Just as the dividing line between Church and world grows dim in the first view, so does that between Christian and non-Christian in the second. If the secular world, outside the Church, is the arena of God's activities, the same should apply to the religious world outside Christianity. If it is no longer necessary to transfer people from the world to the Church, it is also superfluous to transfer them from paganism to Christianity. We should therefore no longer accept that the fulfillment of God's plan with the non-Christian peoples depends on the question of whether they get converted to Christianity and join one of its many denominations. The aim of our mission should not be to incorporate people into the Church but rather to liberate them for a saving contact with the best in their own religious traditions . . . The Christian mission therefore has really no other responsibility in respect of adherents of other religions than to help the Hindu become a better Hindu and the Buddhist a better Buddhist . . ." (Bosch, *Witness*, 38–39).

Bosch cautioned, however, that the WCC has never explicitly affirmed universalism, as some loosely charge. Rather, the official ecumenical view is *ambiguous* on the question of the eternal salvation of non-Christians. Bosch acknowledged that various pronouncements, especially from the 1960s, seem to lean in the direction of universalism, yet since Nairobi there has been a movement in the opposite direction, away from universalism. No WCC statement can be found where universalism is officially endorsed or taught.[154] For Bosch, it would be more true to say ecumenicals have affirmed two contrasting concepts without seeking to work out the theological tensions inherent between them. Ever since the 1928 Jerusalem meeting of the IMC, "statements admitting a true knowledge of God and genuine religiosity in non-Christian religions are to be found side by side with affirmations on the indispensability of Christ for our salvation."[155]

The Ethos of the Conferences

Between Melbourne and Pattaya, Bosch sensed a marked difference in the ethos or "style" of the meetings. Despite his deep criticisms of Melbourne, the meeting was more open than Pattaya, which appeared to Bosch to be a "pre-packaged" affair. Bosch cited the criticism of fellow South African Derek Crumpton in this regard, about how Pattaya was an exercise in programming the conclusions before the commencement of the meeting.[156] Because of its strictly evangelical constituency, Pattaya lacked the spectrum of Melbourne. It also allowed for no plenary discussions or interaction, even when the final documents were presented to the conference. The leadership of the conference let it be known from the beginning that there would be no discussion of divisive theological issues; the conference was to focus exclusively on strategy. In this sense, Pattaya chose not to risk making itself vulnerable to criticism.[157]

Melbourne, however, was significantly different. Bosch mentioned that more real dialogue occurred at Melbourne, with the opportunity for interaction from the floor between speakers and participants. There seemed to be no inhibitions as the

---

154. Bosch, "Behind Melbourne and Pattaya," 32–33.

155. Ibid. 33.

156. Bosch, "In Search of Mission," 17.

157. Ibid. Bosch commented: "Many felt that they were recipients rather than participants, that they had to trust the Conference leadership blindly, as it knew best. One had the impression that there were no unsolved problems left, apart from those regarding practice and strategy. The attitude was that the theological homework had been done at Berlin (1966) and Lausanne (1974) and that only *application* and *strategies* were now required. On the opening night Saphir Atyal [sic], deputy chairman of LCWE stated explicitly, 'We are not here to focus on issues; rather we are here to study the peoples to be reached and how to reach them.' Hence the consultation's theme 'How shall they hear?'. . . The participants were all already safe in the life-boat and were now devising strategies to throw out the life-line to drowning men. Nothing was said about conditions in the life-boat itself—it had been decided in advance that the renewal of the Church was not a subject for discussion. Those in the life-boat were the haves reaching out to the have-nots, not beggars telling other beggars where to find bread" (ibid.).

Part Two: Bosch's Theology of Mission and Evangelism

various participants spoke their minds. At Melbourne, "people agonised together, acknowledged that they differed, sought for a way ahead." In particular, when the debate became particularly tense over the subject of the Russian intervention in Afghanistan, Bosch noted that Melbourne experienced a moment of profound crisis, agony, and soul-searching. It was "a moment when Melbourne was, somehow, at the crossroads, when it could go either way. I felt that, in spite of my criticisms, there was an open-endedness about Melbourne, a willingness to take risks."[158]

A Summary

In summary, Bosch lamented that Melbourne and Pattaya had become symbols of a deep theological conflict between two worldwide constituencies of Christians, and that both sides had failed to develop an adequate theology of mission for our day. He faulted the evangelical movement for promoting an "emaciated gospel,"[159] and the ecumenical movement for advocating a "diluted gospel."[160]

Resolving the Tensions Between Evangelicals and Ecumenicals

Divisions in the Body of Christ

With sadness, Bosch admitted that Melbourne and Pattaya both failed to speak with a clear, united voice about the role of the church of Jesus Christ in the contemporary world. In both the evangelical and ecumenical movements, "we have a church which—in ways which are admittedly opposite—has conformed to the world. Each defines the church according to what it believes itself to possess and the other to lack. Each tends to be over-confident of itself."[161]

Both Melbourne and Pattaya, despite their best intentions, were "captive to their own biases." Bosch found both meetings helpful but inadequate.[162] At bottom, they

---

158. Bosch, "In Search of Mission," 15–17.

159. Bosch's full critique of the evangelical theology of mission can be found in the chapter "An Emaciated Gospel" in *Witness*, 202–11.

160. Bosch's full critique of the ecumenical theology of mission can be found in the chapter "A Diluted Gospel" in ibid., 212–20.

161. Bosch, "Evangelism and Mission: The Contemporary Debate," 5. Cf. Bosch, "Melbourne and Pattaya: The Left Foot . . . ?," 1. Elsewhere, Bosch also chided both sides in this unfortunate division for frequently displaying "an unfortunate tendency towards self-righteousness . . . as well as a lamentable lack of self-criticism" (Bosch, "Theologies of Mission," [21]). Cf. Bosch, "Crosscurrents in Modern Mission," 78.

162. Bosch commented: "I went to Melbourne and Pattaya with much expectation. I found that both conferences taught me a great deal, that both were made up of sincere, devout Christians who want to serve the Lord with all they have. But I also found that the strength of Melbourne was the weakness of Pattaya and vice versa. I found that the convergence between ecumenicals and evangelicals which I had thought was beginning to develop after Lausanne 1974 and Nairobi 1975, was hardly in evidence. Too many people were captive to their own biases. In the words of the General Secretary of the Church

betrayed an unconscious dualism that prevented the necessary theological dialogue from occurring, further dividing the body of Christ. The approaches of Melbourne and Pattaya

> ... [operated] from an either-or mentality—either the deed, or the word; either societal ethics or individual ethics; either humanisation or conversion; either liberation or redemption; either the cry of the poor or the cry of the lost; either a this-worldly utopia or an other-worldly kingdom, and so forth. My problem is that these positions are, in fact, mirror images of each other and that both are indefensible, as both have succumbed to . . . [an] insidious dualism in which, ultimately, nature remains opposed to grace, justice to justification, the body to the soul, society from the individual, creation to redemption, earth to heaven, the deed to the word, and social involvement to evangelism.[163]

Despite his profound criticisms, Bosch believed that the divisions between ecumenicals and evangelicals were not as permanent as they appear. First, he wondered whether H. W. Gensichen's "dimension"-"intention" distinction helped explain Melbourne and Pattaya. Could it be that Melbourne, and the ecumenicals generally, were inclined to stress the broad missionary and evangelistic *dimension*, whereas Pattaya and the evangelicals tended to emphasize the more *intentional* nature of mission and evangelism?[164] Perhaps the evangelical and ecumenical movements are (or can be) mutually *enriching* movements, each reminding the other of the indispensability of both intentional and dimensional aspects of mission.

Second, Bosch noted that serious divisions emerged not only *between* Melbourne and Pattaya, but *within* both of them as well.[165] At both conferences, deep tensions surfaced among participants. In the case of Melbourne, Bosch mentioned the tensions between the theology of Section III and the predominant outlook of the other three sections. At Pattaya, there was clearly a strong disagreement between the signatories of "A Statement of Concerns" and the conference majority. Perhaps these intra-conference tensions provided evidence that the disaffected minorities at both constituencies are but a reflection of a yearning on the part of many Christians for *a way beyond* the impasse between the ecumenical and evangelical theologies of mission.

A New Alternative?

What is the alternative to the present polarization in Protestant mission? Despite the fact that the 1980 conferences seemed to represent a hardening of conflicting theological positions, Bosch noted numerous positive signs of rapprochement between some

---

Missionary Society, Simon Barrington-Ward, who also attended Melbourne and Pattaya, 'In both places we sang in our chains'" (Bosch, "In Search of Mission, 18).

163. Bosch, "Evangelism and Mission: The Contemporary Debate," 13–14.
164. Bosch, *Theology 201*, 180.
165. Bosch, "The Melbourne Conference: Between Guilt and Hope," 513.

Part Two: Bosch's Theology of Mission and Evangelism

evangelicals and ecumenicals. Such missionary statesmen as Stephen Neill, James Scherer, Emilio Castro, Waldron Scott, Mortimer Arias, Arthur Glasser, Johannes Verkuyl, and John Stott[166] were but a sample of leaders whose irenic and self-critical attitudes had contributed to a lessening of tensions on both sides. Beyond these leaders, moreover, there was positive evidence of movement among both groups. Bosch argued that since the Nairobi Assembly, there has been a renewed emphasis upon the centrality of evangelism among ecumenicals. An even more significant indicator, however, was the publication (in 1982) of the document *Mission and Evangelism: An Ecumenical Affirmation*. Its compilers solicited strong input from a whole variety of traditions: ecumenical Protestant, Roman Catholic, Orthodox, and evangelical Protestant. The resulting document reflected a significant convergence of opinion regarding numerous central tenets of modern mission, including the necessities of proclamation and conversion, contextualization, mission and unity, and the gospel in relation to the poor. A key to this convergence was undoubtedly the change that has occurred within the leadership of the WCC itself. Emilio Castro, the chief architect of the statement, became, in 1984, the General Secretary of the WCC.[167]

Among evangelicals too, Bosch discerned positive signs of rapprochement. He contended that the Lausanne Congress "did much to dispel false ideas the ecumenical movement had of evangelicals."[168] Lausanne also had a catalytic effect upon evangelicals themselves, challenging them with increasing urgency to "propound a comprehensive gospel."[169] Following Pattaya, two significant gatherings helped to further a less dualistic, more holistic theology of mission among evangelicals. The Grand Rapids Consultation on the Relationship of Evangelism and Social Responsibility (1982), sponsored jointly by the LCWE and the WEF, issued a report which viewed evangelism and social concern not as competitors or even as separate partners. They were related as two partners in a marriage, in which the two belonged to and depended on one another. Both were acknowledged to have their grounding in the Gospel of Christ itself.[170] The following year brought Wheaton '83, a WEF-sponsored event consisting of three simultaneous consultations concerning the nature and mission of the church. One of the consultations, "The Church in Response to Human Need," produced a significant statement on mission as social transformation. In the statement, evangelism was not defined in narrow terms as a separate and "primary" task of the church but rather "as an integral and inalienable part of the church's total mission in the world."[171] A crucial factor in this changing approach among evangelicals was the

---

166. Bosch, "Crosscurrents in Modern Mission," 80.

167. Bosch, "Theologies of Mission," [22]. One could also mention the positive contribution of such ecumenical leaders as Mortimer Arias and Raymond Fung to the evangelical/ecumenical dialogue.

168. Ibid., [21].

169. Ibid.

170. Cf. Bosch and Sugden, "From Partnership to Marriage," 75–77.

171. Bosch, "Theologies of Mission," [21]. Bosch was involved in both consultations, including the drafting committee of the Transformation statement.

emergence of the so-called "radical evangelical" movement, towards which Bosch was quite sympathetic.[172]

These signs of convergence were heartening, but did not, by the time of Bosch's death, represent the fundamental reshaping of the evangelical and ecumenical mission movements.[173] Many still passionately defend their own viewpoints, and remain acidly critical of the other's point of view. Others lamely seek some sort of synthesis between the two approaches, taking the best of both worlds.[174] Yet, according to Bosch, neither of these options were viable.

> Neither of these two approaches really satisfies, however; the first is too self-righteous, the second too easy. We need a position—no, a way—beyond either *and* beyond both . . . Simply to mix the two [evangelical and ecumenical positions] is no solution. Waldron Scott suggested at Pattaya that Melbourne might be the left foot of the Church and Pattaya the right. This metaphor is appropriate as far as it goes. What happens, however, when the feet march in opposite directions? It might involve our having to do something about the two feet themselves; drastic surgery, for instance![175]

Bosch, of course, would have been the first to admit that there are no easy answers towards resolving the current dispute; and yet his vision to move beyond the present impasse was firm and urgent.

Steps Toward Resolving the Conflict: Theological and Practical

In order for the church in mission to move beyond the evangelical/ecumenical conflict, Bosch urged three fundamental changes: attitudinal changes on the part of all concerned; a deeper, more comprehensive theological framework for mission today; and more practical cooperation at all levels.

---

172. Although Bosch never formally described himself as a "radical evangelical," he was deeply sympathetic to their approach. In his writings, Bosch has given a positive evaluation of major "radical evangelical" themes. It is perhaps significant that Tokunboh Adeyemo, who was *not* entirely sympathetic to the radical evangelical position, perceived Bosch to be a member of the movement. See Adeyemo, "A Critical Evaluation of Contemporary Perspectives," 54–56, 60. For Bosch's understanding of the radical evangelical movement, see "Melbourne and Pattaya: The Left . . . ?," 14–15.

173. For example, the Wheaton '83 Congress refused to address the tensions within evangelicalism over different understandings of evangelism, mission and social concern. The Conference was divided into three separate "tracks," so that the "radical evangelicals" tended towards one track, and traditional evangelicals the other two. Thus each track was not representative of evangelicalism as a whole, but of "special interest groups" within it. As Bosch himself put it: "Wheaton was not a true dialog. [Because of the three-track approach] it *did* mean that the statement that came out of our group was considerably stronger than the Grand Rapids statement. But one should not see this as progress" ("Interview").

174. Bosch, "Melbourne and Pattaya: The Left . . . ?," 3.

175. Ibid.

Part Two: Bosch's Theology of Mission and Evangelism

In terms of *attitudinal changes*, Bosch called for a recognition, first, that there is more that unites evangelical and ecumenical Christians than divides them,[176] and second, that divergences in mission theology and practice need *not* always be divisive. Divergences "should not in themselves be regarded as matters of regret; they may also be signs of life and guarantors of renewal and enrichment."[177] The creative tension between evangelicals and ecumenicals should be looked upon as a source of mutual enrichment, whereby the whole church can grow.

Finally, however, Bosch called for repentance and renewed trust in the Lord by all sides. Evangelical and ecumenical Christians all too frequently have been overly critical of one another, labeling the others' views as "sub-Christian" or even "anti-Christian." Both movements have conformed themselves to the world in different ways, failing their Lord through the sin of self-sufficiency.[178] Evangelicals and ecumenicals must recognize their need of one another, lest they both lose the gospel![179] Both sides are called to a new vision of the church, God's kingdom community, and to a renewed trust in the crucified and risen Lord, in whose own body the dividing wall between evangelicals and ecumenicals has been broken down.[180] Only as they kneel in humility at the foot of the cross, will evangelicals and ecumenicals find sufficient common ground to integrate their varying concerns.

Bosch also sought to overcome the ecumenical/evangelical conflict by a strenuous *re-thinking of the fundamental theological framework* of contemporary missiology. He developed four theses that represent points of "creative tension" between

---

176. Besides a common heritage of "one Lord, one faith, one baptism," Bosch listed many points of convergence between the two movements, including the commitment to fostering indigenous Christian churches, the acceptance of the key role of the laity in all areas of church life, and the recognition of the need to "contextualize" the gospel into every cultural milieu (ibid., 15).

177. Ibid., 15–16.

178. Bosch commented: "Perhaps, however, the problem is not located in the two feet, but in the body, the Church. In both manifestations we have a Church which—in ways which are admittedly opposite—has conformed itself to the world. Each defines the Church according to what it believes itself to possess, and the other to lack. Each is over-confident of itself. Each is in need of repentance" (ibid., 16).

179. As early as 1970, at the apex of the evangelical/ecumenical polarization, Bosch noted that: "it is therefore, my conviction that 'ecumenicals' and 'evangelicals' *need* each other . . . and need one another desperately. I believe that the present ecumenical movement is embarking on a dangerous course which will ultimately prove to be disastrous. I also believe that 'evangelicals' are in danger of reacting so violently against ecumenical convictions that they, too, may miss the essence of the gospel. The present hardening of the two fronts may easily lead both groups astray. Only when both groups are humble enough to be prepared to be corrected and influenced by one another can there be any hope of worth-while ecumenical action" (Bosch, "Possibilities and Limitations of Ecumenical Action in South Africa," 23).

180. After noting the apocalyptic context of mission in the 1980s, Bosch concluded: "We are facing a future that is terrifying . . . Yet to allow ourselves to be overcome by despondency is inexcusable. Genuine modesty, and genuine trust in what the Lord can do, go hand in hand. Then, as the contours of the Kingdom take shape within the fragile body of the Church, it will be granted the ministry of emulating its Lord who 'in his own body of flesh and blood has broken down the enmity which stood like a dividing wall between them' (Eph. 2:14)" (Bosch, "Melbourne and Pattaya: The Left . . . ?," 16).

The Historical and Theological Context of Mission

evangelical and ecumenical missiologies. They form a tightly constructed "skeletal outline" for a contemporary theology of mission.[181]

1. Proceeding from the indissoluble unity of world history and salvation history, we shall have to say that the two are nevertheless not the same.

2. Affirming that the church is a part of the world and with it *en route* to salvation, we shall continue to believe that the church is, at the same time, the unique Body of Christ and as such separate from the world; after all, both the church's mission and its being are of crucial importance.

3. Affirming that we are called to a historical and worldly engagement for the sake of all people, we nevertheless avow that the world is transient and that the faithful are called to persevere in it.

4. Realizing that it is impossible to speak only of a purely personal salvation since that would leave social sin untouched, we nevertheless do not speak exclusively of social salvation, because that would leave untouched the personal root of sin.

With these four carefully nuanced theses, Bosch sought to move beyond present day evangelical and ecumenical missiologies by developing a new, alternative theological model. They emphasize the *eschatological, ecclesiological,* and *soteriological* framework upon which a holistic, contemporary theology of mission could be built. In chapters 7–9, we shall see how Bosch incorporated these concerns into his own theology of mission.

A final step in overcoming the evangelical/ecumenical conflict would be to see an increase in *practical cooperation* at all levels. Beginning at the local level, Bosch urged joint cooperation between differing groups of Christians in areas of mutual need. As Christians work together, Bosch affirmed, they begin to grow in unity, love, and humility.[182] Practical cooperation pays dividends that go far beyond the pragmatic concern to cooperate for the sake of efficiency and good stewardship.

> Somewhere along this road we may even learn to love each other, to pray for and with each other, to work together for the glory of our Lord, to develop a sense of responsibility to the greater Body of Christ. We may also learn some humility and come to realize that we can be taught a lot by those of the "other fold." This does not mean that we shall have no more differences. I don't

---

181. The following theses are taken from Bosch, "Mission and Evangelism: Clarifying the Concepts," 187. Cf. Bosch, "Theologies of Mission," [22–23].

182. We recall that it was precisely through such "grassroots" ecumenical contact that Bosch's own horizons were widened in the Transkei. Bosch described the cooperative ecumenical work of the Transkeian Council of Churches in his "Possibilities and Limitations of Ecumenical Action in South Africa," 24. Remarkably, for the South African context, there was a good working relationship between black and white Christians, as well as between the various denominations (Dutch Reformed, Anglican, Methodist, Presbyterian, Moravian, and Baptist). The Council initiated a great variety of activities, including joint work camps and conferences, an ecumenical Xhosa hymn book, community development, famine relief, hospital and health care work, and theological education by extension.

believe in utopias . . . But I do believe that we have more in common than we often think we do. And I do believe that, while cooperating in some limited objective activities, we may come to trust one another enough to speak the truth in love.[183]

Beyond seeking practical cooperation at the local level, Bosch was also active in promoting evangelical/ecumenical cooperation at the national and international levels. The PACLA and SACLA gatherings, where Bosch played a crucial role, were supremely events of practical evangelical/ecumenical cooperation. In 1987, Bosch was intimately involved in a WCC's Stuttgart Consultation on Evangelism that brought together evangelical and ecumenical leaders. One significant result of the conference was a pointed call (endorsed by Bosch) for the WCC, WEF, and LCWE to commit themselves to a greater degree of cooperation with one another at the level of joint study and action in evangelism.[184]

THE FIRST WORLD/THIRD WORLD MOTIF

That the evangelical/ecumenical tension exists and that it shapes the current missiological discussion is widely acknowledged. Many, however, would dispute whether it should be the *primary* optic for analyzing the meaning of mission in our day. Without denying the essential validity of the ecumenical/evangelical motif, Bosch, particularly in his later years, devoted increasing attention to Third World Christianity, and its relationship to the church in the First World.[185]

Terminology

For our purposes, "Third World" represents those non-aligned, non-industrialized "underdeveloped" nations in Africa, Asia, and Latin America that share a common heritage of endemic poverty and economic dependency, as well as the legacy of Western sociopolitical colonialism. More than this, however, the Third World is a "state of mind," an "emerging consciousness on the part of deprived and relatively powerless people, wherever they live—an emerging awareness of their condition and a growing conviction that it need not and must not continue."[186] The "First World" in Bosch's day represented the industrialized, wealthy nations of Western Europe and North America (along with Japan). Bosch was not completely happy with this terminology,

---

183. Bosch, "Possibilities and Limitations of Ecumenical Action in South Africa," 24.

184. See the WCC/CWME's *Monthly Letter on Evangelism* No. 10/11 (October/November 1987).

185. We cannot here enter into the merits or drawbacks of the such terms as "First World" or "Third World." For a discussion of the derivation of the terms, see Anderson and Stransky, *Mission Trends No. 3: Third World Theologies*, 1–2; Bühlmann, *The Coming of the Third Church*; Daneel, Kritzinger, and Saayman, *Third World Theologies*, xii–xiv.

186. Anderson and Stransky, *Mission Trends No. 3: Third World Theologies*, 2.

although he used it because of its common usage.[187] Bosch also abbreviated these concepts, occasionally contrasting the church and culture of the "west" with that of the "south."[188]

Besides his qualified use of the terms "First World" and "Third World," Bosch also frequently made reference to the "older" and "younger" churches. These terms, he noted, gained currency during the 1928 Jerusalem Conference. Interestingly, both terms have positive and negative connotations. "Older" suggests greater insight and experience, but also hints at aging and decay. "Younger" suggests power and dynamism, but also subordination and inferiority.[189] Bosch cautiously affirmed Stephen Neill's definition that a "younger church" is "one which exists as a minority in the midst of a non-Christian majority, the culture of which has never at any time been deeply influenced by the Christian gospel."[190] Bosch felt that the terms should continue to be used, because a more adequate terminology has not yet been developed.[191]

Criticisms of Bosch

During his lifetime, numerous reviewers criticized Bosch for ignoring Third World theological concerns and giving nearly exclusive attention to Northern European and North American missiology.[192] Before the publication of *Transforming Mission*, three sympathetic critics stood out: Orlando Costas, M. L. Daneel, and Adrio König. These scholars maintained Bosch had frequently failed to do justice to his own "context" (Third World, African, and South African, respectively) in his own theologizing.

Orlando Costas in particular took Bosch to task for this oversight. In his review of *Witness to the World*, Costas complained that Bosch's predominant use of the

---

187. See Bosch, *Church 301*, 117–19. In this section, Bosch also rejected the old DRC terminology of "mother" and "daughter" churches as theologically indefensible and hopelessly paternalistic. He also rejects Dürr's terminology of "sending" and "becoming" churches, and the still-common terms "church" and "mission-church" (as in the "Coloured" N. G. Sending Kerk) as unhelpful. All churches should be sending, missionary churches, in the process of becoming. To tie these labels to the younger churches alone implies subordination and dependency, which is unhelpful for all concerned. Also, to speak as if the older churches have "arrived" and are now complete, "adult" churches is misleading. If mission today is "mission in six continents," then all churches, in first, second and third worlds, are in a missionary situation and must struggle equally hard to contextualize the gospel in their respective cultures. See Bosch, "Vision for Mission," 12.

188. For a diverse survey of the different ways in which modern missiologists have depicted the missiological "shape" of the world, including the aforementioned terminology, see the special issue devoted to "the future of mission" in the January 1987 edition of the *IRM*.

189. Bosch, *Church 301*, 119.

190. Ibid.

191. Ibid.

192. After Bosch's death, similar concerns were echoed by Verstraelen, "Africa in David Bosch's Missiology"; Sugden, "Placing Critical Issues in Relief"; as well as Ahonen, *Transformation*; and Kritzinger and Saayman, *David J. Bosch*. For an early example of Bosch's very Eurocentric survey of mission theology, see his "Kaleideskoop van die Na-Oorlogse Sendingwetenskap," 13–34.

Part Two: Bosch's Theology of Mission and Evangelism

evangelical/ecumenical paradigm obscured the reality of the Third World in the missiological discussion.

> It is doubtful . . . whether the evangelical/ecumenical controversy is as universal as Bosch assumes. For one thing, the most prolific debaters are by and large Westerners. The Church in the Third World does not seem to be half as concerned with this sort of question as its First World counterpart, and if it is, it formulates the issue in different terms. Indeed, a more realistic and universal issue would be the debate between Christian mission as seen from the 'under' and 'upper' sides of history—i.e., from the perspective of the Third or First Worlds . . .
>
> The book reflects a relative silence in regard to Third World theologies of mission. With the exception of D. T. Niles, Stanley Samartha, and M. M. Thomas . . . there is hardly any interaction with Asian mission theologians. A similar flaw occurs with Africa. With the exception of a passing reference to John Mbiti, John Gatu, Byang Kato, and a quote from Burgess Carr, African theologians are given a similar treatment . . . It can be asserted that, by and large, Bosch does not take seriously into account Third World perspectives on mission. Those Third World theologians that are mentioned are usually brought into the discussion in connection with the evangelical/ecumenical controversy and not in the light of their own mission theories.
>
> By the same token, Bosch reflects a bias against Southern European missiology. His sources are basically Dutch, German, Scandinavian, and Anglo-Saxon (British and North American). There is hardly any contact with the French, Italian and Iberian missiologists. This reflects a typical blind spot among many (not all) Euro-North American missiologists who seem to think that missiology begins and ends with Northern Europe and Northern America.[193]

Bosch acknowledged the validity to Costas' critique of *Witness*, admitting that when writing the book in 1978, the evangelical/ ecumenical tension was uppermost in his mind. "I had this struggle [the ecumenical/evangelical debate] going on in my own theological mind and my own existential heart."[194] In an unpublished paper concerning his then-upcoming *Transforming Mission*, Bosch acknowledged this lacuna.

> In *Witness to the World* I . . . paid very little attention to the understanding of mission in Third World churches and in Third World Theologies such as Contextual Theology, Liberation Theology, Black Theology, Minjung Theology, and the like. I now realize that this was a serious omission. This time I'll try my level best to enter into dialogue with these movements . . . The

---

193. Costas, Review of Bosch's *Witness to the World*, 83.
194. "Interview."

The Historical and Theological Context of Mission

church-in-mission has, to my mind, not really begun to establish what these movements and their understanding of the gospel entail for mission today.[195]

Prof. M. L. Daneel, one of Bosch's colleagues at UNISA and a world authority on the African Independent Churches, also criticized Bosch for not bringing his missionary experience to bear more directly in his missiological writings. "His own African background does not seem to enter in."[196] Daneel readily acknowledged the valuable contribution Bosch has made as an "encyclopedic missiologist," but feels it is a pity that Bosch had not devoted more of his energies to "grassroots" concerns of the African Church, such as the theological significance of African traditional religions, the nature of power, magic and witchcraft, the place of ancestors in the Christian community, and communication with the dead.[197]

In a related fashion, another one of Bosch's colleagues at UNISA, Prof. Adrio König, criticized *Witness to the World* for neglecting to probe the *concrete implications* of Bosch's missiological agenda for the South African context. Says König:

> One searches in vain for examples from the ecclesiastic, social, or political life in South Africa. I find this peculiar, particularly in view of the fact that Bosch is famous for his insistence on contextual theology, hence a theology expressed concretely in terms of the present situation. Due to this lack of South African examples it is in fact questionable whether Bosch has really come across. How often Christians are in heartfelt agreement on theoretical points and only really sit up and take notice, and start arguing, when the theory becomes concrete.[198]

The criticisms of Costas, Daneel and König imply that Bosch has frequently failed to do justice to his own "context" (Third World, African, and South African, respectively) in his own theologizing.

It would be unfair, however, to conclude that Bosch neglected to address issues related to the life and faith of the "Third Church," and particularly the church in South

---

195. Bosch, "Some Random Thoughts," 3. Elsewhere, Bosch stated that he would not make the evangelical/ecumenical issue the uppermost motif in his future writings, although it would still be an important one. "I will try to go about it *thetically* next time rather than *antithetically* or *sythetically*, the way I did in *Witness to the World*. I'm still not sure I am going to handle this issue because I think it's a very real issue. There are people, particularly some of the continental European reviewers, who thought that I introduced an issue which was non-existent, and I think they were living in a sense in a 'fools paradise' if they think it's non-existent. I think Americans are aware of the fact that that tension is there. So I think I had to address it . . . I've addressed it subsequently in other articles, but [in my new book] I will go about it in another way" ("Interview").

196. Prof. M. L. Daneel, interview held at the University of South Africa, Pretoria, September 1986. In another context, John de Gruchy has made a similar criticism. In his essay on South African Christian spirituality, De Gruchy highlights Bosch's book *A Spirituality of the Road*, but comments that while it is a South African contribution to the spirituality of mission, it "is not specifically rooted in the South African situation" (*Cry Justice*, 16).

197. Interview with Prof. M. L. Daneel, September 6, 1986.

198. König, "David J. Bosch: Witness to the World," 14.

Part Two: Bosch's Theology of Mission and Evangelism

Africa. This is far from the case. Since his earliest years, Bosch expended considerable energy on numerous aspects of Third World Christian theology and practice. In particular we note his contributions in the following seven areas: African concepts of God and the gospel;[199] African concepts of sin, evil, healing, and the vexing problem of witchcraft;[200] the various dimensions related to the communication of the gospel in Africa, including "contextualization" and "Africanization";[201] numerous theoretical and practical problems concerning the "selfhood" of the "younger" churches and their relationship to the "older" churches, including missionary paternalism and moratorium;[202] a theological evaluation of Black and Liberation Theologies;[203] the theology of religions;[204] and comprehensive surveys of the church scene and of the theological literature in various Third World settings.[205] As can readily be seen, Bosch devoted significant energies to these topics. Unfortunately for the non-specialist, however, many of Bosch's writings concerning First World/Third World, "older church"/"younger church" issues were either unpublished or in written in Afrikaans or available only in obscure journals. An example of this is Bosch's major work on

199. Bosch, "God through African Eyes," 11–22, which also appeared under the same title in Becken, *Relevant Theology for Africa*, 68–78; and Bosch, "God in Africa: Implications for the Kerygma," 3–21.

200. See the following essays by Bosch: "'n Missionêre Dilemna in Afrika: Die Probleem van die Kwade," 173–98; "The Traditional African Understanding of Evil as a Missionary Challenge"; and "The Problem of Evil in Africa: A Survey of African Views on Witchcraft and of the Response of the Christian Church," 38–62.

201. See the following by Bosch: "Die Probleem van die 'Aanknoping,'" 19–27; *Sodat Hulle Kan Verstaan: Kommunikasie as sendingprobleem in Afrika*; "Communicating the Gospel to Africa Today"; "Inheemswording, Afrikanisasie en Swart Teologie," 103–15; "Onderweg na 'n Theologia Africana," 160–179; "The Contextualization of the Gospel"; "Christian Community in Africa, Part I and II"; "Erneuerung christlicher Gemeinschaft in Afrika," 183–88; "Renewal of Christian Community in Africa Today," 92–102; and "The Gospel in African Robes: Toward the Africanization of the Gospel."

202. See the following by Bosch: "Die Selfonderhoud van die Inheemse Kerk—Is dit vir ons waarlik 'n saak van erns?," 481–504; "Die 'Selfstandigwording' van die Inheemse Kerk en die Plek en Taak van die Ampsdraers Darrin," 63–77; "Possibilities and Limitations of Ecumenical Action in South Africa," 20–24; *Gemeenteopbou in Afrika*; *Ampsbediening in Afrika*; "Jongkerke en Ekumene . . .," 473, 476; "Geestelike opbou en Ekumeniese Betrekkinge by die Ned. Geref. Dogterkerke," 129–39; "The Feasability of Moratorium in the South African Context," 25–33; *Church* 301; "Towards True Mutuality: Exchanging the Same Commodities or Supplementing Each Others' Needs?," 284–96; "Le Paternalisme Missionaire—Une Réponse à Roger Mehl," 14–30; "The Missionary: Exemplar or Victim?," 9–16; and "Eenheid Binne die 'Familie' van Nederduitse Gereformeerde Kerke—Waarheen?" 45–73.

203. See the following by Bosch: "Inheemswording, Afrikanisasie en Swart Teologie," 103–15; "The Case for a Black Theology," 3–9; "Schwarze Theolgie in Südafrika," 77–84; "Currents and Crosscurrents in South African Black Theology, 1–22, and appearing under the same title in Wilmore and Cone, *Black Theology: A Documentary History, 1966–1979*, 220–37; and "The Church and the Liberation of Peoples?," 8–47.

204. See the following by Bosch: *Theology of Religions MSR 303*; and "The Church in Dialogue: From Self-Delusion to Vulnerability," 131–47.

205. See the following by Bosch: "Die Sendingsituasie Vandag—Verleentheid of Geleentheid?," 149–64; *Sendingwetenskap Vandag: 'n Terreinverkenning*; "Missiological Developments in South Africa," 9–30; "Die Wêreldkerk Vandag en Môre: Lig en Skadu," 1–18; "Brief Comments on 'the State of the Church in Africa'"; "Missionary Theology in Africa," 161–91; also republished under the same title in *JTSA* 49 (December 1984), 14–37; and "Contextual Missionary Theology from Orbis," 121–31.

contextualizing the gospel in Africa, *Het Evangelie in Afrikaans Gewaad* [The Gospel in African Robes] written in Dutch.[206] In his forward to *Het Evangelie*, Johannes Verkuyl commented that the book is an important guide to the study of African Christianity.[207] So the criticisms of Costas and Daneel, while acknowledged by Bosch, are only partially true.

At this point, we shall highlight three areas where Bosch believed the concerns of the First and Third World churches intersect: the relation between older and younger churches in mission; Black theology; and the contextualization of the gospel.[208] This should demonstrate Bosch's familiarity with prominent concerns of Third World Christianity, and his understanding and use of the First World/Third World paradigm as a valid model for missiology.

Relationships in Mission

Churches are called to strive for mature relationships with one another, working together on a cooperative basis and sharing resources as equal partners, in order to further the mission of Christ in the world and to manifest their unity in him. Yet this is much easier said than done. Tensions with regard to this issue have been acknowledged since the 1928 Jerusalem Conference., and have been epitomized in such slogans as "paternalism," "partnership," and "moratorium." Hans-Ruedi Weber has summarized the tension as follows: "How to give without humiliating and creating dependency? How to receive in freedom without resentment? These are perhaps the most urgent questions which arose from the first interchurch aid project and which are still unanswered today."[209]

Bosch wrote at some length on the continuing tensions in mission/church and "mother church"/"daughter church" relationships. He addressed the issue at both the local level (concerning the relationship between the DRC, NGSK, NGKA, and RCA) and the global level.[210] In our review, we briefly highlight Bosch's understanding of the roots of the tension and his proposed way forward.

---

206. Published in Kampen by J. H. Kok, 1974. Only two of the four essays in *Het Evangelie* have been published in English.

207. Bosch, *Het Evangelie*, 6–7.

208. Another issue relevant to the First World/Third World paradigm treated elsewhere is the relationship of "older" and "younger" churches, including the need for mutuality and partnership between them. See chapter 6.

209. Weber, *Empty Hands*, 36.

210. See footnote 201 for a list of Bosch's works on the subject.

Part Two: Bosch's Theology of Mission and Evangelism

From Paternalism to Moratorium

Bosch frequently referred to the missionary movement's historical alliance with the forces of Western colonialism.[211] The resulting legacy of Western paternalism and attitudes of cultural superiority have "cast a long shadow over all missionary endeavour originating in the West."[212] This legacy is something that cannot be denied, but only confessed and repented of.[213] The long shadows of dominance and dependence have become institutionalized within many of the mission/church structures and relationships. Bosch noted that every ecumenical missionary conference since Jerusalem 1928 has sought to address the issue of older church/younger church relations. Such phrases as Whitby's "partnership in obedience"; Mexico City's "joint action for mission"; Uppsala "multi-lateral relations"; and "ecumenical sharing of personnel"; and Bangkok's "mature relationships," all exemplify this trend.[214]

Yet in the eyes of many Third World church leaders, the slogans about partnership had failed. By 1971, John Gatu of Kenya and Emerito Nacpil of the Philippines were calling for a moratorium on Western missionary involvement in Africa and Asia. Bosch attributed the emergence of the call for a moratorium to a number of factors:[215] First was the issue of *authority*. The younger churches resented the fact that the older churches were very slow in devolving any real power and authority to them. Bosch noted that there remained an unquestioned assumption that "ecclesiastical sovereignty, like its political counterpart, was something that could be subject to negotiation, or in the event of the older church being unwilling to give up control, something which could be obtained by a kind of UDI [Unilateral Declaration of Independence]."

Second was the problem of the *Western "donor mentality."* In the New Testament, mission usually flowed up from the have-nots to the haves. But the Constantinian legitimation of the church turned the church into a power base and bastion of the status quo. In this climate, and despite language about new relationships, the younger churches were being overwhelmed by the amount of missionary personnel, finances and other resources flowing in from Western churches, with little say over how the resources are to be used. In the minds of many Western Christians, this created the view that the younger churches are "a Kindergarten for the mother church and a poorhouse

---

211. See Bosch, "Le Paternalisme Missionaire" 14–15; and Bosch, "Missiology," 3rd ed., 266–67.

212. Bosch, "Missiology," 3rd ed., 266.

213. Bosch, "Le Paternalisme Missionaire," 16. Bosch, however, was not as judgmental as some other critics. He observed that the scourge of paternalism has not been limited to modern Western Christian missions. Paternalism is an ancient phenomenon that has existed in many cultures. Bosch believed that the paternalistic drive stemmed from the fact that "the technological and political expansion of the West (whether "capitalist" or "socialist") had a *religious* foundation. Western nations believed they had a (divine?) *mission* to proclaim the message of "salvation," as they interpret it, to the entire world (ibid., 14).

214. Bosch, "Towards True Mutuality," 285–86.

215. The following, including all quotations, is taken from Bosch, "Towards True Mutuality," 288–90. For more on Bosch's evaluation of the moratorium issue, see his "The Feasibility of Moratorium in the South African Context," 25–33; and *Church 301*, 129–53.

The Historical and Theological Context of Mission

for the exercise of her charity" [Bühlmann]. Western Christians remained captive to a "donor mentality."

Third was the related problem of creating *a "receiver mentality" on the part of the younger churches*, creating an unhealthy relationship of dependency. It was understandable, said Bosch, that most of the younger churches desired to accept Western "generosity," even if it preserved a relationship of dependency. Yet these temporary benefits of Western assistance tended to stifle the growth and maturity of the younger church.

Fourth was the longstanding problem of *Western denominationalism*. Denominationalism guaranteed continued dependence on the West. In Africa, each denomination in almost every African country has its own structures (e.g., seminaries, publishing house, church headquarters). Meanwhile "various pastors from competing churches work in the same village, each with a small, hardly viable congregation. So these little churches can, in fact, only operate as long as they remain dependent on overseas help. But would they not, perhaps, if left alone, be forced to unify their efforts and rationalize their activities?"[216]

The heart of the moratorium call, said Bosch, was a cry from the church in the Third World for Western Christians to take their concerns *seriously*, and to relate to them in an *adult* manner.[217] Bosch's response to the subject was not simply to endorse the moratorium concept,[218] but to affirm that the churches must strive for true mutuality in their ecumenical relationships.

The Challenge of True Mutuality: A Way Forward[219]

As the Body of Christ, the younger and older churches have an obligation to seek a true mutuality in their relationships. All churches agree that to have mature relationships without paternalism, *both* parties need to be able to give and receive. The resources or "commodities" which the churches share should flow in both directions. The trouble is that traditionally, the West has defined the commodities being given and received primarily in terms of skilled personnel, financial and material aid, and technological assistance. If ecumenical sharing between churches is seen in these terms only, then *the churches in the West are automatically ahead and Third World churches permanently*

---

216. Bosch, "Towards True Mutuality," 290.

217 Bosch commented that "At its deepest [the call to moratorium] was a cry that says, 'Please hear us! Please take us seriously! . . . The Bangkok conference also put it well: 'The whole debate on the moratorium springs from out failure to relate to one another in a way which does not dehumanize.' If we don't solve the issue at this level, other arguments are beside the point" (ibid., 291).

218. Bosch noted at least four arguments against the moratorium, including the immense needs of the poor across much of the Third World, and the continued obligation to evangelize the more than three billion non-Christians. Also, the missionary serves an important role as a symbol of the universality of the church, and functions as a check against any church becoming overly nationalistic or isolationistic (ibid., 290).

219. The following is a summary of arguments made by Bosch in "Towards True Mutuality," 291–95; and Bosch, "Le Paternalisme Missionaire," 22–26.

Part Two: Bosch's Theology of Mission and Evangelism

behind. Because of the West's material abundance and the Third World's poverty, there is no equality of sharing. The "traffic" of resources is still predominantly one-way, from the older to the younger churches. This in turn leads to Western spiritual arrogance and to the perpetuation of paternalistic mission patterns, indefinitely postponing the quest for mature ecumenical relationships. It is self-deceptive, said Bosch, to think that mutual sharing and mature relationships exist because a few Third World persons are on loan to Western churches, while the West continues to send huge financial and human resources into the Third World. The imbalance is too great.

At its root, this approach is erroneous because it assumes that two-way reciprocal sharing implies the exchange of the *same kind* of commodities. The global church must to strive toward a true mutuality of giving and receiving by use of the concept of "complimentarity." Western churches must continue giving aid to the Third World, but all the churches must ask the crucial question of what resources do the younger churches have to offer the church in the West? This is a troubling question to many Western Christians, who have for so long conducted mission out of affluence. Many Western churches do not really believe that the Third World church has anything to offer.

Yet the older churches stand in desperate need of the gifts that the younger churches offer. The younger church has given the churches of the West a vision of the worldwide body of Christ. Indeed "the modern ecumenical movement, in both its conciliar and evangelical manifestations, was born on the erstwhile mission fields and to this day still draws its greatest inspiration from the younger churches."[220] The younger church has helped free the churches of the West from their confessional isolation and scholastic theological formulations. It has given the older churches the opportunity to read and understand the message of the Bible in a new way. The very process of cross-cultural mission exposes the older churches to new and unexpected understandings of the Bible and of the gospel itself.[221]

Indeed Bosch noted that if the older churches measure the gifts the younger churches have given to them, versus those that the older churches have given, it is an open question as to who is really the beneficiary and who is the benefactor. "The point is that we need the younger churches just as badly as they need us. No church can demand total autonomy for itself. If it does, it becomes a mere service station for its own clientele and thus a pseudo-church."[222]

Bosch affirmed that true love does not merely involve self-giving, which might lead to objects of such love to feel inferior or worthless. True love also means admitting

---

220. Bosch, Le Paternalisme Missionaire," 27–28.

221. One thinks of the Base Christian Community movement in Latin America, with its many implications for the worldwide church in the areas of worship, the role of the laity, a new approach to ecclesiology, the integral relation between faith and action, evangelism and social concern. Western Christians have many lessons to learn from the survival of the persecuted church in China; from the continued growth and evangelistic zeal of the church in Korea; and from the church's crucial role in the sociopolitical transformation of nations like the Philippines.

222. Bosch, "Towards True Mutuality," 294.

The Historical and Theological Context of Mission

one's *dependence* upon the other, and expecting to *receive* something from them in return. This was the experience of the apostle Paul.

> Most of us probably take it for granted that Paul only *gave* to the Gentile congregations that came into existence through his missionary efforts, without *receiving* anything back. But does this view tally with reality? Would it not be more correct to accept that Paul received (almost?) as much as he gave? For instance, are not the differences between Paul and Peter to a large extent due to the fact that Paul had discovered something of the truly universal meaning of the Gospel from his Gentile converts in the very act of his proclaiming the Gospel to them? Was his attitude about the, at most, relative value of the Torah simply due to his own theological insights revealed directly to him by God, or was it also the result of his interchange with Gentile Christians? Moving to the modern era: is there anybody who has been a missionary in the true sense of the word, who has returned unchanged from the "mission field"?[223]

The real challenge, then, is for Christians to change their perspective. Western Christians must not only see the churches in the Third World in terms of what can be *given* to them, but also what can be *received* from them, and how impoverished the churches in the West would be without partnership of these churches. "If we really succeed in infusing this awareness and this spirit into our students and constituencies, we will, I believe, have solved not only the moratorium problem but also the whole delicate matter of what partnership and mutuality mean. We will have convinced the younger churches that we cannot go ahead without them, that they should not turn their backs on us but share their riches with us."[224]

Black Theology

Beginning in the late 1960s the voice of Black Theology emerged, becoming an increasingly important factor in the life of the church in South Africa. It has encompassed a wide theological terrain, attempting to speak out of the spiritual experience and the social situation of black Christians. Bosch was a long-time observer of this movement, and one of a few Afrikaner theologians to have made a serious attempt to grapple with its implications for the life and mission of the church in South Africa.[225] Bosch's knowledge of the movement is not simply theoretical but experiential. By the mid-1980s, four of Bosch's colleagues at UNISA were advocates of Black Theology,[226]

---

223. Bosch, Le Paternalisme Missionaire," 24–25 (Bosch's translation).

224. Bosch, "Towards True Mutuality," 295.

225. For an insightful evaluation of Black Theology in Southern Africa, including the response of David Bosch and other white theologians, see Kretzschmar, *The Voice of Black Theology in South Africa*, esp. 94–109.

226. Bonganjalo Goba, Simon Maimela, T. A. Mofokeng, and Lebamang Sebidi. See Bosch, "Missionary Theology in Africa," 131.

Part Two: Bosch's Theology of Mission and Evangelism

and Bosch long maintained a close relationship with a number of Black Theology's leading exponents, including Desmond Tutu.

Bosch wrote frequently on the subject of Black Theology (hereafter cited as "BT").[227] As early as 1972, Bosch discussed BT as one dimension of the broader subject of the indigenization or "Africanization" of the gospel.[228] He gave a qualified but essentially positive evaluation of the movement, because it represented an authentic attempt by Black Christians to break out of the pietistic theology which they had inherited from Western missionaries, towards a more holistic understanding of salvation. Later that year, Bosch reviewed the later banned *Essays in Black Theology*.[229] The review contained many curious gaps due to the government's banning of all quotations from the book itself. He applauded BT's emphasis on the all-encompassing nature of God's salvation ("redemption," "liberation") that involves the renewal of humankind in every sphere of personal and corporate life. BT is concerned with humankind in the totality of their needs, liberating persons from all conditions that dehumanize and oppress. Yet Bosch criticized BT's tendency toward a one-sided "horizontalism." Too often, BT seemed to be a mirror image of the Pietist distortion of Christianity when it reduced the meaning of salvation to exclusively *this-worldly* categories. The transcendent dimension of life seemed lost in BT's concern for the sociopolitical struggle. Bosch also criticized BT for its "utopianism." BT underestimated the power and radical extent of sin in human life, and thus appeared to have an over-idealistic vision of man's capabilities in a liberated, "post-apartheid" South Africa. As Bosch put it: "Man is depraved, selfish, egocentric. Even those liberated by Christ still experience the power of evil in their lives; how much more this would be true of those not liberated by him!"[230]

Bosch also urged BT to remain self-critical: the tendency to over-idealize one's own culture and impose it on others is a constant temptation that must be resisted. Here Bosch specifically criticized Steve Biko's essay that gave a "starry-eyed picture of traditional African religion," in contrast to "western imperialistic religion." As Bosch summarized it: "This Western arrogance of seeing its culture as the solution to all the

---

227. See footnote 202 for a list of Bosch's works on the subject.

228. Bosch, "Inheemswording, Afrikanisasie en Swart Teologie," 103–15. Bosch carefully distinguished between "African Theology" and "Black Theology" as follows: "If one moves away from the more specifically historical studies one soon notices that an area of growing importance in the African scene is the one identified by the catchword 'African theology'. One encounters the concept 'Black Theology' with almost equal frequency (in fact, in the southern part of the continent 'Black Theology' is far more common) . . . African Theology and Black Theology represent two distinct though by no means unrelated approaches to the theological scene on the African continent. The first is, admittedly, more explicitly a theology of culture, the latter a theology of sociopolitical relevance. Perhaps it is best to say that *all* relevant theologising [in] Africa moves 'between culture and politics,' as Theo Sundermeier called his German collection of essays on African and Black Theology" (Bosch, "Missionary Theology in Africa," 112).

229. Bosch, "The Case for Black Theology," 3–9.

230. Ibid., 7.

world's problems is untenable. But when blacks today glorify their cultural values and heritage as the answer to the world's ailments they fall essentially into the same arrogance as that of Westerners. Reality is much more complex and ambivalent than all this. We are merely clouding the issues if we look in one direction for all mistakes and in another for all solutions."[231] Nevertheless, Bosch urged whites to study BT sympathetically, and noted certain similarities between the Black Consciousness movement and the history of the *Afrikaner* nation.

In 1973 Bosch wrote a short essay on BT for the German *Evangelische Missions Magazin*[232] that emphasized how BT reflected both a discovery of black self-identity and a rejection of white paternalism and racism. Bosch criticized BT along the lines mentioned above, but expressed appreciation for BT's insistence that the Christian faith is a matter of active, praxis-oriented obedience and not merely a quietistic and privatized system of belief. Bosch also believed the existence of BT to be a sign of the health, creativity and maturity of Black South African Christians, who were beginning to break out of the system of white domination and speak freely as Christian believers and theologians.

In 1974, Bosch wrote a wide-ranging review of Black Theology[233] that emphasized many of the aforementioned concerns. Significantly, Bosch noted that South African BT, as distinct from its North American cousin, manifested a genuine love and concern for whites. Whites were the oppressors, but, in the words of Lutheran Bishop Manas Buthelezi, blacks must come to feel a genuine concern for whites, in order that they might truly evangelize white people and liberate them from their sin of racism.[234]

In Bosch's evaluation of BT, he drew attention to three abiding theological issues which have far-reaching implications.

First, Bosch noted that BT is a "situational theology" and does not intend to be anything else. Its validity is dependent upon the social situation in which blacks find themselves. As Bosch put it:

> Theo Sundermeier is therefore correct when he asserts that Black Theology does not belong among the theological disciplines of Systematic Theology or Exegesis, but in that of *Hermeneutics*. Black Theology has an apologetic-pastoral and socio-ethical purpose. It aims at influencing and changing people's consciousness. It intends to be proclaimed and experienced . . . Black Theology intends to interpret the experience of the black man with the aid of the

---

231. Ibid., 8.
232. Bosch, "Schwarze Theolgie in Südafrika," 77–84.
233. Bosch, "Currents and Crosscurrents in South African Black Theology," 220–37.
234. Bishop Buthelezi's important address from the 1973 South African Congress on Mission and Evangelism has been reprinted as "Six Theses: Theological Problems of Evangelism in the South African Context," in Anderson and Stransky, *Mission Trends No. 2: Evangelization*, 136–38.

Bible *coram Deo*. Black Theology, as a hermeneutical key, focuses the light of Scripture on the black man's experience of reality.[235]

Second, Bosch noted that BT was increasingly recognizing the need to become *self-critical* in its formulations and theologizing. BT could never overtly identify *its* cause with God's cause in an uncritical manner. Even though blacks were indeed an oppressed people, they were sinners like everyone else. These insights, from among the ranks of Black theologians themselves, were evidence of an increasing maturity in the movement, in Bosch's estimation.

Finally, Bosch noted that BT calls for a response from the rest of the church, especially the white church. Since theology is ecumenical, white Christians must also respond to BT, albeit in "hushed and humbled voices." Whites must neither idolize nor reject BT. Rather it should prompt them to a profound self-examination. BT should move white Christians to rethink their theology and reread their Bibles with new eyes and open hearts. Bosch reminded his readers that until we turn our theological attention to the oppressed, we will never understand the gospel. The challenge of BT is that "nothing less than a new *metanoia* is expected of us, a new and radical conversion."[236]

These three issues (the recognition that all theologies are contextually shaped; the need for theological humility and self-criticism; and the need for continual conversion to the demands of the gospel) are the hallmarks of authentic theology. Although Bosch's essay was written in 1974, he affirmed a decade later that he believed that much of his evaluation and critique still held true.[237]

Contextualization and the Challenge of Third World Theology

Bosch addressed a cluster of issues that revolve around the concept of the contextualization of the gospel, with the challenges these pose for First World Christians. For many years now, missionaries have attempted to "indigenize" or "adapt" the gospel among the various peoples they have served, so that the Christian faith could be more adequately related to the traditional cultural forms and worldview of the people. More recently, however, there developed a concern to "contextualize" the gospel. This entailed a broader, more profound process of "accommodating the gospel to the total life of a people."[238] Contextualization seeks to relate the meaning and implications of Christian faith into the total context of a culture at a given moment in time. The contextualization process recognizes that every culture is, under God, being shaped by the dynamic of its own history, as it looks back upon its *past* and forward towards its *future*. Contextualization seeks to relate the transforming dynamic of the gospel

---

235. Bosch, "Currents and Crosscurrents in South African Black Theology," 233.
236. Ibid., 235.
237. See Bosch, "Missionary Theology in Africa," 131.
238. Bosch, "An Emerging Paradigm for Mission," 495. Cf. also his "The Contextualization of the Gospel," 2.

of God's kingdom into that culture, in all the various dimensions of its existence (i.e., political, religious, economic, social). Contextualizing the gospel is a *continuing process*, a dialogue between the total reality of one's situation and the Christian gospel, with the goal of transforming the situation in the light of the Gospel. As a missionary strategy, contextualization thus seeks to enable the church to incarnate itself into the total culture where it exists, and be a more effective witness to Christ from within it.[239]

Bosch commented that few would question the validity of the concept of contextualization. A difficulty has arisen, however, because many in the "older churches" view the entire issue as a *problem for Third World churches only*. They speak as if Western churches and Western theology have no need to contextualize *their* theology and *their* understanding of the gospel. Believing that modern Western culture is somehow normative and absolute, they fail to recognize the cultural conditioning of their own worldview, *including their theological formulations and perceptions of the gospel itself.* The gospel, Bosch maintained, is *always* perceived from within a particular sociocultural worldview. The absolutist mindset of much Western theology—still believing in the superiority of its own methods and perspectives—is no longer tenable. The gospel must come to be seen as an active, subversive agent within *every* culture, including modern Western culture. The gospel must become the leaven that liberates the secular, scientific culture of the Western world, just as much as it transforms the cultures of the non-Western world.[240]

Bosch believed that the theological perspectives emerging from the Third World through this new understanding of the contextual nature of the gospel poses numerous challenges for the churches of the First World. In particular, Third World Christians criticize four tendencies within Western culture that have detrimentally influenced Christian theology and church life.[241]

Third World theology challenges, firstly, the *dualism* of Western culture and theology. Western Christians, according to Bosch, inherited a dualistic orientation to reality that has deeply affected their understanding. Western Christians live with a worldview in which "the soul remains opposed to the body, redemption to creation, the word to the deed, evangelism to social action, the invisible to the visible, the abstract to the concrete, the sacred to the secular, theology to ethics and religion to society."[242]

---

239. For an expansion upon the contextualization idea, see Coe, "Contextualizing Theology," 19–24; Costas, "Contextualization and Incarnation: Communicating Christ amid the Oppressed," in his *Christ Outside the Gate*, 3–20. Costas' essay was first delivered at the SACLA Conference in 1979.

240. See Bosch, "An Emerging Paradigm for Mission," 495–97; and Bosch, "Vision for Mission," 13. This immensely challenging subject is the focus of attention in the writings of Andrew Walls and Lesslie Newbigin. See Walls, "The Gospel as the Prisoner and Liberator of Culture," 39–52, and republished in *Missionalia* 10/3 (November 1982), 93–105; Walls, "The Old Age of the Missionary Movement, 26–32; Newbigin's *Foolishness to the Greeks*.

241. Bosch discussed the following four issues in Third World theology in his "An Emerging Paradigm for Mission," 497–501.

242. Ibid., 498.

Part Two: Bosch's Theology of Mission and Evangelism

This dualism has emerged as a devastating result of Enlightenment thinking upon the Western mind, to the point where it has become an endemic problem in Western theology. Reality has been subdivided into the sacred and profane, and these two realms are not to be mixed.[243] The problem has been compounded through the Christian missionary movement, whereby the church has exported its dualism into cultures where dualism was not a problem.[244]

Bosch believed that the evangelical/ecumenical controversy, to a large extent, was simply an example of Western dualism at work.[245] He urged three practical steps to help Western Christians in this regard. First, Bosch maintained that key missiological works like Newbigin's *Foolishness to the Greeks* should be required reading for Western Christian leaders, in order to see how insidious dualistic thought is in Western culture. Second, he urged Christian pastors and laity in the West to develop friendships with Third World Christians, thereby gaining a non-dualistic perspective on Christian faith and life. Third, he implored pastors and theologians to "go to school in Africa and Asia and Latin America" to rediscover a holistic, non-dichotomous gospel. This might be done quite literally, through spending time in a Third World context, or alternatively through a sympathetic study of some aspects of Third World theology and church life.[246]

---

243. Bosch illustrated this dualism by noting the skepticism which many whites regarded the work of Martin Luther King. "During my previous visit to the Unites States, in 1965, I often saw glimpses of Martin Luther King's protest marches on television. One night, as I was watching television with a white American couple, we saw the whole group of marchers all of a sudden kneel down in the street and pray. I remember the white Americans saying to me that they thought that was artificial, something calculated to create effect. It was clear, though, that for King this was genuine and natural. The trouble with us Westerners is that usually the pious are not politically inclined and the politically inclined are not pious. Politics and prayer do not mix! So, deep down we remain dualists, true to our Greek spiritual ancestors." In this way, Martin Luther King managed to integrally link the "spiritual" and "political." Bosch believed King had something of the wholeness of the African mind which many dualistic Westerners simply cannot understand. See Bosch, *A Spirituality of the Road*, 16; and "Interview."

244. "Interview." Bosch illustrated the devastating results of this approach from the work of missionaries in Africa. Because of their dualistic orientation, they concluded that Africans had no religion. "After all, Africans had no religious buildings and objects, no set times or separate days for religious worship and no religious figure comparable to the pastor in the western church. What these missionaries could not comprehend was that African thinking was integrative, or looked at from another angle, *monistic*. Reality was of a piece. Opposites were not denied but regarded as polar complements. In the Western church religion usually comprises only a segment of life—and a very small segment at that. That is what we have communicated to Africa, with the result that we frequently left African Christians helpless in the face of the day-to-day challenges they encountered" (Bosch, "An Emerging Paradigm," 498).

245. Bosch admitted that inasmuch as his own *Witness to the World* presupposed and was addressed to the evangelical/ecumenical controversy, he also has participated in this dualism! Bosch commented: "If you go to most Third World people . . . these things are not an issue to them . . . . My *Witness* . . . presupposes dualism; it presupposes that you have evangelicals and you have ecumenicals. And you see, Third World people don't have that problem . . ." Bosch admits that some of the Black PhD. students at UNISA with whom Bosch worked had criticized *Witness* for precisely this reason; the divisions his book presupposes are not really true of African Christianity. See "Interview."

246. Ibid.

The younger churches also challenge the one-sided *spiritualities* that Western culture and theology have fostered. Traditionally, the Western churches have elevated the spiritual dimension of life over the physical. In this scheme, which Bosch labeled the "Pilgrim's Progress Model" of spirituality, the world is perceived as a threat to one's spiritual health; it is "a contagion from which the Christian must keep himself free." Conversion is a decisive break from this world and a flight from the "wicked city." To be saved is an exclusively spiritual, otherworldly experience; we are saved *from* the world.[247] Bosch noted that Western traditions of spirituality have been strongly tinged with the two heretical tendencies of docetism and monophysitism. They have been docetic in that they have viewed matter as essentially evil, unspiritual and something to be avoided; they have been monophysitic, in that they have emphasized only the divine nature of Christ, preferring to forget his human nature.[248] Alternatively, and in reaction to the above-mentioned spirituality, many modern Western Christians have reversed the traditional hierarchy, and have emphasized the absolute priority of the physical over the spiritual. Salvation has come to be located almost exclusively within this world, and the quest for social justice polarized with the concern for personal justification. In some circles, Bosch maintained, "[Spirituality] is now being defined exclusively as involvement in the world. Where church and world used to be neatly distinguished one from the other, there is now a complete absence of any tension between church and world. The gospel has a complete absence of any tension between church and world. The gospel has become a completely secular message, whereas it used to be entirely religious. The idea of spirituality has either been dropped completely or it has come to be synonymous with secular humanism."[249]

In both cases, whether this world is perceived as a threat or as the only true reality, Western Christianity reveals a striking polarization between the spiritual and physical worlds.[250]

Bosch believed that spirituality was an essential dimension of being truly human, but it "can never be isolated from the rest of our existence." The Bible teaches a different understanding of spirituality from either of the aforementioned models. The biblical distinction between "flesh" and "spirit" does not refer to two components of our lives, the former relating to the outward and worldly, the latter relating to the

---

247. See Bosch, *A Spirituality of the Road*, 12–13. Bosch credits Newbigin with the concept of the Pilgrim's Progress Model. See Newbigin's *The Good Shepherd*, 96. Cf. Bosch, "An Emerging Paradigm," 498.

248. Bosch, *A Spirituality of the Road*, 12–13. While granting that the modern charismatic and Pentecostal movements, with their emphasis upon divine healing and glossalalia, are basically a healthy phenomenon, since they break down the division between the spiritual and physical "worlds," Bosch believed these movements all too easily manifest a dualistic spirituality, in which one lives dichotomously in two completely separate realms. All too easily the Western Christian divides reality into sacred moments when one immerses oneself in the world of miracles and the supernatural, and then switches into a "secular mode of existence," when one approaches life and work without reference to the spiritual dimensions of existence. See Bosch, "An Emerging Paradigm," 498–99.

249. Bosch, *A Spirituality of the Road*, 15.

250. Bosch, "An Emerging Paradigm," 498.

inward and the otherworldly. They refer to two essentially conflicting *life orientations*, two basic *modes of existence*. To be spiritual means to be "in Christ," whether we are working or praying, acting, or contemplating.[251] In the biblical view, then, our involvement in the world leads to a deepening of one's relationship to God, and a deepening of this relationship should lead to a greater involvement in the world.[252]

Bosch maintained that a way beyond this dilemma could be found by affirming the *paradoxical* nature of our Christian existence in the world. He quotes the famous statement of the 1952 Lund meeting of the Faith and Order Commission of the WCC, that the church is always and at the same time "called out of the world and sent into the world." Bosch then elaborated: "These are not two separate movements but one. The idea is therefore not one of balance but rather of tension. It is not a case of the establishment of equilibrium. Rather, the church's being called out of the world sends her into the world; her being sent into the world calls her out of the world."[253]

This description of the church's existence in the world is merely an extension of the model that God revealed in the cross of Christ. The cross paradoxically unites the spiritual and the physical, the "worldly" and the "other-worldly" in a profoundly deep revelation of the heart of God. As Bosch characterized it: "The cross is, in one sense, a sign of total identification with the world: Jesus was never more worldly than on the cross. In another sense it is a sign of radical separation from the world: Jesus never stood over against the world more clearly than here. And spirituality is both of these at the same time."[254]

This concept of spirituality as simultaneously world-engaging yet world-denying is not new to most Third World Christians, Bosch maintained. "One only has to know somebody like Desmond Tutu or Emilio Castro to know how these two things [the vertical and horizontal dimensions of the faith] can be truly integrated into a wholeness."[255] We must learn from their examples if Western Christianity is to break out of its one-sided spiritualties.

Another issue where Third World theology has posed a challenge to the West concerns the *intellectualism* of Western culture and theology. For far too long, Bosch maintained, Western Christianity has been, in the words of John Taylor, a "classroom religion." Western churches and theology has emphasized the cognitive, conceptual, propositional nature of the faith to the extent that many Christians have been

---

251. Bosch, *A Spirituality of the Road*, 13.

252. Bosch cited the example of Mother Theresa and her Missionaries of Charity as a striking example of this principle in action. And yet this is a difficult concept for most Protestants to grasp, since Protestantism has historically maintained an infinitely radical tension and conflict between God and humanity, between the glory of God and humankind's deepest desires (ibid., 13–14).

253. Ibid. 15. For an insightful critique of the dualism inherent within so much of Western thought and spirituality, see Berger and Neuhaus, *Against the World for the World*.

254. Bosch, *A Spirituality of the Road*, 15–16. Bosch again credits Newbigin with this insight. See Newbigin, *The Good Shepherd*, 98.

255. "Interview."

impoverished as a result. This impoverishment manifests itself in two ways. First, we have lost sight of the experiential, ecstatic, and ultimately mysterious nature of religion. Again citing Taylor, Bosch noted "Christianity has come as a daylight religion of reason and reasonableness set over against the darkness of superstition. This has come at a price: 'By confining the Kingdom of God within the protective walls of the conscious and the rational it has left untouched the great deep of the subliminal . . . the incalculable has been left out of account . . . the mystery glossed over.'"[256]

In this regard Bosch endorsed the new approaches being taken in the areas of "narrative theology" and "oral theology" as a legitimate *complement* (but not alternative) to conceptual theology.[257] It is no longer epistemologically adequate to ground theology in rational doctrine and logical consistency. Theological knowledge must not only be rational but also *experiential* and *participatory*. Descarte's *cogito ergo sum* must be supplemented with "I experience and I participate, therefore I am."[258]

Intellectualism has also stifled Western theology by ignoring the concrete and practical nature of Christian doctrine and practice. Bosch credited Third World liberation theologians for reminding the Christian church that theology is not simply an abstract reflection upon the truth but instead is theology for the sake of mission. Theology must be an exercise in world-transforming praxis. Theology is not simply written; it is *done*.[259] Bosch expanded on this in a review of current African theology:

> Gustavo Gutierrez and other Latin American theologians have taught us that what is being perpetrated in the studies of Western theologians, in splendid isolation from the world out there, hardly deserves to be called "theology." Authentic theology . . . deals with life and death issues and therefore constantly takes risks. This kind of theology is worth shedding blood for; not, however, the sterile scholastic theology traditionally propounded in the West. No theologian in the early Church—including the authors of the New Testament books—wrote theology for the sake of theology. With the exception of Origen, they wrote theology for the sake of mission.[260]

Bosch believed this is precisely what has been happening in Africa, Asia, and Latin America. Third World Christians are increasingly being *compelled* to do theology. They are "doing theology on the frontiers, where there are many dangers, where ambushes await one and where one can easily take a wrong turn." But it is precisely because they are reflecting on the faith from within their turbulent contexts that their

---

256. Bosch, "An Emerging Paradigm," 499. Bosch is here citing Taylor's *The Primal Vision: Christian Presence amid African Religions*.

257. Bosch, "An Emerging Paradigm," 500.

258. Ibid.

259. Ibid., 499.

260. Bosch, "Missionary Theology in Africa," 107–8.

Part Two: Bosch's Theology of Mission and Evangelism

theologizing is so exciting and worthwhile.[261] Western theologians have much to learn in this regard.

Finally, Third World Christianity is challenging the West with regard to its *individualism*. Christianity as exported by the missionary movement often portrayed the Christian life as an individual affair between individuals and their God. Conversion and salvation were private matters located in the realm of one's personal experience. The church was a collection of consenting individuals who agreed to form a church. While noting that such individualism is actually a *recent* phenomenon in Western culture, Bosch reminded his readers that Westerners have forgotten this fact, acting as if life has always been thus.[262] "We have . . . overlooked the biblical reality of the body as being more and greater than the sum total of all its members. We have missed the significance of Holy Communion and Baptism as both being sacraments of incorporation into the corpus, the living Body of Christ. Our hymnbooks are replete with 'I-hymns' to the almost total exclusion of 'We-hymns.'"[263]

Again, Third World Christians are now helping Western Christians appreciate the importance of the social nature of human existence and of the communal nature of the church itself.

To summarize, Bosch believed that Third World Christian theology posed a clear and urgent challenge to Western Christians to overcome the inadequacies that have plagued them: their tendencies towards dualism, one-sided spiritualities, intellectualism, and individualism.

How, then, can First and Third World Christians and churches begin the vitally necessary task of overcoming our theological and ideological blind spots, such as those mentioned above? Bosch called for recognition of and a creative interaction between "local theologies."[264] All theologies are "local," in the sense that they are written from within a specific context, and must be understood in that light. Only when we begin to recognize the limitations of our own theological formulations will the church begin to work together towards a truly ecumenical and "catholic" theology. As Bosch summarized it:

> What we are in need of, therefore, is creative interaction between different "local" theologies, in the first and third worlds. In that way we may tentatively advance towards a truly "catholic" theology, which is not to be a new monolithic superstructure, but a "zone" in which we can communicate creatively with one another. Once again, it is only "together with all God's people" that we shall discover how broad and long, how high and deep Christ's love is. If we proceed in isolation from one another, distortion and heresy are inevitable.[265]

---

261. Ibid., 108.
262. Bosch, "An Emerging Paradigm," 500.
263. Ibid.
264. For more on this subject, see Schreiter, *Constructing Local Theologies*, esp. 1–94.
265. Bosch, "An Emerging Paradigm," 501.

The Historical and Theological Context of Mission

Of course, Bosch readily admitted there are dangers inherent in the creative interaction between First World–Third World Christianity. There is a fear expressed by some that Third World theology will be uncritically elevated to a normative position.[266] Others are rightly concerned about the danger of "over-contextualization," whereby a theology becomes subservient to a group's self-interests. Bosch acknowledged this to be a valid concern, although somewhat hypocritical, since Western theology has viewed itself for centuries as *the* normative theology for the global church. And again, have not *Western* theologies in particular been guilty of overcontextualizing theology to protect the racial, political, or economic interests of some? All theology is indeed subject to distortions and inadequacies. So Third World theology can never become the norm for the entire worldwide church, but *Western theology can no longer be the norm either!* Instead, Western Christians are called to begin a new, mutually enriching relationship with their Third World sisters and brothers, free from the attitudes of cultural or theological superiority that have plagued their relationship in the past. When Westerners do speak—and they should—they should address their African, Asian, and Latin American colleagues "with modesty and in subdued tones."[267]

In this chapter, we have analyzed three basic motifs that David Bosch used in his missiological writings to portray the fundamental dynamics of mission today. Although he continued to view the evangelical/ecumenical tension as a dominant reality within the global missiological debate, he devoted increased attention to the First World/Third World paradigm, and to the emerging perspectives on mission that were emerging from the "undersides" of history in Africa, Asia, and Latin America. We now turn from the historical and theological context of mission today to the biblical foundation for mission. It is only as the whole church, evangelical and ecumenical, First World and Third World, hears and responds to the voice of her Lord as found in the Bible that she can find her bearings as an inherently missionary community, sent into the world to cross all human frontiers in the name of Christ.

---

266. In this regard, Bosch noted the tongue-in-cheek remark of Professor Andrew Walls: In light of the explosive growth of Christianity in the Third World and its continued decline in the West, Walls has commented that perhaps in the near future Third World theologies will be the only theologies worth bothering about, since the majority of Christians will be living there! (Bosch, "Missionary Theology in Africa," 106).

267. Bosch, "An Emerging Paradigm," 502.

5

The Biblical Foundation for Mission

IN ITS MISSIONARY ENDEAVORS, the church has given a central place to the Bible. The Bible has served as a stimulus both to evangelistic action and missiological reflection.[1] Indeed, Willem Visser 't Hooft once stated "the future of missions and the future of the ecumenical movement will in the last analysis depend on the solidity of their biblical foundations."[2] David Bosch, like all missiologists, sought to ground his theology of mission in the witness of the Bible. In this chapter we shall consider Bosch's contribution to the biblical theology of mission by describing his critique of traditional approaches to the subject, and outlining the fundamental elements in his own approach. It also serves to inform later perspectives Bosch developed on this theme in the first section of *Transforming Mission*.

THE BIBLICAL FOUNDATION FOR MISSION: HERMENEUTICAL ISSUES

Why a "Biblical Foundation for Mission"?

Bosch noted it is customary, especially for Protestants, to begin their exposition of the theology of mission with a section on the biblical foundation. "As soon as this 'biblical foundation' has been firmly laid, one may move ahead to elucidate the practice of mission (the descriptive task) and evaluate it critically in light of the Bible (the normative task)."[3] The theologian who attempts to develop biblical foundations for

---

1. For a fascinating historical survey of the place of the Bible in evangelism, see Chirgwin, *The Bible in World Evangelism*. This volume served as a contribution to the WCC's Evanston Assembly.

2. I have been unable to trace the origin of this quotation. It appears on the back cover of Harry Boer, *Pentecost and Mission*.

3. Bosch, *Witness*, 42. Cf. Bosch, "The Why and How," 33. In another context Bosch elaborated on the justification for rooting one's theologizing in the Scriptures. Speaking to African theologians about

mission is not only interested in the historical questions of the way that the biblical authors understood "mission"; he or she seeks "to help the church discover a sound theological foundation for its missionary involvement in today's world."[4] It is a study of the Bible *for* mission rather than simply mission *in* the Bible. The study of the Bible *for* mission seeks to understand "how the Bible becomes a source of meaning and motivation for us—how we . . . see the Bible as our charter or sending document undergirding our enterprise."[5]

In practice, however, this task has often been neglected or relegated to a secondary place. Bosch acknowledged that the early Pietists and Moravians gave little serious study to the biblical foundation for mission.[6] William Carey was one of the earliest Protestants to develop a real biblical foundation for the missionary enterprise with his famous *Enquiry*, but based his entire argument upon a single text of Scripture (Matt 28:16–20). Even the great fathers of modern missiology, Warneck and Schmidlin, manifested certain diffidence with regard to building a theology of mission exclusively upon a biblical base.[7]

In the mid-twentieth century, the need for a biblical foundation for mission had been served by Johannes Blauw's work *The Missionary Nature of the Church*. It functioned as the standard introduction to the subject. Bosch acknowledged, however, that Blauw's work had become outdated.[8] The church in the final decades of the twentieth century understood its missionary obligation to the world in substantially different ways from that of the 1950s. Also, advances in biblical studies had thrown some of Blauw's conclusions into question. The need to construct a theology of mission upon a biblical base was acknowledged by missiologists, but severe problems remained.

---

the nature of God, he admitted: "I can find no other point of reference or point of departure than God's revelation to us all as it has been delivered to us in the pages of the Old and the New Testament. If we ever hope to encounter him, we must encounter him there and not in the pages of dogmatic treatises of white theologians. I cannot prove to you that my point of departure is correct. it is a claim based on faith, which is a certainty of realities we do not see (Heb 11:1). This my point of departure cannot be defended or rationalised, but only accepted or rejected. I can, however, offer no apology for it." See his "God Through African Eyes, 12.

4. Bosch, "Mission in Biblical Perspective," 532.

5. Schreiter, "The Bible and Mission," 427. Bosch endorses Schreiter's approach. See his "Mission in Biblical Perspective," 532.

6. Bosch, "The Why and How," 33–34.

7. See Bosch, *Witness*, 42; Bosch, *Theology 201*, 23–24. Ferdinand Hahn has made the same point. "In our day it is widely agreed that only a biblical foundation for mission is legitimate, and that nothing else can provide the theological basis of all missionary work. This is not so self-evident as it may sound, for the missionary theory of the nineteenth century took very different paths." He notes how Gustav Warneck, in his *Evangelische Missionslehre*, tried to develop ecclesiastical, historical and ethnological foundations for mission, in addition to the biblical and theological foundations (Hahn, *Mission in the New Testament*, 167).

8. Bosch, "Mission in Biblical Perspective," 531–32.

Part Two: Bosch's Theology of Mission and Evangelism

Problems with the Traditional Approach to the Biblical Foundation for Mission

Bosch made five criticisms of the ways in which theologians have traditionally approached the biblical foundation for mission. First, some persons approach the biblical record with a pre-critical, "proof-text" methodology, looking to justify what they already assume "mission" to be. "What happens all too frequently—when missiological publications open with a section on the biblical foundation—is that the author proceeds from the assumption that his readers already know what mission is (their definition tallies with his own!) and that his primary task now is to establish what the Bible has to say about mission, thus defined."[9]

In this approach, we come to the Scriptures with a pre-understanding of what mission is. We then turn to the Scriptures and seek what we are already predisposed to find. We find some isolated texts that justify our own viewpoint. Other biblical material that does not conform to our pre-understanding of mission is ignored, consciously or unconsciously. We thus find a justification for our own biases or current mission practices without ever seriously grappling with Scripture.

For example, one could assume that mission is activistic, involving the crossing of remote geographical frontiers with God's word. With this preconceived idea of mission, the Old Testament and the ministry of Jesus have almost no missionary significance![10] Ultimately this approach begs the question of what mission is. We must allow our understanding of mission to emerge out of the whole Bible.

According to Bosch, another problem in the traditional approach to the biblical foundation for mission was the tendency to overlook the historical gap between the world of the Bible and the world of today. Between these two worlds there lies a chronological, cultural and historical chasm; there can never be a simple one-to-one correspondence between these two worlds. All too frequently, however, this is precisely what happens. Contemporary missionary practices are justified with a facile appeal to certain biblical teachings or examples, without ever dealing with the historical gap. According to Bosch, this approach is illegitimate, because "[t]he contemporary

---

9. Bosch, *Witness*, 45.

10. Bosch alludes to this danger in an early essay. "Maar nou moet ons baie versigtig wees om nie die Nieu-Testamentiese sendingbegrip ook in die Ou Testament is sending voorwaar iets anders as in die Nuwe Testament. Wanneer ons hierdie feit misken, sal ons ongetwyfeld in verleentheid raak met die Ou Testament" [We must be very careful to to go looking for the New Testament concept of mission in the Old Testament. In the Old Testament, mission is indeed something different from the New Testament. When we fail to appreciate this, we will undoubtedly get into trouble with the Old Testament] (Bosch, "Jeseja en die Sending," 35, hereafter cited as "Jeseja").

Bosch also criticizes Ferdinand Hahn and Adolf von Harnack on this account. "When theologians with preconceived ideas about mission . . . look at the Bible, it is obvious that they would judge that at least the Old Testament reveals a 'thoroughly passive character' as far as mission is concerned [Hahn]. The same verdict has often been made about the Jesus of the gospels; the idea of a mission to the pagan world lay entirely outside his horizon. Adolf von Harnack was one of the first scholars to have come to this conclusion, and since then many others have followed suit. I believe, however, that the definition of mission which underlies this interpretation is open to question" ("The Why and How," 36). See also Bosch, *Witness*, 47–48.

missionary enterprise in all its ramifications and with all its paraphernalia is so vastly different from what the New Testament calls 'mission' . . . that it is plainly dishonest to appeal directly to the latter as a justification for what we do today."[11]

A related problem in the traditional approach to the biblical foundation for mission is the tendency to ignore the contextual shaping of one's own perspective. Bosch posited that one's theology of mission, indeed one's understanding of the Bible itself, is profoundly shaped by his or her particular vantage point. Although some persons believe that "we can without further ado know precisely what a biblical text meant in its original context," the situation is far more complicated than that.[12] Understanding a biblical text is affected by such factors as church tradition; culture; personal experience; understanding of religion; and social position (e.g., whether we are members of the privileged or underprivileged sector of society).[13] There is no completely "neutral" ground for establishing the biblical foundation for mission. All persons involuntarily read the Bible from within a specific historical and social context that colors their understanding of the text.[14]

A fourth problem in the traditional approach to the biblical foundation for mission was the unresolved tension between biblical scholars and missiologists, with their differing approaches to the Bible. Bosch posed the problem as follows:

> *Biblical scholars*, on the whole, tend to emphasize the diversity of the biblical message and the historical conditioning of each text. This makes them very reticent to draw a direct connection between the biblical text and today's missionary enterprise. The biblical text functions, at most, as a metaphor, model or paradigm for our own involvement, and there always remains a large range of alternative possibilities; we should, therefore, refrain from any single-option reductionism. In addition, biblical scholars tend to point out that the books of the bible were not written as guides for Christian mission (not even the Book of Acts) so they cannot become that twenty centuries later.[15]

---

11. Bosch, "Vision for Mission," 9. Walter Brueggeman has drawn similar conclusions, urging that "There are no simplistic or obvious moves [from the Bible] to contemporary missional practice, for the Bible does not function in such a direct way. Rather it can open a field of metaphors for a fresh perception of social reality and social possibility" (Brueggeman, "The Bible and Mission," 408).

12. Bosch, *Theology 201*, 24.

13. Ibid. Bosch goes on to give a practical example of this difficulty. Referring to Ernesto Cardenal's *The Gospel in Solentiname*, in which a group of Nicaraguan peasants reflect on the meaning of certain biblical passages in the context of the brutal Somoza regime, Bosch comments: "The average privileged, affluent white South African reader of these conversations cannot but wonder at times at what these impoverished Nicaraguans manage to find in the scriptural passages. It is not a matter of whether their exposition is legitimate (in fact, they could ask the same about the exposition of the privileged whites!), but that our own context colours—even determines—our interpretation of the Bible" (ibid.).

14. Bosch, *Witness*, 43.

15. Bosch, "Mission in Biblical Perspective," 532. He draws attention to this same tension in "Towards a Hermeneutic for 'Biblical Studies and Mission,'" 65–78.

Part Two: Bosch's Theology of Mission and Evangelism

Although Bosch credited biblical scholars for helping in the essential task of understanding the biblical text in its original historical setting, he goes on to fault their approach. They "frequently fail to show whether, and if so, how, the Bible can be of significance to the church-in-mission and how, if at all, a connection between the biblical evidence and the contemporary missionary scene can be made."[16]

On the other hand, Bosch was equally critical of much missiological writing on the biblical foundation for mission.

> By contrast *missiologists* . . . tend to err in the opposite direction. Even where they are sufficiently sophisticated not to use the Bible as a handy reference file of quotations to justify their own group's actions, they do have a tendency to operate with a very large brush. On the one hand, they are inclined to overlook the rich diversity of the biblical record and therefore to reduce the biblical motivation for mission to one single idea or text (for instance the great commission or, more recently in liberation theology circles, Jesus' appeal to Isaiah in Luke 4); on the other hand, they tend far too easily to read back into the Bible aspects of the missionary enterprise in which they are involved today.[17]

Biblical scholars and missiologists approach and use the Bible in quite different ways. For Bosch, this dilemma created a significant gap that needed to be bridged if the church's missionary involvement is to have biblical integrity.

A final problematic factor in one's approach to the biblical foundation for mission is the debate over a proper theological methodology. Bosch discerned a hermeneutical conflict within the worldwide church concerning the proper method of interpreting the Bible. Broadly speaking, Bosch saw two different hermeneutical procedures operating: the "inductive" and "deductive" methods. What follows is an abbreviated sketch of this complex issue.

---

16. Bosch, "Mission in Biblical Perspective," 532. Bosch cites French missiologist Marc Spindler's criticisms of much contemporary biblical scholarship, and notes: "I share Spindler's misgivings about the kind of biblical scholarship which perceives the New Testament writings primarily as the rendition of beliefs which belong to another era or as documents of 'a struggle between different Christian parties and theologians' [Fiorenza] . . . in the process missing the point that biblical theology (at least New Testament theology) has first and foremost to be regarded as missionary theology since it was the early church's missionary involvement that gave rise to its theological reflection" (Bosch, "Towards a Hermeneutic for 'Biblical Studies and Mission,'" 71). Bosch favorably reviewed some works in biblical studies that attempted to bridge the gap between the biblical evidence and the praxis of mission today. See his "Mission in Biblical Perspective," 535–37, where he reviewed, among others, Senior and Stuhlmueller, *The Biblical Foundations of Mission*; and Kertelge, *Mission im Neuen Testament*.

17. Bosch, "Mission in Biblical Perspective," 532. In his review, Bosch criticized American missiologist F. DuBose's *God Who Sends*, as being reductionist and hermeneutically deficient. DuBose focuses on the term "send" and declares it to be *the* key verb in the Bible, and proceeds to construct an entire biblical theology of mission around it. Bosch attacked the idea that any one concept or word is absolutely central to the biblical theology of mission. This inevitably led to distortions of the text as other, equally valid words or concepts are ignored. "Sending" becomes an over-arching concept which DuBose finds everywhere in the Bible, thus threatening to swallow up everything in its path. See ibid., 533–34.

The Biblical Foundation for Mission

In the *inductive method* one takes the situation in which one stands as the hermeneutical starting point. God's will is determined *"from* a specific situation rather than *in* it."[18] The Bible is then read, interpreted and applied in light of the situation. The context, therefore, becomes "the hermeneutical key which makes possible [one's] 'correct' understanding of the Bible."[19] This approach, according to Bosch, has been the method usually used in "ecumenical" circles. An example of this approach is the oft-quoted statement from the 1968 Uppsala Assembly: "The world provides the agenda."[20] Bosch was critical of this method because of its fundamental ambivalence. "Historical events and personal or group experience are too ambivalent to serve as [the] key for the interpretation of a biblical text."[21] In the *deductive method* one takes Scripture as the point of departure. The interpretive task involves establishing precisely what Scripture teaches on a certain subject, and then deriving normative guidelines that the believer can apply to his present situation.[22] Bosch linked this approach to the "evangelical" movement. The difficulty with this methodology is that it ignores the historical gap between our era and the biblical era, and downplays the impact of theological and historical traditions upon one's understanding of Scripture. Using the deductive method alone, we are "blinded by the presuppositions lurking behind our own interpretations."[23]

Bosch concluded that both methods, practiced in isolation, betray a selective use of Scripture in which the reader refers only to "the biblical data which particularly appeal to him or provide the 'answers' he is looking for."[24] Bosch labeled this the "Bible as a 'mine' approach."[25] The interpreter comes to the Scriptures seeking to dig out missionary texts, searching for "nuggets" that conform to his or her pre-understanding of mission.

Bosch believed these five interrelated factors (uncritical proof-texting, the historical gap between the Bible and today's mission, ignorance of the contextual nature of one's theology, the polarization between biblical studies and missiology, and differing hermeneutical approaches) prevent the church in discovering a sound biblical foundation for her missionary task in the world.

---

18. Bosch, *Witness*, 38.

19. Ibid., 45. For defenses of the "inductive" hermeneutical method and a critique of the "deductive" approach, see Casalis, *Correct Ideas Don't Fall From the Skies*; and Chikane, "Doing Theology in a Situation of Conflict," 98–102.

20. Bosch, *Witness*, 45.

21. Ibid., 44. Cf. Bosch's critical review of G. Casalis' "inductive approach" in his "Contextual Missionary Theology from Orbis," 122–23.

22. Bosch, *Witness*, 43. For a clear example of this approach, see the work of Reformed theologian Louis Berkhof, esp. his *Introduction to Systematic Theology* and *Systematic Theology*.

23. Bosch, *Witness*, 44.

24. Ibid., 45. Bosch attributes the ongoing evangelical/ecumenical debate largely to this factor, that both sides often use Scripture selectively. "As a result, it inevitably happens that a canon develops with the canon; what is not to the liking of a particular group is simply ignored" (ibid.).

25. Ibid., 45–46.

Part Two: Bosch's Theology of Mission and Evangelism

Bosch's Hermeneutical Approach to the Biblical Foundation for Mission

Presuppositions

Bosch put forward a number of hermeneutical presuppositions that are essential to developing an adequate biblical foundation for mission.[26] First, a true biblical foundation for mission must be *historically informed*. It must seek to sympathetically yet critically analyze the church's historical missionary self-understanding. The missiologist should be aware of the ways that the church down through the centuries has understood the relationship between the Bible and the missionary task.[27] Only after looking closely at the different ways in which the church, down through the centuries, has interpreted an issue or biblical text, will we be able to break out of the tyranny of our own context and see the relativity of our own approach.[28]

Second, a true biblical foundation for mission must be *grounded in the reconciling event of God in Christ*, not simply in an authoritative biblical commission. The person and ministry of Jesus was the catalyst that "triggered the missionary consciousness of the early church and shaped its basic message . . .."[29] Although Matt 28:18–20 and other biblical pronouncements are significant, these texts are not the decisive point of the biblical witness. Rather, it is what God has done in Christ. Bosch echoed the sentiments of Martin Kähler that "[t]he content of the Biblical witness, viz. the message about Jesus Christ, urges the church to its universal mission."[30]

Finally, a true biblical theology of mission must assert that *mission is at the heart of the church's being and nature*. To affirm that the church by its very nature is missionary is to acknowledge that the church's historical documents, including the Bible, must be seen in this light.[31] It is to affirm, in the words of two Catholic biblical scholars, that "approaching the Bible from the vantage point of mission [leads] to the center of its message."[32]

---

26. For an early attempt by Bosch at linking hermeneutics with mission, see his "Hermeneuse in 'n sendingsituasie," 220–40.

27. Bosch, "The Why and How," 33.

28. Ibid.

29. Senior and Stuhlmueller, *The Biblical Foundations for Mission*, 141, cited approvingly by Bosch in "Mission in Biblical Perspective," 536.

30. Bosch, "Systematic Theology and Mission: The Voice of an Early Pioneer," 171. Bosch refers the reader to Martin Kähler, *Schriften zu Christologie und Mission*, xxii–xxvi. For Kähler, mission is rooted in the atonement. "As an indispensable means, decreed by God, for the comprehensive evangelisation of the world, *mission is an aspect of the full implementation of the reconciliation of the world with God; therefore God's saving grace is its foundation and the encompassing of the whole of humanity is its purpose* . . ." Because the Christian has replaced his debt of sin with a debt of gratitude to God, he is compelled to witness. "Mission has its fundamental motivation in the necessity to witness . . . Witness is the fundamental moving force of the church of Christ" (ibid., as cited by Bosch in "Systematic Theology and Mission," 169).

31. Bosch, "Vision for Mission," 10.

32. Senior and Stuhlmueller, *The Biblical Foundations for Mission*, 4.

A Thematic, Integrative, Cooperative Approach

Beyond these theological preconditions, Bosch's approach to the Biblical foundation for mission can be summarized by four words: thematic, integrative, cooperative, and "postmodern." We shall simply take note of the first three concepts and then probe more deeply into the final one.

First, in approaching the Bible the central thrust of its message must be emphasized, not just certain biblical pronouncements and stories. "What is decisive for the Church today," Bosch emphasized, "is not formal agreement between what she is doing and what some isolated biblical texts seem to be saying but rather her relationship with the essence of the message of Scripture."[33] The central themes of both the Old and New Testaments should be the building blocks upon which a biblical theology of mission is constructed.[34]

Second, Bosch urged an *integrative* approach in addressing the tension between the inductive and deductive traditions of biblical interpretation. To pose the two methods in strictly antithetical terms is a false dichotomy. Bosch admitted there is no easy way out of the tension between the biblical word and the contemporary situation. "We can only, with full awareness of the limitations and relativity of 'deductive' *and* 'inductive' approaches, make use of both."[35]

Third, Bosch called for a cooperative approach between biblical scholars, missiologists and other theologians in developing a biblical theology of mission. Speaking with reference to an ongoing research project on biblical studies and mission of the International Association of Mission Studies, Bosch urged "a concerted effort in which scholars from various disciplines, confessions and cultures cooperate," affirming that this approach would "help us uncover for our own time what has traditionally been referred to as the 'biblical foundations for mission.'"[36] Yet he admitted that this goal is elusive. Recent works in both missiology and biblical studies only show "how far removed we [are] from gaining clarity on this issue."[37]

---

33. Bosch, "The Why and How," 35.

34. This does *not* imply a desire to uncritically harmonize the biblical material into a neat package, however. Bosch frequently states that the Bible is a varied collection of literature, with numerous and at times competing perspectives. See Bosch, *Witness*, 48.

35. Bosch, *Witness*, 44. Bosch approvingly cites French Protestant theologian Georges Casalis in this regard: "Theology, nurtured by the word of God, reflects on a historical situation in which we are wholly and responsibly involved . . . The situation is not God's word; God's word is not outside the situation; only a reference back to both the analysis (of the situation) and the word permits the discovery of all dimensions of the situation" (ibid.).

36. Bosch, "Toward a Hermeneutic for 'Biblical Studies and Mission,'" 65.

37. Ibid.

Part Two: Bosch's Theology of Mission and Evangelism

A "Postmodern" Approach to Scripture

As a solution to this dilemma, Bosch affirmed the need for a "postmodern" approach to Scripture that would liberate the church from both the rationalistic excesses of the historical-critical method, and the pre-critical biblicism of many evangelicals and fundamentalists.

THE INADEQUACY OF THE HISTORICAL-CRITICAL METHOD

Bosch posed the problem as follows.[38] Ever since the advent of the modern historical-critical method in biblical research, it has been assumed that the goal of biblical scholarship was to find the original meaning of a text, the meaning being what the author intended for his first readers. A text had only one meaning, and the scholar's task was to rid himself of presuppositions and get to the original meaning of author. Although the primary loyalty of biblical scholars was supposedly to the text itself (and to the believing community), many surrendered their primary loyalty "to the guild of biblical scholars who in turn submitted to the dictates of the spirit of the Enlightenment."[39] The Enlightenment approach to Scripture, which emphasized the human origins of the Bible and an anti-supernaturalist bias, has "distanced" the biblical text from the ordinary modern reader.[40] While Bosch acknowledged the positive benefits of the historical-critical method, he declared that the positivism of the historical-critical method had gone too far in the opposite direction.[41] Rather than assisting people of faith, critical biblical scholarship has frequently been perceived as *preventing* people from understanding and appropriating the biblical message. The biblical message, due to the uncertainties created by historical-critical method, has been seemingly deprived of its power.

A NEW "POSTMODERN" PARADIGM

In the midst of contemporary theological and hermeneutical confusion, Bosch saw signs of hope. He believed a new "postmodern" paradigm in theology and biblical studies was emerging that was striving to go beyond the sterile alternatives of pre-critical fundamentalism or historical-critical rationalism. It had emerged out of the revolution in twentieth century science, particularly physics. As a result of the massive

---

38. The argument that follows is found in ibid., 71–72.

39. Ibid., 71.

40. Ibid., 72. Bosch elaborates on this point as follows: "The time-span between the text and the modern reader grew larger. Scripture was rendered 'into a strange object to be dissected and examined instead of acknowledging it to be the Word that must be heard and obeyed in the present moment'. The orientation was one-directional: *backwards* towards the past—an approach that encouraged a kind of 'spectator exegesis'" (ibid.).

41. Ibid.

changes in the way scientists perceive the nature of the physical universe, all other realms of knowledge, including theology and biblical studies, have been undergoing a similar shift. They are moving away from a mechanical, "critical" understanding of reality toward a holistic, "post-critical" worldview.[42]

Bosch saw evidence of this shift in two realms. He discerns a postmodern approach in the realm of *systematic theology*. Theologians such as Hans Küng and David Tracy had begun to apply Thomas Kuhn's work on "paradigm changes" to theology. Küng posited there have been five major "paradigm shifts" in the history of Christian theology.[43] With the advent of dialectical, existential and Third World theologies, the present "modern Enlightenment" paradigm has been fundamentally challenged, and now a new "postmodern" paradigm is emerging whose concrete shape is not yet clear.[44]

Second, Bosch discerned a new "postmodern" approach emerging in *biblical studies* (although it is admittedly far too early to view this approach as a distinct "school" in current biblical scholarship). Bosch believed that this "postmodern" approach is exemplified in a new journal with which he was involved. Along with such theologians as C. K. Barrett, Horton Davies, Nicholas Lash, Howard Marshall, Ben Meyer, David Steinmetz, Peter Stuhlmacher, and Anthony Thistleton, Bosch served as an editorial consultant for Princeton Theological Seminary's *Ex Auditu*, devoted to the theological interpretation of Scripture. "This annual," declared Bosch, "heralds . . . a new era in biblical scholarship which can take us out of the impasse created by the historical critical school and its rationalistic approach."[45] Bosch saw an interesting and significant convergence between Küng and Tracy's work on the postmodern paradigm, and the work that the *Ex Auditu* project was doing.[46]

THE POSTMODERN PARADIGM AND THEOLOGY

What are the essential tenets of this postmodern paradigm? At its heart, the postmodern paradigm in hermeneutics and biblical studies argues that a text must be understood not only in terms of its pre-history and *Sitz im Leben*, but also its

---

42. For a full explication of the radical implications of this approach in the realm of biblical studies, see Martin, "Towards a Post-Critical Paradigm," 370–85; and Outler, "Toward a Postliberal Hermeneutic," 281–91. In a broader sense, this has been the burden of Michael Polanyi in the philosophical realm, and T. F. Torrance in the theological realm. See, respectively, *Personal Knowledge: Toward a Post-critical Philosophy*; and *Transformation and Convergence in the Frame of Knowledge: Explorations in the Interrelationships of Scientific and Theological Enterprise*.

43. Bosch, "Vision for Mission," 8. In their jointly edited *Theologie wohin? Auf dem Weg zu einem neuen Paradigma*, Küng and Tracy posit five paradigms, viz. the early Christian apocalyptic, the Hellenistic Byzantine, the medieval Roman Catholic, the modern Enlightenment, and the postmodern or contemporary paradigm.

44. Bosch, "Vision for Mission," 8.

45. Bosch, "Some Random Thoughts on a Writing Project," 1.

46. Ibid., 3.

"post-history."⁴⁷ One can only understand what a text "originally meant" when we also seek to understand what it might mean today. Bosch cites the work of Gadamer in this regard. Gadamer speaks of how "the application ('*Anwendung*') of a text is integral to the whole experience of understanding it."⁴⁸ This insight has significant implications for doing theology.

> The biblical scholar no longer has a monopoly on the meaning of the text, a meaning which he (grudgingly?) passes on to other theologians (*if* he does!). Rather, he is as dependent upon other theologians (including missiologists!) as they are upon him. There are, in fact, two poles in the interpretative process: the biblical text and the contemporary community of faith. These two poles are no threat to each other, but are interdependent, in mutually creative tension . . . The historical-critical method taught us that the biblical interpreter must escape from his or her own historical "horizon" and enter that of the biblical author. Gadamer tells us that to do . . . this is not only undesirable but, in fact, impossible if we truly wish to understand the text. Such an understanding can only occur when the horizon of a particular present meets the horizon of the past, namely that of the text.⁴⁹

Bosch went on to point out how Gadamer labeled this interpretative event as a *Horizontverschmelzung*, a "fusion of horizons." At the *Horizontverschmelzung*, theologians of all stripes can meet and supplement one another.⁵⁰ We should not seek to *escape* our historical context, for only by standing *within* it can we understand the biblical word.

This "postmodern" approach to exegesis does *not* mean an end to the historical-critical method. Bosch affirms that the "pastness" of the text must still be taken seriously. There can be no return to a "pre-critical" world.⁵¹ But no longer is the biblical text the exclusive province of the historical-critical scholar, either. The Bible is "the book of the Church, of the community of faith."⁵²

This means there must be a fundamental break with the Enlightenment principle of elevating doubt rather than faith as the first principle of knowledge. Among the numerous advocates of this new approach, Bosch proffered two prominent examples: missiologist Lesslie Newbigin and biblical scholar Peter Stuhlmacher. Newbigin (who had been profoundly influenced by the work of Michael Polanyi), claimed that "all knowledge of reality rests upon faith-commitments and that this is as true for the scientist as for the Christian believer."⁵³ Doubt is an essential element in doing the-

---

47. Bosch, "Towards a Hermeneutic for 'Biblical Studies and Mission,'" 72–75.
48. Bosch, "Vision for Mission," 9.
49. Bosch, "Towards a Hermeneutic for 'Biblical Studies and Mission,'" 74.
50. Ibid. Bosch cites Gadamer's *Truth and Method*, 269–74.
51. Bosch, "Towards a Hermeneutic for 'Biblical Studies and Mission,'" 74.
52. Ibid., 75.
53. See Newbigin's *The Other Side of 1984* and *Foolishness to the Greeks; The Gospel and Western*

ology, but should play a secondary role. Faith is the essential, primary prerequisite. Stuhlmacher said much the same thing in his programmatic essay *Historical Criticism and the Theological Interpretation of Scripture*. Stuhlmacher urged the theological community to give primacy to a "hermeneutic of consent," and relegate the "hermeneutic of suspicion" to a necessary but secondary role.[54]

Implications of the postmodern paradigm for the biblical theology of mission

Bosch saw at least two implications of the postmodern paradigm for the biblical theology of mission.[55] In order to understand the Bible correctly, Bosch argued, one must establish both what a text *means* today as well as what it *meant*. If this is true, then the guild of biblical scholars must be open to contributions from other fields, including missiology, in order to understand to Bible better. Missiologists, Bosch contended, "may be in a position to save [biblical scholars] from turning theology into religious archeology."[56] On the other hand, biblical scholars can help missiologists remain faithful to the original intentions of the text as they develop their mission theologies and strategies. Biblical scholars can assist the missionary enterprise by asking if its praxis is consonant with the biblical message.

Another implication of the postmodern paradigm is that missiologists should not attempt to construct a biblical theology of mission that is exactly *identical* with the message of the Bible, but rather to construct a theology that is *consonant* with what the text meant.[57] This is a crucial distinction. Bosch claimed that any communicated message, in order to be properly understood in a different era or context, must be stated *differently* in order for it to make sense to the hearer. A simple repetition or literal, wooden translation of the message will probably mislead the hearer.[58] But a dynamic

---

Culture; and *The Gospel in a Pluralist Society* for elaborations of his argument.

54. Bosch, "Towards a Hermeneutic for 'Biblical Studies and Mission,'" 75, citing Stuhlmacher, *Historical Criticism and the Theological Interpretation of Scripture*, 84–85.

55. Bosch outlines the two implications in "Towards a Hermeneutic for 'Biblical Studies and Mission,'" 75–78; and "Vision for Mission," 8–10.

56. Bosch, "Towards a Hermeneutic for 'Biblical Studies and Mission,'" 76.

57. Ibid. As far back as 1969, Bosch was arguing for an essentially similar approach. Noting the radical overuse of form-criticism, Bosch urged a basic reorientation in synoptic studies. Its goal should be "not so much to try to isolate authentic sayings of Jesus from the additions and transformations of the early Church and the theology of the evangelists, but rather to put the question in a new way: Is the evangelists' handling of the gospel material a legitimate interpretation of the mind of Jesus or not?" (Bosch, "Jesus and the Gentiles," 7).

58. Bosch relies here on the work of Hugo Echegaray. Echegaray points out the hermeneutical dangers of a simple transposition of the biblical material into our later era. It is necessary to "take account of the insurmountable historical distance separating us from [Jesus'] world. Between his time and ours irreversible qualitative changes have occurred. This fact forbids us to make mechanical transpositions from the one period to the other; to do so would be proof only of naiveté. If we unconsciously project our own situation into the past, we necessarily distort the past. If, conversely, we attempt a literal revival

retelling of the message, taking into consideration the worldview and experiences of the intended audience, will more likely be a faithful theological interpretation of the message. For a proper biblical foundation for mission, therefore, more must be done than simply an accurate analysis of what individual texts meant; "theological consonancy" with the biblical text must be sought.[59]

The above-mentioned approach is precisely the method of the Bible itself, and of the Christian church. Bosch illustrated this truth with three examples.

> When the New Testament authors used the Old Testament, this was far more than mere citation of or allusion to Old Testament language or application of Old Testament prophecy in order to substantiate Jesus' claims. Rather, where they referred to the Old Testament this was a wholly creative handling that proceeded from a sure understanding of the Old Testament for those New Testament authors in their context . . . Similarly, when Martin Luther transformed Psalm 46 into his famous "Ein feste Burg ist unser Gott"—in this process letting it refer to the church's battle against Satan and also bringing Jesus Christ onto the stage—he was not distorting the original meaning of the psalm but creatively reinterpreting it in a way that was consonant with its original intention. The two horizons were fused. A similar process took place with reference to Jesus in the New Testament itself. The message of and about this Jesus was creatively reinterpreted within the circumstances of Christians in Jerusalem, Antioch, Rome and Corinth. Putting it differently: Jesus inspired his disciples to prolong the logic of his own ministry in an imaginative and creative way amid historical circumstances that were in many respects new and different. The traditions were retained carefully but they were also modified to meet new circumstances.[60]

Thus the Biblical text is the point of departure, but understanding the text is a *creative process*. Different readers in different contexts may discern numerous, equally valid interpretations of a single text, so long as each interpretation is consonant with the intention of the text.[61]

Bosch used this hermeneutical approach in his previous writings to a limited degree, but *Transforming Mission* incorporated this approach much more explicitly. In an unpublished prospectus of the book, Bosch explained that his approach would "not be pre-critical, but, if anything, post-critical . . . I will not attempt to develop one, definitive 'biblical theology of mission' but, rather, try to show how different biblical

---

of the past in our own day, we shall be weakening its real power without realizing it." See his *The Practice of Jesus*, 34.

59. Bosch, "Towards a Hermeneutic for 'Biblical Studies and Mission,'" 76.

60. Ibid., 76. Bosch here develops the work of Echegaray. See Echegaray, *The Practice of Jesus*, xv–xvi.

61. Bosch, "Towards a Hermeneutic for 'Biblical Studies and Mission,'" 76. This hermeneutical principle of "consonance" has been developed more fully in Bosch's exegetical analysis of the Lord's Prayer: *The Lord's Prayer: Paradigm for a Christian Lifestyle*, esp. 1–2.

perspectives, trailing from different authors and periods, can help us to arrive at different although mutually complementing 'biblical theologies of mission.'"[62]

There are risks to Bosch's "postmodern" methodology. He acknowledged that with this approach the interpreter might overemphasize his or her context, thereby "distorting or muting what the texts say." All too easily, Bosch noted, we can divorce ourselves from the text and the critical challenge it poses to us.[63] But this is a constant danger in all theological work. Even when the right hermeneutical methods are followed, there is still no guarantee that one has interpreted either the biblical word or the existential situation correctly.[64] Thus "the practice of theology remains a risk. We can engage in theology only haltingly."[65]

The only safeguard we have from the risk of absolutizing our own interpretations is the Christian community, according to Bosch. The church is an "ecumenical, intercultural fellowship of brothers and sisters in the faith."[66] And only by working together in the ecumenical community of faith can we learn to humble ourselves, listen to one another, and begin to see the relativity of our own contexts.[67]

ELEMENTS IN BOSCH'S BIBLICAL THEOLOGY OF MISSION

We shall now outline the fundamental elements in Bosch's biblical theology of mission. Recalling his admonition to seek out the central thrust of the Bible rather than specifically "missionary" pronouncements,[68] we will examine six essential elements that, for Bosch, exemplify the missionary dimension of both the Old and New Testaments. They are: 1) history as the horizon for God's mission; 2) the relationship between God, Israel, and the nations; 3) the ministry and mission of Jesus; 4) the "Great Commission"; 5) the biblical model of mission as *martyria* (suffering/witness); and 6) *missio Dei*, the lordship of God himself in mission. Bosch admitted that there are undoubtedly other valid elements to a biblical foundation for mission that he did not highlight.[69] Nevertheless, these elements were the central tenets of Bosch's own biblical theology of mission.

---

62. Bosch, "Some Random Thoughts on a Proposed Writing Project," 1–2.
63. Bosch, "Towards a Hermeneutic for 'Biblical Studies and Mission,'" 78.
64. Bosch, *Witness*, 45.
65. Ibid.
66. Bosch, "Towards a Hermeneutic for 'Biblical Studies and Mission,'" 78–79.
67. Ibid. In another article, Bosch makes the same point and shows its striking relevance to the South African scene. See his "Racism and Revolution," 19–20.
68. "We want to employ a different method, namely, that of trying to establish the central thrust of the message of Scripture" (Bosch, *Witness*, 48). Cf. Verkuyl, *Contemporary Missiology*, 89–90.
69. Bosch, *Witness*, 45.

Part Two: Bosch's Theology of Mission and Evangelism

History as the Horizon for God's Mission

The first essential tenet of Bosch's biblical foundation for mission is an acknowledgement of the decisively *historical character* of the biblical religion. Although biblical "pre–history" in Genesis 1–11 is a universal description of human beginnings, from Genesis 12 onwards the biblical story concentrates on the offspring of Abraham, the people of Israel. History, by its very nature, is specific, localized, and particular.[70] This fact would appear to be a hindrance rather than a help to the missionary enterprise. If the Christian faith is to be a worldwide, universal phenomenon, should not the discussion begin with *universal and eternal truths* rather than the *historical particularities* of an obscure Semitic people? Bosch pointed out that many people see the historical, "particularistic" nature of the Bible as a stumbling block to the concept of a worldwide mission. They say, in effect: "We should so much have preferred the Bible to concern itself not only with Israel, but with all humanity . . ."[71] According to Bosch, this impulse for a universalistic approach revealed a fundamental misunderstanding of the nature of history and of revelation in the Bible.[72] Biblical revelation happens in the midst of certain historical events and personalities, which implies particularity. God reveals himself to a *particular* person in a *particular* place. Yet this particularity is filled with universal, missionary significance.[73] It is this biblical particularism that Bosch recognized as the source of the missionary heart of the Bible. Without it, Bosch noted, Yahweh's salvation would have been ahistorical.[74]

Building on the work of Mircea Eliade, Bosch elaborated on the *historical* character of the biblical religion by contrasting two essentially disparate concepts of religion: the "hierophantic" versus the "historical."[75] Both of these religious "types" have struggled with the meaning of history, and have emerged with opposing conclusions.

Hierophantic religions are those faith traditions that emphasize "ritual practices which were primarily related to problems experienced by a predominantly agrarian population, practices in which the king as earthly representative of the gods played an

---

70. Ibid., 58.

71. Ibid.

72. Bosch normally uses the terms "universalist" and "universalistic" *not* in the doctrinal sense, i.e., that all people will eventually be saved, but in the more general sense of being *universal or worldwide in scope*, i.e., that God's loving concern is global and comprehensive rather than limited and finite.

73. Bosch comments that: "A careful reading of the Old Testament . . . reveals the enormous missionary significance of Yahweh's dealings with Israel. This becomes apparent in the call of Abraham (Gen. 12:1–3). This event refers back to the Babel episode in Gen. 11. Man's attempt at obtaining salvation has failed miserably; now God begins with a new thing. What Babel lost, is promised and guaranteed in the history of Abraham's election. Genesis 12 follows Genesis 11. The entire history of Israel is nothing more than a continuation of God's dealings with the nations." See Bosch, "The Why and How," 39.

74. Ibid.

75. For more on the hierophantic religions and their contrast with the historical, see Eliade, *The Myth of the Eternal Return*.

important role."[76] Reality is viewed in cyclical terms based upon seasonal and annual events. By ritually reenacting certain primordial events from the past (e.g., the world's creation, the birth of the universe), the mythical time is made contemporaneous with the worshippers. In hierophantic religions, reality is essentially static. The emphasis is on continuity, repetition, remembrance, and the stability of the status quo. Consequently, there is a fundamental orientation to the past, with little concern for the possibilities of change, progress or development.[77]

Historical religions, such as Judaism, challenge the hierophantic religions' view of reality.[78] Yahweh is the God of history, of the Exodus, of cause and effect.[79] History is not cyclical but oriented toward the future. History is a creative, dynamic process, filled with meaning.[80]

Bosch granted that the OT contains numerous elements of the hierophantic, cyclical religions of the ancient Near East. But the religion of Israel, with its prophetic, self-critical element, never allowed its faith in Yahweh to be completely identified with the static "nature cycles" of the hierophantic religions.[81] Faith in Yahweh fundamentally challenged the seasonal "nature cycle" of birth, growth, decay, death, resurrection, new birth.[82] Even where the Hebrews celebrated religious feasts associated with past events or seasonal festivals, their concern was not primarily the commemoration of the past but "a forward movement towards the future."[83]

Another significant tension between the hierophantic and historical religions is their understanding of the nature of truth. Is religion grounded in eternal truths or historical encounters? In the hierophantic religions, truth is seen as the correct formulation of eternally and universally valid principles or ideas. In the historical religions, however, truth is more a matter of personal encounter and personal relationship, grounded in a particular historical revelation of God.[84] The Bible rarely deals with questions abstractly or theoretically; persons know the truth as they encounter

---

76. Bosch, *Witness*, 58.

77. Bosch, *Theology 201*, 36. See also Bosch, *Witness*, 58–59.

78. In particular, the faiths of Judaism, Christianity and Islam challenge the hierophantic outlook.

79. Bosch commented that: "The biblical cult is an 'exodus celebration', ever again a new journey into the future. Its concern is not with festivals of remembrance or with a return of a one-time appearance of God in a mythical, primordial time (a hierophany), because man is not caught up in passive commemoration, directed to the past. The Bible speaks predominantly in terms of personal relationships . . . and hardly ever treats any question abstractly . . ." (Bosch, *Witness*, 59).

80. On this (essentially Hebraic/Christian) concept of history as a meaningful, creative process, see Hendrikus Berkhof, *Christ the Meaning of History*, esp. 17–56.

81. Bosch, *Witness*, 59.

82. Ibid.

83. Bosch, *Theology 201*, 36. Elsewhere, Bosch has noted that many African concepts of God, like the hierophantic religions, tend to stress God as a Creator who is uninvolved in present history. In biblical revelation, God is presented as Creator as well. "But his creative activity is always intimately bound up with his redemptive activity in history, and is of only secondary importance" (Bosch, "God in Africa: Implications for the Kerygma," 19).

84. Bosch, *Theology 201*, 36–37. See also Bosch, *Witness*, 59.

Part Two: Bosch's Theology of Mission and Evangelism

God and enter into vital relationship with him. This is particularly true in the New Testament, where Truth is a historical person, Jesus Christ (John 14:6).[85]

Bosch illustrated the profound tension between these two differing understandings of the relationship of religion and history by citing an incident in the life of Bishop Lesslie Newbigin. When Newbigin told a learned master of the Ramakrishna Mission that he was prepared to stake his entire Christian faith on the essential reliability of the New Testament historical records about Jesus, the master was astonished. "To him it seemed axiomatic that such vital matters of religious truth could not be allowed to depend upon the accidents of history. If the truths which Jesus exemplified and taught are true, then they are true always and everywhere, whether a person called Jesus ever lived or not."[86]

A final tension between the hierophantic and historical religions is the contrasting emphasis between the ceremonial and the ethical. The hierophantic faiths place a high emphasis on cultic ceremonies and rituals, based on the cyclical, commemorative nature of their worship. But in the Bible the accent is on ethics, the behavior of the community in the here and now.[87] This does not mean that the cultic and the ceremonial were dispensed with in either the Old or New Testaments. But Bosch maintained that they receive their significance only inasmuch as they foster an encounter of faith with God, a God who is calling them to journey with him into the future. The ceremonial is legitimate inasmuch as "it serves to improve the believer's conduct here and now." The cultic and the ceremonial *"strengthen* Christian faith, but they do not *embody* it."[88] Thus in three key areas (history as static versus dynamic; truth as eternal versus historical encounter; and religious devotion as ceremonial versus ethical), Bosch exposed the radical difference between biblical faith and the other faiths of the ancient world.

> This concept of the *historical* character of biblical revelation is an essential aspect of a biblical theology of mission. Beginning with Abraham, the Bible portrays God as calling a particular people out of their cyclical existence and *into* history, *into* the world.[89] Abraham is called out of Ur for a journey into the

---

85. Bosch, *Witness*, 59. D. T. Niles has spoken of this contrast in his affirmation that the biblical revelation cannot be taught but only proclaimed. "The Christian evangelist announces that something has happened which is of both immediate and ultimate significance . . . The adherents of other religions . . . expound the teachings of their own religions as the true interpretation of the meaning and responsibilities of life." See Niles, *Upon the Earth*, 242–43, quoted in Bosch, *Witness*, 59.

86. Newbigin, *The Finality of Christ*, 50, as quoted in Bosch, *Witness*, 59. This is, of course, essentially the same dilemma that G. E. Lessing has posed: How can the "accidental truths of history" ever become "the proof of the necessary truths of reason"? For both Lessing and the Ramakrishna master, historical events could not form the basis for authentic religious faith. It is only in the rational or metaphysical realm that the key to proper religious belief is found. See Heron, *A Century of Protestant Theology*, 18–21.

87. Bosch, *Theology 201*, 37. Bosch notes that "time and again this is the charge leveled against Israel by the prophets: that they observe the ceremonial rites meticulously but ignore the ethical . . . The same is true of Jesus' rebukes to the Pharisees . . ." (ibid.).

88. Ibid.

89. Bosch, "The Why and the How," 39.

unknown, with the promise that through his offspring, all the nations of the world would be blessed.[90] Israel is called out of Egypt for a journey through the wilderness into a promised land, in order to be a light to the nations. Most significantly, God descends from heaven to reveal and incarnate himself in the history of one particular man, Jesus, for the salvation of the world. And then early Church is called out from the world and then sent back into it as God's ambassadors, in the power of the resurrection and Pentecost. In each case, Scripture maintains that what was merely "historical" and "particular" became a vessel that God infused with cosmic, missionary significance. For Bosch, "only a historical religion can be truly missionary. If, on the other hand, we discover in the Bible nothing but 'eternal, immutable truths', the missionary dimensions will be quickly dissipated."[91]

God, Israel, and the Nations

It is significant that Bosch, in developing his biblical theology of mission, devoted major attention to the OT. Frequently this is neglected, at the risk of condensing and reducing the full biblical vision of what mission is.[92] So far we have shown how Bosch emphasized the centrality of the *historical* character of revelation, and how this historical particularism is at the heart of the universal, missionary message of the OT. In biblical history, this tension between the particular and the universal was worked out by means of the election of Israel from among the nations (particularism), in order to actualize God's purposes of salvation for the nations (universalism). Israel lives by the grace of God with a distinct responsibility for the nations. For Bosch, this sense of *responsibility*, rooted in both the particularism of God's election of Israel and universalism of God's saving compassion for all the nations, was central to the OT concept of mission.[93] This section will trace how Bosch unfolded this complex relationship between God, Israel and the nations, and its missiological significance.

---

90. "With Abraham's call God embarks upon a history. The patriarch is snatched from the cyclical stranglehold of the Amorite and Sumerian religious world and called to journey into the unknown—an event that symbolizes that what follows in Abraham's life is truly 'history,' something new, where something different may happen at any time, a transcending of the predictability of the cyclic thought world" (Bosch, *Witness*, 61).

91. Bosch, "The Why and the How," 39. Bosch comments that the cultic, cyclical religions of the nations surrounding Israel constituted a permanent threat to believers. "In the early period this threat came especially from the Canaanite fertility cults as personified in the Baalim and the Asherim. In the New Testament period it usually assumed the form of the Greek mystery religions or Gnosticism, which agreed in at least one respect: their ahistorical understanding of reality" (Bosch, *Witness*, 59–60).

92. Bosch, "Sendingperspektief in die Ou Testament," 285–86, hereafter cited as "Sendingperspektief." Cf. Bosch, "Der Alttestamentliche Missionsgedanke," 174, hereafter cited as "Alttestamentliche." It is an irony that *Transforming Mission* neglected this rich theme, particularly since Bosch had reflected and written much on the subject.

93. Bosch, "Jeseja," 35, Bosch, "Sendingperspektief," 290–91.

Part Two: Bosch's Theology of Mission and Evangelism

The Universalist-Particularist Tension

In Genesis 1–11, we encounter a God who is involved with the whole world. The unity of humankind is unquestioned, and the genealogical lists in Genesis 10 give no hint that the forebears of Israel are set apart.[94] In Genesis 12, however, God zeros in on one man, Abraham, and immediately the Bible moves into the story of one nation and one people. The story of Abraham's calling contrasts sharply with the Babel story. And yet, as Bosch saw it, there is a crucial link. "In Babel man's attempt to procure salvation fails miserably. Thereafter God begins something new. What Babel has lost, is promised and guaranteed in the history of Abraham's election. Genesis 12 follows on Genesis 11—the history of Israel is a continuation of God's dealings with the nations. Precisely as the elect the patriarch, and with him Israel, is called into the world of nations."[95]

Bosch goes on to point out how every one of the Abrahamic stories touches upon the relationship between Abraham (and thus Israel) and the nations. Throughout the rest of the OT, we see this truth emphasized again and again. God reigns over the whole earth. Although God has particularly chosen Israel to be his instrument, he has the salvation of the nations as his ultimate object. Salvation, in the biblical sense, must be historic and concrete; God is bound to begin with a particular person and a particular people. But this historical "boundedness" of salvation is not antithetical to God's desire for a universal salvation. In the world of the Bible, the latter can only emerge as a result of the former.[96]

Bosch showed how this universalistic element emerges especially in the Psalms. God holds all the nations in his hands; he is the keeper of all creation (Pss 33:5; 104:27–28; 145:15–16; 147:8–9); he is the God who rules as king over all the earth (Pss 22:28; 47:3, 8; 59:14); he is the judge over all the nations (96:10, 13); even the pagan nations are urged to praise him, for he is their God as well (Pss 47:2; 66, 117).[97] God is truly the Lord of the nations as well as Israel. it is only from this vantage-point of God's universal concern that we may properly understand the significance of Israel's history.

Israel's Election and the Compassion of God

By the time of Israel's sojourn in Egypt, the descendants of Abraham had lost their earlier sense of destiny. They had become an oppressed and enslaved people. It is precisely here, at their point of deepest need, that God revealed himself as the one who has compassion on the poor, the afflicted, the weak, the oppressed, and the outcast.[98]

94. Bosch, *Theology 201*, 39.

95. Bosch, *Witness*, 61–62.

96. Bosch, "Sendingperspektief," 295–97; Bosch, "Alttestamentliche," 183–85; and Bosch, *Jesus, die Lydende Messias, en ons Sendingmotief*, 25–28; subsequently referred to as *Lydende*.

97. Bosch, *Theology 201*, 43.

98. At the outset, we should note that Bosch contrasts "compassion" from mere "sympathy." "Compassion is not the same as sympathy, as we understand it today. But 'sympathy' has come to mean: having

The Biblical Foundation for Mission

Other ancient gods placed an emphasis upon order, harmony and the status quo; but Yahweh revealed himself as the God of change, the rescuer of the poor and needy.[99] Bosch cited Ezekiel's moving description of Israel's election by Yahweh. "Israel is portrayed as the child of an Amorite father and a Hittite mother, who, after birth, was discarded in the open field, unwashed and uncared for. Yahweh, however, had compassion on this foundling: 'Then I came by and saw you kicking helplessly in your own blood; I spoke to you, there in your blood, and bade you live.'"[100]

This graphic description of Israel's helplessness and Yahweh's empathetic response exemplifies the nature of God's election of Israel: it is grounded solely in the compassionate, gracious love of God.[101] It is no wonder, according to Bosch, that the Exodus event therefore became "the corner-stone of Israel's confession of faith. It is this *compassion for the unworthy* which distinguished Yahweh from the other gods . . ."[102]

Who then, was Israel? She was simply a heathen nation like her neighbors, but as a result of God's loving election, she was a nation "set apart," obliged to live in tension with them. "The distinction [between Israel and the surrounding nations] does not come from ethnic differences but only from the fact that Israel is a 'heathen' nation whom God has called to salvation, whereas those outside of Israel are foreigners for whom this salvation is not yet valid . . . Israel is what she is on the basis of God's gracious covenant."[103]

The Purpose of Election and Israel's Covenant Responsibilities

God revealed himself as a God of compassion, and elected Israel to be his covenant people. But this covenant also carried responsibilities and obligations. The God of

---

pity from a safe distance, in a condescending manner. True compassion is, however, a suffering with the other, sharing in His suffering, suffering on His behalf. And that is the amazing thing about sharing: if I share in His grief, that grief is halved" (Bosch, *TCAC*, 29).

99. Bosch comments: "Whereas the gods of the predominantly hierophantic religions stressed order, harmony, integration and the maintenance of the status quo, the violation of which would provoke fury, Yahweh revealed himself as the God of change, the God who comes to the rescue of the poor and needy" (Bosch, *Witness*, 50). Cf. Bosch, "The Why and How," 38; Bosch, *Theology 201*, 28.

100. Bosch, *Witness*, 50.

101. "Israel's election is to be attributed to this divine compassion, not to any good qualities Israel might have possessed . . . The basis for God's election of Israel was to be found throughout in his spontaneous and unmerited mercy . . ." Bosch cites Deut 7:6–8 in this regard: "For you are a people holy to the Lord your God. The Lord your God has chosen you out of all the peoples on the face of the earth to be his people, his treasured possession. The Lord did not set his affection on you and choose you because you were more numerous than other peoples, for you were the fewest of all peoples. But it was because the Lord loved you and kept the oath he swore to your forefathers that he brought you out with a mighty hand and redeemed you from the land of slavery, from the power of Pharaoh king of Egypt" (ibid., 51).

102. Ibid., 50 (my emphasis). Here Bosch cites significant biblical evidence for this contention, including Exod 20:2; Ps 68:5–6; and Deut 4:32, 34–35.

103. Bosch, "Sendingperspektief," 287–88 (my translation).

Part Two: Bosch's Theology of Mission and Evangelism

compassion elected a people to be set apart and holy.[104] What is significant for the missionary thought of the OT, however, is that *Israel was to live out her holiness by being like Yahweh*, namely by showing the same compassion upon others as Yahweh had shown upon her. Election was for service.[105]

The responsibility that Israel bore as God's covenant partner has many aspects, but Bosch highlights two. First, Israel had a specific obligation to accept and help those strangers and aliens within her midst, especially the poor and oppressed, widows and orphans. Israel herself had been a stranger in Egypt, and so she was to have "compassion on the stranger in her midst. The constitutive element here was neither ethnic, nor the biological, nor the cultural; the stranger who lived in Israel had to be accepted completely and without reserve."[106]

Second, Israel had a more general obligation to the nations. She was called to understand her national existence in a larger perspective. Through her election, God was laying hold of all the tribes and nations of the earth. She was thus a symbol of what God's plan was for *all* the nations.[107] "Israel was not to distance herself from other nations, but was made responsible for them. God's concern is with the whole world. Israel's special position is not grounded in anything other than the fact that she is called to be his instrument by which he can bless and witness to the nations."[108]

Even in the making of the holy covenant between Yahweh and Israel (which was the very act that set her apart from the other nations), the role of the nations figured prominently.[109] In all her actions, both toward her own people and toward her neighbors, Israel was called to model the same compassion that her Lord had for her.[110]

---

104. Bosch, "Jeseja," 34. See Lev 11:44–45 for a link between God's holiness and Israel's obligation to be holy, rooted in the fact that he is *their* God, their liberator from Egypt.

105. "It was characteristic of Yahweh that he expected his elect to reveal the same compassion which he himself possessed. The purpose of election was service and where this service was withheld, election lost its meaning. Israel's besetting sin was precisely that she interpreted election as favoritism. However, election was not primarily privilege but rather responsibility" (Bosch, "The Why and How," 38). Cf. Bosch, "Sendingperspektief," 292; and Bosch, "Alttestamentliche," 180–81.

106. Bosch, *Witness*, 52. Cf. Bosch, "The Why and How," 38. Bosch cites Num 9:14; 15:14–16; and Josh 20:9 as examples of legal statutes in Israel designed to help the stranger.

107. Bosch, "Sendingperspektief," 292.

108. Ibid. (my translation).

109. In Bosch, *Theology 201*, 41–43, Bosch examines the missiological significance of "the nations" by expounding the arguments made by W. Vogels in his "Covenant and Universalism: Guide for a Missionary Reading of the Old Testament," 25–32. The article sees "the nations" as having a pivotal role in the covenant between God and Israel found in Exod 19.

110. Bosch repeatedly emphasizes the cardinal importance of the biblical theme of compassion. "There is an intimate link between God's compassion and mission" (Bosch, *Theology 201*, 27). "A religion in which compassion occupies so central a position, cannot but be a missionary religion" (Bosch, *Witness*, 57).

Israel and the Betrayal of Her Election

Israel was a very imperfect model of God's compassion. The covenant was perverted. All too frequently she began to attribute her election not to the unmerited grace of God but to her national achievements, or her superior character, or her extraordinary merit. "Instead of God's faithfulness to Israel being contingent on her obedience to his law, the Israelites came to feel that God was unconditionally committed to preserving Israel because of their superiority to the heathen nations."[111]

Bosch illustrated how in the so-called Late Judaism era, the roles had become reversed and history rewritten, to the effect that God needed Israel, and Israel had "elected" God! Israel' holiness became an attribute of her being rather than a constant gift from God. She assumed that her election was permanent, her holiness inextinguishable. Even if she sinned grievously, she remained God's people.[112] This sense of ethnic nationalism led to a changed attitude toward the "heathen." Interest shifted away from the desire to make proselytes of non-Jews, and toward racial purity and exclusivism.[113]

Again and again, Bosch noted, the prophets spoke out against such misconceptions. Israel owed her very existence to God, and was called to obey him in showing compassion to others. Her election was pointless if she merely gloried in her own salvation and neglected the service of others.[114] Yet with similar frequency, many Jews ignored their "missionary calling" to service and witness.

How does one account for the tensions within the Jewish self-understanding of their election? Bosch found an answer in the ambivalence of the term "Israel" in the OT. Israel was at once a theological entity, God's people in the world; but she was also an ethnic and political entity. "Because of Israel's struggle for existence—a small nation surrounded by powerful empires—it was, humanly speaking, difficult for them to impart a message of love and generosity to the surrounding nations. There was always a tendency automatically to regard one's political enemies as religious opponents as well; it was, in fact, practically impossible to distinguish between the two types of opponents."[115]

---

111. Bosch, *Witness*, 51.

112. Ibid., 51–52; Bosch, *Theology 201*, 28. For more details, see Bosch, *Heidenmission*, 31–35.

113. "The emphasis shifted increasingly away to racial purity which led to a dwindling zeal for absorbing proselytes.... This entailed too great a risk since they were not children of Abraham after the flesh and therefore had certain inherent weaknesses. On the strength of the story of Ruth many Jewish authors claimed that it was unnecessary to go out consciously in search of proselytes. At most they should, like Ruth, present themselves—in which case they could be accepted, but even then they should be discouraged rather than encouraged. A proselyte is never wholly on a par with a native Jew, for something of his former life will always cling to him . . ." Bosch adds a contemporary warning, particularly relevant for South Africa: "Incidentally: we must not judge this Jewish attitude too harshly! Our own churches are not always innocent of a similar approach. Possibly we have merely learnt to disguise this more cleverly than the Jews of old" (Bosch, *Theology 201*, 29).

114. Ibid.

115. Bosch, *Witness*, 62. Cf. Bosch, *Theology 201*, 40–41.

Part Two: Bosch's Theology of Mission and Evangelism

This ambivalence about the calling and identity of Israel obscured the missionary dimension of Israel's existence, but never entirely defaced it. Even in times of severe faithlessness, she was reminded of her calling to compassionate service. Through the ministry of the prophets, there always remained the awareness that "... not all descendants of Israel are truly Israel" (Rom 9:6).[116]

The Exceptional Example of Jonah

Perhaps no other book has been more frequently used and less understood in this regard than the book of Jonah. Jonah is frequently held up in missiological works as the only OT book that gives a decisive "New Testament" understanding of mission. For here we have an evangelist going out to a distant land to proclaim God's message to pagans. It is true that, superficially at least, this is the meaning of the book. In this sense Jonah is an exception to the OT rule.[117] The crucial message of the book of Jonah, however, concerns the conversion of *Israel*, not Nineveh. Little interest is shown in the reaction of the Ninevites; rather the attention is on Jonah himself. The entire story is an ironic satire against the pride of Jewish particularism and an object lesson of God's compassion.[118] In the narrative, we see Jonah (and in him, all Israel) as a very atypical missionary. He is a missionary without a missionary's heart. Ironically, Jonah knows that God "is a gracious and compassionate God, slow to anger and abounding in love, a God who relents from sending calamity" (Jonah 4:2), but his pride keeps him from admitting that this love extends beyond Israel to the other nations of the earth. It is also ironical that the pagans (who are objects of God's wrath in Jonah's eyes) did what Israel (who is the object of God's mercy) usually failed to do, namely turn to God in repentance and faith. As Bosch summarized it: "The emphasis of the Jonah story is therefore not on the conversion of Nineveh; it is a call to Israel to allow themselves to be converted to a compassion comparable to that of Yahweh. The story's missionary significance does not lie in the physical journey of a prophet of Yahweh to a pagan country but in Yahweh's being a God of compassion—a compassion which knows no boundaries. What is being castigated is Jonah's and Israel's exclusivistic appropriation of God's favour and compassion to themselves."[119]

---

116. Bosch, *Witness*, 62.

117. Bosch, "Sendingperspektief," 294; Bosch, "Alttestamentliche," 183.

118. For a further elaboration of what follows see Bosch, "The Why and How," 38; and Bosch, *Witness*, 52–53. For an excellent discussion of the missiological significance of the book, see Verkuyl, *Contemporary Missiology*, 96–100.

119. Bosch, *Witness*, 53.

Mission in the Bible as Centrifugal and Centripetal

Mission in the OT is clearly *not* confined to Jonah. But how was Israel to carry out her mission to the world? If mission was not defined as journeying to faraway places, what was the nature of mission in the OT? Bosch answered this question by making use of Bengt Sundkler's now familiar terminology "centripetal" and "centrifugal." Sundkler introduced the terms into modern discussion in 1936, in order to do away with the notion of an apparent antithesis between particularism and universalism in the Bible.[120]

Simply stated, "centrifugal mission" is active. It is mission that emphasizes sending people journeying out from a central point, in which physical boundaries are crossed. "Centripetal mission" is more passive. It is mission that draws people in from the outside toward a central point, in which certain actions or events attract and impel outsiders to come. Bosch noted that the OT sees mission primarily (but not exclusively) in centripetal terms (drawing in), whereas the New Testament sees mission primarily in centrifugal terms (sending out).[121] We will return to this distinction in later sections; now we simply highlight the nature of Israel's *centripetal* mission task.

Israel's missionary self-understanding focused primarily on drawing the nations into Jerusalem, into Zion, where God's truth and righteousness were made known.[122] This theme is found throughout the later literature of the OT (Pss 22:27, 47:9, 72:9–11, 86:9, 87; Isa 2:2–4, 19:23, 25:6–8, 45:14, 56:7, 66:18; Jer 3:17; Ezek 38:12; Mic 4:1–4; Zeph 3:9; Zech 8, 14:16).[123] In the OT, Israel stood at the center of salvation-history. Her mission was not to take this salvation out to the Gentiles, but simply to allow God to work out his purposes of holiness, peace, and justice in her national life, before the eyes of the world. Her most essential missionary contribution was therefore simply to remain *faithful* to her Lord. As God worked in Israel, she would serve as a sign to the Gentiles, as "a light to the nations" (Isa 42:6; 49:6).[124] As Israel was obedient to God, she would gather the Gentiles in, journeying to her by means of the light that radiated out of her. "Israel must simply and truly be Israel, to be exactly that which God has called her. Israel, in her history and her experience, is herself the proclamation [verkondiging] . . . Israel's missionary task is to remain faithful to Yahweh, her God, to

---

120. See Sundkler, "Jésus et les Païens," 462–99. Also see Bosch's discussion of Sundkler in *Heidenmission*, 21; and more fully in his essay "Jesus and the Gentiles," 3–5.

121. Early in his career Bosch emphasized that the Old Testament was almost exclusively centripetal, the New almost exclusively centrifugal. See Bosch, "Sendingperspektief," 295; and "Jeseja," 35. Later Bosch modified his views, affirming the presence of both dimensions of mission in both testaments. See Bosch, "The Why and How," 40; and Bosch, *Witness*, 76.

122. Bosch, *Witness*, 76.

123. Bosch, "Sendingperspektief," 295–97.

124. Bosch, *Theology 201*, 68. On the metaphor of light, Bosch notes: "The metaphor of light in Isa 42.6, 49.6 and elsewhere, is particularly appropriate to give expression to both a centripetal and a centrifugal movement. A light shining in the darkness draws people towards it, centripetally, yet at the same time it goes outward, crossing frontiers, allowing, in the words of Isa 49.6, God's salvation to reach 'to earth's farthest bounds'" (Bosch, *Witness*, 76).

Part Two: Bosch's Theology of Mission and Evangelism

remain true. God himself manifests and proclaims his own lordship, and Israel must only be a 'witness' . . . This happens when Israel recognises and affirms the Lordship of God over herself, and gives her praises to the glory of God."[125]

The Witness of Israel and the Witness of the "Servant of the Lord"

In concrete terms, how was Israel to be God's witness? Bosch returned to the theme of witness often, and we shall develop this later in the chapter. Here we simply highlight Bosch's understanding that Israel was a witness of the Lord, but not in the traditional, evangelistic sense of the word. The OT understanding of "witness" bears little resemblance to the New Testament or Christian connotations of the word. Witness in the OT usually has to do with a *judicial* witness in a courtroom.[126] In Isa 42–43, Bosch noted that Israel appeared as God's witness in the court case between Yahweh and the nations. Ironically, she was an "impossible witness," being deaf, blind, and dumb (Isa 42:18–20; 43:8–13). She witnessed to the nations about Yahweh "simply through her experiences and her very existence."[127] When Israel spoke, she usually did so through the mouths of the prophets *to her own people*. As long as she remained faithfully obedient to the prophets and their words from God, God empowered Israel to live. It is the behavior of *God* toward *Israel* that provided the witness, not vice versa.

God himself was the true witness; he alone was the source and stimulus for Israel's witness to the nations. This emphasis comes out clearly in Bosch's interpretation of the "Servant of the Lord" concept in Isaiah.[128] With the advent of the Servant of the Lord, God's salvation for the nations became more explicit. The Servant's task of mediating salvation to the nations did not consist in what he said or did, but *in what God did in and through him*. When he preached, he spoke to Israel rather than the nations. The heathen were simply invited to come and see what God was doing in Israel. The only "proclamation" that the Gentiles would receive were the *events* that would unfold through his ministry and sufferings. Through him, God would cause justice to go out to the nations (42:1). God would mediate the Covenant and enlighten the nations through him (42:6). God would bring salvation to the ends of the earth through him (49:6). He would bear the sins of many and intercede for sinners (53:12). Yet despite the immense missionary significance of the Servant of the Lord, salvation in the full

---

125. Bosch, "Sendingperspektief," 295–96 (my translation).

126. Bosch, "Jeseja," 35–36.

127. Bosch, "Sendingperspektief," 293; Bosch, "Alttestamentliche," 182. "The whole point seems to be that the message of this dumb and blind witness does not consist in verbal proclamation but that merely by his existence and his experiences he is a witness for Yahweh. His mission consists in his being there for others" (Bosch, "The Why and How," 40).

128. For a further elaboration of what follows see Bosch, "Jeseja," 36; Bosch, "Sendingperspektief," 293–94; and Bosch, "Alttestamentliche," 182–83. Bosch refuses to identify the "Servant of the Lord" with any particular Old Testament figure, but contends that Christians are right to see Jesus as the true fulfillment of this historical character, whoever he might have been.

sense of the word was not yet given to the nations; this would have to wait for a future time (cf. Isa 60–66).

The Eschatological Character of the Old Testament

From all that has been said, Bosch maintained that mission, in the centripetal sense of active outreach to non-Jews, was still something that belonged to the future. An active missionary witness among the nations was not yet possible for the people of God in the OT, for the Messiah had not yet come.[129] This does not mean that God's eschatological judgment and salvation were far off; the OT prophets spoke often that these were imminent, present-day realities and not in the far-off future. This consciousness of the imminence of God's salvific judgment provided a strong motivation for Israel to take the present seriously because, in truth, she *already* stood under the Day of Judgment and salvation.[130] God's ultimate missionary purposes, however, still belonged to the future.

> In some mysterious fashion [mission] is related to the coming of the Messiah who—however incomprehensible this may seem—would unite in himself the prophecies of the suffering and reviled Servant of the Lord (Is. 53) and of the royal Son of man (Dan. 7:13–14). Only then would the way to active mission be opened, something which the Old Testament could express only through vague intimations. Thus the prophets anticipated a day when the peoples would acknowledge Yahweh as God, even as Israel was doing (or should do). How this is to happen remains hidden. For the present this glorious future is at best celebrated liturgically in worship and in song. The Psalms in particular call the peoples to universal worship, though the peoples themselves are not present... Provisionally, therefore, mission exists in Israel's songs of praise![131]

In the OT, the vision for mission remained strongly centripetal. Israel, and Jerusalem in particular, were to serve as the "reintegration center" for the nations of the world as they came to receive God's law (Isa 2:2; Mic 4:1).[132] And yet there remained seemingly inexplicable alternative visions within the OT, distinct from the centripetal view, which posited a salvation for the nations that was *not* tied to Jerusalem and the Temple (Isa 19:19–24; Zeph 2:11; Mal 1:11). These alternative visions of salvation for the nations were crucially significant, for they promised a day when true worshippers would worship God in spirit and in truth, irrespective of place (John 4:19–24), but these visions belonged to a future era.[133]

---

129. Bosch, *Theology 201*, 45.
130. Bosch, "Sendingperspektief," 297–98; Bosch, "Alttestamentliche," 186–87.
131. Bosch, *Theology 201*, 44.
132. Ibid.
133. Ibid., 45.

Part Two: Bosch's Theology of Mission and Evangelism

We conclude this section on the complex relationship between God, Israel, and the nations with eight theses. Although they are drawn from Bosch's essay "Isaiah and Mission," we believe they summarize Bosch's thinking concerning the missionary significance of the OT.[134]

1. Israel is God's chosen people, called to be holy.

2. Although the OT is chiefly concerned with Israel, it reveals a God who has not forgotten the Gentiles. The earth is indeed the Lord's and he is its only Lord.

3. Israel, as God's people, has a missionary responsibility for the nations, although her mission is primarily centripetal not centrifugal.

4. Israel is merely God's instrument; Yahweh himself is the primary missionary.

5. Israel is the "witness" of Yahweh to the nations, not primarily through her words, but by her very existence as God acts upon and through her.

6. The witness *par excellence* is the "Servant of the Lord." Through his work, witness and especially his suffering, it is promised that justice will shine out from Israel, giving light to the nations.

7. Real mission is still in the distant future, in "the last days." But an eschatological vision is announced, particularly in Isa 66, which proclaims that God himself will gather all the nations together to see his glory.

8. God constantly judges Israel, with only a remnant remaining faithful. This remnant will get increasingly smaller, until only one man is left, the Messiah, who will incarnate the true faithfulness of God's people.

Jesus and Mission

Any Christian theology of mission must grapple with the decisive significance of Jesus for mission. As the central figure of the church's inner life and outer witness, the person, words and actions of Jesus loom large on the horizon. In this section, we can only summarize some of the most important avenues that Bosch pursued concerning Jesus and the biblical foundation for mission.[135]

---

134. Bosch, "Jeseja," 34–37.

135. For a fuller treatment of the subject, readers are referred to Bosch's doctoral thesis on Jesus and the Gentile mission, *Heidenmission*, and also to his *Lydende*. See also Bosch's expansive treatment of the subject in *Transforming Mission*, 15–124.

Judaism in Jesus' Day

Jesus came into a Jewish world that was remarkably different from the world of the OT. Although the subject is vast, Bosch highlighted six specific aspects of Judaism in Jesus' day that are foundational for a proper understanding of mission in the New Testament.[136]

First, the Jews were living under the rule of Rome. Despite various wars, uprisings and exiles, the Jews of Jesus' day were living as an occupied nation, with no real political independence. This meant "the traditionally close link between Israel, the political entity, and Israel, the people of God, gradually loosened. Increasingly the Jews became primarily a religious group" (p. 45).

Second, Jewish religion was still fanned by the flame of nationalistic aspirations. Bosch commented upon different Jewish religious groups of the day who defined themselves in relation to the state. These groups included: the Sadducees, the status-quo conservative "realists" who sought a compromise with Rome in order to preserve some independence; the Pharisees, the zealous and legalistic "pietists" of their day, with their concern to safeguard themselves and the Jewish nation from all Gentile contamination; the Zealots, an underground, religiously-oriented liberation movement that sought, by violent means, to liberate the Jewish nation from her Roman overlords; and the Essenes, an isolationist, millenarian group who withdrew from the world, waiting for the judgment of God to fall upon the Gentile world. Bosch added that the very existence of so many different, identifiable groups within Judaism "points to a radically new situation, compared to the Old Testament period" (p. 46).

Third, Bosch mentioned the very significant emergence of synagogues by the phase of Jewish history. After the destruction of the temple and with the dispersion of the Jews throughout the ancient Western and Near Eastern worlds, Jews began to meet on the sabbath for religious exercises. What had begun as an emergency measure had developed, by the time of Jesus, into a normal pattern of "congregational" worship throughout the Roman Empire, with crucial consequences for the early spread of Christianity.

Fourth, with the dispersion came the decline in the use and comprehension of Hebrew and Aramaic. Many Jews learned the Greek language and customs, leading to the translation of the OT into Greek (the *Septuagint*), as well as other Jewish religious literature.

Fifth, the Jews by this time lived in a multi-faith context with people of other nations and religions. Bosch commented "Judaism, with its strict monotheism and lofty moral code, proved attractive to pagans" (p. 46). Many Gentiles became "proselytes," converts to Judaism. Even though the Jews did not maintain an explicit evangelistic program, a significant number of proselytes entered into the faith of Abraham.

---

136. The following section is adapted from Bosch, *Theology 201*, 45–48. All citations are taken from these pages. For more on Bosch's understanding of Judaism in Jesus' day, see his *Heidenmission*, 43–75.

Part Two: Bosch's Theology of Mission and Evangelism

Finally, a profoundly pessimistic historical and eschatological outlook marked the era. Jews believed that "God would at the end of the ages bring the nations flocking to share in the salvation of Israel" (p. 47). The emphasis was on *God's* action. Although some Jews witnessed to pagans and welcomed converts into their synagogues, "they were never able to free themselves from the exclusivism of their national consciousness" (p. 47). Thus in the Judaism of Jesus' time, Bosch found "a tension between the universal and exclusive approaches, between attraction and rebuff, between openness and isolation. There may have been differences of emphasis, but these two poles were always there" (pp. 47–48).

The Ministry of Jesus

Given this understanding of the context of Jesus' life and times, what distinctive traits emerge from his ministry that contributes to a biblical foundation for mission? Bosch summarized it as follows: "Unlike the other teachers of his day Jesus did not recruit disciples to teach them the tôrâh, but in order that they might 'follow' him. He questioned traditional Jewish values at decisive points, especially by turning to the outcasts of society and by proclaiming to them the message of God's compassion. Simultaneously he radicalised the ethical demands of the tôrâh by focusing on the command to love, especially to love the enemy. And in his miracles his concern was the totality of human need—poverty, sickness, hunger, sin, demonic oppression."[137]

In what follows, we highlight three aspects of Jesus' ministry that Bosch discerned to be of crucial significance to the biblical theology of mission: Jesus' boundless compassion toward all persons, especially "outsiders"; his comprehensive, holistic service to others; and his proclamation of the kingdom of God with its call to an ethically demanding discipleship. Taken together, these three traits set Jesus apart from the other religious groups of his day.

Jesus was a loyal and faithful Jew, yet his life and words frequently failed to conform to standard Jewish piety. Whereas many Jewish leaders tried to base their human righteousness before God on the basis of their achievements, works and national heritage, Jesus grounded all true righteousness on the free, universal love of the Father.[138] Whereas the Pharisees attempted to isolate themselves from "worldly" influences and Gentile contamination, Jesus mixed freely with pagans and disreputable people, and felt a compassion toward the multitudes. Whereas the Pharisees regarded all Gentiles and even most of their fellow Jews as "sinners, the rabble who know nothing of the Law," Jesus turned primarily to these very outcasts of Jewish society as the focus for his ministry and as his primary audience. To them he "proclaimed the possibility of a new life on the basis of the love of God."[139]

---

137. Bosch, *Witness*, 54.
138. Bosch, "The Why and How," 41.
139. Ibid. Cf. Bosch, *Witness*, 54.

This burden to proclaim the good news of God's compassionate love to his own people, especially the outcasts, is seen most clearly in Jesus' programmatic Nazareth sermon (Luke 4:14–30). Bosch noted that Luke (unlike Matthew or Mark) places this pericope at the very beginning of Jesus' ministry, in order to highlight its significance. "In this unique event," Bosch contended, "the entire future pattern of Jesus' ministry unfolds itself."[140] The sermon also provides the reader with insight into both the nature and extent of Jesus' compassion.

In the course of worship in the synagogue, Jesus read from the scroll given to him by the attendant. The reading was a messianic text from Isaiah 61:1–2. "The Spirit of the Lord is upon me, because he has anointed me to preach good news to the poor. He has sent me to proclaim freedom for the prisoners and recovery of sight to the blind, to release the oppressed, to proclaim the year of the Lord's favor."

Bosch noted three things with regard to this incident.[141] First, Jesus personalized and temporalized the messianic prophecy. In contrast to John the Baptist, who announced that the kingdom was near, Jesus announced that the kingdom, in his own person and ministry, had arrived. "Today, in your very hearing this text has come true." Second, Jesus clarified the breadth of the mission that had been given him by the Spirit. His ministry was to be comprehensive (including preaching, healing, liberation), and aimed primarily toward the outsiders, the outcasts of Israel. Third, Jesus proclaimed that vengeance had been superseded and that God's compassion was paramount, thereby showing the true nature of his mission. This was illustrated when Jesus deliberately broke off his reading of Isaiah 61 before the words "and a day of vengeance of our God" (Isa 61:2). Bosch noted that in the synagogue preaching of Jesus' day "it was customary to put the whole emphasis precisely on these words—that God's vengeance on his (and therefore Israel's) enemies. Jesus, however, does the unimaginable: He reads only the portion on grace, not the one on vengeance! This was unforgivable, especially as it implied that the same attitude might be expected of his followers."[142] Because of Jesus' action, a storm of controversy ensued. Far from admiring his words, the people in the synagogue were furious that he spoke only of God's compassionate mercy and neglected the words of God's vengeance.[143]

Bosch cited further evidence of this "compassion principle" at work in the later encounter between Jesus and the disciples of John the Baptist in Luke 7:22–23 (cf. Matt 11:5–6). When asked whether he was "the one who was to come," Jesus answered by citing three messianic passages from Isaiah (29:18–20; 35:5–6; 61:1–2). Curiously,

---

140. Bosch, *Witness*, 55.

141. For a full discussion of what follows, see Bosch, *Witness*, 55–56.

142. Ibid., 55.

143. Bosch followed the exegesis of Jeremias and Grundmann here, suggesting that verse 22 has usually been mistranslated. According to his exegesis, the passage should read: "They protested with one voice and were furious, because he only spoke about [God's year of] mercy [and omitted the words about messianic vengeance]." More recent exegesis, Bosch contended, supported this interpretation of Jeremias and Grundmann, including studies by Ralph Martin and A. A. Trites. See Ibid., 56, 252 n. 6–9.

Part Two: Bosch's Theology of Mission and Evangelism

however, he omitted any reference to the eschatological day of vengeance, which was a part of all three passages. Surely this was intentional, argued Bosch. Then Jesus added "... and happy is the man who does not find me a stumbling block" (Luke 7:23; Matt 11:6). In other words, concluded Bosch: "Blessed is everyone who does not take offence at the fact that the era of salvation differs from what he has expected, that God's compassion on the poor and outcast has superseded divine vengeance!"[144] Like Jonah of old, many Jews in Jesus' day found it impossible to conceive that the compassion of God was wider in scope than their narrow, nationalistic horizons. Yet for Jesus, the compassion of God was the heart of his total ministry.

To whom was this compassion to be directed? Bosch believed that Jesus evinced a special concern for the "outsiders," those on the periphery of Jewish society. The following categories of people are specifically mentioned by the gospel writers as receiving the compassionate care of Jesus: the poor, the blind, the cripple, the leprous, the hungry, those who weep, the sick, the little ones, the widows, the captives, those who are last, those who are weary and heavily burdened with religious legalism, the lost sheep, the Gentiles, the Samaritans, a Roman Centurion, women, children, tax gatherers, women of bad reputation, one's enemies.[145] Bosch noted particularly how Jesus' compassion extended (scandalously) beyond the "poor and oppressed" Jews; he showed a concern even for traitors and the enemies of Israel![146]

The teaching of Jesus is also replete with examples of boundless compassion toward outsiders. Bosch singled out two stories for special attention: the parable of the lost son, that cut at the root all human attempts at self-justification by works and pride of achievement, and the story of the Good Samaritan, that criticized all national self-righteousness and pride of descent, and called the hearer to love one's enemies.[147]

In concrete terms, then, how was the compassion of Jesus harnessed and acted out? Of what did Jesus' ministry consist? First, it was a ministry focused upon *human need*. Throughout the gospels Jesus is portrayed as one who showed a profound concern with the whole gamut of human needs; from divine healing of diseases to the forgiveness of sins; from relief from hunger and poverty to release from demonic oppression. This concern extended beyond mere sympathy for the needs he encountered.

---

144. Ibid., 56.

145. Ibid., 54. Cf. Nolan, *Jesus Before Christianity*, 21–29.

146. Bosch elaborates: "Jesus violated the definitions of communion and solidarity of all four [Jewish] groups at certain crucial points . . . (1) Unlike any of these groups, he contacted and helped the useless—the blind, the lame, the leprous in particular, who were the most pathetic members of society. (2) Unlike them he incorporated traitors and exploiters of the people—the odious tax-collectors, Jews who had sold out to the Romans. (3) Unlike them, he embraced 'the enemy'—the Samaritans and the Romans specifically. This prompted his injunction to love one's enemies (Mt. 5:44; Lk. 6:27-29) and his prayer on the cross: 'Father forgive them for they know not what they do.' Behind all this is his boundless compassion" (Bosch, *Theology 201*, 31).

147. Bosch, *Witness*, 54–55.

The Biblical Foundation for Mission

Jesus actively served people, meeting them at their point of deepest need, and encouraged his disciples to do likewise (Mark 10:45; Luke 22:27).[148]

And yet Jesus was no mere miracle-worker. His service to others, particularly in his ministry of healing, had a deeper purpose. Acts of *diakonia* were to function as a sign of God's coming kingdom. The works of compassion performed by Jesus and his disciples intended to point beyond themselves, giving witness to the reality of the complete healing and salvation that God intended for all persons and for the world. The ultimate purpose for Christ's service was thus not simply the alleviation of human need. As signs of the lordship of God over all of life, they had a signifying, witness-bearing function.[149]

The second way that Jesus acted out his ministry of compassion was through his proclamation. It was a ministry focused upon *the gospel concerning the kingdom of God*. This gospel of the kingdom was both a liberating and a demanding word. It spoke of good news, of an abundant life filled with love, peace, freedom and joy. But it also spoke of demands, of a radical reorientation of one's life, including self-renunciation, service to others and even suffering. We note three crucial elements of Jesus' proclamation.

Jesus' proclamation was firstly a call to *recognize the kairos of God*. In the Gospels, Bosch maintained, there is a special understanding of time, a new view of history that not everyone discerns. With the advent of Jesus, something decisive happened; it was the decisive moment, the fateful hour, the turning point in history, the *kairos*. "History is *filled time*, now, in the present.[150] This understanding of time as being filled, pregnant with new possibilities, contrasted sharply with the essentially closed, empty views of history that the other Jewish sects maintained. "If the present is empty, as the Pharisees, Essenes and Zealots believed, then you can only flee into the memory of a glorious past recorded in codes (Pharisees), or you can, with folded arms, sit and wait for God's vengeance on your enemies (Essenes), or you can play God yourself by violently liquidating the empty present thus trying to make the utopian future a present reality (Zealots), or you can enter into an uncomfortable compromise with the status quo (Sadducees)."[151]

In the person and proclamation of Jesus, however, Bosch discerned a radically different eschatology. The kingdom of God, in a real sense, has been inaugurated. Jesus spoke of a God who was decisively working in *contemporary* history.[152] It was this awareness that impelled Jesus and his band to mission. Neither Jesus nor the disciples could remain silent, for the coming of the new age demanded a response. "Either one

---

148. Bosch and Jansen, *Sending in Meervoud*, 12–13; 38–40.
149. Bosch, "Die Diens van die Genesing in Sendingperspektief," 170.
150. Bosch, *Witness*, 64.
151. Ibid., 64.
152. Bosch cites Matt 11:11; 12:41–42; Mark 2:10; Luke 4:21; 10:17–18, 24; 11:20; 17:21 as examples. Ibid., 64; Bosch, *Theology 201*, 48–49; Bosch, *The Church as the Alternative Community*, 16–17.

accepted Jesus and the dawning of an entirely new age, or one became so annoyed by Him that it became a battle unto death. But nobody could remain neutral."[153]

This leads us to another tenet of Jesus' proclamation: the call to *conversion*.[154] The good news of Jesus demanded a specific response. Jesus' first words in Mark 1:15 provide a good example of this. "The right time (*kairos*) has come and the Kingdom of God is near! Turn away from your sins and believe the Good News" (GNB). Jesus' proclamation linked repentance and conversion together, calling men and women to deny themselves and transfer their allegiance to God and his kingdom. This conversion implied a new relationship to God and to neighbor, which was to be worked out as one followed Jesus, journeying with him into the unknown future of God.

The final tenet of Jesus' proclamation follows on from the first two: the call to *community*.[155] People who heard the good news of God's new order and were converted were not to remain isolated in their faith. Jesus called them to a new life together, a life of solidarity with one another, where the artificial, human barriers between people were broken down. The new community that Jesus gathered was based not on a common language, race, class, political outlook, religious affinity, or any other human principle of organization, but solely in the desire to follow Jesus. Their unity was grounded in a common discipleship.

This, then, was the shape of Jesus' ministry. It was a ministry that was grounded in the boundless, compassionate love of God; made active through selfless service to others, and explained in terms of the good news of the kingdom of God with its call to costly discipleship.

The Mission of Jesus: Historical Particularity and Universal Significance

Besides analyzing the shape of Jesus' ministry, Bosch also devoted significant attention to the missionary practice of Jesus. How did Jesus' self-understanding influence his "missionary strategy"? Why were the Jews his particular focus? Did he have any concept of a mission to Gentiles? And how did Jesus' understanding of the eschatological Reign of God influence his understanding of the intended *audience* of the good news? To ask these questions is to return to the particularist/universalist tension, but from a new angle. Within the person and ministry of Jesus there existed two apparently contradictory emphases, the understanding of which Bosch saw as crucial to a proper biblical foundation for mission.

When the reader of the New Testament encounters the Gospels, he or she confronts an immediate problem. How are we to understand the seeming contradictions in the gospels concerning Jesus' relationship to Jews and Gentiles? Within each gospel there is a tension between, on the one hand, the exclusively *Jewish* focus of his

---

153. Bosch, *The Church as the Alternative Community*, 17.
154. Ibid., 18–26.
155. Ibid., 10–15.

mission, and on the other hand, the words and actions of Jesus that imply a worldwide, universal mission.

Examples of this tension abound.[156] Bosch noted that in Matthew's gospel, Jesus forbade his disciples to go to Gentiles and Samaritans (10:5–6), and later he tells the woman from Cana that he was sent "only for the lost sheep of the house of Israel" (15:24). Yet later Jesus tells his disciples that the Gospel shall be preached "to the whole world" (24:14), and Matthew ends with the call to go into *all the world* and make disciples of *all nations* (28:18–20). Mark is similar to Matthew. Jesus in Mark 7:27 appears to think as a "Jewish-particularist," but even this verse is set in the context of a journey into a Gentile area (7:24ff). Mark also records Jesus' prophecy of one day when the gospel will be preached worldwide.

Luke's gospel appears much more "universalistic." Jesus' genealogy begins with Adam (3:38) rather than Abraham (Matt 1:2). Luke portrays Jesus as being extremely open to Gentiles: at his Nazareth sermon (4:16–30) Jesus implies that the Gentiles will be receptive to his message; he shows a special compassion on Samaritans (10:25–37; 17:11–19). And yet Luke is at pains to show the significance of *Israel* for salvation-history. The Temple occupies a central place in his Gospel (2:21–52; 19:45–48). Jesus heals a crippled woman, and bases his action on the fact that she "is a daughter of Abraham" (13:16). He brings salvation to Zacchaeus using the same argument (19:9). And Luke (alone among the synoptic gospels) fails to mention Jesus' tours of the Gentile areas of Tyre, Sidon, and Caesarea Philippi.

John's gospel has similar elements as the other three. John frequently seems to use an anti-Jewish polemic (1:11; 8:12–59). And yet John portrays Jesus, when speaking with the Samaritan woman, affirming "salvation is from the Jews" (4:22).

In light of the evidence, three common resolutions to the problem have been suggested.[157] Some have argued that Jesus, from the beginning of his ministry, was more attracted to the Gentiles than his fellow Jews. He was a "universalist" from the start. And yet, Bosch argues, this ignores the fact that again and again the Jews stood at the center of Jesus' actions and attitudes. There can be no denial that he spent the vast amount of his ministry with Jews, proclaiming the good news to them.

Others have argued that Jesus restricted himself to working with the Jews for a time but, finding their hearts hardened, he consciously turned away from them and toward the Gentiles. Therefore mission to the Gentiles was really a stop-gap measure to make up for his abortive attempts to convert the Jews. And yet, according to Bosch, this is no solution.

> According to the tradition there are numerous "universalistic" elements in the early ministry of Jesus—think of Mt. 8:11–12 and Luke 4:25. On the other hand the gospels also tell of "particularistic" elements in the later ministry of

---

156. See Bosch, *Lydende*, 6–7.
157. Ibid., 6.

Jesus. Think of their deliberate concentration on Jerusalem and their precise emphasis on this city . . . (Mt. 5:35) and on bringing faith to its inhabitants (Mt. 23:37; Lk. 19:41–44; 23:28). Yes, even the cross proclaimed that this Jesus was "the King of the Jews" (Mt. 27:37). A careful study brings to light that in his early ministry he was no less universalistic, and in in later ministry he was no less Jewish-particularistic.[158]

Still others have argued that the biblical material cannot be harmonized. Jesus, during his entire ministry, focused exclusively on the Jews. He was consistently a "particularist." Only with the apostles came the (fabricated) idea to preach the gospels to the Gentiles, and the New Testament documents were adjusted to suit a mission to the Gentiles.[159] But this approach, argues Bosch, forces one to disregard the historical reliability of many texts (Matt 21:43; 24:14; 18:18–20; Mark 13:10, etc.), and attribute them solely to the later Christian community. It simply reduces the issue to the preference of the theologian concerned; the theologian determines which sayings of Jesus are "false" and which are "true."[160]

All too often the particularistic and universalistic strands of the biblical material have been posed as irreconcilable, opposing views. But Bosch argued that in the Bible itself, the two themes are not mutually exclusive. They are intertwined. He cites the work of Julius Schniewind in this regard, who posits that almost every tradition regarding Jesus can be read simultaneously in a Jewish-rabbinic conservative light, *and* in a universalistic light. What is an irreconcilable tension for modern minds was, in the person of Christ, an inseparable unity.[161] The whole discussion concerning universalism and particularism is a false antithesis. Rather they are mutually *inclusive*. For Bosch, this is the key contribution of Bengt Sundkler. Many before Sundkler had acknowledged that Jesus was sent exclusively to "the lost sheep of the house of Israel" and that he was chiefly occupied with Jerusalem and the temple. "But never before had it been so forcefully argued that exactly this exclusive tension on Israel, Jerusalem and the temple has such a profound meaning for the eventual world-wide mission, or . . . that "particularism" and "universalism" could not be regarded as mutually exclusive realities but rather as mutually inclusive."[162]

Bosch thus resolved this tension within the gospels by returning to theme of the historical character of God's revelation, making use of Sundkler's work on particularism

---

158. Ibid., 7 (my translation).

159. Bosch cites Harnack as an early exponent of this approach. In his *Mission and Expansion of Christianity in the First Three Centuries*, "he put forward the thesis that a mission to the Gentiles had been altogether outside the sphere of ideas of Jesus, that we could at best speak of his 'implicit' universalism which illustrated itself in his attitude toward publicans, sinners and Samaritans, and that therefore the missionary command of Matt. 28:18–20 could be considered authentic 'only in an ideal sense'" (Bosch, "Jesus and the Gentiles," 3).

160. Bosch, *Lydende*, 7.

161. Ibid., 8.

162. Bosch, "Jesus and the Gentiles," 4, 8–9.

and universalism. It is through this hermeneutical "lens" that Bosch made sense of the seemingly contradictory New Testament data. God, at creation, began with the whole world, but in order to work out his salvific purposes in history, he choose one nation, Israel. Through time the remnant of the faithful in Israel became progressively smaller, until only one person was left: Jesus of Nazareth.[163] In Jesus, salvation history becomes extremely specific. The paradox of God's revelation is that through the particular history of this one person, God was touching all of humankind. In *Christ*, God was reconciling the *world* to himself (2 Cor 5:19). "God's revelation is incarnated and concentrated in the history of this one Man. In his entire ministry he remains true to Israel . . . This does not, however, mean that his ministry is without meaning for the rest of the world. On the contrary. His very concentration on Israel—or to express it differently: precisely the historical specificity of his ministry—has cosmic-missionary significance. As Bengt Sundkler puts it: He was 'universalist' precisely because, in fact, only because he was 'particularist.'"[164]

Mission to the Jews? Mission to the Gentiles?

In light of the above, how did Bosch understand the nature of Jesus' mission to the Jewish people? And in what sense, if any, can we talk about a "Gentile mission" in the life and ministry of the historical Jesus?

In his life and ministry, Jesus never left the framework of Judaism. He was sent to his own people Israel, and his earthly life, as attested in the gospel records, bears witness to an almost exclusive preoccupation with the lost sheep of the house of Israel. He viewed Jerusalem and the temple as the "axis of the cosmos," the center of the world.[165] He remained Israel's Messiah, even unto death (see Matt 10:5–6; 15:24; 19:28; 23:37; Mark 11:15–18; Luke 19:41–42; 23:38; 24:49; John 4:22). Therefore Jesus stands in a relationship of profound *continuity* between Yahweh and Israel. Yahweh declared his relationship with Israel would endure eternally, and Jesus is the fruition, the full embodiment of Yahweh's promise to Abraham.[166]

On those occasions when Jesus entered into non-Jewish territory, Bosch observed that "he never penetrated deeply into it, almost as if he were hesitant to do so—as it were by way of experimentation and as a sign of what was to come—only to return to Jewish terrain soon after."[167] Bosch illustrated this by citing John 12:19–23. Here the Pharisees despair that "the world has gone after him [Jesus]" (12:19). Im-

---

163. Bosch, "Jeseja," 5. See also Bosch, *Lydende*, 24–25, where he pays tribute to Oscar Cullmann for developing this concept of the "progressive reduction" of salvation-history, culminating in Jesus.

164. Bosch, *Witness*, 63. Also see the section "War Jesus Partikularist oder Universalist?" in Bosch's *Heidenmission*, 111–15; and Bosch, *Lydende*, 24–28.

165. Bosch, "Jesus and the Gentiles," 4–5.

166. Bosch, *Lydende*, 8.

167. Bosch, *Theology 201*, 48.

Part Two: Bosch's Theology of Mission and Evangelism

mediately following this, a group of Greeks sought Philip's aid in arranging a meeting with Jesus, as if to say, "If the Jews do not want you, come to us!" Yet Jesus turned down their request and proceeded directly to Jerusalem and the Cross, remaining faithful to *Israel*.[168] Yet Jesus' particular emphasis on Israel had universal implications for the Gentiles. Bosch brought out four aspects of Jesus' relationship to the Gentiles, which can be summarized as follows: his ministry to the Gentiles was *compassionate, indirect, centripetal*, and *"periodized."*

The foremost aspect of Jesus' relationship with Gentiles was his *compassion*. Bosch commented that what distinguished Jesus from his contemporaries was not the concept of a Gentile mission as such, since the Pharisees had a missionary program and were zealous for converts (Matt 23:15). Nor was it found in an extensive ministry among Gentiles, for he said very little about them and had relatively little contact with them. Rather, the real basis for Jesus' ministry among Gentiles was his boundless compassion for them.[169] Jesus' relationship to Gentiles, however, was primarily *indirect*. In his earthly ministry, he concentrated his time and energies on Israel. Jesus called his people to be faithful to their true destiny as the nation through whom the entire world would be blessed. His immediate task was "to create a community within Israel to transform the life of this people, in the faith that a transformed Israel would transform the world."[170] In true "centripetal" fashion, the Gentiles came to Jesus and not the reverse, much like the OT notion of the nations coming to Jerusalem. Bosch recalled Sundkler's work in this regard, explaining the centrality of Israel for Jesus and shows how this understanding affected Jesus' view of the nations.

> This centrality of Israel in the thought of Jesus is of overriding importance. The drama of redemption was enacted in Jerusalem, in the centre of the entire cosmos. But what happened in the centre would naturally have consequences also for the periphery; to interfere in the centre is to transform the whole organism . . . To illustrate the fundamental relation between Israel as the centre and the surrounding world, Sundkler refers to various passages in the Old Testament (Ps. 24, 47, 67, 87). . . From Mount Zion, the navel of the earth (Ezek. 38:12), the converging point of the nations (Is. 2:2–4), living waters will flow in all directions (Zech. 14:18ff.) . . .
>
> From this Old Testament background Sundkler then formulates his thesis that the mission of Jesus was basically a centripetal one. His actions were confined to Israel, but nevertheless had consequences for the entire world. He never left the holy land. The Wise Men from the East came to him (Matt. 2); the Roman centurion came to him (Matt. 8, as did those Greeks who wished "to see Jesus" (John 12:20 f.). Looking at his earthly life from this point of view, the cleansing of the temple also acquires a new significance. The cosmic

---

168. Ibid., 48.
169. Bosch, *Witness*, 54. Cf. ibid., 50–57 for more on Jesus' compassion on the Gentiles.
170. Bosch, "Jesus and the Gentiles," 10–11.

transformation which it was the Messiah's mission to effect, had to begin at the axis of the cosmos, namely Israel, Jerusalem, the temple . . .[171]

Regarded in this light, Bosch contended that this indirect, centrifugal relationship between Jesus and the Gentiles has profound missionary implications. In his ministry and passion Jesus is bound in two directions simultaneously. "'Geographically' Jesus journeys to the temple to Jerusalem and his death; 'theologically' he is bound for the nations."[172] *He* becomes the temple, the New Jerusalem, the place where God encounters the nations. Just as the OT promised that the nations would meet God at Mt. Zion, the gospel affirms that God calls us to meet him in Jesus Christ.[173]

Finally, Jesus' relationship to Gentiles can be understood in terms of a *"periodizing"* of his ministry. By periodizing Bosch meant that any "mission to the Gentiles" was possible only *after* certain presuppositions had been fulfilled. The OT spoke of at least two "pre-conditions" for the salvation of the Gentiles: 1) the Gentiles turning to the faith of Israel would be preceded by a hardening of Israel's heart; and 2) this conversion of the pagans to Israel would occur mysteriously through the suffering of the *Ebed Yahweh*, the Servant of the Lord.[174] It seems clear, according to Bosch, that in the life and ministry of Jesus, particularly in the events surrounding his passion, these two preconditions were fulfilled. From a Christian perspective, real mission to the Gentiles was possible only *after* Jesus' rejection of by the Jews and his sacrificial death on the cross.

That being said, however, Bosch went on to affirm that we *could* discern some indications of a future mission to the Gentiles in the conduct of the earthly Jesus.

> While the Messiah of Late Judaism was expected to destroy the sinners—whether they be Jews or Gentiles—Jesus, by turning to sinners and tax collectors broke through the barriers of religious particularism of his time and thus prepared the way for opening the door to Samaritans and Gentiles as well. Through his ministry God appeared as the seeking and inviting God—as is evident in his miracles, his opening sermon in Nazareth (Luke 4:17–27) and his parables (those of growth, of the talents, the marriage feast, the good Samaritan, the lost coin and sheep, the prodigal son, etc.). Even Jewish scholars . . . recognized the uniqueness of his concern for sinners and outcasts. In every case the conventional barriers were broken down. This is what Harnack meant by his term 'implicit universalism'! And even the most skeptical scholar would have difficulty in maintaining that all these elements are 'products of an early

---

171. Ibid., 4–5.

172. Bosch, *Witness*, 63.

173. Ibid. Bosch notes that this concept is developed further in Martin-Achard's *A Light to the Nations*.

174. Bosch, *Theology 201*, 51–54.

Part Two: Bosch's Theology of Mission and Evangelism

> Church? Is it then in the light of all this, so inconceivable that the earthly Jesus could have expected and foretold a future mission to the Gentiles.[175]

Seeing Jesus' ministry as "periodized" helps resolve the seemingly contradictory statements in the gospels with which we began this section. It explains how glimmers of a future world mission can spring up frequently in the words and attitude of Jesus, without denying the essentially Jewish thrust of his message and mission. When one reads the gospels, one frequently observes an unfolding sense of destiny, of *kairos*. Bosch cites Verkuyl's conclusion of the matter as his own. According to Verkuyl, all of Jesus' encounters with non-Jews "vibrate with the holy impatience of him, who, while temporarily limiting himself to the lost sheep of the house of Israel, is yearning for the day when salvation will in its fulness go out to the nations."[176]

> What is the significance of Jesus' attitude to a Gentile mission, then? Bosch commented that all too frequently, missiologists have attempted to ground the legitimacy of the missionary mandate of the church upon the sayings and attitude of the historical Jesus toward Gentiles. It then becomes a necessity to "prove" that Jesus really did seek to evangelize Gentiles, in order to justify our own missionary practice today. Bosch deemed this approach unhelpful. While affirming that Jesus' attitude toward Gentiles is certainly a significant theological issue, it is of no more than secondary importance to the biblical foundation for mission. "There would have been a post-Easter Gentile mission even if Jesus had never been in contact with non-Jews and never said anything about them. That he did meet non-Jews and did say some surprising things about them should not be interpreted as a motive for the Church to engage in a Gentile mission but as a consequence of the essentially missionary dimension of God's revelation in him."[177]

The Way of Mission and the Way of the Cross

Jesus' ministry to both Jews and Gentiles was noteworthy but, for the biblical writers, quite secondary. The unanimous testimony of the New Testament posits that the decisive turning point of Christ's mission did not come at the beginning of his ministry but at the *end*, in the events of the crucifixion, resurrection, ascension, and the pouring out

---

175. Bosch, "Jesus and the Gentiles," 16–17.

176. Bosch, "The Why and How," 42. Cf. Verkuyl, *Contemporary Missiology*, 104. It is noteworthy that this concept of "yearning" for the salvation of God among the nations and for the growth of his church, is the central theme of a massive work on the ecclesiology of the Church Growth movement, Van Engen's *The Growth of the True Church*, esp. 486–507.

177. Bosch, "The Why and How," 40. Elsewhere, Bosch noted how this represents a change in his thought, ". . . the attitude of the historical Jesus to a mission to the Gentiles will not be of decisive importance for our subject. To me this represents something of a shift away from an earlier position when I still believed . . . that the positive attitude of the historical Jesus towards the Gentile mission was basic to a scriptural foundation for mission. Today I would put it differently . . ." (Bosch, *Witness*, 48).

the Holy Spirit. Bosch cited German missiologist Walter Holsten in this regard: "What is decisive for mission is not what the historical Jesus said about the pagans, but the fact that it was for the pagans and for their salvation that he was crucified and rose again."[178] The way of salvation was opened to the Gentiles through the passion of Christ. Here the heart of mission is revealed. There is an inescapable relationship between God's *via missionis* to the nations and the *via dolorosa* of the Messiah of Israel. World mission is authentic only as it derives its meaning in the light of the cross.[179] Bosch, again reflecting the thought of Sundkler, commented as follows on this relationship: "In a profound sense the way of the cross was the way of mission . . . When Israel was hardened and had rejected the offered salvation, only one conclusion could be drawn. Jesus had to go to the cross, thus bringing the kingdom of God to the 'others' (Matt. 21:43). Jesus could therefore not have conceived of his relationship with the Gentiles in the horizontal dimension of . . . universalism, but only in the vertical dimension of salvation history. He was 'universalist' precisely because He was 'particularist.'"[180]

In the Bible, the power of God is thus revealed at the point of maximum *weakness*. Jesus was most truly a missionary, said Bosch, not when he was successfully preaching to the masses, nor when he was performing healing miracles, but precisely in his suffering and death.[181]

But the gospel does not end with the death of Christ, because Jesus was raised from the dead. What appears to be an unmitigated disaster turns out to be God's salvific victory. Bosch comments that Jesus' resurrection has crucial missiological significance in the New Testament. "Throughout the New Testament the resurrection of Christ is regarded as the legitimization and affirmation of his 'death for the many' on the cross . . . Every encounter between the risen Christ and his disciples is in the context of mission, and that . . . mission is universal."[182]

The "Great Commission"

Many of the aforementioned issues come into sharper focus when we turn to the so-called "Great Commission" of Matthew 28:16–20. Many mission enthusiasts have raised this passage up as the heart and core of the biblical foundation for mission since the days of William Carey. It continues to function as the primary foundation for mission in many circles today.[183] Because so many people attach crucial significance to the

178. Bosch, *Theology 201*, 54.
179. Bosch, *Lydende*, 20–23, 32.
180. Bosch, "Jesus and the Gentiles," 5.
181. Bosch, *Witness*, 72.
182. Bosch, *Theology 201*, 54.
183. As examples, Bosch mentions the Constitution of the Evangelical Foreign Missions Association in the U.S. and the student pledge of 1980 Student Consultation on Frontier Missions in Edinburgh. The pledge reads: "By the grace of God and for His glory, I commit my entire life to obeying His commission of Mt. 28:18–20 wherever and however He leads me, giving priority to the peoples currently beyond

"Great Commission" (particularly evangelicals), we will analyze Bosch's discussion of the passage at some length.[184]

In his review of the many attempts to expound this passage, Bosch clearly demonstrated the hazards of eisegesis. Many well-meaning Christians "read their own presuppositions into the text rather than allowing the text to say what it intends to say within its own context."[185] Indeed Bosch urged a thorough study of the history of the exegesis of this passage in relation to the church's mission. Such a study would tell us little about the meaning of Matthew 28, but reveal much concerning the church's missiological self-understanding down through the ages.[186]

A Command to Obey?

At the outset, Bosch attempted to deal with two major misconceptions about the passage. First, he noted that nowhere in the New Testament does the Great Commission function as the primary foundation or motive for mission. In none of the traditional parallels to Matt 28:16–20 (Luke 25:45–49; John 20–21; Acts 1:8) do we find a *command* to do mission work. The Great Commission is nowhere appealed to or referred to by the early church.[187] Instead, the early church's mission emerged as "a natural consequence of their understanding of the ministry of Jesus within the situation of contact with Gentiles in which they lived"[188] and as "an expression of the inner law of their lives."[189] Christian

---

the reach of the Gospel . . ." See Starling, *Seeds of Promise: World Consultation on Frontier Missions, Edinburgh '80*, 219.

184. Bosch deals with this topic in the following works: *Heidenmission*, 184–92; *Lydende*, 28–32; *Witness*, 66–70; "The Structure of Mission: An Exposition of Matthew 28: 16–20," 218–48; and "The Scope of Mission," 17–32. In "The Structure of Mission" Bosch provides a long bibliography of material related to Matthew 28. Curiously, he neglected to mention the Barth's essay on the subject. Bosch and Barth came to numerous similar conclusions. See Barth, "An Exegetical Study of Matthew 28:16–20," 55–71.

185. Bosch, *Witness*, 69. Elsewhere, Bosch has commented on the proper hermeneutical procedure for biblical interpretation: "Naturally any Christian can read and understand the Bible, but in this process 'short-circuiting' inevitably occurs. It then becomes the theologian's responsibility to call the reader back to the context and intention of the biblical author and to draw attention to the distance that separates the present situation from that of the biblical story. A creative tension must be maintained between these two contexts, and we do ourselves a disservice if we immediately read our own situation back into the Bible. If we accept that the Bible is the historical document about God's dealings with his people, then its historical dimension must be taken seriously. What Matthew wrote in his Gospel was primarily intended for his first readers. It has a meaning for us only in a derived sense. What is more, the better we know the original setting and identify with Matthew's first readers, the better we will be able to make the transition to our own time and to model *our* mission in such a way that it is true to the intention of the evangelist, who here interprets his Lord's Word to the church" (Bosch, "The Structure of Mission," 226–27).

186. Bosch, "The Structure of Mission," 218.

187. Ibid., 219. Bosch noted: "It is quite clear that the early church did not embark on a mission to Jews and Gentiles simply because it had been told to do so. This would have placed mission in the context of legalism. Mission would then have been depersonalized" (ibid.).

188. Bosch, "The Why and How," 43.

189. Bosch, "The Structure of Mission," 220. Bosch elaborated on this concept, building on the work of Paul Minear and Lesslie Newbigin. The "obligation" of "debt" towards all people of which Paul speaks

The Biblical Foundation for Mission

mission was not sparked off by the command of Jesus but by two events: the resurrection of Jesus and the sending of the Spirit to his followers at Pentecost. These two historical events assured the early church of the continued presence and activity of Jesus in their own lives and in the world, and empowered them for mission.[190]

A Creation of the Early Church?

Another misconception concerning the passage is the debate over the "historicity" of the Great Commission. Some have maintained that the Commission is simply a creation of the early church, while others have believed that it represents the *ipsissima verba* of Jesus. Bosch warned that it is improper to approach the issue with these two stark alternatives.[191]

The first group maintains that the tradition surrounding the Great Commission passage is unreliable and, in all likelihood, a creation of the early church in order to justify her mission to Gentiles. Proponents of this view (following Harnack) argue that the gospels portray Jesus as a particularist; the universalist element in Jesus' ministry is simply a later addition. They also point to the fact that the early church was slow in developing a conscious program of evangelizing Gentiles, thus arguing against the authenticity of an original command from Jesus himself.

Bosch contended that neither of these arguments seriously challenges the essential reliability of the Great Commission tradition, arguing that the universalist/particularist tensions within the gospels can be explained in terms of "periodizing." Both streams of material stand together without the need to question the authenticity of either tradition.[192] And while it is true that an *organized* mission to the Gentiles started comparatively late, Gentile individuals and families were coming to faith in Christ from the very beginning of the church's life.[193] The real issue in the early church was *not whether Gentiles could be evangelized* and brought into the community, for the Jews already allowed this. The issue was rather whether these Gentile converts could enter the Christian community without being circumcised and obliged to keep Torah. This debate grew out of a concern that the Jewish character of Christianity would be in jeopardy with the large influx of Gentile converts.

(in Rom 1:14) is not a debt of duty but of *gratitude* (Minear). "We have [wrongly] regarded witness as a demand laid upon us instead of seeing it as a gift promised to us" (Newbigin) (ibid.).

190. Bosch, *Witness*, 65–66; and Bosch, *Theology* 201, 55–56. For more on the link between mission and the sending of the Spirit, see Boer's classic work *Pentecost and Missions*.

191. For a detailed elaboration of what follows, see Bosch, "The Structure of Mission," 220–26.

192. Bosch, "The Structure of Mission," 224–25. Bosch, however, does not see this "periodizing" as absolute, since even in the earlier Matthean material (chapters 1–21) "Jesus in principle transcended the narrow confines of contemporary Judaism" by exhibiting concern for the poor, the unclean, women and Gentiles.

193. Even at the earliest stage, Bosch argues, "Gentiles felt accepted and at home in the Christian community." Bosch mentions Nicolas of Antioch, a Gentile convert (Acts 6:5) as evidence of this acceptance (ibid., 224).

Part Two: Bosch's Theology of Mission and Evangelism

> The overwhelming majority of early Jewish Christians, both Aramaic- and Greek-speaking, originally regarded the new movement as a renewal movement within Judaism, with a smaller or larger Gentile contingent. There was nothing in Jesus' conduct and words, as they understood them, that could have led them to believe otherwise . . . It was only because of the rapid growth of a distinctly Gentile Christianity in Antioch that their eyes were opened to a development that they had not forseen . . . The fact of the late start of the Gentile mission is thus not itself a convincing argument against the reliability of the tradition behind the Great Commission . . .[194]

Ipsissima verba or ipsissima intentio?

Others, however, maintain that the Great Commission sayings are not only reliable, but in fact must be the *ipsissima verba* of Jesus. Without a sure and certain command from the risen Lord, they say, the church has no sure biblical foundation for mission. This approach is often found in conservative evangelical literature on the subject, and is typified by the work of Samuel Zwemer, the noted missionary to the Muslim world and professor at Princeton Seminary. He tried to prove the verbal accuracy and authenticity of the Great Commission, based on the conviction that "the command of our Risen Lord" is the "primary basis of missions."[195]

Bosch argued that Zwemer's approach to the meaning and authority of the Great Commission (which is typical of many conservative evangelicals) is inadequate. There is clear and unambiguous evidence that Matthew redacted the tradition handed down to him. In every detail, the passage attests to the particular language and style of Matthew.[196] But does this mean that because we may not have the exact words of Jesus, we therefore have only a fabrication of Jesus' words on the part of a later author, and that mission is therefore without a biblical foundation? Bosch commented that it is irrelevant to ask whether the commission gives us the exact words of Jesus or not. Instead, he wants to emphasize that *the biblical foundation for mission does not depend on the verbal accuracy of this passage.*[197] As Bosch put it: "History is not a matter of

---

194. Ibid. Here he appeals to the conclusions of Hubbard, *The Matthean Redaction of a Primitive Apostolic Commission.*

195. See Zwemer, *"Into All the World": The Great Commission: A Vindication and an Interpretation,* 89–90, as cited by Bosch, "The Structure of Mission," 224.

196. Bosch comments: "*Matheteuein* (to make disciples), *terein* (keep), and *entellesthai* (command) are typical Matthean concepts. The key word is *matheteusate*, make disciples. For Matthew Jesus is the rabbi *sui generis*, the incomparable. Therefore the theme of discipleship, of following, is central in this gospel . . ." Bosch goes on to show how Matthew's concept of Jesus' kingship is emphasizes more than any other gospel, and this is reflected in imagery of Jesus' universal kingship in Matt 28:18–20 (Bosch, *Witness,* 68).

197. It is interesting to note Bosch's citation of the famed Anglican missionary theologian Roland Allen in this regard. Allen, a favorite of many conservative evangelicals, argued forcefully that mission does not depend on the Great Commission at all. "Had the Lord not given any such command, had the Scriptures

bare facts but of appropriating and assimilating what has happened. To quote Jesus' words literally has in itself little meaning. To make them one's own is another matter, but in the process those words inevitably acquire the stamp of the narrator of the event concerned..."[198]

This does not mean, however, that the Great Commission is a fictitious creation of a later Christian author. Bosch affirmed that the Great Commission sayings *are* rooted in the ministry of the historical Jesus.[199] But in the transmission process of the traditions regarding Jesus, it was only normal that these traditions would have been shaped by Matthew to meet the specific needs and context of the community to which he was writing.

> It was inevitable that Matthew, writing in the crucible of the moment, would tell the Jesus story in such a way that it would help his community to understand what it meant to be Christians in the changing milieu of postwar [A. D. 70] Judaism.... This does not imply that Matthew was unfaithful to the tradition; only by retelling the story in such a way that it became contextual for his own community was he really faithful to the tradition. This is as true of the Great Commission as it is of every other pericope in Matthew's gospel. Therefore, instead of asking whether Matthew recorded the ipsissima verba of Jesus and the ipsissima facta about him, we should rather ask whether he was faithful to the ipsissima intentio—the true intention—of Jesus...[200]

For Bosch then, the issue is not whether the Great Commission in Matthew corresponded exactly to the original words of our Lord; rather it is to understand how Matthew creatively interpreted the message of Jesus into a new and different situation. Only through a creative retelling of the words could they come alive in the hearts of his readers.[201]

---

never contained such a form of words... the obligation to preach the Gospel to all nations would not have been diminished by a single iota. For the obligation depends not upon the letter, but upon the Spirit of Christ; not upon what He orders, but upon what He is, and the Spirit of Christ is the Spirit of Divine love and compassion and desire for souls astray from God." See his *Missionary Principles*, 31.

198. Bosch, *Witness*, 67–68.

199. "Whereas a few scholars do indeed believe that the entire pericope is the creation of the evangelist... most, after a critical analysis, come to the conclusion that Matthew definitely used an earlier tradition... even if it is no longer possible to reconstruct it..." (Bosch, "The Structure of Mission," 221).

200. Bosch, "The Structure of Mission," 221. Cf. Bosch, "Jesus and the Gentiles," 6–7.

201. Bosch, "The Structure of Mission," 220. This is exactly the same approach Bosch takes with regard to the Lord's Prayer. Matthew creatively interpreted the message of Jesus into a new and different situation. He did this precisely to be true to the original intentions of Jesus; any mere one-to-one, mechanical transposition of the exact words of Jesus into Matthew's situation would have actually *distorted* the message of Jesus, and prevented his readers from understanding him! See Bosch, *The Lord's Prayer: Paradigm for a Christian Lifestyle*, 1–2.

Part Two: Bosch's Theology of Mission and Evangelism

Some Exegetical Comments

The central theme of Matthew's gospel is the concept of following, of making disciples, of discipleship; this is the central theme of the Great Commission as well.[202] Although biblical scholars disagree as to the literary form (*Gattung*) of Matt 28:16–20, there is a broad consensus that this pericope is the key to the understanding of the whole book.[203] Bosch also noted a scholarly consensus regarding the three main elements of the passage. There is "a statement concerning Jesus' exaltation and authority, a missionary charge, and a promise of Jesus' abiding presence," with typical Matthean language used throughout.[204] Without recounting Bosch's full exegesis of the passage, we note a few crucial interpretative issues he raised.[205]

Referring to verse 17, Bosch juxtaposed the contrasting sentiments of the disciples: they stood between doubt and worship. Citing French missiologist Jacques Matthey, Bosch noted how the disciples' doubts, even at this time, were not completely removed: "It is precisely those disciples who submit themselves to [Jesus] but still have fundamental doubts that Jesus sends out in mission. The Great Commission is not only addressed to those who have overcome their doubt. Christians are called to mission as people who confess Jesus as Son of God and King, but who also experience crises in their faith."[206]

In verse 18, Bosch noted that the call to universal mission is grounded in Christ's universal lordship. While on earth, Jesus' power and authority to heal, teach and forgive was localized and limited. But as the risen Lord, he has been given authority *on heaven and on earth*, with the implication that a totally new era has been inaugurated, an era of global dominion and worldwide mission. The connection between his universal lordship (verse 18) and the worldwide mission (verse 19) is made explicit by the word *oun* ("therefore," verse 19). His universal mission flows from his universal authority.[207]

In verse 19 we come to a crucial part of the commission that is frequently misinterpreted. Many have believed the key idea of the Great Commission is found in the word *poreuthentes*, usually translated as "Go!" According to Bosch, this notion has

---

202. Bosch, *Witness*, 68.

203. Bosch, "Jesus and the Gentiles," 12. Cf. Bosch, "The Structure of Mission," 222; Bosch, *Witness*, 66–67.

204. Bosch, "The Structure of Mission," 222.

205. In particular, we shall ignore Bosch's extensive comments on the much-disputed concept of "all the nations" (v. 19). This will be discussed in depth in a later section on Bosch's evaluation of the Church Growth movement.

206. Matthey, "The Great Commission according to Matthew," 165.

207. Bosch, *Witness*, 68; Bosch, "The Structure of Mission," 228. Bosch goes on to highlight the personal nature of the commission. "The word *oun* ('then', 'therefore', v. 19) ties this missionary responsibility indissolubly to the authority granted to Jesus (v. 18). The Great Commission, says Max Warren, is *not an ethical demand, but a person*: 'Jesus . . . is the Great Commission.'" See Bosch, *Witness*, 68 (my emphasis).

produced a mistaken concept of mission in the West that is unnecessarily geographical and activistic.[208]

What does Matthew mean when he uses *poreuthentes*? The verb *poreuthentes* (going into all the world) is an auxiliary verb, reinforcing the action of the main verb *matheteusate* (make disciples).[209] *Poreuthentes* should be translated not as a separate command, but as "adding emphasis and urgency to *matheteusate* . . ." With this understanding of verse 19, Bosch commented: "Mission then refers to bringing people to Jesus as Lord, wherever they may be . . . Mission then loses its preoccupation with the geographical component and becomes mission in six continents."[210]

The heart of the Great Commission is the concept of making disciples, of discipleship. But how are we to understand the command to make disciples? In Matthew, there is a link between discipleship and the kingdom of God. Bosch cited Lohmeyer in this regard: "When the Master still walked this earth, proclaiming the Kingdom or the gospel were appropriate terms; now he is himself the Kingdom and the Gospel." Bosch believed that the task of Jesus' followers is not only to proclaim a kingdom, but to enlist people into a new fellowship, calling them to a commitment both to Jesus and to one another.[211]

Discipleship and Justice

Bosch also highlighted another neglected aspect of the Commission; *the pursuit of justice* is an integral part of the mission of Christ's disciples. Matthew consciously links the making of disciples (v. 19) with the admonition to teach them to observe all that Jesus had commanded (v. 20). But what did Jesus teach his disciples? What did he "command"? In his teaching, Jesus linked the correct *interpretation* of the law with the *doing* of the law. This law was "more than the moral and ceremonial law or than a purely religious, otherworldly rule of life. It is nothing less than the command to love God and people."[212] Referring to the rich young man in Matthew 19, Bosch commented:

---

208. Bosch comments: "Due to the standard Western translations of *poreuthentes* as 'Go ye (therefore)!' . . . a peculiar conception of mission developed. The emphasis tended to be on the 'going' rather than on the 'making disciples' . . . The locality, not the task, determined whether someone was a missionary or not; one qualified if one was commissioned by an agency in one locality to go and work in another. The greater the distance between these two places, the clearer it was that the individual was a missionary . . . In addition, the imperative voice appealed to an activist people. It was easy to rally popular support around the vision of conquering unknown territory and pioneering on distant frontiers . . ." (Bosch, "The Structure of Mission," 229–30).

209. Bosch, "The Why and How," 43; Bosch, "The Structure of Mission," 229. Bosch notes an analogy between Matt 28:16–20 and Phil 2:6–11. Both refer to the exaltation and the universal rule of Christ after his humiliation. The Philippians text adds that "every knee shall bow . . ." *not* as a command but as a *logical consequence* of Jesus' accession to the throne. In the Great Commission "the historical *kairos* for the Gentile mission has come and it needs no explicit command" (Bosch, "The Why and How," 43).

210. Bosch, "The Structure of Mission," 230.

211. Ibid., 232–33. The Lohmeyer quotation is taken from his *Das Evangelium des Matthäus*, 418.

212. Bosch, "The Structure of Mission," 234. "Protestant Christians . . . may feel embarrassed by

Part Two: Bosch's Theology of Mission and Evangelism

> In the story of the rich young man, Matthew has edited Mark thus: "If you would enter life, keep (*tereson*) the commandments (*tas entolas*)" (Mt. 19:17). The words in Matthew 28 are a clear allusion to those in Matthew 19 . . . But Jesus radicalizes these commandments in a specific direction: To love one's neighbors means to have compassion on them . . . and to see that justice is done. Thus *dikaiosyne* (justice) becomes another key concept in Matthew's Gospel. The disciples are challenged to a life of righteousness (=justice) which infinitely surpasses that practiced by the Pharisees (Mt. 5:20) and to seek God's Kingdom and his justice (Mt. 6:33). Justice is, as in the Old Testament, practically a synonym for compassion or almsgiving, as the famous parable in Matthew 25:31–46 demonstrates . . .[213]

What has all this to do with the Great Commission and the command to make disciples? Bosch affirmed (with Waldron Scott) that Christians must place the Commission in a wider context than they often do. God's ultimate mission, his larger mission, is the establishment of justice.[214] He also endorsed Jacques Matthey's conviction that in Matthew's Great Commission, "it is not possible to make disciples without telling them to practice God's request of justice for the poor."[215]

If Bosch's exegesis of Matthew 28:18–20 is correct, then the making of disciples has a deeper significance than is often acknowledged. It involves commitment to the King *and* to his kingdom of justice. It is not merely an initial evangelistic invitation but also a call to a new lifestyle. "To become a disciple is to be incorporated into God's new community through baptism and to side with the poor and oppressed. To put it differently, it is to love God and our neighbor. That is what Jesus has commanded his disciples (Matt 28:19). And of course, for Matthew this obedience is determined not by a conformity to any impersonal commandment but by the relation to Jesus himself."[216]

Biblical Foundation for Mission in the Other Gospels

Bosch argued strenuously that Matthew's concept of mission is grounded in his understanding of discipleship and rooted in God's concern for justice. What is frequently overlooked is that the other gospel writers also have unique perspectives on mission.

---

this emphasis on commandments that have to be observed, as it suggests the possibility of salvation by works. It should, however, be pointed out that Matthew uses these expressions in a fierce polemic against (Jamnia) Pharisaism. In doing so, Matthew consciously uses the Torah according to the Jewish tradition, but in such a way that the discrepancy between teaching and doing on the part of his opponents is exposed. The issue at stake is therefore the correct interpretation of and obedience to the law: The true teacher of the law, says the author in 13:52, is one "who has been discipled unto the kingdom . . ." (ibid.).

213. Bosch, "The Structure of Mission," 234.

214. Ibid., 234, citing Scott, *Bring Forth Justice: A Contemporary Perspective on Mission*, xvi.

215. Bosch, "The Structure of Mission," 234, citing Matthey, "The Great Commission according to Matthew," 171.

216. Bosch, "The Structure of Mission," 234.

The Biblical Foundation for Mission

Throughout Mark, the emphasis is on the intimate relationship between the disciples (the "fishers of men") and their Lord, Jesus. These disciples are called to go into the world and "proclaim release from unbelief, evil powers and sickness."[217] This authoritative proclamation (*kerussein*) of the good news of salvation (*euangelion*) is a key concept in the book. Bosch added that "Mark's rendering of the Great Commission is not to be looked for in the unauthentic ending of his Gospel, but in 13:10: '. . . before the end the *euangelion* must be proclaimed to all the nations.'"[218]

In Luke's gospel the accent is on the "Gospel of the poor," emphasizing the message of forgiveness and the possibility of new relationships. This is seen in Luke's special concern for the less privileged groups on the periphery of society: women, children, Gentiles, Samaritans, the tax-gatherers, the "lost" (Luke 15). "It is therefore understandable," Bosch concluded, "that in [Luke's] rendering of the Great Commission (24:46–49) conversion and forgiveness are central."[219] Also important to Luke's gospel is the notion that mission is is to be understood as "*witness in the power of the Holy Spirit.*"[220]

John's gospel emphasizes the centrality of Christology, and his understanding of mission must be seen from this perspective. "The mission of the Son by the Father establishes contact between God and the world; the mission of the Church continues this contact: 'As the Father sent me, so send I you' (20:21)."[221] This Christological foundation for mission (which Jesus embodies and his disciples are to exemplify) is rooted in John's unique concept of "sending." Bosch contrasted John with the synoptic gospels in this regard. "In the synoptic tradition, the authors' concern is with Jesus being sent *in* the world, whereas in the fourth gospel, the emphasis is on being sent *into* the world." More than the synoptics, John's gospel evaluates the "world" very negatively, as a realm that is over against and estranged from God. It is into this evil "world-system" that Jesus and his followers are "sent" to be a witness, through their mutual love, service and unity.[222]

Mission as Martyria: the Biblical Model of Suffering/Witness

In the Bible, there is a close connection between mission, witness and suffering. This element of mission is often neglected in Western missiological thought, but when one turns to the Old and New Testaments, one cannot help but be struck by the profound ways in which God uses failures, weaknesses, and suffering in his mission to the nations. Bosch pointed out that the biblical word *marturía* has two distinct

217. Bosch, "Theologies of Mission," 45.
218. Bosch, *Witness*, 69–70.
219. Ibid., 70.
220. Bosch, "Theologies of Mission," 45.
221. Bosch, *Witness*, 70.
222. Bosch, "Mission in Biblical Perspective," 533.

Part Two: Bosch's Theology of Mission and Evangelism

connotations: that of "witness" and of "martyrdom" or "suffering." The fact that both meanings reside in the same root word illustrates a basic biblical theme: that there is "an inextricable link between suffering and mission, witness and opposition, victory and the cross."[223]

The Greek word *mártus* originally meant a "legal witness," related to giving evidence in a courtroom. But Bosch maintained that the meaning of the word began to change as far back as the second century A.D., so that *mártus* increasingly came to mean a "blood witness" or "martyr": one who gave a witness by suffering and laying down his or her life for the beliefs he or she held. In our day, the word "martyr" has lost any attachment to the idea of a witness, but throughout the history of the church, this link has always been preserved. Martyrdom and mission belong together.[224]

Bosch highlighted the link between martyrdom/suffering and mission by analyzing three themes in Scripture: the exilic sufferings of the people of Israel, particularly as it manifested itself in Isaiah's Suffering Servant of the Lord; the passion and death of Christ; and Paul's mission theology as it is revealed in 2 Corinthians.

In Isaiah 40–55, we find the high point of the universalistic motif in the OT, yet remarkably, this section was written when Israel was in exile in Babylon![225] Bosch believed that this was not accidental. Israel became the most universalistic in her outlook, the most mission-oriented, precisely when she was in the midst of suffering, failure and humiliation. "Completely contrary to what Israel always imagined, it now appears that the possibility of witness finds expression not in national triumph but in national adversity."[226] Bosch continued:

> Israel believed that she could truly achieve God's purpose for herself only as long as she was powerful and was feared and respected by the nations. What is remarkable, however, is that, the mightier Israel became, the less was there an indication of a missionary dimension to her existence—the nations moved into the background, they remained at a distance . . .
>
> Conversely, the more Israel was stripped of all earthly power and glory, the more clearly her prophets spoke of the missionary dimension of her existence. Deutero-Isaiah deals with a period in her history when she was, politically speaking, completely insignificant. She had apparently failed miserably in playing any significant role as a priestly presence among the nations. She had become the refuse of the earth, abhorred by every people, a slave of tyrants (49:7). Nevertheless, precisely at this moment of deepest humiliation

---

223. Bosch, *Witness*, 71. The integral relationship between mission, service and suffering in 2 Corinthians is fully explored in Bosch's *A Spirituality of the Road*, esp. 58–90.

224.. Bosch, *Witness*, 73; Bosch, *Theology 201*, 61. Later, Bosch cites the dictum of Tertullian as an illustration of the witness potential of martyrdom in the life of the church: *Semen est sanguis Christianorum*, which eventually became the famous slogan: "The blood of the martyrs is the seed of the church" (ibid., 62). See also Bosch, "Confession and Believing: the Sneezing and Inhaling of the Church," 1.

225. Bosch, "The How and Why," 39; Bosch, *Witness*, 71.

226. Bosch, *Witness*, 72.

The Biblical Foundation for Mission

(and self-humbling) there was the possibility of kings and princes bowing down, "because of the lord who is faithful, because of the Holy One of Israel who has chosen you" (49:7).[227]

Bosch considered the apex of God's witness in the OT is found in Isaiah 53. Here we see mission revealed at its highest and deepest dimensions. What is intriguing is that Isaiah 53 reveals a servant who serves as a witness not so much by his words as by his silent suffering that he endures for others.[228] He who is the priest for others becomes the sacrifice, and in his suffering comes forgiveness and salvation.[229]

Turning to the New Testament, Bosch saw this same idea at work. True mission is at its zenith at the point of the most suffering—in the cross of Christ. On the cross, the Son of Man gave his life as a ransom for many (Mark 10:45). What seemed an unmitigated disaster was turned into God's victory.[230] Bosch affirmed that for this reason, the early church saw the suffering servant of Isaiah 53 as the archetype of Jesus of Nazareth. Here, then, is the paradoxical heart of mission in the Bible: "Not in Jesus' successful preaching to the masses, neither in the sometimes overwhelmingly positive reaction to his miracles, *but in his suffering and death* he became the true Missionary."[231]

Bosch drew two conclusions from this for Christian mission today. First, by its very nature, Christian mission may frequently involve suffering and, at times, even martyrdom. But more importantly, the *cross* should mark the Christian's daily life, preaching, witness, and service. Christian theology should be a *theologia crucis*, a theology of the cross. This does not mean that the church should always focus on the crucifixion, but rather that "the cross should leave an indelible mark on our manner of being a church."[232] The church can accept failures and setbacks in stride. She does not depend on "success stories" to find her justification. Her justification lies in God's mercy alone; she is called to be faithful to her Lord.[233]

---

227. Ibid., 71–72. Bosch expands upon this concept, and devises an intriguing "law" showing the inverse relationship between authentic mission and power. ". . . When Israel was powerful and great it largely lost its missionary dimension. The ambivalence of the concept Israel is again pointed out—both [as a] political entity and [as the] people of God . . . Perhaps we could express it thus: the more of a political entity Israel became, the less it was God's people; conversely, the more it was God's people, the less of a political entity it became. This has certain implications for the church today. The more the church becomes an important, prestigious, even powerful force in society, the less missionary it is in the true sense of the word. Of course the church may (and does!) expand greatly when it occupies a privileged and dominant position, and can then exercise an ever greater influence on society. But can such expansion and influence in fact be called *genuinely missionary*?" (Bosch, *Theology 201*, 63).

228. Elsewhere, Bosch commented that at times, *silence* can be a very evangelistic action! For more on the missiological implications of silence, see Bosch, "The Church without Privileges."

229. Bosch, *Lydende*, 20–23; Bosch, "The Why and How," 39; Bosch, *Witness*, 71.

230. Bosch, "The Why and How," 43.

231. Bosch, *Witness*, 72 (my emphasis).

232. Bosch, *Theology 201*, 63.

233. Ibid.

Part Two: Bosch's Theology of Mission and Evangelism

In a similar way, this "crucified lifestyle" was to be the most effective means of witness by the apostles and early church leaders. They were to identify with Christ's sufferings when they themselves encountered suffering, affliction, and weakness.[234] This is best exemplified, according to Bosch, in the life of the apostle Paul, particularly in his second letter to the Christians in Corinth. In this letter, the apostle rejected any concept of mission that involved demonstrable success and triumphalism. By contrast, he glories in his weakness, affliction and suffering as the ground of his own true apostleship. It is these qualities that distinguish him from "those superlative apostles" (11:5; 12:11).[235] Indeed, "suffering and affliction are normal experiences in the life of the apostle, but for those who can only think in terms of success categories, they are a skandalon, a stumbling block. True mission only manifests itself in a church which agonises with the victims of the world. The difference between the Pauline mission and that of his opponents in Corinth lies in the Cross."[236] Mission can only be authentic if it is mission *in Christ's way*, in which we identify with the cross of Christ, and take it up daily upon ourselves as we follow him.[237]

On a larger scale, this is to be the lifestyle of the church as well. Bosch noted that many of the metaphors for the church in the New Testament are expendable items (salt, yeast, light). In fact, they are only of use when they are *used up*; if they are saved, their true purpose is frustrated. In a striking image, Bosch cited N. P. Moritzen, who highlights that it was (and still is) essential that God uses a *weak* witness, a *powerless* representative to deliver his message. The people who are to be won and saved, are those who are able to *crucify* the witness of the gospel! This is exactly what happened to Jesus and the early church. In their weakness and vulnerability, the bearers of the gospel became living witnesses of God to the people to whom they were sent, even through their deaths. The church today, all too frequently, finds this concept alien and strange. She acts as if her own survival was her goal, when in fact she is called to be, in Bonhoeffer's phrase, a "church for others," a suffering church, a church that bears the word of reconciliation and salvation to the world.[238]

---

234. Bosch, "The Why and How," 43.

235. Bosch, *Witness*, 72. Cf. Bosch, *A Spirituality of the Road*, 75–90.

236. Bosch, "The Why and How," 43–44.

237. Bosch, *Witness*, 73. In an interesting aside, Bosch develops the idea that, according to Paul, there may be real *salvational* value in our sufferings as we identify with Christ. Bosch admits that Christ's death is unrepeatable; He alone is our Substitute. But Bosch believes that in numerous passages, esp. Col 1:24, Paul teaches that his sufferings help to make Christ's death *effective* in building up the church. Sufferings as a result of witness for Christ are sure to come into his life and others' lives, and it is only through these sufferings that the church can be built up. Thus Paul ascribes salvational value to his own sufferings, believing that without them, "the full tale of Christ's sufferings remains incomplete" (Col 1:24). His suffering is "for the sake of the gospel" (2 Tim 1:8). To the Corinthians, he says "If distress be our lot, it is the price we pay for your consolation, for your salvation" (2 Cor 1:6). Bosch concludes: "Obviously, these Pauline sayings do not mean that he, Paul, became co-mediator with Christ. Christ is far to central in Paul's preaching for that. Yet Paul sees a real connection between his own *martyria* and Christ's, one which is significant for mission" (Bosch, *Theology 201*, 64).

238. Bosch, *Witness*, 73.

The Biblical Foundation for Mission

Missio Dei: God's Mission and Our Responsibility

The final essential tenet of Bosch's biblical foundation for mission is the conviction that God is the true subject and author of mission. Mission is God's work, the *missio Dei*. The witness that is given in word and deed has its origin not in the human witness himself, but in God. This does not mean that the human witness is excluded from the process of God's mission, but God alone remains its true author.[239]

The *missio Dei* is readily seen in the OT. Yahweh is the source and subject of mission, but he works through Israel to proclaim his message and name to the ends of the earth.[240] This is exemplified in the concept of "centripetal mission" that we analyzed previously. Bosch cited Zechariah 8 as a classic example of the centripetal dimension of the *missio Dei*. When the text is analyzed, we see a creative tension between mission as the work of God and the responsibility of humans.

> It is Yahweh who, after the exile, gathers his scattered people from the nations (vv. 7–8) and instructs them (vv. 9–19). The nations observe this and spontaneously express the desire to go to Jerusalem. As many as ten men "from nations of every language" will pluck the robe of a Jew and say: "We will go with you because we have heard that God is with you" (v. 23). It is not Israel's faith, example and witness that act as a magnet here; it is God's faithfulness to Israel that causes the nations to come. And yet, not for a single moment does this suggest that Israel's faith, example and witness are dispensable. Far from it . . . Israel herself is fully involved in God's mission to the nations. She was a pagan whom God elected to salvation; but she retains her new and special position as "non-pagan" only in so far as she accepts and lives up to her responsibility in the world. Primarily, this means remaining true to Yahweh; but then this implies remaining true to the world, in letting her light shine forth, in being an example to the world, indeed, in witnessing by word and deed.[241]

Another example of the *missio Dei* principle at work arises in the book of Isaiah. Bosch argued how the figure of the Servant of the Lord personalizes the nature of Israel's witness to the nations. Many therefore argue that the Servant is the "missionary figure" in chapters 40–55. And yet the events associated with the Servant in those chapters serve to show that it is really *God himself* who is at work.

> The "servant" is . . . not an active missionary sent out to the nations . . . It is not the servant's own activities which are emphasized, but the fact that God works in and through him. He is, we are told, brought into the courtroom to witness in the case between God and the nations. He is, however, a very remarkable and, according to our standards, useless witness, for he can neither see nor speak (Isa. 42:18–20; 43:8–13). The purpose of this metaphor is, once

---

239. Ibid., 75.
240. Bosch, "Jeseja," 35; Bosch, "Sendingperspektief," 295.
241. Bosch, *Witness*, 77 (my emphasis).

Part Two: Bosch's Theology of Mission and Evangelism

again, not to say that the witness is indeed blind and deaf, but that, in the final analysis, Yahweh himself is the Witness.[242]

The Servant of the Lord is a paradigm for Israel. Her election has no goal in itself, but serves as the instrument through which God involves himself with the nations. Through her "God stretches his hand out to the world."[243] Israel is the servant, called to make God's truth and righteousness known among the nations. "God himself remains the real 'missionary,' but Israel—in as far as she is God's obedient servant—is most directly involved in this."[244]

In the New Testament too, God reveals himself as the primary missionary. In his doctoral thesis, Bosch affirmed this truth. "Der auferstandene und erhöhte Herr missioniert selber in der Gestalt des Heiligen Geistes durch seine Boten."[245] Yet *people are intimately related to his mission.*

Bosch criticized the theories of Albert Schweitzer and Joachim Jeremias in this regard. Schweitzer believed that Jesus was captivated by an apocalyptic worldview that held that God's work excluded any human involvement, particularly with regard to any mission to the Gentiles. At most, God himself would call and prepare the Gentiles for the messianic era, but Jesus could do nothing; he simply awaited the imminent arrival of the kingdom. In a somewhat different context, Jeremias argued that the calls in the gospels to proclaim the good news to all the nations (Matt 24:14; Mark 13:10, 14:9) totally excluded any "human mission work." The salvation of the Gentiles would come only as a result of an eschatological act of God's power at the end of time.[246]

Bosch argued that Schweitzer and Jeremias were wrong for assuming that Jesus believed that God's work excluded the work of humans. By their logic, people will either stand by idly with a sense of "blind unbending fate" (since God is sovereign, and working out his purposes apart from us) or they will become "fanatics and arrogant zealots," acting as if everything depended on them and their efforts. Instead, Bosch urged, we should look at the example of Jesus. He lived and worked and relaxed in serene dependence upon God. There was no contradiction in his life between God's work and his own. He lived with this mysterious and creative tension, and so should his followers. As believers recognize their existence "in Christ," they overcome both of the above-mentioned debilitating alternatives.[247]

---

242. Ibid., 75–76, (my emphasis); Cf. Bosch, "The Why and How," 40; Bosch, *Theology 201*, 68.

243. Bosch, *Witness*, 76.

244. Ibid., 77.

245. "The risen and glorified Lord himself does the missionary work in the form of the Holy Spirit through his envoys" (Bosch, *Heidenmission*, 199). Cf. Bosch, *Theology 201*, 70.

246. Bosch here cites Jeremias' *Jesus' Promise to the Nations*, 70.

247. Bosch notes that this false dichotomy between God's work and our work has been seriously detrimental to the church down through the ages. The Bible knows no such distinctions. In *Witness*, 80, Bosch elaborates: "The disciples are seed (Mt. 13:38) and at the same time labourers bringing in the harvest (Mt. 9:37–38); they are members of the flock (Mt. 10:16; Lk. 12:32; Jn. 10:1–16) but also shepherds (Mt. 10:6; Jn. 21:15–17); they are in need of absolution (Mt. 18:23–27) but they also give absolution to

The Biblical Foundation for Mission

There can be no polarization between mission as the work and God and mission as the work of humans. Mission, even centripetal mission, is never a *passive* event in which people have no role to play. The elements of God's work and the work of humans must be held in a dialectical and creative tension, for this is how they exist in the Bible.[248] God's activity is not a contradiction of human freedom; in fact the more a Christian surrenders to God the more truly free that man or woman is. The same principle is operative when it comes to the church's mission. "In light of the gospel (and the Old Testament!) . . . the more we recognize that the church's mission is God's activity, the more we may properly speak of it as our activity."[249]

MOTIVES, CONCLUSIONS, AND OBSERVATIONS

Bosch closed his major exposition of the biblical foundation for mission in his *Witness to the World* with a discussion of the biblical *motive* for mission.[250] Throughout church history, different missionary motives have been operative.[251] Biblically speaking, however, one motive stands above all others. Mission is "in Christ." The deepest missionary motive is not found in obeying a command or pitying the lost but the

---

others (Mt. 16:19; 18:18; Jn. 20:23). God has revealed to them the 'secrets of the Kingdom' (Mt. 13:11), yet they have to seek the Kingdom (Mt. 5:20; 6:33; Lk. 13:24). They are God's children (Mt. 17:26), yet have to become that by loving their enemies (Mt. 5:44–45). They have received eternal life (Jn. 3:16–17; 11:25–26) yet they still have to go through the gate that leads to life (Mt. 7:14). Because they have done what Jesus expected of the rich young ruler, they are 'perfect' (Mt. 19.21; cf. Mk. 10:28), yet have to keep watch and pray so that they will not fall into temptation (Mt. 26:41). The believers must work out their own salvation in fear and trembling, *for*(!) it is God who works in them (Phil. 2:12–13). Therefore Paul can, quite unselfconsciously, call them 'God's fellow-workers' (I Cor. 3:9). The key to these apparently complete paradoxes lies in the New Testament expression 'in Christ:' 'By God's grace I am what I am, nor has his grace been given to me in vain; on the contrary, in my labours I have outdone them all–not I, indeed, but the grace of God working with me' (I Cor. 15:10)."

248. Bosch comments that it is unfortunate that many theologians unnecessarily *polarize* the Old Testament and New Testament concepts of mission. In the former, mission is perceived in exclusively passive, centripetal terms. In the latter, mission is perceived in activistic, centrifugal terms. But this distinction is artificial and unhelpful. Bosch readily grants that in the Old Testament, mission is primarily understood as centripetal, centering on Jerusalem and Zion. But an absolute distinction between the two is artificial for three reasons: 1) elements of centripetal and centrifugal mission exist in *both* testaments; 2) pressing this distinction may lead to the false idea that "real" mission is centrifugal only, that it is merely the crossing of geographical barriers to give a verbal proclamation to pagans. But biblical mission is much more than this; 3) it tends to view Old Testament mission as God's work, and thus see New Testament mission, in which people are more actively involved, as "man's work." But these distinctions are unnecessary. God and humans, centripetal and centrifugal, Old Testament and New Testament are not competing categories, but complementary ones. See Bosch, *Witness*, 77–79.

249. Bosch, *Witness*, 79. Bosch cites the work of John Deschner in this regard, as found in Anderson, *Christian Mission in Theological Perspective*, 223.

250. Bosch, *Witness*, 81–83.

251. Verkuyl devotes a chapter to this issue, dividing the motives for fulfilling the missionary task into "pure" and "impure" categories. Among the pure motives are obedience, love, mercy, doxology, personal conviction, and haste. Impure motives include the imperialist, cultural, commercial, and the colonialistic (Verkuyl, *Contemporary Missiology*, 163–75).

Part Two: Bosch's Theology of Mission and Evangelism

result of experiencing the grace of God. Mission is "the result of an encounter with Christ. To meet Christ, means to become caught up in a mission to the world. Mission is a privilege in which we participate. Thus Paul introduces himself to the church in Rome as somebody who, through Christ, has 'received the privilege of a commission in his name to lead to faith and obedience men in all nations' (Rom. 1:5)."[252]

Citing other Pauline texts, Bosch urged that mission be seen as a "predicate of Christology." In the christological hymn of Phil 2:6–11, Bosch noted that while there is no reference to a missionary command, it is nevertheless clear that a worldwide mission is assumed: ". . . that at the name of Jesus every knee should bow . . . and every tongue confess, 'Jesus is Lord.'"[253] In 2 Cor 5:18–20 and Eph 2:14–18, mission is christologically founded as well. "[M]ission is christologically founded as the message of the reconciliation of the world with God; the 'service of reconciliation,' entrusted to the Church, proceeds from the fact that Jesus, with regard to Jews and Gentiles, has broken down, 'in his own body of flesh, the enmity which stood like a dividing wall between them', thus creating 'out of the two a single new humanity in himself.'"[254]

If the church is "in Christ," she is, by definition, involved in mission. Her whole *existence* takes on a missionary character.[255] This is seen most clearly in the book of 1 Peter.

> Her conduct as well as her words will convince the unbelievers (1 Pet. 2:12) and put their ignorance and stupidity to silence (1 Pet. 2:15). "God's scattered people'" to whom 1 Peter is addressed (cf. 1:1), are a chosen race, a royal priesthood, a dedicated nation, and a people claimed by God for his own. This new status in Christ has a clear purpose: to proclaim the triumphs of him who has called them out of darkness into his marvelous light (cf. 1 Peter 2:9). Because of this new life in Christ, mission "happens", so to speak, for we read about unbelievers calling upon the Christians for an explanation of the hope that is in them (1 Pet. 3:15).

The church finds herself engaged in mission because she finds herself in relationship to the crucified and risen Christ, not simply because Jesus made certain universalistic claims.[256]

---

252. Bosch, *Witness*, 81–82. Elsewhere Bosch elaborates on this theme. "The church's involvement with mission is not the result of obedience to a command, but rather a logical outcome of the grace of God experienced by the faithful. Let us consider the familiar text Jn. 3:16 in this connection . . . Nowhere in this text are we told *how* we will discover that God had loved the world and sent his Son. It merely says that those who believe in him will be saved. Yet it is manifestly *assumed* that there will be people to tell the tale, bearers of the message, 'missionaries.' It is apparently not considered necessary to state this explicitly; after all, it is simply *logical* that anyone who has experienced the love of God will tell others about it. Mission is the outcome of grace" (Bosch, *Theology 201*, 70).

253. Bosch, *Witness*, 82. Bosch also notes that 1 Tim 3:16, another ancient hymn, exhibits the same character.

254. Ibid.

255. Ibid.

256. Bosch, *Theology 201*, 70.

Bosch concluded that both the Old and New Testaments are permeated with the idea of mission; they exhibit the essentially *missionary dimension* of the Scriptures. Throughout its pages, the Bible reiterates the same basic themes. These themes, as we have seen, are very closely interrelated. One could even say that these themes are simply different aspects of the same primary subject of the Bible; *God himself in his salvific relationship to the world*. As Bosch summarized it:

> The God who has compassion on stranger, orphan and widow in Israel, and through Jesus of Nazareth on all discarded people, is also par excellence the God of history who uses the history of Israel as arena for his activities among the nations and the history of Jesus as the gateway to the world. He is also— precisely as compassionate God and God of history—the One who turns all human categories upside down: he uses the weak, the suffering, and those of no consequence as his 'witnesses' in the world. In the final analysis it is he himself who works among the nations, through Jesus Christ, in whom the believers exist and live.[257]

Bosch's work in the biblical foundations for mission is quite impressive, both for its sheer comprehensiveness as well as its theological depth. Few missiologists have dealt as extensively with the biblical material as Bosch, and even fewer have brought the sustained, critical insight into the text that Bosch brought. (It is helpful to recall that Bosch's doctoral work was in New Testament studies and not missiology). We agree with Orlando Costas' assessment, who, in reviewing *Witness to the World*, wrote: "It is not often that one sees in contemporary missiological circles such a qualitative treatment of the biblical material."[258] The originality of Bosch's contribution to the biblical foundation for mission is revealed in two ways.

First, Bosch admirably emphasized the *continuity of the two testaments*, showing how they are dynamically related to one another. Bosch has showed that both testaments reveal a fundamental *unity* with regard to certain basic missiological themes, including: the significance of history; the universalist/particularist tension; the compassionate nature of God; God's concern for justice, particularly for the poor and outcast; the inevitable link between witness and suffering; and God's worldwide salvific intentions. This insight is significant, for it shows that Bosch, true to his Reformed heritage, emphasized the continuity rather than the discontinuity of the two testaments.[259]

Second, Bosch drew deeply from the work of biblical theologians. He used the various standard "biblical theologies" (von Rad, Eichrodt, Jeremias, Hahn, etc.) in order to serve as the foundational materials for his biblical theology of mission. Although this approach hardly sounds unique, it is (regrettably) all too rare among

---

257. Bosch, *Witness*, 83.

258. Costas, Review of *Witness to the World*, 84.

259. For representative examples of the Reformed approach, see Barth, *Church Dogmatics I/2*, 55–56, 481–85; and Berkhof, *Christian Faith*, 249–51, 257–61.

Part Two: Bosch's Theology of Mission and Evangelism

missiologists. All too frequently, as we have already noted, missiologists tend to overlook the rich diversity within the Bible, reducing the biblical vision for mission to a few key texts or emphases. By focusing on central, foundational elements of the Bible and showing the missiological dimension inherent within them, Bosch provided the Christian world mission a much broader foundation. Again, Costas complimented Bosch's approach, noting that Bosch's treatment liberated mission from both "the militaristic (commandment) language of traditional evangelical theologies of mission and the tendency toward anthropocentrism in traditionally liberal missiological circles."[260]

We now raise two questions regarding Bosch's approach. The "biblical theology" movement and Protestant neo-orthodox theology, as we have seen, decisively shaped Bosch. This is especially noticeable in his understanding of "truth as encounter."[261] He appealed to Karl Barth as a positive example of the theological exegesis of Scripture. Even the fact that Bosch chose to study at Basel under Cullmann and Barth rather than the Free University of Amsterdam (the traditional place for young Afrikaner theologians to pursue postgraduate studies outside of South Africa) sheds some light on his basic theological approach to the Bible.

In his later writings, however, Bosch made a creative missiological appropriation of the hermeneutical approach of Gadamer. He set high hopes on the new "postmodern" paradigm for biblical studies, which attempts to steer clear of the rationalistic excesses of Bultmannian radicalism and pre-critical fundamentalism. But it remains to be seen whether this "postmodern" approach to Scripture is truly a new, theologically unifying paradigm, or just another failed attempt at overcoming the massive impasse between traditional Christian belief and the historical-critical method. How will this new "postmodern" approach to mission look any *different* from the present approaches? Will it be able to draw upon the radically disparate "theologies" (and "missiologies"!) that are emerging around the world today, through a common, shared hermeneutical approach? Bosch's *Transforming Mission* attempted to deal with this subject in depth, but it remains to be seen whether this approach will bear fruit in missionary obedience in the decades to come.

Second, we note that Bosch was extremely critical of the "command" element in traditional missiology. He sought to base the church's missionary motivation in the grace of God acting in the believer rather than the command of God acting upon the believer, in the "gospel" rather than the "law." Surely this is a right and proper emphasis. And yet was Bosch, at times, not too extreme in his total rejection of the "command" element in the Bible? While we readily grant that the *primary* missionary motive is grounded in the believer's gratitude to God, can there *no* positive role for the motive of *obedience* in the church's missionary existence? We suspect that Bosch's attitude emerged from a deep suspicion of any language that elevates "command," "law," "duty," or "obligation," and this suspicion has arisen quite apart from the biblical

---

260. Costas, Review of *Witness to the World*, 85.
261. Brunner, *Truth as Encounter*.

material. In the apartheid-era Afrikaner world, particularly in church circles, there was a very positivistic attitude toward the law. Law, command, and obligation had become all-powerful influences in the decision-making process, revealing a tendency to regard the present situation, whatever the circumstances, as inevitable because God had willed them so.[262] It is clear that in the South African context, these concepts were frequently used to justify many harmful actions by the state as well as the church. Bosch, in his reaction against this approach to the law, gave an overly negative evaluation of the role of obedience in the church's missionary task. Perhaps this is simply evidence of the contextual shaping of Bosch's own theology.

---

262. Bosch, "Racism and Revolution: Response of the Churches in South Africa," 16.

6

Mission, Evangelism, and Church Growth

HAVING REVIEWED BOSCH'S UNDERSTANDING of the historical and theological context of mission today and outlined the main themes in his biblical foundation for mission, we turn to consider his theology of mission. In this chapter, we shall consider four pivotal issues which have shaped the missiological discussion in our era, and to which Bosch devoted significant energies: the relationship between mission and evangelism; the meaning of mission; the meaning of evangelism; and an evaluation of the church growth movement.[1]

ELUCIDATING THE RELATIONSHIP OF MISSION AND EVANGELISM

The Impasse of Differing Understandings of Mission and Evangelism Today

The words "mission" and "evangelism," and their theological relationship, have been a focal point of theological discussion in recent years.[2] Both terms have been used with an increasing frequency in ecclesiastical and academic circles[3] An unfortunate result of the proliferation in the use of these words is the emergence of a wide variety of differing understandings of the two terms. The resulting terminological and theologi-

---

1. Space forbids us from expounding other topics that Bosch addressed elsewhere, including the history of the theology of mission; missionary spirituality; the theology of religions, and the relationship of church and mission.

2. Bergquist, "Evangelism in Current Ferment and Discussion," 59.

3. Evidence of this trend is to be found in the veritable landslide of publications on the two subjects in the last dozen years. David Barrett calculated that between 1960–69, some 1200 items were published related to the task of evangelization. From 1970–79, the number had increased to 2,410 publications, and from 1980–89, some 2,950 items. See his *Evangelize!*, 37. Also see Bergquist, "Evangelism in Ferment and Discussion," 59–70.

cal confusion is exemplified in the theme of an issue of the *International Bulletin of Missionary Research*: it is entitled "Evangelism: Why the Endless Debate?"[4]

Bosch wrote extensively on the subject and developed a typology of the divergent understandings of the meaning and relationship of evangelism and mission.[5] Broadly speaking, he distinguished between those who view "mission" and "evangelism" as equivalent, synonymous terms and those who, in some way, distinguish between the two terms.

Mission and Evangelism as Synonymous Terms

Among those who speak of "mission" and "evangelism" as synonyms, Bosch discerned six variations, ranging all the way from strict fundamentalism to a secularized political theology.

First, mission/evangelism is defined narrowly and exclusively in terms of the verbal proclamation of the gospel, the goal of which is to "win souls" from eternal damnation. Typical of this approach, said Bosch, is the viewpoint expressed in South African evangelist Reinhard Bonnke's book *Plundering Hell*. The church's mission is about "making sure that as many people as possible get 'saved' from eternal damnation and go to heaven."[6] In this scheme, social involvement of any type is a *betrayal* of the church's missionary outreach. Bosch linked this outlook to a strict fundamentalist and premillennialist viewpoint.

Second, mission/evangelism is defined, like position one, as "saving souls," yet concedes that "it would be good—at least in theory—to be involved in some other good activities at the same time, activities such as relief work and education."[7] However these involvements generally serve as a *distraction* from mission, and are considered *optional* activities. Bosch believed this approach is typical of many in the conservative wing of evangelicalism.[8]

Third, mission/evangelism is again defined as "soul-winning." With this position, however, service ministries have a legitimate (albeit utilitarian) function, inasmuch as they serve as a means to an end: drawing people to hear the gospel of Christ. Bosch cited the words of Harold Lindsell in this regard. "Service," says

---

4. *IBMR* 11/3 (July 1987).

5. See Bosch's "Evangelism: Theological Currents and Cross-Currents Today," 98–99. This was originally a paper presented at the South African Council of Churches' Seminar on "The Relevance of Evangelism in South Africa Today" at Hammanskraal, January 27–31, 1986. Bosch has developed this subject in *Witness*, 11–20; "Mission and Evangelism: Clarifying the Concepts," 166–68; and his article "Evangelisation, Evangelisierung," 102–5.

6. Bosch, "Evangelism: Theological Currents," 98.

7. Ibid.

8. Bosch named Trinity Seminary's Arthur Johnston as an exponent of this approach. Johnston, in his *The Battle for World Evangelism*, strongly criticized the leadership of the LCWE (and John Stott in particular) for undermining world evangelization because of their emphasis on social responsibility as a legitimate dimension of the church's mission to the world.

Part Two: Bosch's Theology of Mission and Evangelism

Lindsell, "is a means to an end. As long as service makes it possible to confront men with the gospel, it is useful."⁹

Fourth, mission/evangelism is understood as preaching the gospel of repentance and conversion. Mission/evangelism relates to social responsibility as a *seed to fruit*. Social responsibility is an important outgrowth of conversion, a necessary but secondary *result of mission*, but *not a part* of mission or evangelism. As Bosch summarized it: "Once [persons] have accepted Christ as Savior, they will be transformed and become involved in society as a matter of course. In the words of Elton Trueblood, 'The call to become fishers of men precedes the call to wash one another's feet.' Jesus did not come into the world to change the social order: that is part of the result of his coming. In similar fashion the church is not called to change the social order: redeemed individuals will do that."¹⁰

Fifth, mission/evangelism is defined in broad terms as the total Christian ministry of the church in the world. Evangelistic preaching and the call to conversion are included here, but clearly there is much more involved than simply the verbal proclamation of the gospel message. For position five, mission/evangelism involves "the whole church taking the whole gospel to the whole world," in the classic formulation of the 1928 Jerusalem IMC meeting. This has been the dominant position in the ecumenical movement. According to Bosch, this understanding of mission and evangelism as *interchangeable concepts* is reflected in the name "Commission on World Mission and Evangelism" and has informed the ecumenical literature on the subject.¹¹

Sixth, mission/evangelism is defined here, like position five, as the church's total involvement in the world, but does not insist that mission/evangelism must include a call to repentance and faith in Christ. It is reduced to an exclusively "this-worldly" sociopolitical program, and emphasizes the "horizontal" dimension of faith to the exclusion of the "vertical." Bosch cited the work of American theologians Gibson Winter and George Pixley in this regard. Winter, a theologian from the "secular Christianity" movement of the 1960s, defined salvation as humanization and stated: "The categories of biblical faith are freed from their miraculous and supernatural garments . . . Why

---

9. Bosch, "Mission and Evangelism: Clarifying the Concepts," 167; Bosch, "Evangelism: Theological Currents," 98. He is citing Lindsell, "A Rejoinder," 439.

10. Bosch, "Evangelism: Theological Currents," 98. Bosch is citing Quaker theologian Elton Trueblood's *The Validity of the Christian Mission*, 98.

11. Bosch noted that "[w]hen the International Missionary Council merged with the World Council of Churches (WCC) at its New Delhi meeting in 1961, it became one of several divisions of the WCC and was renamed Commission on World Mission and Evangelism. Both words, 'mission' and 'evangelism,' were thus included in the title, not because they meant different things but precisely because they were, by and large, understood to be synonyms. Another synonym was the word 'witness,' which is also often used in the New Delhi report. Phillip Potter is correct when he wrote, in 1968, that 'ecumenical literature since Amsterdam (1948) has used "mission," "witness" and "evangelism" interchangeably.'" See his "Evangelism: Theological Currents," 98. Cf. Bosch, *Witness*, 13–14; *Theology 201*, 173. Bosch is citing Potter's "Evangelism and the World Council of Churches," 176.

are men not simply called to by human in their historical obligations, for this is man's true end and his salvation?"[12]

Winter's approach was echoed in the preparatory documents of the WCC's 1968 Uppsala Assembly with its affirmation: "We have lifted up humanization as *the* goal of mission."[13] Similarly, said Bosch, the Baptist liberation theologian George Pixley defined the kingdom of God "exclusively as a historical category. The Palestinian Jesus movement, which was, according to him, a wholly political movement, was completely misunderstood by Paul, John, and others, who spiritualized Jesus' political program. In Pixley's thinking, then, salvation becomes entirely this-worldly, God's kingdom a political program, history one-dimensional, and mission/evangelism a project to change the structures of society."[14]

Mission and Evangelism as Distinct Terms

Bosch also discerned at least three different understandings among those who hold that "mission" and "evangelism" are distinct concepts.

Some continue to distinguish between mission and evangelism on the basis of geography, in terms of the *recipients* or *objects* of gospel. This view, to which many European missiologists in the Reformed, Lutheran, and Roman Catholic churches subscribe, is based in the old geographic distinction between "mission," which is the sending of people "overseas" to communicate the gospel to those who are foreign to it (i.e., the Third World), and "evangelism," which is the communication of the gospel in the West to nominal Christians who are estranged from the gospel. This distinction is supported by Dutch Reformed thinkers such as Verkuyl and Van Ruler[15] and used in the documents of the Second Vatican Council.[16] It is grounded theologically in the fact that there is a difference between those who have been raised in nations that have never been Christian and those who have grown up in a so-called "Christian" nation.[17]

12. Bosch, *Witness*, 215. Cf. Bosch, "Evangelism: Theological Currents," 98. See Winter's *The New Creation as Metropolis*, 60–61.

13. Bosch, *Witness*, 215.

14. Bosch, "Evangelism: Theological Currents," 98. He refers the reader to Pixley's *God's Kingdom*, 88–100.

15. See Bosch, *Missiology 101*, 55.

16. In his *Witness*, 13, Bosch noted that Roman Catholics have frequently linked "mission" with those in the Third World who are "not-yet-Christian," and "evangelism" with nominal Catholics in the West. The Vatican II documents *Lumen Gentium* and *Ad Gentes* reflected this approach.

17. Bosch summarized Van Ruler's argument as follows: "God-in-Christ . . . has walked a long way with the peoples of the West and they cannot undo this history, even if they wished to. In Europe God himself is (in a way quite different from that which obtains in Asia) the point of contact for the gospel. A secularised, de-Christianised European is not a pagan. The Westerner *cannot*, in fact, revert to paganism for that has been totally destroyed in Europe. He can never again become pre-Christian (or pagan), but at the most post-Christian. For precisely this reason we have to maintain the difference between mission and evangelism" (Bosch, *Witness*, 13).

Part Two: Bosch's Theology of Mission and Evangelism

Other groups, particularly progressive Roman Catholics, have expanded the meaning of "evangelization" to include such tasks as development, peace-making, and the struggle for liberation and justice.[18] Evangelism becomes an "umbrella concept" for the whole way in which the gospel takes root in the life of people. They have either dropped the word "mission" out of their vocabulary (because of its link with colonialism), or have redefined it as a purely theological concept, giving the theoretical foundation to the various "evangelistic" tasks described above.[19]

Particularly since the pronouncements on mission of the 1970s, many have articulated a third position; that the term "mission" is a comprehensive concept and "evangelism" is a narrower one. Mission describes all that God sends the church into the world to do, and evangelism describes that dimension of mission that involves the communication of the gospel and the invitation to Christian discipleship. Yet Bosch maintained there are three distinct sub-groups within this general position.[20] First, there are those who would affirm the mission is made up of two component parts, evangelism and social responsibility. Both parts of mission are essential, but evangelism maintains the place of priority. This is the position of John Stott and the Lausanne Covenant. Second, there are those who believe that mission consists of evangelism and social involvement, but hold that in light of the social context today, social responsibility should take precedence over evangelism. Finally there are those who affirm that evangelism and social concern are "equally important but genuinely distinct aspects of the church 's total mission." There can be no permanent prioritizing of the one above the other. This position is usually associated with Ron Sider and the so-called "radical evangelicals."[21]

Bosch's Understanding of the Relationship of Mission and Evangelism

Bosch's first major statement on mission and evangelism came in 1968 in his *Sending in Meervoud*.[22] It was during the 1970s, however, that Bosch believed he came

18. Bosch cites the work of John Walsh and Segundo Galilea in this regard. See the former's *Evangelization and Justice*; and the latter's *The Beatitudes: To Evangelize as Jesus Did*.

19. Bosch, "Evangelism: Theological Currents," 99.

20. For a summary of these three approaches, see ibid.

21. Bosch did not mention the distinctly *Anabaptist* approach to mission and evangelism in "Evangelism: Theological Currents." In his "Mission and Evangelism: Clarifying the Concepts," 167, however, Bosch discusses the Anabaptist perspective. For Anabaptist theologians, "the primary mission of the Church is simply to *be* the Church. 'The very existence of the church is her primary task' [Yoder]. This position reflects, to some extent, the radical anabaptist understanding of mission/evangelism and—though for very different theological reasons—also the view of the Eastern Orthodox Churches."

22. In *Sending in Meervoud*, Bosch explored the relationship between word and deed in mission under the rubric of *diakonia*, service. He maintained that mission can never be defined solely in terms of evangelistic proclamation, for this illegitimately reduces the work of medical mission to a secondary level. Mission must include diaconal ministries of healing and social concern in its self-definition. On the basis of biblical and theological considerations, Bosch concludes that the concept of mission can be adequately expressed only as *both* word and deed, *kerygma* and *diakonia*. That explains the title of the

to greater conceptual clarity regarding the meaning and relationship of mission and evangelism. He attributes this to three sources: his own theological reading and study; his involvement in the South African debate; and his participation in a variety of local and international mission conferences (SACME, Lausanne, PACLA, SACLA, Melbourne, Pattaya, and CRESR).[23]

Since 1980, Bosch devoted extensive attention to clarifying the meaning of the terms "mission" and "evangelism" and describing their proper relationship. Bosch aligned himself with those (such as James Scherer and John Stott) who view mission as a *wider* concept than evangelism.[24] Mission is "the total task that God has set the church for the salvation of the world."[25] Mission deals with the church as it crosses a myriad of frontiers and barriers into all the world with the message of God's salvation. Evangelism, for Bosch, is an *essential dimension* of mission, which is concerned to cross the frontier between belief and unbelief.[26] Evangelism "consists in the proclamation of salvation in Christ to nonbelievers, in announcing forgiveness of sins, in calling people to repentance and faith in Christ, in inviting them to become living members of Christ's earthly community, and to begin a life in the power of the Holy Spirit."[27]

We make three observations about Bosch's basic position. First, Bosch *deplored the recent tendency to define mission (and evangelism) too comprehensively*. Too often in some ecumenical circles, mission "becomes a collective noun for everything God does as well as for everything Christians believe they should be doing."[28] Rather, mission is only *one* aspect of the church's existence. "Mission and evangelism," said Bosch, "both have to do with that aspect of the Church's life where she crosses frontiers towards the world. This is not the only feature of her existence. She is also a worshipping presence, providing for the building-up of her members (oikodome) through liturgy

---

publication *Sending in Meervoud* [Mission in the Plural]. Any permanent theological division or prioritization between them leads to a false understanding of the church's missionary task. Bosch approvingly cites the 1952 Willingen declaration that "this *witness* is given by *proclamation, fellowship* and *service*" (Bosch and Jansen, *Sending in Meervoud*, 14). For more on *Sending in Meervoud*, see chapter 2.

23. Bosch, "How My Mind has Changed: Mission and the Alternative Community," 7. His two major essays on the subject during this period were "The Question of Mission Today," 5–15; and "Crosscurrents in Modern Mission," 54–84.

24. Bosch clarified his approach in *Witness*, 16–17; "Evangelism: An Holistic Approach," 47; "In Search of a New Evangelical Understanding," 79; "Mission and Evangelism: Clarifying the Concepts," 169, 172–73; and "Evangelism: Theological Currents and Cross-Currents," 100. For an explanation of their perspectives, see Scherer, *Gospel, Church, and Kingdom*, 243–44; and Stott, *Christian Mission*, 15–34.

25. Bosch, *Witness*, 17. See also his "Evangelism and Mission: The Contemporary Debate," 10; "Mission and Evangelism: Clarifying the Concepts," 169; and "Evangelism: Theological Currents and Cross-Currents," 100.

26. Bosch, *Witness*, 19–20.

27. Bosch, "Mission and Evangelism: Clarifying the Concepts," 170.

28. Bosch, *Witness*, 15.

(leitourgia), fellowship (koinonia) and teaching (didaskalia). We may therefore not call everything the Church does 'mission' or 'evangelism.'"[29]

This is similar to the distinction Bosch made between the "dimensional" and "intentional" aspects of mission. As Bosch summarizes it: "The Church's whole being and nature . . . is characterized by a missionary dimension, but not all that it is or does is explicitly or intentionally missionary. To put it another way: the Church is always 'missionary', but not always 'missioning'. And so it is most important to maintain a dynamic, creative tension between dimension and intention."[30]

Second, Bosch made clear that *mission and evangelism can never be separated or truncated from one another*. Even though they are *distinct* realities, they are inseparably *linked*. Both terms "refer to God's salvific intervention in the world."[31] This was true of Jesus' own understanding of his mission in Luke 4:18–19 and Matthew 11:4–5. "Taken together," says Bosch, mission and evangelism "represent Christ's onslaught against the power of the Evil One; taken together they also define the task and vocation of the church in the world."[32]

This distinction is similar to the one made by Douglas Webster at the SACME '73 Congress. Webster asserted "there was a distinction between "Evangelism" and "Mission." The former, he said, is the preaching of the Word. The latter, however, involves the whole task of the church, from care of the sick to the proclamation of justice and righteousness in the community. Evangelism, he said, is part of mission, but not all of mission is evangelism. In a nutshell, Canon Webster was saying that both mission and evangelism are vital in the church and that they are inextricably interlinked.[33] We can surmise that Webster's proposal influenced Bosch's own approach to the topic.

Third, Bosch was concerned *to avoid "compartmentalizing" mission into easily divisible components*. While endorsing Stott's general approach,[34] Bosch was critical of the way Stott separates mission into two separate *segments* or *components*: evangelism and social concern. Mission is "something more dynamic than the sum total of evangelism and social action."[35] If mission is merely the joining together of two separate "compo-

---

29. Bosch, *Witness*, 17 (my emphasis). Also see his "Contextual Evangelism," 22.

30. Bosch, "Missiology," 3rd ed., 276. Bosch is here relying on the work of Gensichen, *Glaube für die Welt: Theologische Aspekte der Mission*, 80–95.

31. Bosch, "Evangelism: An Holistic Approach," 47.

32. Bosch, *Missiology 101*, 64. Indeed, Bosch admitted "If evangelism is incarnational, contextual, then it comes close to a description of mission." He approvingly noted Paul Löffler conclusion that "when referring to its theological meaning, 'evangelism' is practically identical to 'mission.' When referring to the evangelistic witness, 'evangelism' more specifically means 'the communication of Christ to those who do not consider themselves Christian' . . . Thus evangelism is sufficiently distinct and yet not separate from mission" (Bosch, *Witness*, 19). He was quoting Löffler's "The Confessing Community," 341.

33. Bosch, "Mission and Evangelism: An Historic Congress [SACME '73]," 16.

34. See Bosch, *Witness*, 16–17; "In Search of a New Evangelical Understanding," 79; and "Evangelism and Mission: The Current Debate," 10–11, 18.

35. Bosch, *Witness*, 16.

Mission, Evangelism, and Church Growth

nents," a dualistic tension between evangelism and social action emerges, and the two become isolated from one another. This results in a battle for supremacy between proponents of each.[36] Instead, Bosch preferred to speak of evangelism and social concern as "*dimensions* of the one indivisible mission of the church."[37] Bosch chose the word "dimension" because it is a more flexible metaphor than "component," and because he believes it to be more true to the biblical witness about the nature of mission.[38]

WHAT IS MISSION?

In raising the question of Bosch's understanding of the meaning of mission, we arrive at the core of his thought. There are numerous ways to respond. For example, we could sketch out the way Bosch understood different theological models or paradigms of mission operating down through the history of the church.[39] Alternatively, we could detail the changes in Bosch's thought regarding the nature of mission, beginning with his earliest work up to his final perspectives in *Transforming Mission*. For our purposes, however, it is sufficient to summarize four foundational theses that delineated his understanding of the question.[40] We will then approach the issue from a different angle, highlighting three "metaphors" of mission that Bosch developed, each metaphor giving a unique and slightly different perspective on the same object (mission). Taken together, these metaphors provide a fuller understanding of how Bosch answered the question: "What is mission?"

Four Theses Concerning the Nature of the Christian Mission

First, mission is fundamentally rooted in *God's concern for the salvation of the world*. "The scope of mission," Bosch said, "is as wide as the scope of salvation; the latter determines the former."[41] Bosch affirmed that the Bible understands "salvation" in broad, cosmic terms, not merely in individualistic, "spiritual" categories.[42] Sin has alienated persons from God, from themselves, from their neighbor, and from the creation. Sin

---

36. Bosch argues that this is precisely what happened at Pattaya. This is also a major source of conflict between evangelicals and ecumenicals. See his "In Search of a New Evangelical Understanding," 79; "Evangelism and Mission: The Current Debate," 17–18; and *Missiology 101*, 60.

37. Bosch, "In Search of a New Evangelical Understanding," 81. See also *Witness*, 18; *Missiology 101*, 60; and "Evangelism and Mission: The Current Debate," 20.

38. Bosch, "Interview." Bosch corresponded with Stott and met with him on numerous occasions. Bosch noted: "I think we're much closer to each other. I think he would not use the word 'components' anymore. I just felt that that was a very unfortunate concept to use. It is *too* precise" (ibid.).

39. This is the approach Bosch takes in *Transforming Mission*.

40. These theses are explored at length in our interpretation of Bosch's missiology in chapters 7–9.

41. Bosch, "Mission and Evangelism: Clarifying the Concepts," 173.

42. "According to Scripture," Bosch says, "salvation is cosmic; it is much more than delivering souls from eternal damnation" (ibid.).

results in broken lives, destructive relationships, evil structures, and death. God, however, has intervened decisively in Jesus Christ to bring full salvation to the cosmos. God in his reconciling love seeks to overcome sin and evil in its personal, social and cosmic dimensions. This salvation involves the re-creation and restoration of the entire created order, including humankind. Various dimensions of God's complete salvation include "healing, reconciliation, salvation, liberation, justice, transformation, peace . . ."[43] Mission, since it is intimately linked to salvation, has its proper scope the totality of God's redemptive purposes.

Second, mission focuses not on the church but *on the kingdom of God*. The kingdom of God alone provides the proper orientation and goal for the Christian mission. The kingdom of God relates to every facet of human existence. It is "the Biblical term for God's caring control of the whole of life, for shalom, for reconciliation between God and His people and between people themselves for justice and equity."[44] Jesus understood his own mission in terms of the kingdom of God, and Christians are to carry on his mission in this light.[45] Christian disciples are sent out in mission to manifest Christ's reign through their lives and words and deeds.[46] In a very real sense, then, mission is "kingdom work," concerned with the transformation of the entire world into what God intends it to be, participating in the extension of the reign of God into all the world and every context.[47]

Third, mission is *an expression of God's compassionate love for the entire world*. It is from a perspective of *fervent love* for the world and *humble solidarity* with it that the church carries out its mission as a witness to the reconciling work of God in Christ. Citing Hans Margull, Bosch defined mission as "simply and solely being sent to *witness to the love of God* in the crucified and the risen Lord Jesus Christ."[48] The church's mission is to extend a gracious invitation to those who are "outside." But this in no way implies any sense of superiority on the part of those who are "inside."[49]

---

43. Ibid.

44. Bosch, "Mission—An Attempt at a Definition," 10.

45. Bosch affirmed "we are to carry on His work of proclaiming, healing, teaching, working for justice and peace, and breaking down barriers of prejudice and discrimination. 'As the Father has sent me, I am sending you' (John 20:21). Our mission is to participate in the mission which Jesus began, the mission of inaugurating God's Kingdom" (ibid.).

46. Ibid., 11.

47. Ibid., 10. Bosch commented that "Since the early days of Protestant mission it has been customary to refer to mission work as the 'extension of the Kingdom of God.' In recent years many people have begun to decry this motto as presumptuous—who are we to think that our puny missionary efforts could extend God's Kingdom? In spite of such objections, however, this traditional Protestant motto has a degree of validity. Mission is indeed Kingdom work. It is concerned with the total reality that has to be transformed into what God wishes it to be" (ibid.).

48. Bosch, "Missiology," 3rd ed., 275 (my emphasis).

49. Bosch commented: "When we [invite those who are outside], we do not suggest that we are, in ourselves, better and more pious than those outside. As a matter of fact, we do not invite anybody to take up his residence in *our* ecclesiastical house where *we* are the hosts and where *we* have all sorts of commodities to offer. We rather invite them to enter through the open door of the house of the Father—the

The varieties of witness vary immensely, but there is a single goal for Christ's ambassadors as they go out in mission: to hold up Christ for the entire world to behold,[50] to "be a witness to the reconciling work of God in Christ, seeking to reconcile persons to God . . ."[51] There is also only one acceptable attitude as the church goes out in mission—*in a spirit of loving servanthood and in deep humility*. Like Christ himself, the church is always sent to be a servant.[52] "If we are in Christ," said Bosch, "we cannot not witness, but we do so with a trembling heart and a penitent spirit."[53]

Finally, mission is always *contextual; different contexts determine the "shape" of the gospel*. The church in every locale must determine how the good news of the gospel affects their particular society. To contextualize the gospel is to identify those sinful attitudes, practices and problems that beset a particular people in a specific place, and address persons at the point where the gospel message speaks to that issue.[54] This means, therefore, that the concrete expression of mission will vary from place to place and from situation to situation, if the context is taken seriously.[55]

Three Metaphors to Portray the Christian Mission

We now turn to consider three metaphors or models that Bosch used to describe the Christian mission. Each model provides a clearer understanding of Bosch's perspective. The first model Bosch used was the concept of *prismic refraction*.[56]

---

house in which we also live solely by his grace and through his kindness . . . A true Christian life is always an invitation. It cannot be lived without open windows and a wide horizon, without a view of the world which God loves" (Bosch, "The Question of Mission Today," 15).

50. Bosch, "Mission and Evangelism: Clarifying the Concepts," 173.

51. Bosch, "The Church in South Africa—Tomorrow," 181.

52. Bosch, "Mission—An Attempt at a Definition," 11. Cf. Bosch, *Witness*, 71–74, 248.

53. Bosch, "The Church in South Africa—Tomorrow," 181.

54. Bosch, "Mission and Evangelism: Clarifying the Concepts," 173. See also Bosch, "The Contextualization of the Gospel," 2.

55. Bosch, "Mission and Evangelism: Clarifying the Concepts," 173.

56. See Bosch, "Mission—An Attempt at a Definition," 10. Also Jonsson, "An Elliptical Understanding of Mission and its Roles," 6–7.

Part Two: Bosch's Theology of Mission and Evangelism

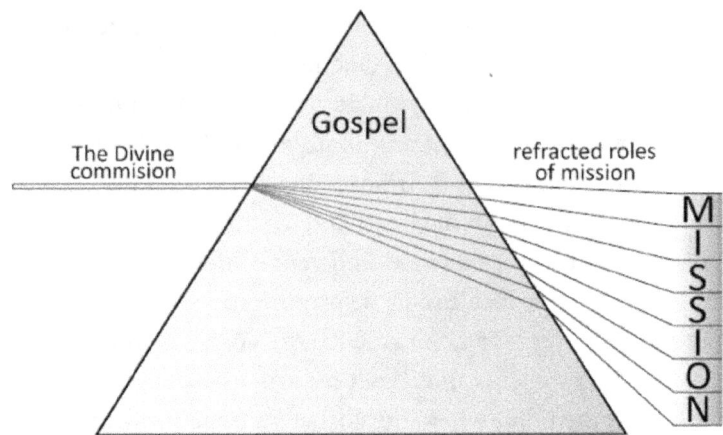

In this model, the analogy involves rays of sunlight which, when they strike a prism, produce the seven different colors of a rainbow. "Each colour is distinct from the others, yet they all issue from the same source and form a unity."

In an analogous way, "as the light of the Divine commission (the *missio Dei*) passes through the prism of the Gospel of the Incarnate Christ, that light refracts into different missionary roles." The church is called to take the whole gospel to the whole world. However the precise missionary priorities are determined by the contextual realties that arise out of that particular place and time. While professing that the work of mission will always involve a call to repentance and conversion, Bosch affirmed that

> we may—in a given context—get involved in mission as evangelism, healing, development, prophetic witness, social involvement, work for justice and peace, diaconal aid, etc. These would be the different spectral colours into which the missio Dei is refracted. And each of these roles is as integral to mission as any other. Our involvement in development and in issues of justice is not less missionary that our evangelistic preaching. Much less may we regard such involvement as merely a trail-blazer for what we regard as our "real" mission. All these roles, taken together, signify our missionary activity as Kingdom work, and they are mutually inter-dependent.

The strength of the *prismic refraction* model is that it preserves the essential unity of the gospel of the kingdom, while allowing for many different expressions of missionary commitment. These differing, contextually shaped missionary roles are complementary rather than competitive. No single role can lay claim to being the *whole* gospel, any more than one color in the spectrum can claim to be light in its fullness.

The second model Bosch used was the (Anglican) Church Mission Society Model.[57]

---

57. See Bosch, "Mission—An Attempt at a Definition," 10–11. All quotations in this section come from ibid.

Mission, Evangelism, and Church Growth

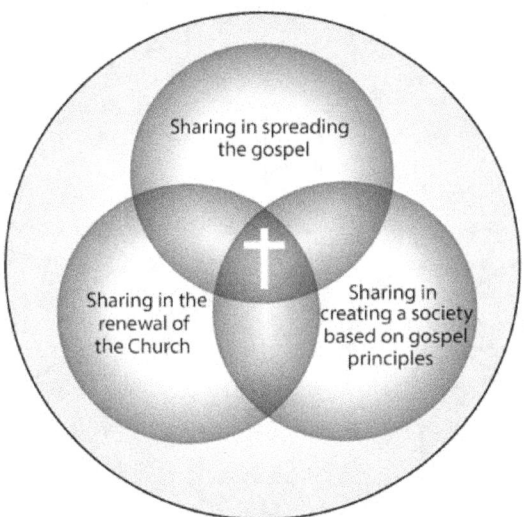

The encompassing circle represents "the church-in-mission." The three smaller circles represent three equally indispensable dimensions of the church's total mission. The first circle, sharing in the spreading of the gospel, is evangelism—the proclamation of the gospel of Christ, to the end that "people are called to faith in and personal commitment to Christ as Lord and Savior and into a fellowship of believers." Without this dimension, according to Bosch, the missionary enterprise ceases to be *Christian* mission.

The second circle, sharing in the renewal of the church, goes hand in hand with spreading the gospel. Bosch observes that it is futile to argue about which circle should come first.[58]

The third circle, sharing in creating a society based on gospel principles, is a call to take the social dimension of the gospel seriously. Mission involves "calling people to involvement in the fabric of society" both locally and internationally. It includes "getting involved in issues of justice, peace, development and charity, in issues of the the family, the community, the nation, the world."

Bosch drew two conclusions from the CMS Model. He emphasized that mission, biblically defined, is the combination of *all three circles*—if any one dimension is excluded, it is not really mission in its fullness. Second, Bosch wanted to emphasize that these three circles must never be isolated from one another. They "interlock" in the person and ministry of Jesus Christ. This is the significance of the symbol of the cross at the center.

---

58. Bosch commented: "A renewed church gets involved in mission and evangelism; a church-in-evangelism experiences renewal—that is, if both the evangelism and the renewal are authentic, because it is possible that they are not. If a church is evangelising without experiencing renewal, it is not engaged in evangelism but propaganda., that is, increasing its own numbers and extending its own sphere of influence. Similarly, if a church claims to have been renewed but is not involved in authentic evangelism, its so-called renewal is counterfeit: it has only grown fatter spiritually, not fitter" (Bosch, "Mission—An Attempt at a Definition," 11). Bosch here had Kähler's distinction in mind. See Bosch, *Witness*, 138.

Part Two: Bosch's Theology of Mission and Evangelism

The third model Bosch uses is the metaphor of "crossing frontiers."[59]

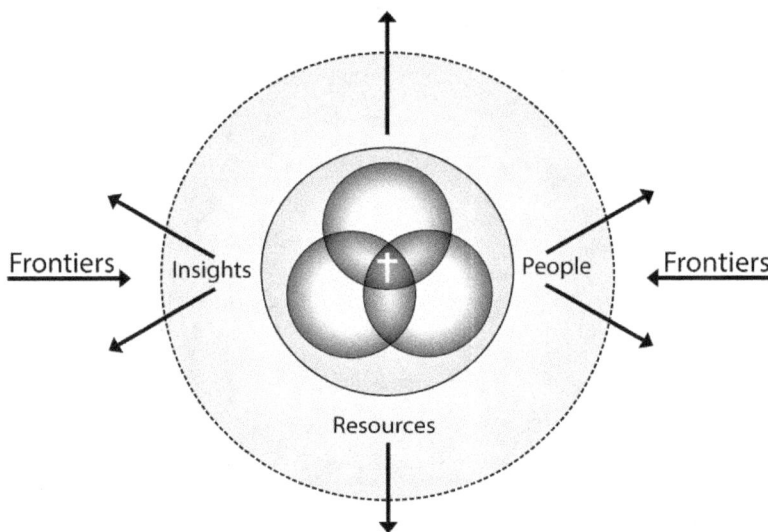

Bosch used this model for mission, first popularized by Bengt Sundkler, extensively.[60] It is characterized as "a ministry of crossing frontiers, of breaking down barriers" into all the world. While the first two metaphors focus attention on the unified yet diverse content of the church's gospel mission, the frontier-crossing metaphor focuses attention on *the world* in its varied dimensions and divisions. It unfolds specific *contexts* in which the church must minister and to which the church must speak. This model also defines and narrows the proper scope of mission.[61]

Bosch identified seven specific frontiers or barriers: geography, religion, culture, ideology, social class, racism and tribalism, and denominationalism. Some of these frontiers deserve special comment. By the frontier of *ideology*, Bosch was concerned that the church not become captive to a Western capitalist worldview, with its emphasis on individualism and personal consumption.[62] By the frontier of *social class*, Bosch sought to highlight the profound changes that are taking place in this century, as the church around the world becomes more and more and church of the

59. See Bosch, "Mission—An Attempt at a Definition," 11; and Bosch, *Witness*, 17–20, 248. Unless otherwise noted, all quotations describing the metaphor of crossing frontiers come from Bosch, "Mission—An Attempt at a Definition," 11.

60. Bosch, "Missionary Theology in Africa," 167.

61. Reacting to Stephen Neill's concern that mission has recently been defined too broadly, Bosch commented: "We must try to establish that characteristic property of mission which allows a particular church activity to be designated 'mission.' This characteristic aspect is the *crossing of frontiers*. Mission is essentially concerned with the Church's moving beyond itself, with the crossing of . . . boundaries. So the *science* of mission may be defined as the theology-of-the-Church-crossing-frontiers" (Bosch, "Missiology," 2nd ed., 240).

62. Bosch noted that "the origins of our faith . . . lie in a society which was fundamentally different from the modern so-called free enterprise system; it was a society which was more participatory in nature and which cared more about people than about material possessions. Today we are rediscovering some of those ancient roots of faith" ("Mission—An Attempt at a Definition," 11).

poor. This has profound missiological implications.[63] By the frontier of *racism and tribalism*, Bosch addressed his own context most deeply. He acknowledges the natural inclination of people "to hide behind the barricades they erect to keep strangers out" and "to nurture their own ethnic interests." Yet the church can never succumb to this temptation. To do this would make the church not the body of Christ but a "club for religious folklore."

Bosch brought together these theses and models concerning the meaning of mission in a series of three brief definitions.[64] Taken together, they helpfully summarize the main themes of his approach. Mission is "the total task which God has set the church for the salvation of the world." It is "the church's ministry of stepping out of itself, into the wider world, in this process crossing geographical, social, political, ethnic, cultural, religious, ideological and other frontiers or barriers." Mission is "the whole church bringing the whole gospel to the whole world."[65]

WHAT IS EVANGELISM?

Now that Bosch's approach to mission has been explored, we turn to consider his perspectives on evangelism. In what follows, we shall review Bosch's critique of the dominant models of evangelism in the late twentieth century, and explore the central tenets of Bosch's theology of evangelism.

Models of Evangelism

Since the 1970s, "evangelism" has gained renewed prominence in the global Christian community.[66] Yet evangelism, like mission, has become an over-worked, impre-

---

63. Bosch commented that in the emerging century, the church was again becoming "a church without privileges, a church not of the wealthy, but of the poor, not of the powerful but of the powerless, not of those in the centre, but of those on the periphery. This state of affairs is so new in many parts of the world that the church is still at a loss how it should respond to it. We [in the West] are used to mission out of affluence and power. How do we adapt to an entirely different reality? We are often reminded that there are still about 3,000,000,000 people in the world who do not believe in Christ. . . . Of late we have slowly begun to discover that the majority of those non-Christians are also poor and oppressed or, putting it the other way around, that by and large the poor are non-Christian. The same people who need to come to faith in Christ also need food and shelter" (ibid.).

64. We should mention another model that Bosch developed, derived from Barth's threefold understanding of the church in volume IV of his *Church Dogmatics*. Barth conceived of the church as the community of Christ that is gathered (IV/1), built up (IV/2), and sent out (IV/3) by the Holy Spirit. This structure of the *gathering, upbuilding*, and *sending* of the church has been developed by Bosch to contrast his own viewpoint with what he labels the "ultra-evangelical" and the "ultra-ecumenical" positions. See Bosch, "Evangelism and Mission—The Contemporary Debate," 10–11; and Bosch, "In Search of a New Evangelical Understanding," 76–82.

65. Bosch, "Evangelisation, Evangelisierung," 103 (Bosch's translation).

66. Bosch attributes this, in part, to the influence of Lausanne, Nairobi, and the Catholic Bishops' Synod on Evangelization. See *Witness*, 11–12. Al Krass also makes this point in *Evangelizing Neo-Pagan North America*, 46–68.

Part Two: Bosch's Theology of Mission and Evangelism

cise term, with a wide variety of perceived meanings.[67] Using the work of George Hunter as his point of departure, Bosch outlined five prominent contemporary models of evangelism.[68]

The first model, which Bosch called "presence evangelism," is built on the premise that the church must "be there" in a very deep sense before it can speak in an evangelistic way. This evangelistic approach is characterized by Hunter's slogan: "let us help you." Citing the work of Mother Theresa and the French "worker-priest" movement, Bosch believed that the strategy of compassionate presence is a deeply evangelistic approach. Considering the human need in places like Calcutta, Bosch asked "whether there *can* really be any other way of evangelizing there but by living a life of deep compassion for Christ's sake."[69] Likewise, the French worker-priest movement emerged in Le Havre because the church had become totally irrelevant to the daily lives of the dockworkers. So the worker-priests said, in effect, "we first have to *create room* for our witness by *identifying* with the workers, otherwise they are *unable* to hear the gospel."[70]

Yet Bosch criticized those who assume that presence *alone* is adequate as an evangelistic strategy. *Verbal* witness remains an indispensable part of evangelism. "The verbal witness . . . remains indispensable, not least because our deeds and our conduct are ambiguous; they need elucidation. The best we can hope for is that people will deduce from our behavior and our actions that we have 'a hope within' us. Our lives are not sufficiently transparent for people to be able to ascertain whence our hope comes. So we must name the Name of him in whom we believe (I Pet. 3:15)."[71]

The second model, which can be characterized as "power evangelism," is built on the premise that God, through direct, divine intervention, desires to meet the psychological, emotional and/or physical needs of persons. God brings healing, miracles, and blessings as persons turn to Him in faith. Their evangelistic slogan may be characterized as: "let God help you." Bosch cited Oral Roberts and Kathryn Kuhlmann as representatives of this approach.[72]

With Hunter, Bosch was critical of this approach on a variety of grounds. First, those who seek divine aid through such an evangelistic approach may indeed receive God's help, but never actually become *followers* of Jesus Christ. Or they may "follow Christ only because of what they get out of it." Also, the techniques of some proponents of this model are very manipulative. However Bosch did not dismiss this approach.

---

67. See Bosch's summary of the several different (conflicting) interpretations of evangelism in his "Evangelisation, Evangelisierung," 102–3.

68. See Bosch's unpublished lecture "Contextual Evangelism," 22–29. Bosch was responding to Hunter's *The Contagious Congregation: Frontiers in Evangelism and Church Growth*, 19–34.

69. Bosch, "Contextual Evangelism," 23.

70. Ibid.

71. Bosch, "Evangelism: Theological Currents and Cross-Currents Today," 101.

72. Bosch notes the popularity of this approach in South Africa, citing numerous "super-churches" in the Witwatersrand area. See his "Contextual Evangelism," 24. This approach has been popularized in the teachings of John Wimber. See his *Power Evangelism* and *Power Healing*.

Many persons have become Christians through the Pentecostal and charismatic renewal movements. Also, it is good for people to be reminded that God is sovereign, and "is able to do much more than we can ever ask for, or even think of (Eph. 3:20)."[73]

The third model, which Bosch called "proclamation evangelism," is built on the premise that evangelism is essentially verbal proclamation of the gospel, of telling the good news. This evangelistic approach is characterized by the slogan: "Hear the Word!" Bosch denotes J. I. Packer, John Stott, and the Lausanne Covenant as exponents of this approach.[74]

Bosch affirmed "proclamation evangelism" as a legitimate approach, particularly in light of the appalling ignorance of many converts who have undergone an emotional "conversion experience" but have no real understanding of what following Christ involves, with little understanding of what they believe or why they believe it. As Bosch put it (echoing the phraseology of Stott): "Because they know little about the 'objective bedrock of Jesus Christ' they flounder on the 'quicksands of subjectivity.' They are being converted not to the Christ of Scripture but to the Christ of their own imagination and subjective visions."[75]

Yet Bosch could not fully endorse this approach. He believed it relies too strongly on the Western "rational" tradition. Communicating the gospel is much more than the correct verbal explanation the way of salvation and carefully reasoned theological argument; faith is much more than intellectual assent.[76]

The fourth model, which Bosch calls "persuasion evangelism," is built on the premise that evangelism, whether done individually or in mass "crusades," is essentially an appeal to "make a decision." Exponents of this very prevalent viewpoint include Billy Graham and Campus Crusade for Christ, to name but two prominent examples.

Bosch criticizes "persuasion evangelism" on three grounds. First, this approach tends to be "ultra-Arminian." In its extreme form, "Man ultimately becomes his own saviour since he is completely capable of making the right decision. God is little more than the great Inviter, begging man to let Him in. Much depends on the evangelist's

---

73. Ibid.

74. Bosch argued that the Lausanne Covenant's paragraph on evangelism endorses this approach, when it states that ". . . evangelism itself is the *proclamation* of the historical, biblical Christ as Saviour and Lord" ("Evangelism: An Holistic Approach," 50).

75. Ibid., 26. Bosch refers the reader to Stott's *Christian Mission*, 45.

76. Bosch criticizes "proclamation evangelism" for unnecessarily restricting the *communication of the gospel*. ". . . [I]n many cultures, the appropriate way of communicating is not that of logical argument, nor even of proclamation as it is traditionally understood in the West. Story is more important than argument. So Walter Hollenweger pleads the case for what is called 'narrative theology' rather than 'conceptual theology.' In narrative theology, as in the Bible, the medium of communication is 'not definition, but description, not thesis, but dance, not doctrine but hymn, not learned book, but history and parable, not the formulation of concepts, but the celebration of banquets.' We should, in our evangelistic outreach, make far more use of plays, music, singing, discussion and storytelling than we have been accustomed to do" (Bosch, "Contextual Evangelism," 26). Bosch is citing, in translation, Hollenweger's *Erfahrungen der Leibhaftigkeit*, 80–81.

Part Two: Bosch's Theology of Mission and Evangelism

abilities to argue persuasively. If he is truly eloquent, employing the right psychological and rhetorical devices, the force of his argument will persuade his listeners."[77]

Second, this approach may turn the gospel into a "consumer product," focusing exclusively on the *benefits* the recipient of the gospel will obtain rather than on the *costs* of becoming a follower of Christ. The ever-present danger with this approach is that the gospel becomes "adulterated" and "diluted" in the evangelists' efforts to make their message more acceptable.[78]

Third, this approach often reduces Christ and his gospel to a "psychological panacea" to meet the needs of the affluent Western world. Bosch recalled an incident at Lausanne that illustrates this point. "I still remember how . . . some 400 of us met on the Sunday evening following the Billy Graham rally in the stadium. During our discussion an Indian took issue with an evangelistic approach which concentrates on questions such as, 'Are you satisfied? Do you want peace of mind? Are you fed up with yourself? Do you need love, joy, peace in your heart?' This approach, the Indian said, may be all right for the affluent and comfortable people of Europe, but in India such a message would be completely irrelevant because it neatly bypasses all the real issues."[79]

Yet for all these criticisms, Bosch granted that "persuasion evangelism" can be a legitimate strategy, particularly among the "spiritually poor" in the affluent West. "There is so much personal tragedy, emptiness, loneliness, physical and mental agony, estrangement, meaninglessness, boredom and weariness all around us, particularly among those who are well off. They are also the poor, in a very special sense. Many of them just cannot let go, they are consumed by frustrations and anxieties, they are suffocated by the many burdens they carry. To people suffering from these . . . maladies the Gospel indeed comes as peace, comfort, fullness, joy, rest. It is therefore perfectly in order that it be presented to them as an answer to their felt-needs."[80]

The fifth model, which Bosch calls "disciple-making evangelism," is built on the premise that one must make *disciples* rather than mere converts. People are called to be "life-time followers of Jesus Christ as their Lord" who live obediently under his lordship; and they must be "incorporated into Christ's body—the church or messianic

---

77. Bosch, "Contextual Evangelism," 27.

78. Bosch cites Latin American preacher Juan Carlos Ortiz in support of this point. All too often persuasion evangelism becomes ". . . the gospel of the big offer. The gospel of the hot sale. The gospel of the irresistible special deal . . . We have told people, 'if you accept Jesus you will have joy, you will have peace, health, prosperity . . . Our gospel is like Aladdin's lamp; we think we can rub it and receive everything we like. No wonder Karl Marx called religion the opiate of the masses." Ortiz's words come from Scott, *Bring Forth Justice*, 209, as cited by Bosch in his "Contextual Evangelism," 27.

79. Bosch, "Contextual Evangelism," 27. Bosch also noted this same tendency in much of the campus evangelism in North America. This psychological approach is popular because it meets the "felt needs" of very affluent students. Citing Waldron Scott again, Bosch commented: "Salvation must be offered to [the students] in relevant terms. What needs do rich people have other than psychological needs? Consequently we tend to present a spiritualized salvation based on a psychologically-oriented gospel" (ibid.).

80. Ibid.

community."⁸¹ Exponents of this viewpoint include George Hunter and the Church Growth movement.

Bosch agreed with the main thrust of this model, particularly that evangelism involves calling persons to live out the implications of Christ's lordship over *all* realms of life, but he was critical of Hunter for being too dependent on Church Growth theory. Hunter and others have overemphasized the significance of numerical growth in regard to evangelism.⁸²

Each of these five models of evangelism (presence, power, proclamation, persuasion, church growth) has its strengths but all of them remained inadequate for Bosch. We shall now spell out his own understanding of evangelism and outline the central themes of his approach.

Essential Aspects of Evangelism

Biblically speaking, Bosch emphasized that the words "evangelism" and "evangelization," (derived from the verbs *euangelizein* and *euangelizesthai*) have as their basic meaning "the proclamation of the inauguration of the Kingdom of God in the person and ministry of Jesus and a call to repentance and faith."⁸³ Bosch also noted that Luke's preferred term *euangelizesthai* can be regarded as a synonym for *keryssein* in Matthew and Mark and for *martyrein* in John.⁸⁴ "Evangelism" refers to those activities involved in spreading the gospel as well as theological reflection upon those activities, while "evangelization" refers to "the *process* of spreading the gospel or the *extent to which* it has been spread.⁸⁵

The following eleven theses, drawn from a number of his publications, will summarize the main themes of his theology of evangelism.

First, evangelism is *an integral dimension* and *the abiding heart* of Christian mission.⁸⁶ In 1984, Bosch defined evangelism as "the core, heart or center of mission: it consists in the proclamation of salvation in Christ to non-believers, in announcing forgiveness of sins, in calling people to repentance and faith in Christ, in inviting them to become living members of Christ's earthly community, and to begin a life in the power of the Holy Spirit . . . The heart of the matter . . . is calling people to a personal encounter with the living Christ. [Evangelism] aims at conversion, which means a switch of allegiance to Christ and his Lordship."⁸⁷ Evangelism, understood as

---

81. Ibid. The phrases come from Hunter, *The Contagious Congregation*, 24.
82. Bosch, "Contextual Evangelism," 29.
83. Bosch, "Evangelisation, Evangelisierung," 102 (Bosch's translation).
84. Ibid.
85. Ibid. Cf. Bosch, *Theology 201*, 173.
86. This is a recurring theme for Bosch. See his "Evangelism: Theological Currents and Cross-Currents Today," 100; *Witness*, 18; "Mission and Evangelism: Clarifying the Concepts," 170; "Evangelisation, Evangelisierung," 104; and "Contextual Evangelism," 35.
87. Bosch, "Mission and Evangelism: Clarifying the Concepts," 170. Bosch also approvingly cites

the calling of persons to repentance and faith and new life in Christ, is the perpetual vocation of the church. Mission without evangelism would be like a body without a heart; it would be lifeless.[88]

Second, *evangelism has salvation and conversion as its aim*, but these realities are to be understood in *broad* rather than narrow categories. Bosch affirmed that the goal of evangelism is to call persons to repentance, faith, and new life in Jesus Christ. Evangelism inherently involves coming to Christ personally and being reconciled to God.

> We do indeed need new men and women if we are to hope for a new world; and in order to become such new men and women, individual people have to experience a personal and life-giving encounter with the risen Christ. To dispense with repentance, redemption and faith is to divest the Gospel of its central significance. A genuine, personal renewal is called for—a renewal so far-reaching and decisive an experience that Jesus referred to it as "being born all over again" (John 3: 3–8) and Paul described it as "putting on the new self which is created in God's likeness" (Eph. 4: 24). True evangelism aims at that kind of personal renewal.[89]

But the aim of true evangelism does not stop here. God's work of conversion is not mere "soul-winning." This would make God's salvation too *atomistic* and too *individualistic*. Evangelism and salvation have the *whole person in community* as the proper scope of their concern, not just the inward, "spiritual," non-material dimension of life. Salvation is "individual," but also "social" and "corporate." Bosch endorsed the *Response to Lausanne* document at this point: "[T]he new birth is not merely a subjective experience of forgiveness. It is a placement within the messianic community, God's new order which exists as a sign of God's reign to be consummated at the end of the age."[90]

He also approvingly cited Lesslie Newbigin, who wrote that it was biblically untenable to have as our evangelistic aim the salvaging of eternal souls from a perishing world; this is a "Hindu solution." "In the sharpest possible contrast to this attempt, the Bible always sees the human person realistically as a living body-soul whose existence cannot be understood apart from the network of relationships that bind the person to family, tribe, nation, and all the progeny of Adam."[91] Evangelism, for Bosch, could

the words of *Evangelii Nuntiandi* § 9, with its clear emphasis on the centrality of evangelism in Christ's salvific mission. "As kernel and centre of the good news, Christ proclaims salvation, this great gift of God which is liberation from everything that oppresses people but which is, above all, liberation from sin and the Evil One, in the joy of knowing God and being known by Him, of seeing Him and of being turned over to Him" (ibid.).

88. Bosch, "Evangelism: Theological Currents and Cross-Currents Today," 100.

89. Bosch, "Evangelism: An Holistic Approach," 53.

90. Ibid., 55–56, (Bosch's emphasis). We recall that this was the Response to Lausanne document was the creation of the so-called "radical evangelicals" at Lausanne.

91. Newbigin, "Cross-Currents in Ecumenical and Evangelical Understandings of Mission," 149, as

not be reduced to either individual or spiritual categories. To do so was to deny "the corporateness of salvation as well as the incarnational character of the gospel." Evangelism's aim is calling "human beings of flesh and blood, in *all* their relationships" to faith in Christ.[92]

The previous point leads naturally to the third thesis: evangelism *seeks to bring people into the visible community of believers*.[93] Bosch commended the WCC's *Mission and Evangelism—an Ecumenical Affirmation* for its forthright endorsement of this evangelistic aim.[94] Yet authentic evangelism that seeks to bring people into the visible community of believers is *not* the same as the recruitment of church members. Membership recruitment *may* simply be an evidence of proselytism,[95] or a desperate gimmick when membership is declining. As Bosch put it: "We tend to regard [evangelism] as a gimmick to achieve results. Says Michael Green: 'Sometimes when a church has tried everything else—in vain—it comes reluctantly round to the idea that if it is to stay in business it had better resign itself to an evangelistic campaign.' That, however, is not evangelism. It is propaganda. Unless something happens to the church itself, this kind of activity is utterly futile. We then resemble the farmer who carries his harvest into his burning barn."[96]

Evangelism may turn into "propaganda" when a church promotes its own particular doctrines or promotes self-expansion for its own sake. Too often, said Bosch, both the traditional Roman Catholic and Church Growth approaches have fallen into this trap of "institutional self-aggrandizement."[97] If measured by its faithfulness to the proclamation of the gospel, "authentic evangelism may in fact cause people *not* to join the church, because of the cost involved."[98]

Fourth, evangelism is grounded in the work of *God* in the past, present and future.[99] It is not a call for humans to put something into effect, but to respond to *God's*

---

cited by Bosch, "Evangelism: Theological Currents and Cross-Currents Today," 100.

92. Bosch, "Evangelism: Theological Currents and Cross-currents Today," 100.

93. See Bosch's "Mission and Evangelism: Clarifying the Concepts," 170; "Evangelism: Theological Currents and Cross-currents Today," 100; and "Evangelisation, Evangelisierung," 102.

94. Bosch, "Evangelism: Theological Currents and Cross-currents Today," 100. Bosch draws from ¶ 25 of the *Ecumenical Affirmation*: "It is at the heart of the Christian mission to foster the multiplication of local congregations in every human community. The planting of the seed of the Gospel will bring forward a people gathered around the Word and sacrament . . . This task of sowing the seed needs to be continued until there is, in every human community, a cell of the kingdom, a church confessing Jesus Christ." Ibid.

95. Bosch, "Evangelisation, Evangelisierung," 104.

96. Bosch, "Contextual Evangelism," 35–36. Bosch refers to Green's *Evangelism—Now and Then*, 15.

97. Bosch, "Evangelism: Theological Currents and Cross-Currents Today," 100–101.

98. Ibid., 101; Cf. Bosch,"Mission and Evangelism: Clarifying the Concepts," 170.

99. See Bosch's "Evangelism: An Holistic Approach," 49; "Mission and Evangelism: Clarifying the Concepts," 170; "Evangelisation, Evangelisierung," 104; and "Evangelism: Theological Currents and Cross-Currents Today," 101.

Part Two: Bosch's Theology of Mission and Evangelism

initiative in the sending, life, death and resurrection of Jesus Christ. Bosch summarized the Christocentric content of the good news as follows:

> This is the good news (*euangelion*): the Kingdom has come; God has manifested his justice through Jesus Christ (cf. Rom. 3: 21–27); He has conquered the powers of darkness (cf. Col. 1: 13) and triumphed over the power of death (cf. 2 Tim. 1: 10); He has, in Christ, broken down the middle wall of partition between Jews and Gentiles (Eph. 2: 14–17), which means that He has shattered all the barriers that divide the human family and has made possible a new community. What He has done once and for all in Christ, He is still doing today . . . [Evangelism] begins . . . with what God has done, is doing, and will do. Only then can the rest follow. When Jesus commenced his public ministry, He began by proclaiming, "The time has come; the Kingdom of God is upon you", and only then did he proceed to say, ". . . repent, and believe the good news". If we turn this sequence around, then the Gospel will be replaced by the Law. So evangelism is not a call to put something into effect but to respond to what has already been put into effect.[100]

Fifth, evangelism involves "*witnessing* to what God has done." Although evangelism begins with God, it is given to humans to be God's "witnesses."[101] Bosch was critical of the traditional viewpoint that evangelism is equivalent to "the verbal proclamation of the gospel." Evangelistic witness is *far more than verbal proclamation*. He based his argument on three grounds.

The teaching of the New Testament. Both the ministry of Jesus and Paul's teaching in the book of Galatians imply a much broader interpretation of *euangelizomai* than an exclusively verbal presentation of the gospel. Following the work of Richard Cook, Bosch argued that *euangelizomai* should not be translated "to preach the gospel" but rather "to live the Gospel" or "to embody the Gospel in your midst."[102]

---

100. Bosch, "Evangelism: An Holistic Approach," 49–50.

101. See Bosch's *Witness*, 18; "Evangelism: An Holistic Approach," 50–52; "Mission and Evangelism: Clarifying the Concepts," 171; "Evangelisation, Evangelisierung," 104; and "Evangelism: Theological Currents and Cross-Currents Today," 101.

102. See Bosch, "Contextual Evangelism," 31–32; and "Evangelism: An Holistic Approach," 50–53. Cf. Cook, "Paul, the Organizer," 485–98. Bosch's comments are worth repeating here, taken from "Contextual Evangelism," 31–32.

"In [Galatians] the verb *euangelizomai* appears seven times out of the twenty-one times it is used in all the Pauline epistles together. So surely, if we want to find out how St. Paul employs it, this is the place to look! Galatia was, in a particular sense, the place where the very heart of St. Paul's understanding of the Gospel was in jeopardy. In this epistle . . . he wanted to demonstrate that the gospel was more than a new teaching or a new law, but a radically new way of living . . .

Now in this epistle, *euangelizomai* should not simply be translated "preach the Gospel". "Preach", in contemporary English, implies the delivery of a sermon, as any dictionary will tell us. It simply does not convey the range of meanings that *euangelizomai* had for St. Paul. Gal. 1:11 is normally rendered as follows: "I must make clear to you . . . that the Gospel you heard me preach is no human invention". Perhaps, however, it should read: "I must make clear to you . . . that the Gospel *which I embodied in your midst* is no human invention". Elsewhere in this epistle *euangelizomai* may perhaps be translated "present the Gospel", or "live the Gospel before you". this kind of translation is given further credence by the fact that St. Paul thought

The practice of the early church. Relying on C. F. D. Moule's work in Acts, Bosch maintained that the early church gave their witness through their *actions*, their *words*, and their *community life*. "In the early church's outreach to the world . . . deeds, words and community life blended into one. In a similar vein Michael Green tells us that the early Christians evangelised by means of their example, their fellowship, their transformed characters, their joy, their endurance, and their power . . . At no stage and under no circumstances was it possible to divorce their evangelistic preaching from their total martyria."[103]

Our understanding of the communication process. Bosch believed the communication process was much more than an oral affair. To communicate a message, including the gospel, a variety of nonverbal forms are often used. Communication happens with the aid of the printed word, pictures, films, drama, deeds of love, a Christian home, a changed life. The message is conveyed through all these means.[104]

With these arguments, Bosch was not trying to downplay the indispensability of verbal witness; the meaning of deeds remains ambiguous without verbal elucidation. The Name must be named.[105] But Bosch sought to redress the balance by stressing that evangelistic witness is "by word *and* deed, proclamation *and* presence, explication *and* example."[106]

Sixth, the ministry of evangelism is a *privilege rather than a duty*. The ground of the Christian's evangelistic witness flows from his gratitude to God rather than from his obedience to a burdensome law.[107] Bosch contended that Paul understood his witness to Jesus Christ in this light. The constraining love of Christ left Paul no choice but to witness (2 Cor 5:14); his evangelistic vocation was a profound *privilege* (Rom 1:5).[108] Authentic evangelism, then, is nothing but "an overflow from Pentecost." It is "the contagion of a joy that cannot but communicate itself."[109]

---

of himself as somehow physically representing and expressing the crucified Christ to the Galatians. Christ was "openly displayed on the Cross" before their eyes (3:1) and St. Paul himself bore the marks of Jesus branded on his body (6:17). St. Paul did not conduct evangelistic "campaigns" or "crusades" in Galatia. Rather he was, in himself and his conduct, the embodiment of Christ crucified. To translate *euangelizomai* throughout with "preach the gospel" or "conduct a mission", has revivalistic overtones completely foreign to St. Paul's ministry. As a matter of fact, this entire contemporary interpretation of evangelism presupposes Christendom—a society in which it is popular to be a Christian, in which the church is a respected part of society because it does not 'turn the world upside down.' Evangelism, as it emerges from the pages of St. Paul's epistles is, however, something that involves the entire person and often takes the shape of silent suffering and compassion rather than amplified rhetoric."

103. Bosch, "Contextual Evangelism," 35. Cf. Bosch, *Witness*, 18. Bosch is relying on Moule's *Christ's Messengers*; and Green's *Evangelism in the Early Church*, 178–93.

104. Bosch, *Missiology 101*, 61.

105. Bosch, "Evangelism: Theological Currents and Cross-Currents Today," 101.

106. Ibid.

107. Bosch, "Mission and Evangelism: Clarifying the Concepts," 171.

108. Ibid. Cf. Bosch, *Witness*, 82, 246. Bosch is relying here on the argument of Paul Minear in his essay "Gratitude and Mission in the Epistle to the Romans," 42–48.

109. Bosch, "Mission and Evangelism: Clarifying the Concepts," 171. The phrases come from

Part Two: Bosch's Theology of Mission and Evangelism

Seventh, authentic evangelism includes a *positive invitation*, offering good news, salvation, joy, and freedom. The "attractions of Christ"—and not coaxing or threats—should draw people to him.[110] Bosch was critical of two common evangelistic approaches that focus on the negative. Some evangelize by seeking to inculcate guilt feelings in people, so that—motivated by despair—they will turn to Christ to be saved from their awful sinfulness. Others attempt to scare people into repentance and conversion with stories about the horrors of hell. Bosch responded that people should turn to God because they are drawn to him by his love, not because they are pushed to him for fear of hell.[111]

Eighth, authentic evangelism is "risky" because the evangelist has no control over how the gospel will impact its hearers.[112] Bosch affirmed that the gospel often "comes alive" among its hearers in entirely unexpected ways. Indeed, as the good news permeates a culture or a people, *new insights into the gospel itself* will emerge, changing the *evangelist* and *the sending church* just as much as it changes the recipients. Bosch referred to the biblical examples of Peter[113] and Paul[114] as examples of this truth. The

---

Newbigin's "Cross-Currents in Ecumenical and Evangelical Understandings of Mission," 148.

110. See Bosch's *Witness*, 18; *Missiology 101*, 62–63; "Mission and Evangelism: Clarifying the Concepts," 171; "Evangelism: Theological Currents and Cross-Currents Today," 101; and "Evangelisation, Evangelisierung," 104.

111. Bosch, "Evangelisation, Evangelisierung," 104. In "Evangelism: Theological Currents and Cross-Currents Today," 101, Bosch expands upon his strong revulsion to evangelistic "scare tactics." The citations in the quote are taken from Newbigin's "Cross-currents in Ecumenical and Evangelical Understandings of Mission," 151.

"A variation of interpreting evangelism as the inculcating of guilt feelings is to scare people into repentance and conversion with stories about the horrors of hell. Lesslie Newbigin comments on this approach: '. . . to make the fear of hell the ultimate motivation for faith in Christ is to create a horrible caricature of evangelism. I still feel a sense of shame when I think of some of the "evangelistic" addresses I have heard—direct appeals to the lowest of human emotions, selfishness and fear. One could only respect the toughminded majority of the listeners who rejected the message.' Such an appeal indeed degrades the gospel of free grace and divine love. People should turn to God because they are drawn to him by his love, not because they are pushed to him for fear of hell. Newbigin elaborates: 'It is only in the light of the grace of God in Jesus Christ that we know the terrible abyss of darkness into which we must fall if we put our trust anywhere but in that grace.' Furthermore, '[T]he grave and terrible warnings that the New Testament contains about the possibility of eternal loss are directed to those who are confident that they are among the saved. It is the branches of the vine, not the surrounding brambles, that are threatened with burning.'"

112. See Bosch's "Mission and Evangelism: Clarifying the Concepts," 172; "Contextual Evangelism," 34–35; and "Evangelism: Theological Currents and Cross-Currents Today," 101–2.

113. In the story of Peter's proclamation of the gospel to the Gentile Cornelius (Acts 10), Bosch notes that while the story has been referred to as the conversion of Cornelius, it could just as well have been titled 'The Conversion of Peter.' "The person facing the toughest decisions here is not the pagan Cornelius but the Rev. Simon Peter. Walter Hollenweger comments correctly: 'The real evangelist cannot help but take the risk that in the course of his evangelism his understanding of Christ will get corrected.' For this is precisely what happened to Peter. In Cornelius's house he did not just receive some additional theological insights, No, he began to understand Christ in a new way." See Bosch, "Evangelism: Theological Currents and Cross-Currents Today," 102. The Hollenweger quote comes from his *Evangelism Today*, 17.

114. Bosch makes a similar evaluation of the apostle Paul as Peter. Citing Catholic missiologist José Comblin, Bosch comments: "When the Spirit sent Paul to the Greeks, it was not just to evangelize them;

evangelist and the sending church must be ready to take a risk, to have their perception of Christ and his gospel modified in the course of their evangelistic outreach.[115]

Ninth, authentic evangelism is inextricably linked to the renewal of the church. It is impossible to divorce the church's evangelistic proclamation from her total witness in the world. All too often, however, this is *precisely* what the church does. When the church lacks a winsome lifestyle and societal relevance, it frequently resorts to what Bosch called "cheap evangelism."

> [Cheap evangelism] is due to the poverty of the lives of our churches. Instead of drawing people to our churches like a magnet, we repel them. Instead of causing people to stare in amazement at the newness and sparkle of our community life, we irritate those outside because we are more like them than they are themselves, or we make them yawn because we bore them through irrelevance. So we have to stage evangelistic campaigns and other special programmes in order to boost our membership and to make our tarnished image a bit more respectable. But precisely these programmes often become self-defeating because of the shallowness of the life of the church into which we receive the new converts.[116]

Only when the lifestyle of the church is *credible*, living out its faith as God's alternative community, will its evangelism be effective. Bosch pointed to the example of the early church in this regard.

> Evangelism is possible only when the community that evangelizes—the church—is a radiant manifestation of the Christian faith and has a winsome lifestyle . . . If the church is to impart to the world a message of hope and love, of faith and justice, something of this should become visible, audible, and tangible in the church itself. According to the book of Acts, the early Christian

---

it was also to make it possible for Paul himself to see the real heart of his message . . . The Spirit reveals to the Church through the mediation of new Christians . . . that many old things are not necessary, that they actually obscure the truth of Jesus Christ" (Bosch, "Evangelism: Theological Currents and Cross-Currents Today," 102). He is quoting Comblin's *The Meaning of Mission*, 107.

115. Bosch observes that this is usually not the case. "Usually when the church sends out missionaries and evangelists, it is in the firm conviction that we, the believers, are in possession of the whole truth, whereas those to whom we go, the so-called pagans, sit in darkness and are doomed. not for a moment does the church-in-evangelism and its evangelists expect that they themselves will change; all necessary changes has to take place at the 'receivers' ' end. After all, we go out to help others get converted, not to be converted ourselves!" (Bosch, "Evangelism: Theological Currents and Cross-Currents Today," 102). Bosch also notes that the evangelist who comes to see that his own understanding of Christ and the gospel will be modified in the course of his evangelistic work frequently finds himself *in conflict with the church that sent him to evangelize*. "When Peter returned to his home-base in Jerusalem those who were of Jewish birth began quarreling with him (Act 11:3). When the frontiers are crossed, when new dimensions of faith are discovered, it seems that quarrel in the church is inevitable! Usually the church takes a long time to come round to a proper understanding of evangelism. The empirical church is by nature not interested in evangelism, but in propaganda, that is, in producing carbon copies of itself. Part of the true evangelist's calling is to help the church see what evangelism really involves" ("Contextual Evangelism," 35).

116. Bosch, "As I See It," 2.

Part Two: Bosch's Theology of Mission and Evangelism

community was characterized by compassion, fellowship, sharing, worship, service, and teaching (Acts 2:42–47, 4:32–35). Its conspicuously different lifestyle became in itself a witness to Christ.[117]

Those who are evangelized do not encounter Jesus directly, but as he is mediated through the evangelist. In a very real way, the "attractiveness" of Jesus Christ is contingent upon the "attractiveness" of his messengers. Echoing Marshall McLuhan, Bosch observed that the evangelizing church is not just an *agent* of evangelism, but is *itself* part of the message.[118]

A tenth thesis (related to the previous one) is that authentic evangelism is *contextual* or *incarnational*.[119] Bosch used these terms to signify that evangelism is not merely the communication of an objective body of religious truths, but a personal, historically specific encounter between the risen Christ, the person with whom the good news is shared, and the evangelist. Bosch defined contextualization as follows:

> The *euangelion* is . . . never good news in general, but always quite concretely and contextually good news over against "bad news" which threatens and governs the lives of the addressees. Evangelism is thus never merely the proclamation of "objective" truths, but of what Emil Brunner used to refer to as "truth as encounter" . . . The gospel takes shape concretely in the witness, in the church, and is never a general, objective, immutable revelation. True evangelism is incarnational. The situation of the person to whom the gospel is being brought and the involvement, with that situation, of the one who brings the gospel, concretely determine the content of evangelism—naturally nurtured by the Scriptures.[120]

And again: "[T]he gospel is good news, but it is always good news as against the bad news of that specific society. One has to ascertain what the bad news in this society is before one is able to interpret the good news to it. It is bad news which differs from society to society. As Rev. Gottfried Osei-Mensah has pointed out, 'In various situations, sin manifests itself in various ways.'"[121]

---

117. Bosch "Evangelism: Theological Currents and Cross-Currents Today," 102, (my emphasis). Cf. Bosch "Evangelism: An Holistic Approach," 61–63; and "Evangelisation, Evangelisierung," 104.

118. See Bosch, *Missiology 101*, 63; and Bosch, *Witness*, 19. Elsewhere, he has elaborated on this point. "In evangelism . . . the first question is not *what:* what do I have to preach? What is the message I have to transmit. Neither is the first question *how:* which methods should I employ? How do I have to go about it? I believe the first question is *who:* Who am I, the evangelist? Do I embody the Christ I proclaim? How real is he to me? Am I truly his ambassador? Marshall McLuhan has taught us that the medium is the message. If this is true in communication in general, it is pre-eminently true of the church and of the evangelist" ("Contextual Evangelism," 33).

119. See Bosch's *Witness*, 18–19; "The Contextualization of the Gospel," 2; "Contextual Evangelism," 30–39.

120. Bosch, *Witness*, 18–19. This conception of the church's witness as "incarnational," as personal encounter has long been an emphasis in Bosch's writings. See his early "The Christian and the World of Today," 239.

121. Bosch, "The Contextualization of the Gospel," 2. Contextualization of the gospel should not be confused with the older missionary concern of *indigenization*. Indigenization is the concern to relate

If any evangelistic outreach is to effectively address the needs of a person or a group, the context must be allowed to "shape" the gospel. Differing contexts should draw out different facets or dimensions of the gospel. This was true of Jesus' own evangelism,[122] and should be true of the church's present missionary proclamation.[123]

If contextualization means identifying the bad news in each society in order to interpret the good news to it, then what, according to Bosch, does a contextualized evangelism imply for South Africa? Bosch affirmed clearly that ". . . the basic issue in South Africa is our racial dividedness. This is the bad news to which we have to bring the good news."[124]

The evangelist who would share the good news in a contextually relevant fashion needs discernment, sensitivity and the guidance of the Spirit to know the right approach for each context; when to emphasize the "comfort" of the gospel and when to emphasize its "challenge."[125] The evangelist also needs to be *willing to suffer*. Evangelism that seeks to proclaim the gospel in the manner of Jesus presupposes that the missionary will embody or incarnate the message he or she is preaching, even to the point of great personal sacrifice. The evangelist must be willing to be a victim rather than an exemplar.[126] True evangelists must be willing, like Paul, to identify with those among whom they minister, to the point of bearing "the marks of Jesus" in their embodiment of the gospel.[127] This, then, for Bosch, was the deepest meaning of contex-

---

the gospel to the traditional *culture* of a people. Contextualization, however, is the concern to relate the gospel to "the entire existential context of a group, in which the cultural element may be playing a very insignificant role." Because it deals with the life issues of a people, it is much more like to create controversy. See Bosch, "Crosscurrents in Modern Mission," 83.

122. Bosch emphasizes that the ministry of Jesus provides many examples of contextual evangelism. The bad news of Jesus' day included the legalism of the Pharisees, the inferior position of women, the ostracism of certain classes of people (e.g., lepers), the attitudes of Jews towards Gentiles. Bosch concludes: "In his ministry . . . Jesus challenged those things which were considered to be the very pillars of Jewish society. If he had been preaching in such a way that everything remained intact, there would never have been an uproar, there would never have been resistance and there would never have been a crucifixion" ("The Contextualization of the Gospel," 2). For examples of Jesus' contextual approach (the woman caught in adultery, Nicodemus, Zacchaeus) see Bosch, "Contextual Evangelism," 30–31. Cf. Yoder, *The Original Revolution*, 17.

123. Citing the example of Paul in Acts 14 and 17, who took a very different evangelistic approach among Gentiles than among Jews, Bosch affirms that "[I]n our proclamation of the gospel we will have to meet people on their own ground; we will have to bring the gospel *into* their religious world. And then it is unlikely that we shall be able to begin immediately with the message concerning Christ . . . Simply to repeat in our preaching the New Testament words and phrases will not take us anywhere. It will merely cause us to make one of the basic mistakes in verbal communication, viz. the confusing of words with the things they try to describe. The gospel is something God has done and is still doing, not a series of phrases . . . It has to be verbalised in a different way in every new setting" ("God in Africa: Implications for the Kerygma," 18–19).

124. Bosch, "The Contextualization of the Gospel," 2.

125. Bosch, "Contextual Evangelism," 30.

126. See Bosch, "The Missionary: Exemplar or Victim?," 9–16. Also see Bosch's five-part series "Die Lewe van die Sendingwerker."

127. Bosch, "Contextual Evangelism," 30. This is the central theme of Bosch's *A Spirituality of the Road*.

tual, incarnational evangelism: the privilege of evangelizing is *costly* because authentic evangelism involves *bearing the cross of Christ*.[128]

Finally, authentic evangelism should do more than inviting people to accept Christ as a personal savior; it should also inform them as to what following Jesus as Lord requires.[129] Bosch was highly critical of the tendency to make the personal enjoyment of salvation and the promise of eternal blessedness the center of one's evangelistic approach. While these benefits are a valid and significant result of evangelism, they should not be the primary focus.

> It is . . . not the primary purpose of evangelism to impart to people such guaranteed happiness, neither in this world or the next . . . Christ gives people joy, hope, trust, vision, relief, and courage in this life, as well as a blessed assurance for all eternity. But if the offer of all this gets center-stage attention in our evangelism, if evangelism becomes the offer of a psychological panacea, then the gospel is degraded to a consumer product and becomes the opiate of the people. Then evangelism fosters a self-centered and self-serving mind-set among people and a narcissistic pursuit of fulfilled personhood.[130]

Bosch appealed to Karl Barth in this regard. In Vol. IV/3 of *Church Dogmatics*, Barth criticizes the tendency of believers to focus upon their own personal enjoyment of grace, salvation, and their own relationship with God. This development is, according to Barth, unbiblical and egocentric; it reduces God to a dispenser of blessings. The biblical conversion stories do not emphasize the personal enjoyment of salvation. This does not mean that the enjoyment of salvation is wrong or unimportant, but that it is incidental and secondary.[131]

"What makes someone a Christian is not his personal experience of grace and redemption, but his ministry: God and his fellow human beings 'have become more important to him, and indeed qualitatively more important, than he can be to himself' . . . Indeed, he receives forgiveness, justification and sanctification in order to

---

128. René Padilla's words exemplify Bosch's call for a genuinely contextual, incarnational evangelistic approach: "It was thus—from within the situation of sinners, in an identification with them that he carried to its final consequences—that God in Christ reconciled the world to himself once and for all. This was the vertical movement of the gospel, the movement that in the Cross reached its darkest point. This is the heart of the gospel. But it is also the standard for evangelism. If God worked out reconciliation *from within the human situation*, the only fitting evangelism is that in which the Word becomes flesh in the world and the evangelist becomes "the slave of all" in order to win them to Christ (I Cor. 9:19–23). The first condition for genuine evangelism is the crucifixion of the evangelist. Without it the gospel becomes empty talk and evangelism becomes proselytism" (Padilla, *Mission Between the Times*, 25; my emphasis).

129. See Bosch, "Evangelism: An Holistic Approach," 56–61; "Mission and Evangelism: Clarifying the Concepts," 172; "Evangelisation, Evangelisierung," 104; and "Evangelism: Theological Currents and Cross-Currents Today," 102–3.

130. Bosch, "Evangelism: Theological Currents and Cross-Currents Today," 102.

131. See Bosch, "Evangelism: An Holistic Approach," 57–58; and Bosch, "Evangelism: Theological Currents and Cross-Currents Today," 102. The appropriate section in Barth is found in *Church Dogmatics* IV/3, 561–614.

be serviceable . . . Being called by God to faith in Christ means being simultaneously commissioned by God to perform a task in the world."[132]

Bosch used a series of contrasting images to distinguish between these two contrasting understandings of evangelism. "The Church exists for the world, not the world for the Church." Persons are called to Christ not "as an expression of favouritism but as election to service." People are called to become Christians "not exclusively to *receive* life . . . but rather to *give* life." They are to live "exocentric" rather than "egocentric" lives. They are to discourage "religious navel-gazing" and encourage "Kingdom-expectation and Kingdom-participation."[133]

Evangelism's deepest aim, then, is to call people to a commitment to Jesus the King, but this commitment is expressed through positive involvement in the world, through "a commitment to the purposes of the King in history."[134] Bosch affirmed Waldron Scott's call for a broader "discipleship evangelism": "An evangelistic invitation oriented toward discipleship will include a call to join the living Lord in the work of his Kingdom. It will point to specific needs in the larger world beyond the individual's private concerns. It will direct attention to the aspirations of ordinary men and women in society, their dreams of justice, security, full stomachs, human dignity, and opportunities for their children."[135] Evangelism, then, must never be understood in contradistinction to social concern. Compassionate action can never be juxtaposed against preaching a message of individual salvation.

Based upon these eleven theses, Bosch evolved a comprehensive definition of evangelism that succinctly summarizes the main themes of his approach.

> Evangelism may be defined as that dimension and activity of the church's mission which, by word and deed, offers every person, everywhere, a valid opportunity to be directly challenged to a radical reorientation of their lives, which involves, inter alia, deliverance from slavery to the world and its powers, embracing Christ as Saviour and Lord, becoming a living member of his community, and being incorporated into his service of reconciliation, peace and justice on earth and integrated into God's purpose of placing all things under the rule of Christ.[136]

---

132. "Evangelism: An Holistic Approach," 57–58. Cf. Barth, *Church Dogmatics* IV/3, 592–93.

133. All these phrases come from Bosch, "Evangelism: An Holistic Approach," 58.

134. Ibid.

135. Bosch, "Evangelism: An Holistic Approach," 58.

136. Bosch, "Evangelisation, Evangelisierung," 104–5, (Bosch's translation). Curiously, Bosch's pronouncement on the definition of evangelism in English is slightly different from the aforementioned definition in the German *Lexicon Missions-Theologischer Grundbegriffe*. In his "Evangelism: Theological Currents and Cross-Currents Today," Bosch omits the phrases "by word and deed," "deliverance from slavery to the world and its powers," and the final phrase beginning "and integrated . . ." He adds, however, that evangelism offers people "a valid opportunity to be directly challenged by the gospel of explicit faith in Jesus Christ, with a view to embracing . . ."

Part Two: Bosch's Theology of Mission and Evangelism

ASSESSING THE CHURCH GROWTH MOVEMENT

Beginning in 1954 with the publication of *Bridges of God*, and in 1970, his magnum opus *Understanding Church Growth*, Dr. Donald McGavran pioneered the increasingly influential missiological approach known as the "church growth" movement. McGavran tirelessly emphasized that the essential heart of Christian mission involves the tasks of "winning the lost" (calling people to be converted to Christ), and of planting local congregations of Christian believers in every culture. The basic conviction of church growth advocates has been that God desires the church to grow, and the church must do everything in her power to "gather in the harvest" among those peoples which are responsive to the gospel. Out of McGavran's years of missionary experience in India, he began to research why some churches experienced rapid growth while others appeared stagnant. The typical "mission station" approach tended to isolate new converts from their native culture and inculcated them with the "foreign" values and attitudes of the Western missionaries. This effectively cut them off from their own social group, and rendered them useless in evangelizing their own neighbors. Churches grew at a very slow rate.

McGavran found, however, that people became Christians more easily when they did not have to cross racial, linguistic, or class barriers. When whole homogeneous groups of people converted in a short span of time, churches grew more rapidly. Such "people movements," where the decision to convert was a corporate decision of the group or of its leaders, tended to preserve the social relationships of the community. Indigenous structures of leadership and organization remained intact, thus making it easier for the gospel to penetrate rapidly throughout that social group.

McGavran also believed that the traditional missionary approach retarded the growth of the church because of its failure to understand three distinct priorities in Jesus' Great Commission in Matt. 28: 16–20. Christian missions were called to "disciple" and "baptize." "Teaching" the converts all that Jesus had commanded was an essential but secondary concern, and could be done only after they had become members of the church. In McGavran's view, the traditional "mission station" strategy, with its emphasis on hospitals, schools, and social programs, hindered the rapid growth of the church. In such situations, the missionaries were devoting most of their time wrongly to "perfecting of the saints" (through the maintenance of mission institutions) rather than to the essential, top-priority task of "discipling" (e.g., evangelizing the lost).

The "church growth" movement has been centered around but not limited to the School of World Mission (now School of Intercultural Studies) at Fuller Theological Seminary. Thousands of students from all six continents have studied the principles of church growth at Fuller and elsewhere. Hundreds of books and unpublished graduate research studies have emerged. Numerous periodicals have been established, dedicated to spreading the church growth perspective. Many other institutes, schools and study centers have emerged across the world devoted to research, planning and mobilizing the church for growth. Two distinctive traits of the movement have been its emphasis on research and publication, and its extensive appropriation of the social sciences (especially anthropology). Such research serves as a tool to better understand those factors that foster or hinder growth.

Our brief overview does little justice to this dynamic and multifaceted movement. It has developed a legion of admirers, as well as many critics.[137] Bosch described himself as a "friend" of the Fuller School of World Mission, and his understanding of the church's mission overlapped to a considerable extent with the SWM.[138] More particularly, Bosch regarded Donald McGavran one of the remarkable missiological figures of the twentieth century, whose contribution to the theory and practice of mission was incalculable.[139] In his review of McGavran's *Understanding Church Growth*, Bosch applauded McGavran's encyclopedic knowledge of the church around the globe, his passionate concern for the growth of the church, his emphasis on the continual need for Christian missionaries to cross cultural barriers with the gospel, and his criticism of those who rationalize their own church's negligible growth rate by maintaining that "good growth is necessarily slow growth."[140] Bosch believed all these emphases are valid and timely.

While he did not claim to be an "expert" on the subject,[141] and while he never developed his criticisms in a systematic, comprehensive manner, Bosch remained a friendly but persistent critic of church growth missiology. In what follows, we shall summarize his most salient criticisms.

---

137. For a retrospective look at the Church Growth movement from the perspective of its advocates, see Glasser, "Church Growth at Fuller," 401–20; Wagner, *Church Growth and the Whole Gospel*; and also his pamphlet *The Church Growth Movement: A 30th Anniversary Assessment*, a privately published inaugural lecture at Fuller Theological Seminary, November 6, 1984). The most substantial critiques of the movement are found in Conn, *Theological Perspectives on Church Growth*; Costas, *The Church and Its Mission*, 87–149; Kraus, ed., *Missions, Evangelism, and Church Growth*; Newbigin, *The Open Secret*, 135–80; Shenk, *The Challenge of Church Growth*; and Shenk, *Exploring Church Growth*.

138. In a 1987 address to the Fuller School of World Mission, Bosch confessed that "I come as a friend, as somebody who shares much of what all of you share and who sees the mission of the church—at least to some extent—in the same terms. In our Department of Missiology at the University of South Africa we have a full course at the honors level on church growth. And the purpose of the course is not at all simply to attack church growth; in fact, the course was first developed by Johan Kritzinger, who spent a long time here at Fuller. Also, the Southern African Missiological Society is not averse to church growth . . . Our 1986 meeting was devoted to the theme, 'Living Churches Challenging the World,' and one of the major presentations was on the church growth movement, by a Fuller graduate, Chris R. de Wet . . . So you see I really do not really hail from the camp of the enemy—although I was once accused by a friend of the SWM of being an 'ecumenical evangelical'!" ("Church Growth Missiology," 13–24).

139. Personal Interview with the author, September 7, 1986.

140. Bosch, "Review of D. A. McGavran's *Understanding Church Growth*," 93.

141. Bosch, "Church Growth Missiology," 13.

Part Two: Bosch's Theology of Mission and Evangelism

Polemical Style

At a general level, Bosch criticized the *overly polemical approach* of some church growth advocates (particularly McGavran), which led to unnecessary polarization, particularly between themselves and the ecumenical movement.[142] Bosch traced this approach back to 1968, when McGavran blasted the WCC's Uppsala Assembly for "Betraying the Two Billion."[143] While Bosch believed McGavran was right to call attention to the WCC's neglect of evangelism, McGavran's intolerant outbursts lacked both historical perspective and humility.

> I would like to plead for a larger and broader historical perspective. While it is true that we live and have to act in the here and now, should we not see ourselves and what we do and believe in a broader context? Should we not be more tolerant of one another if, in a given moment, the other does not see things the way I see them? Should we not allow for shifts, for changes of emphasis, for the pendulum swinging first this way and then the other? Should we not be able to concede that—again in a given moment—my brother or sister may have priorities other than my own, and acknowledge that those priorities may be as valid as my own? Referring specifically to the WCC in the 1960's and early 1970's: Could we not, even if we do not agree with the answers given then, a least agree that they were genuine (although perhaps, misguided) attempts at grappling with the real issues?[144]

Beyond this, Bosch discerned important signs of rapprochement between ecumenicals and evangelicals since 1975, and asked whether such a shift proved so long in coming precisely because the two groups remained intolerant of one another, consigning one another to the "enemy camp."[145]

---

142. One can detect this tension between polemical and irenic attitudes very clearly by comparing the contributions of McGavran and Glasser in their jointly authored volume *Contemporary Theologies of Mission*. Comparing Glasser's work in chapters 5, 7, and 10, with McGavran's work in chapters 1, 3 and 4, the contrast in tone is striking.

143. Further, McGavran maintained "They [the WCC] do not believe that it makes an eternal difference whether men accept the Lord Jesus and are baptized in His name. They do not believe that in the Bible we have the authoritative, infallible Word of God. They cannot but oppose church growth strategy; their theology allows them to take neither the Church nor the salvation of men's souls seriously." See McGavran's "Church Growth Strategy Continued" as cited by Bosch, "Church Growth Missiology," 14.

144. Bosch, "Church Growth Missiology," 14.

145. Bosch believed evidence of such rapprochement could be found in such evangelical landmarks as the 1974 Lausanne Congress, the 1982 CRESR gathering, and the Wheaton '83 deliberations. On the ecumenical side he notes the WCC's 1982 Ecumenical Affirmation on Mission and Evangelism, and the 1987 Stuttgart Consultation on Evangelism. Bosch feels particularly grieved over those evangelicals who "break off relations with our brothers and sisters" and who judge ecumenicals "as having forsaken the gospel." Perhaps referring to such harsh critics as Peter Beyerhaus, Bosch concluded: "I therefore cannot but express my deepest sadness because of those evangelical brothers and sisters for whom the WCC always *has* to be wrong, since they believe they themselves can only be right if the WCC is proved to be wrong" (ibid., 15–16).

One manifestation of this polemical style that proved offensive to Bosch is McGavran's and others' extensive use of *military terminology* in describing the nature of the Christian mission. This "antagonistic" motif surfaces repeatedly in McGavran's writings. McGavran, in "A Giant Step in Christian Mission" (published in the WCC's *Monthly Letter on Evangelism* in August 1985), used such expressions as "victories of the cross," "mobilization," "task forces," "campaigns," "evangelizing forces," "enemy territory," "beachheads of saving faith," and "liberated areas" of "Bible-believing and Bible-obeying Christians."[146] One wonders how the objects of such "campaigns" regard this terminology!

Cultural Captivity to North American Pragmatism and Values

Bosch noted that American missiology has always had a pragmatic and not theoretical bent, in contrast, for example, with Germany.[147] Many perceive that in church growth missiology, this emphasis is not only acknowledged but celebrated.[148] Bosch acknowledged that he saw nothing wrong with pursuing a practical approach whose primary concern is the growth of the church. "We are all deeply indebted to the work the SWM has done to uncover reasons for slow growth, to use statistics properly, to evaluate existing models of evangelism critically, and to explore issues such as nominality, leadership selection and training, cross-cultural communication particularly in frontier situations, etc."[149]

Bosch believed, however, that many critics perceive that church growth missiology allows *pragmatism* to reign supreme over theological principle. Pragmatism, according to Bosch, "suggests an approach according to which everything is in order as long as it works and where the end justifies the means." In missiology, such pragmatism has been perceived as "an approach where practice has shut itself off from the critique of theology and has become a law unto itself."[150] Bosch deemed the charge of rampant pragmatism to be a somewhat unfair criticism, but he urged church growth advocates to be more circumspect in their theorizing.

---

146. Bosch questioned this use of militaristic language to describe the church's mission, as if Christians are "at war" with the world, seeking to "conquer" it. If military terms are to be used at all, they should not describe fighting solely on the frontier between belief and unbelief. They should be used in conjunction with the coming of the Kingdom of God, God's reign of peace and justice. Other frontiers such as poverty, hunger, oppression, injustice, etc. are also evils that must be attacked as well. Citing some of McGavran's terminology, Bosch concludes: "Let us by all means take a giant step forward and 'furiously organize' Christian 'task forces,' but let them then be in the forefront of the struggle on *all* the frontiers between the kingdom of God and the kingdom of evil" (Bosch, Kritzinger, Meiring, and Saayman, "Response to Donald McGavran," 8–9).
147. Bosch, "Missiology," 161–62.
148. Cf. Wagner, "Consecrated Pragmatism" in *Church Growth and the Whole Gospel*, 69–86.
149. Bosch, "Church Growth Missiology," 18.
150. Ibid.

Part Two: Bosch's Theology of Mission and Evangelism

Many church growth advocates place too high a premium on numerical growth alone. In the minds of many critics, says Bosch,

> There is something typically capitalistic and American in Church Growth theory. Two very secular motifs appear to lie behind the theory: the one is that one should invest one's money where the greatest dividends are promised; the concomitant motif is that "free enterprise" is the key to achieving our objectives: the more new agencies and specialised ministries we can devise for different "target audiences", the surer we may be of success. In contrast to this, so it appears to me, genuine . . . evangelism will not always be successful if measured quantitatively. In fact, it may even lead to a numerical decline in membership.[151]

Bosch believed that the differing contexts of various countries and situations militated against making the *numerical* growth of the church a permanent top priority. "There are situations," said Bosch, "where the church can evangelize boldly and others where it can not."[152] Depending upon how the church is perceived by the society, differing priorities emerge at different times. Bosch recalled the contribution of Halina Bortnowska at the 1980 Melbourne Assembly, where she contrasted the church in Poland, where it was regarded as a *sign of hope*, with the church in Holland, where it had become a *sign of guilt*, where Christians perceived themselves to be a part of the problem of their society. In the former, a quest for maximal church growth is a viable option; in the latter, it is not. Bosch thought that since 1949, the church in China has served as a great *sign of hope* for many. It is this factor that helps explain the massive numerical growth of the church in that land. It now has legitimacy and credibility to proclaim the gospel with great effectiveness and power. In South Africa, on the other hand, the White church had become a *sign of guilt*. In such a context the emphasis must be different; *not* on the numerical growth of the church, but "showing solidarity with the weak, the marginalised, and the oppressed . . ." Bosch passionately believed that such a stance would be profoundly evangelistic, "leading to church growth at another moment in history." Even in America there are places that are "over-evangelised," where the central priority of the church must be "a demonstration of the authenticity and depth of our Christian faith."[153]

Church growth missiology's emphasis on "responsiveness" also comes in for criticism by Bosch. Persons and societies deemed "resistant" to the gospel are all too frequently devalued or ignored. Resources and energy are to be poured into more responsive areas. This approach, says Bosch, was too pragmatic. The history of mission is filled with examples "where missionaries had laboured faithfully for decades without any registrable results, only to see the next generation come pouring into the church."[154]

---

151. Bosch, "Contextual Evangelism," 29. Cf. Bosch, "The Church in South Africa—Tomorrow," 174–75.

152. Bosch, "Church Growth Missiology," 18.

153. Ibid., 18–19. Cf. Bosch, "The Melbourne Conference Between Guilt and Hope," 512–18.

154. Bosch, "Church Growth Missiology," 19. Bosch repeats the story of German missiologist Walter

A final way Bosch believed that North American values had pervaded the church growth movement was its emphasis on technology and financial resources in the missionary enterprise. On this basis, the impetus of missionary advance will remain in the hands of the wealthy countries of Europe and North America rather than the impoverished "South." This however, ignores the fact that it is precisely in lands where the church has *suffered* the most, and has had the *least* technological and financial resources available to it, where church growth has been strong (e.g., China and the Soviet Union). This emphasis also perpetuates the idea that mission does not really happen in all six continents. Missionary "traffic" becomes a "one-way" rather than multi-directional affair.[155]

Simplistic Hermeneutic

Bosch criticized the church growth movement for failing to develop an adequate biblical foundation. "Hermeneutically," he said, "there is in the church growth movement . . . the tendency to handle the biblical material too self-confidently and to build on one text the whole mystery of mission."[156] This inadequacy revealed itself, exegetically speaking, in two ways. In McGavran's exegesis of Matt 28: 16–20, he made a specious distinction between "discipling" and "perfecting," and he interpreted the *panta ta ethne* clause ethnologically rather than theologically.

A Disjunction Between "Discipling" and "Perfecting"

In his understanding of the Great Commission mandate, McGavran's distinguished between "discipling"—an initial conversion experience of an individual or a people, where they turn from non-faith to faith in Christ and incorporation into his church— and "perfecting"—the ethical instruction given to Christians to become an informed and socially responsible follower of Christ.[157] "Discipling" is essentially a synonym for "evangelizing," while "perfecting" involves the total "Christianization" of the evangelized group. Bosch criticized McGavran on two counts. First, the biblical text does not allow his separation of "discipling" and "perfecting" into two successive and separate activities. The very act of "making disciples" involves "teaching." Second, McGavran's definition of "discipling" (*matheteuein*) is not consistent with Matthew's own understanding of the word. There is an inseparable link between discipleship, a personal

---

Freytag, who visited a Lutheran mission post in Egypt in the 1950s. "At the time of his visit the missionaries had already been labouring there for 52 years. And all they could show for their labour was one convert who, in the meantime, had disappeared. Freytag commented: 'Only then did I understand what mission really is: to praise the Lord Jesus in the midst of the nations, irrespective of the results'" (ibid.). Cf. Bosch, *Witness*, 173–74.

155. See Bosch et al., "Response to Donald McGavran," 9.
156. Bosch, "The Structure of Mission," 241.
157. Bosch, "The Structure of Mission," 230–31. Cf. McGavran's *Understanding Church Growth*, 169–72.

Part Two: Bosch's Theology of Mission and Evangelism

relationship to Jesus, and the pursuit of God's justice. Based on Bosch's own exegesis of Matt 28:16–20, Bosch concluded that "neither McGavran's juxtaposition of discipling and perfecting as two consecutive stages, nor his definition of making disciples as calling a people to an initial turning to Christ, is tenable. To become a disciple is to be incorporated into God's new community through baptism and to side with the poor and oppressed. To put it differently, it is to love God and our neighbour. This is what Jesus commanded his disciples (Mt. 28:19). And of course, for Matthew this obedience is determined not by a conformity to any impersonal commandment but by relationship to Jesus himself."[158]

This disjunction between discipling and perfecting in McGavran's missiology is important because it leads to a false understanding of mission and evangelism. For McGavran, Wagner, and other church growth advocates, the "evangelistic mandate" (discipling) takes priority over the "social mandate" (perfecting). Evangelism is the "seed," whereas social concern is the "fruit"; personal regeneration is the key to social transformation.[159] Any approach, they maintained, that puts social responsibility on an equal plane with evangelism is bound to blunt the effectiveness of the church's missionary outreach.[160] As we have seen in the preceding sections of this chapter, Bosch believed that the concern to prioritize verbal proclamation above all other missionary activities was a faulty way of understanding of mission and evangelism. It is biblically indefensible and unnecessarily polarizing. Everything that the church does should have an evangelistic *dimension*, but this does not mean that always and everywhere, verbal proclamation is to be given top priority. Likewise, when the church reaches out in responsible social involvement, it is *implicitly* involved in evangelism.[161]

A Misreading of panta ta ethne

In McGavran's exegesis of the Great Commission mandate, he also misunderstood the concept of *ethne* ("nations"), interpreting the word in terms of its ethnological and sociological sense—as homogeneous units of people with common affinities. This was a *crucial* interpretation for McGavran, because it provided the heart of his missionary methodology, the "homogeneous unit principle" (HUP). McGavran argued that because people *like* to become Christians without having to cross racial, linguistic, or class barriers, and because numerical church growth is the top priority of mission, then Christian missionaries must adopt a strategy of evangelizing and planting churches among the world's peoples *within all the existing homogeneous units*. Peter

---

158. Bosch, "The Structure of Mission," 234–35.
159. Bosch, "Church Growth Missiology," 16–17.
160. Cf. Wagner, *Church Growth and the Whole Gospel*, 50–68, 87–129.
161. Bosch, "Church Growth Missiology," 17. Bosch comments that "during the 1950's and 1960's the American south produced two great men of God, both Baptists—Billy Graham and Martin Luther King, Jr. Was only Graham an evangelist? Was King not, in a profound way, also evangelising, calling people to faith, to a commitment, to solidarity with the Kingdom of God and its cause?" (ibid.).

Wagner's subsequent work *Our Kind of People* built on this basic concept, concluding that the HUP is the hermeneutical key to the New Testament that explains Jesus' exclusivism during his earthly ministry and provides a model for ethnically distinct homogeneous congregations.[162]

Bosch fully agreed that the gospel must be communicated in an intelligible way to its hearers; it must be "contextualized in the culture of the people who are being evangelized."[163] He acknowledged that at the local level, specific congregations should function "primarily within the orbit of one cultural context—as long as we do not define that cultural context too narrowly."[164] Yet Bosch remained strongly critical of the HUP for two reasons.

First, the wording of the Great Commission does not justify the modern proposition that Jesus commissioned his followers to "disciple" the various ethno-linguistic nations in their separate "homogeneous units." This modern problem of missionary strategy, Bosch believed, had been *read back into the text*.[165] The *ethne* in Matt 28:19 were interpreted by McGavran, Wagner and Tippett in ethnic terms. As McGavran put it: "[Jesus] had in mind the families of mankind—tongues, tribes, castes and lineages of men. That is exactly what *ta ethne* means . . . in Matthew 28:19."[166] In his exegesis of verse 19, Bosch argued against this interpretation.[167] *Ethne* refers to Gentiles (and perhaps to the Jews as well) not in a socio-ethnic but in a *religio-ethical* sense. The context makes clear that Jesus had in view the entire world of humanity, the *oikoumene*. Other Greek words would have been more suitable for Matthew if he had meant to refer to "nations" in the sociological sense of separate ethnic units. All of the parallels to the Great Commission and other related passages in the gospels confirm

---

162. It must be acknowledged that church growth proponents have *never* endorsed the establishment of *segregated* churches, officially excluding members of other ethnic groups. They condemn this as racism. They do affirm, however, that as a *penultimate evangelistic strategy*, the HUP provides a helpful tool in evangelizing the thousands of distinct "people groups" around the world. It is simply a tool. Wagner admits, however (in his *Church Growth and the Whole Gospel*, 169), the danger of the HUP in the South African context. Wagner comments: "It appears to some that encouraging the formation of homogeneous unit churches is implicitly placing a seal of approval on segregation, discrimination, racism, the caste system, and apartheid. Much to the dismay of church growth leaders, it has, at times, been used for those ends. Ralph D. Winter made a plenary session presentation that incorporated the homogeneous unit principle. A few weeks later we heart that some white South African participants had played tapes of Winter's address on the radio to prove that Lausanne had endorsed apartheid. Approving apartheid was so far from Winter's mind that the whole affair seemed ludicrous. But just as a knife can be used as an instrument of mercy in a surgical operation or as an instrument of horror in a murder, the homogeneous unit principle can be used for good or bad. Properly applied, it can be an effective force to reduce racism; wrongly applied, it can support racism. It must be admitted that the principle carries with it an element of risk."

163. Bosch, "The Structure of Mission," 236.

164. Bosch, "Nothing But a Heresy," 34.

165. Bosch, "The Structure of Mission," 236.

166. McGavran, *Understanding Church Growth*, 56.

167. Bosch, "The Structure of Mission," 235–40.

Part Two: Bosch's Theology of Mission and Evangelism

this interpretation.[168] The real point of mentioning "all nations" is to emphasize that in the Christ-event, God's salvation-history has been universalized. God's redemption has crossed into the whole world, no longer restricted to the confines of Judaism.[169] In Bosch's view, the word *ethne* was thus "completely unrelated to the question of homogeneous units."[170]

Second, the HUP bears a striking if unintentional resemblance to one line of late nineteenth and early twentieth-century German missiology. Gustav Warneck, Bruno Gutmann and Christian Keysser) emphasized *Volkschristianisierung*, the conversion of a people as a homogeneous ethnic unity.[171] In the approach of such missiologists, the *Volk* concept took on an extraordinary importance. As Bosch put it:

> German missiology would show a remarkable parallel development with German political thinking in general. The concept Volk, deeply influenced by Romanticism, was given a theological weight that could not but secularize the theological and biblical concept. It derived its content not from Scripture but from the contemporary scene... For Gutmann the fellow-Christians are hardly distinguishable from the compatriots; through their sharing in the urtümliche Bindungen (primordial ties) they are sociologically circumscribed. There is therefore an abiding connection between church and Volk (Hoekendijk). Thus "the foundations of the Church are sought as much in anthropological as in soteriological considerations, and in the end the anthropological elements crowd the soteriological into a corner (Boer)."[172]

Historically speaking, this perspective was very influential among Afrikaner theologians.[173]

Bosch objected strenuously to this German missiological approach because it elevates ethnic differentiation into a theological principle. One's ethnic heritage becomes a constituent factor in the formation and structure of the church. As Bosch put it: "Class prejudices and people's alienation from each other only becomes more deeply ingrained

---

168. Ibid., 236.

169. In another context, Bosch points out how Martin Kähler long ago affirmed that "it is not nations as ethnic entities that are called into the Kingdom, but *humanity*, through individuals." See his "Systematic Theology and Mission," 174.

170. Bosch, "The Structure of Mission," 237.

171. "Bosch, Nothing But a Heresy," 26–28; "The Structure of Mission," 238–40; and Bosch et al., "Response to Donald McGavran," 7–8. Cf. Bosch, *Witness*, 134.

172. Bosch, "The Structure of Mission," 238. Bosch refers to the major works of Johannes Hoekendijk and Harry Boer here. See the former's *Kerk en volk in de duitse zendingswetenschap*; and the latter's *Pentecost and Missions*.

173. Bosch notes that "German missiology and Keysser in particular, with their concept of an 'ethnic church' had a great influence on the Dutch Reformed Church's policy of constituting racially separated churches in South Africa. In fact, it can be argued that they provided a great deal of the theological justification for this policy. For this reason Keysser, Gutmann and others have been studied extensively by South African scholars..." (Bosch et al., "Response to Donald McGavran," 7).

in the human heart where ethnicity is regarded as an intrinsic feature of the church..."[174] Although the *Volkschristianisierung* approach did not set out to create racially exclusive churches, "the tragic reality is that [this] approach eventually provided the theological justification for racially separated churches, e.g. in South Africa."[175]

While acknowledging there are important differences between church growth missiology and the German *Volkschristianisierung* missiology,[176] Bosch remained profoundly uneasy with church growth proponents in this regard. He pointed out that Wagner, in his apologetic for Jesus' supposed ethnic exclusivism in *Our Kind of People*, makes precisely the same argument that Gutmann made long ago. Keysser's major work *Eine Papua Gemeinde* has been "rediscovered," translated, and published by the Church Growth movement. McGavran once described Keysser as a "genius" whose approach to mission is tremendously important.[177] In light of these developments, Bosch concluded that

> As South African missiologists we are therefore not convinced that the "unreached peoples' approach" is simply a practical tool to speed up the evangelization of the world; this same argument was used in 1857 when the white DRC in South Africa took its momentous decision to introduce racial separation into the church... [A] seemingly admirable evangelistic practice can become an heretical ideology in a world where racism is still too prevalent... Until the serious theological questions about the people's approach have been taken seriously, we cannot be enthusiastic about a scheme such as McGavran proposes.[178]

Inadequate Ecclesiology

A final, related criticism concerned the inadequate ecclesiology of the church growth movement. This brings us to the crux of Bosch's critique. Church growth theory in general (and the HUP in particular) neglects and downplays the fundamental theological significance of the *unity of the church*, which compromises the very heart of the gospel. This is not a coincidence, for Bosch believed that Protestants in general

---

174. Bosch, "The Structure of Mission," 239; and Bosch et al., "Response to Donald McGavran," 8.

175. Bosch et al., "Response to Donald McGavran," 7.

176. "This is not to suggest that what the Church Growth movement has in mind with its interpretation of *panta ta ethne* is in all respects the same as that which German missionary thinkers in the latter part of the nineteenth and early twentieth century read into this expression. At an early stage of the development of the Church Growth movement Harry Boer already cautioned that by 'peoples' McGavran did not have in mind an anglicized version of the German concept of *Volk*, with its idea of the socially unifying and integrating power that arises from the bonds of common blood and common soil" (Bosch, "The Structure of Mission," 239). Bosch refers here to Boer's *Pentecost and Missions*, 169, 179.

177. See Bosch, "The Structure of Mission," 239; and Bosch et al., "Response to Donald McGavran," 7. The Keysser work and McGavran's preface can be found in McGavran, *A People Reborn*.

178. Bosch, "Response to Donald McGavran," 8. It is important to note that the HUP has been a much-disputed missiological concept, even within evangelical missiology. See Stott, ed., *The Pasadena Consultation—Homogeneous Unit*.

Part Two: Bosch's Theology of Mission and Evangelism

and evangelicals in particular have a "low" view of the church. Unity is rarely a major concern, and when it is, it is primarily sought for functional, pragmatic reasons.[179]

Bosch was particularly disturbed at McGavran's disregard for the unity of the church, fearing that McGavran's writings displayed a tendency of reading church growth principles and categories back into the Bible. He also questioned whether McGavran had really come to grips with the *biblical* demands of discipleship and conversion.

> I must . . . confess that I was deeply disturbed when I read in the revised edition of Dr. McGavran's *Understanding Church Growth*: "Sometimes a church splits and both sections grow" (pp. 3–4, 159). Apparently, in this view, growth is more important than unity. But may we ever juxtapose the two? Should our concern not be for the growth of the one church . . . Can we really argue—with reference to the slowness with which the early church came to a missionary involvement among Gentiles—that it was "only after the one-people Church grew strong among the Jews" that the Holy Spirit "led it out to win the Gentiles"? (p. 241). Would it not be equally (if not more!) valid to argue that it was because of a lack of understanding of what the gospel was all about that they did not go to the Gentiles sooner?
>
> Dr. McGavran does not seem to be disturbed by the fact that the "Jewish caste had no dealings with the half-breed Samaritans" (p. 231 . . .). But was not Jesus' entire ministry a sustained critique of this attitude? On the same page Dr. McGavran suggests that there are "no reasons to believe that Christian Jews started to interdine" with Samaritan and Gentile converts—but it this was so, what is Galatians 2 all about? Again, Dr. McGavran seems to show understanding for "would-be Jewish converts" who found "the racial and cultural barriers too high and turned sorrowfully away" when they discovered that becoming Christians might mean "joining a house church full of Gentiles and sitting down to agape feasts where on occasion pork was served" (p. 231). Now, if this kind of attitude is condoned, what were Paul's many passionate pleas for unity all about? Dr. McGavran rightly states that biblical barriers must not be played down when people are called to faith, but isn't not accepting others as brothers and sisters also a "biblical barrier" we dare not circumvent? Can we really just relegate all of this to the "fruits" of conversion: once people grow in the faith, they will gradually accept others as equals and as brothers and sisters? Does not the reality of the churches around us point in the opposite direction? Is it not true that many churches gradually develop into clubs for religious folklore

---

179. Bosch noted Protestantism's weak ecclesiology in "Church Growth Missiology," 20, noting that: "We have a lamentable history of splits upon splits, mostly, I fear, for very questionable reasons. We are not strong on the centrality of the unity of the church. I have seen, in my own denomination, how a weak ecclesiology has opened the door to racially segregated churches and what this has done to the credibility and evangelism of the church. I have seen other denominations—particularly Anglicans and Roman Catholics—where their White members were also racially prejudiced, no less than the Dutch Reformed Church members, *yet they found themselves incapable of giving up on the unity of the church. That unity was not something on which they decided or could decide. It was a given, it was part of the gospel itself*" (my emphasis).

and become increasingly introverted, xenophobic, and victims of ethnic, class or cultural captivity? And if this is the case, is it not because something went wrong far back, perhaps right at the beginning of such a church?[180]

We cite this lengthy passage because it reveals Bosch's central critique of church growth missiology: *it distorts our understanding of the church and of the gospel itself.* The church, in McGavran's thought, is too often viewed in merely functional categories, and he betrays very little concern for the church's credibility in the world.[181] McGavran would have had great difficulty with Bosch's emphasis on the church as God's new, alternative community, where a crucial dimension of the good news is precisely that the existing walls between peoples have been broken down in Christ. The act of reconciliation with God *simultaneously* involves joining a community where people no longer find their identity in their race, sex, culture or class, but in Jesus Christ.[182]

Despite these critical comments, Bosch affirmed that the church growth school presents many valid challenges to the Christian world mission in our era. Missionaries and church agencies who ignored the challenges McGavran's posed did so at their peril.[183] He believed the Fuller School of World Mission had "an absolutely crucial role to play in years to come,"[184] and that with the addition to the Fuller faculty of such missiological scholars as Eddie Gibbs[185] and Charles Van Engen,[186] the SWM had taken steps towards resolving some of the theological and ecclesiological issues raised by Bosch's critique.

---

180. Bosch, "Church Growth Missiology," 20–21. Cf. Bosch, "Review of D. A. McGavran's *Understanding Church Growth*," 93–94.

181. Bosch, "Review of D. A. McGavran's *Understanding Church Growth*," 94. On the same page, Bosch cites McGavran's unfortunate comment that "The student of church growth . . . cares little whether a Church is credible; he asks how much it has grown."

182. See chapter 8 for an elaboration of this point.

183. At the end of his review Bosch challenges all missiologists to take McGavran's work with the utmost seriousness, and to strengthen those areas where church growth theology is inadequate. "We should not throw out the proverbial baby with the bathwater. There are so many *valid* challenges in McGavran's book, challenges which all of us *ought* to hear and take up, so much of what this grand and intrepid old man is drawing our attention to is of the utmost importance, so many missionaries and churches are guilty of the mistakes and shortcomings he identifies, that we ignore at our peril his passionate pleas for a reorientation of much of what we do as churches. I firmly believe that the essence of what McGavran stands for can be integrated into a theologically sounder framework. Let those of us who differ from him, not be found wanting in remedying those maladies he diagnoses so correctly" ("Review of D. A. McGavran's *Understanding Church Growth*," 94).

184. Bosch, "Church Growth Missiology," 23.

185. Dr. Eddie Gibbs is a British pastor and theologian from the Church of England. His *I Believe in Church Growth*, attempted to provide a deeper theological foundation for church growth thinking, and dealt extensively with the relation of the church and the kingdom of God.

186. Dr. Van Engen is a missiologist from the Reformed Church in America, with missionary experience in Latin America. His doctoral thesis "The Growth of the True Church" (under Johannes Verkuyl at the Free University of Amsterdam) is a critical study of the ecclesiology of the church growth movement.

Part Three

Crucial Theological Dimensions
for a Missionary Church

Introduction

The Missionary Nature of the Church as the Theological Horizon for Bosch's Missiology

WE HAVE OUTLINED THE historical and theological context out of which David Bosch emerged. We have briefly examined his theological methodology and surveyed the major motifs in his thought. We have detailed the way he develops a biblical foundation for his theology of mission, and analyzed certain pivotal issues in his theology of mission and evangelism. In the next three chapters, we will probe into the theological structure of Bosch's missiological thought, and attempt to show its relevance to the apartheid-era South African situation in which Bosch lived and worked.

Bosch defined mission as "the total task which God has set the Church for the salvation of the world."[1] Every word in this statement is filled with meaning. What is the fundamental theological relationship between God, church, salvation, and world? In the following chapters we will attempt to unpack Bosch's understanding of the meaning of this statement, highlighting three Christian doctrines that emerge therefrom: eschatology, ecclesiology, and soteriology. These doctrines provide a vital framework for Bosch's thought, and serve as a springboard into the heart of his theology of mission.[2]

We want to avoid two errors as we approach our task. First, we want to avoid positing any single word or concept as "the key" to understanding Bosch's theology of mission. No such word—for example, "witness" or "salvation" or *"missio Dei"* or "alternative community"—can do justice to the various dimensions of his missiological

---

1. Bosch, "Evangelism: An Holistic Approach," 47.

2. The idea to ground our reflections upon Bosch's theology of mission in the doctrines of eschatology, ecclesiology, and soteriology doctrines derives from Bosch himself, and his four theses which arise out of the "creative tension" between evangelicals and ecumenical mission theologies. There are doubtless other doctrines that could be used to unfold Bosch's theology of mission, but we judge these three to be the most central.

Part Three: Crucial Theological Dimensions for a Missionary Church

thought. Bosch was always sharply critical of reductionist approaches that oversimplify the issues involved, flattening out all subtle differences and creative tensions.[3] Approaching his theology of mission from a number of different theological approaches or "angles" will be a safeguard in this respect.

Second, we do not want to isolate these three doctrines unnecessarily. Rather we seek to bring out a tripartite theological structure that is discernable (albeit implicitly) within the writings of David Bosch. We seek to examine a single reality—Bosch's understanding of the church in mission—from three different standpoints. The motifs of eschatology, ecclesiology, and soteriology provide three distinct "points of entry" into his theology of mission.

This tripartite framework of Bosch's theology of mission stands, however, within the larger context of *the missionary nature of the church*. This concept has gained increasing prominence as a result of the work of Karl Barth[4] and Emil Brunner[5] (among Protestants) and Vatican II (among Roman Catholics).[6] Protestant missiology has reflected this understanding of the "missionary nature of the church" since the 1952 Willingen Conference. Johannes Blauw's influential work *The Missionary Nature of the Church* was also influential in this regard. Lutheran missiologist James Bergquist goes so far as to affirm "the widespread recognition of the essentially missionary character of the church" is "the most important development in the current theology of mission."[7]

Even a cursory reading of Bosch shows that "the Church as a missionary community" lay at the very heart of Bosch's missiological agenda. His writings repeatedly called attention to the church as God's missionary community on earth. The church's

---

3. This is Bosch's major criticism of DuBose's work *God Who Sends*, and also his complaint against some aspects of the 'BISAM' project of the International Association of Mission Studies. They reduced mission to the concepts of "send/sending" and "witness," respectively. See Bosch, "Mission in Biblical Perspective," 533; and Bosch, "Towards a Hermeneutic for 'Biblical Studies and Mission,'" 65–79.

4. See Scott, *Karl Barth's Theology of Mission*, 16–25 Cf. Bosch, *Witness*, 164–67.

5. Brunner's dictum that "the Church exists by mission as fire exists by burning" is a classic statement of the position. See his *The Word and the World*, 108.

6. See Power, *Mission Theology Today*, 33–58. Cf. the Vatican II Decree *Ad Gentes*.

7. Bosch, "Evangelism in Current Ferment and Discussion: A Bibliographical Survey," 59. Two theologians who attempted to spell out the theological and practical implications of conceiving the church to be essentially missionary in nature are Carl Braaten (Lutheran) and John Piet (Reformed). Braaten links the missionary nature of the church with its true identity. He states: "The doctrine of the Church needs to be reconceived within the larger horizon of the eschatological mission of God in world history. *The very being of the church is shaped by its missionary calling to go into the uttermost parts of the world*. The missionary structure of the church derives from its apostolic origin . . . A church with an identity crisis can do no missionary good. But *its true identity is precisely a missionary one*. The church's identity does not lie in itself. It can only find itself by losing itself and define itself while being *en route*. It is always in an eccentric position" (Braaaten, *The Flaming Center*, 57; my emphasis).

Piet echoes Braaten's concern. "The chief concern of the church today is mission—the call to solve the tremendous problems of society, and the cry of man for authentic life. *The church must describe itself anew in terms of its essential nature and develop a theology commensurate with the church's reason for being*. This procedure will create a method whereby the church looks to God and the world and then to itself as the people of God in the world, people who are God's agents of reconciliation" (Piet, *The Road Ahead*, 12; my emphasis).

The Missionary Nature of the Church as the Theological Horizon for Bosch's Missiology

whole existence has a missionary character; she is missionary by her very nature.[8] We believe Bosch unfolds his entire theology of mission in relation to the church as an essentially missionary community. The goal of the following chapters, therefore, is *to show how Bosch interpreted the meaning of the doctrines of eschatology, ecclesiology, and soteriology from the standpoint of the church in mission.*

In what follows, therefore, we shall expound how Bosch linked the three aforementioned doctrines to an integral understanding of the church as God's missionary community. We turn first to the eschatological dimension of the missionary church—the church as *the kingdom community*. In this dimension of her existence, she acts as an instrument of and witness to the present and future Reign of God. Here we explore the creative tension between such eschatological concepts as kingdom, church, and world. Next we turn to the ecclesiological dimension of the missionary church—the church as *the alternative community*. In this dimension of her life, she is set apart from the world and called to a life of costly discipleship. She is set apart, however, precisely for the sake of the world. As God's alternative community, she exemplifies to the world the radical implications of the new age, and acts as a servant and witness to the world. Finally, we turn to the soteriological dimension of the missionary church—the church as *the reconciled and reconciling community*. In this dimension of her existence, she serves as a sign and agent of God's reconciliation. She embodies in her own life and actions the costly, reconciling love of God in Christ, and thus, in a real sense, participates in the very life of the triune God.

---

8. For example, see Bosch *Witness*, 82–83, 98–99, 245; Bosch, "Missiology," 3rd ed., 272–76; and Bosch, "Vision for Mission," 9–10. This perspective developed extensively in Bosch's writings was a foundational precursor to the contemporary missional church movement, whose proponents were mentioned in the introduction. It is significant here to note that along with Lesslie Newbigin, David Bosch must be seen as a foundational source for the theological foundations of the missional church perspective in contemporary missiology.

7

The Eschatological Dimension of the Missionary Church

The Church as Witness to the Kingdom of God

ESCHATOLOGY AND MISSION

Introduction

WHEN THE WORD "ESCHATOLOGY" is used in theological discourse, at least two things are signified.[1] Traditionally understood, eschatology means the doctrine of "last things," pointing to the end of time (the finis of history). It has traditionally been understood in terms of the Second Coming of Christ, the resurrection of the dead, the final judgment, the coming of the kingdom, and the future states of heaven and hell.[2] Within much of modern theology, however, eschatology is used to refer to the power of God in Christ through the Spirit working out his purposes within world history as well as beyond it. It refers to the meaning of historical events and the goal of world history (the telos of history).[3] In these newer Christian eschatologies, the kingdom remains the goal of God's work in history, and the church is an instrument—although not the only instrument—through which God's reign in Christ is established. Both traditional and revisionist eschatologies are unified, however, in their quest to under-

---

1. On this point, see Kuzmic, "History and Eschatology: Evangelical Views," 136; and Marshall, "Slippery Words: Eschatology," 264–69.

2. Representative works of "traditional" eschatology are Bloesch, *Essentials of Evangelical Theology*, 2:174–234; and Hoekema, *The Bible and the Future*.

3. Representative works in this approach would include Berkhof, *Christ the Meaning of History*; and Moltmann, *The Theology of Hope*.

The Eschatological Dimension of the Missionary Church

stand and provoke "the transition from the old order of things that is breaking down to a new order in which peace, righteousness, and love will reign." They desire to know the "personal, social and cosmic dimensions of salvation which the gospel promises will be realized in the fullness of God."[4] We now turn to consider the relationship of mission and eschatology in recent Protestant missiology.

The Eschatological Framework of Twentieth-Century Mission Theology

Lutheran theologian Carl Braaten has that remarked "No history of twentieth-century theology could be written without taking into account the variant meanings of eschatology. The diversity runs the gamut from Karl Barth to Rudolf Bultmann and from Wolfhart Pannenberg to Gustavo Gutierrez. It is not surprising then that eschatology has placed its stamp on the theology of mission that comes out of the twentieth century."[5]

It is beyond the scope of this thesis to provide a detailed historical and theological survey of the eschatological framework of twentieth-century missiology.[6] We seek only to sketch out the main lines of recent developments, in order to set the context for understanding Bosch's contribution to the debate.

At the beginning of the twentieth century the missionary approaches of Gustav Warneck and John R. Mott held sway, which emphasized an almost unbroken continuity between Christian (Western!) civilization and the gospel. Missions were optimistic about the growth of Christianity across the globe. Mott himself discerned many propitious "signs of the times" (linked to the advance of Western science and technology) that were serving to advance the gospel on many fronts.[7] Evidence of this spirit of optimism can readily be found in the proceedings of the Edinburgh 1910 World Missionary Conference, and the hopeful slogan of the Student Volunteer Movement "The evangelization of the world in this generation." One has only to read Warneck, Mott and other authors of the period to see the radically different worldview that held sway at the time. Indeed, the Edinburgh conference—despite its occurrence in 1910—could well be considered the last of the great

---

4. Both citations are from Braaten, *The Flaming Center*, 52–53.

5. Ibid., 29.

6. Numerous helpful expositions of the subject exist. Besides Bosch's discussion of the subject (in *Witness*, 140–95 passim) we note the following treatments: see Braaten, *The Flaming Center*, 9–63; Kuzmic, "History and Eschatology: Evangelical Views," 135–63; Kwak, "Eschatology and Christian Mission"; Saunders, "Christian Eschatology: The Ground and Impetus for Mission," 3–10; Smith, "The Eschatological Drive of God's Mission," 209–16; Strothmann, "Eschatology and the Mission of Christianity"; and Wiedenmann, *Mission und Eschatologie*.

7. See his *The Decisive Hour of Christian Missions*. The very title of the book exhibits the challenging sense of eschatological optimism that prevailed in Mott's mind.

Part Three: Crucial Theological Dimensions for a Missionary Church

nineteenth-century missions conferences, with its indefatigable optimism about the progress of the gospel in the world.[8]

World War I shattered this spirit of optimism. Theologically speaking, two other events challenged this optimistic, "progress-oriented" missiology. First was the rediscovery of the eschatological message of Jesus in the theology of the New Testament. The radical, apocalyptic nature of the kingdom, uncovered by such scholars as Weiss, Kähler, and Schweitzer, helped to dispel any notion that it was realizable through the ethical and evolutionary progress of humankind. Allied to this was the emergence of Karl Barth's dialectical theology, with its emphasis on the radical distinction between heaven and earth, between God's transcendental kingdom and humankind's transitory efforts. In Barth's approach, all human endeavors, including the Christian mission, are provisional and limited. Mission belongs to God alone.[9]

The Barthian approach began to influence continental missiologists, particularly Hendrik Kraemer. Kraemer's classic work *The Christian Message in a Non-Christian World*, with its strong Barthian overtones, profoundly influenced the third World Missionary Conference at Tambaram, India in 1938. In a time of increasing global crisis, Tambaram emphasized—in clear biblical categories—its understanding of man as a sinner, in rebellion against God and his fellows. Similarly, the kingdom was not viewed as a coming gradual evolutionary improvement in human societies, but rather as a reality that was at once already present but still to come. In Jesus the kingdom had dawned, yet the fullness of the kingdom lay in the future, determined by God alone. Thus the kingdom would not come merely as leaven, fermenting the present order, but as dynamite, transforming it.[10] The German delegation, mindful of the increasingly powerful and despotic Third Reich, released a powerfully worded declaration at Tambaram (the so-called "German Eschatological Declaration") that emphasized this eschatological tension even more fully. The Declaration warned the church against equating the kingdom of God with any set of goals or ideals that could be attained on the earth (e.g., Nazism). The kingdom would be achieved "by a creative act of God himself." The church stood "between the epochs which God has appointed." Christians were to acknowledge that they were "citizens of two world orders," and were not

---

8. For more on the eschatological import of Edinburgh, see Bassham, *Mission Theology: 1948–1975*, 15–20; Bosch, *Witness*, 159–61; Hogg, *Ecumenical Foundations*, 98–142; and Shivute, *The Theology of Mission and Evangelism in the International Missionary Council from Edinburgh to New Delhi*, 25–41, hereafter cited as *The Theology of Mission*.

9. See Bosch, *Theology 201*, 110. Johannes Aagaard goes so far as to label Barth "the decisive Protestant missiologist in this generation." This is not because he wrote works of missiology but because Barth was the herald and backbone of the theological reorientation in Protestant theology in general, which affected missiology as it did other fields. See Aagaard, "Some Main Trends in Modern Protestant Missiology," 238–39. For more on the impact of Barth on missiology, see Bosch, *Witness*, 164–67; Braaten, *The Flaming Center*, 29–31; Manecke, *Mission als Zuegendienst*; and Scott, *Karl Barth's Theology of Mission*.

10. Bosch, *Theology 201*, 111–12. Cf. Bosch, *Witness*, 168–71.

to strive for "a social programme for a new ordering of the world, or to establish a Christian state."[11]

A more liberal approach to eschatology, emphasizing the "social gospel," continued to influence many Anglo-American mission circles. But the events of World War II had a profound influence on Protestant missiology, particularly in Germany. The apocalyptic events associated with the war drove a new generation of post-war missiologists to an even deeper eschatological framework for mission. Building on the exegetical work of Oscar Cullmann, Walter Freytag. and Karl Hartenstein adopted the salvation-history approach, and attempted to relate it to mission. Freytag believed that "the significance of this time [the interim period between the 'already' of Jesus resurrection and the 'not yet' of his parousia]; lies in the gathering together of the community which awaits the coming of the Lord. This significance of the pause in the history of salvation finds its full expression in the missionary enterprise."[12]

Freytag and Hartenstein exercised a strong influence in the post-war IMC, yet their profoundly pessimistic eschatological and historical outlook (influenced by Germany's experience of the 1930s and '40s) caused them to divide history in a dualistic manner. As Bosch summarized it, they "concentrated solely on salvation history and left secular events to take their course, occupying themselves with the church and withdrawing from the world."[13]

The perspective of other senior missiologists was not as gloomy, however. Particularly influential in this regard was the contribution of Max Warren, who linked the eschatological hope with a more balanced concern for the responsibility of the church in this world, grounded in the reality of the present lordship of God over his

---

11. The German Eschatological Declaration is found in *The Authority of the Faith*, 183–85. For evaluations of the eschatological dimensions of Tambaram, see Hogg, *Ecumenical Foundations*, 290–303; Schoonhoven, "Tambaram 1938," 299–315; and Shivute, *The Theology of Mission*, 66–90.

12. Freytag, "Mission im Blick aufs Ende," as cited by Schorzmann, "Eschatology and Mission," 191. Cf. Cullmann, "Eschatology and Mission in the New Testament," 42–54. Perhaps more than any other missiologist, Freytag focused on the link between missions and eschatology. Bosch summarizes Freytag's approach as follows: he insisted that missions not focus merely on social upliftment. "To regard it as such would be to re-admit the entirely unacceptable Anglo-American approach of forging a direct link between our human culture, history and civilization on the one hand and God's revelation on the other. The goal of mission in the end time was essentially the gathering of the congregation. The 'congregation' which was gathered—the church—was not, however, the same as the kingdom of God, but simply a sign of the kingdom. We are not to 'enthuse about an impending world church' but rather await the end, the coming kingdom" (Bosch, *Theology 201*, 116). Freytag had a pessimistic view of history. "All history was viewed as merely human history, the 'progress' of which was, at best, a multiplication of catastrophes. The Church was regarded as living between the 'already' of Christ's first coming and the 'not yet' of the Second Advent. Only one thing, Freytag said, gave meaning to this interim period: mission! In the 'salvation-historical pause' between the Ascension and the parousia, mission held the walls of history apart . . . This view implies an unbridgeable gulf between 'world history' and 'salvation history.' The one is, by its very nature, a product of man, the other an act of God. We can therefore not apply world-historical categories to mission, which is a salvation-historical event. 'Success especially is no category with which mission can operate. Mission does not advance through the world as victor but, like its Lord, as servant and sufferer, without striving for success and results" (Bosch, *Witness*, 173–74).

13. Bosch, *Theology 201*, 116–17. Cf. Wiedenmann, *Mission und Eschatologie*, 131–56.

creation. As an Anglican, Warren stressed the missiological implications of the incarnation as an essential perspective from which we view the meaning of mission.[14] Warren strongly influenced the missiological discussion during and after the 1947 Whitby IMC conference, coining the influential phrase "expectant evangelism" as an expression of the confident hope that Christians were to possess in the present "in between time."[15]

By the time of the 1952 Willingen Conference, the growing link between eschatology and mission took on a new development: the missio Dei motif.[16] With the renewed emphasis on eschatology, it became possible to see the missionary enterprise as the activity of God himself. It was not humans at the center stage of missionary outreach but God who was the principal agent of mission. The theological foundation for mission was to be found not in the church or in a biblical command, but in the eternal will of the triune God, as revealed in the cross of Christ. In the purposes of God's salvation-history, the church played an essential role; she was the bearer of mission, but God was the subject of mission. Again, we note the profound influence of Karl Barth here, with its trinitarian, God-centered emphasis. Also, we emphasize that the original missio Dei perspective was firmly rooted in the Cullmannian Heilsgeschichte model.[17]

Willingen represented the end of one era and the beginning of a new one. Bosch observed that from Tambaram to Willingen, missiology was characterized by "a new emphasis on the eschatological understanding of mission, a rediscovery of the Church's calling to world-wide mission, and the integration of mission with theology. The most important stimulus towards this process was the theology of Karl Barth, the missiological implications of which were adapted to missiology by Walter Freytag and Karl Hartenstein. The Willingen Conference of 1952 may be regarded as the crown of this development."[18]

---

14. Bosch summarizes Warren's position of calling for Christian social responsibility in this world because—in Warren's thought—"Salvation in Christ has to be realised in the world now already—this is the logical consequence of the Incarnation" (Bosch, *Witness*, 174).

15. Warren's classic work with regard to eschatology and mission is *The Truth of Vision: A Study in the Nature of the Christian Hope*. In one noteworthy passage, dealing with the relation of eschatology and social involvement, Warren countered the popular Christian attitude of historical pessimism. "The real reason for the failure of Second Adventism to win support lies in the fact that it affronts the moral conscience of the Church by its virtual abandonment of responsibility for the things of this world in deference to its preoccupation with the imminent return of the Lord and the end of history . . . On this view, salvation is salvation of the soul alone. No serious attempt is made to consider the soul's environment . . . Its despair of the world seems to be based on a too thorough-going dualism. This world may indeed be 'enemy-occupied territory' but the Enemy has got no property rights in it. He is a thief and a liar. Our responsibility as Christians is to be good stewards of the King's property" (ibid, 53).

16. For more on the deep link between eschatology and mission at Willingen, see Bassham, "Seeking a Deeper Theological Basis for Mission," 329–37; Rosin, *Missio Dei*, 6–23; Shivute, *The Theology of Mission*, 111–51.

17. Rosin, *Missio Dei*, 23. The use of the *heilsgeschichte* approach in discussing the *missio Dei* can clearly be seen in Georg Vicedom's influential *The Mission of God: An Introduction to a Theology of Mission*.

18. Bosch, "Crosscurrents in Modern Mission," 54. This is essentially the same viewpoint Andersen's *Towards a Theology of Mission*. The eschatological framework of Whitby and Willingen undoubtedly

The Eschatological Dimension of the Missionary Church

At Willingen, however, there emerged an alternative understanding of the missio Dei, grounded in a rejection of the old Heilsgeschichte model. God's missionary activity, some urged, was to be seen in relation to the whole of human history, and not simply within the narrow band of "salvation history." Leaders of this movement—notably the Dutch missiologist Johannes Hoekendijk—maintained that the center of God's concern was not the church but the world. If the Christian mission was really God's mission, and if God was working outside the church in the whole of world history (in the American civil rights movement or political liberation movements, for example), then the church's responsibility was to find out where God was at work in the world and join with him in the pursuit of shalom.[19]

Numerous factors contributed to the profound change in post-1960 missiology.[20] Taken together, they resulted in a newer world-centered theology that was to profoundly influence the missiological perspective of the 60s and beyond.[21] Lesslie Newbigin highlighted the essential tension as follows:

> The theological problems which the 1952 Willingen conference had recognized but failed to solve were to dominate the scene during the 1960's . . . The central issue was that of the relation between 'salvation history' and world history. The dominant theology of the 1950's had placed its emphasis on the former: in the centre of the picture was the Church as the bearer of salvation. In the 1960's the emphasis was upon the later, upon the world as the place

---

influenced the fledgling World Council of Churches as well. The theme of the WCC's 1954 Evanston Assembly, whose theme was "Christ—the Hope of the World," and whose preparatory volume *The Christian Hope and the Task of the Church* raised numerous issues which related eschatology to the church's life and witness. See Bassham, *Mission Theology: 1948–1975*, 37–40.

19. See Rosin, *Missio Dei*, 24–32; and Aagaard, "Some Main Trends in Modern Protestant Missiology," 251–59.

20. Bosch notes the influence of Hoekendijk, whose broader interpretation of mission and anti-ecclesial stance marked him as the crucial ecumenical missiologist of the 1960s. Second, he highlights the work of such "political theologians" as Paul Lehmann, Richard Shaull, and others, whose writings emphasized the presence of the kingdom now, in history, with a corresponding lack of interest in eschatology as a futuristic and other-worldly concern. Third, Bosch believes that the growth in communication and cross-cultural interaction led to an increase in relativistic thinking with regard to absolute convictions (e.g., the absolute *heilsgeschichtlich* distinction between church and world). Fourth, Bosch comments on the demise of post-war optimism among Western nations. Empires were collapsing as the era of political colonialism came rushing to an end. The Cold War appeared to be a permanent rather than a transitory situation. Marxism continued to expand its hold over many. The rapidly changing social and political scene, particularly in the Third World, began to force the church to realize that she lived in a revolutionary era of rapid technological, social and political change. See Bosch, *Witness*, 182–93; and "Crosscurrents in Modern Mission," 54–58. For two other (distinctly different) evaluations of the profound changes within ecumenical thought during the 1960s see Arthur Glasser's chapter "Conciliar Perspectives: The Road to Reconceptualization," in his and Donald McGavran's *Contemporary Theologies of Mission*; and Margaret Nash, *Ecumenical Movement in the 1960s*.

21. Bosch, "Crosscurrents in Modern Mission," 54–58. Bosch notes that Dietrich Bonhoeffer was a vital influence and pioneer in this transition.

Part Three: Crucial Theological Dimensions for a Missionary Church

where 'God was at work', and where the Church must go to find him and co-operate with him. This was supremely the decade of the secular.[22]

The alternative missio Dei framework began to manifest itself by the time of the IMC-WCC integration in 1961, at the WCC's New Delhi Assembly,[23] and again at the 1963 Mexico City meeting of the newly formed CWME. At Mexico City some continued to affirm the centrality of the Christian community as the primary means by which the redeeming power of Christ was made active in the world. Others argued strongly that "God is at work also in the activities of secular agencies."[24] In a candid admission of deep theological division, one of the section reports brought the old and new missio Dei perspectives into sharp contrast:

> Debate returned again and again to the relationship between God's action in and through the Church and everything God is doing in the world apparently independently of the Christian community. Can a distinction be drawn between God's providential action and God's redeeming action? If the restoration and reconciliation of human life is being achieved by the action of God through secular agencies, what is the place and significance of faith? If the Church is to be wholly involved in the world and its history, what is the true nature of its separateness? We were able to state thesis and antithesis in this debate, but we could not see our way through to the truth we fell lies beyond this dialectic. Yet we believe that all attempts to adapt the structures or the thinking of the Church to match the great changes that are taking place in the world will be doomed to paralysis until we can find the way through to a truer understanding of the relation between the world and the Church in the purpose of God.[25]

Throughout the 1960s this division grew. God was perceived to be purposefully and positively involved in world history, particularly in the process of Western secularization.[26] Certain proponents of the new missio Dei theology radically criticized traditional mission theology and practice. Two influential WCC reports issued in 1967 spoke disparagingly about the traditional Christian understanding of evangelism and mission. Evangelism was condemned as mere "proselytism." Any desire to see the church grow numerically was an illegitimate form of "self-aggrandizement." Instead, a theology of

---

22. Newbigin, "Recent Thinking on Christian Beliefs," 261.

23. We are thinking here of American Lutheran theologian Joseph Sittler, whose controversial presentation at made use of the "cosmic Christ" concept. See Visser 't Hooft, *The New Delhi Report*, 15; and Bosch, *Witness*, 187–88. For the eschatological stance of New Delhi, see Shivute, *The Theology of Mission*, 164–86.

24. Orchard, *Witness in Six Continents*, 157.

25. Ibid. (my emphasis).

26. Two very significant works in this regard were Van Leeuwen's *Christianity in World History*; and Cox's *The Secular City*.

presence was advocated as the sole legitimate missionary posture, with dialogue replacing evangelistic proclamation as the appropriate missionary strategy.[27]

With the arrival of the 1968 Uppsala Assembly of the WCC, a head-on clash occurred between the various conflicting eschatological viewpoints. The "Renewal in Mission" section became the theological battleground. Was the goal of mission "world evangelization" or "humanization"? Was the proper missionary method to be found in "proclamation" or "presence"? With regard to the theological relationship of God to the world, what was the proper sequence: "God—church—world" or "God—world—church"?[28] In the original draft of "Renewal in Mission," mission was nearly equated with the largely secular purposes of God in world history.[29] Donald McGavran and other evangelicals accused the new ecumenical mission theology with "betraying the two billion" who had not yet heard the gospel message. Hoekendijk and others attacked McGavran and his cohorts as Christians who were content to live in the past with outdated missionary structures and imperialistic missionary methods. Moderate ecumenical statesmen at Uppsala such as Lesslie Newbigin, John Coventry Smith, John Taylor, and W. A. Visser 't Hooft tried and failed to reconcile the extreme positions of the two groups.[30]

Uppsala proved to be the apex of the ecumenical theology of secularization. It exuded confidence that its sociopolitical vision, rooted in a theology of human development, would succeed.[31] Yet the lack of consensus at Uppsala highlighted certain fundamental theological conflicts, grounded in differing conceptions of the relationship of eschatology and history. Evaluations of the new missio Dei theology differ.[32] There can be no doubt, however, that this set in motion a radical rethinking of the nature of the missionary task in the current era.

By 1970, Peter Beyerhaus and other German theologians set forth "The Frankfurt Declaration on the Fundamental Crisis in Christian Mission," which sharply attacked

---

27. The European and North American reports on the "Missionary Structure of the Congregation" were published as *The Church for Others*. Newbigin criticized the controversial perspectives these documents advocated: "From the point of view of [the European and North American reports] the Church as an institution is only of peripheral interest. A line of thought which had begun with the conviction that "the Church is the Mission", had led into a missiology from which the Church was practically eliminated" (Newbigin, "Recent Thinking on Christian Beliefs," 261).

28. Throughout *The Church for Others* these positions are contrasted, with a strong bias to the latter conceptions. See World Council of Churches, *The Church for Others*, esp.15-22, 69-71.

29. See Bosch, *Witness*, 189-90; and Bosch, *Theology 201*, 132-34.

30. Visser 't Hooft, for example, urged the assembly to produce a balanced and holistic understanding of mission. See his speech "The Mandate of the Ecumenical Movement," 317-18. For more on Uppsala's contribution to mission theology see Bassham, *Mission Theology: 1948–1975*, 79-83.

31. Bosch compared Uppsala 1968 and Edinburgh 1910 in this regard: both conferences were extremely confident, indeed naively confident, about their ability to influence and change the world. See Bosch, *Witness*, 189-90.

32. Rosin, for example, believed the new *missio Dei* theology was a "Trojan horse," infiltrated into ecumenical mission thought by certain American theologians. It went far beyond the intentions of Hartenstein and Freytag. See Rosin, *Missio Dei*, 26.

Part Three: Crucial Theological Dimensions for a Missionary Church

the ecumenical movement's mission theology.[33] Johannes Hoekendijk, who was then teaching at Union Theological Seminary, New York, responded in kind. Hoekendijk declared, "this [the Frankfurt Declaration] is the challenge that has been issued, the gauntlet that has been thrown down. This is what we have to address more than anything else. It challenges at its very root everything we have for the last decades been doing."[34]

At the next World Mission Conference, in Bangkok in 1973, the conference theme was "Salvation Today." There was some disagreement, particularly from the evangelical and Orthodox participants, with the main thrust of the preparatory documents. Was salvation to be understood primarily in individual terms as personal liberation from sin and death? Or was it to be viewed as a corporate reality, and as a social phenomenon that could be experienced primarily in this world? Some participants appeared to affirm that mission was primarily a call to become involved in God's work of sociopolitical liberation, and that traditional concepts of evangelism were outmoded. Particularly influential in this regard was the opening address at Bangkok by M. M. Thomas. Others, such as Peter Beyerhaus, fiercely attacked Bangkok for failing to face the theological questions raised by the 1970 Frankfurt Declaration. Many others, however, found in the final documents from Bangkok, and particularly Section II, a positive and holistic perspective on mission and salvation.[35] Again, a strong tension emerged at Bangkok concerning the unresolved relationship between salvation and social justice, rooted in differing understandings of the eschatological relationship between the church, the world, the kingdom and history.[36]

By the time of the 1974 Lausanne Congress and the WCC's Nairobi Assembly, the sharp polemics of the 1960s began to die down. On the one hand, evangelicals were beginning to develop an integral theology of mission, including a commitment to social justice, as evidenced supremely in the Lausanne Covenant, which affirmed "evangelism and socio-political involvement are both part of our Christian duty."[37] On the other hand, the ecumenical movement seemed chastened by its failure to

---

33. The declaration stated that "the 'primary tasks' of mission had been 'displaced', the motives and goals of mission had been 'insidiously falsified' by the ecumenical movement . . . The Bible had been 'surrendered' as the 'primary frame of reference' in favor of 'a one-sided outreach of missionary interest toward man and his society.' The uniqueness of Christ and the gospel had been 'abandoned' in favor of 'a humanitarian principle'. The 'essential difference' between the church and the world had been obscured. Instead of mission and evangelism, Christian presence and dialogue had been advocated. This . . . led to 'syncretism' and to positively 'antichristian directions'. The churches had been seduced by an 'enthusiastic and utopian ideology falsely equating messianic salvation with progress, development, and social change.'" This is Al Krass' summary of the Frankfurt Declaration. See his *Evangelizing Neopagan North America*, 46–47. A full text of the declaration is found in ibid., 179–86.

34. Ibid., 48–49.

35. Bosch, *Witness*, 190–92. The most balanced critique of Bangkok is found in Costas' *The Church and Its Mission: A Shattering Critique from the Third World*, 265–301.

36. Bosch, *Theology 201*, 134–38.

37. This famous line is found in para. 5 of the Covenant. Further evidence of this ferment can be found in Padilla, *The New Face of Evangelicalism*; Kirk, *A New World Coming*; Padilla and Sugden, *Texts on Evangelical Social Ethics*; and Padilla, "Evangelism and Social Responsibility," 27–33.

The Eschatological Dimension of the Missionary Church

implement the radical developmental changes that Uppsala called for. The Nairobi Assembly, according to Bosch, reflected a sober eschatological realism rather than the euphoric utopianism of the '60s.[38]

In particular, we note the contribution of Bishop Mortimer Arias at Nairobi, who made a passionate call for the WCC to give renewed attention to evangelization as a permanent and essential priority of the ecumenical movement.[39] Arias' speech found an echo in the report of Section 1, "Confessing Christ Today."[40] This report, looked at from the point of view of eschatology, appears strikingly different from Uppsala's "Renewal in Mission" report. It clearly distinguished between the church and the world, while affirming the church's solidarity with the world.[41] It made clear that conversion to Jesus Christ and discipleship in his way lay at the heart of the gospel (paras. 7–20). It affirmed a forthright call to mission and evangelism, but emphasized the wholeness of the gospel that could not be divided (esp. paras. 17–20, 57–65).[42] The gospel was

> . . . good news from God, our Creator and Redeemer. On its way from Jerusalem to Galilee and to the ends of the earth, the Spirit discloses ever new aspects and dimensions of God's decisive revelation in Jesus Christ. The gospel always includes: the announcement of God's Kingdom and love through Jesus Christ, the offer of grace and forgiveness of sins, the invitation to repentance and faith in him, the summons to fellowship in God's church, the command to witness to God's saving words and deeds, the responsibility to participate in

---

38. By Nairobi, Bosch believes that problems with the new missio Dei theology were being recognized. "The dream of a 'theology of development' as key to the solution of the world's problems was shattered. The years since Uppsala produced more failures than successes, both for the WCC and its member churches. The 'theology of history', that is, the idea that God's will can be deduced directly from world events and that we are expected to join in these events, which had become the fashion since New Delhi, had proved to be more ambiguous than many had at first expected. The programme of dialogue with other religions had in many respects run into a blind alley. The one-sided idea of salvation as humanisation or shalomisation had proved to be too restricted a base for the Church's involvement in the world" (Bosch, *Witness*, 192).

39. See Paton, *Breaking Barriers: Nairobi 1975*, 17–19. The full text of his speech "That the World May Believe" is found in Anderson and Stransky, *Mission Trends No. 3: Third World Theologies*, 84–103.

40. See Paton, *Breaking Barriers: Nairobi 1975*, 43–57.

41. In Paton, *Breaking Barriers: Nairobi 1975*, 52–53, the following paragraphs from the report provide excellent examples.
"52. We confess Christ in the perspective of the Kingdom. His Spirit is the Spirit of the New Age. This vision makes us both sober and hopeful. None of the achievements as individuals, churches, societies will in themselves inaugurate the messianic era. Never can men and women be justified by works. Yet the promise of the Kingdom is valid and encourages Christians to respond in prayer and action. Confessing Christ shall not be in vain.
60. The world is not only God's creation; it is also the arena of God's mission. Because God loved the whole world, the Church cannot neglect any part of it—neither those who have heard the saving Name nor the vast majority who have not yet heart it. Our obedience to God and our solidarity with the human family demand that we obey Christ's command to proclaim and demonstrate God's love to every person, of every class and race, on every continent, in every culture, in every setting and historical context."

42. Ibid., 45.

the struggle for justice and human dignity, the obligation to denounce all that hinders human wholeness, and a commitment to risk life itself.[43]

The Lausanne and Nairobi conferences reflected a cautious missiological convergence among Protestants. Along with the 1974 Roman Catholic Synod on "The Evangelization of the Modern World," the 1970s seemed to signify a renewal of interest in evangelism across the world.[44] Despite their considerable differences, Roman Catholics, Orthodox, Protestant ecumenicals and Protestant evangelicals were beginning to think, pray and sometimes work together in the Christian world mission.

By 1977, no less an evangelical spokesperson than John Stott asked whether—in light of signs of recent convergence in Roman Catholic, Protestant ecumenical and Protestant evangelical thought—some forms of joint Christian witness were warranted.[45] From the ecumenical side, too, there came positive signs of convergence in missiological understanding. The CWME's "Ecumenical Affirmation on Mission and Evangelism" represented the culmination of a long process of bridge building between a wide variety of theological persuasions and church traditions. Under the guiding editorial hand of Emilio Castro, the statement weaves together a coherent vision of mission and evangelism that has been well received. The search for a "common missiology"—whereby the unique insights of ecumenical, evangelical, Catholic, and orthodox Christians can be harnessed for mission—remains an elusive goal. Yet to the extent that all Christians are called to serve in the world and to share in God's one mission to the world, they must strive towards a common missiology grounded in a common eschatological vision, a common call to witness to the kingdom.[46]

Two Conflicting Eschatological Models

Now that we have sketched out the main developments in the relationship of eschatology and mission in modern Protestant theology, we now turn briefly to the contemporary missiological situation. Notwithstanding the significant convergences mentioned above, it remains true that Christians remain sharply divided over what constitutes an adequate contemporary theology of mission. We recall the tensions that surfaced at

43. Ibid., 52.

44. See Marty, "What's Ahead for Evangelism?," 76–83; Krass' chapter "New Understandings of Evangelism and an Unfinished Agenda," in his *Evangelizing Neopagan North America*, 46–68; and Rosin, "Worldwide Interest in Evangelism/Evangelization."

45. Basing his argument on three representative statements related to world evangelization, Stott identified ten common affirmations about the missionary task: 1. The church is sent into the world. 2. The church's mission in the world includes evangelism and social action. 3. The content of the gospel is derived from the Bible. 4. The gospel centers on Christ crucified and risen. 5. Salvation is offered to sinners in the gospel through Jesus Christ. 6. Conversion is demanded by the gospel. 7. True conversion invariably leads to costly discipleship. 8. The whole church needs to be mobilized and trained for evangelism. 9. The church can evangelize only when it is renewed. 10. The power of the Holy Spirit is indispensable to evangelism. See Krass, *Evangelizing Neopagan North America*, 234–39.

46. See Verstraelen, "World and Mission: Towards a Common Missiology, 34–47.

the 1980 Melbourne and Pattaya meetings as symptomatic of this trend toward continued polarization in mission. According to Bosch, the heart of this division—which reveals itself whenever one discusses the meaning of such concepts as evangelism, social involvement, salvation, the church and the kingdom—is grounded primarily in differing "eschatologies," differing conceptions of the way in which historical action and eschatological hope is related.[47]

In this regard, the work of Thomas Kramm is of particular interest. Kramm developed two interpretive models (Interpretationsmodelle) that shed light on the eschatological framework of contemporary mission theology. Kramm labeled the first approach heilsgeschichtlich-ekklesiologisch (the salvation-historical, ecclesiological model) and the second geschichtlich-eschatologisch (historical-eschatological model).

The salvation-historical, ecclesiological model reveals the following characteristics:

1. It proceeds from a strict separation between salvation history and world history.

2. God is active in history, but only in the realm of the church, the words of the Bible and the sacraments.

3. God's promises apply only to believers.

4. Church and world are antithetical to one another, leading either to salvation or damnation.

5. The focus of this missiological approach is the *existence* of the church.

6. The goal of missions is to draw all people into the universal church, standing steadfast against the world.[48]

In contrast, *the historical-eschatological model* reveals a very different vision of the Christian mission:

1. It proceeds from the unity of salvation and world history.

---

47. In his retrospective "How My Mind Has Changed," 8–9, Bosch wondered "whether the real difference between 'ecumenicals' and 'evangelicals' (and, may I add, between different brands of 'evangelicals'), does not lie in the area of eschatology. This became abundantly clear at the recent Consultation on the Relationship between Evangelism and Social Responsibility (CRESR) in Grand Rapids (June 1982). Until we clarify our convictions on eschatology, we will continue to talk at cross purposes." Bosch has also told an anecdote about the eschatological views at CRESR. In his discussion group, they found themselves continually divided over the relationship of evangelism and social involvement. One day they decided to reveal their respective eschatological positions. He was amazed that the premillennial and amillennial division within the group corresponded exactly with their fundamentally conflicting views regarding the importance of social responsibility. Differing eschatologies were at the root of the conflict ("Interview").

48. "(1) ausgeht von der strikten Trennung von Heilsgeschichte und Weltgeschichte. (2) Gottes Handeln ereignet sich zwar innerhalb der Weltgeschichte, aber ausschließlich im Sonderraum der Kirche, im Wort der Bibel und im Sakrament. (3) Gottes Verheißung betrifft die Menschen nur, insofern sie Glaubende sind. (4) Kirche und Welt bestehen im Gegensatz von Heil und Unheil. (5) Das Sein der Kirche steht im Mittelpunkt dieses missionstheologischen Denkens. (6) Ihr missionarischer Auftrag besteht in der Heimholung aller Menschen zur Weltkirche in standhafter Beharrung gegen die Welt" (Kramm, *Analyse und Bewährung theologischer Modelle zur Begründung der Mission*, 13; my translation).

Part Three: Crucial Theological Dimensions for a Missionary Church

2. God's activity not *identified with* the course of historical events, but manifests itself in the events of world history and can only be experienced in and through them.

3. God's promises are for the whole world

4. The church is part of the world and, with the world, on the way to salvation.

5. The focus of this missiological approach is the *mission* of the church.

6. The goal of missions is historical, this-worldly salvation of all humanity[49]

The first model derives from the more classic Christian theologies of Barth and Cullmann, while the second finds its basis in the more "history-oriented" theologies of Pannenberg, Moltmann, and Metz. Kramm believes these two models reflect the deep division in mission theology today, within both Protestantism and Roman Catholicism (Kramm is a Roman Catholic).[50] The models embody sharply contrasting understandings of such crucial theological themes as humanity, world, church, history, salvation-history, salvation, dialogue, and the missio Dei.[51]

The advantage of Kramm's approach is that it draws the reader away from the sterile and misleading "evangelical"/"ecumenical" categorization and probes into the deeper theological issues that divide Christians across the ecclesiastical spectrum. What is significant about Kramm's work, for our purposes, is that his analysis is in broad agreement with Bosch's; and the division Kramm highlights is essentially a disagreement about the nature of Christian eschatology, about the precise relation between eschatological hope and historical action. Although he focuses too narrowly on European missiology, and too easily categorizes almost all missiologists within one of his two models,[52] Kramm renders a service for the Christian mission by clarifying those issues where further theological work needs to be done. In the following sections we will give an exposition of Bosch's understanding of the relation between eschatology and mission, highlighting those aspects of his thought that move missiology beyond Kramm's two-model approach.

---

49. "(1) ausgeht von der Einheit von Heils- und Weltgeschichte. (2) Gottes Handeln wird nicht einfach mit dem Ablauf der geschichtlichen Ereignisse identifiziert, manifestiert sich aber in Ereigneissen der Weltgeschichte und ist nur in ihr und durch sie erfahrbar. (3) Gottes Verheißung gilt der Welt als ganzer. (4) Kirche ist Teil der Welt und mit dieser auf dem Weg zum Heil. (5) Die Sendung der Kirche steht im Mittelpunkt dieses missionstheologischen Denkens. (6) Ihr missionarischer Auftrag ist der geschichtlich-welthafte Einsatz für das heil des ganzen Menschen" (ibid.).

50. As advocates of the former model, Kramm names such representative mission theologians as Georg Vicedom, Klaus Bockmühl, John Stott, and Peter Beyerhaus (Protestant), Josef Amstutz, and André Seumois (Catholic). Advocates for the latter model include Manfred Linz, Paul Aring, Hans-Werner Gensichen (Protestant), Ludwig Rütti and Josef Schmitz (Catholic). Ibid., 13–15.

51. Ibid., 95–190.

52. One wonders, for example, how Kramm would categorize the WCC's "Affirmation on Mission and Evangelism" or the writings of radical evangelical theologians like Orlando Costas, René Padilla, Chris Sugden, or Andrew Kirk. His models are not ultimately satisfying, in that he does not include these mediating perspectives.

THE MEDIATING APPROACH OF BOSCH[53]

Preliminary Observations

Ever since his thesis (*Die Heidenmission in die Zukunftsschau Jesu*) Bosch reflected a strong interest in eschatology. One sees the influence of eschatology on Bosch's thought most clearly in Witness to the World and in his presentation at SACLA "The Kingdom of God and the Kingdoms of this World." More obliquely, however, one sees the pervasive influence of eschatology throughout his writings. It permeates his theologizing, and determines his fundamental theological stance with regard to the relationship between the church and the world.[54]

The Influence of Cullmann

Bosch's linkage of eschatology and mission undoubtedly reflects the influence of Oscar Cullmann, Bosch's Doktorvater, whose work linking eschatology and mission in the New Testament has been so influential.[55] Cullmann influenced Bosch in at least two ways. First, he provided Bosch with the heilsgeschichte theological framework that Bosch used until the 1970s. Cullmann sharply distinguished between "salvation history" and "world history," and saw the salvific work of God in the world as essentially contiguous with the ministry of the church. Bosch made use of the heilsgeschichte approach as late as 1967.[56] In later years, however, Bosch abandoned drawing such sharp

---

53. We use the term "mediating approach" in describing Bosch's work in this area not because Bosch is a "mediator," in the sense of arbitrating a dispute by seeking a happy middle ground. Rather we mean that Bosch evidences an ecumenical breadth of perspective and an openness to learn from different theological traditions, while remaining firm about his own missiological convictions. His missiological perspective is based on the conviction that "a creative tension between Kramm's two models [is] the way forward in missiology" (Bosch, "Mission and Evangelism: Clarifying the Concepts," 187).

54. We believe Carl Braaten captured this facet of Bosch's theological perspective when he wrote: "Eschatology cannot be isolated from other themes of faith and dealt with in a treatise on 'the last things.' Instead it determines the horizon of all Christian understanding and is thematically structural for all the contents of faith and action" (Braaten, *The Flaming Center*, 39).

55. Indeed, in a festschrift for Bengt Sundkler, Bosch notes that Cullmann and Sundkler were the first New Testament scholars to work out the eschatological perspective of mission. "To my knowledge Oscar Cullmann was the very first . . . Before Cullmann and Sundkler the connection between mission and eschatology was the monopoly of some enthusiastic missionary groups . . . In fact, before the 'thirties there was little in common between the theology of mission and that of the New Testament. Since then the picture has changed radically. The studies of New Testament scholars like Cullmann and Sundkler brought new life to the theology of mission, especially because of their contributions to the theme 'mission and eschatology.' This aspect gradually became the distinguishing mark of continental missionary theology" (Bosch, "Jesus and the Gentiles," 18–19).

56. See Bosch, "Heilsgeschichte und Mission," 386–94 where Bosch reviews the work of Moltmann, Cullmann, and Linz. In this publication Bosch was still interacting almost exclusively with European theology.

Part Three: Crucial Theological Dimensions for a Missionary Church

distinctions, believing that "salvation history" cannot be made a completely separate dimension of history.[57]

Cullmann also influenced Bosch with regard to his concept of the "already" and "not yet" dimensions of the kingdom. Cullmann argued that there is both a realized and a future element within the eschatology of the New Testament. Writing of the current age, Cullmann states:

> It is already the time of the end, and yet is not the end. This tension finds expression in the entire theology of Primitive Christianity. The present period of the church is the time between the decisive battle, which has already occurred, and the "Victory Day". To anyone who does not take clear account of this tension, the entire New Testament is a book with seven seals, for this tension is the silent presupposition that lies behind all that it says. This is the only dialectic and the only dualism that is found in the New Testament. It is not the dialectic between this world and the Beyond; moreover, it is not that between time and eternity; it is rather the dialectic of present and future.[58]

In the coming of Jesus, the Old Testament promises have been fulfilled and the "last days" have begun. The kingdom has already been inaugurated with the coming of its King, but it still awaits its consummation when Jesus returns again at the end of time. We now live "Zwischen den Zeiten," in the interim period between the "already fulfilled" and the "not yet completed" of the kingdom, between the first and second comings of Christ. It is a time of profound tension yet deep hope.[59] Bosch adopted this perspective after reading Cullmann's *Christ and Time*, and acknowledged it to be "one of the few theological insights that have remained absolutely constant in my thinking."[60]

---

57. Bosch summarized the change in his thinking: "In *Witness*, I did not distinguish in [Cullmann's] way between 'salvation history' and 'world history'. I would not do it any more . . . I now recognize God at work outside of the Church much more readily than I would have done twenty years ago. And the moment you say that God is at work outside of the Church, in other religions, in events of history, you have in fact given up *heilsgeschichte* as a separate, identifiable thread in history, in juxtaposition to world history. I think it is a cul de sac to try to unravel the two, and to try to detect where God is at work and where he is not at work, and to say that this is *heilsgeschichte* and this is secular history" ("Interview").

58. See Cullmann, *Christ and Time* and *Salvation in History*, 145–46. Manson has summarized this tension in his *Eschatology in the New Testament*, 6.

59. Rottenberg illustrates the tension and hope that Christians find in the promise of the kingdom. "Redemption has been fully accomplished in Christ and is present in the fullness of the Spirit. But the power of the new age is still engaged in a struggle with the principalities and the powers of this world. The 'already' and the 'not yet' aspects of the Christian faith are both essential elements in the hope that it inspires, and they both give that hope its peculiar quality. Rather than being placed in opposition to each other, they must be seen as reinforcements to each other" (Rottenberg, *The Promise and the Presence*, 43).

60. Referring to the tension between the "already" and the "not yet," Bosch acknowledged that "I first picked this up during my B.D. studies in Pretoria when I read *Christus und die Zeit*. This 'already' and 'not yet' element of the Kingdom, I think, is very, very important. This is probably one of the few theological insights that have remained absolutely constant in my thinking. I still work with that model. It has been refined, it has grown stronger, but I still hold on to the 'already' and the 'not yet' of the Kingdom" ("Interview").

Eschatology and Apocalyptic

Bosch defined eschatology as "the living hope that God, who has already intervened in history in Jesus Christ . . . is now conducting history to its conclusion."[61] Beyond this general definition, Bosch acknowledged the various eschatological views held by many in the church (including the premillennial, postmillennial, amillennial, and dispensational schemes of interpretation).[62] He pled, however, for the church to move beyond these well-worn labels, for "a position beyond the sterile duality of pre- and postmillennialism," urging Christians to seek "a position where we take seriously both the present and the future of the kingdom."[63]

Up until the writing of *Transforming Mission*, Bosch drew a sharp distinction between eschatology and apocalypticism.[64] All too often in the history of the church, there has been a tendency toward apocalypticism, which in Bosch's view conveyed an outlook on history that was completely pessimistic, void of any hope for the historical future.[65] Bosch regarded apocalypticism as unbiblical. In apocalyptic thought

> the world is evil and continues to deteriorate. The present is empty. The past is a Golden Era for which people yearn nostalgically but which is not constitutive for the present. The future comes as a deus ex machina, catastrophically; it is the complete reversal of the present. This is how every apocalyptic functions, be it Christian or non-Christian. Examples are first century Jewish apocalyptic, as well as countless variations of Christian apocalyptic, from the Montanists in the second century, up to the Millerite movement in the nineteenth century and various groups in our own time.[66]

---

61. Bosch, *Missiology 101*, 95.

62. Bosch, *Theology 201*, 89–91.

63. Bosch, "In Search of a New Evangelical Understanding," 72. In another article, however, Bosch admits to that he has moved "from a mildly pre-millenialist position to what could probably be called an a-millenialist stand." Even here, though, he claims not to be defending an eschatological "system" but rather emphasizing the need to live in the tension between the 'already' and the 'not yet' of the kingdom. See Bosch, "How My Mind has Changed: Mission and the Alternative Community," 9.

64. In *Transforming Mission* Bosch developed a more nuanced approach, having been strongly influenced by the writings of Princeton biblical theologian J. Christiaan Beker. Beker sought to redeem the category of "apocalyptic" in the New Testament writings from its more extreme and unhealthy manifestations in theology and church history.

65. For a full review of this subject and a critique of Bosch, see König, "David J. Bosch: Witness to the World," 14–18. König criticizes Bosch for failing to distinguish between Jewish apocalyptic, which is illegitimate because of its complete denial of the world, and Christian apocalyptic, which is essentially positive and world-affirming. König cautions Bosch not to lump all apocalyptic theologies together and reject them all. Apocalyptic thought does not always teach there is no hope for the historical future. For Bosch's rejoinder see his "Salvation Tomorrow and Today," 21–26.

66. "Salvation Tomorrow and Today," 24. Bosch admits that within the New Testament documents, one can detect traces of apocalyptic thinking, just as one can trace material related to Gnosticism or the Greek mystery religions. Yet he believes the New Testament does not, in his understanding of the word, have an apocalyptic worldview. It is essentially hopeful, filled with confidence that the Kingdom is both a present and future reality, and thus the historical future is open rather than closed. The New Testament must not be interpreted apocalyptically.

Bosch believed that when the "already–not yet" tension is abandoned and the emphasis is placed exclusively on the future, then authentic Christian mission is paralyzed.[67]

Bosch contrasted apocalyptic thought with biblical eschatology. As he characterized it, the eschatological perspective of the New Testament focuses on the present and coming kingdom. The present and future dimensions of this kingdom stand in creative tension.

> The future . . . has been cleft in two by Christ. The future is already present. In apocalyptic the future remains entirely future. Christian eschatology, however, is future-in-the-process-of-being-fulfilled . . .
>
> The end does not—as apocalyptic would have it—immediately come in its entirety; it is divided into two. Or even better: from now on everything is "end". In the events regarding Jesus of Nazareth the end is inaugurated . . . The "new creation" has already begun, not merely in the personal lives of individuals, but in a cosmic sense. Kaine ktisis in 2 Cor. 5:17 should therefore not, with almost all the older translations, be interpreted as referring to "new creature", but rather as the N.E.B. does it: "When anyone is united to Christ, there is a new world; the old has gone, and a new order has already begun." This is not apocalyptic language![68]

Thus in the Christ-event, the future has proleptically become present. Everything should now be perceived from this future perspective—"im Blick aufs Ende," to use Freytag's phrase. This has tremendous consequences for the church's life and mission today, as we shall soon see.

The Centrality of the Kingdom of God

The central ingredient in Bosch's understanding of the missionary church as an eschatological community was the kingdom of God. The gospel of Jesus Christ that Christian mission proclaims is none other than the good news of the kingdom. The reign or rule of God, as proclaimed and embodied by the crucified and risen Christ, and as proleptically and provisionally present in the world through the power of the Spirit, serves as the essential, trinitarian foundation for the Christian mission.[69] In this section we will summarize Bosch's understanding of the role the kingdom has played within the history of mission. We shall then highlight the centrality of the kingdom

---

67. Bosch approvingly cites the comments of René Padilla in this regard. Padilla states that "the one-sided emphasis on the 'not yet' of the Kingdom has kept the Church from discovering in the 'already' of the Kingdom the basis for responsible social action. We have fallen into the same trap as the first-century apocalyptical Jews and consequently suffer from an eschatological paralysis that prevents our actively committing ourselves to man in his concrete historical situation" (Padilla, "The Kingdom of God and the Church," 10, as cited in Bosch, "Salvation Tomorrow and Today," 25).

68. Bosch, "Salvation Tomorrow and Today," 25.

69. See Ridderbos, "Church, World, Kingdom," 17–18; Verkuyl, *Contemporary Missiology*, 5.

The Kingdom in the History of Mission

Bosch outlined four competing—and incomplete—understandings of the role the kingdom motif has played in the history of missions. Nearly all Christian groups have affirmed a close link between mission and the kingdom, although they have differed with regard to its meaning and implications. Bosch noted there is "a close connection between a group's ecclesiology, missiology and eschatology."[70]

The first model nearly identifies the kingdom with the visible church. This has been the traditional viewpoint of pre-Vatican II Roman Catholicism, Anglicanism, and some Protestant denominations. Here the stress is on the institutional character of the church, and upon its unity and visibility. The goal of mission is defined as the planting and extension of the church into all the world. The world and the church are viewed as mutually exclusive, competing entities. The church's goal becomes the "churchification" of all areas of life, so that mission means "more and more church, and less and less world." The kingdom, in this approach, is de-eschatologized. The idea of the kingdom as co-extensive with the church leads to neglect of the future dimension of Christian eschatology, flattening out the tension between the present reality and the "not yet" of the kingdom.[71]

Bosch countered that while the church is surely not identical with the kingdom, this model is right in affirming that there is—or should be—a strong relationship between church and kingdom. The church is called to be a reflection of the kingdom, "God's experimental garden,"[72] a fragment of the kingdom living in this world. Inasmuch as the church remains faithful to the King and his kingdom, she is God's "new creation," "a house where God lives through his Spirit" (Eph 2:22). The church can thus never identify itself with God's kingdom, but neither can it be completely separated from the kingdom. By faith, the church exists as a reflection of and witness to the kingdom.[73]

The second model views the kingdom as invisibly present in the hearts of true believers—with a corresponding lack of interest in the institutional church. This viewpoint emerged particularly at the time of the Pietist renewal movement within Protestantism. In contrast to Protestant orthodoxy's disdain for mission, the Pietists pioneered cross-cultural missions among Protestants. In contrast to Rome's

---

70. Bosch, "The Kingdom of God in Mission—Eschatological Motifs and Their Functions," 1.

71. Ibid., 2–4.

72. This is Hendrikus Berkhof's phrase, which Bosch uses regularly. See Berkhof's *Christian Faith*, 244–46, 421–22.

73. Bosch, "The Kingdom of God in Mission—Eschatological Motifs and Their Functions," 11. For more on the integral relationship between church and kingdom, see Verkuyl, "My Pilgrimage in Mission," 154.

Part Three: Crucial Theological Dimensions for a Missionary Church

identification of the kingdom with the institutional church, they affirmed that the kingdom was an inward rather than external reality. It was "a spiritual and invisible entity and only to be found in the hearts of true believers." This Pietistic model dramatically influenced later mission theory and practice.

The Pietists believed that the "true church" was invisible, and was to be distinguished from the visible but nominal churches of Christendom. The "true church" was the ecclesiola in ecclesiae, the small, authentic church within the larger institutional church. As the Pietists developed a missionary consciousness, they formed independent missionary societies, separate from their own Lutheran and Reformed churches.[74] Because of their distrust of the formal churches, and also because of their independent, "non-churchly" status, the Pietist missionary societies did not seek to plant churches. Instead, they attempted to convert individuals and form small communities of "true believers." Likewise, they usually perceived the meaning of the kingdom—and thus the heart of mission—in "spiritual" terms only. With their radical distinction between the outer, visible realities and the inner, invisible ones, the Christian mission was essentially a "spiritual mission," and not primarily concerned with bodily needs and societal problems.[75] In this model, the eschatological kingdom of the future was a glorious reality, but the present dimension of the kingdom was privatized: the kingdom became an individual, inward and invisible experience of the believer with his or her Lord.[76]

In his criticism of the Pietist model, Bosch argued that it is biblical indefensible to limit the kingdom to the realm of man's heart alone. It is surely a larger reality than that. Yet Bosch admits that the Pietist emphasis on personal faith in God and his kingdom are indispensable. The strength of the Pietist model was their joyful confidence in the good news of salvation in Christ. God had to take possession of individuals' lives in a deep, personal way if the kingdom was ever to be established. The Pietists' weakness, however, was that they remained content to limit the kingdom to these inward dimensions.[77]

---

74. In fairness, they often did this because the institutional churches betrayed no interest whatsoever in evangelizing beyond their own ecclesiastical and national boundaries.

75. This does not mean that Pietists were uninterested in the physical needs of people. Their example is noteworthy. Yet their theological presuppositions relegated physical and social concerns to a secondary place in their theology of mission.

76. Bosch, "The Kingdom of God in Mission—Eschatological Motifs and Their Functions," 4–6. Bosch elaborates on the Pietist theological perspective. ". . .[It] was not the ecclesia (the formal, established Church) which was important, but the ecclesiola (the spontaneous, unorganised group of true believers). The entire emphasis fell on conversion. All missionary activities were merely aids serving this overriding primary goal. This theological perspective explains why Moravians, and to a slightly lesser extent the Pietists, had precious little interest in any cultural mandate in mission. The concentration on the individual and his soul caused the cultural, national and social life to fall completely outside the purview of mission. The Kingdom of God was for all practical purposes limited to the sphere of converted souls" (Bosch, *Witness*, 131).

77. Bosch, "The Kingdom of God in Mission—Eschatological Motifs and Their Functions," 12.

A third model that Bosch found in the history of missions was completely opposite from the Pietist view, namely that this world will become the kingdom. The postmillennial viewpoint arose in the United States and later in Europe, reflecting the confident nineteenth-century worldview of social progress and optimism. Inasmuch as the theory of evolution began to reflect the scientific and social outlook of the day, so the Social Gospel was its theological manifestation. This model affirmed that God was actively at work not only in hearts and souls (Model 2) nor even in the church (Model 1) but also in the world at large. God was shaping world history towards the realization of the millennial kingdom within this world.

In this scheme of things, mission meant building up of the kingdom throughout the entire world, through a variety of means (e.g., education, social programs, medical, and developmental assistance). The goal of mission was perceived not so much in evangelistic terms (to move people to confess Christ and join the church) but humanitarian (to help people "share in the benefits of the better world"). Eschatology, in this view, became a process of realizing God's will in this world. The kingdom was sure to progress "through a process of evolution, and through the efforts of man, under the guidance of God." In this scheme, the theological distinction between the church and the world became essentially unimportant.[78]

Bosch criticized the postmillennial, "Social Gospel" model for its naive optimism. The twentieth century, with its numerous social upheavals, destroyed many grand schemes for the transformation of this world into God's kingdom. Bosch did credit the postmillennial movement, however, for its affirmation that Christians are "called to be faithful stewards of God in this world, to permeate society." While they can never establish God's kingdom in this world, they are called, in faith, to create "signposts" of the kingdom, "approximations" of God's reign in the world.[79]

The final model of the kingdom that Bosch found in missions history—that the kingdom is an entirely future reality—developed in Adventist circles in the nineteenth century as a reaction to the optimistic evolutionary model discussed above, and continues to influence the perspective of many Christians. Models 3 and 4 stand in direct opposition to one another in numerous ways. While the former makes no fundamental theological distinction between God's work in the church and in the world, the latter makes a clear, radical distinction. While the former reduces the coming kingdom to a "realizable" dimension of the historical process, the latter removes the kingdom entirely from this world, believing it to be a completely future reality that cannot be realized, even partially, in history. While the former evaluates the world in very positive terms (believing that moral and social transformation of societies and nations is possible), the latter sees the world as being in the grip of the Evil One, completely impervious to the transforming power of the gospel.

---

78. Ibid., 7–8. Cf. Bosch, "Theologies of Mission," [11–12]. All citations of this article are taken from the unpublished version of this paper.

79. Bosch, "The Kingdom of God in Mission—Eschatological Motifs and Their Functions," 12.

Part Three: Crucial Theological Dimensions for a Missionary Church

The Adventist model downgrades the church into a "waiting room" for the eternal, other-worldly kingdom. Mission, in this schema, is the collection of people into such waiting rooms. Bosch also uses the analogy of the church as a lifeboat. The church's job, as a tiny lifeboat, is to pick up survivors adrift in the sea. The only valid task for the church is to row around, picking up other survivors. Existence in the lifeboat is essentially meaningless; it is simply a time of waiting for their future day of rescue. While on the lifeboat, the survivors develop an organization to provide for their survival until their rescue; but such an organization is simply a necessary evil, an unwanted but necessary institution to guarantee their existence while they wait. What is the relationship between the "lifeboat" (church) and the "sea" (world)? "The sea . . . is hostile and evil and always threatening." The lifeboat has no relationship to the sea, apart from a struggle against its constant threat.[80]

Bosch found this understanding of the kingdom seriously deficient. The kingdom, to a greater or lesser degree, has already come with the advent of Christ. We must acknowledge that our present-day existence is meaningful because there are "signs of the kingdom" already present in this world. We are not called abandon the world and flee from our societies. The Adventist model does serve one positive purpose, however. It reminds the church that the kingdom will not come in its fullness and glory before the return of Christ. The kingdom cannot be established by human efforts; its coming rests solely in the hands of God. Yet the Adventist response is inadequate to the reality of the presence of the kingdom in world history.[81]

What, then, did Bosch conclude from this historical survey of perspectives on the kingdom in relation to Christian mission? He was obviously unhappy with all four models, yet each retains an element of truth. "[All] are wrong . . . but at the same time: all are right. Each has a degree of validity. It is only if we hold on to all four together that we can be really true to our calling."[82]

Bosch affirmed that all four models stand in creative tension with one another. The church as the eschatological "kingdom community" has the tasks of "planting the Church, as the firstfruits of God's Kingdom; winning over people's hearts to Christ, and to a total commitment to him; going into the world to change structures of injustice and to help the poor, the afflicted and the suffering; and hoping for the day when the Kingdom will be fully consummated in all its glory."[83]

Only within this creative tension could the missionary dynamic of the God's reign emerge.

---

80. Ibid., 9–10. Cf. Bosch, "Theologies of Mission," [12–13]; and Bosch, *Witness*, 32.
81. Bosch, "The Kingdom of God in Mission—Eschatological Motifs and Their Functions," 13.
82. Ibid., 11.
83. Ibid., 13.

The Eschatological Dimension of the Missionary Church

The Kingdom of God in Contemporary Missiology

Bosch's emphasis on the kingdom is indicative of a convergence of opinion about the centrality of the Reign of God idea in contemporary missiology, including evangelicals,[84] ecumenicals,[85] and, to a lesser degree, Roman Catholics.[86] Arthur Glasser, a senior statesman of evangelical missiology, heartily affirmed Howard Snyder's contention that "the recent partial recovery among evangelicals of the kingdom of God theme is surely one of the most important theological developments of this decade—perhaps of this century."[87] Likewise WCC General Secretary Emilio Castro, in a survey of contemporary theology, concluded that "Today it would be difficult to come across a theological search for a missionary clarity that is not conducted from the perspective of a kingdom theology. Practically all contextual theologies of the third world attempt to interpret their reality—historical, cultural and political—in terms of visions of the future within a kingdom perspective."[88]

The motif of the kingdom provides, according to Johannes Verkuyl, "the hub around which all our mission work revolves."[89] But this affirmation of the centrality of the kingdom does not mean that all Christians agree about what the kingdom signifies. As we have shown, some of the deepest disagreements at the 1980 Melbourne and Pattaya conferences centered on contrasting evaluations of the nature and content of the kingdom, as it exists in and beyond world history.

It is particularly significant that the kingdom motif has been an important emphasis in Bosch's own Reformed tradition. Jerald Gort of the Free University of Amsterdam helpfully delineated the main themes in the Reformed understanding of the Christian mission. Gort argues that the kingdom theme has always been central for Reformed thought, and that the gospel of the messianic kingdom serves as "the central integrating theme, the cutting edge, the heart and perspective, the beginning

---

84. Among evangelicals, one could mention the work of Howard Snyder, René Padilla, and Andrew Kirk. Snyder's post-Lausanne works relating church and kingdom have been especially noteworthy. See his *The Community of the King* (1977), *Liberating the Church: Towards an Ecology of Church and Kingdom* (1983), and *Kingdom Lifestyle: Calling the Church to Live Under God's Reign* (1985). See also Padilla's *Mission Between the Times: Essays on the Kingdom*; and Kirk's *A New World Coming*. It is significant that the opening plenary session at the global evangelical "summit meeting" at Wheaton in 1983 was concerned with "The Church and the Kingdom of God" delivered by the Croatian theologian Peter Kuzmic. See also Dyrness, "The Kingdom is our Goal."

85. The following representative works emerged from persons related to the WCC's CWME: Mortimer Arias, *Announcing the Reign of God: Evangelization and the Subversive Memory of Jesus*; Emilio Castro, *Freedom in Mission: The Perspective of the Kingdom of God*; and Isaac Rottenberg, *The Promise and the Presence: Toward a Theology of the Kingdom of God*. Besides these works, also noteworthy was the 1980 Melbourne conference with its theme "Your Kingdom Come."

86. For descriptions of the role the kingdom in Roman Catholic thought, see the official missiological documents *Evangelii Nuntiandi*, esp. paras. 8–9; and the report of the 1981 "SEDOS Seminar on the Future of Mission," 34–52.

87. Glasser, The Evolution of Evangelical Mission Theology since World War II," 9.

88. Castro, *Freedom in Mission*, 64.

89. Verkuyl, *Contemporary Missiology*, 203.

and end of Christian mission."⁹⁰ Gort summarizes the Reformed view of the kingdom as follows:

> Briefly put, the New Testament concept of the gospel of the kingdom is understood as God's announcement of total human salvation through the reestablishment of his liberating rule in the earth. This kingdom gospel has, in the Reformed view, direct application to every single aspect of human life and living: religious, cultural, social, economic, and political. It applies to individual persons but also to the micro- and macro-structures created by people to organize their life in the world; it applies to the inner but also to the outer life of human beings. Its concern is with the relief not only of the spiritual but also of the physical burdens of men, women, and children. It has to do with the forgiveness of sins but also with the sanctification of life, with the restoration of the relationship between God and human, but also with the setting right of relations between individuals, between people and the surrounding natural world, between the sexes and generations, the nations and the races.⁹¹

With the kingdom understood in this light, Reformed theology permits no permanent divisions between the spheres of church and state, religion and politics, individual and society, spiritual and material, heaven and earth, soul and body are all tied together under the lordship of God the Creator and Redeemer.⁹²

The church receives its missionary focus and orientation from this "kingdom perspective." In light of the gospel of the kingdom, the task of the Christian mission is broad and comprehensive. It is good news about the total liberation of all persons from all that oppresses, enslaves and dehumanizes. Inasmuch as human life is a complex unity of various dimensions of existence, salvation in Christ is likewise a total and comprehensive reality, addressing the whole range of humankind's needs. Differing missionary priorities may emerge as the situation demands, so long as the broad vision of the kingdom is maintained.⁹³

The Kingdom and Its Relation to God, the World, and the Church

Emerging from a Dutch Reformed background, Bosch would have heartily affirmed Gort's Reformed perspective on the kingdom of God. Throughout his writings, the kingdom served as a fundamental dimension of his missiological approach.⁹⁴ Mis-

---

90. Gort, "Contours of the Reformed Understanding of Christian Mission," 156–57.

91. Ibid., 156.

92. Ibid. See also Lutheran Carl Braaten's similar conclusion in his *The Flaming Center*, 54–55.

93. Gort, "Contours of the Reformed Understanding of Christian Mission," 158. Also see Verkuyl, *Contemporary Missiology*, 197–204; Emilio Castro, *Freedom in Mission*, 76–88; and Padilla, *Mission Between the Times*, 22–25.

94. In particular see Bosch, *Witness*, 209–11, 221, 224–25, 236–38, 241, 244, 246; and Bosch's SACLA address "The Kingdom of God and the Kingdoms of This World," 3–13.

sion is nothing less than "the church-crossing-frontiers, witnessing to the Kingdom of God."[95] In what follows, we shall sketch out Bosch's understanding of the kingdom in its relation to God, the world, and the church.

The Kingdom in Relation to God

The kingdom motif provided Bosch with an understanding of the source of mission, which is God himself. The heart of the theocentric emphasis in mission theology since Willingen springs from the fact that the triune God, the King of the kingdom, is the author of mission.[96] Just as God is the central source and agent of the kingdom, so God is the chief source and agent of mission. The missio Dei is logically rooted in the regnum Dei.

Moreover, from Bosch's perspective, the theocentric character of the kingdom provide the essential boundaries of mission. Inasmuch as the rule of God extends over all creation, his mission is likewise universal in scope, seeking the redemption of all creation. This is made even clearer when we consider the intimate relationship between the kingdom of God and the lordship of Christ.

Early on in the life of the church, the kerygmatic focus shifted from the proclamation of the kingdom to the announcement that Jesus was Lord. In his SACLA address, Bosch expanded on this.

> It is interesting to note that the theme of Jesus' message, according to the Gospels, was "the Kingdom of God" or the "Kingdom of heaven". It was his theme even after his resurrection, as we read in Acts 1:3. After his ascension there came a subtle change. The early church seldom explicitly proclaimed the "Kingdom of God". Her message was: "Jesus is Lord". Jesus Christ himself became the focus of the message. He himself was, after all, the Kingdom of God, in person. He could therefore say to the Pharisees that it was useless to exclaim, "Look, here is the Kingdom!" or, "There it is!" for, said Jesus, "The Kingdom of God is in your midst" (Luke 17:21). In the person of Jesus the Kingdom was present among men, yet they were unable to recognize it.[97]

This switch in the early church from the "kingdom of God" to the "lordship of Christ" was not an unwelcome intrusion but a natural development that the early church was driven to make as it reflected on the meaning and significance of Jesus Christ. If the reign of God is none other than the lordship of Christ, then there can be no fundamental separation between the kingdom and the King. To divide the two would do violence to the essential biblical connection between eschatology and

---

95. Bosch, "Theologies of Mission," 41.
96. Bosch, *Witness*, 239–44.
97. Bosch, "The Kingdom of God and the Kingdoms of This World," [5]. Bracketed page references refer to the unpublished version of this paper.

Part Three: Crucial Theological Dimensions for a Missionary Church

Christology.[98] The kingdom, understood in relation to Christ, thus provides a comprehensive vision of the scope of God's mission.

The Kingdom in Relation to the World

If God is the center of the kingdom, then the world, for Bosch, is the arena or object of the kingdom. God's kingdom stands in fundamental relation to God's creation. The biblical vision of the kingdom envisions an eschatological transformation of the world ("the kingdoms of this world") into the kingdom of God.[99] There is an inescapable tension between the world and the kingdom, however, because of the estrangement and alienation between the world and God himself.

God loves the world. This is the first and fundamental reality in the relation between his kingdom and the world.[100] Yet the world is manifestly not the kingdom, nor does it seek the kingdom, for it is in sinful rebellion against God and estranged from him. It stands under God's judgment. Bosch summarizes this relationship between the God and the world as follows: "On the Cross God revealed that he took the world seriously, in that he judged the world. He not only judged the world, however; on the Cross, as well as in the Incarnation and Resurrection, he claimed the world for his Kingdom, he reconciled the world to himself."[101]

The Christ-event thus graphically embodies God's dialectical relationship with the world. The whole world stands under his judgment, yet the whole world has, in Christ, been reconciled to him. The entire created order stands under his gracious, judging reign.

The Kingdom in Relation to the Church

If God is the center and source of the kingdom, and the world is the arena and object of the kingdom, then the church, in Bosch's appraisal, exists as a witness to and instrument of the kingdom. She is different from both the kingdom and the world around her. Eschatologically speaking, she lives in a profound tension with both the kingdom and the world.[102] She exists—in the words of Dutch theologian O. Noordmans—"too

---

98. On the relationship of eschatology and Christology, Bosch comments: "'Present' and 'future' are no longer contrasted as two distinct times . . . Christ has cleft that future in two. That is why [Witness to the World] accentuates the intimate connection between eschatology and Christology. Eschatology is rooted in Christology—it is only as a result of the life, death and resurrection of Jesus Christ that eschatology exists, for through these events the future entered the present. Whenever eschatology is divorced from Christology—even if only momentarily—we lapse into one of three untenable positions" archaism, futurism or escapism . . ." (Bosch, *Theology 201*, 200).

99. Bosch, "The Kingdom of God and the Kingdoms of This World," [6].

100. Bosch, *Witness*, 240.

101. Ibid., 240–41 (emphasis mine).

102. Bosch, *Church 301*, 23, 42.

early for heaven and too late for the earth."[103] We shall consider this tension between church, kingdom and world more fully in our analysis of Bosch's conception of the church as the "alternative community." For the moment, we simply note that Bosch's "alternative community" concept is firmly rooted in the Cullmannian eschatological emphasis that the kingdom is already present but not yet complete.[104]

The church is, first of all, a witness to the kingdom. We recall that the theme of "witness" was important for Bosch.[105] Through the resurrection of Jesus and the gift of the Holy Spirit, the church has been empowered, commissioned and thrust into the world by God as his witnesses.[106] The church serves as a witness to the kingdom by her very existence, as she lives "in Christ" in the midst of unbelievers.[107] She serves as a witness to the kingdom through "her conduct as well as her words."[108] She serves as a witness to the kingdom when she is weak (rather than strong and self-sufficient), for it is precisely in her weakness that she most resembles her King, following the the Suffering Servant all the way of the cross.[109]

Bishop Newbigin uses an analogy that exemplified Bosch's understanding of the nature of the church's witness to the coming reign of God. Newbigin speaks of the Holy Spirit as the arrabon ("firstfruit," "foretaste") of the kingdom. The Spirit is,

> on the one hand, a real foretaste of the love and joy and peace which are the very substance of God's rule. But—on the other hand—it is not yet the fullness of these things. It is the solid pledge which gives assurance that the fullness is coming. And this is what constitutes the witness. It is not the lantern which the traveller in the dark carries in his hand; it is the glow on his face which reflects the coming dawn. It is pure gift. It is not an accomplishment of the one who bears witness but rather a gift which comes from beyond him and so directs men's attention away from the bearer to the source of the gift—to the light in the eastern sky. In this sense one must say that the Church is not the author of the witness; it is not that the Church bears witness and that the Spirit helps the Church to do so. This kind of language completely misses the point. The point is that the Church is the place where the Spirit is present as witness. The witness is thus not an accomplishment of the Church but a promise to the Church.[110]

---

103. Bosch refers to Noordman's words frequently, including *Witness*, 222; "Renewal of Christian Community in Africa Today," 98; and "The Kingdom of God and the Kingdoms of This World," [8].

104. Bosch, *Church 301*, 23.

105. See chapter 4, "Mission as Martyria: The Biblical Model of Suffering/Witness."

106. Bosch, *Witness*, 64–66.

107. Ibid., 81–82.

108. Ibid., 82–83.

109. See ibid., 71–74, 211.

110. Newbigin, *Sign of the Kingdom*, 37–38 (my emphasis). This short work by Newbigin is a masterful statement of the fundamental theological relationship of God, church and world from the perspective of the Kingdom. See Bosch's "An Emerging Paradigm for Mission," 508 for his endorsement of Newbigin's perspective.

Part Three: Crucial Theological Dimensions for a Missionary Church

The church therefore has no reason to boast. She is not superior to the world when she gives witness to the coming kingdom; rather she speaks and lives in solidarity with the world.[111] She serves as a witness, a pointer, a sign of the coming kingdom.

Besides serving as a witness to the kingdom, the church is also called to be an active instrument of the kingdom, according to Bosch. "Because the Church knows that she is a commissioned witness of the coming new order," said Bosch, "she has to erect signs of the Kingdom already."[112] On the basis of Christ's resurrection, the church is impelled to work for the transformation of the world by the standard of God's kingdom. Bosch readily acknowledged that the personal and social transformation demanded by the standards of the kingdom remain empirically unattainable in this world. Yet the church has no choice but to strive to embody the values of the kingdom if she wants to remain faithful to her Lord. In broad terms, Bosch summarized the church's role as God's instrument as follows:

> Someone who knows that God will one day wipe away all tears, cannot with resignation accept the tears of those who suffer and are oppressed now. If we believe that one day all disease will vanish, we cannot but begun to anticipate here and now the victory over disease in individuals and communities. If we accept that the enemy of God and man, the devil, will ultimately be completely conquered, we cannot but begin at once to unmask his strategems in the individual, family and society. We believe in God not because we despair of the present and future; rather, we believe in the present and future of both man and the world because we believe in God. Precisely because we hope for the eternal and ultimate things, we also hope for the temporary and provisional.[113]

For Bosch then, the kingdom stands as a central reality in the life of the church. A proper understanding of God's eschatological reign provides her with the essential theological orientation she needs to live faithfully in the world.

Mission as an Eschatological Event

We can characterize Bosch's understanding of the relationship between eschatology and mission by means of seven theses.[114]

First, mission as an eschatological event assumes that the church's worldwide mission does not and cannot hasten "the end." Some have mistakenly assumed, on the basis of Matt 24:14 and Mark 13:20, that a worldwide preaching of the gospel is a "prerequisite" for the Second Coming. In this view, mission tends toward a Pelagian

---

111. Bosch, *Witness*, 246.
112. Ibid., 246.
113. Ibid., 247.
114. Bosch has developed these seven theses in *Witness*, 234–38. For his final ruminations on the subject, see Bosch, *Transforming Mission*, 510–522.

activism, whereby "we can hasten [the parousia] through our missionary activities."[115] It is as if the end cannot come until certain conditions are fulfilled; and that the end must come as soon as they are.[116] Bosch further objected that this approach resembles the Jewish apocalyptic thought of Jesus' day, where the crucial questions were "how" and "when" the kingdom would come—precisely the questions that the Scriptures forbid its readers from asking. Bosch believed that where mission is linked to "the end" in the New Testament, it is presented as the missio Dei, "the missionary activity of God, which . . . is not susceptible to human calculations and manipulation."[117] God in his sovereign love, not humankind in its strivings, will determine the time and the form of the parousia.

Second, mission as an eschatological event prevents the church from turning in on itself; mission pushes the church outward into the world. God's people have constantly been tempted to abandon the world and become an isolated "ghetto community." Mission, seen in light of the reign of God, has served as a constant reminder to the church that it cannot do this. The church can never renounce her calling and responsibility for apostolic action in the world. Her Lord has sent her to the ends of the earth. Thus mission—in light of the coming kingdom —replaces "apocalyptic self-preservation" as the central motive of the church's historical existence.[118]

Third, mission as an eschatological event reminds the church that her mission is never finished; eschatology serves as a perpetual stimulus for mission. Not only is the church called to the ends of the earth; she is called to the end of time. God reveals his plan for the salvation of the world precisely in and through the church's missionary involvement with the world.[119]

Fourth, mission as an eschatological event proceeds from the certainty that the kingdom is not only a future but also a present reality, thus rendering the present age

---

115. Bosch, *Theology 201*, 71. In contrast, Bosch notes that in mission passages like Matt 28:18–20; Luke 24:46–49; John 20:21–23; and Acts 1:8 there is no sense of eschatological fervor. This is also true in the Paul's missionary labors. Bosch comments that "human activities do not bring the end to pass. Hence there is no reason to interpret Paul's missionary zeal . . . as if he were dashing around the countries of the Mediterranean to proclaim the gospel to all the peoples before Christ's imminent return. Paul did not see such a close connection between his own missionary activities and the coming of the end" (ibid., 72).

116. Bosch, *Witness*, 235. Bosch notes that this was one of Martin Kähler's central criticisms of much of the missionary movement of his day. Kähler discovered some missionaries who more concerned with the eschatological "timetable" than with a compassionate concern for the lost. They had divorced Christology from eschatology, to the extent that the fate of the multitudes mattered little, so long as God's timetable and Christ's return was precipitated. Cf. Bosch, "Systematic Theology and Mission: The Voice of an Early Pioneer," 172–74.

117. Bosch, *Theology 201*, 71.

118. Bosch, *Witness*, 235–36. Carl Braaten makes a similar point about how mission kept the early church's apocalypticism in check. See *The Flaming Center*, 13.

119. Bosch summarized it thus: "While believers carry the message across all frontiers, the mystery unfolds itself to them. The Church's mission into the world is Jesus' only reply to the question about the date of the coming of the Kingdom (Acts 1:6–8). To wait for the end never implies passivity but rather intense activity in the here and now. Involvement in the world is one of the chief ways of preparing ourselves for the parousia" (Bosch, *Witness*, 236).

meaningful rather than empty. In the Christ-event, the future has invaded the present age. In the New Testament, eschatological time is divided into the past, present and future. Israel believed her eschatological salvation would come entirely in the future. But with the Christ's coming, the future has flowed into the present.[120] This means that the present era is filled and not empty; historical time is rendered meaningful and consequential. Salvation has already come upon the world. Life in the reign of God has already begun, and Christians are to live in light of its "nearness" and presence.[121]

Fifth, mission as an eschatological event reminds us that even as we live and work in light of the kingdom's presence, the kingdom can never be completely attained in this world; its fullness is still to come. This is the converse of the previous point. While it is important to affirm that the present era is not void of the presence of God's reign, neither can the present era bring in the kingdom in its fullness. Complete salvation is not possible in the here and now.

Bosch maintained that many in today's church had forgotten that the salvation that the kingdom embodies is a reality that is wrought by God himself.

> Wherever we lose sight of the merely relative and variable nature of this world and act as though it is perfectable, we are in fact turning out backs on the divine Kingdom and our faces towards the passing world. We then operate with blueprints we have ourselves drawn up, with plans we are ourselves going to execute. We then easily exclaim in euphoria: "Eureka!", in the belief that our blueprint is finally being translated into reality. This blinds us to the pock-marks of sin which disfigure event the most perfect human community. It becomes an easy boast that what we do is nothing but God's work. Our crusader mentality demands that the whole of society be re-created in our image. Our religion becomes a mechanism to control God. Salvation is made dependent upon the right kind of religious, moral and political activity and we forget that the "authorities and powers" will not be finally dethroned before Christ returns. We are unable to recognise the tragic imperfection of even the best of our human attempts.[122]

---

120. Ibid., 236; cf. 64–66. Christians can never posit that salvation is an entirely future reality; if they do they are upholding a pre-Christian position.

121. Bosch qualifies this "presence of the Kingdom" in two ways. It is admittedly a hidden kingdom, perceived only with eyes of faith. It is also only a partial manifestation of the kingdom, inasmuch as the full presence of the kingdom will be revealed only in the eschaton. Bosch also acknowledges that the Christian believer exists in a profound tension between the "already" and "not yet." This tension is inescapable but bearable. Bosch comments: "The believer is already a naturalised citizen of the New Age and yet he still lives fully in this world. There is, in other words, an admittedly dualistic element here. 'A person with an eschatology in the midst of this world is willy nilly a citizen of two worlds' and the only reason why he can endure this almost unbearable tension is to be found in the fact that these two worlds overlap in Christ, that the new has arrived while the old has not yet passed away" (Bosch, *Witness*, 237). The quotation in this paragraph is from Braaten's *The Flaming Center*, 47.

122. Bosch, *Witness*, 243.

The Eschatological Dimension of the Missionary Church

Bosch commented that the ecumenical movement in particular is prone to forget this truth.[123] This tendency, however, is not confined to the WCC; he has criticized the example of some African Christian theologians in this regard as well.[124] Instead, the church must be reminded that it is the hope of God's intervention—and not merely human efforts for social improvement or the "salvation of souls"—which drives Christian mission forward into the world.[125] The kingdom should therefore serve as critical category for the church's mission, but never be reduced to a mere political, social, or ideological program. The kingdom is always something beyond what can be realized in this world.[126]

Sixth, mission as an eschatological event means infusing the world with hope. Any eschatological perspective that is grounded in the Bible is, by definition, a "theology of hope," for the biblical teaching reveals an unshakable confidence in God's purposes for the future of this world. Hope in the Bible, declared Bosch, always means two things. First, it is an affirmation that God is the Lord, and that his kingdom will ultimately triumph. Second, it is a call to God's people to act on the strength of this

---

123. Bosch has commented: "There is still an eschatological reservation we have to uphold. We can never ever have here [in this world] a full manifestation of the Kingdom . . . I think Melbourne overstepped the boundaries in several of the four reports in identifying [certain places and political systems] with the Kingdom of God. I remember Julia Esquivel who just explicitly said that 'this is the Kingdom of God coming to Nicaragua.' I was immediately disturbed when that was done, because I felt—How do you critique the situation there if things go wrong? How do you now say this was the Kingdom but it isn't the Kingdom any more? You should say from the beginning: 'This isn't the Kingdom, by definition it can never be the Kingdom, because the Kingdom is something qualitatively and essentially different.' That to me is the eschatological reserve I want to hold open. And it is a problem in the ecumenical movement . . . It is constantly under pressure and it frequently disappears" ("Interview").

124. Too often, says Bosch, "the church in many African countries was frequently very prophetic before liberation but then after independence they ceased to be so. The problem was that before liberation, they had committed themselves irrevocably with the alternative to the colonial system, and the moment the colonial system was removed, they could not disentangle themselves. This is what I see happening in [South Africa] too. I for one would say 'sure, we should plead for justice—and we should be very clear on that—but the moment it is empirically realized, in other words the moment it becomes concrete, it has to be critiqued again. And I think this is what many of my black colleagues . . . would not do.'" The Church in Zambia, according to Bosch, is an example of what the church should be. Confronted by an anti-religious campaign which threatened the rights of Christian believers, church leaders produced the document "Scientific humanism and Christianity," which challenged the state to withdraw or revise its new policies. Church leaders brought a critique to the state before independence, but remained critical after independence too. "We have to uphold an 'eschatological reservation'. We can never ever have here a full manifestation of the Kingdom of God" ("Interview").

125. Bosch, *Witness*, 237. "It is precisely mission which should keep alive the hope for a divine fulfillment of the Kingdom. Where the expectation of God's intervention withers, mission loses its true character and eschatology is reduced to ethics. It then becomes either merely humanitarian improvement without a transcendent dimension or a private affair where the concern is not with the renewal of the entire creation but simply with individual salvation, a living on after death" (ibid.).

126. Bosch notes that this understanding of the kingdom grew out of his interaction with Karl Barth. "The church can never endorse anything . . . Karl Barth said in one of his writings that 'the church can never endorse any political system, even if it were democracy.' He said we should not even call democracy the 'Christian' way of government, because even democracy can be twisted and manipulated" ("Interview").

knowledge. The ultimate hope in God's purposes for the world serves to call the people of God to leave nothing unchanged within the world and to become involved in its transformation.[127]

Seen in this eschatological light, Bosch defined Christian mission as a faithful "hope in action," because a true eschatological hope always manifests itself in action.[128] This hope has significant consequences for the scope of Christian mission. It is precisely because of the church's confident hope about the future that it can act responsibly in the present. Because God is Lord over the "ultimate" things—life and death, heaven and hell, the redemption of the world, the church can become confidently involved in penultimate ministries—including healing, development, relief work, and social action. The church is active in these penultimate areas "not because she has abandoned her hope in the ultimate, but for the very reason of that hope."[129] This understanding is at the heart of the Christian hope.[130]

Seventh, mission as an eschatological event preserves the church from despondency. A proper eschatology drives the church into a deep and sacrificial involvement with the world, erecting signs of the coming kingdom in the present age. It also preserves the church, however, from succumbing to feelings of disappointment, disillusionment and frustration when the church falls short of the mark. A realistic biblical eschatology acknowledges the very real gap between the ideal and the real, between the world as it is and the world as it will one day become, under God.[131] This perspective is absolutely essential if the church is to live out the reality of its identity as the eschatology community of God.

Tensions Between Eschatology and History in the Church's Missionary Practice

As we have seen above, the doctrine of eschatology has broken out of the confines of an exclusively "futurist" and otherworldly orientation. Thanks to the contribution of

---

127. Bosch, *Theology 201*, 201.

128. See Bosch, *Witness*, 237. Bosch refers the reader to Barth's section "Life in Hope" in *Church Dogmatics* IV:3, which is the source of his emphasis on mission as hope in action. Cf. Margull, *Hope in Action: The Church's Task in the World*. This theme became the final element of Bosch's emerging ecumenical paradigm in *Transforming Mission*, 510–522.

129. Bosch, *Witness*, 238.

130. Ibid. Bosch comments: "The penultimate may be neither despised nor neglected for the sake of the ultimate. The idea that things may stay the way they are, is the absolute antithesis to the gospel. The Christian who concerns himself only with 'ultimate things', arguing that the present things are no more than provisional and passing away, does not understand the Christian hope" (ibid.).

131. Bosch elaborates: "The message of the transcendent Kingdom and the knowledge that, in the final analysis, everything is in God's hands, gives us the necessary distance and austerity towards everything in the world. God is the One who prepares the feast; we are but the servants who distribute the invitations. The awareness of this determines the horizon of our expectations . . . If we lose this perspective, the gospel ceases to be a gift and becomes law. A restiveness and nervousness then appears in our activities because everything seems to be dependent on us. This danger is not an imaginary one. Only a healthy eschatological perspective can fortify us against it" (ibid.).

such eschatologically oriented theologians as Cullmann, Pannenberg, and Moltmann and the liberation theologians, it has become crucial to relate eschatology to present history. The future still remains a critical dimension of eschatology, but it is the future as it penetrates and shapes the present, the future as it gives guidance as to the meaning and purpose of history today. This, in turn, has had dramatic implications for the church's understanding of the nature and content of her missionary task.

Bosch affirmed this basic shift in theological perspective. Eschatology relates to the historical future of this world, as well as to the meta-historical. Modern eschatology asks: "How do we evaluate the meaning of contemporary historical events theologically?" What does it mean when we say that God is "at work" in certain persons, events or nations? What are the criteria for discerning the work of God from the work of other forces? What constitutes a proper Christian theology of history for our day?

One look at the polarization in mission theology—with different groups discerning radically different "signs of the times"—supplies abundant evidence that a Christian theology of history is a controversial affair. Bosch criticized evangelicals and ecumenicals alike for their misunderstanding of the relationship of eschatology and history.[132] In fact, Bosch argued, both evangelicals and ecumenicals are operating from the same model, even though they arrive at conflicting conclusions. All too often, both groups wrongly attribute to the providence of God what is, in fact, simply various sociological forces at work. "Both evangelicals and ecumenicals . . . are subjectivistic. There was a time, for instance, when the colonial programme of European countries was regarded as divine providence, as 'salvation history'. Today, on the contrary, decolonization is regarded as proof of God's direct intervention. In the past, capitalism was labelled 'Christian'; today the same is said of socialism. Time and again the tendency thus is to ascribe to divine providence the sociological forces dominant in a particular period. Behind this lies historical positivism."[133]

It is too easy, Bosch maintained, to read God into historical events. Whatever the event—be it a natural disaster or a human political revolution, the rise of an Adam Smith or a Karl Marx—we cannot uncritically ascribe to God what may very well be the work of other social or historical (or demonic!) forces. Bosch provided four twentieth-century examples of such false theologies of history.

132. Evangelicals tend to polarize world history and salvation history. They quarantine God's work to the realm of salvation history only. World history remains under the grip of Satan. It becomes significant only when God's missionary church expands into the world and "conquers" a segment of it. God's plan for the world is that the church grow larger and larger, and the world smaller and smaller. The missionary expansion of the empirical church thus provides the hermeneutical key to the eschaton. In this scheme, Christians can "deduce from the geographical progress of mission what time it is on God's watch and how close we are to the final unfolding of salvation history" (ibid., 230). In reaction, ecumenicals have neglected salvation history. They have preferred to emphasize how God is at work in the realm of politics, nation-building, and other faiths and ideologies. God has sometimes been perceived to be at work everywhere except in the institutional church! Bosch notes that this "desacralization of salvation history" has gone hand in hand with a "sacralization of world history." All too often in the ecumenical scheme, world history becomes salvation history! See ibid., 231.

133. Ibid., 231 (my emphasis).

Emmanuel Hirsch hailed the "German turning-point" of 1933 unreservedly as divine intervention. Bruno Gutmann exalted ethnicity and the so-called urtümliche Bindungen (primordial ties) of any specific people as inviolable data of creation and declared everything that serves and upholds the people, to be in accordance with God's will. Elsewhere adventists incorporate national disasters and all manner of world events into an apocalyptic understanding of history. Or, violent revolutions are interpreted by liberation theologians as a direct extension of the biblical exodus event.[134]

While decrying these false "theologies of history," Bosch did not mean to imply that God is uninvolved in the historical process. If this were so, the believer would be in the same skeptical position as a deist or an atheistic existentialist. Rather, Bosch roundly criticized all one-dimensional interpretations of history—interpretations which both evangelicals and ecumenicals are prone to make.[135] We can thus summarize Bosch's own theology of history as follows:

Bosch believed that God acts in history, and that his acts are interwoven into secular history. Thus "salvation history" (i.e., the creative and redemptive actions of God in Jesus Christ by the power of the Spirit) cannot be isolated or divorced from world history.[136] The God of the Bible does not act only on a narrow "spiritual" plane, or solely among the redeemed in the church. God is concerned for and involved with the whole of humankind, in every dimension of existence. The Old Testament provides ample evidence of the universal scope of God's concern.

Yet God's activity, as revealed in the Bible, is radically particular in nature. God's historical involvement with the world is centered on the person of Jesus Christ.[137] The doctrine of the incarnation stands as the supreme example of the "interweaving" of God's history and human history. God sent his Son into the concrete historical context of first-century Palestine. The radically particular nature of the Christ-event shows that God takes human history seriously. The incarnation is God's Yes to the significance of human history; he takes humankind seriously enough to enter into its history. Yet the coming of God in Christ also represents a No to human history. The lordship of God in Jesus Christ relativizes the claims of all other human persons, movements and nations. Through the presence of God's Spirit in the world, God's Yes and No towards human history continues. As Bosch put it: "In, through, and among

---

134. Ibid., 231.

135. Ibid., 231–32.

136. Ibid., 232; Bosch, *Theology 201*, 198. We note that this is a definite break from the Cullmannian Heilsgeschichte paradigm with which Bosch used to operate. He has elaborated as follows: "In Witness, I did not distinguish in the same way between salvation history and world history . . . I now recognize God at work outside of the church much more readily than I would have done twenty years ago. And the moment you say that God is at work outside of the church, in other religions, in events in history, you have in fact given up heilsgeschichte as a separate, identifiable thread in history in juxtaposition to world history. I think it is a cul de sac to try to unravel the two, and to try to detect where God is at work and where he is not at work, and to say that this is heilsgeschichte and this is secular history" ("Interview").

137. Bosch, *Witness*, 63–64.

the events of this world God is operating, in such a way that these events are deprived of all absoluteness and become as it were second-rate or relative."[138]

Bosch therefore argued that mission is the focal point of God's involvement in world history. God's purposes in human history are ultimately missionary in nature. Out of God's love, he seeks to redeem a fallen world, to save a lost world, to bring shalom to a world that is fragmented and alienated. All of God's actions in the world must be seen from this redemptive, missionary frame of reference. This is most clearly seen in the person and work of Jesus Christ, who is the central figure of God's missionary involvement with the world.

But what about God's activities in the present world? How do we discern the presence (or absence) of God's action in contemporary history? Here we come to the heart of the missio Dei debate of the 1960s. Bosch maintains that God's action in history is discernible only by faith. The death and resurrection of Christ, along with the guiding presence of the Holy Spirit allows the corporate church as well as every Christian believer to perceive something of the mystery of God's providence in the midst of human confusion.[139] Yet Bosch remained profoundly skeptical of any theology which claims to discern the hand of God, fully understanding and explaining the "signs of the times." To interpret the providential acts of God in history remained, for Bosch, an ambivalent enterprise, fraught with danger. Even for believers, the meaning of history is often hidden. "God's activities cannot be derived directly from history. History is full of contradictions, gaps, discontinuities, puzzles, surprises, mysteries, temptations, and confusions. After all, not only God, but also the counter-forces are at work in it. God's activities in history are therefore for the eye of faith simultaneously revealed and hidden."[140]

Despite his deep skepticism, Bosch did not abandon the attempt to faithfully interpret the meaning of history in our day. With Hendrikus Berkhof, Bosch affirmed that we cannot evade our responsibility to attempt to understand what God is doing in our history.[141] The "signs of the times" must be discerned, but always with deep humility and vigilance. Bosch urged that Christians be "very modest" in their efforts. "We may never simplistically distinguish between light and dark—especially since our interpretation [of history] is easily determined by our own prejudices and predilections; we see God at work only when and where it suits us."[142] In this regard, Bosch believed the parables of vigilance in Matthew 24–25 were instructive. We must seek interpret the meaning of history with caution, but also with a courageous confidence in the Lord who sends us into history to participate with him in his mission.

138. Bosch, *Theology 201*, 198.
139. Bosch, *Witness*, 232–33.
140. Ibid., 233.
141. In *Witness*, 233, Bosch refers the reader to Berkhof's defense of this proposition in his *Christ the Meaning of History*, 194–205.
142. Bosch, *Witness*, 233.

Part Three: Crucial Theological Dimensions for a Missionary Church

> People who stay alert are people who do not know what course events will take. They continue to wait for the unveiling and do not anticipate the final judgment. They must interpret the reality in which they live, yet not so much by judging as by keeping their lanterns burning and making the most of their talents. While doing this, they develop an "instinct" which enables them to discern, however imperfectly, who their fellow servants are and who are in need of their help (cf. Matt. 25.31–46). The one who watches, thus interprets the facts of history, albeit fallibly. Such a person has the courage to take decisions, even if they are relative. He knows, however, that the best way of interpreting history is to allow God to send him into the world. Mission is an exegesis of history.[143]

In the final analysis, according to Bosch, the best way to interpret history was to become personally involved in God's mission. It is precisely because Christians live in hope of the future kingdom with its comprehensive vision of salvation that they can become "involved in the struggles of this world and begin to erect signs of the coming kingdom."[144] Bosch asserted the vital need for Christians to seek to discern how God is working in today's world, and to work for a better world of increasing peace and justice. Christians, of all people, are obliged to strive alongside others of goodwill to create concrete political and social models that will enhance the vision of a more just society.[145] It is precisely the Christian's eschatological hope which drives them to this earthly activism.

> We live in the tension between the "already" and the "not yet", a tension that, by its very nature, remains almost unbearable, as we seek to allow something of the 'not yet' to take shape in the here and now. In practice this perspective means, inter alia, that anybody who believes that one day God will wipe away all tears, cannot acquiesce in tears and sorrow now, anybody who knows that one day swords will be turned into plough-shares and former

---

143. Ibid., 233–34.

144. Bosch, "Mission and Evangelism: Clarifying the Concepts," 184–85. Bosch has elaborated on how the expectation of the End gives meaning to the present as follows: "The expectation of the end (together with the 'already') gives meaning to the interim. . . . Nevertheless—the emphasis for the church-in-mission should not fall on the future but on our responsibility in the here and now. And this is what I [have] tried to highlight. The imminence of the future Kingdom should be approached on the basis of the reality of the present Kingdom" (Bosch, "Salvation—Tomorrow and Today," 25).

145. "Interview." Orlando Costas criticized Bosch precisely at this point. In his review of *Witness to the World*, he faulted Bosch for failing to be more historically concrete about the specific historical and political ideologies with which the church must align itself, in order to work for a more viable social order. Costas believed a mixed or socialist economy to be the most just alternative in today's world, and liberation theology the most effective response that the church can give to those who find themselves in situations of oppression. In my interview with Bosch, he affirmed the need strive for social justice and to be historically concrete about the various sociopolitical options available. Yet Bosch felt that Costas, along with other theologians of liberation, were not critical enough. Too often, many such theologians simply endorse a specific political programme without qualification. They fail to see the need for the church to keep a critical distance, criticizing every political programme as soon as it becomes concrete.

enemies become friends, cannot but work for peace and reconciliation now. Precisely our faith in the Coming Kingdom leads to our involvement in the world here and how.[146]

Characteristically, Bosch affirmed the need to live in a creative tension, neither despairing about this world by placing "all our stakes in the Coming Kingdom," nor giving up all hope in a Coming Kingdom by trying "to build utopia here and now with our bare hands." We must live in the tension between the "already" and the "not yet" in order that "something of the 'not yet' may take shape in the here and now."[147]

---

146. Bosch, "How My Mind Has Changed," 9.
147. Ibid.

8

The Ecclesial Dimension of the Missionary Church

The Church as God's "Alternative Community"

THE TENSION BETWEEN THE CHURCH AND THE WORLD

IN THE PREVIOUS CHAPTER, we reviewed how Bosch understood the missionary church from the standpoint of eschatology. The church of Jesus Christ exists as a witness to and instrument of God's kingdom. She is called to be a community that is distinct from the world, yet deeply involved with the world. She is to live in the world as a concrete sociopolitical institution in relation to the rest of human society. As the body of Christ, however, she is called out of the world, and set apart to live a qualitatively different lifestyle.

Drawing on the work of Hendrikus Berkhof, Bosch emphasized that the church exists *simultaneously* as a theological entity and as a sociological entity. She is a unique, transcendent, Spirit-led community, but also an earthly institution with inherent social and political interests.[1] As Bosch put it:

> Through the eyes of the world the Church recognises that she is doubtful, disreputable, shabby; in the eyes of the faithful, that she is a mystery. Christ breathed his Holy Spirit into a very earthy, dusty group of disciples. And so his Church is an inseparable union of the divine and the dusty, of the spiritual and the physical. Sometimes one part seems more apparent than the other. We can be utterly disgusted, at times, with the earthiness of the Church; yet we can be

---

1. Bosch, "The Church in South Africa—Tomorrow," 171–72; and Bosch, "The Church as the 'Alternative Community,'" 3. See Berkhof, *The Christian Faith*, 344–45.

transformed, at times, with awareness of the divine in the Church. The Church moves, as tiny Israel did, dependent on the guiding finger and daily solicitude of her God—good men, weak men, hesitant men, but essentially men on the move, seeking, questing, experimenting, dust-stained but somehow still rejoicing. Of the Church it is pre-eminently true that beauty lies in the eyes of the beholder.[2]

All too often, however, the church falls prey to dualism. She forgets one of these dimensions of her existence, breaking the delicate tension between them. "One group," Bosch lamented, "stands against the world, at the risk of not being in it, irrelevant and isolated. The other stresses being for the world yet risks being of the world—being absorbed and liquidated into it, thus losing the Church's transcendental dimension."[3]

Bosch acknowledged the difficulty of being *for* and *in* the world without being *of* the world, but urges that the church must.[4] Only in this double relationship, distinguishable from the world but also in solidarity with the world—existing as a *theological* entity as well as a *sociological* entity—can the church truly be a *missionary community*.[5]

How can the church live faithfully in relation to both God and the world? To answer this question Bosch made extensive use of the image of the church as the "alternative community." We shall outline the sources from which Bosch has drawn this concept; then expound the main themes of the "alternative community" concept, and finally show its significance within the South African context in which Bosch lived and served.

SOURCES OF THE "ALTERNATIVE COMMUNITY" CONCEPT

In his development of the "alternative community" concept (hereafter called "AC"), Bosch drew upon at least four separate sources. Each source explicitly or implicitly informs his major writings on the subject.

The earliest influence on Bosch's thought is undoubtedly the *"biblical theology movement,"* including the work of such men as Oscar Cullmann, Otto Piper, and Paul Minear. As a result of their efforts, says John Howard Yoder, "it became thinkable that there might be about the biblical vision of reality certain dimensions which refuse to be pushed into the mold of any one contemporary world view, but which stand in

---

2. Bosch, "The Church in South Africa—Tomorrow," 172. This essay is as an excellent introduction to Bosch's ecclesiology. See also Bosch, *Witness*, 93–95 on the dual nature of the church in the world.

3. Bosch, *Witness*, 221. Also see Bosch, "The Church as the 'Alternative Community,'" 3.

4. Bosch, *Witness*, 221.

5. Ibid., 222. Bosch comments that "[the church] lives in a double relationship: to the *world*, for she is part of this world and of secular history; and to *God*, as an expression of his saving love reaching towards a perishing world. These two relationships are interdependent. Without a faithful and sustained contact with God the Church loses her transcendence. Without a true solidarity with the world she loses her relevance" (ibid.).

Part Three: Crucial Theological Dimensions for a Missionary Church

creative tension with the cultural functions of our age or perhaps of any age . . . [The "biblical realist" movement] led to a renewal of concern for ecclesiology and for eschatology without which neither ecumenical developments since then nor Christian thinking about hope since then would have been understandable."[6]

Bosch undoubtedly stood critically yet solidly in this theological tradition. His studies under Cullmann, as well as his career-long interest in ecclesiology and eschatology as they impinge on the Christian mission, bore witness to this. It is precisely at the intersection of these two concerns, of church and kingdom, that the AC concept has its roots, as we shall see.

Second, and more explicitly, Bosch attributed the emergence of the AC idea to his exposure in the early 1970s to the thought of *John Yoder and other Mennonite theologians*.[7] Bosch first met Yoder in Basel, where both men were taking their doctorates. As Bosch put it in his 1982 retrospective: "Perhaps it would be correct to say that, in the course of time, the essence of my thinking in this area has crystallised in the concept of the church as the 'alternative community'. The expression was not coined by me; it originated, I think, in American Mennonite circles."[8]

Bosch goes on to explain his rationale for adopting this concept. Despite all the historic tensions between the Reformed and the Anabaptist viewpoints, Bosch believed that numerous intrinsic similarities exist between Reformed and Anabaptist ecclesiologies. Both groups have *sought to know how the church is to relate to the world*. Bosch tried to develop and build on this commonality through his use of the AC concept.

> Reformed ecclesiology, particularly in its early manifestations (and despite Calvin's own warnings in Book 4 of the Institutes) perhaps tended to draw too direct a line from the church to the world. Anabaptism, on the contrary, tended to reject the world and withdraw into the church as an almost self-contained entity. On the surface, then, it may be said that there are very few similarities between these two ecclesiologies. A closer look, however—and Anabaptists and Calvinists, particularly in the U.S.A., are becoming increasingly aware of this—reveals that the concerns of both groups are intimately related. The more identifiably separate and unique the church is as a community of believers (Anabaptism) the greater significance it has for the world (Calvinism) . . . The church has tremendous significance for society precisely because it is a uniquely separate community.[9]

---

6. Yoder, *The Politics of Jesus*, 5.

7. Bosch refers to a variety of Mennonite theologians in this regard. He was been most influenced by John Howard Yoder. See especially his *The Original Revolution*; *The Politics of Jesus*; and *The Priestly Kingdom*. Kraus' *The Community of the Spirit* and *The Authentic Witness* should also be mentioned here.

8. Bosch, "Mission and the Alternative Community," 8. See also Bosch, "Mennoniete Trap Diep Spore in Kerkgeskiedenis," 12, 16.

9. Bosch, "Mission and the Alternative Community," 8.

The Anabaptist emphasis upon costly conversion and discipleship, community-oriented Christian lifestyle, and the redemptive power of suffering and nonviolence, all figure prominently in the Bosch's vision of the AC.

The third influence on Bosch's conception of the AC is the *Reformed tradition*, particularly recent Reformed theology related to the nature of the church and its relation to the world. At the very outset of his discussion of the AC concept in *Witness*, Bosch began by citing the Heidelberg Catechism and Belgic Confession, both key doctrinal/confessional summaries within the Reformed tradition.[10] Bosch, of course, stood within the "Dutch" branch of the Reformed movement, and it is thus no surprise that the work of systematic theologian Hendrikus Berkhof of Leiden has influenced Bosch a great deal.[11] Along with Berkhof, we discern the influence of fellow Dutchmen A. A. van Ruler and J. Hoekendijk. Behind these figures, however, we note the looming presence of Karl Barth.[12]

The final major influence upon Bosch's understanding of the church as AC was a variety of Catholic and Protestant *biblical scholars*. In particular we mention the work of Dominican Albert Nolan, whose *Jesus Before Christianity: The Gospel of Liberation* was frequently cited by Bosch; and of Protestant scholar Martin Hengel, who wrote extensively on the historical and social framework of first-century Palestine.[13]

MAIN THEMES IN THE "ALTERNATIVE COMMUNITY" CONCEPT[14]

A Question About the Church

In his writings on the AC, Bosch was deeply concerned to answer the fundamental question: *What is the appropriate model for the church's existence in the world?* This, of course, is not a new question. Theologians have probed this issue from the earliest days of the Christian faith, as Niebuhr's *Christ and Culture* makes clear. Bosch believed, however, that it is essential to go *behind* the answers to this question that the different church traditions have developed. The life and ministry of Jesus, understood in relation to the sociopolitico-religious context of his day, reveals a model for the

---

10. Bosch, *Witness*, 223.

11. Bosch frequently refers to Berkhof's major dogmatic work, *Christian Faith*. We note that Berkhof's major section on ecclesiology (339–422) is titled, significantly, "The New Community."

12. For example, see the influence of these Reformed theologians in Bosch's "The Church and the Liberation of Peoples?," 13–29.

13. A work by another Roman Catholic biblical scholar substantiated many of the theses Bosch makes regarding the AC concept. See Gerhard Lohfink's *Jesus and Community: The Social Dimension of Christian Faith*.

14. Bosch's writings on the church as "alternative community" are found only in African journals and books. In this section, we shall be summarizing Bosch's approach based on his "The Renewal of Christian Community in Africa" (hereafter abbreviated as "Renewal"; *The Church as Alternative Community* (hereafter abbreviated as *TCAC*); relevant sections in *Witness*; and from his 1975 *JTSA* article "The Church as the 'Alternative Community.'"

church's existence in the world. Indeed, Bosch affirmed that the approach Jesus and the early church took toward society remains *normative* for Christians today, inasmuch as the situation faced by Jesus is analogous to our day.[15] The social context of Jesus' day bore a striking resemblance to the South African situation of Bosch's day.[16] Bosch acknowledged there is a risk involved in moving from the *descriptive* to the *prescriptive*, from the historical data about Jesus and the early church's relationship to society to its contemporary meaning and application, but that is the risk of all theologizing.

The Four Options Jesus Rejected[17]

Bosch pointed out that the era in which Jesus lived was filled with social conflict. During the decades before Christ, the Jewish nation had been torn apart by internal divisions, political scandal, and corruption. Differing factions battled among themselves for power and leadership. It was in this weakened condition that the Romans, with all their military might, conquered Palestine in 63 B.C. The Roman rule over the Jews was orderly, but even more oppressive.[18]

In Bosch's words, first-century Palestine was "a world pregnant with revolution and violence and it was impossible for any public figure not to take a stand on the issues of the day. Jesus of Nazareth was no exception . . ."[19] Citing Mary's Magnificat and Zechariah's song from Luke 1, as well as Jesus' own inaugural sermon in Luke 4, Bosch concluded:

> It was virtually impossible for anyone hearing such words not to understand them with the political framework of the day. Revolution was in the air. Whispers about freedom did the rounds. For this reason few of Jesus'

---

15. Bosch, *TCAC*, 2. Bosch here aligns himself with the approach of Yoder. Yoder makes a strong case for the argument that the teachings and ministry of Jesus represent a coherent, relevant approach to the Christian church's life in the world, i.e., social ethics. This approach has been set aside by much of mainline Protestant and Catholic theology. See his *The Politics of Jesus*, 11–25, 99–114.

16. Bosch, *TCAC*, 2–3. Bosch acknowledges that such an approach is problematic. There is a constant danger of allowing the biblical narrative, which emerged out of a very different historical context, to uncritically govern one's actions today. He explains the problem as follows: "Even if we accept the Bible as normative for today—and all Christians do that, in one way or another—our problems are in no way solved. There remains the danger of reading our own attitudes into the Bible. Or the danger of trying to build theological positions on isolated texts, out of context . . . What we need, therefore, is a great degree of discernment: to be able to relate 'text' and 'context', the Biblical text, within its own context, to the 'text' of our own situation . . . This means that we have to get behind the mere 'face value' of Biblical pronouncements. This may involve new formulations for new times" (ibid.).

17. See ibid., 1–10. Bosch's line of thought was apparently adopted from Yoder's typology in *The Original Revolution*, 18–27.

18. Standard works concerning the social and religious dynamics of first-century Palestine referred to by Bosch included the works of Bruce, *New Testament History*; Cullmann, *Jesus and the Revolutionaries*; Hengel, *Victory over Violence*; Hengel, *Christ and Power*; Jeremias, *Jerusalem in the Time of Christ*; and Lohse, *The New Testament Environment*.

19. Bosch, *TCAC*, 4.

contemporaries could have thought of Him as an eminently religious man who steered clear of politics. That kind of thing was just not possible. "For the unsophisticated Jewish population, it was almost entirely a history of oppressive exploitation . . . indescribable brutality and disappointed hopes." So everybody was preoccupied with the political situation. And everybody had to work out his own reaction to the political set-up. Neutrality was out. Also for Jesus. There are many indications in the gospel narratives that He was challenged to take a stand on the political issues of the day.[20]

In this first-century maelstrom, there evolved in the Jewish community four separate "models" or religio-ideological responses to the fundamental question of how the people of God were to relate to the society around them. Humanly speaking, these four groups represented the available social options for Jesus.[21]

First there was the model of the Sadducees and their allies, the Herodians. Theologically, the Sadducees were socially conservative political "realists." It seemed impossible to overthrow the Roman rulers by force, so they adapted to Roman rule and worked out a compromise: as leaders of the Jewish community they tried to maintain order in return for a certain degree of freedom. In their own way they were working for justice and change, but *within* the system. Theirs was a *theology of the status quo*. The problem with the Sadducees is that they identified themselves with the existing sociopolitical order to such an extent that they found it impossible to criticize "the system"—even when criticism was necessary. The Sadducees opposed Jesus because his activities jeopardized the peace and the balance of power they had so carefully worked out.

The second model Jesus had open to him was the Pharisees, the party of the scribes. They despised the worldly Sadducees because of their cooperation with the Roman authorities. To a pious Pharisee, politics was something to be shunned. The Pharisees sought to be rigidly faithful to the religious law, and thus spent much time and energy classifying the whole of life as "clean" or "unclean," holy and unholy. Every person they met, every object they were about to touch, had to be judged clean or unclean. And since one never knew if he had accidentally touched some unclean thing, the Pharisees developed elaborate rituals to keep the body and soul clean. In the eyes of the Pharisees, Jesus committed a mortal sin because he did not observe many of the ceremonial rules and rituals. Not only did Jesus reject their views on "clean" and "unclean" objects, he also associated with unclean *people:* sinners, publicans, prostitutes, and pagans.

As the zealous guardians of God's law, the Pharisees exercised a powerful authority over the common people. Yet the common people lived under a burden of guilt, since they were constantly reminded of their inadequate devotion to God in comparison to the legalistic righteousness of the Pharisees. If the Sadducees advocated a theology of the status quo, the Pharisees were the *legalistic Pietists* of their day. They

---

20. Ibid., 4–5. The quotation is from Hengel's *Victory Over Violence*, 71.
21. The following descriptions are based on Bosch, *TCAC*, 5–8; and Bosch, "The Church as the 'Alternative Community,'" 4–5.

lived in the midst of society but tried to stay pure from all forms of contamination. By retreating into legalism and avoiding contact with dirty things and dirty people they thought they could earn God's approval. Although they sought to avoid political involvements, their actual theological position implied an acceptance of the status quo. To avoid politics meant, tacitly at least, that they took the side of the establishment.

The third model available to Jesus was the Zealot party. The Zealots, an underground, revolutionary movement, sought to overthrow the Roman oppressors and set up their own Jewish state once again. They perceived themselves as Yahweh's freedom fighters, making holy war against the Roman pagans. They refused to cooperate with "the system" and despised the Sadducees and others who did. They believed that by overthrowing their Roman oppressors, they could hasten the coming of the kingdom of God. Theirs was a *theology of revolution.*

Bosch made the significant observation that Jesus was probably more attracted to the Zealot option than to the Sadducees or the Pharisees. More of his disciples came from the Zealot group than from any other part of Palestinian society. Jesus was perceived by many people, including some of his own disciples, as being sympathetic to the Zealot cause. He spoke their apocalyptic language; he took sides with the poor as they did; he condemned the same evils they did; he created a disciplined community of committed followers as they did; he prepared himself, as they did, to die for a divine cause; he was crucified for his alleged political activities. Why then, did Jesus not choose the path of the Zealots? Bosch approvingly cites Yoder's answer.

> He rejected the Zealot path not, as some of us might, because, being secure, we stand to lose in a revolution, or because, being squeamish, we want to avoid social conflict.... [No], His rejection of their righteous violence had another kind of reason.... What is wrong with the violent revolution according to Jesus is not that it changes too much but it changes too little; the Zealot is the reflection of the tyrant whom he replaces by means of the tools of the tyrant... What is wrong with the Zealot path for Jesus is not that it produces its new order by means of illegitimate instruments, but that the order it produces cannot be new. An order created by the sword is at the heart still not the new peoplehood Jesus announces.[22]

Ironically, although Jesus stood in close sympathy to many of the concerns of the Zealots, it was a former Zealot, Judas, who eventually turned him over to the authorities.

The final model presented to Jesus was that of the Essenes. Like the Zealots, these "sons of light" believed that the Roman pagans and the Jewish collaborators were oppressive "sons of darkness," and that violent change was necessary. Unlike the Zealots, however, they believed that the impending judgment was God's alone to invoke. The present world order could only be changed by means of God's apocalyptic

---

22. Yoder, *The Original Revolution*, 23–24; as cited by Bosch, "The Church as the 'Alternative Community,'" 4–5.

intervention. The Essenes, therefore, retreated to the desert as God's faithful remnant, uncontaminated by the world. They lived for the day when God's judgment would fall upon their enemies. Theirs was an ascetic *theology of the ghetto*, believing that God wanted his people to be physically and spiritually isolated from the wicked world around them. Jesus also rejected the Essene model. The Scriptures teach that Jesus deliberately journeyed to the cities and mixed with all varieties of people. Rather than retreating to the comforts of the countryside, Jesus set out quite consciously for the city, for Jerusalem, with all the conflicts that were sure to meet him there. A self-imposed life in a ghetto was not Jesus' idea of the new community.

According to Bosch, these were the four available social options that were available to Jesus. "There was either the more or less opportunistic accommodation to the establishment of the Sadducees, or the armed revolution of the Zealots, or the patient passive endurance of the Essenes and the Pharisees."[23] Yet Jesus refused to adopt any of them. Proof of this is found in the fact that in the end of Jesus' ministry the Sadducees, the Pharisees, and the Zealots all cooperated to get rid of Jesus.[24] In the end, these four groups, as different as they were from one another, had more in common with each other than with the new community that Jesus sought to form.

> They all sensed that the alternative Jesus offered, was so radically different that it would cut the ground from under their very feet unless they did something about it. What distinguished them from one another was mere squabbles compared to what distinguished them all from Jesus. The options they represented were all of the same order. What Jesus offered, belonged to another order, on a totally different level. And therefore this man from Nazareth was so insufferable and disgusting. They had to get ride of Him at all costs, so as to be able, once again, to continue undisturbed with their own trivialities and mutual squabbles. Therefore they declared war on Jesus, total war.[25]

We now turn to the radical new alternative that Jesus offered, a new possibility, in the words of Martin Hengel, "to break out of the vicious cycle of violence and counter-violence, opportunistic complicity, and apathetic resignation . . ."[26]

---

23. Bosch, *TCAC*, 8–9.

24. Bosch comments: "The Sadducees saw in Him a threat to the status quo: 'If we let Him go on in this way . . . the Roman authorities will take action and destroy our temple and our nation!' (John 11:48). The Pharisees, who used to enjoy the esteem of the masses, saw in Him a devastating threat; He was evidently doing everything just the other way round from what they regarded as decent, and it looked as though this appealed to the people. The Zealots considered His demand for love of enemies and renunciation of violence to be in extreme opposition to their ideal of revolutionary zeal; how can you kill your enemy if you love him? So Jesus was, simultaneously, a competitor and a traitor. This meant that both the extreme right and the extreme left rejected Jesus as an intolerable provocation; His death was undoubtedly welcomed by both wings" (Bosch, *TCAC*, 9).

25. Ibid.

26. Hengel, *Victory Over Violence*, 72, as cited in Bosch, *TCAC*, 10.

Part Three: Crucial Theological Dimensions for a Missionary Church

The New Option Jesus Offered: a New Definition of Community—the Old Barriers are Torn Down![27]

First, Jesus called his followers to a radically new understanding of community and solidarity. In the traditional Jewish framework, including all four above-mentioned groups, fraternal solidarity extended only to fellow Jews. All others were outsiders. The one exception to this rule, the Gentile proselytes, were a small group within Judaism, and never very influential. Jewishness was defined by a certain set of rules, dietary laws, and institutions peculiar to Jewish people. In this, the Jews were no different than other human communities. Human solidarity is normally grounded on the *differences* between peoples. These differences serve to identify a particular people, and define who they are over against other groups.

Jesus called for a solidarity that transcended all of these differences. Jesus drew together his disciples from across the social and political strata of Palestinian Judaism. He not only taught Jews to love their fellow Jews, beginning with their neighbors, but urged his listeners to love even their enemies (Matt 5:43; Luke 6:28). In his inaugural sermon in Nazareth (Luke 4), Jesus omitted any reference to the Lord's vengeance upon the Gentiles and read only the section about God's gracious salvation.[28] He taught that even the most solid family loyalties needed to be transcended (Mark 3:31–35). Many of his parables —those concerning Samaritans, sinners, the unclean, the lost—repeatedly emphasized that God, not one's nation or ethnic group, defined the meaning and limits of human solidarity. To pious Jewish ears, this must have sounded incredible—and sometimes enraging. As Bosch summarized it: "The enemy has to become a friend. The excluded have to be included. This means a fundamental regrouping according to new criteria . . . Not hatred, but love brings the victory. Not exclusivism but inclusivism is the answer. Not the limiting to the own group but the transcending of that groups is the way we should go."[29]

Jesus called his hearers to a new life together, where the artificial barriers between people were broken down. The AC that Jesus gathered was based solely in the desire to follow Jesus rather than any principle of human differentiation. Their unity was grounded in a common discipleship. When Jesus set his face toward Jerusalem to endure his passion, Jesus' followers still hoped that he would become a sociopolitical liberator of Israel (Mark 10:37; Luke 24:21). He refused to fulfill their expectations. Ultimately, he was rejected—even by his disciples—on the cross. He refused to fulfill the ideological dreams of his Jewish compatriots. In his death on the cross, according to Bosch, "he was undermining all the values upon which religion, economics, politics and society were based."[30]

---

27. For a full discussion of what follows, see Bosch, *TCAC*, 10–15.
28. See chapter 5, "The Ministry of Jesus."
29. Bosch, *TCAC*, 11.
30. Ibid., 15.

Only in light of the post-Easter experience of the risen Lord, however, did the full implications of the inclusive nature of the AC begin to be realized among the disciples. Beginning with Pentecost, the Spirit began to reveal the true nature and extent of the new community that Christ had inaugurated. Peter registered genuine surprise at Cornelius' house that God had no favorites (Acts 10:34). Paul marveled that Gentiles and Jews were heirs together, sharing in the blessings of Christ (Eph 3:6); and that in the new community there was now no difference between Jews and Gentiles, slaves and free persons, men and women—all were one in their union with Jesus Christ (Gal 3:28). In an expansive description, Bosch described the church as

> . . . God's new creation, the messianic community, the "single new humanity" in Christ, who has broken down the dividing wall and has reconciled Jew and Gentile "in a single body to God through the cross" (Eph. 2:14–16). The mutual solidarity within this community is not prescribed by the loyalties and prejudices of kinship, race, people, language, culture, class, political convictions, religious affinities, common interests, or profession. It transcends all these differences. There was room in the early church for simple fishermen from Galilee, for erstwhile Zealots such as Simon and one-time tax collectors of who Matthew was typical, for the likes of Paul, an erudite Pharisee, for members of the nobility such as Manaen who grew up with Herod, for Jews and Greeks, for blacks from Africa, among them the eunuch from Ethiopia and Simon called Niger who served with Paul as an elder in Antioch, for the slave Onesimus but also for his master Philemon, for prisoners no less than members of the imperial guard, and for a captain in the Roman army.[31]

For Bosch, the new community is rooted in the reconciling work of Christ, which began with his earthly ministry and which found its ultimate fulfillment on the cross. The old solidarities have been broken down. By the power of the Spirit, relationships are transformed into an open, inclusive community with Christ as the Head.

The New Option Jesus Offered:
A New Interpretation of the Present—the New Age has Come![32]

The second way that Jesus dramatically differed from the other groups of his day was his evaluation of the present moment, his *eschatological outlook*. If we return to the other groups during Jesus' day, we find that they had a one-sided view of history, an "eschatological paralysis." God had acted in the past. God would act one day in the future. But for the present, all they could do was endure as a hated, persecuted minority among the Gentiles.

---

31. Bosch, *Witness*, 223.
32. See Bosch, *TCAC*, 15–18.

Part Three: Crucial Theological Dimensions for a Missionary Church

Particularly among the Essenes and Zealots, Israel's sacred past—especially the reign of David—was glorified beyond all recognition. The present era in which they lived was dismal, filled with suffering, and essentially meaningless. When they pondered the future, they hoped for a restoration to the glories of Israel's past. Then all the nations would journey to Israel, looking to Jerusalem rather than Rome as the seat of earthly power.[33]

Jesus, however, viewed the present age in radically different terms. The present era was filled with meaning. Jesus urged his hearers to *recognize the kairos of God*. With the advent of Jesus, something decisive had happened; it was the decisive moment, the fateful hour, the turning point in history, the *kairos*. Present day history had become *filled time*, pregnant with meaning.[34]

This new awareness of the *kairos* was a result of Jesus' eschatological outlook. Jesus spoke of a God who was decisively working in *contemporary* history.[35] But more than that—he was consciously aware that, in his deeds and his very person, the promised kingdom of God had been inaugurated (Matt 11:5; 11:11; 12:28–29; 12:41–42; Mark 2:10; Luke 4:21; 10:17–18; 10:24; 11:20–22; 17:21). For the early Christian community, this awareness that God had filled the present age with meaning through the advent of Jesus impelled them to mission. Nothing could ever be the same again. The new age had dawned.[36]

The experience of the early church at Pentecost confirmed this. The resurrection of Jesus and the gifts of the Holy Spirit were visible manifestations or "first fruits" of the new age. As Bosch explained it: "Jesus' resurrection was tangible evidence of the fact that the new age has invaded the old. Of course, they knew that the kingdom would come in its fullness only at Christ's return, but the resurrection of Jesus and the presence of the Spirit in the church were visible signs that it made sense to begin living according to the standards of the new age."[37]

This is a crucial point. The kingdom, God's new order, has now become manifest in the church, although not yet in the world. Here we return to the heart of the tension with which Bosch repeatedly deals: the church's dual relationship to God and the world. Members of Jesus' community, Bosch affirmed,

> live in an unredeemed world, but they walk with their heads held high; they know that the Kingdom is coming because it has already come. The church

---

33. As Bosch summarizes it in Bosch, *Witness*, 64: "If the present is empty, as the Pharisees, Essenes and Zealots believed, then you can only flee into the memory of a glorious past recorded in codes (Pharisees), or you can, with folded arms, sit and wait for God's vengeance on your enemies (Essenes), or you can play God yourself by violently liquidating the empty present thus trying to make the utopian future a present reality (Zealots), or you can enter into an uncomfortable compromise with the status quo (Sadducees)."

34. Ibid.

35. Ibid. Cf. Bosch, *Theology 201*, 48–49; Bosch, *TCAC*, 16–17.

36. Bosch, *Witness*, 64–65; Bosch, "Renewal," 94–95.

37. Bosch, *TCAC*, 17.

as the Jesus community lives in the creative tension between the "already" and the "not yet". She is no longer what she used to be and not yet what she is destined to be. She is too early for heaven and too late for this world. She lives on the borderline between the already and the not yet. She is a fragment of the world to come. She is God's colony in man's world, God's experimental garden on earth. She is a sign of the world to come and at the same time a guarantee of its coming. And she is all this because of the indwelling of the Holy Spirit. She was given the Spirit as "firstfruits of the harvest to come", as "pledge of what is to come" (2 Cor. 1:22; 5:5; Eph. 1:14), as God's first installment. This new life in the Spirit is a present reality which puts everything on earth in a new perspective.[38]

Two important implications follow from the fact that the kingdom has now become manifest in the church. Positively, *it is imperative that the church live according to the extraordinary new standards of God's Reign.* The church's conduct is determined by the standards and values of the kingdom rather than the old age. Members of the community are to live "extraordinary" lives (Matt 5:47); they are to allow themselves to be remade and transformed by God's Spirit rather than adopting the patterns of the old world (Rom 12:2). In the old world, Jesus says, the kings lord it over their subjects, but he categorically adds: "Not so with you" (Luke 22:26).[39]

Negatively speaking, *in light of God's reign, everything in the old order has been relativized.* This means that all institutions—social structures, human traditions, governing authorities—have lost their claim to absoluteness. In the new community, there are no human institutions which are deemed divinely ordained and therefore inviolable. If any existing structure of society is perpetrating an injustice, it can and should be changed, and not treated as if it were sacrosanct.[40]

Entering the Alternative Community: Repentance and Conversion[41]

One of the fundamental tenets of Jesus' teaching and preaching was that it demanded a response.[42] The whole process of response to the gospel is called conversion. It is through repentance and conversion that one becomes—and remains—a member of the God's alternative community. Bosch decried the common Western reduction of the meaning of conversion into mere individualistic, spiritualistic and emotionalistic categories. Conversion, Bosch affirmed, certainly involves the individual, the spiritual,

38. Ibid., 18.
39. Bosch, "Renewal," 95.
40. Ibid.
41. See Bosch, *TCAC*, 18–27.
42. "Either one accepted Jesus and the dawning of an entirely new age, or one became so annoyed by Him that it became a battle unto death. But nobody could remain neutral" (ibid., 17).

and the emotional. But it includes much more than that. In the biblical narrative, conversion always includes at least seven elements.[43]

1. Conversion always involves a turning *from* (repentance) as well as a turning *to*.

2. The call to conversion goes out not only to unbelievers, but *to believers also*. This was particularly true in the Old Testament. The call to repent and be converted was normally addressed to *Israel*.

3. Conversion is *always "contextual."* It is linked to a specific moment in time (God's *kairos*), to a particular person or group, to a particular place or situation.

4. "Conversion always implies a *transfer of loyalty* or allegiance. It implies an exchange of lords. It means becoming citizens of the kingdom of God."

5. Conversion always involves an element of *self-denial*. Conversion is exactly the opposite of entering a state of relaxation and rest, for it involves losing oneself, leaving the self behind.

6. Conversion is a *journey into the unknown*. To follow Jesus implies a certain insecurity and homelessness (Matt 8:20). This "pilgrim existence" corresponds to God's pattern of leading his people Israel through the desert, in order that they might remain dependent upon God daily.

7. Conversion simultaneously implies *new relationships with both God and humankind*. It is both vertical and horizontal, spiritual as well as societal (Jas 2:19–20; Hos 12:6).

Conversion, then, involves a whole new way of life, a turning away from other loyalties to follow Christ. It means abandoning those things to which one is most attached and devoted. The fruits of repentance and conversion are as diverse as are the contexts in which the conversions take place. For some, like the Apostle Paul, conversion meant a new attitude toward human relationships, so that he treated people in a new way, with love and respect (2 Cor 5:17). For others, like Zacchaeus, conversion was linked to abandoning his unjust practices and his obsession with material wealth.[44]

Bosch cautioned against selective or "cheap" conversion. All too often only *certain parts* of the gospel are really accepted, and thus whole areas of life —consciously or unconsciously—remain unconverted.[45] Cheap conversion allows one to make some

---

43. These seven elements of conversion are taken from ibid., 19–20. All quotes come from this source.

44. Bosch noted that "I acknowledge without hesitation that I am embarrassed by these sayings of Jesus and that I cannot clearly tell how they ought to be translated and contextualised in our complex modern world. But I do believe that they mean *at least* the following: that there should be a carefreeness about material possessions among us and not the compulsiveness which is so typical of us. It also implies that our life style should be simple, sober, without extravagance" (ibid., 23).

45. As an example of this, Bosch cited a letter in an Afrikaans newspaper about a DRC dominie who preached a fiery sermon on South Africa's national Day of Prayer in 1976. His sermon was based on the text Amos 5:12: "Israel, prepare to meet your God!" The letter continued: "[The dominie] explained that the disasters they had experienced did not yet lead the people of Israel to repentance. So God Himself

peripheral sacrifices without being forced to come face to face with the costly, absolute demands of God. Cheap conversion compels people to "pass the sermon on as easily as if it were the collection plate," so that they think that the message God is speaking if for someone else rather than themselves.[46] Cheap conversion allows people to blame others when change does not come—rather than changing themselves. Cheap conversion, said Bosch, remained at the heart of the polarization between Black and White in apartheid South Africa. The question must be: "Only until *I* am prepared to change, moving to the foot of the Cross, will it possible for some other people to make a similar move."[47]

Becoming a member of God's new community is a risky affair, because it means being ruthlessly honest with one another. It means demolishing all of the walls that protect us, and opening ourselves to God and to others.

Who is able to do such things? In their own strength no human is capable of such a radical conversion. Bosch affirmed, therefore, that conversion is ultimately *the work of God alone.*

> No man can come to Jesus unless he is drawn by the Father (John 6:44). Nobody can repent and be converted unless he experiences a change of heart. This is so far-reaching and decisive an experience that Jesus refers to it as "being born over again" (John 3:3–8) and Paul as a "putting on the new self which is created in God's likeness" (Eph. 4:24). What is more: it can only be sustained when the Spirit directs our lives (Gal. 5:16), and when we meet around the Word and the Sacraments. Human selfishness is so tenacious, that unless God transforms a man and sustains him, he will soon resemble the old human self, however much he may decorate himself with a beautiful Christian varnish. Only the Spirit provides the antidote against the temptations and tensions that will arise.[48]

---

would deal with them. This was his declaration of war. What should we repent of today, here in South Africa? The packed audience waited with rapt attention. The preacher continued: 'We have to repent of the culture in which we pride ourselves, we have to repent of our pleasure, such as boxes full of alcoholic drinks at our festivities, of our carefree comfort, of our afternoon naps.' I began to wonder: when was he going to mention the most conspicuous sin which Amos chastised? That was, after all, the oppression and exploitation of the poor by the rich. Why did the preacher refer to our afternoon naps instead of race relations?" (ibid., 24).

46. Ibid., 25.
47. Ibid., 24–26.
48. Ibid., 27. Cf. Bosch, "Renewal," 96–97.

Part Three: Crucial Theological Dimensions for a Missionary Church

Living in the Alternative Community: Discipleship Under the Cross[49]

Compassion

The reality of the new community is to transform every dimension of one's life.[50] There is one overriding feature of the Christian disciple, however; a life of *compassion*. Compassion is the test of true discipleship. Here we reiterate what we observed in a previous chapter: Bosch understood *compassion* to be at the very center of Jesus' ministry.[51] A compassionate approach to life is opposite from the world's approach. According to Bosch, Paul constantly drew a contrast between the behavioral patterns of the world (inward-looking, self-assertive, self-centered) with the new life of Christ: (outward-looking, out-going and other-centered). "Compassion," Bosch said, is ". . . a suffering with the other, sharing in His suffering, suffering on His behalf."[52] It is no surprise, then, that the compassionate love of Jesus led to his suffering and death for the sake of others. This is the inexorable logic of compassion itself.

Ministry

In her compassionate love for the world, the new community is called to a mission of *ministry* to the world. She has been "saved" not simply to enjoy her salvation, but in order to minister for God in a needy world.[53] Her identity, inasmuch as she finds it in Jesus,

---

49. See Bosch, *TCAC*, 27–34.

50. In ibid., 29–30, Bosch commented on the remarkably all-embracing vision of the radical implications of life in the new community, citing the work of Roman Catholic theologian Juan Mattheos. "The characteristics of the group of disciples were first, love of the brethren, then joy, peace, tolerance, kindness, generosity, loyalty, simplicity and self-control (Gal. 5:22–23; Col. 3:12–13). It is a group without privileges, either racial, national, social, or of class or sex (1 Cor. 12:13; Gal. 3:28; Col. 3:11); a group where all barriers have fallen, in which all hostility has vanished, because Jesus Christ has made peace (Eph. 2:13–16). Thus is created the community in which there is no one on top or beneath, but all are last and first at the same time (Matt. 19:30), brothers with one Father, servants with one Lord, disciples with one Master, poor men whose only riches and security are in God Himself (Matt. 6:19–21). Here there is no mine or thine (Acts 4:32). It is a group filled with perfect joy (John 15:11; 16:24), mutual affection (Rom. 12:10; Col. 3:12), swift and unlimited pardon (Matt. 18:21–22; Col. 3:13); where no rivalry or partisanship exists, but all are united in love (Col. 3:14) and reciprocal support (Matt. 5:7). Each one shoulders the burden of the others (Gal. 6:2), the qualities of each are at the service of all (Rom. 12:3–8; 1 Cor. 12:4–11; Eph. 4:11–13), and authority means greater service not superiority (Luke 22:16–17)." Bosch then admits that this is a tall order indeed. Although we are very far from this ideal, we must not forget that because of what Christ did, all this has now become a possibility.

51. We note Bosch's strong dependence upon Nolan's *Jesus Before Christianity* in this section. Nolan acknowledged that compassion is a central feature of the biblical revelation of God and Jesus Christ. See ibid., 27–29, 67, 71, 79–81, 84, 95–98, 113–14, 124–25, 141.

52. Bosch, *TCAC*, 29.

53. Bosch, *Witness*, 225–26. Newbigin made the same point in his "The Future of Missions and Missionaries," 217: "The baptism which the Church gives is the act by which we are incorporated into that baptism of Christ with its focus on the cross. It is not baptism just for our own salvation . . . Rather, it is our incorporation into the one baptism which is for the salvation of the world. To accept baptism, therefore, is to be committed to be with Christ in his ministry for all men."

is inextricably bound up with the call to servanthood. The gospel, Bosch contended, is perfectly clear on this matter. "The church stands in this world as servant and not as lord. The church is the church for others. The church is, in the words of William Temple, 'the only society in the world which exists for the sake of those who are not members of it.' Everything is centred on the world; indeed it was the world that God loved (Jn. 3:16) and the world which he reconciled with himself in Christ (2 Cor. 5:19)."[54]

In his 1975 address to the SACC, Bosch developed a fourfold schema—of intercession, faithful witness, hope-filled prophecy, loving service—that highlights the church's unique responsibilities toward the world. In each of these tasks, the church, as God's AC, ministers to the world in ways that the world cannot do for herself.[55]

First, the church *intercedes* for the world, by praying for its needs. For this intercession to be credible and efficacious, however, two things are presupposed. First, it presupposes an essential *difference* between the church and the world. As Bosch put it, "The world cannot pray. Only believers, the Church, can."[56] Second, it also presupposes that the church is firmly *anchored in Christ* and nourished by him. She must be in a continual state of repentance before the Lord, asking if the peace and love and justice for which she is petitioning the Lord for the world has yet been adequately manifested in the *church itself*.[57]

Second, the church *witnesses* to the world, through her words and her deeds. In this way she is God's vehicle to grant persons his gift of faith and salvation. Her witness is grounded not in any sense of superiority but in deep solidarity with the world. She, like the world, exists only by the grace of God. She serves as a witness in a variety of ways. In her election as the people of God, as God's "experimental garden" (Berkhof), she serves as a model of what God's intentions are for the whole earth.[58] She serves as a witness through the extraordinary quality of her life, which amazed the first-century non-Christian world.[59] She witnesses to God through her suffering in the world, by following in the footsteps of her Lord, by being "a Church without privileges."[60] Finally, she witnesses to the world through her words. This form of witness is absolutely essential, but is also dangerous for the church. All too often, this verbal witness is visibly contradicted by the lamentable quality of Christians' lives.[61]

---

54. Bosch, *Church 301*, 42. Cf. Bosch, *Witness*, 225.

55. See Bosch, "The Church in South Africa—Tomorrow," 179–85; and Bosch, *Witness*, 219, 244–48. Bosch adapted this schema from Berkhof, *Christian Faith*, 416–18.

56. Bosch, *Witness*, 219.

57. Bosch, "The Church in South Africa—Tomorrow," 180–81.

58. Ibid., 180. Cf. Mott, *Biblical Ethics and Social Change*, 135–36.

59. Bosch, *TCAC*, 30–32.

60. Bosch, "The Church in South Africa—Tomorrow," 181. Cf. Bosch, "The Church as the 'Alternative Community,'" 11; and Bosch, "The In Between People," 10.

61. Bosch, *Witness*, 229.

Part Three: Crucial Theological Dimensions for a Missionary Church

In order for verbal witness to be authentic and credible to the world, the community of Christ must seek to be credible in the world's *eyes* as well as its *ears*.[62]

Third, the church *prophecies* to the world, and especially the fallen powers, concerning the Christian hope of the present and coming kingdom of God. In this prophetic ministry, the Christian community does not address people in order to convert them. Rather, said Bosch, "It aims at people as personifications of institutions and situations which perpetuate circumstances that are contrary to the will of God for this world. In her prophecy the Church confronts the powers that be and challenges them to employ their power for the sake of greater justice, peace and freedom. In this way she humanizes society, as Jesus did in respect of Samaritans, tax-gatherers, women and lepers in the society in which he lived."[63]

It is the certain hope of the coming kingdom that enables the church to work *now* for the values of the new order. Because the church is not only a witness but also an *agent* of the coming kingdom, she has to erect visible *signs* of the kingdom's presence in the world.[64] But again, it is essential that if the church wants to give the world a message of hope, something of that hope and of the new order must take shape in the church herself. The church is itself a part of the message.[65]

Fourth, the church *serves* the world by embodying the love which God himself has for the world. This is a love that ignores all human barriers, reaching out with genuine concern to meet the concrete needs of men, women and children. The essence of the church's service is the model of humility seen in Christ's sacrificial death on the cross. The disciples were moved to confess their belief in the Lord when they recognized the scars on Jesus' hands and side. In the same way, the world will be moved to believe when it observes the sacrificial scars that the church bears, as she witnesses to the Lord through a life of service to others.[66]

---

62. Bosch, "Renewal," 100.

63. Bosch, "The Church in South Africa—Tomorrow," 182.

64. Ibid., 183. Bosch also summarized this link in "Renewal," 98: "The Church has been saved in hope. Yet her present life already belongs to the time of hope. Christian hope is both possession and yearning, repose and activity, presence and journey. She dreams about the future by working to make it come true. Her temporal activity is a form of anticipating here and now the kingdom of God. She therefore allows herself not a moment's relaxation (Phil. 3:2–14). It flows from this that the Church cannot be indifferent to the wrongs of society. She cannot leave the world undisturbed in its injustice. She may not spend her time in quibbling about trivialities, while neglecting 'the weightier demand of the Law: justice, mercy and good faith' (Mt. 23:23). She may not allow her hope for an ultimate future consummation to paralyse her actions in the here and now. On the contrary: because she knows that Christ has said 'Behold, I make all things new!' she can be a constant disturbance in human society *now*. Someone who knows that God will wipe away all tears, will not accept with resignation the tears of those who are tormented *now*."

65. Bosch, *Witness*, 247. Cf. ibid., 224; and Bosch, *Theology 201*, 193.

66. Bosch, "The Church in South Africa—Tomorrow," 184–85.

A New Value System

Emerging out of this lifestyle of compassionate ministry in the world, Bosch highlighted four specific tenets of life in the AC: a new value system with regard to money, glory, power and violence. In Bosch's 1976 PACLA address, he spelled out the first three of these tenets.[67]

With regard to money, the AC must emphasize sharing rather than hoarding. Jesus expected his followers to have a detached, carefree attitude with regard to their money and possessions. Jesus expected "a giving up of their surpluses, a simple lifestyle, and compassionate giving," in order that no member of the community would ever be in need. It follows then, that "any society that is so structured that some suffer because of their poverty and others have more than they need, is a part of the kingdom of Satan."

With regard to glory, the AC must emphasize equality rather than selfish ambition. Jesus took exception to the Pharisees at precisely this point: they sought out places of honor, esteem and importance for themselves. In the AC, no one was allowed to divide people into inferior and superior categories. "Those who were not prepared for this," said Bosch, "who could not bear to have beggars, former prostitutes, servants, women, children and Samaritans treated as their equals, would simply exclude themselves."

With regard to power, the AC must emphasize service rather than domination. Rulers seek to make their subjects feel the weight of their authority, lording it over them. But Jesus says that greatness in his community consists of being a servant or a slave to all, leaving the self behind (Mark 10:42–45; Matt 6:24). This "selfless" life of following in the footsteps of Jesus involves suffering and persecution, even the taking up of a cross.

Finally, with regard to violence, Jesus set an example which most of the world, and even most Christians, have failed to follow. Bosch described how Plutarch once described Alexander the Great as "the universal author of peace" and as a "reconciler of the world." But how did Alexander do this? He brought all men together "in unity *by words and force of violence.*"[68] Bosch then pointedly asked whether the force of violence is ever a sufficient basis of reconciliation for those who follow Jesus. The New Testament does not speak this language at all. Rather,

> Jesus works reconciliation in a way that is the absolute antithesis of what Alexander and Augustus did: not by inflicting violence but by suffering violence. The motivating force is not lust for power, but love, indeed: love for enemies. In Romans 5 Paul indicates that we perceive the depth of divine love only when we see that Jesus died for His enemies. ". . . when we were God's enemies, we were reconciled to Him through the death of His son . . ." (5:10 NEB). Love for enemies, even love unto death, is not just part of Jesus' teaching, it is at the heart of His atonement. If we reject the Biblical imperative to follow Jesus

---

67. Bosch, "Renewal," 95–96. All quotations in the next three paragraphs are taken from these pages.
68. Bosch, *TCAC*, 34 (emphasis original).

Part Three: Crucial Theological Dimensions for a Missionary Church

at precisely this point, then we in effect express disbelief in the validity or effectiveness of God's way of reconciling enemies. But to do that is to express disbelief about reconciliation itself.[69]

Bosch here arrived at what appears to be a pacifist position. In both its tone and its logic, it resembles the nonviolent approach of John Howard Yoder and Ron Sider.[70] We will postpone consideration of the issue of violence, however, until later in this chapter.

The Church's Priestly, Pilgrim Existence

Clearly, life in the AC poses a radical challenge to the world around it. The New Age has relativized the old order. The church, by her very *existence* as God's AC, is a *sign of judgment*. She is "a sign of the devastating criticism which God has pronounced on the world."[71] By being true to her essence and origins, the AC antiquates the old society around her and threatens the continued existence of the status quo. Inevitably, Bosch believed, a church that lives out the values and relationships of the kingdom will have to endure a confrontation with the power structures of the society in which she lives.[72]

This should come as no surprise to followers of Jesus. Down through biblical history, people who lived in faithfulness to the promises and law of God have encountered deep opposition. The same will be true for any church today which begins to assume its role as the AC: the church will not easily fit into the patterns of behavior and the structures of this world. It will be perceived as a threat to the status quo and treated as such.[73]

It is with good reason, then, that Bosch emphasized the "pilgrim" nature of the church. The church, according to the book of Hebrews, is not settled community within this world.

> She is, at most, being granted a "sabbath rest" (Heb. 4:9). She has no permanent home here, but is "seeking after the city which is to come" (Heb. 13:14). She is looking forward "to the city with firm foundations, whose architect and builder is God" (Heb. 11:10). Her members confess that they are "no more than strangers or passing travellers on earth" (Heb. 11:13). She is, by definition, in Dietrich Bonhoeffer's phrase, "the church without privileges". She has been led into the desert, made to live under tents, where God can speak to her heart more directly (cf. Hosea 2:14; 12:9).[74]

---

69. Ibid.
70. See fn. 7 of this chapter for some of Yoder's works. Also see Sider, *Christ and Violence*.
71. Bosch, "Renewal," 97.
72. Bosch, "The Church as the 'Alternative Community,'" 9.
73. Ibid., 7–9.
74. Bosch, "Renewal," 98. See also Bosch, "The Church without Privileges," 2–3; and Bosch, *Church 301*, 23–24.

Life in the AC is marked not by "success"[75] but faithful obedience to the radical implications of the cross. Bosch recalled at the 1973 SACME gathering, Hans-Ruedi Weber reminded the delegates that reconciliation in the Bible occurs in the clash between two opposing forces, and someone gets crushed in the middle. This is precisely what happened to Jesus on the cross. In God's AC this principle still holds true. "Unless this cross becomes visible in us, there will be no reconciliation and the church's mission will remain incomplete . . . Without thorns and pain and nails there can be no new life."[76]

In this way, the church lives out its calling to be a reconciling community of *priests*. The church exists as a "priestly Kingdom"[77] whose members offer *themselves* as offerings and sacrifices in the service of others for Christ's sake. The priestly character of the church's self-identity is a reminder to its members that it has been called into existence by God to serve his mission to the world—even to the point of "getting crushed in the middle." The primary purpose of the pilgrim community can never be its own self-preservation, but rather a sacrificial life of service to God and his world.[78]

This, then, is the net result of life in the new community. It involves a new understanding of community and solidarity; a new evaluation of the present moment; a continual conversion to Jesus; and a costly discipleship marked by compassion for others, even to the point of suffering and the cross.

THE FUNCTIONS OF THE "ALTERNATIVE COMMUNITY" CONCEPT WITHIN THE CONTEXT OF BOSCH'S MISSIOLOGY

Now that we have reviewed the main features of Bosch's conception of the church as the alternative community, we need to show how it functioned within the larger framework of Bosch's thought. What are the "questions" that the AC is attempting to address? We believe the AC idea functioned in Bosch's missiological perspective in at least two ways. First, it offered an answer to the vexing theological question of the proper relationship of church and world. Second, it provided a conceptual and practical strategy in the struggle for justice in South Africa.

The AC as a Theological Response to the Church-World Issue

The AC concept is an attempt to resolve the question, first raised in our discussion of Bosch's eschatology, of the proper relationship between the church and the world.

---

75. In *TCAC*, 33, Bosch cites the comment that Bishop Tutu made at a meeting of the South African Council of Churches. Tutu observed that the church has been so inveighed by the "success ethic" that she forgets that, in many ways, she was meant to be a *failing community*.
76. Bosch, "The Church as the 'Alternative Community,'" 11.
77. This is the meaning behind the title of Yoder's book *The Priestly Kingdom*.
78. See Bosch, *Church 301*, 20–24.

Part Three: Crucial Theological Dimensions for a Missionary Church

At first glance, the AC concept appears to be a very *ecclesiocentric* notion. Bosch acknowledged that the church is in constant danger of shifting away from its concern for the world, isolating itself from the world and gravitating to selfish concern for self-enhancement and institutional survival.[79]

Bosch, however, believed that it is vital—for the sake of the world—that the church exist as a self-consciously distinct "alternative community." Indeed, the whole AC idea flows out of a deep concern and love for the world, as Bosch made clear in his 1982 retrospective.

> In my understanding . . . we have to work consistently at the renewal of the church—the alternative community—and precisely in that way at the renewal of society. It is for this reason that so much of what I have written in recent years in fact concentrates on the church. It is not a concentration on the church merely for the sake of the church but, rather, for the sake the world. If the "alternativeness" of the church is not apparent, the world loses its point of reference. I am not saying that the world can or even should copy the church—it remains, by definition, unable to be copied—and yet the church is called to be a permanent challenge to the world and its values.[80]

And again:

> The more identifiably separate and unique the church is as a community of believers . . . the greater significance it has for the world . . . The church is entirely different from the world, the "place where God lives through his Spirit" (Eph. 2:22 GNB) and in which, therefore, things are possible which would not even be considered in the world . . . [T]he church is also God's "experimental garden" on earth, his bridge-head into the world. Therefore, what happens in the church has tremendous significance for society, admittedly not on a one-to-one basis but at least in such a way that those who are members of the One Body cannot—as citizens of society—be and act in a way inconsistent with their life in the alternative community.[81]

It is absolutely essential that the church remain a unique community.[82] Only when the church as the AC is truly distinguishable from the world can she resist and

---

79. Ibid., 25–27. In Bosch, *Witness*, 226–27, Bosch elucidates the insight of Stephen Knapp that the church does not become a ghetto by being an alternative community, but by "spiritualizing" and "de-materializing" the gospel: "What makes the church into a ghetto . . . is not the idea of a separate community as such, 'but the tendency of communities to slip over into spiritualism, into a de-materialization and de-politicization of the Gospel.' Knapp argues that this tendency manifests itself precisely where the true distinctiveness of the Church grows dim and the Church becomes a captive of culture and politics. To solve the problem by deliberately relinquishing the distinctiveness of the Church and integrating her into the world, is likewise self-defeating." See Knapp, "Mission and Modernization," 168.

80. Bosch, "Mission and the Alternative Community," 9.

81. Ibid., 8.

82. Bosch is very careful to refute any suggestion that the church must be an alternative *society*. The church must always exist *within, yet different from,* the world around her. See Bosch, "Mission and the

challenge "the homogenizing power of the world." Only as the AC can she remain faithful to her role as a prophetic minority within society.[83]

This approach was not unique to Bosch, of course. Many Christians from diverse theological traditions have argued in recent decades that if the church is to remain true to her nature as the Body of Christ and have a redemptive impact on the world, she must maintain a distinct identity from the surrounding culture. The church is continually tempted to adopt "the ways of the world," the *zeitgeist* of the culture in which she lives. This was the burden of the provocatively titled work by Peter Berger and Richard Neuhaus, *Against the World for the World*.[84]

The 1952 Lund meeting of the WCC's Faith and Order Commission stated the issue with beguiling simplicity: "The Church is always and at the same time called out of the world and sent into the world." The dilemma has been how to live out both these affirmations simultaneously. Bosch,—and others—found in the concept of the church as AC a valuable resource with which to hold together these two affirmations.

Dr. J. J. Kritzinger of UNISA made the valuable suggestion that Bosch's use of the AC concept was an attempt to reconcile two very different ecclesiologies. On the one hand there is the traditional approach of the church as a divine institution, focused on God and called out from the world. On the other hand, there is the newer emphasis of the church as a pilgrim people sent into the world, in order to be "the church for others." The former emphasized the church's central role of mediating God to the world. The latter viewed the church merely as a "hyphen" between God and the world. Bosch's AC ecclesiology emerged out of a dialogue between these two approaches, seeking to integrate the abiding truths of both.[85]

Bosch would surely have concurred with the American Methodist theologian William Willimon regarding the proper relationship between the church and the world.

> The crucial political question for the church, is therefore, what kind of community do we need in order to be faithful to our Christian convictions? The church exists as a congregation, a congregating of those who have been called forth to live the truth which is not a new philosophy but the truth which is this Jew from Nazareth.

Alternative Community," 8; and Bosch, *Theology 201*, 193.

83. Bosch, *Witness*, 224.

84. Berger and Neuhaus, *Against the World for the World*. For more advocates of this trend, we refer the reader to the works of Yoder and other Mennonite theologians. From the evangelical tradition, see Mott, *Biblical Ethics and Social Change*, esp. his chapter on "The Church as Counter-Community." From the mainline Protestant perspective, see Haurwas, *The Peaceable Kingdom*, esp. his chapter "The Servant Community: Christian Social Ethics"; Willimon, *What's Right with the Church*; and Hauerwas and Willimon, *Resident Aliens*.

85. Bosch, *Missiology 101*, 182. Likewise, the AC concept seeks to integrate the abiding truths found in Kramm's *geschichtlich-eschatologisch* and *heilsgeschichtlich-ekklesiologisch* models. See Kramm, *Analyse und Bewährung theologischer Modelle zur Begründung der Mission*.

Part Three: Crucial Theological Dimensions for a Missionary Church

Our primary task is not to give advice to Congress or to help the president keep running things smoothly, as if America were the key to the truth of Jesus Christ. Our first political task is to be the church, to keep criticizing our message and mission and life together, so that we become a people who are formed and reformed by our dominant convictions.

> The primary question is not whether what we advocate is effective or acceptable or practical, because it normally is not. The question is whether or not what we advocate is true to the gospel. We criticize the world best by being the church, by being an alien people who belong to another kingdom.[86]

The AC as a Response to the Struggle for Social Justice in South Africa

The AC idea also functioned in Bosch's writings as a conceptual and practical strategy in the struggle for justice and peace in South Africa. The AC represents a particular—and distinctly Christian—socio-ethical stance in relation to the goal of the social transformation of South Africa. The church, said Bosch, could be a pillar of the status quo—*or* a major force for social change.[87] The tragedy is that while the DRC (arguably one of the most influential institutions within South African society) should have been on the *vanguard* of such change, it remained so long as a bulwark *against* any change in the apartheid system. It often appeared to drag its feet more resolutely than other elements of Afrikaner society—even the National Party government.[88] Bosch argued that only when the South African church, *including the DRC*, began to embody the values of the AC would there be any real possibility of a nonviolent social transformation in South African society.[89] Indeed, Richard John Neuhaus commented that even Bosch's opponents recognized Bosch's vision of social transformation through the AC model represented "a way of substantive change short of the revolutionary apocalypse."[90]

As we showed above, Bosch credited his adoption of the AC concept, in large measure, to Mennonite theologians such as Yoder.[91] Yoder passionately believed in the church's capacity to contribute to social justice and peace in the world as she lived out the implications of being God's AC. In Yoder's words, "the primary social struc-

---

86. Willimon, "A Crisis of Identity," 27.
87. Bosch, "Racism and Revolution," 20.
88. Hope and Young, *The South African Churches in a Revolutionary Situation*, 181.
89. Bosch, *TCAC*, 24–25, 26–27, 30–33.
90. Neuhaus, *Dispensations*, 155.

91. Besides the influence of his books, Yoder journeyed to South Africa on numerous occasions, and his influence among South African Christians outside the traditional Anabaptist subculture was noteworthy. See, for example, the strong influence of Yoder on John de Gruchy's writings, including *The Church Struggle in South Africa*, 195–237; and "Radical Peace-Making," 173–85. Yoder's significance for issues facing South African Christians was critically analyzed in an unpublished doctoral thesis by South African Anglican, David Russell. See his "A Theological Critique."

ture through which the gospel works to change other structures is that of the Christian community."[92] While Yoder would hasten to add that the social transformation of the world order is not be the church's *primary* function, it is nonetheless one of her essential functions.

Bosch would surely have acknowledged other legitimate strategies for social change besides the AC model. Bosch himself discussed the possibilities of peaceful reform through such tactics as civil disobedience and political action,[93] and would undoubtedly have agreed with ethicist Stephen Mott that "the creation of an alternative community has validity in itself, but is inadequate to express fully the biblical images of executing justice in the gate and breaking every yoke. The demonstration of Christian community is a facet of social change, but as the single expression of social justice it is inadequate."[94]

Bosch would have hastened to add, however, that the AC concept was essential and foundational to all other strategies for social change. At this point, we will not enter into a critique of the AC concept. We merely seek to show that the AC concept, as a Christian strategy for social transformation, gained currency among Christian thinkers both inside and outside South Africa;[95] and that Bosch developed this particular sociopolitical stance of the AC on the basis of *theological* considerations. The reality of the church as God's new community—and not merely pragmatic political considerations—determined the shape of his sociopolitical vision.

THE SACLA EVENT AS THE CONCRETE EMBODIMENT OF AC CONCEPT

We now turn to analyze one key event which embodied, better than any essay, Bosch's understanding of the church functioning as the AC within South African society: the interdenominational and interracial South African Christian Leadership Assembly (SACLA), held in Pretoria from July 5–15, 1979. Bosch helped to shape—and was profoundly shaped by—the SACLA experience.

The SACLA Event

The vision for SACLA emerged out of a concern among the South African delegates to the 1976 PACLA conference for some kind of follow-up gathering in South Africa. There was also an intense enthusiasm for such a gathering among many who had not

---

92. Yoder, *The Politics of Jesus*, 157.

93. Bosch discussed nonviolent civil disobedience in two unpublished addresses: "Violence," and "Burgerlike Ongehoorsaamheid."

94. Mott, *Biblical Ethics and Social Change*, 139.

95. See Wink, *Violence and Nonviolence in South Africa: Jesus' Third Way*.

Part Three: Crucial Theological Dimensions for a Missionary Church

attended PACLA.[96] SACLA was organized (as was PACLA before it) under the auspices of Africa Enterprise.[97] It sought to reach out to all the major ecclesiastical constituencies within the nation. This goal was a monumental task in itself, considering the polarization between the various churches in the land. SACLA's stated objective was "to discover together what it means to be faithful and effective witnesses to Jesus as Lord in South Africa today."[98] Bosch was involved in the SACLA preparations from the outset and served as Chairman of the SACLA Executive Committee.

Even before it was held, however, many roundly condemned SACLA. From one side, a some Afrikaner and English-speaking whites were disturbed by SACLA's vision. Some saw SACLA as a religious facade for a WCC-sponsored "political agenda"; others feared it would disturb the status quo and lead to further religious and political conflict.[99] Some of the attacks were quite scurrilous.[100] Others exhibited a deep paranoia that anything that attempted to bring Christians together across racial and theological lines must be a covert attempt to destroy Afrikaners.[101] The DRC leadership was deeply divided about participating. We recall the remarks of the Northern Transvaal *Moderamen* in this regard.[102] In order to secure any participation by White Dutch Reformed pastors and laity, a compromise arrangement had to be struck with the DRC leadership: SACLA would be a one-time event, with no continuation committee.[103]

From the other side, numerous younger leaders from the Black churches criticized the event as being a symbol of false reconciliation. SACLA did not go far enough, in their eyes, to justify their participation. Sam Buti of the NGKA and Allan Boesak of

---

96. For the full rationale behind the origins and goals of SACLA, see Bosch's "Why SACLA?".

97. Africa Enterprise is an evangelical, interdenominational mission agency headquartered in Pietermaritzburg, Natal. It was founded in 1961 by Michael Cassidy and funded in part by Fuller Theological Seminary. For the complete story, see Cassidy's *Bursting the Wineskins*.

98. In his "Why SACLA?" speech, 3–5, Bosch affirmed the goal of SACLA was to help put the divided Christian constituencies in touch with one another. As he put it: "The Church of Christ in this country is ecumenical *and* evangelical, Black *and* White, charismatic *and* non-charismatic, whether we like it or not. If we call ourselves Christians, we are brothers and sisters to one another, whether we like it or not." The church, says Bosch, was called to defy the "laws of logic" which assume that Blacks and Whites are a threat to one another, and to rebuild the bridges of communication among the body of Christ in South Africa. Cf. Bosch's unpublished paper "The In Between People," 8.

99. See "SACLA Preparations in Top Gear Despite Attacks," 1–2; and "South African Leadership Assembly Stirs Up Controversy," 1482–83.

100. We are speaking here of the tragically misinformed attacks on SACLA by the so-called "Christian League of Southern Africa" and some ad-hoc Afrikaner groups. See "Is SACLA Ecumenical or Evangelical?," 1, 4; Jooste, *SACLA?*; and *SACLA: Die Verkeerde Weg*. During the conference, the SACLA billboard outside the venue of the meetings was painted with a hammer and sickle sign by an unknown vandal.

101. Dr. J. D. Vorster, former DRC moderator, was reported to have told an audience that the SACLA event was "nothing more than another ecumenical front organization which liberals and Communists were using to destroy the Afrikaner." See "South African Christian Leadership Assembly Stirs Up Controversy," 1482.

102. See chapter 1, footnote 175.

103. Bosch, "Interview."

the NGSK declined to participate.[104] Bosch commented that the intense opposition to SACLA, particularly from elements within his own DRC, was one of the most difficult experiences of his life.[105]

SACLA did occur, however. Over 5,000 Christians of all races participated in the ten-day event, 15 percent of whom came from the DRC.[106] SACLA was structured to accommodate various audiences: church leaders, students, school children, politicians, and civic leaders. The overall theme of the conference revolved around the concept of "witness," with daily sub-themes bringing out different aspects of the topic.[107] Speakers at SACLA included Archbishop William Burnett, Bishop Manas Buthelezi, Michael Cassidy, Derek Crumpton, Abel Hendricks, Willie Jonker, Desmond Tutu, and, from the political arena, Chief Gatsha Buthelezi and National Party cabinet minister Piet Koornhof. Non-South African speakers included Orlando Costas, John Gatu, Ron Sider, Hendrikus Berkhof, and John Howard Yoder. The program involved plenary sessions, small discussion groups, times of worship, and informal interaction over the ten-day period.

SACLA was judged in positive terms by most observers, including most of the Afrikaans press.[108] Never before had so many Christians from so many different theological and ethnic backgrounds gathered for a time of sustained—and at times heated—dialogue on the church's role in South Africa. Within the confines of this work, we cannot detail the SACLA story any further.[109] Instead, we are concerned to show, inasmuch as Bosch was a crucial leader at SACLA, that the event served as a *call to* the church to be the AC, and functioned as a living *embodiment of* the AC concept.

SACLA as a Call for the Church to Become the AC

Bosch gave four major addresses at SACLA:[110] The first, "Earthen Vessels, But Containing a Treasure!," was given at a service of dedication for SACLA at St. Alban's

---

104. "South African Christian Leadership Assembly Stirs Up Controversy," 1482.

105. Bosch, "Interview."

106. Hope and Young, *The South African Churches in a Revolutionary Situation*, 180.

107. SACLA's seven-day program consisted of the following sub-themes: The Focus of Witness (Jesus Christ); The Community of Witness (Fellowship); The Message of Witness (The Kingdom of God); The Dynamic of Witness (The Holy Spirit); The Scope of Witness (The Great Commission); The Bearers of Witness (Incarnational Ministry); and The Acts of Witness (Worship and Evangelism). See Cassidy, *Bursting the Wineskins*, 239.

108. Bosch, "Interview." Cf. Hope and Young, *The South African Churches in a Revolutionary Situation*, 181.

109. The full story of SACLA has never been written, although Prof. Bosch perservered an extensive amount of materials related to all aspects of the event. The best brief accounts of SACLA are found in Lee, *Guard Her Children*; and in "Forging a Fragile Togetherness in the Land of Apartheid Rifts," 39–40. See also the appraisals of SACLA in the following South African publications: *JTSA* 29 (December 1979); *JTSA* 30 (March 1980); *Dimension* 10/8 (August 5, 1979); *DRC Africa News* 4/7 (July 1979); and *New Vision* (September 1979).

110. Bosch, "The Kingdom of God and the Kingdoms of this World" was subsequently published in the *JTSA* 29 (December 1979), 3–13. The other three were never published and exist in photocopied

Part Three: Crucial Theological Dimensions for a Missionary Church

Cathedral in Pretoria on June 24, 1979. "For Such a Time as This" and "The Kingdom of God and the Kingdoms of This World" were delivered at the Assembly. His "Blessed are the Peacemakers!" was delivered to 7,000 people at the Rally of Witness on July 15, 1979. Each of the four addresses make explicit or implicit reference to the major themes we have examined related to the AC concept: the four options which Jesus rejected;[111] Jesus' new understanding of community;[112] Jesus' interpretation of the present as being "filled time," the *kairos* of God;[113] the unconditional compassion of Christ toward others, especially the poor and powerless;[114] costly reconciliation and discipleship;[115] nonviolence;[116] the eschatological "kingdom" basis for the new community's standards and lifestyle, and its relationship to the world;[117] and the AC as an agent for social transformation.[118] Bosch's addresses at SACLA must be viewed, in large part, as an attempt to communicate his vision of the church as God's AC.

Other main speakers besides Bosch addressed subjects that touched upon themes related to the AC concept.[119] Orlando Costas' "Contextualization and Incarnation" dealt at length with the compassion of God toward the poor and oppressed. Ron Sider's "Words and Deeds" was a call for the church to be an agent for evangelization and social justice. Bishop Manas Buthelezi's "Violence and the Cross in South Africa Today" implored Christians to take seriously the call to costly discipleship, which involves suffering and a renunciation of violence. Hendrikus Berkhof's "The Holy Spirit and the World" spoke of the transforming work of the Spirit in the life of the world and in God's church. John Howard Yoder's "The Spirit of God and the Politics of Men" was a clear call for the church as the new community to live out the kingdom mandates of justice and peace within its culture.[120] With the exception of Yoder, none of the speakers specifically sought to address the AC concept. Yet the cumulative effect of

---

form only.

111. Ibid., [4–10]. Bracketed page references refer to the unpublished version of this paper.

112. Bosch, "For Such a Time as This," 8; Bosch, "Blessed are the Peacemakers!," 5–6.

113. Bosch, "Earthen Vessels, Indeed, But Containing a Treasure!," 5–6; Bosch, "For Such a Time as This," 1–2, 13–14; Bosch, "The Kingdom of God and the Kingdoms of this World," [5–6].

114. Bosch, "For Such a Time as This," 12; Bosch, "The Kingdom of God and the Kingdoms of this World," [11–13].

115. Bosch, "Earthen Vessels, Indeed, But Containing a Treasure!," 5; Bosch, "For Such a Time as This," 14; Bosch, "Blessed are the Peacemakers!," 6–9.

116. Bosch, "Blessed are the Peacemakers!," 1–9; Bosch, "For Such a Time as This," 14.

117. Bosch, "Earthen Vessels, Indeed, But Containing a Treasure!," 2–3; Bosch, "The Kingdom of God and the Kingdoms of this World," [8–14].

118. Bosch, "Blessed are the Peacemakers!," 6; Bosch, "The Kingdom of God and the Kingdoms of this World," [13–14].

119. The following addresses were all contained in the special SACLA issue of the *JTSA* 29 (December 1979).

120. In passing, we note that it is certainly no coincidence that two of the theologians who profoundly shaped Bosch's vision of the church as the alternative community—Yoder and Berkhof—were main speakers at SACLA.

all these SACLA addresses—Bosch's in particular—was a call for the church in South Africa to reconceive her identity as God's alternative community.

SACLA as the Embodiment of the Church as the AC

SACLA served as a call for South African Christians to become the alternative community of God. Yet it was also—in a limited but nonetheless real way—a true *embodiment* of the church as the AC in South Africa. Some criticized SACLA because it stressed politics too much.[121] For others, relevant discussion concerning South African political and social conditions was precisely what they found lacking at SACLA: it was not political enough![122] Both sets of critics, however, could be criticized in turn for misunderstanding the *nature* and *purpose* of SACLA. If SACLA was meant to be an embodiment of God's new community, understood in the way Bosch outlined, then the most effective and faithful way she could challenge the values and standards of South African society would not be by "being political," but simply by *being the church*. SACLA, according to Adrio König,

> was a rare but true embodiment of the church in its truest sense for the very reason that it constituted such a vast variety of denominations, traditions, convictions and ways of experiencing Christ. This is the church, the children of God. Whoever wishes to belong to it should in principle be prepared to worship and associate with all Christians . . . To me the prime merit of SACLA was that no one could accept everything that he encountered there, that everyone came across elements that troubled him, people with whom he could maintain his unity in Christ only by dint of unsparing effort. That is the true church.[123]

To be the AC, where Christian believers make "unsparing efforts" to live out their unity in Christ, where the barriers of language, sex, theological perspectives, and especially *race* have been broken down, has transforming social implications. Bosch described some of these as follows: "The mere fact that SACLA happened is a breakthrough. All apartheid legislation was suspended—eating rooms, toilets, everything was integrated . . . Blacks were put up in White homes in Pretoria. We just informed the authorities that they were staying there, and the authorities accepted it, although it was against the law . . . For most Whites it was the first time they'd had Blacks in their homes. Also, it was the first time that many of the English-speaking Whites had been guests in Afrikaner homes—and vice versa."[124]

---

121. See fn. 100 in this chapter.
122. See Wells, "Raising Power Against the Power Structures," 63–67.
123. König, "SACLA: A Rare but True Embodiment of the Church?," 80.
124. Hope and Young, *The South African Churches in a Revolutionary Situation*, 180–81 (my emphasis).

Part Three: Crucial Theological Dimensions for a Missionary Church

The actions of SACLA thus spoke louder than its words. SACLA, by embodying the values of God's new order, served as a witness to South African society. It exhibited a vision of what South Africa could be. It also relativized the human laws of the Republic of South Africa which stood in conflict with the values of God's new community. While SACLA obviously did not miraculously change the societal structures, it surely had a more subtle impact, changing the attitudes and dispositions of many of the participants. Changed attitudes alone do not change the structures of society, of course, but surely the goals of working to transform *personal attitudes* and *structures of society* need not be polarized. Both were essential in the struggle to conform South Africa more fully to the image of Christ.

Bosch's Evaluation of SACLA

It is impossible to judge the ultimate significance of SACLA, although surely it made its own unique contribution to the fundamental change experienced by South Africa as it moved into a post-apartheid era. In the immediate aftermath of SACLA, Bosch made the following evaluation.[125] On the positive side, Bosch comments that the impact of SACLA had been considerable. "I still meet people today who say to me SACLA changed my life. They say it as clearly and directly as that. There was a movement of the Spirit throughout the country. Because the size of SACLA, it could not be ignored. We had regularly 5,000 to 7,000 people every day, from morning to evening, in Pretoria, of all places, in the capital of the country. So nobody could ignore it, and it did make a tremendous impact."

Bosch's greatest regret, however, is that the SACLA team was not able to get the DRC officially involved. Unofficially, there were hundreds of DRC participants. There was great concern, however, that if SACLA was perceived to be an ongoing structure, then the DRC would have pronounced a synodical decision dissociating the church from SACLA, and demanded that no DRC person participate, much like what the DRC did to Beyers Naudé and others with regard to the Christian Institute in the 1960s. Through the work of Frans Geldenuys, the Executive Committee of the DRC encouraged people to go and participate, but with the clear understanding from the SACLA leadership that there would be no ongoing SACLA movement.

Bosch deeply regretted that SACLA did not build an infrastructure and continue to work at the grassroots. Reflecting on the matters seven years later, Bosch acknowledged: "With the NIR,[126] we are now picking up the threads [from SACLA],

---

125. This is a summary from my interview with Bosch. All quotations come from the interview. Also see the following unpublished evaluations of SACLA by Bosch: an untitled document drawn up for the Northern Transvaal Synod entitled "Opgestel vir Voorlegging (deur ds. J. G. du Plessis) aan 'n tydelike kommissie van die Noord-Transvaalse Sinode"; and ". . . And how Vast the Resources of His Power Open to Us Who Trust in Him" (SACLA Follow-up meeting, Johannesburg, 10 November 1979).

126. Africa Enterprise's National Initiative for Reconciliation. See ch. 1. In 1988, Bosch became the National Chairman of the NIR.

and therefore the NIR is going to be an ongoing concern. It is struggling to get off the ground. It is very, very difficult, because the tensions in the country are incredible now compared to what they were in '79. I think had we decided to follow a strategy similar to the NIR it could and would have grown to be a formidable factor within the country. We did not, so we did not exploit what was there."[127]

Bosch was doubly disappointed when he learned the results of a sociological study done at SACLA. Dr. Bob Koenig, a sociologist at Harvard University, conducted a detailed survey of SACLA participants to judge which groups were most deeply influenced and affected by the experience. "On almost every count," Bosch says, "the people who were most deeply influenced and affected were the Afrikaner church leaders. When those results came out, I was even more sorry, because it meant that people were brought up to a peak, and then just dropped. And that was truly a tragedy. We should have had a structure to exploit that and to build them up."[128]

A QUESTION CONCERNING THE AC CONCEPT

Bosch's vision of the church as God's AC, grounded in the central Anabaptist themes of costly discipleship, the church as a servant community, and a christologically centered social ethic, is powerful and compelling. It provides a credible paradigm to the vexing theological issue of the proper relationship between the church to the world. It also gave the church a biblically-grounded model for confronting social injustice in South Africa. Numerous criticisms of the AC concept emerged, however. We shall highlight one of these, namely the implicit *pacifism* of the AC and the question of *violence*.

The question of violence, both revolutionary and institutional, was a deeply troubling issue for Christians in South Africa. Beyers Naudé noted that "In South Africa we have never yet had a thorough discussion of the issue of violence or nonviolence. It is vitally important to form a legitimate theological position regarding that question."[129]

Various South African theologians assessed the nature and causes of violence in South Africa, analyzing both the violence *of* apartheid (including the repression which the state exercises in its enforcement of the apartheid system), and the violence

---

127. Interestingly enough, there was also resistance to make SACLA an ongoing structure from the opposition direction: because of the South African Council of Churches. Bosch noted: "It was difficult to see how we could have an ongoing structure which would not compete with the SACC, which is the official body of church representatives. I think we fooled ourselves, we misjudged the situation, because the kind of work we could have done and which is now being done by the NIR, is not something that the council of churches is doing. The Council is a council of *churches* . . . They run some programmes, but they do not have this network in the regional areas . . . They have local regional councils of churches, but again, they operated too officially and with too much official issues. SACLA and NIR, however, are based on relationships rather than structures. In that sense it would not really have competed, and I don't think the SACC would really have worried" (Bosch, "Interview").

128. Bosch, "Interview."

129. As quoted by Wink, *Violence and Nonviolence in South Africa*, vii.

Part Three: Crucial Theological Dimensions for a Missionary Church

used by those who feel led to take up arms to fight against apartheid.[130] Bosch, of course, had strong views on the subject. We have already argued that Bosch understood the AC concept to be a *legitimate* Christian strategy for social transformation, grounded on theological principles rather than pragmatic political considerations. A central dimension of the AC was its focus on *nonviolence*.

There are some who would ask whether the implicit pacifism of the AC was not merely a pragmatic response to social pressures in South Africa. They would point out a seeming inconsistency among the English-speaking churches. Why, they ask, have these churches, who stood firmly in the "just war" tradition and supported the Allied forces in two world wars, begin making quasi-pacifist statements, particularly since the rise of black liberation movements? Was the growing pacifist stance of these churches, and also of Afrikaner reformers like Bosch, indicative of a genuine change in theological convictions, away from the "just war" position and toward the Anabaptist position of nonviolence? Or could their behavior be explained as a *pragmatic* response to social pressures, as English-speaking Christians attempt to withdraw from the increasingly violent social conflict between a militarized Afrikaner state and the Black liberation movements?[131] Seen in this light, some viewed the perceived pseudo-pacifism and neutrality of these churches as a flight from their Christian social responsibility.[132]

We cannot answer for the English-speaking churches. We do not believe, however, that Bosch's adherence to the nonviolent lifestyle of the AC was grounded in such pragmatism. For Bosch and for the Anabaptists, their nonviolent stance was deeply rooted in their theology. As John de Gruchy puts it, the Anabaptist's pacifist position "arose out of a Christology and ecclesiology which took seriously the fact that the church is a community which has been called out of the world to bear witness to the gospel of Jesus Christ . . . For . . . the Anabaptists, the prime issue is not one of obedience to rules or principles, but the following of Jesus the suffering Messiah."[133]

De Gruchy notes that the early Anabaptists made no overt attempts to change the social order. Instead, they devoted their efforts to keeping their own fellowship alive. "Their witness to the world, and therefore their testimony to God's order for the world, derived from their struggle to be the church."[134] In time, this social stance laid the Anabaptists open to the criticism that they were simply "neutral" with regard to the things of this world: their refusal to become involved in the political arena sometimes meant an escape into an "alternative society" that resembled the ancient Essene community more than the community of Jesus Christ. Some critics maintained that

---

130. See the articles in Villa-Vicencio, *Theology and Violence: The South African Debate*; and Russell, "A Theological Critique of the Christian Pacifist Perspective with Special Reference to the Position of John Howard Yoder."

131. See De Gruchy, "Radical Peace-Making," 174.

132. This is one of the strong criticisms of the Kairos document against so-called "Church Theology."

133. De Gruchy, "Radical Peace-Making," 182.

134. Ibid., 183.

Bosch's AC model was similar: it served as a retreat from the active struggle for social justice in South Africa into mere "neutrality."

Yoder and other Anabaptist theologians have criticized their tradition's social isolationism. In contrast, they have emphasized that

> the Anabaptist vision requires socio-political engagement, but a way of engagement which derives from the gospel rather than secular norms, values and pragmatism. In particular, the Christian and the church are called to take sides with the oppressed in the struggle for justice, but in ways which are consonant with the cross of redemptive suffering. The "enemy" is always to be regarded as a human being for whom Christ died, and therefore the goal for Christian witness is not only justice for the oppressed but also redemption for the oppressor. The Christian's position in the struggle for justice is therefore not neutral; sides have to be taken, but in taking sides Christians may well find themselves caught in the crossfire of opposing forces. It is a form of radical peacemaking through a willingness to suffer for the cause of the right.[135]

This summary of Anabaptist social strategy could well have described Bosch's own position. In the church's prophetic witness, she *must* indeed stand on the side of justice. Sociopolitical engagement is an obligation for the church of Jesus Christ. She must not, however, resort to worldly methods and means but must adopt the way of the cross, which *suffers* rather than *causes* violence. As Bosch put it:

> And what if the powers that be reject the Church's prophetic witness? Does she then try to force her ideas upon the world by applying the means and methods of the world? Does she try to conquer where she has failed to persuade? Does she attack the world on its own terms? If she did, she would become thoroughly worldly and therefore utterly redundant. Triumphalism is an ever present temptation for the Church.
>
> So what must she do? If her prophetic witness is rejected, she has only one way to go: on the road of the Cross. This will be the new form of her prophetic witness, characterised by silence rather than garrulity. But will this have any effect? That is, in the last analysis, none of her business. She is called to be faithful, not effective. Success and failure are in any case very relative concepts in the Kingdom of God.[136]

This firm position regarding the nonviolence of the AC helps explain Bosch's criticism of the Kairos document in particular, and of liberation theology in general. While Bosch affirmed much of what Kairos declares (e.g., that reconciliation cannot exist without justice, that a false type of reconciliation has often been preached by the church in order to subdue people), he believed Kairos was wrong in "laying a psychological basis for hatred and its tacit support for revolutionary violence, or at

---

135. Ibid., (my emphasis).
136. Bosch, "The Church in South Africa—Tomorrow," 184.

Part Three: Crucial Theological Dimensions for a Missionary Church

least suggesting that responding with violence to violence is inevitable."[137] To advocate or condone such an approach would inevitably contaminate the church itself with the same hatred that characterizes the oppressor. According to estimates by both the ANC and the South African Security Police, between three and four million people would have died in an all-out liberation struggle in South Africa. Was this really the option that the church wished to endorse, Bosch asked?[138]

Bosch believed that the church must declare and exemplify an *alternative to violence* in her quest for the liberation of South Africa. "The church will always be tempted to follow the ways of the world but . . . it is called to resist this temptation. Unless the church in South Africa does this, it will just, with the rest, sink deeper into the quagmire and find it even more difficult to be a symbol of better values. It is called to find a way of resolutely showing solidarity with the poor and oppressed while at the same time preaching and practicing a transcendent love. Unless it follows this course, the spectre of violence and ruin and hatred will always be with us, both now and after liberation."[139] This desire to work for social change without compromising the nonviolent character of the gospel lay at the heart of Bosch's approach to violence.[140]

In the final analysis, the efficacy of the nonviolent ethos of the AC would have to be proved not by the *words* of its advocates, but by their *deeds*. In reference to people like Prof. Bosch, John de Gruchy has made this point clear. "For those who do adopt [Yoder's] position and seek to be the 'alternative community' in South Africa, it must be said that the proof of their position will not be made primarily in argument but in example and witness. Even if not all Christians are willing to espouse such pacifism, it is surely of vital importance that there be such communities of Christians in South Africa who can point to an alternative witness and way to justice in which violence is overcome not only as an end but also as a means."[141]

For David Bosch, as for countless other South Africans, the cost of being part of God's alternative community was lived out daily in the choices they made and the actions they took.

---

137. Bosch, "The Christian Church in a Revolutionary Situation," 15.

138. Ibid., 15. The estimate Bosch cites is to be found in Neuhaus, *Dispensations*, 286.

139. Bosch, "The Christian Church in a Revolutionary Situation," 17 (my emphasis).

140. Bosch made essentially the same argument in 1972 to the (Indian) Lenasia congregation of the Reformed Church in Africa. In his unpublished lecture "Violence," Bosch argues forcefully that, when faced with a situation of social injustice, various nonviolent strategies for social change (following the example of Jesus and as practiced by such men as Gandhi and Martin Luther King) are preferable to violent, revolutionary change. See also Bosch's unpublished text prepared for a July 1985 television interview, "Burgerlike Ongehoorsaamheid" [Civil Disobedience].

141. De Gruchy, "Radical Peace-Making," 184. Emilio Castro, General Secretary of the WCC, argued along similar lines in referring to the violence/nonviolence debate in Latin America. "In the urgency of the Latin American situation," Castro says, "there is no time to lose in discussions on violence and non-violence. Those who are committed to non-violence should prove the efficacy, the validity of their approach, not by discussing it with those who do not share their conviction, but by struggling with the factors of oppression in society" (Castro, *Amidst Revolution*, 68).

9

The Soteriological Dimension of the Missionary Church

The Church as a Sign and Agent of God's Reconciliation

WE NOW TURN TO the soteriological dimension of the church's witness in the world—the church as *the reconciled and reconciling community*. In this dimension of her existence, she serves as a sign and agent of God's salvation. She is called to embody in her own life and actions the costly, reconciling love of God in Christ, and thus, in a real sense, participate in the life of the triune God. An essential way this soteriological dimension of the missionary church had to be expressed in South Africa, according to Bosch, was by striving for a visible, structural *unity across the racial lines of the Dutch Reformed "family" of churches*. This concern should be seen as the logical outgrowth of the atonement.[1]

THE RECONCILING ACTION OF THE TRIUNE GOD AS THE SUBJECT AND FOUNDATION OF BOSCH'S THEOLOGY OF MISSION

Bosch's Approach to the Subject

In contemporary missiology there is a consensus that the Christian mission is rooted not only in a biblical mandate or an ecclesiastical obligation but in the very being and action of the triune God. The church undertakes her mission as a response to the prior, foundational mission of God in Christ, through the power of the Holy Spirit, in the world.[2] Such theologians as Abraham Kuyper, Gustav Warneck, and Karl

---

1. For an analysis of the doctrine of the atonement from the standpoint of the church's mission, see John Driver, *Understanding the Atonement for the Mission of the Church*.

2. Bassham, *Mission Theology*, 331–37; Stott, *Christian Mission*, 21–25; Verkuyl, *Contemporary*

Part Three: Crucial Theological Dimensions for a Missionary Church

Barth alluded to a trinitarian basis for mission.[3] Karl Hartenstein and Walter Freytag expounded it at the 1952 Willingen conference.[4] It was later popularized through the work of Lesslie Newbigin and Georg Vicedom,[5] and through the emergence of the *missio Dei* terminology of the 1960s and 1970s.

Bosch clearly agreed with describing mission in these terms. The title of his final chapter in *Witness to the World* is "Missio Dei: Mission in Trinitarian Perspective." He explained there that "Mission has its origin neither in the official Church nor in special groups within the Church. It has its origin in God. God is a missionary God, a God who crosses frontiers towards the world. In creation God was already the God of mission, with his Word and Spirit as 'Missionaries' (cf. Gen. 1:2–3). God likewise sent his incarnate Word, his Son into the world. And he sent his Spirit at Pentecost. Mission is God giving up himself, his becoming man, his laying aside of his divine prerogatives and taking our humanity, his moving into the world, in his Son and Spirit."[6]

Yet Bosch acknowledged a *danger* in founding the theological basis of mission upon "God's mission" or the *missio Dei*. Too often this had been done in a vague and theologically imprecise way. The original intent of the *missio Dei* theology as developed by Hartenstein was to safeguard to conviction that God alone was the Subject of mission, and that the initiative for the church's mission sprang from God himself. In the 1960s, the *missio Dei* concept was reinterpreted to focus on God's hidden actions in the world *apart from the church*, so that the church was obliged to identify and participate in those arenas of social conflict where God was "at work."[7]

Taking his cues from Martin Kähler, Karl Barth, and Max Warren, Bosch sought to anchor the trinitarian foundation for mission firmly in the doctrine of *reconciliation*, in order to protect it from some of the more speculative implications of the reinterpreted *missio Dei* theology of the 1960s. Bosch approvingly notes that Kähler organized his entire theology around the doctrine of reconciliation. It was "precisely from this central place occupied by soteriology in his theology, from the doctrines of justification and reconciliation, [that] Kähler had profound things to say about the church's mission."[8] For Kähler, mission was founded on the central fact of the atonement. God's reconciling grace was the ground of mission and the salvation of all humanity was its goal.[9]

Missiology, 197–204; and *Mission and Evangelism: An Ecumenical Affirmation*, paras. 1–5, 10, 15, 20.

    3. Bosch, *Witness*, 167, 240; and Bosch, *Theology 201*, 85.

    4. Rosin, *Missio Dei*.

    5. See Newbigin's *The Relevance of Trinitarian Doctrine for Today's Mission*; and Vicedom's *Missio Dei: Einführung in eine Theologie der Mission*.

    6. Bosch, *Witness*, 239.

    7. Ibid., 179–80. Cf. Bosch, "The Church in South Africa—Tomorrow," 178.

    8. Bosch, "Systematic Theology and Mission: The Voice of an Early Pioneer," 169.

    9. Ibid., 169, 174–75.

Bosch also noted that reconciliation is the central feature of Barth's trinitarian foundation for mission. It is significant that Barth chose to ground his discussion of mission in his volume on the doctrine of *reconciliation* (*Church Dogmatics* IV:3). As early as 1932, Barth argued for a trinitarian basis for the Christian mission. True to his Christocentric theological method, however, Barth concentrated his focus upon the person and work of Christ. As Bosch puts it, Barth's foundation for mission had a clear trinitarian basis, but it had a *christological concentration*.[10]

Barth's approach had a major impact at Willingen, through the influence of Max Warren's paper "The Christian Mission and the Cross." Warren proposed that the starting point for a theology of mission was found not in the church but in the triune God himself, not in ecclesiology but Christology. Warren, echoing Barth, emphasized ". . . the doctrine of the Trinity [be] interpreted on the basis of the atonement. Mission could be derived from the doctrine of the Trinity only indirectly. If soteriology, or more specifically the Cross, was taken as the starting point, it could however be derived directly. This explains why the Willingen report was not published under the original conference theme ["The Missionary Obligation of the Church"] but with the title Missions under the Cross (1953)."[11]

Bosch, following the lead of Barth and Warren, clearly believed that the proper grounding of the *missio Dei* perspective was Christology, in the reconciling work of Christ in his incarnation, death, and resurrection, and that tethering it to a Christological foundation would preserve the *missio Dei* from becoming a speculative and ambiguous enterprise.

The Triune God in His Reconciling Actions

The reconciling action of the triune God has three distinct dimensions. Each provided an insight into Bosch's understanding the missiological significance of the Holy Trinity. First, there is the mission of the Father, exemplifying *God's compassionate love*. No deeper foundation for mission can ever emerge than that God loves the world. As Bosch put it: "Mission has its origin in the *fatherly heart of God*. He is the fountain of sending love . . . It is not possible to penetrate any deeper: there is mission because God loves man."[12] This gracious compassion provides the basis for all his interaction with the world, including the sending of the Son and the Spirit. Jesus, in his teachings and parables, spoke frequently of his loving Father who had sent him for the sake of the salvation of the world.[13]

---

10. See Barth, "Die Theologie und die Mission in der Gegenwart." Cf. Bosch, *Theology 201*, 121; Bosch, *Witness*, 241.

11. Bosch, *Witness*, 179.

12. Ibid., 240. Cf. ibid., 50–53.

13. Ibid., 240.

Second, there is the mission of the Son, embodying *God's costly atonement*. Bosch believed there is indeed a "christological concentration" in the doctrine of the Trinity[14] Echoing Barth and Warren, Bosch argues that Christology—and most supremely the event of the Cross—provides the hermeneutical key to understanding the *missio Dei*, the mission of the triune God in this world.

> The Incarnation, Cross and Resurrection compel us to take history seriously, and thus also mission as historical involvement in this world. On the Cross God revealed that he took the world seriously, in that he judged the world. He not only judged the world, however; on the Cross, as well as in the Incarnation and Resurrection, he claimed the world for his Kingdom, he reconciled the world to himself. Mission thus indeed has a trinitarian basis, but in such a way that it has a christological concentration, because it is precisely Christology that accentuates God's entrance (his mission) into the world.[15]

Jesus Christ, in the uniqueness of his person and work, also reveals both the *definitive salvation* of God, and the *absolute model* for the church's mission. He is, firstly, God's final, definitive response to the world. As Bosch puts it: "Since Christ came we can no longer expect a salvation other than that which he inaugurated. Neither can we expect another Saviour."[16] Second, Jesus, as the Obedient Man and Missionary *par excellence*, reveals the model for the church's mission as she emulates her Lord. The incarnation provides a permanent paradigm for missionary theology and practice.

Finally, there is the mission of the Spirit, expressing *"God in action toward the world."* The significance of the pneumatological dimension of the trinitarian foundation for mission has emerged only recently.[17] Bosch emphasized two ways that the Spirit is foundationally related to mission. First, the Spirit labors to continue the mission of Jesus Christ, through the mission of Christ's disciples in the world. He is not a replacement for Christ; "his presence *is* the presence of Christ."[18] (Cf. John 20:21–22; Luke 24:49; Acts 1:8). In this role, the Spirit serves as the Enabler and Helper of the missionary church.

---

14. Bosch, *Theology* 201, 204. Bosch even goes so far as to argue, in refering to various Pauline texts, that mission is "a predicate of Christology" (Phil 2:6–11; 1 Tim 3:16); and is "christologically founded (2 Cor 5:18–20; Eph 2:14–18). See Bosch, *Witness*, 82.

15. Bosch, *Witness*, 240–41 (final emphasis mine).

16. Ibid., 241.

17. Bosch elaborates on this in ibid., 242. "Although the missionary dimension of Pneumatology was rediscovered at the time of the birth of the Protestant missionary movement in the eighteenth century, it played no significant role in Protestant theology. Pneumatology continued along more or less traditional avenues. Roland Allen was one of the first to protest against this. Subsequently Harry Boer made a thorough study of the close relationship between the Holy Spirit and mission. As far as systematic theology is concerned, it was particularly Karl Barth who, in the fourth volume of his *Church Dogmatics*, in which he treated Soteriology, discussed the missionary dimension of Pneumatology."

18. Bosch, *Witness*, 241.

The Soteriological Dimension of the Missionary Church

The Spirit of God, however, is not confined to working in the individual as an internalized Sanctifier, or only in the life of the church. The Spirit is, in the words of Gerardus van der Leeuw, "the Holy Spirit whom we may never hem in."[19] Bosch noted that the Spirit in the New Testament is seen as the driving, historical force behind the renewal of the entire world. The Spirit is the one who is paving the way, crossing frontiers, changing the attitudes and hearts of both believers and non-believers to make them more receptive to the message of the gospel. The Spirit is also changing society, nurturing in many human hearts the desire to see the world completely changed. The Spirit, as the "firstfruits" and "guarantee" of God's promises, is the one who provides believers with a vision of God's new world. It is precisely this vision for the renewal of the world that the church is called to live out, through its own inner life and missionary outreach.[20] Bosch approvingly cited Berkhof's missiologically potent definition of the Spirit: He is "God-in-action towards the world."[21]

For Bosch, then, the work of mission is the work of God himself, in his self-revelation as Father, Son, and Spirit. Since the Christian mission is anchored firmly on this trinitarian base, it can be nothing but *missio Dei*.

Clearly, God alone is the author, source, ground and subject of mission.[22] Hartenstein promulgated his *missio Dei* theology in order to safeguard this conviction, and Bosch stood in basic agreement with his approach.[23] Mission is not simply an activity that some human agent organizes but God's work. Yet it clearly *does* involve the energies and devotion of men and women. Mission, as we stated earlier, exists in creative tension as the work of God and as the joyful response of humans. Mission as *missio Dei* does not imply a passive quietism—or a frantic activism—on the part of humans. Rather God, through his body, the church, is laying claim on the whole world for his coming kingdom. Mission flows out from the church as she testifies to her experience of God's grace, revealed in the reconciling work of God in Christ. Thus God graciously acts, the church responds, and witness arises out of the interplay.[24]

WHAT IS RECONCILIATION? TWELVE THESES

So far we have shown that Bosch emphasized the centrality of the reconciling activity of God in the life of the missionary church. We now turn to analyze more fully what

---

19. Ibid., 199.
20. Bosch, *Theology 201*, 97–98.
21. Bosch, *Witness*, 242. See Berkhof, *Christian Faith*, § 52–55 ("The Renewal of the World") esp. pp. 507–8.
22. See Bosch, *Witness*, 77, 242–43; Bosch, "Sendingperspektief in die Ou Testament," 295; Bosch, "Jeseja en die Sending," 35; Bosch, "The Why and How of a True Biblical Foundation for Mission," 40.
23. "Faithful to Hartenstein's original intention we have to maintain that mission is concerned with God's Kingdom, that it exists on the basis of an expectation of that Kingdom, and that the salvation belonging to that Kingdom is wrought by God himself" (Bosch, *Witness*, 242–43).
24. Bosch, "The Church in South Africa—Tomorrow," 181–82.

Part Three: Crucial Theological Dimensions for a Missionary Church

Bosch meant by "reconciliation" in the challenging South African context in which he lived. Reconciliation has been a problematic word in South Africa because of its frequent misuse. Allan Boesak noted that ". . . there are many black Christians who frown when someone talks of reconciliation—not so much because reconciliation is regarded as unnecessary but because 'reconciliation', 'forgiveness', 'love' are words that have been glibly used by 'Christian' authorities to frustrate opposition and protest."[25]

Boesak did not, on this account, drop the word from his vocabulary. Rather he sought to clarify the proper meaning of the word in its full biblical context, redeeming it from those who have misused and cheapened it. We believe that Bosch, in his writings on the subject, attempted to do the same.[26]

In what follows, we shall summarize twelve theses propounded by Bosch about the meaning of reconciliation. Bosch first expounded these theses in a major address at the launching of the National Initiative for Reconciliation in November 1985.[27] Many of the themes Bosch proposed at the inaugural of the NIR are familiar to those who know his thinking with regard to the church as the AC or the theology of conversion. In fact, Bosch used the terms "conversion" and "reconciliation" almost interchangeably in some of his essays.[28] Both words describe that divine process whereby humans are put right in their relationships with God and their fellows.

1. "Cheap reconciliation is the deadly enemy of the church." Reconciliation can become a cheap, worn-out term through indiscriminate use, much like the "cheap grace" of which Bonhoeffer spoke. There are three aspects to cheap reconciliation. First, it costs very little. It allows deep-seated differences between persons to be papered over with a facade of Christian unity. Second, it assumes that since Christians have been reconciled to Christ, they are *automatically* reconciled to one another and that deep divisions no longer exist between different groups. Third, it reduces reconciliation to spiritual categories alone; everyday social relationships remain unaffected.[29] As Bosch put it: "Cheap reconciliation means tearing faith and justice asunder, driving a wedge between the vertical and horizontal. It suggests that we can have peace with God without having justice in our mutual relationships . . . Cheap reconciliation means applying a little bit of

---

25. Boesak, *The Finger of God*, 63.

26. The following published essays lay out Bosch's understanding of reconciliation: "Processes of Reconciliation and Demands of Obedience in South Africa: Twelve Theses," 12–13; reprinted in *Hammering Swords into Plowshares: Essays in Honour of Archbishop Desmond Tutu*, 159–71; and "Reconciliation—An Afrikaner Speaks," 60–65. Also see the following Bosch's unpublished essays: "As I See It"; "Polarisation or Reconciliation—Which Way?"; "Blessed are the Peacemakers!"; and "The In Between People."

27. The twelve theses and the main themes in the following section are taken from Bosch's "Processes of Reconciliation and Demands of Obedience in South Africa: Twelve Theses."

28. See, for example, Bosch's "As I See It."

29. As an illustration of this, Bosch tells the story of overhearing a white pastor say "All we need is to be truly born again, then all our problems will get solved." To this a black pastor answered, "Brother, my greatest frustrations come from born-again Christians!" (Bosch, "Processes of Reconciliation," 161; cf. Bosch, "As I See It," 8).

goodwill and decency to South African society, but that is like trying to heal a festering sore with sticking plaster or treating cancer with an aspirin."[30]

True Christian reconciliation in South Africa or anywhere else presupposes that people have to be reconciled, firstly, to *themselves*. Bosch mentions Boesak's book *Farewell to Innocence* in this regard. Boesak pointed out that Blacks needed to be reconciled to who they are, as Black people created in God's image. Bosch believed this insight was the major contribution of the Black Consciousness Movement. To be reconciled to others, one must know and understand oneself as one really is. This, said Bosch, is the teaching of the New Testament. Only those persons who have "found" themselves have the capacity to truly give themselves to others.[31]

True Christian reconciliation also presupposes open communication, honesty, even confrontation with those with whom we need to be reconciled. But it also assumes a love and commitment to the other party, a willingness to go the extra mile. Bosch elaborated that

> It is part of my Christian duty to tell my brother when I believe him to be wrong or misled, without writing him off. It is also part of my Christian duty to listen to my brother when he tells me that, without writing him off. Let us differ, by all means, but let's keep the channels of communication open . . . In Black-White relationships, so I believe, there are especially two emotions that have to be exposed: the White man's fear and the Black man's bitterness. Any attempt at reconciliation . . . that stops short of dealing with these two [issues] will be doomed to failure even before it got off the ground.[32]

2. *"All of us are prisoners of history, and are, as such, challenged to become prisoners of hope."* Bosch believed that the legacy of racial and cultural factionalism in South Africa had created an imprisoned society. Every ethnic group constructed an invisible defensive stronghold between itself and the other groups. In time, however, these fortresses had become prisons, and South Africans became prisoners of their own history.[33] The legacy of history cannot be reversed, no matter how much one might want. It cannot be shaken off. "We take our history with us into our future," said Bosch. And yet he believed these various, competing histories represented in the

---

30. Bosch, "Processes of Reconciliation," 161.

31. Bosch, "As I See It," 7–8.

32. Ibid., 9.

33. Also see Bosch, "Prisoners of History or Prisoners of Hope?," 14–18. Elsewhere, Bosch compares the racial polarization in South Africa to the divided city of Berlin, with its massive wall. "I think every city in South Africa is a divided city. There are invisible Berlin walls separating us from one another. Every morning Soweto spews its inhabitants into the White city of Johannesburg and swallows them up every evening. In the hours inbetween Blacks and Whites mingle in our streets, our offices, our shops, our factories, but the invisible walls remain intact. There is little true communication, little encounter on the human level, little real understanding of the world of the other, of his anxieties and hopes and frustrations" (Bosch, "Polarisation or Reconciliation—Which Way?," 3).

maelstrom of South Africa could actually provide a key to unlock the prison doors that had kept South Africans imprisoned.

> History is indeed a prison that locks us in. But it is, paradoxically, also the key that can open that prison for us. Then we move from being prisoners of history to being "prisoners of hope"—this is a phrase used by the prophet Zechariah to refer to the Judean captives in Babylon who are awaiting liberation (Zech. 9:12). Only by taking both the guilt and the grandeur of our history upon us, can we transform that history en route towards our common hope. Some people take only the guilt of their history with them . . . Others take only the grandeur of their history with them; then they absolutize it and make it normative also for the future. In neither case do they escape from their prisons.
>
> Let me say it by means of a metaphor—that of a bird in a violent storm. If the wings of that bird are set wrongly, it will be smashed against the cliff. But if the wings are set correctly, the storm itself will lift that bird above the danger of the cliff and it will soar towards the sun. We do not need new wings, then. It is the setting of our wings that matters. That has to be made new. God takes us as we are, together with our histories and he "sets" our histories in a new way. Indeed, our histories could have smashed us against the cliffs. But they can also, under God, help us to soar into true freedom. If there had been no wind, no storm, the bird would never have been carried into the blue.[34]

For Bosch, the key was neither denying nor glorifying one's own history, but rather allowing God to transform those personal and collective histories into something new. The obligation upon people, therefore, was *to be open to God's transforming power in the midst of their situation*, in order that God might work in a new way.

3. *"The biblical concept of reconciliation has as its corollaries the concepts repentance and forgiveness."* One cannot speak of reconciliation without focusing attention on repentance and forgiveness. These concepts clarify what reconciliation is all about. It is significant that the title of Bosch's major essay on reconciliation included the words "demands" and "obedience." Although God's reconciling, gracious love is free and unmerited, the proof of reconciliation is found in concrete, costly steps of obedience. True reconciliation demands true, heartfelt changes in all the parties of the reconciling process.

4. *"In ordinary inter-human communication people are usually more aware of the sins of others than of their own sin."* Here Bosch noted the human tendency to see the best in oneself and one's own group, and the worst in others (Luke 6:41–42). In the polarized South African situation, this tendency had been exacerbated. "In white circles the tendency is to blame everything that went wrong in our country on the blacks, or on Communist infiltrators or agitators, or on hooliganism. In black circles the opposite tendency prevails: whites are regarded as the authors of every conceivable evil in society."

34. Bosch, "Processes of Reconciliation," 162–63.

The Soteriological Dimension of the Missionary Church

The result of this approach led to increasing alienation between the various groups, with reconciliation a virtual impossibility, as both sides hardened their positions. This is precisely what occurred among the South African delegation at the 1976 PACLA conference, according to Bosch.[35] Bosch urged those who seek reconciliation to speak the truth to one another, but to speak the truth in *love* and *solidarity*, lest they block the way to true reconciliation.

5. *"In the context of the Christian faith, by contrast, we judge ourselves before we judge others."* This thesis states in a positive way what the previous thesis stated negatively. We can criticize others only when we have first criticized ourselves. The Christian is called to identify with the sin and guilt of his or her adversaries, irrespective of whether they do the same for us. The Christian must be ready to carry the guilt of the other party, forgiving them wholeheartedly.

6. *"If we are followers of the One who was crucified we too will have to be cross-bearers."* In this thesis, Bosch affirmed that the atoning work of Christ on the cross has demanding ethical implications for the church in South Africa. Reconciliation occurs when two opposing forces come into conflict, and someone gets crushed in between. This is precisely what happened to Jesus on the cross when he reconciled Jew and Gentile, making them into one new humanity (Eph 2:14–17).[36] Yet Jesus not only died an atoning death. In a real sense, his entire life and ministry was a reconciling, atoning action. He constantly embodied a "crucified lifestyle."

> Look at this man as he walks the dusty roads of Palestine and ministers to the crowds! He could also—as we often do—present argument upon argument to show that the people have only themselves to blame, that the Jews only got what they deserved or that the Romans were wicked and cruel. Jesus does not adopt this line, however. He disarms himself. He stands with a bleeding heart before Jew and Roman, black and white. He invites all of them in, even if it might mean that they would exploit him, trample upon him and deceive him. He accepts all of them unconditionally. He is the good Samaritan who risks his life for a Jew who is really supposed to be his arch-enemy. He is the good Shepherd who puts his own life in jeopardy for every obstinate sheep. He is the Servant who washes the feet even of his traitor. He is the Master who loves the rich young ruler while knowing that the young man would not be prepared to pay the price of discipleship. He is the one who reinstates Peter in his office, even if Peter has denied him in the hour of trial. He is the Master

---

35. Blacks and Whites were divided, with each group calling the other side to repent and change, convinced as they were of the rightness of their position. Then Michael Cassidy commented that both groups were confronting each other with two different "muscular Christs." Bosch summarizes Cassidy's line of thought as follows. "We tend to confront one another with a very muscular Christ. And if one group's Christ becomes too muscular, the others get frightened and go back into their shells. That is the end of community, the end of communication. And if Christ becomes too muscular, it will be hard to rehabilitate Him back to Calvary. The print of the nails tends to disappear behind the flexing of those powerful muscles" (Bosch, "As I See It," 9–10. Cf. Bosch, "Processes of Reconciliation," 163–64).

36. Ibid. Hans-Ruedi Weber made this point at the 1973 SACME gathering.

who trusts his disciples sufficiently to send them to the ends of the earth, even while knowing that they have all deserted him and fled in the hour of trial. Ultimately, he is the One who prays for those who crucify him: "Father, forgive them, for they do not know what they are doing."[37]

This sacrificial lifestyle and reconciling death of Jesus provides a costly path for those who would follow him. Bosch put this demanding lifestyle in deeply moving, lyrical terms:

> It is of such a Man that we are called to be disciples. And it is totally out of the question that we shall be his disciples without getting hurt ourselves. Moreover, unless I get hurt, I can't help others who hurt. It is only through wounds that wounds can be healed. Isn't that what the prophet said? ". . . he was pierced for our transgressions, he was crushed for our iniquities; the punishment that brought us peace was upon him, and by his wounds we are healed" (Isa. 53:5). The early Christian church took up this ancient word from the prophetic tradition: it was Jesus, they said, who was pierced for our transgressions; it is by his wounds that we are healed. The soldiers mocked him, "He saved others; he cannot save himself." But that is just the point. This Christ who saved others but did not save himself reveals the fundamental character of the true God. False gods save themselves; they do not save others. By implication the same is true of false Christians; they save themselves, not others. True Christians, however, bear on their bodies "the scars of Jesus" (Gal. 6:17), inflicted by other people. They carry around in their mortal bodies the death of Jesus (2 Cor. 4:10). They are like people condemned to death in the arena, a spectacle to the whole universe, fools for Christ's sake (1 Cor. 4:9–10). Where the world demands violence, they bring peace. Where the world cries for vengeance, they offer forgiveness. They thus turn everything upside down, almost as if nothing makes sense any longer! According to 2 Cor. 6:8–10 . . . it is imposters who speak the truth, the unknown people whom all people know. It is the dying who still live on and the sorrowful who have always cause for joy. It is the poor who bring wealth to many and the penniless who own the world. This is the paradox of the Christian life: it is when we are weak that we are strong (2 Cor. 12:10).[38]

We cite these passages in full because they set forth the heart of Bosch's understanding of reconciliation. The paradox of Christian discipleship is the paradox of the crucified God himself. God's reconciliation is grounded in the kenotic, forgiving, sacrificial love of Christ, and it is worked out as the world recognizes the very scars of Jesus in the lives of his disciples.

---

37. Ibid., 164–65.

38. Ibid., 165. Cf. Bosch, The Church as the "Alternative Community," 11; Bosch, "As I See It," 10–13. As in so many of Bosch's writings, we note here an implicit "creative tension" in the Christian faith and life.

The Soteriological Dimension of the Missionary Church

7. *"Repentance and conversion always affect those elements in our lives that touch us most deeply, which we are most attached or devoted to, without which—so we believe—we simply cannot exist."* Bosch here made the argument that an inherent dimension of the reconciliation process—which he links to the subject of conversion—is a renunciation of all our earthly securities and loyalties. Too easily these can become idols, things to which we become so devoted that we cannot imagine life without them. Yet the scriptural call to self-denial is clear: "If anyone wishes to be a follower of mine, he must leave self behind" (Matt 16:24, NEB). As evidence, Bosch cites the biblical examples of Abraham and Paul. Abraham, when called by God to sacrifice his son Isaac, had to deny himself and his own plans in order to be open to *God's* future for him. Paul, when confronted by the claims of Jesus, had to deny himself by abandoning his dependence upon his beloved Jewish heritage—counting it as nothing—in order to gain Christ (Phil 3:3–11).[39]

With these biblical precedents, Bosch moved on to apply this thesis to his own nation. Bosch refused to speculate whether his words had any implications for his black and English-speaking whites. Instead, he addressed his fellow Afrikaners directly.

> The gospel . . . challenges us to be willing to give up our privileges. As a matter of fact, the gospel goes further than that. It challenges us to "leave self behind", that is, to deny ourselves. It reveals to us that, in taking it upon ourselves to regulate the lives of other people in the minutest details, we have overstepped all limits. It urges us to stop all this and put it right now, regardless of the consequences. We know that, at least as we perceive it, this involves tremendous risks. But the gospel challenges us to do justice now, even if the world comes to an end—our world. We know that only if we accept this and get up and do it, shall we really be free to obey. We remind ourselves of Bonhoeffer's words: Only the one who believes, obeys; only the one who is obedient, believes. We know that God does not ask about the extent of our successes but about the depth of our obedience.[40]

Bosch believed that this path of self-denial and costly reconciliation might cost the Afrikaners everything —their freedom, their privileges, "all those things to which we have clung for dear life." It might even involve living under a corrupt and oppressive Marxist regime or suffering or perhaps even martyrdom for some.[41] Yet only in this path would Afrikaner Christians find *true freedom*—the freedom of the children of God. Afrikaner Christians will then be liberated from the guilt of privilege and from their bad conscience. Even if they became empty-handed, it would be as free

---

39. Bosch makes the same argument in "As I See It," 4–7.

40. Bosch, "Reconciliation—An Afrikaner Speaks," 64.

41. Bosch is not in any sense welcoming a Marxist-oriented regime, but simply reminding his Afrikaner brethren that much worse *could* befall them. God's church continues to survive and even grow in Russia and China. To the Afrikaner's utter surprise, he says, they may even get a *good* regime! See ibid., 64. We note that this last sentence is omitted from the other editions of this address.

Part Three: Crucial Theological Dimensions for a Missionary Church

men and women, "under God's wide open heaven." Bosch acknowledged his own fears about the South Africa's possible future, but affirms the mysterious providential action of God even in the midst of a seemingly hopeless situation.[42]

8. "Confession of guilt and repentance cannot be imposed by others but is a gift of the Holy Spirit." This thesis is intimately related to the previous one. God's Spirit must convict a person of sin; the Spirit alone enables confession, repentance, and conversion by changing that person's heart. Demands from other parties for someone to repent will fall on deaf ears. When someone seeks to impose this sense of guilt from the outside, the reconciliation process is usually short-circuited.[43]

It is for this reason that Bosch firmly believed that attempts by non-Afrikaners to bring Afrikaners to repentance accomplishes little.

> If . . . the challenge to confess our guilt comes from black South Africans, this might be counter-productive. We might argue that they stand to gain from our confession and this might harden us. Neither should the challenge to Afrikaners come from white English-speaking South African Christians. Afrikaners will simply label them hypocrites, in light of their own history of oppression and exploitation. Least of all should the challenge come from Christians outside South Africa; from their comfortable positions they make demands on us which cost them nothing, and precisely for that reason we will dismiss those demands with contempt. I daresay the main reason Afrikaner Christians have been so slow in confessing their guilt is precisely that others—for whom nothing was at stake—have tried so frequently to bludgeon us into it.[44]

Yet Bosch believed fellow Afrikaner Christians who shared in the privileges of South African society, were in a strategic position to challenge their fellows to change. Ideally, he said, it should be "Afrikaner Christians who challenge fellow-Afrikaners to come to the recognition that we all share in the guilt of the sins we

---

42. Bosch comments: "I am saying all this truly with fear and trembling, not only because I know that what I am saying may be misunderstood and misreported, but also, and perhaps particularly, because I know myself and my own weakness too well to make in confidence this kind of statement about willingness to be a servant in a context where I am the underdog and the oppressed. I can only say I will do it . . . may God have mercy on me! Like the father of the boy with an evil spirit, I can only say: 'Lord, I believe . . . help me overcome my unbelief' (cf. Mark 9:24). 'Lord, I am willing . . . help me overcome my unwillingness.' We are, after all, not only talking about 'processes of reconciliation', but also about 'demands of obedience'. This was the terrible lesson Abraham had to learn, and Saul of Tarsus. They saw their entire world crumbling down, before a new world could be rebuilt, out of the ruins, piece by piece. Can we expect to get by with less? . . . Naturally, we would have preferred all these changes to come about because of the promptings of God's Spirit rather than because of the terrible events around us—biblically speaking, that change should come about because of the repentance of Israel, not because of the batterings of Assyria. But this is often the way God works: if our hearts are hardened to his Spirit, he uses other means. And the executors of his judgment may surprise us" (Bosch, "Processes of Reconciliation," 168).

43. Newbigin makes a similar argument about the Spirit's overarching role in repentance and forgiveness in his *The Open Secret*, 147–57.

44. Bosch, "Reconciliation—An Afrikaner Speaks," 64. Curiously, parts of this section are missing from the reprint of the essay in *Hammering Swords into Plowshares*. This is an unfortunate error, for it distorts the meaning of the thesis.

have committed, that we should recognise that guilt for what it is, confess it, and take deliberate steps at making restitution."[45] Bosch went on to applaud the 1985 confession of guilt concerning the injustice of apartheid by the Presbytery of Stellenbosch as a step in the right direction.[46]

Despite this inadequacy, Bosch also affirmed that Afrikaners—and all other groups—must never make their confession and repentance *conditional upon the response of others*. To do so would be to deny the nature of God's grace itself. "No longer dare we argue that the others also have guilt and that they, too, must confess their guilt and repent. Perhaps they have guilt. But that is of no consequence to us. We dare not make our confession of guilt and repentance subject to, of dependent upon, theirs. We dare not even demand forgiveness; we may not withdraw our confession of guilt if the other party fails to forgive us. Confessing our guilt is in itself a supreme blessing and a sign of grace. It opens up the fountains of new life and cleanses us."[47]

This was precisely the reason Bosch had trouble with elements of the Kairos Declaration, which tended to make forgiveness and reconciliation conditional upon the response of the South African government. Kairos declared "Reconciliation, forgiveness and negotiations will become our Christian duty in South Africa only when the apartheid regime shows signs of genuine repentance."[48] Bosch agreed with Kairos that complete reconciliation is impossible without justice for all concerned, and yet insisted the duty of the Christian disciple is to begin the reconciliation process, and to continue in the path of forgiveness and costly, sacrificial love even when other parties are *not* admitting their guilt or their need to repent and be forgiven.[49] In the language of Calvin and Reformed theology, there is a distinction between "legal repentance" and "evangelical repentance." In "legal repentance," human repentance is made a *condition* of God's forgiveness. "Evangelical repentance" on the other hand, emphasizes that repentance is a *response* to God's grace and the forgiving power of the word of the Cross. In this understanding, forgiveness is logically *prior* to repentance.[50]

9. *"Our most terrible guilt is that of which we are unaware."* Not only is one more conscious of the sins of others than of one's own (thesis 4 above). Those who regard themselves as the most innocent are in reality the most guilty. Bosch noted that many of Jesus' parables which relate to forgiveness and mercy were focused not upon

---

45. Bosch, "Processes of Reconciliation," 168.

46. Cf. fn. 115 in this chapter.

47. Bosch, "Processes of Reconciliation," 169. Torrance argues along similar lines in his critique of the Kairos document. See his "The Kairos Debate: Listening to Its Challenge," 42–45.

48. *The Kairos Document: Revised Second Edition*, 10.

49. For two opposing viewpoints on the issue of forgiveness, reconciliation, and justice in South Africa, compare Torrance, "The Kairos Debate: Listening to Its Challenge" and Snook, "Forgiveness and Justice in South Africa", 18–21.

50. See Calvin, *Institutes of the Christian Religion*, Book III, 3.3. Also see the unpublished paper by James Torrance, "Interpreting the Word by the Light of Christ or the Light of Nature? Calvin, Calvinism and Karl Barth," 13.

"sinners" but upon those who thought they were innocent, righteous, blameless, and "spiritually healthy." The imagined innocence of the Pharisees and the rich man who oppressed Lazarus "did not lessen their guilt but aggravate[d] it."[51] This is the lesson Jesus drew when he told the parable about the final judgment in Matt 25. "The people in Jesus' last parable in Matthew (25:31–46) who did not minister to the hungry and the naked for the simple reason that they never consciously 'saw' those unfortunate victims of society, are not acquitted by Jesus for not being aware of the others' needs; on the contrary, they are pronounced guilty and sent into eternal punishment. All these are cases not of innocence but of pseudo-innocence."[52]

Bosch linked this pseudo-innocence to the Afrikaner churches. "If a pastor today attacks a colleague for referring to injustices in our society and then claims that he is totally unaware of any injustice in South Africa, he is not just ignorant, he is misguided and blind."[53] Ignorance provides no excuse; the personal guilt of which one is unaware may be the worst guilt of all.

10. "God forgives us our debts as we also forgive our debtors." Here Bosch referred to the fifth petition of the Lord's Prayer, confirming that reconciliation with God and reconciliation with neighbor are intimately linked. God's forgiveness is unconditional; God does not forgive us *if* we forgive our debtors. Any sinner who honestly confesses his guilt can be assured of the forgiveness of God. Yet Bosch affirmed it was impossible "to receive God's forgiveness and remain unyielding to our human debtors." Bosch's argument is comparable to the relationship of faith and works in Christian theology. Salvation is by grace through faith alone. Yet there can be no real faith without the authenticating evidence of works. It is impossible to maintain two contradictory attitudes. Bosch affirmed that we cannot expect the unconditional pardon of God when we have a radically *different* attitude towards our neighbor, an attitude which is restricted and conditional upon whether the neighbor properly repents. Citing the work of Leonardo Boff, Bosch concludes that ". . . if we have really had the radical experience of forgiveness of our sins and our debts, if we truly have felt the mercy of God at work in our sinful life, then we are also impelled to forgive without limits, without reservations . . . We have no right to God's forgiveness if we do not want to forgive our neighbours."[54]

11. "If we reject the road of reconciliation we are crucifying Christ anew." The duties of repentance, forgiveness, and reconciliation are not optional but mandatory for

---

51. Bosch, "Processes of Reconciliation," 170.

52. Ibid. In his *The Lord's Prayer: Paradigm for a Christian Lifestyle*, Bosch expands on this concept of pseudo-innocence, and affirms the argument made by Alan Boesak in his doctoral thesis *Farewell to Innocence*. Boesak, says Bosch, argues that the privileged groups in South Africa go to extraordinary lengths to prevent themselves of becoming aware of what is really going on in their country. This pseudo-innocence plagues many good and pious people who are simply totally unaware of their guilt towards other human beings. See Bosch, *The Lord's Prayer*, 35.

53. Bosch, "Processes of Reconciliation," 170.

54. Ibid. Cf. Bosch, *The Lord's Prayer*, 31–32. Bosch is citing Boff, *The Lord's Prayer*, 94–95.

the disciple of Christ. To refuse to repent, forgive, and be reconciled is tantamount to declaring that what Christ did on the cross—when he broke down the human barriers that divide the world—was of no consequence. It is as if Christ had never come at all. "Not to believe in the possibility of reconciliation," said Bosch, "and not to act as people who have found and embraced one another, [who] act justly toward one another, actually means reinforcing and buttressing the wall that divides us."[55] To refuse to act on the divine mandate for interpersonal reconciliation is a denial of the Lord, because true reconciliation with God necessarily involves being reconciled with those around us.

12. "Reconciliation is not a human possibility but a divine gift." Reconciliation, like conversion, is ultimately the work of God himself. Left to ourselves, human beings would be incapable and powerless to effect the reconciliation which God demands. Yet it is part of the mysterious grace of God that he calls together a powerless, despairing group of disciples, infuses them with the hope of the resurrection and the power of the Holy Spirit, and sends them into the whole world with a ministry of reconciliation. In one sense reconciliation is the work of God's ambassadors, as they build bridges with the gospel of Christ to all those around them. In the deepest sense, however, Bosch stated that we are not so much bridge-builders as bridge-*crossers.* "The Bridge is already there—our Lord, who in his own body of flesh and blood has broken down the enmity which stood like a dividing wall between us. *He* is the Bridge over which we cross to each other, again and again."[56]

In conclusion, we make two observations about Bosch's theology of reconciliation. First, Bosch saw the "processes of reconciliation and the demands of obedience" as an urgent call *to the church*. "True reconciliation," said Bosch, "is really a challenge to us as the Church, not the world outside. If there is no reconciliation, it is because we have not been the church. It is as simple as that."[57] Here we see a crucial link between Bosch's theology of reconciliation and his concept of the church as the alternative community. In the ministry of reconciliation, the church must *embody* in herself what she envisions for the world. The church is a distinct alternative to the surrounding society precisely because it is the one community where love for one's enemies is an assumed obligation of membership. Costly, reconciling compassion for others is not simply the heart of Christ's atonement but the heart of his new community.[58]

Second, Bosch's understanding of reconciliation provided the theological foundation for his practical ministry within South Africa. In particular, it defined and shaped his response to the policies of his own denomination—the DRC. Bosch attacked the DRC's tacit support of apartheid most severely because it *undermined the true identity of the church*. The church was called to be a community of reconciliation. The ideology of apartheid threatened this foundational truth.

55. Bosch, "Processes of Reconciliation," 171.
56. Bosch, "Reconciliation—An Afrikaner Speaks," 65.
57. Bosch, "As I See It," 14.
58. Bosch, *TCAC*, 34.

Part Three: Crucial Theological Dimensions for a Missionary Church

THE MISSIONARY CHURCH AS THE RECONCILED AND RECONCILING COMMUNITY

The Integral Relationship Between Reconciliation, Unity, and Witness

The doctrine of reconciliation is the touchstone of the church's unity and witness. Whenever the New Testament refers to the unity or mission of the church, it does so in the broader context of the death and resurrection of Christ.[59] We shall now briefly spell out the relationship between reconciliation, unity and witness. We believe it summarizes Bosch's essential stance.

The missionary church is called to be a *sign* of reconciliation in the world. It serves as a sign of reconciliation when it lays claim to the implications of Christ's gracious sacrifice for *its own inner life*. She is to strive, in faith, to be God's family, his alternative community. The church exists in an amazing variety of forms: e.g., different languages, cultures, theological approaches, and liturgical styles. Yet as a sign of God's reconciliation, she is to retain a fundamental unity of fellowship and mind and purpose. The divisions that exist within the church's life, to the extent that they are based *solely* on racial, economic, nationalistic, or other human distinctions, are a result of sin and must be eradicated in the name of the gospel. Here we emphasize the *unitive* dimension of Christian reconciliation: she must be *internally reconciled within herself*.

The missionary church is also called to be an *agent* of reconciliation in the world. As an agent of reconciliation, the church witnesses to others about God's saving work in Christ. By word and deed she points people to God's grace. She speaks and acts within the society around her to lift up Christ and his kingdom, with all its demanding values and standards. God has entrusted a part of his reconciling work on earth to the church, and equips her to be his unique emissary in the world. Here we emphasize the *missional* dimension of Christian reconciliation: she must be a *reconciling agent within and on behalf of the world around her*.

As the church moves toward greater unity, based on the gracious gift of the reconciling cross of Christ, she moves into a deeper understanding of the gospel itself, and her witness to the world will be enhanced. As George Yule summarizes it: "Every true move to unity is . . . a move towards a deeper understanding of the gospel. As we become one we leave behind the uniformity of isolation for the enrichment of community. For in unity that is based on the love of God, Father, Son and Holy Spirit, as displayed in the death and resurrection of Christ, the church will bear the marks of a reconciled family, and its witness and its life will be one."[60]

We could equally emphasize that only as the church moves out in faithful witness, proclaiming and embodying the message of reconciliation, will she discover the

---

59. Yule, *Mission and Unity in Christ*, 5. Yule's work probes the relation between reconciliation, mission and unity.

60. Ibid., 11.

unity that she desperately needs. The church's unity and mission are thus inextricably linked, grounded as they are in the reconciling act of the cross of Christ. They must never to be divided from one another.[61]

In his writings, Bosch never tired of calling attention to the tremendous and varied missiological implications of the doctrine of reconciliation. In what follows, we shall not, however, attempt to comprehensively summarize all that Bosch said about the church as a community of reconciliation. Rather we analyze a critical issue—the quest for structural church unity across racial boundaries within the Dutch Reformed Church family in South Africa. This allows us to draw on Bosch's understanding of unity and witness, and of the church as sign and agent of reconciliation, in a concrete way. It also clarifies how Bosch's theological reflection on reconciliation was worked out in practice. According to Bosch, apartheid threatened the very heart and nature of the church as the community of reconciliation, and it is on this level that he attacked apartheid most severely.

The DRC Family's Unity Across Racial and Cultural Boundaries as the Test of Faith in South Africa

We recall that even in the apartheid era, most South African churches claimed to be multiracial, at least at the synodical or national levels.[62] Within the DRC "family," however, there developed a system of ethnically separate white, black, coloured, and Asian churches (the DRC, NGSK, NGKA, and RCA, respectively).[63] Early on, this division was justified missiologically on the grounds that each ethnic and linguistic group needed to hear the Word in its own idiom. There was no doubt, though, that the Afrikaner DRC modeled its ecclesiological stance in correspondence with the racial prejudices of white South Africa. In turn, the political and social apartheid policies of the National Party were a logical extension of the DRC's ecclesiastical divisions.

This lack of unity across racial boundaries within the DRC was a bone of contention in South Africa for many years. The general principle was spelled out clearly by the 1961 Cottesloe Conference. "No one who believes in Jesus Christ may be excluded from any Church on the grounds of his colour or race. The spiritual unity among all

---

61. See *Mission and Evangelism: an Ecumenical Affirmation*, paras. 20–27. For a missiological analysis of the concept of unity and mission, see Saayman, *Unity and Mission*.

62. De Gruchy notes, however, that racial divisions were a problem for every major South African church. While the DRC and NHK have been explicitly divided along racial lines, the English-speaking churches have tolerated an unofficial and implicit division. De Gruchy, *The Church Struggle*, 93–94.

63. We recall that historically, there were two other white Reformed bodies with similar segregationist tendencies. The Nederduitsch Hervormde Kerk, in its constitution, explicitly states that it allows white members only. The small Gereformeerde Kerk in Suid Afrika (the "Dopper Kerk"), has a separate black "daughter" church.

Part Three: Crucial Theological Dimensions for a Missionary Church

men who are in Christ must find visible expression in acts of common worship and witness, and in fellowship and consultation on matters of common concern."[64]

Most non-Afrikaner church bodies endorsed this statement, and followed it up with pronouncements and reports of their own.[65] For the white Dutch Reformed Church, however, Cottesloe's emphasis on the visible unity between black and white believers was totally unacceptable.[66] It led to a break in relations with the WCC, an increasing isolation from other Reformed bodies worldwide, and a breakdown in communication with the "English-speaking" churches in South Africa.[67] Those few Afrikaners who dared to affirm the Cottesloe position, like Naudé, were eventually forced out of the DRC.

In the final years of the apartheid era, numerous persons *within* the DRC strongly dissented from their church's policies of ecclesiastical apartheid, and called for church unity across racial boundaries.[68] David Bosch was been one prominent voice.[69] He exhibited his own desire for unity among the divided members of the DRC family by joining the *Broederkring*, an interracial fellowship of blacks and whites within the DRC family who seek social justice and church unity in South Africa.[70] He also repeatedly called for a single, multiracial church. Typical of such calls was his speech to the Student Christian Association: "We seem to think, even in 'progressive' and 'verligte' circles, that racially open Christian communities are a kind of 'optional extra'. If we can have it, fine, but we are not going to go out of our way to achieve it. It seems to me, however, in the light of Scriptural evidence, that this is not just something expendable, that it belongs to the essence of the church that she includes people from all ranks, and that it is abnormal when this is not the case."[71]

In what follows, we shall summarize three of Bosch's public critiques of the DRC's membership policies that surely contributed to the rejection of apartheid within the DRC. His analysis was rooted in his understanding of ecclesiology and soteriology, i.e., that the church was to be a community of reconciliation.

---

64. This is the sixth point of the 1961 Cottesloe Consultation statement.

65. See the appendix in De Gruchy, *Apartheid is a Heresy*, 144–84 for a representative sample.

66. Lückhoff, believes this factor to be one of five Cottesloe resolutions which provoked the wrath of the Afrikaner community. See his *Cottesloe*, 154–56.

67. Saayman, *Unity and Mission*, 121–25.

68. In this regard, see the symposium volume edited by Meiring and Lederle, *Die Eenheid vand die Kerk*; and *Die Eenheid van die Kerk van Christus*.

69. We also think of Nico Smith, Willem Nicol, Adrio König, Willem Saayman, and Jaap Durand, to name but a few.

70. Hope and Young, *The South African Churches in a Revolutionary Situation*, 180.

71. Bosch, *TCAC*, 30.

1982 Congress on the Church in the Eighties

In January 1982, Bosch delivered a paper at the Congress on the Church in the Eighties, held in Pretoria. In his address, entitled "Church Unity Amidst Cultural Diversity: A Protestant Problem,"[72] Bosch argued that the current system of racially segregated churches within the DRC family was a heresy and an abrogation of the Reformed tradition.

First, Bosch compares Catholic and Protestant attitudes towards church and culture. Historically speaking, the issue of the church's unity in relation to its ethnic and cultural diversity has not been a major problem with the Roman Catholic tradition. The Pope served as a visible embodiment of the church's unity. Also, the Latin Mass, with its emphasis on liturgical activity rather than the proclamation of the Word, downplayed the significance of the spoken word in defining the identity of the church.

In contrast, Protestantism has emphasized the centrality of the proclamation of the Word. The Reformed ideal was that each worshipper should hear the Word of God preached in his or her own language. By definition, this meant a differentiation in worship services between various linguistic groups. Bosch has noted the early example of a 1578 Reformed synod at Dort, which determined that French and Dutch-speaking Reformed Christians should have their own Synods.[73]

Bosch then reviews how this ethno-linguistic differentiation was, in the South African context, transformed from a simple missiological expedient into a primordial theological principle. The temporary differentiation *within* a single church became a permanent division between the so-called "mother" and "daughter" churches.[74] Bosch retraces the decisions of numerous DRC synods, and criticizes the way they consistently legitimated the creation and continued existence of racially separate denominations. Bosch grants that white racism helped create separate church structures, yet he argues that nineteenth-century *Pietism* and *denominationalism* also played a part. The pietistic emphasis on individual salvation and the invisibility of the true church (with its corresponding *lack* of emphasis on the corporate and empirical dimension of the church) discouraged interest in the unity of the church. Denominationalism spawned all sorts of new groups, as theological and cultural differences became an excuse to form separate denominations. On this basis, Bosch argues that DRC's membership

---

72. The original paper was entitled "Church Unity Amidst Cultural Diversity: A Protestant Problem," and published in *Missionalia*. It was subsequently republished as "Nothing But a Heresy" in De Gruchy et al., *Apartheid is a Heresy*, 24–38.

73. Bosch cautions the reader not to see a similarity between this ruling and the South African situation. Individual Dutch- and French-speaking Christians in the Netherlands were free to join the congregation of their choice, and pastors could be called to any congregation. The Reformed Church was structurally unified. This is *not* true of the South African DRC family. See Bosch, "Nothing But a Heresy," 36–37.

74. We have expounded the essence of Bosch's argument in this regard in our earlier sections on the development of separate mission churches and the influence of German missiology. See chapter 1.

Part Three: Crucial Theological Dimensions for a Missionary Church

policies, theologically speaking, resulted primarily from an *inadequate understanding of the nature of the church.*

Bosch locates the source of this inadequate ecclesiology in the perennial tension between church and culture. Bosch believes that cultural diversity plays a vital role in the church. Cultural differences should be regarded "as mutual enrichment, as aids to a broadening of our horizons, as object lessons on the richness of the unfolding of God's works among people."[75] He admits that linguistic differences must be accommodated, because the Reformed principle of an intelligible hearing of the Word is important. This is simply a basic form of contextualizing the gospel. Yet

> . . . cultural diversity should in no way militate against the unity of the Church. Such diversity in fact should serve the unity. [Diversity] belongs to the well-being of the Church, whereas unity is part of its being. To play the one off against the other is to miss the entire point. Unity and socio-cultural diversity belong to different orders. Unity can be confessed. Not so diversity. To elevate cultural diversity to the level of an article of faith is to give culture a positive theological weight which easily makes it into a "revelation principle".[76]

This had become the root of the problem for the DRC. Because of its all-consuming desire to preserve Afrikaner identity, such theologians as F. G. M. Potgieter taught that when it comes to church membership, cultural differences were a more decisive factor than the sharing of the same confession. Using this rationale, structural unity between ethnically divided churches was an optional extra.[77]

Bosch sharply attacked this viewpoint from biblical and theological angles. First, the concern for church unity across ethnic boundaries lies near the heart of the New Testament doctrine of the nature of the church and the meaning of salvation. In the early church, Jew and Gentile had been made one through the cross of Christ; the Judaizers' denial of this fundamental truth was, in reality, a denial of the sufficiency of the Cross as the sole basis of God's salvation.

> Paul and his co-workers passionately contended that the crucified and risen Messiah had superseded the Law as the way of salvation, and therefore to demand the circumcision of Gentile converts to the Christian faith was, in effect, crucifying Christ anew. Paul still accepted the principle of division of labour as far as the mission to Jews and Gentiles was concerned (cf. Gal. 2:7), but

---

75. Bosch, "Nothing But a Heresy," 34.
76. Ibid., 30. Also see Bosch, "How My Mind Has Changed," 9–10.
77. Bosch summarizes Potgieter as follows: "Within the same ethno-cultural grouping there is no room for more than one Church (denomination) for people sharing the same confession. On the other hand, Christians of the same confession but of different cultural backgrounds should be divided into different denominations. The implication is clear: cultural differences count for more than the sharing of the same confession." Bosch is referring to Potgieter's contribution to the edited work by Vorster, *Veelvormigheid en Eenheid*, 29–30.

the theological (or "salvation-historical") difference between the two had been abrogated: the Law was a "tutor" only until Christ came (Gal. 3:24).

. . . [A]n unbiased reading of Paul cannot but lead one to the conclusion that his entire theology militates against even the possibility of establishing separate Churches for different cultural groups. He pleads unceasingly for the unity of the church made up of both Jews and Gentiles. God has made the two one, "a single new humanity", "a single body" (Eph. 2:14–16, NEB). This was the mystery revealed to him, "that through the Gospel the Gentiles are heirs together with Israel, members together of one body and sharers together in the promise in Christ Jesus" (Eph. 3:6, NIV). Paul could never cease to marvel at this new thing that had caught him unawares, something totally unexpected: the Church is one, indivisible, and it transcends all differences. The sociological impossibility (Hoekendijk) is theologically possible. And so the New Testament describes the Church as first-fruit, as new creation, as the one body of Christ, the "one new man".[78]

Bosch also attacked Potgieter from the perspective of Reformed theology. Adopting the arguments of Jaap Durand and Henry Lederle, Bosch insisted that Reformed ecclesiology has always held a high view of the church and its unity.[79] Citing the Heidelberg Catechism (Question 54) and the Belgic Confession (Article 27), Bosch made clear that Reformed thought emphasizes that "only faith in Christ and not biological descent or cultural distinctiveness constitutes the precondition of admission to the church. What we find today in Potgieter and other Reformed exponents of the doctrine of the plurality of ethnic churches is a later development, and as such an aberration."[80]

At the root of the matter, then, is the issue of the gospel itself. *Breaking down barriers between peoples is an inherent part of the gospel.* True reconciliation with God simultaneously includes incorporation into God's church, the alternative community, "where people find their identity in Jesus Christ rather than in their race, culture, social class, or sex."[81] On this basis Bosch declared that inasmuch as the DRC closes its doors to other worshippers from other cultural backgrounds, it was placing cultural distinctives above the cross of Christ and thus falling captive to a non-Christian ideology.[82] The Afrikaans Reformed Churches, like the Jews mentioned in 2 Cor 3:14–16, had had a veil placed over their eyes and ears so that they could not hear what the Bible says about the unity of the church.[83] Furthermore, he labelled the DRC's then-practice of all white membership to be "nothing but a heresy." "The Afrikaans Reformed Churches have only to return to their roots to discover that what

78. Bosch, "Nothing But a Heresy," 29.
79. See their contributions in Meiring and Lederle, *Die Eenheid van die Kerk*.
80. Bosch, "Nothing But a Heresy," 35.
81. Ibid. Bosch here uses René Padilla's phrase, taken from Padilla's "The Unity of the Church and the Homogeneous Unity Principle," 24.
82. Bosch, "Nothing But a Heresy," 34.
83. Ibid., 35–36.

they now cherish is nothing but a heresy that strikes at the very foundation of the church. Because of this heresy the Afrikaans Reformed Churches have designed a missiology tailor-made 'for Churches and institutions whose main function in society is to reinforce the status quo', where the Church becomes little more than a pale reflection of its environment."[84]

In this address, Bosch implored the DRC to renounce its worldliness and to rethink its stand on church membership. He called for an acknowledgment that unity in Christ across racial barriers was not optional but an *essential* dimension of the true church. It is perhaps significant that Bosch labeled the DRC's stand as "nothing but a heresy" eight months *before* the WARC's similar pronouncement in Ottawa at General Council meeting in 1982.

1982 Ope Brief

Following the 1982 WARC General Council came the release of the *Ope Brief*, the "Open Letter." It is significant for our study of Bosch because he was one of its authors and a key leader in the subsequent discussion about it.[85] It takes on added significance because Bosch identified the *Ope Brief* as representing the heart of his theological convictions. In his ten-year retrospective article "How My Mind Has Changed," Bosch affirms that

> I find much of my theological concern, as it has evolved during the past decade, expressed in the Open Letter to the Dutch Reformed Church which was signed by 123 DRC pastors and published in June this year [1982]—particularly in the Open Letter's emphasis on the unity of the Church and on its prophetic calling. Both of these flow from the central thrust of the Gospel, which is unconditional acceptance and reconciliation. As a missionary and a missiologist I would like to add that I believe that all these matters are intimately related to the very heart of the Church's mission.[86]

The *Ope Brief* linked together a concern for church's unity, her prophetic calling and her witness to the world—and grounded all three in the Christian doctrine of reconciliation. In a helpful manner, the letter discussed both the theological basis and the necessary practical implications of the concern for reconciliation in South Africa. In numerous ways, it resembles two other pronouncements from 1982: the WARC's Statement on Racism and South Africa; and the Sendingkerk's Statement on

---

84. Ibid., 36 (my emphasis). Bosch again cites Padilla at this point.

85. The official text and discussion concerning the *Ope Brief* are contained in Bosch, König, and Nicol, *Perspektief op die Ope Brief*. For Bosch's analysis of the DRC's seeming lack of response to the letter, see his chapter "Die Ope Brief in Konteks," 33–52. Cf. De Gruchy, "Towards a Confessing Church," in De Gruchy et al., *Apartheid is a Heresy*, 89.

86. Bosch, "Mission and the Alternative Community," 10 (my emphasis).

Apartheid and Confession of Faith.[87] All three deplored the effects of apartheid for creating a dehumanizing, oppressive and unjust system of inequalities and alienations. All three documents noted that apartheid threatened the unity and witness of the church of Jesus Christ. All three stressed that the Christian doctrine of reconciliation undermines any theological legitimation of apartheid and provides for a true sense of equality between persons of all races and cultures.

The documents differ, however, in that the "Open Letter" emanated from *within* the DRC. In that sense, the Letter is a *cri de coeur* from Bosch and other Afrikaner Christians pleading for a genuine recovery of the gospel by the DRC. Bosch's influence is detected throughout the letter (particularly § 1.1.2; 1.1.5; 1.2.2; 2.1.3; 2.1.4). Because of its avowed significance for Bosch, we cite the central portion of the letter in full.

> We, ministers and ordinands of the DRC, state as our conviction that genuine reconciliation in Christ between individuals and groups is the greatest single need in the Church and so also in our country and society. We believe that the Church of Jesus Christ in South Africa has a particular contribution to make in this connection by (1) giving ever more explicit expression to reconciliation and the unity of the church, and (2) by exercising its prophetic calling towards society.
>
> 1. Concerning the reconciliation and the unity of the church
>
> 1.1 We are convinced that the primary task of the church in our country is the ministry of reconciliation in Christ.
>
> 1.1.1 In the first place this means that it is the inalienable privilege of the church to proclaim the message of reconciliation between God and man. Without this aspect of reconciliation, the whole point at issue would lose its deepest meaning and significance.
>
> 1.1.2 Simultaneously, it is also inalienable privilege of the church to proclaim the message of reconciliation between people—even between those who had formerly been enemies—and to bear witness that, for believers, Christ has put an end to human enmity and has united us by creating "a single new humanity" (Eph. 2:15–16).
>
> 1.1.3 We confess that the unity of the church is both a gift and a command from God. Like reconciliation, the church's unity was brought into being by God and it is therefore our responsibility to give it visible expression. The church will therefore oppose factors which threaten her unity. This includes factors like heresy, lovelessness, self-righteousness, exclusivism, prejudice, and placing one's personal or group interests first.

---

87. A rather literal, wooden English translation of the Open Letter can be found in Serfontein's *Apartheid, Change and the NG Kerk*, 275–78. The WARC and Sendingkerk statements are found in De Gruchy et al., *Apartheid is a Heresy*, 168–73, 175–82.

Part Three: Crucial Theological Dimensions for a Missionary Church

1.1.4 There is room within the unity of the church for a diversity of languages and cultures. Precisely because of reconciliation, this diversity provides mutual enrichment not division.

1.1.5 Unity, however, belongs to a different category than diversity. Unity is primary, diversity secondary. Unity is normative and is confessed (in the Apostles' Creed and the Nicene Creed); diversity is not.

1.2 This has the following concrete implications for the church in South Africa:

1.2.1 That no particular church (denomination) can afford to neglect discussion and fellowship with other churches, or close its doors to others.

1.2.2 That the church can lay down no condition for membership other than the confession of true faith in Jesus Christ (Belgic Confession, Art. 27).

1.2.3 That the various churches within the family of Dutch Reformed Churches, who adhere to the same Confession of Faith and who originated from the same church, ought to do everything within their powers to give visible expression to the unity which they confess.

1.2.4 That immediately, while negotiations for a closer structural unity are under way, all members of churches within the family of Dutch Reformed Churches should be welcome at any meeting of any of these churches.

1.2.5 That members of the one Body of Christ: accept one another as brothers and sisters, without questioning one another's Christian faith; that they concern themselves with each other's welfare; esteem the other higher than oneself; bear one another's burdens; show mutual love in word and deed; and intercede for one another in prayer.

2. Concerning the prophetic calling of the church

2.1 We are convinced that the calling of the church to exercise a ministry of reconciliation extends beyond the four walls of the church. We therefore reject the opinion that the church should concern itself only with so-called 'spiritual matters' and withdraw from other areas of society.

2.1.1 Reconciliation includes a prophetic witness towards the whole of societal life, and therefore the church dare not remain silent concerning such matters as moral decay, family disintegration and discrimination.

2.1.2 The church will always bear witness that an arrangement of society based on the fundamental irreconcilability of individuals and groups cannot be accepted as a basic point of departure for the ordering of society.

2.1.3 The church has the wonderful opportunity to be God's experimental garden in the world. This means that God wants to demonstrate something to the world, through the life of the church, concerning that unity, mutual love, pace, understanding, sharing and justice which God intends to be present in the whole of society.

2.1.4 Naturally, all this is revealed in the church only in a defective way! This admission must not, however, push the prophetic task of the church in relation to society into the distant future, as if the church is made responsible only when her integrity has been completely established.

2.2 For the concrete situation in South African society, the above comments imply the following:

2.2.1 That the church must exercise its prophetic witness in South African society with great boldness. We live in a state which explicitly calls itself Christian, and therefore, together with the church, wishes to listen to the Word of God.

2.2.2 That a social order which elevates irreconcilability to a principle of social life, and which alienates different sections of the South African population from one another, is unacceptable.

2.2.3 That such a system makes it virtually impossible for the inhabitants of South Africa to really learn to know each other, trust one another, and be loyal to one another.

2.2.4 That the laws which have become symbols of this alienation, including those concerning mixed marriages, race classification, and group-areas, cannot be defended scripturally.

2.2.5 That justice, and not simply law and order, should be the guideline and point of departure for the ordering of society. We believe that the occurrence of the forced removal of people; of the disintegration of marriage and family ties as a result of migrant labor; of the inadequate expenditure on black education; of insufficient and inadequate housing for black people; and of the low wages paid to such people cannot be reconciled with the biblical demands for justice and human dignity.

2.2.6 That all people who regard South Africa as their fatherland ought to be included in the process of negotiating a new order for society.

2.2.7 That this system ought to be built on order and peace which is the fruit of justice. This means that all people ought to enjoy equal treatment and opportunities.[88]

The letter ends in an attitude of humility, confessing that the signatories have often failed in these areas as well. It also goes out with the prayer that the letter might clarify the church's vision regarding her unique calling, and that the process of realizing a new social order may be quickened as a result. We call particular attention to § 2.2.1–2.2.7, where virtually every important principle of political and ecclesiastical apartheid is repudiated.

In the short term at least, the effect of the *Ope Brief* was mixed. At the autumn 1982 DRC General Synod it was studiously ignored by the leadership. Yet the Open Letter gave the lie to any notion that the DRC no longer had any theologians and pastors in its ranks opposed to apartheid. If anything, it represented a slow but steady *growth* in anti-apartheid sentiment among younger Afrikaner churchmen, with 123

---

88. This is my own translation is the Open Letter, as found in *Perspektief op die Ope Brief*, 13–16.

Part Three: Crucial Theological Dimensions for a Missionary Church

DRC ministers and professors as signatories of the document. Its effect was minimal, however, beyond DRC circles. Although it was a significant document to emerge from within DRC ranks, it was overshadowed by the WARC and Sendingkerk pronouncements of the same year. It was never publicized outside of South Africa.

1986 Pretoria Theological Conference

Four years later, Bosch made another impassioned attempt to argue for structural unity between the DRC church family, this time at a conference on church unity sponsored by the Theology Faculty at the University of Pretoria. Theologians and church leaders of the three Afrikaner Reformed churches (DRC, NHK, GKSA) gathered to discuss the subjects of unity and ecumenical relationships.[89] Professor Willie Jonker of Stellenbosch and Johan Heyns of Pretoria presented challenging papers calling for the churches to acknowledge apartheid as a theological error, and to take a lead in negotiating a union between themselves and their "sister" Reformed bodies in the black and coloured communities.

Bosch's paper, titled "Eenheid Binne die "Familie" van Nederduitse Gereformeerde Kerke—Waarheen?" [Unity within the "Family" of Dutch Reformed Churches—Whither?], was an extensively documented historical survey of the struggle for unity within the DRC family.[90] He began by noting that one could discuss church unity without reflecting on the DRC's past development of the theology of apartheid. Until the DRC acknowledged this and consciously changed its course, any talk of unity was shortsighted and doomed to fail.[91] He also acknowledged he still loved his wayward church. Bosch still saw evidence within the DRC of "much that is evangelical," so "it is worth the effort to call this church back to its origins." Bosch retained love and affection for his church, and remained formally as a member of it out of deep conviction.[92]

---

89. A report on this conference from a North American perspective is found in Anderson, "South Africa: Kairos or Crisis?," 17–20. Ray Anderson from Fuller Seminary and James Torrance from the University of Aberdeen were invited observers, and gave brief responses at the end of the conference.

90. The thirty-eight-page paper included a bibliography of fifty-nine different works, almost all of which were Afrikaans sources. It was subsequently published in *Die Eenheid van die Kerk van Christus*, 45–73.

91. "Ek vind dit egter onmoontlik om oor die begeerde eenheid te praat—d.w.s. oor eventuele toekomstige eenheidstrukture—sonder om ook—een eers—oor die verlede te pratt. Sonder 'n nugtere analise van die verlede en 'n ruiterlike erkenning ten opsigte van wat daar verkeerd gegaan het, het dit weinig sin om oor die toekoms te praat. Deur my navorsing oor hierdie onderwerp het ek toenemend daarvan oortuig geraak dat die N.G.K. dedurende die afgelope vyftig jaar 'n gesofistikeerde apartheidsteologie ontwerp en ontplooi het wat ook vir ons tema van vandag verreikende gevolge gehad het; tensy ons van hierdie ontwikkelinge kennis neem en doelbewus 'n ander koers inslaan, het dit weinig sin om oor eeheid in die N.G.K.-'familie' te besin" (Bosch, "Eenheid binne die 'familie,'" 1). This and subsequent quotes are taken from the original unpublished lecture.

92. "Daar is soveel wat eg evangelies in hierdie kerk is dat dit oor en oor die moeite werd is om die kerk na sy oorsprongs terug te roep. Ek sê dit met deernis en liefde vir die kerk waarvan ek nog steeds en uit oortuiging lidmaat is en bly" (ibid., 2).

Bosch then reviewed the legacy of the nineteenth century, particularly following the fateful Synod decision of 1857[93] and explored the white racial prejudice that marked the nineteenth and early twentieth century. Typical of this paternalistic era was the implicit assumption that the younger black and coloured churches were *"onvolledige"*—incomplete. They needed supervision, oversight, and guidance by the white "mother" church. In this way, the control of the younger churches stayed firmly in the hands of the white leadership. Under the influence of Pietism, it became popular to affirm that there was an *invisible* unity between the churches, and there was therefore no need to move towards greater *structural* unity.[94] This loose, "low" understanding of the empirical church in South Africa made it quite a simple matter to argue for racially segregated churches. This pragmatic, paternalistic approach was typified in the approach of Johannes du Plessis, the great DRC missiologist.

By the 1930s, however, there began to emerge the ideology of Afrikaner *"volksnationalisme."* Bosch outlined the impact of European romanticism and nationalism on the early pioneers of Afrikaner nationalism (Malan, Diederichs, Meyer, Cronjé) and explained the immense appeal of the Nationalist ideology to the emerging Afrikaner nation. During the economically bleak 1930s, the ideology of Christian Nationalism gave a firm theoretical foundation to the aspirations of the Afrikaner people, who, for the most part, remained a defeated underclass in South Africa. In particular, Bosch identifies seven new elements which entered the life and thought of the DRC as a result of the growth of the apartheid ideology.[95]

1. Up until the 1920s there existed an uncertainty about the solution to the issue of segregation between the races. By the 1930s the church became more assured and convinced that apartheid was the answer, and that it would succeed. The DRC's vision became more concrete, and she petitioned the government to establish specific apartheid legislation.

2. The earlier view of cultural superiority over blacks was now replaced by a biologically based sense of racial superiority. Cultural segregation now became racial apartheid. The fear of *gelykstelling* (equalization, a leveling of differences) and of *rassevermening* (racial mixing) were explicitly mentioned in the 1935 policy statement of the DRC Mission.

3. For the first time, self-justifying *apologias* for apartheid were now made, such as the following: "Proportionally, our church has done more, in both manpower and money, for the colored peoples of Africa than any other church" (Strydom);

---

93. Ibid., 2–11.

94. Typical of this approach was the viewpoint of A. B. du Preez, who maintained "that a spiritual unity existed between believers from different cultural and colour groups by the ministry of the Holy Spirit and that this unity would only take on a visible form when history had come to an end" (Van der Merwe, *The Road Ahead*, 33).

95. The following seven elements are found in Bosch, "Eenheid binne die 'familie,'" 15–23.

that "apartheid as a church policy has had blessed results for the non-white peoples in South Africa" (Hanekom); and that apartheid had ensured "order and peace" in the church.[96]

4. Afrikaner intellectuals and theologians now began to stress the uniqueness of the Afrikaner people and their traditions. The existence of the *volk* as a separate nation, with its own language and identity, was now becoming normative, almost revelatory. In the words of Groenewald: "History . . . verifies the truth that the nations which have maintained their identity, in the name of the Lord, have been able to bring benefits for themselves and their neighbors."[97]

5. The development of a scriptural foundation for racial apartheid began in the 1940s (and *not* earlier). Before that, ideas about racial segregation in the DRC were founded out of practical necessities rather than eternal principles. As late as 1941 the Federal Council of Dutch Reformed Churches emphasized that the church's race policies were based on practical rather than scriptural grounds. It was J. D. du Toit of Potchefstroom and E. P. Groenewald of Pretoria who first developed the scriptural foundations for apartheid.

6. The biblical story of the Tower of Babel became central to the developing apartheid theology. Many Afrikaner theologians began their scriptural justification of apartheid with Gen 10–11, where the nations of the earth were divided. These theologians read the Babel story back into the *creation story*. In this way, the permanent division of the races became an implicit dimension of creation itself. The existence of separate nations was seen as a *skeppingsbevel*, a creation ordinance. In this way, racial separation between various nations became a positive virtue, the will of God for the entire world.

7. The capstone of all this came in the development of the concept of *veelvormigheit* or *pluriformiteit* (pluriformity). If the existence of separate nations and peoples was an eternal and inviolable principle, present from creation itself, then it was legitimate, even *mandatory* that separate churches for separate ethnic-linguistic groups be maintained. Pluriformity rather than unity became the dominant ecclesiological emphasis. In this view, institutional church unity across national (racial/ethnic) boundaries was to be vehemently rejected; the nation remained the absolute boundary that determined the membership of the various churches.[98]

---

96. These are my own translations of Strydom and Hanekom, as cited in ibid., 16–17.

97. "Die geskiedenis . . . bevestig ook die waarheid dat die volke wat hul identiteit bewaar het, in die Naam van die Here in staat was om voordeel vir hulself en hul buurvolk te bring" (ibid., 17). Bosch is citing E. P. Groenewald's "Apartheid en voogdyskap in die lig van die Heilige Skrif" in Cronjé, ed., *Regverdige Rasse-Apartheid*, 48.

98. One attempt to justify such a position is found in Vorster, *Veelvormigheid en Eenheid*.

After surveying the story of the theological legitimation of apartheid, and highlighting the DRC's glaring lack of interest in unity with her "sister" churches, Bosch laid out his theological response.

First, Bosch reminded his audience of the *primacy of the unity of the church*. This is the clear teaching of the New Testament. In his letters, Paul strives passionately to defend the unity of the church. This unity, which is given in Christ, is the cement that binds believers together in this present age. The church's unity does *not* exist simply in the far-off eschatological future, as some Afrikaner theologians (e.g., Boshoff, Du Preez, Hanekom) have argued. It is called to exist in such a unity *in this present age*. With Jonker, Bosch affirmed that

> The question is not . . . whether there has ever existed, since the time of the apostles, a visible, undivided church; the question is rather whether such a church ought to exist. If something is true in Christ yet it almost never happens, then this has only one cause: sin. Certain things are reserved for the eschaton: the renewing of our bodies, the disappearance of death and suffering, etc. Church unity, however, is not a matter of the proper dispensation but of obedience or disobedience. For example, the church was also never completely holy, yet the command of sanctification remains, and we may never be content in the absence of complete holiness.[99]

We may *recognize* the reality of division within the church, said Bosch, but we may never *approve* of it; we may *cry* about it but we must never *rejoice* over it.[100]

Second, Bosch denied that his plea for the unity of the church was in any way a call for *uniformity*. The Reformed principle of hearing the Word in one's own language is entirely proper. But Bosch criticized the policies of the DRC for assuming that this good Reformed principle necessarily implies *separate churches* for different peoples. This makes the missionary task of *verinheemsing* ("indigenization") incompatible with the unity of the church. Bosch argued that the DRC's then-current *Algemene Sendingreglement* (General Rules for Mission) was theologically invalid at this point. Article 2.4 stated: "In order that everyone can hear and understand the mighty acts of God in his own language, separate churches must be formed out of separate population groups." This proposition, claimed Bosch, was logically inconsistent. The conclusion (separate independent churches for separate peoples) does not follow logically out of the premise (understandable preaching in one's own language.)

> Rather this is only a logical result if the presupposition is . . . that the gospel should not transcend the boundaries of a particular volk. This only follows if the idea of many peoples becomes a non-negotiable law for church formation, and indigenization is thereby lifted up to become a timeless, eternal part of the essence of the church. This only follows when not Christology but instead the

---

99. Bosch, "Eenheid binne die 'familie,'" 26 (my translation).
100. Ibid., 26 (my translation). Cf. Bosch, "Die kerk in die branding," 6–7, 11.

doctrine of Creation becomes the basis upon which the church is understood. Thereby, everything is turned around. Then unity and diversity become realities which exclude each other . . .[101]

This was the position of Potgieter and numerous traditional DRC theologians, with many dangerous consequences. When the doctrine of creation rather than Christology controls our understanding of the church, the church becomes "a 'fortress of the nation,' a piece of ethnic heritage, a cultural possession which is endangered when it encounters other cultures. Then the task of the church is to be sympathetic towards the nation, and to serve it."[102]

Instead, Bosch urged that we must allow Christology, and not the doctrine of creation, to be the hermeneutical criterion by which we derive the nature and structure of the church of Jesus Christ. There always must be a critical distance between the church and the nation, lest the primordial ties of race or blood or language determine the church's form.

With some exceptions, the DRC throughout the apartheid era never maintained this critical distance. In the words of Jonker, the DRC paid a high price for this confusion between Christian church and Afrikaner nation. The DRC ". . . has, to a very large extent, become impoverished in her koinonia. The fact of separate churches brings with it the fact that white Christians know very little about the life and problems of Christians from the other population groups. They are never confronted with the real world of their fellow brothers and sisters on the other side of the dividing line of color [kleurskeidlyn]."[103]

Bosch fondly hoped that the DRC would give the highest priority to ending the divisions within the immediate DRC family. He considered it a marvel that in spite of the growing tensions, all three of the DRC "daughter" churches still desired union—not only with one another—*but with the DRC!*

Bosch was aware that there are some DRC leaders who would rather give a higher priority to unification between the three white Afrikaner churches—the DRC, NHK, and GKSA. Here Bosch pointed out the hypocrisy of such a position.

> The 1978 General Synod of the DRC made the decision that everything should be done in order to realize a visible, organic unity between the three [white] Afrikaans churches. Why is a "spiritual unity" never enough in the case of the Afrikaans churches, but in the case of the younger churches, a "spiritual unity" is sufficient? Why will the DRC Synod never accept the ecclesiastical divisions of 1852 and 1859 [when the NHK and GKSA were

---

101. Bosch, "Eenheid binne die 'familie,'" 27–28 (my translation).
102. Ibid., 28 (my translation).
103. Ibid., 29 (my translation). Bosch is citing Jonker's "Afsonderlike kerke vir afsonderlike bevolkingsgroepe?," 12.

formed]. . . but accept and even welcome the divisions which occurred in 1857 because of the "weakness of some"?[104]

Bosch was *not* against striving for unity among the Afrikaans churches; he simply wanted to emphasize that the DRC's priority when it came to church union must necessarily focus on the members of its own "family" first.

The most important reason Bosch believed in giving the highest priority to unity within the DRC "family" was that *in the present South African situation, unity between the DRC "family" of churches has become the touchstone for the church's witness concerning the kingdom of God*. The truth of the gospel was being attacked in South Africa at the crucial point of ethnic and racial loyalty: Did loyalty to Jesus Christ really break down racial and ethnic barriers, or not? Was the fellowship of Jesus Christ to be a multiracial church, or a separate collection of "national" churches? Here Bosch invoked the famous saying of Martin Luther: "Even if I confess with a loud voice and if I recognize most fervently every part of the truth of God except that very small part which the devil and the world are now at this moment attacking, then I did not confess Christ, no matter how loudly I proclaimed Christ."[105]

Luther was declaring that a small, neglected aspect of biblical truth can become, in certain contexts, the very *heart* of the gospel. Bosch illustrated this principle with the struggle between Peter and Paul in Galatians 2. "Peter's apparently harmless social behavior in Antioch—not eating together with the Gentile Christians—was seen by Paul as something that was not peripheral. No; according to Paul, with this act Peter had 'deviated from the straight path of the truth of the gospel' (Gal. 2:14). This was the point at which the heart of the gospel was at stake, in Antioch at that moment."[106]

Bosch believed that an open, multiracial church was precisely the point at which the heart of the gospel was at stake in South Africa. It was supremely for this reason that he worked for the unification of the DRC family of churches: the credibility and the power of the gospel is at stake. "It does not require a miracle to allow Afrikaners to worship together and to be one church . . . But the true miracle is when Greeks and Jews, or Afrikaners and Blacks, who are enemies in their daily life, or who at least appear to be so to outsiders, unite 'in a community of love and service, living together so that they regard the other's interest as being higher than their own; this is a miracle. Therefore the unity of the church is a proof of God—a proof of the power of the Holy Spirit.'"[107]

Finally, Bosch turned to the question of how this structural unity should come about. He believed that because the unity of the church was being torn apart by ideological and theological reasons, there was a need for strong, structural unity. He also believed there was a need for a joint confession of guilt for the sinful divisions in the Dutch

---

104. Bosch, "Eenheid binne die 'familie,'" 31 (my translation).

105. Ibid., 31–32 (my translation).

106. Ibid., 32 (my translation).

107. Ibid. (my translation). The quotation is taken from König, "In gesprek met prof. F. J. M. Potgieter" in Bosch et al., *Perspektief op die Ope Brief*, 121.

Reformed family. Beyond this, however, he was not willing to be specific. This was not because he has no opinions on the matter, but because Bosch believed that the emerging structure could be found only as the four churches entered into dialogue together.

Bosch ended with a stirring challenge to the gathered theologians, students and church leaders. "We call ourselves a Reformed church; is not the issue of the unity of the DRC 'family' perhaps the issue whereby God is testing us? Is this issue not perhaps in our day the very point on which we will be challenged by God to put into practice our motto: ecclesia reformata, semper reformanda est?"[108]

Bosch received an openly enthusiastic response from the meeting.[109] He found the warm reception to his and Willie Jonker's papers very encouraging, noting "it indicated the way the younger, theologically-trained pastors were thinking."[110] But he noted sadly these were not the ones who went to the DRC's General Synod. At the time, Bosch did not expect the 1986 General Synod to take any significant steps forward, although he retained hope of some change.[111] Perhaps symbolic of the rift in Afrikanerdom was the contrast between the theologians' enthusiastic response to Bosch, and the antipathy towards Bosch by the official representatives of the three Afrikaner Reformed churches. Bosch and Jonker's papers, in the words of one critical Afrikaner church leader, were "a betrayal of the theology, ethos, and essence of the church as God had ordained it."[112]

Conclusion: "First Crocuses in the Snow?"

As we have seen, Bosch's understanding of the church as the sign and agent of God's reconciliation has led him to argue forcefully for the unity of the Dutch Reformed churches across racial barriers. Bosch believed this issue of church unity highlighted the concrete meaning of the gospel for Afrikaner churches in his day.

> For the Afrikaner churches at the moment, this [the unity of the church across racial barriers] is the doctrine which is at stake, which is becoming, or which is in fact, the gospel . . . In other words, this is not simply a social issue; this is a deeply theological issue where the gospel as such is at stake . . . And this is what the World Alliance of Reformed Churches was trying to say, and the Sendingkerk was trying to say with its status confessionis . . . At the Pretoria conference, I pushed the issue that church unity is the absolute minimum and the first step . . . Of course, naturally, when once we have that, we'll get into all the other things, the social and political issues as well. But ecclesiologically,

---

108. Bosch, "Eenheid binne die 'familie,'" 34 (my translation).
109. Anderson, "South Africa: Kairos or Crisis?," 18.
110. "Interivew."
111. Ibid.
112. Anderson, "South Africa: Kairos or Crisis?," 18.

theologically, the unity of the church is the thing that has to be put right. Otherwise we do not have any credibility.[113]

What was the response of the DRC? Beginning with the 1986 General Synod and accelerating in the years that followed, the DRC began a slow but steady move away from its policies of racial exclusivism.[114] The election of more moderate theologian Johan Heyns as the DRC Moderator in 1986, along with various critical resolutions that emanated from some regional presbyteries and synods, gave evidence of a clear shift within the self-understanding of the DRC.[115] At a meeting in March 1989 meeting in Vereeniging, official representatives of the DRC produced a document entitled "The Testimony of Vereeniging" which condemned apartheid as sinful, and the scriptural defense of apartheid a heresy. "We confess with humility and sorrow the participation of our church in the introduction and legitimation of the ideology of apartheid and the subsequent suffering of people . . . [Apartheid] in all its forms [is] a sin and irreconcilable with the Gospel."[116]

Allen Boesak, who attended the meeting in his capacity as the President of the World Alliance of Reformed Churches, exclaimed after the meeting: "I have never heard these things said in such a way. The church has clearly opened its door to reconciliation."[117]

Were these shifts merely a grudging accommodation by the DRC to new political realities, with no real desire to change from its support of ecclesiastical and social apartheid, or did they represent "the first crocuses in the snow,"[118] a harbinger that the DRC would return to its Reformed and evangelical roots by renouncing the elevation of ethnic interests above the gospel?

Bosch took consolation from the fact that at the 1960 Cottesloe Conference, the DRC's official representatives actually stood up (for an all-too-brief moment) in support of fundamental reforms within the DRC and within South African society. Bosch life was devoted to the hope that history might repeat itself, and it was surely this hope that fueled Bosch's stubborn refusal to leave the DRC and function as a voice for renewal and unity with the Dutch Reformed family.

Bosch remained a member of the DRC out of a *prophetic faithfulness to the gospel of reconciliation* and a *deep love for his own people*. In his 1982 "Nothing But a Heresy"

---

113. "Interview."

114. Cf. Villa-Vicencio, "Report from a Safe Synod," 9–12; and Schrotenboer, "Turning the Tide?," 10–11, 31–32.

115. We note in particular the 1983 resolution by the Synod of the Western Transvaal that criticized separate development and called for an open church in which all races would be welcome; and the 1985 statement of repentance by the Presbytery of Stellenbosch. See Neuhaus, *Dispensations*, 161; and Bosch, "Reconciliation—An Afrikaner Speaks," 64–65, respectively.

116. See "Apartheid is Sinful," 306.

117. "Hopes for Reconciliation Spurred by South African Church's Change," 36.

118. The phrase comes from Bosch, "The Roots and Fruits of Afrikaner Civil Religion," 34.

Part Three: Crucial Theological Dimensions for a Missionary Church

speech in Pretoria, Bosch described the pain he felt in seeing his own people blinded by an anti-Christian ideology.

> In regard to the subject under discussion [the unity of the church] and the way it is viewed by the current white Dutch Reformed Church leadership, I cannot help sharing Paul's agony in respect to his fellow-Jews. In II Cor. 3:14–16 he says that their minds have been made insensitive, for there is a veil that obscures their reading of the Old Covenant. So they cannot see and hear what it really says. I observe a similar veil preventing the Afrikaans Reformed Churches from really hearing what the Bible says about the unity of the Church. I say this not in a spirit of judgement, but of shared guilt and deep concern. Of course, other denominations have their limitations and blind spots too, in regard to other central issues of the Gospel. But my concern here is with a specific blind spot, that of being unable to catch a vision of a Church truly transcending the divisions of mankind.[119]

If it was true that his church and his people had been "blinded," then why did Bosch remain within the DRC? Was it simple ethnic loyalty that kept him from joining the NGSK or NGKA as many of his reforming colleagues like Beyers Naudé, Nico Smith, and others did? Bosch certainly had sufficient reason to leave the DRC. For his public stand that church membership be entirely open across racial barriers, Bosch was charged with heresy, and numerous attempts were made to "discipline" him. Bosch acknowledged having many discussions, particularly with Alan Boesak, about remaining in the DRC. Why would he remain within a body that, as he himself had declared, bordered on being heretical in the eyes of much of the global church because it excluded black members? Bosch gave the following tentative answer:

> Believe me, it would be very easy for me to do as Boesak and Naudé and others say, and just resign and walk away from this. These disciplinary measures would immediately evaporate and, I can assure you, I would be quite happy in a black or coloured church. But I am sorry, I think that would be self-indulgent. Quite frankly I see a more enlightened view on the ascendancy in the Dutch Reformed church . . . .Who can read his own heart aright? It may be, as they say, that my reluctance to leave is tied to group loyalty, ethnic solidarity, and so forth. But I do believe that I see in the Dutch Reformed church that more general, more catholic, Christianity which holds my primary allegiance. I am not ready to give the Dutch Reformed church over to the devil.[120]

For Bosch, the central issue was *prophetic solidarity*, identifying with the guilt of one's people in order to speak to them in a credible way. Although written in the third person, Bosch could well have been describing himself in the following remarks: "The true prophet identifies himself with the sin and guilt of the church. He knows that

---

119. Bosch, "Nothing But a Heresy," 34.
120. Neuhaus, *Dispensations*, 161–62.

he himself is no better. That is, by the way, the difference between the critic and the prophet: the critic criticises from the outside, the prophet confesses from within. The critic accuses, the prophet weeps. Criticism is easy, but also cheap; prophecy is costly, because it flows from solidarity."[121]

It is inappropriate to pass judgment on whether Bosch's remaining within the DRC was the most *faithful* or the most *effective* response to the demands of the gospel in apartheid South Africa. No doubt there are mixed motives in all human decisions. Perhaps in the final analysis, the two options of resigning from the DRC or remaining within it were somehow *complementary* in the slow process of change that the gospel of reconciliation demands.[122] Those who work on the "inside" for change and those who work on the "outside" for change, are, after all, both working to change the status quo. The final judgment on this issue, however, must be reserved for a higher court.

It is supremely sad that David Bosch did not live to see many of the monumental changes that have taken place within church and society in what has now become the multiracial democracy of South Africa. Bosch did witness the unbanning of the ANC and other opposing political parties on February 2, 1990 and the subsequent release of Nelson Mandela. Later that year the DRC Synod meeting at Bloemfontein announced a revision of the *Kerke en Samelwing* (Church and Society) report, declaring and acknowledging its personal guilt and responsibility for the political, social, economic, and structural injustices inherent in South African society. Beginning in 1994, two years after his death, Bosch's dream of seeing unity between the DRC family of churches finally began to bear practical fruit with the beginning of formal conversations towards church unity between the various parties. In November 2006, 127 representatives from the DRC, the Reformed Church in Africa and the Uniting Reformed Church in Southern Africa met in Achterbergh near Krugersdorp to move the agenda of unity forward.[123]

---

121. Bosch, *TCAC*, 26.

122. Neuhaus, *Dispensations*, 166.

123. "NG Kerk" (Dutch Reformed Church) official website, http://www.ngkerk.org.za/index.asp?bodyType=geskiedenis.

10

Epilogue

WE HAVE SOUGHT TO expound the essential tenets of David Bosch's theology of mission and evangelism and to evaluate his contribution to the church in South Africa and to contemporary missiological thought. This is particularly true of Part Three, where the fundamental theological structures of Bosch's theology of mission were analyzed in light of the missionary nature of the church. The church is called to live as the *kingdom* community, as the *alternative* community, and as the *reconciled* and *reconciling* community.

We would like to conclude our assessment by asking a question: What are the abiding contributions that David Bosch made to the theology of mission in our generation, to the church in South Africa, and to the church universal? We want to highlight six areas that deserve special mention.

First, we believe that Bosch made a substantial contribution toward a *deeper biblical foundation for mission*. The missionary movement has yet to develop a common understanding of how the Bible functions as the authority, basis and frame of reference for the church's missionary thought and practice. There is a lack of consensus regarding an adequate biblical hermeneutic among Christians today.[1]

Bosch contributed to a deeper biblical foundation for mission in three ways. First, he has contributed on the *methodological* level of biblical hermeneutics with his critique of traditional approaches to the biblical foundation for mission, and his proposal regarding a "post-critical" approach to scripture. These suggestions warrant serious ongoing study within the IAMS, and among biblical scholars as well. Second, Bosch has contributed to a rediscovery of the intrinsically missionary nature of the church, based on the witness of the Bible. The issue is not so much whether an adequate justification for mission can be found in the Bible, but how the Bible can assist the church in living out her essentially missionary calling in the world.[2] The Bible

---

1. Scherer, *Gospel, Church and Kingdom*, 243.
2. Bosch, "Vision for Mission," 9–10.

functions as a foundational source and standard by which the church understands her identity in Christ, as well as a source of paradigms and models for current missionary engagement with the world. Third, we find Bosch's own contribution to the biblical foundation for mission compelling, particularly such themes as the compassion of God, the link between witness and suffering, the radically historical, particularized scope of God's action in the history of Israel and in Jesus Christ, resulting in universal mission for the salvation of the whole world, and his detailed exegetical interpretation of the Great Commission.

Second, we believe that Bosch helped bring *greater theological clarity to the meaning and relationship of mission and evangelism*. Bosch's various models are helpful illustrations that show the holistic nature of the Christian mission, flowing from the wholeness of the gospel of Christ and the breadth of the biblical witness. "Mission takes place," Bosch affirmed, "where the church, in its total involvement with the world, bears its testimony in the form of a servant, with reference to unbelief, exploitation, discrimination and violence, but also with reference to salvation, healing, liberation, reconciliation and righteousness."[3] Evangelism, understood by Bosch as that essential dimension of mission that is concerned to cross the frontier of unbelief with the announcement of the good news of Jesus Christ, is thus held in vital and creative tension with mission. We also find Bosch's use of Gensichen's "dimension"–"intention" model helpful in clarifying the relationship between the two concepts. Although evangelism and mission are *distinct* entities, they are *inseparably linked*; together they embody the church's life when she crosses frontiers into the world.

Bosch wrote of the desperate need for what W. A. Visser 't Hooft has called "pan-Christians." "Pan-Christians" are those ". . . who are able to embrace both the depth and breadth of the Church's mission and mandate, people who know that there is, by definition, no clash between our calling people to personal faith and commitment to Christ in the fellowship of the Church (evangelism) and our calling those thus committed to cross all kinds of frontiers in communicating salvation to the world (mission)."[4] Bosch identifies such missionary statesmen as John Mott, J. H. Oldham, Nathan Söderblom, Toyohiko Kagawa, and Visser 't Hooft himself as examples of "pan-Christians" in this century. We believe that Bosch, based on the definition above, deserves the label of "pan-Christian" as well.

Third, we believe Bosch rendered valuable service in *clarifying the fundamental issues of theological conflict between the evangelical and ecumenical streams of world mission movement*. We believe his theology to be, in large measure, an existential response to historical and ongoing polarizations in mission, and a creative attempt to move beyond either sterile alternative toward a more genuinely integral mission theology. Although the evangelical/ecumenical paradigm is not the *only* way to analyze the

---

3. Bosch, "Mission—an Attempt at a Definition," 11.

4. Bosch, "Mission and Evangelism: Clarifying the Concepts," 187. Bosch is citing Visser 't Hooft's "Pan-Christians Yesterday and Today," 387–95.

contemporary dynamics of mission in our day, and although Bosch was increasingly conscious of the missiological contribution of Third World theologians, it remains true that the evangelical/ecumenical tension insidiously hinders the life and health of the church—particularly in the Third World—and he sought to address this tension.

Fourth, we believe Bosch is to be commended for *developing and popularizing the "alternative community" concept*. The church is set apart from the world and called to be a church without privileges, a servant community that embodies the radical lifestyle of Christ's new community. Yet the Christian community's "called out" existence is *for the sake of the world*. As Bosch put it: "The church has tremendous significance for society precisely because it [exists] as a uniquely separate community . . . We have to work consistently for the renewal of the church—the alternative community—and precisely in that way at the renewal of society."[5]

The AC concept played two roles in Bosch's missiological stance: it functioned as a credible paradigm for the vexing theological issue of the relationship between church and world; and it served as a distinctly Christian socio-ethical response to the struggle for social justice in South Africa. We have shown how the South African Christian Leadership Assembly provided a concrete embodiment of the AC concept. The implications of the AC concept go far beyond South Africa, however, into all locales where Christians seek to engage and live out their distinct calling to be God's people in the world.

Fifth, we believe that *Bosch's missiological "style" serves as a model for missiological work in our era*. Bosch attempted to be faithful to the witness of the biblical revelation, doing his missiological reflection after a deep and scholarly engagement with Scripture. He was a theologian of ecumenical breadth, whose writings gave evidence of openness to the diverse contributions and insights of the whole church of Jesus Christ—ecumenical and evangelical; First World and Third World; black and white; Catholic, Protestant, and Orthodox. He was a constructive critic, who spoke with courtesy and fairness towards other persons and other theological positions, even while boldly propounding and defending his own approach. One of Bosch's colleagues at UNISA, Adrio König, captured Bosch's essential style well when he wrote: "Bosch does not present his theology in an authoritarian style. His views and approach are characterised by humility, candour and benevolence. He is conscious of the fragmentary nature of theological thinking which is influenced by one's own immediate situation . . ."[6]

Finally, and most directly relevant to South Africa, we would argue against those who criticized Bosch for not taking his South African context seriously enough or for neglecting the "practical" side of the missiological task.[7] We believe that *Bosch's theology of mission and evangelism exemplifies an admirable integration of theological reflection*

---

5. Bosch, "How My Mind Has Changed," 8–9.
6. König, "David J. Bosch," 12.
7. See chapter 4.

and praxis. Throughout this study, we have attempted to show that Bosch is no mere "armchair theologian." His theological reflection is linked to his missionary practice.

His work on the church as the "alternative community" was grounded in events such as SACLA, to which he contributed so much (in spite of the harsh criticism he endured from both "sides"). His theologically grounded call for organic church unity across the racial lines in the DRC family of churches was grounded in the leadership he gave to the *Ope Brief,* one of the most substantial challenge to apartheid from within the DRC in its history. His theological emphasis upon reconciliation was grounded in a long and extensive involvement with the ministry of Africa Enterprise and a multitude of other Christian denominations, ministries, and organizations.

With such dramatic changes evident within the DRC with its final rejection of apartheid, it is at least arguable that fundamental change during the apartheid era began to emerge precisely because of people like David Bosch. He remained *within* the DRC out of a sincere, prophetic desire to speak the truth of the gospel to the Afrikaner people from a position of solidarity with them—even in their sin!

Likewise, some criticized Bosch for emphasizing "reconciliation" instead of "liberation" in the struggle for justice in South Africa. Although it was not aimed at Bosch in particular, the *Kairos Document* criticized "Church Theology" because of its superficial talk about reconciliation and non-violence. In the interests of social liberation, *Kairos* rejected the call for the church to be a reconciling "alternative community"[8] At UNISA's 1986 Institute for Theological Research (devoted to the theme of reconciliation), a major paper expressed doubt that the symbol of reconciliation could play any meaningful role in transforming South African society.[9]

In response to this skepticism about the efficacy of the "reconciliation model" for the social transformation of South Africa, we would affirm, with John de Gruchy, that reconciliation and liberation do not necessarily have to conflict. They actually served as *complementary helpmates* in the quest for justice in South African society. After comparing and contrasting the *Kairos Declaration* and the *National Initiative for Reconciliation Statement,* De Gruchy summarizes his conclusions as follows:

1. In the struggle for a just society, the church cannot be neutral, but there are different, complementary strategies.

2. The church must be the church, but this does not mean that it has its own political program alongside that of the struggle for liberation. It must participate in critical solidarity.

3. The gospel of reconciliation and liberation, as well as the political strategies of negotiation and confrontation, are not antithetical but two sides of the same coin.

4. The suffering witness of the cross, and therefore nonviolent redemptive action, remains the paradigm for the Christian, even though there is an honored

---

8. See De Gruchy, "The Church and the Struggle for South Africa," 239.
9. Smit, "The Symbol of Reconciliation and Ideological Conflict in South Africa," 79–112.

Christian tradition that supports the idea of a just revolution.[10]

From this perspective, Bosch's approach (focusing as he did on the church as the alternative commuity, the gospel of reconciliation, and the role of *martyria*—suffering witness—in Christian discipleship) is to be praised as an essential component in helping South Africa transition in a remarkably nonviolent way from the dark days of apartheid into the multiracial democracy it has become in our time.

Many years ago, John MacKay, then President of Princeton Theological Seminary, wrote *A Preface to Christian Theology*. One chapter was called "Two Perspectives: The Balcony and the Road," where MacKay contrasted two ways of approaching life. The "Balcony Approach" is a symbol of those who seek to know the truth about life by standing as a spectator on a balcony, watching from the sidelines. The person on the balcony betrays aloofness towards the people below, unaffected by what was happening down in the street. It is an immobility of the soul. As MacKay summarizes it: "He lives so much in the world of universals that he loses all contact with the world of concrete reality, and all interest in ordinary people."[11]

MacKay contrasts this with the other approach to life, the pilgrim way of "The Road."

> The Road is the symbol of a first-hand experience of reality where thought, born of a living concern, issues in decision and action. When a man squarely faces the challenge of his existence, a vital concern is aroused within him. He puts to himself the question, what must I do? He is eager to know, not so much what things are in their ultimate essence, as what they are and should be in their concrete existence. He asks insistently such questions as these: How can I be what I ought to be? How can I know God? How can I become related to the purpose of the universe? How can a better order be established than that which now exists? . . . The deepest truths about reality can be known, therefore, only by people who start from a deep concern about life and who are prepared to commit themselves irrevocably to the full implications of the truth that satisfies their concern . . . [R]eligious truth is obtained only on the Road.[12]

We believe that David Jacobus Bosch embodied "a missiology of the road." By remaining in his embattled homeland to live out his discipleship and by attempting to integrate his theology and practice in a contextually relevant fashion within the maelstrom of apartheid South Africa, Bosch provided an exemplary and authentic *martyria*, a witness to the world, that was profoundly evangelistic. Bosch the Afrikaner Christian was a "missiologist of the road" who made a creative and redemptive contribution to the world church.

---

10. De Gruchy, "The Church and the Struggle for South Africa," 240–43. De Gruchy's approach is similar to that taken by Jan Milic Lochman in his *Reconciliation and Liberation: Challengeing a One-Dimensional View of Salvation*.

11. MacKay, *A Preface to Christian Theology*, 43.

12. Ibid., 44–45.

Bibliography

Aagaard, Johannes. "Some Main Trends in Modern Protestant Missiology." *Studia Theologica* 19 (1965) 238-39.

Adam, Heribert, and Hermann Giliomee. *The Rise and Crisis of Afrikaner Power*. Cape Town: David Philip, 1979.

Adeyemo, Tokunboh. "A Critical Evaluation of Contemporary Perspectives." In *In Word and Deed: Evangelism and Social Responsibility*, edited by Bruce Nicholls, 41-61. Grand Rapids: Eerdmans, 1985.

Ahonen, Tiina. *Transformation Through Compassionate Mission: David J. Bosch's Theology of Contextualization*. Helsinki: Luther-Agricola Society, 2003.

Allen, Roland. *Missionary Principles*. London: Lutterworth, 1968.

Allmen, Daniel von. "The Birth of Theology." *IRM* 44 (January 1975) 37-55.

Andersen, Wilhelm. *Towards a Theology of Mission*. IMC Research Pamphlet No. 2. London: SCM, 1955.

Anderson, Gerald. *Christian Mission in Theological Perspective*. Nashville: Abingdon, 1967.

———. "Theology of Mission." In *Concise Dictionary of the Christian World Mission (1492-1969)*, edited by Stephen Neill et al., 594. London: Lutterworth, 1970.

———, and Thomas Stransky, eds. *Mission Trends No. 2: Evangelization*. Grand Rapids: Eerdmans, 1975.

———, eds. *Mission Trends No. 3: Third World Theologies*. Grand Rapids: Eerdmans, 1976.

Anderson, Ray. "South Africa: Kairos or Crisis?" *RJ* 36 (October 1986) 17-20.

"Apartheid is Sinful." *CC* 106 (March 22, 1989) 306.

Arias, Mortimer. *Announcing the Reign of God: Evangelization and the Subversive Memory of Jesus*. Philadephia: Fortress, 1984.

The Authority of the Faith: The Madras Series. Presenting Papers Based upon the Meeting of the International Missionary Council at Tambaram, India, December 12 to 29, 1938. Vol. 7. London: Oxford University Press, 1939.

Barrett, David. *Evangelize! A Historical Survey of the Concept*. Birmingham, AL: New Hope, 1987.

———, ed. *World Christian Encyclopedia*. New York: Oxford University Press, 1982.

Barth, Karl. *Church Dogmatics* IV/3. Edinburgh: T. & T. Clark, 1962

———. "An Exegetical Study of Matthew 28:16-20." In *The Theology of the Christian Mission*, edited by Gerald Anderson, 55-71. London: SCM, 1961.

———. "Die Theologie und die Mission in der Gegenwart." *Zwischen den Zeiten* (1932), as reprinted in *Theologische Fragen und Antworten III*, 100-126. Zollikon-Zurich: Evang. Verlag, 1957.

Bibliography

Bassham, Rodger. *Mission Theology, 1948–1975: Years of Worldwide Creative Tension—Ecumenical, Evangelical, and Roman Catholic.* Pasadena: William Carey, 1979.

———. "Seeking a Deeper Theological Basis for Mission." *IRM* 67 (July 1978) 329–37.

Bavinck, J. H. *An Introduction to the Science of Missions.* Philadelphia: Presbyterian & Reformed, 1960.

Bax, Douglas. *A Different Gospel: A Critique of the Theology Behind Apartheid.* Johannesburg: Presbyterian Church of Southern Africa, 1979.

———. "A Different Gospel." In *Apartheid is a Heresy*, edited by John de Gruchy et al., 112–43. Grand Rapids: Eerdmans, 1983.

Beale, Alex. "Mission Is My Calling." *Crusade Magazine* (August 1976) 19.

Bekele, Girma. *The In-Between People: A Reading David Bosch through the Lens of Mission History and Contemporary Challenges in Ethiopia.* Eugene, OR: Pickwick, 2011.

Berger, Peter. *Introduction to Sociology.* Harmondsworth, UK: Penguin, 1982.

———, and Richard Neuhaus, eds. *Against the World for the World: The Hartford Appeal and the Future of American Religion.* New York: Seabury, 1976.

Bergquist, James. "Evangelism in Current Ferment and Discussion: A Bibliographical Survey." *Word and World* 1 (Winter 1981) 59–70.

Berkhof, Hendrikus. "Berlin versus Geneva: Our Relationship with the 'Evangelicals.'" *Ecumenical Review* 28 (January 1976) 80–86.

———. *Christ the Meaning of History.* Grand Rapids: Baker, 1979.

———. *Christian Faith: An Introduction to the Study of the Faith.* Grand Rapids: Eerdmans, 1979.

Berkhof, Louis. *Introduction to Systematic Theology.* Grand Rapids: Baker, 1979.

———. *Systematic Theology.* Grand Rapids: Eerdmans, 1939.

Beyerhaus, Peter. "The Ministry of Crossing Frontiers." In *The Church Crossing Frontiers: Essays on the Nature of Mission in Honour of Bengt Sundkler*, edited by P. Beyerhaus and C. F. Hallencreutz, 36–54. Uppsala: Gleerup, 1969.

———. *Missions: Which Way? Humanization or Redemption?* Grand Rapids: Zondervan, 1971.

———. *Shaken Foundations: Theological Foundations for Mission.* Grand Rapids: Zondervan, 1972.

Blauw, Johannes. *The Missionary Nature of the Church: A Survey of the Biblical Theology of Mission.* 3rd ed. Grand Rapids: Eerdmans, 1974.

Bloesch, Donald. *Essentials of Evangelical Theology.* 2 vols. New York: Harper & Row, 1978.

Bockmuhl, Klaus. *Was heist heute Mission? Entscheidungsfragen der neuren Missionstheologie.* Giessen & Basel: Brunnen, 1974.

Boer, Harry. *Pentecost and Missions.* Grand Rapids: Eerdmans, 1961.

Boesak, Allan. *Black and Reformed: Apartheid, Liberation, and the Calvinist Tradition.* Maryknoll, NY: Orbis, 1984.

———. *The Finger of God.* Maryknoll, NY: Orbis, 1982.

———. "He Made Us All, But . . . Racism and the World Alliance of Reformed Churches." In *Apartheid Is a Heresy*, edited by John de Gruchy et al., 1–9. Grand Rapids: Eerdmans, 1983.

Boff, Leonardo. *The Lord's Prayer: The Prayer of Integral Liberation.* Maryknoll, NY: Orbis, 1983.

Bosch, David. "The Afrikaner and South Africa." *TT* 43/2 (July 1986) 203–16.

———. "Afrikaner Civil Religion and the Current South African Crisis." *Trans* 3/2 (April-June 1986) 23–30.

———. "Afrikaner Civil Religion and the Current South African Crisis." *Princeton Seminary Bulletin* 7/1 (1986) 1–14.

———. "Afrikaner Civil Religion and the Current South African Crisis." In *The Best in Theology*, edited by J. I. Packer, 1:221–34. Carol Stream, IL: Christianity Today, 1987.

———. "Afrikaner-identiteit só beïnvloed." *Beeld*, September 11, 1984.

———. *Ampsbediening in Afrika*. Lux Mundi 5. Pretoria: N. G. Kerkboekhandel, 1972.

———. ". . . And How Vast the Resources of His Power Open to Us Who Trust in Him." SACLA Follow-up meeting, Johannesburg, November 10, 1979. Unpublished document in private ownership.

———. "As I See It." Address at the Multi-Racial Conference on Reconciliation, sponsored by the Interdenominational African Ministers' Association of South Africa (IDAMASA), Johannesburg, October 1, 1977. Unpublished document in private ownership.

———. "Behind Melbourne and Pattaya: A Typology of Two Movements." *IAMNSN* 16–17 (May-October 1980) 21–33.

———. *Believing in the Future: Toward a Missiology of Western Culture*. Valley Forge, PA: Trinity, 1995.

———. "Blessed are the Peacemakers!" Address given at the SACLA Rally of Witness, Pretoria, July 15, 1979. Unpublished document in private ownership.

———. "Brief Comments on 'the State of the Church in Africa.'" Address at the Annual General Meeting of Africa Enterprise, Pietermaritzburg, April 28, 1977. Unpublished document in private ownership.

———. "Burgerlike Ongehoorsaamheid [Civil Disobedience]." Text prepared for TV interview, July 1985. Unpublished document in private ownership.

———. "The Case for a Black Theology." *Pro Veritate* (August 1972) 3–9.

———. "The Changing South African Scene and the Calling of the Church." *Miss Stud* 8/2 (1991) 147–64.

———. "The Christian and the World of Today." *Kerugma* 9/4 (February 1970) 228–41.

———. "The Christian Church in a Revolutionary Situation." 1987. Unpublished document in private ownership.

———. "Christian Community in Africa, Part I." *Kairos* 9/1 (February 1977) 4–5.

———. "Christian Community in Africa, Part II." *Kairos* 9/2 (March 1977) 5.

———. "Christianity as an Anti-Body and an Alternative Society." *To The Point* (October 21, 1977) 28.

———. "Christian-Nationalism." Lecture presented at a meeting of the Student Christian Association, University of Pretoria, April 21, 1982. Unpublished document in private ownership.

———. "Christians Must Make a Difference to the World." *Dimension* 10/8 (August 5, 1979) 6–7.

———. *Church and Culture Change in Africa*. Lux Mundi 3. Pretoria: N. G. Kerkboekhandel, 1971.

———. *Church and Mission*. Missiology and Science of Religion. Pretoria: UNISA, 1973.

———. "The Church and the Liberation of Peoples?" *Miss* 5/2 (August 1977) 8–47.

———. "The Church as the 'Alternative Community.'" *JTSA* 13 (December 1975) 3–11.

———. *The Church as the Alternative Community*. Potchefstroom, RSA: Instituut vir Reformatoriese Studie, 1982.

Bibliography

———. "The Church as the Alternative Society." *IFES Review* 2 (1979) 3–14.

———. "Church Growth Missiology." *Miss* 16/1 (April 1988) 13–24.

———. "The Church in Dialogue: From Self-Delusion to Vulnerability." *Missiology* 16/2 (April 1988) 131–47.

———. "The Church in South Africa—Tomorrow." In *The Church in South Africa Today and Tomorrow*, edited by B. O. Johanson, 33–48. Johannesburg: South African Council of Churches, 1975.

———. "The Church in South Africa—Tomorrow." *Pro Veritate* 14/4 (August 1975) 4–6; 14/5 (September 1975) 11–13.

———. "The Church in South Africa—Tomorrow." *TE* 9/2–3 (July/September 1976) 171–86.

———. "The Church is to be the 'Alternative Community.'" *Christian Leader* 9/5 (May 1977) 4–5.

———. "Church, State and Power." Paper read at the Rhodesian Christian Leaders' Consultation, Salisbury, November 23, 1977. Unpublished document in private ownership.

———. "The Church: The Alternative Community." *Be Transformed* 2/2 (1977) 3–45.

———. "Church Unity Amidst Cultural Diversity." *EvRT* 8/2 (October 1984) 246–60.

———. "Church Unity Amidst Cultural Diversity: A Protestant Problem." *Miss* 10/1 (April 1982) 16–28.

———. "The Church without Privileges." *Asfacts* (Anglican Students' Federation) 19 (September 1977) 2–3.

———. "The Church's Mission." Two Addresses given at the Rosettenville Methodist Church, Johannesburg, August 14, 1974. Unpublished document in private ownership.

———. "Communicating Christ in a Sick Society." Address to the Lunchhour meeting, Metropolitan Methodist Church Hall, Pietermaritzburg, September 19, 1975. Unpublished document in private ownership.

———. "Communicating the Gospel to Africa Today." Address given at the Southern Natal Missionary Conference, Port Shepstone, April 1971. Unpublished document in private ownership.

———. "Confessing and Believing: The Sneezing and the Inhaling of the Church." Paper presented at a meeting of the signatories of *Die Ope Brief* to discuss the Belhar Confession of the NGSK, Hammanskraal, May 1, 1984. Unpublished document in private ownership.

———. "Contextual Evangelism." Paper read at the Clergy Synod, Church of the Province of Southern Africa Diocese of Cape Town, St. John's Church, Wynberg, September 21, 1982. Unpublished document in private ownership.

———. "Contextual Missionary Theology from Orbis." *Miss* 13/3 (November 1985) 121–31.

———. "The Contextualization of the Gospel." *AEN* (March 1976) 2.

———. "Creatiewe Spanning Tussen Oecumenisch en Evangelisch." In *Verbindend Overleg*, edited by Evangelische Alliantie (Netherlands), 7–34. Arnhem, Neth.: Interlektuur, 1982.

———. "Cross-Cultural Ministry: Pitfalls and Opportunities." Paper given at a Mennonite Students' Conference, Elkhart, Indiana, February 1978. Unpublished document in private ownership.

———. "Crosscurrents in Modern Mission." *Miss* 4/2 (August 1976) 54–84.

———. "Currents and Crosscurrents in South African Black Theology." *JRA* 6/1 (1974) 1–22.

———. "Currents and Crosscurrents in South African Black Theology." In *Black Theology: A Documentary History, 1966-1979*, edited by Gayraud S. Wilmore et al., 220-237. Maryknoll, NY: Orbis, 1979.

———. *De Achtergrond van Melbourne en Pattaya. Een karakteristiek van twee bewegingen*. Breukelen, Neth.: Uitgave Guntersteinberaad, 1981.

———. "Der alttestamentliche Missionsgedanke." *EMM* 100/6 (November 1956) 174-88.

———. "Der Südafrikanische Kirchenrat—Ein Bericht für die Untersuchungs-kommission." In *Bekenntnis und Widerstand*, edited by Gisela Albrecht et al., 137-51. Hamburg: Missionshilfe, 1983.

———. "Derriére Melbourne et Pattaya: une Typologie de Deux Mouvements." *Perspectives Missionaires* 2 (1981) 43-65.

———. *Die Heidenmission in der Zukunftsschau Jesu: Eine Untersuchung zur Eschatologie der synoptischen Evangelien*. Zürich: Zwingli, 1959.

———. "Die 'Nuwe Gemeenskap' rondom Jesus van Nasaret." In *Die Eenheid van die Kerk*, edited by P. G. J. Meiring et al., 1-5. Cape Town: Tafelberg, 1979.

———. "Die 'Selfstandigwording' van die Inheemse Kerk en die Plek en Taak van die Ampsdraers Daarin." *Kerugma* 8/2 (August 1968) 63-77.

———. "Die Diens van die Genesing in Sendingperspektief." *NGTT* 8/3 (June 1967) 153-72.

———. "Die Kerk in die Branding." *Die Kerkbode* 134/20 (May 26, 1982) 6-7, 11.

———. "Die Lewe van die Sendingwerker." *Pro Veritate* 13/11 (March 1973) 7-10; 13/12 (April 1973) 13-16; 14/1 (May 1973) 10-14; 14/2 (June 1973) 18-20; 14/3 (July 1973) 21-24.

———. "Die Ope Brief in Konteks." In *Perspektief op die Ope Brief*, edited by D. J. Bosch et al., 33-52. Cape Town: Human & Rousseau, 1982.

———. "Die Probleem van die 'Aanknoping.'" *Op die Horison* (June 1960) 19-27.

———. "Die Religiöse Situation in Südafrika und die Themen unserer Verkündigung." Jahreskonferenz der Hermannsburger Mission, El Mirador, September 22, 1976. Unpublished document in private ownership.

———. "Die religiösen Wurzeln der gegenwärtigen Polarisation zwischen Schwarz und Weiss in Südafrika." *ZM* 9/2 (1983) 98-105.

———. "Die Selfonderhoud van die Inheemse Kerk—Is dit vir ons waarlik 'n saak van erns?" *NGTT* 3/4 (September 1962) 481-504.

———. "Die Sendingsituasie Vandag—Verleentheid of Geleentheid?" *NGTT* 4/3 (June 1963) 149-64.

———. "Die Sendingwerker en die Sendingdoel." Lesings Gelewer Tydens Kursus in Praktiese Sendingwerk, Aangebied by die Universiteit van Pretoria, Pretoria, February 25—May 5, 1972. Unpublished document in private ownership.

———. "Die Taak van die Kerk in 'n Konteks van Politieke Polarisasie." Lecture presented to the SAAK (Studente Aktuele Aangeleenthede Komitee), Stellenbosch, April 16, 1980. Unpublished document in private ownership.

———. "Die Wêreldkerk Vandag en Môre: Lig en Skadu." In *Die Kerk op Pad na 2000*, edited by P. G. J. Meiring, 1-18. Cape Town: Tafelberg, 1977.

———. "Dissension Among Christians: How Do We Handle Contentious Issues?" In *Healing in the Name of God*, edited by Pieter G. R. de Villiers, 1-8. Pretoria: C. B. Powell Bible Centre, 1986.

Bibliography

———. "Draers van die Boodskap van Heil in 'n Tyd Soos Hierdie." Konferensie Transvaalse Predikantsvroue, Arcadia, February 13, 1979. Unpublished document in private ownership.

———. "Earthen Vessels, Indeed, But Containing a Treasure!" Sermon given at the service of dedication for SACLA, St. Alban's Cathedral, Pretoria, June 24, 1979. Unpublished document in private ownership.

———. "Ecumenical Deadlock or Prophetic Opportunity?" *The Christian Minister* 5/4 (April 1969) 7–10, 18.

———. "'Ecumenicals' and 'Evangelicals': A Growing Relationship?" *ER* 40/3 (July 1988) 458–72.

———. "Eenheid Binne die 'Familie' van Nederduitse Gereformeerde Kerke—Waarheen?" Paper presented at University of Pretoria's D. R. C. Theology Faculty Coninuing Education Course on the Unity of the Church of Christ, Pretoria, August 1986. Unpublished document in private ownership.

———. "Eenheid binne die 'familie' van Nederduitse Gereformeerde Kerke—Waarheen?" In *Die Eenheid van die Kerk van Christus*, edited by P. B. Van der Watt et al., 45–73. Universiteit van Pretoria Teologiese Studies 3. Pretoria: University of Pretoria, 1987.

———. "El Evangelismo: Corrientes y Contracorrientes Teologicas de Hoy." *Misión* 6/4 (December 1987) 6–14.

———. "An Emerging Paradigm for Mission." *Missiology* 11/4 (October 1983) 485–510.

———. "Erneuerung christlicher Gemeinschaft in Afrika." *ZM* 3/3 (1977) 183–88.

———. "Ethics in Contexts of Transition." Paper read at International Committee for Witwatersrand Industrial Mission Conference on "Theology Steps into the Industrial Arena." Potchefstroom University, July 1–5, 1985. Unpublished document in private ownership.

———. "Ethics in Contexts of Transition." *JTSA* 57 (1986) 17–23.

———. "Evangelisation, Evangelisierung." In *Lexicon Missions-Theologischer Grundbegriffe*, edited by Karl Müller et al., 102–5. Berlin: Dietrich Reimer, 1987.

———. "Evangelism." *MF* 9/4 (December 1981) 65–74.

———. "Evangelism: An Holistic Approach." *JTSA* 36 (September 1981) 43–63.

———. "Evangelism and Mission: The Contemporary Debate." Paper read at the Clergy Synod, Church of the Province of Southern Africa Diocese of Cape Town, St. John's Church, Wynberg, September 21, 1982. Unpublished document in private ownership.

———. "Evangelism and Mission—The Contemporary Debate." *Church Scene* (March 8, 1985) 10–11; (March 15, 1985) 10–11.

———. "Evangelism and Social Transformation." *TE* 16/2 (June 1983) 43–55.

———. "Evangelism and Social Transformation." In *The Church in Response to Human Need*, edited by Tom Sine, 271–92. Monrovia, CA: MARC, 1983.

———. "Evangelism and Special Needs." In *I Will Heal Their Land, Papers of the South African Congress on Mission and Evangelism*, edited by Michael Cassidy, 207–12. Maseru, Les.: Africa Enterprise, 1974.

———. "Evangelism, as Defined by Melbourne and Pattaya." *Reformed Ecumenical Synod Mission Bulletin* 1/2 (October 1981) 1–10.

———. "Evangelism: Theological Currents and Cross-Currents of Our Time." Paper presented at the South African Council of Churches' Seminar on "The Relevance of Evangelism in South Africa Today." Hammanskraal, January 27–31, 1986. Unpublished document in private ownership.

———. "Evangelism: Theological Currents and Cross-Currents of Our Time." *Church Scene* (June 6, 1986) 12–14.

———. "Evangelism: Theological Currents and Cross-currents Today." *IBMR* 11/3 (July 1987) 98–103.

———. "Evangelism: Theological Currents and Cross-currents Today." *Reformed Ecumenical Synod Mission Bulletin* 7/3 (September 1987) 8–16.

———. "The Feasibility of Moratorium in the South African Context." In *Out of the Dust: The Moratorium Debate*, edited by Margaret Nash, 25–33. Johannesburg: South African Council of Churches, 1977.

———. "For Such a Time as This (Esther 4:1–16)." Opening address given at the SACLA Conference, Pretoria Showgrounds, July 8, 1979. Unpublished document in private ownership.

———. "Forgive Us . . . As We Forgive . . ." *IRM* 69/275 (July 1980) 330–31.

———. "The Fragmentation of Afrikanerdom and the Afrikaner Churches." In *Resistance and Hope: South African Essays in Honour of Beyers Naudé*, edited by Charles Villa-Vicencio et al., 61–73. Cape Town: David Philip, 1985.

———. "Geestelike opbou en Ekumeniese Betrekkinge by die Ned. Geref. Dogterkerke." *NGTT* 13/3 (June 1972) 129–39.

———. *Gemeenteopbou in Afrika*. Lux Mundi 4. Pretoria: N. G. Kerkboekhandel, 1972.

———. "Gesamentlike Aanbidding." *Die Kerkbode* 27 (June 1973) 819–21.

———. "God in Africa: Implications for the Kerygma." *Miss* 1/1 (April 1973) 3–21.

———. "God through African Eyes." *TE* 6/1 (March 1973) 11–22.

———. "God through African Eyes." In *Relevant Theology for Africa*, edited by H. J. Becken, 68–78. Durban: Lutheran, 1973.

———. "The Gospel in African Robes: Toward the Africanization of the Gospel." Lectures presented at the Overseas Ministries Study Center, Ventnor, New Jersey, March 16–20, 1981. Unpublished document in private ownership.

———. "Hat die Kirche in Südafrika Versagt?" *Frohe Botschaft* 101 (May 1979) 3–4.

———. *Heil vir die Wêreld: Die Christelike Sending in Teologiese Perspektief*. Pretoria: N. G. Kerkboekhandel Transvaal, 1979.

———. "Heilsgeschichte und Mission." In *Oikonomia: Heilsgeschichte als Thema der Theologie (Festschrift für Oscar Cullmann)*, edited by Felix Christ, 386–94. Hamburg: Herbert Reich Evang., 1967.

———. "Hermeneuse in 'n Sendingsituasie." In *Hermeneutica: Feesbundel vir prof. E. P. Groenewald*, 220–240. Pretoria: N.G. Kerkboekhandel, 1970.

———. *Het Evangelie in Afrikaans Gewaad*. Kampen, Neth.: Kok, 1974.

———. "In Gesprek met Dr. P. F. Theron." In *Perspektief op die Ope Brief*, edited by D. J. Bosch et al., 134–42. Cape Town: Human & Rousseau, 1982.

———. "In Search of a New Evangelical Understanding." In *In Word and Deed: Evangelism and Social Responsibility*, edited by Bruce Nicholls, 63–83. Grand Rapids: Eerdmans, 1985.

———. "In Search of Mission: Reflections on 'Melbourne' and 'Pattaya.'" *Miss* 9/1 (April 1981) 3–18.

———. "The In Between People." N.d. Unpublished document in private ownership.

———. "Inheemswording, Afrikanisasie en Swart Teologie." *NGTT* 13/2 (March 1972) 103–15.

———. "Interview." Personal interview with the author. September 8, 1986.

Bibliography

———. "Jesaja en die Sending." *Deo Gloria* (1957) 34–37.

———. "Jesus and the Gentiles." In *The Church Crossing Frontiers: Essays on the Nature of Mission in Honour of Bengt Sundkler*, edited by Peter Beyerhaus and Carl Hallencreutz, 3–19. Uppsala: Gleerup, 1969.

———. *Jesus, die lydende Messias, en ons Sendingmotief*. Kerk en Wêreld 3. Bloemfontein: N. G. Sendingpers, 1961.

———. "Johannes du Plessis as Sendingkundige." *TE* 19/1 (March 1986) 66–76.

———. "Johannes du Plessis: Grondlegger van die Sendingwetenskap in Suid-Afrika." In *Sendinggenade: Sendingwetenskaplike opstelle aangebied aan Prof. W. J. Van der Merwe by geleentheid van sy tagtigste verjaarsdag*, edited by J. Du Preez et al, 42–57. Bloemfontein: N. G. Sendinguitgewers, 1986.

———. "Jongkerke en Ekumene . . ." *Die Kerkbode* (April 12, 1972) 473, 476.

———. "Julle Sal My Getuies Wees." Handleiding vir Sendingwerkkragte, 1967. Unpublished document in private ownership.

———. "Kaleidoskoop van die Na-Oorlogse Sendingwetenskap." In *Sendingwetenskap vandag: 'n terreinverkenning*, edited by David Bosch, 13–34. Pretoria: N. G. Kerkboekhandel, 1968.

———. "Kerk en Politiek in die Suid-Afrikaanse Konteks." In *Storm-kompas*, edited by N. Smith et al., 24–37. Cape Town: Tafelberg, 1981.

———. "The Kingdom of God and the Kingdoms of this World." *JTSA* 29 (December 1979) 3–13.

———. "The Kingdom of God and the Kingdoms of This World." Address given at the SACLA Conference, Pretoria, July 11, 1979. Unpublished document in private ownership.

———. "The Kingdom of God in Mission—Eschatalogical Motifs and Their Functions." Paper given at Andrews Theological Seminary, Berrien Springs, Michigan, May 11, 1978. Unpublished document in private ownership.

———. "La Iglesia: una Nueva Sociedad." *Certeza* 67 (July–September 1977) 74–79.

———. "Le Champ de la Mission." *Panorama InterEglises* (October–December 1985) 53–71.

———. "Le Paternalisme Missionaire—Une Réponse à Roger Mehl." *Perspectives Missionaires* 8 (1984) 14–30.

———. *L'Eglise, une Société Alternative*. Lausanne: Presses Bibliques Universitaires, 1983.

———. *The Lord's Prayer: Paradigm for a Christian Lifestyle*. Pretoria: Christian Medical Fellowship, 1985.

———. "Luke 16: 19–31 & 18: 9–14." Sermon delivered at the Edenvale Methodist Church, September 25, 1983. Unpublished document in private ownership.

———. "Medewerkers in Genesing en Barmhartigheid." *Die Sendingblad* (June 1969) 189–92.

———. "Melbourne and Pattaya: The Left Foot and the Right Foot of the Church?" N.d. Unpublished document in private ownership.

———. "The Melbourne Conference: Between Guilt and Hope." *IRM* 69/276 and 70/277 (October 1980 and January 1981) 512–18.

———. "Mennoniete Trap Diep Spore in Kerkgeskiedenis." *Unisa Bulletin* (August 1978) 12, 16.

———. "Ministry in the Context of Tension and Alienation." Paper given at a Mennonite Students' Conference, Elkhart, Indiana, February 1978. Unpublished document in private ownership.

———. "Missiological Developments in South Africa." *Miss* 3/1 (April 1975) 9–30.

———. "Missiology." In *Introduction to Theology*, edited by I. H. Eybers et al., 159–70. Pretoria: D. R. Church, 1974.

———. "Missiology." In *Introduction to Theology*, edited by I. H. Eybers, et al., 230–43. 2nd revised and enlarged edition. Pretoria: D. R. Church, 1978.

———. "Missiology." In *Introduction to Theology*, edited by I. H. Eybers, et al., 263–86. 3rd revised and enlarged edition. Pretoria: D. R. Church, 1982.

———. "Mission—An Attempt at a Definition." *Church Scene* (April 25, 1986) 10–11.

———. "Mission—An Attempt at a Definition." Paper presented at a seminar on mission organized by the D. R. Mission Church, University of the Western Cape, Belville, April 1986. Unpublished document in private ownership.

———. "Mission and Evangelism: Clarifying the Concepts." *ZMR* 68/3 (July 1984) 161–91.

———. "Mission and the Alternative Community [How My Mind has Changed]." *JTSA* 41 (December 1982) 6–10.

———. "Mission Hospitals—The Challenge of the Future." N.d. Unpublished document in private ownership.

———. "Mission in Biblical Perspective." *IRM* 74/296 (October 1985) 531–38.

———. "Mission in Theological Education." In *Missions and Theological Education in World Perspective*, edited by Harvie Conn et al., xv–xli. Farmington, MI: Associates of Urbanus, 1984.

———. "Missionaarista Teologiaa Kohti." *Kirkkomme Lähetys vår Kyrkas Mission* (Helsinki) 1 (1984) 20–30.

———, ed. *Missionalia: Southern African Journal of Mission Studies*. Vols. 1/1–20/1 (1973–1992). Pretoria: Southern African Missiological Society.

———. "The Missionary: Exemplar or Victim?" *TE* 17/1 (March 1984) 9–16.

———. "Missionary Paternalism: A Response to Roger Mehl." 1984. Unpublished document in private ownership.

———. "Missionary Theology in Africa." *IMR* 6/2 (April 1984) 161–91.

———. "Missionary Theology in Africa." *JTSA* 49 (December 1984) 14–37.

———. "'n Missionêre Dilemma in Afrika: Die Probleem van die Kwade." *TE* 6/3 (September 1973) 173–98.

———. "The Nature of Theological Education." *TE* 25/1 (1992) 8–23.

———. "Navolging van Christus in Suid-en Suid-Wes-Afrika Vandag." In *Swakopmundkonferensie van die Christelike Akademie*, edited by M. Buthelezi et al., 13–22. Johannesburg: Christian Academy, 1974.

———. "Nothing But a Heresy." In *Apartheid is a Heresy*, edited by John de Gruchy et al., 24–38. Grand Rapids: Eerdmans, 1983.

———. *Onafhanklike kerklike bewegings in Afrika*. Sending en Godsdienswetenskap MSR 503–2. Pretoria: UNISA, 1973.

———. "Onderweg na 'n Theologia Africana." In *Teologie in Vernuwing*, edited by I. H. Eybers, et al., 160–79. Pretoria: University of South Africa, 1975.

———. "Ons Geskiedenis in Gevaar." Speech given at a Day of the Covenant Meeting in the Northern Transvaal, December 16, 1950. Unpublished document in private ownership.

———. "Opgestel vir Voorlegging (deur ds. J. G. du Plessis) aan 'n tydelike kommissie van die Noord-Transvaalse Sinode." ["Draft Submission" (through Rev. J. G. du Plessis) to a temporary commission of the Northern Transvaal Synod.] October 25, 1979. Unpublished document in private ownership.

Bibliography

———. "Our Missionary Service: Toward Renewed Confidence and Commitment." Paper presented at the Annual Conference of the Hermannsburg Mission Society, Sierra Ranch, Mooirivier, November 10, 1987. Unpublished document in private ownership.

———. "Perspectives on Evangelism and Social Responsibility in Contemporary Theology: A Response to Tokunboh Adeyemo." Paper presented at the Consultation on the Relationship between Evangelism and Social Responsibility, Grand Rapids, Michigan, June 19–26, 1982. Unpublished document in private ownership.

———. "Polarisation or Reconciliation—Which Way?" Address at the Christian Businessmens' Lunch, Carlton Hotel, Johannesburg, October 19, 1977. Unpublished document in private ownership.

———. "Possibilities and Limitations of Ecumenical Action in South Africa." *Das Gespräch: Jaarblad van die Christelike Akademie* (1970–71) 20–24.

———. "Prisoners of History or Prisoners of Hope?" *The Hiltonian* 114 (March 1979) 14–18.

———. "The Problem of Evil in Africa: A Survey of African Views on Witchcraft and of the Response of the Christian Church." Paper presented at the C. B. Powell Bible Centre's Conference on the Bible, the Church and the Demonic Powers, University of South Africa, Pretoria, July 1986. Unpublished document in private ownership.

———. "The Problem of Evil in Africa: A Survey of African Views on Witchcraft and the Response of the Christian Church." In *Like a Roaring Lion . . . Essays on the Bible, the Church and Demonic Powers*, edited by P. G. R. de Villiers, 38–62. Pretoria: University of South Africa, 1987.

———. "Problems and Progress in South Africa." *Evangelical Newsletter* 4/13 (July 1, 1977) 4.

———. "Processes of Reconciliation and Demands of Obedience in South Africa: Twelve Theses." *Church Scene* (September 20, 1985) 12–13.

———. "Processes of Reconciliation and Demands of Obedience—Twelve Theses." In *Hammering Swords into Plowshares: Essays in Honour of Archbishop Desmond Tutu*, edited by Itumeleng Mosala et al., 159–71. Johannesburg: Skotaville, 1986.

———. "Prof. Bosch on Church-State Relationship." [Submission to the Eloff Commission], *Ecunews* 2 (February 1983) 24–30.

———. "The Question of Mission Today." *JTSA* 1 (December 1972) 5–15.

———. "Racism and Revolution: Response of the Churches in South Africa." *OBMR* 3/1 (January 1979) 13–20.

———. "Reconciliation—An Afrikaner Speaks." *Leadership SA* 4/4 (October 1985) 60–65.

———. "Re-Evangelisation? Reflecting on the Contributions of J. N. J. Kritzinger and S. Mkhatshwa." *JTSA* 76 (September 1991) 122–31.

———. "Reflections on Biblical Models of Mission." In *Toward the Twenty-First Century in Christian Mission*, edited by James Phillips et al, 175–92. Grand Rapids: Eerdmans, 1993.

———. "Religion and the State: Five Models." n.d. Unpublished document in private ownership.

———. "The Religious and Historical Roots of the Present Polarisation Between Black and White." Paper read at the Ecumenical Association of African Theologians, Laverna Conference Centre, September 15–17, 1982. Unpublished document in private ownership.

———. "Renewal of Christian Community in Africa Today." In *Facing the New Challenges*, edited by M. Cassidy et al., 92–102. Nairobi: Evangel, 1978.

———. "Review of D. A. McGavran's *Understanding Church Growth*." *Miss* 9/2 (August 1981) 93.

———. "Romans 13." Sermon delivered at the Sunnyside Methodist Church on "Christian Citizenship Sunday," November 14, 1976. Unpublished document in private ownership.

———. "The Roots and Fruits of Afrikaner Civil Religion." In *New Faces of Africa: Essays in Honour of Ben Marais*, edited by J. W. Hofmeyr et al., 14–35. Pretoria: University of South Africa, 1984.

———. "Salvation Tomorrow *and* Today: A Response to Adrio König." *TE* 13/2–3 (July–September 1980) 20–26.

———. "Schwarze Theologie in Südafrika." *EMM* 117/1-2 (1973) 77–84.

———. "The Scope of Mission." The 1982 CMS annual sermon. London: Church Missionary Society, 1982.

———. "The Scope of Mission." *IRM* 73/289 (January 1984) 17–32.

———. "Sending—'n Prinsipiële Besinning." In *Wat is Sending?*, edited by P. Robinson et al., 109–22. Malmesbury, RSA: Swartland Drukpers, 1986.

———. "Sendingperspektief in die Ou Testament." *NGTT* 3/1 (December 1961) 285–302.

———. "Sendingwetenskap." In *Inleiding in die Teologie*, edited by I. H. Eybers et al., 157–68. Pretoria: N. G. Kerkboekhandel, 1973.

———. "Sendingwetenskap." In *Inleiding in die Teologie*, edited by I. H. Eybers et al., 230–43. 2nd revised and expanded edition. Pretoria: N. G. Kerkboekhandel, 1978.

———. "Sendingwetenskap." In *Inleiding in die Teologie*, edited by I. H. Eybers et al., 275–99. 3rd revised and expanded edition. Pretoria: N. G. Kerkboekhandel, 1982.

———. *Sendingwetenskap Vandag: 'n Terreinverkenning*. Lux Mundi 1. Pretoria: N. G. Kerkboekhandel, 1968.

———. "Seven Theses on Ministry in Southern Africa Today." Africa Enterprise Board Meeting, Pietermaritzburg, April 29, 1976. Unpublished document in private ownership.

———. *Sodat Hulle Kan Verstaan: Kommunikasie as sendingprobleem in Afrika*. Lux Mundi 2. Pretoria: N. G. Kerkboekhandel, 1969.

———. "Some Random Thoughts on a Proposed Writing Project." April 22, 1986. Unpublished document in private ownership.

———. "Speaking the Truth in Love." Address to the St. Andrew's Presbyterian Church, Pretoria, November 5, 1972. Unpublished document in private ownership.

———. *A Spirituality of the Road*. Scottdale, PA: Herald, 1979.

———. "The Structure of Mission: An Exposition of Matthew 28:16–20." In *Exploring Church Growth*, edited by W. R. Shenk, 218–48. Grand Rapids: Eerdmans, 1983.

———. "Südafrika: Fünf nach Zwölf?" *Kontinente: Magazin für Kirche und Gesellschaft in der Dritten Welt* 17/3 (June 1982) 8–9.

———. "Systematic Theology and Mission: The Voice of an Early Pioneer." *TE* 5/3 (September 1972) 165–89.

———. "Theological Education in Missionary Perspective." *Missiology* 10/1 (January 1982) 13–34.

———. "Theologies of Mission." In *Reflecting on Mission in the African Context: A Handbook for Missiology*, edited by H. L. Pretorius et al., 41–55. Bloemfontein: Pro Christi, 1987.

———. *Theology of Mission*. Missiology and Science of Religion MSR 201-1. Pretoria: UNISA, 1980.

———. *Theology of Religions*. Missiology and Science of Religion MSR 303-1. Pretoria: UNISA, 1977.

———. "Three Church Attitudes Towards the State." *AEN* (July 1978) 5.

———. "Thy Will Be Done on Earth." *IRM* 69/275 (July 1980) 303–5.

Bibliography

———. "Too Early for Heaven, Too Late for Earth." *Decision* 18/11 (December 1977) 10.

———. "Towards a Hermeneutic for 'Biblical Studies and Mission.'" *Miss Stud* 3/2 (October 1986) 65–79.

———. "Towards True Mutuality: Exchanging the Same Commodities or Supplementing Each Others' Needs?" *Missiology* 6/3 (July 1978) 284–96.

———. "The Traditional African Understanding of Evil as a Missionary Challenge." Paper read to various theological student groups in England, November-December 1982. Unpublished document in private ownership.

———. *Transforming Mission: Paradigm Shifts in Theology of Mission.* Maryknoll, NY: Orbis, 1991.

———. *Transforming Mission: Paradigm Shifts in Theology of Mission.* 20th anniversary edition. Maryknoll, NY: Orbis, 2011.

———. "Verkondig die Koninkryk." *Deo Gloria* (1954) 51–53.

———. "Vielfalt der Völker und die eine Kirche." In *Wenn wir wie Brüder untereinander wohnten...*, edited by J. de Gruchy et al., 44–58. Neukirchen-Vluyn, Ger.: Neukirchener, 1984.

———. "Violence." Paper read to the Lenasia Congregation of the Reformed Church in Africa, 1972. Unpublished document in private ownership.

———. "Vision for Mission." *IRM* 76/301 (January 1987) 8–15.

———. "The Vulnerability of Mission." *ZMR* 76/1 (January 1992) 201–16.

———. "Wat Baat Sending en Evangelisasie Ons?" In *Sodat My Huis Vol Kan Word: Reformatoriese Perspektiewe op ons Evangelisasieroeping Vandag*, 193–202. Potchefstroom: Potchefstroom University, 1986.

———. "The Why and How of a True Biblical Foundation for Mission." In *Zending op Weg naar de Toekomst, Feesbundel aangeboden aan Prof. Dr. Johannes Verkuyl*, edited by T. J. Baarda et al., 33–45. Kampen, Neth.: Kok, 1978.

———. "Why SACLA?" Address given at the Holiday Inn, Jan Smuts Airport, Johannesburg, November 26, 1977. Unpublished document in private ownership.

———. *Witness to the World.* The Christian Mission in Theological Perspective. Atlanta: John Knox, 1980. Also published in Afrikaans as *Heil vir die Wêreld: Die christelike sending in teologiese perspektief.* Pretoria: N. G. Kerkboekhandel, 1979.

———. "You Can't Go It Alone!" *Unisa Bulletin* (November 1980) 3.

———, M. Buthelezi, J. L. de Vries, and M. Tlhabanello. *Swakopmund-konferensie van die Christelike Akademie.* Johannesburg: Christian Academy, 1974.

———, and G. Jansen. *Sending in Meervoud.* Kerk en Wêreld 5. Pretoria: N. G. Kerkboekhandel, 1968.

———, A. König, and W. Nicol. *Perspektief op die Ope Brief.* Cape Town: Human & Rousseau, 1982.

———, J. N. J. Kritzinger, and P. G. J. Meiring. *Introduction to Missiology.* Missiology and Science of Religion MSR 101-1. Chapters 1 and 4–10 written by Bosch. Pretoria: UNISA, 1980.

———, J. N. J. Kritzinger, P. G. J. Meiring, and W. A. Saayman. "A Response to Donald McGavran's 'A Giant Step in Christian Mission,'" *A Monthly Letter on Evangelism* 10–11 (October–November 1985) 7–9.

———, and W. A. Saayman. *Church and Mission.* Missiology MSR 521-X. Revised issue. Pretoria, UNISA, 1987.

———, and Chris Sugden. "From Partnership to Marriage: Consultation on the Relationship between Evangelism and Social Responsibility (CRESR)." *Themelios* 8/2 (January 1983) 26–27.

———, and Chris Sugden. "From Partnership to Marriage: Consultation on the Relationship between Evangelism and Social Responsibility (CRESR)." *Miss* 10/2 (August 1982) 75–77.

———, and T. D. Verryn. *Church and Mission 301*. Missiology and Science of Religion MSR 301-1. Pretoria: UNISA, 1978.

Botha, A. J. *Die Evolusie van 'n Volksteologie*. Teks en Konteks 4. Bellville, RSA: University of Western Cape, 1984.

Botha, C. J. "Belhar: A Century-Old Protest." In *A Moment of Truth: The Confession of the Dutch Reformed Mission Church*, edited by G. D. Cloete et al., 66–80. Grand Rapids: Eerdmans, 1984.

Braaten, Carl. *The Flaming Center: A Theology of the Christian Mission*. Philadelphia: Fortress, 1977.

Brown, E. *A Historical Profile of the Nederduitse Gereformeerde Kerk (Dutch Reformed Church) in South Africa*. N.p.: University of Zululand, 1973.

Brueggeman, Walter. "The Bible and Mission: Some Interdisciplinary Implications for Teaching." *Missiology* 10 (October 1982) 397–412.

Brunner, Emil. *Truth as Encounter*. Philadelphia: Westminster, 1964.

———. *The Word and the World*. London: SCM, 1931.

Bühlmann, Walbert. *The Coming of the Third Church*. Slough, UK: St. Paul, 1976.

Buthelezi, Manas. "Six Theses: Theological Problems of Evangelism in the South African Context." In *Mission Trends No. 2: Evangelization*, edited by Gerald Anderson et al., 136–38. New York: Paulist, 1975.

Calvin, John. *Institutes of the Christian Religion*. 2 vols. Edited by John T. McNeill. Translated by Ford L. Battles. Philadelphia: Westminster, 1960.

Casalis, Georges. *Correct Ideas Don't Fall From the Skies*. Maryknoll, NY: Orbis, 1984.

Cassidy, Michael. *Bursting the Wineskins*. London: Hodder & Stoughton, 1983.

———, ed. *I Will Heal Their Land: Papers of the South African Congress on Mission and Evangelism*. Maseru, Les.: Africa Enterprise, 1974.

———, and Gottfried Osei-Mensah, eds. *Together in One Place: The Story of PACLA*. Kisumu, Ken: Evangel, 1977.

Castro, Emilio. *Amidst Revolution*. Belfast: Christian Journals, 1975.

———. "Ecumenism and Evangelicalism: Where Are We?" In *Faith and Faithfulness: Essays on Contemporary Ecumenical Themes*, edited by Pauline Webb, 8–17. Geneva: World Council of Churches, 1984.

———. "Evangelical and Ecumenical." *Reformed Journal* 37 (January 1987) 17–22.

———. *Freedom in Mission: The Perspective of the Kingdom of God*. Geneva: World Council of Churches, 1985.

———. "Reflection after Melbourne." In *Your Kingdom Come*, 225–34. Geneva: World Council of Churches, 1980.

"Charter for Mobilising Evangelical Unity." *Trans* 3 (April 1986) 15.

Chikane, Frank. "Doing Theology in a Situation of Conflict." In *Resistance and Hope: South African Essays in honour of Beyers Naudé*, edited by Charles Villa-Vicencio et al., 98–102. Grand Rapids: Eerdmans, 1985.

Chirgwin, A. M. *The Bible in World Evangelism*. London: SCM, 1954.

"Church is Easing Apartheid Stand." *New York Times*, October 26, 1986.

Cloete, G. D., et al., eds. *A Moment of Truth: The Confession of the Dutch Reformed Mission Church*. Grand Rapids: Eerdmans, 1984.

Clouse, Robert, ed. *The Meaning of the Millenium: Four Views*. Downers Grove, IL: InterVarsity, 1977.

Coe, Shoki. "Contextualizing Theology." In *Mission Trends No. 3: Third World Theologies*, edited by Gerald Anderson et al., 19–24. Grand Rapids: Eerdmans, 1976.

Comblin, José. *The Meaning of Mission*. Maryknoll, NY: Orbis, 1977.

Concerned Evangelicals. *Evangelical Witness in South Africa: Evangelicals Critique Their Own Theology and Practice*. Grand Rapids: Eerdmans, 1986. Reprinted in *Trans* 4/1 (January 1987) 17–30.

Cone, James. *God of the Oppressed*. New York: Seabury, 1975.

Conn, Harvey, ed. *Theological Perspectives on Church Growth*. Nutley, NJ: Presbyterian and Reformed, 1976.

Cook, Richard. "Paul, the Organizer." *Missiology* 10 (October 1981) 485–98.

Costas, Orlando. *Christ Outside the Gate: Mission beyond Christendom*. Maryknoll, NY: Orbis, 1982.

———. *The Church and Its Mission: A Shattering Critique from the Third World*. Wheaton, IL: Tyndale, 1974.

———. Review of *Witness to the World*, by David Bosch. *IRM* 71 (July 1981) 82–86.

———. *Theology of the Crossroads in Contemporary Latin America*. Amsterdam: Rodopi, 1976.

Cotterell, Peter. *The Eleventh Commandment*. Leicester, UK: InterVarsity, 1981.

Cox, Harvey. *The Secular City*. New York: Macmillan, 1965.

Cronjé, G., ed., *Regverdige Rasse-Apartheid*. Stellenbosch, RSA: C.S.V., 1947.

Cullmann, Oscar. *Christ and Time*. Philadelphia: Westminster, 1950.

———. "Eschatology and Mission in the New Testament." In *The Theology of the Christian Mission*, edited by Gerald Anderson, 42–54. London: SCM, 1961.

———. *Salvation in History*. London: SCM, 1967.

Daneel, M. L., J. N. J. Kritzinger, and W. A. Saayman. *Third World Theologies MSB 302-G*. Pretoria: UNISA, 1982.

De Gruchy, John W. *The Church Struggle in South Africa*. 2nd ed. London: Collins, 1986.

———. *Cry Justice: Prayers, Meditations and Readings from South Africa*. London: Collins, 1986.

———. "The Church and the Struggle for South Africa." *TT* 43 (July 1986) 229–43.

———. "Radical Peace-Making: The Challenge of Some Anabaptists." In *Theology and Violence: The South African Debate*, edited by Charles Villa-Vicencio, 173–85. Grand Rapids: Eerdmans, 1988.

———. "The Relation Between the State and Some of the Churches in South Africa." *JCS* 19 (Autumn 1977) 437–55.

———. "A Short History of the Christian Institute." In *Resistance and Hope*, Edited by John W. de Gruchy et al., 14–26. Grand Rapids: Eerdmans, 1985.

———. "Theologies in Conflict: The South African Debate." In *Resistance and Hope*, edited by John W. de Gruchy et al, 85–97. Grand Rapids: Eerdmans, 1985.

———. "Towards a Confessing Church." In *Apartheid is a Heresy*, edited by John W. de Gruchy et al, 75–93. Cape Town: David Philip, 1983.

———, and Charles Villa-Vicencio, eds. *Apartheid is a Heresy*. Cape Town: David Philip, 1983.

De Klerk, Willem A. *The Puritans in Africa: A Story of Afrikanerdom*. Harmondsworth, UK: Penguin, 1976.

Driver, John. *Understanding the Atonement for the Mission of the Church*. Scottdale, PA: Herald, 1986.

Du Plessis, Johannes. *Wie Sal Gaan? Die Sending in Teorie en Praktyk*. Cape Town: Bible Union, 1932.

Du Toit, André. "No Chosen People: The Myth of the Calvinist Origins of Afrikaner Nationalism and Racial Ideology." *AHR* 88 (October 1983) 939–47.

DuBose, Francis. *God Who Sends: A Fresh Quest for Biblical Mission*. Nashville: Broadman, 1983.

Durand, Johannes Jacobus Fourie. "Afrikaner Piety and Dissent." In *Resistance and Hope*, edited by John W. de Gruchy et al., 39–51. Grand Rapids: Eerdmans, 1985.

———. "Bible and Race: the Problem of Hermeneutics." *JTSA* 24 (September 1978) 3–9.

Dyrness, William. "The Kingdom Is Our Goal." *Together* 1 (December 1983) 1-3, 39-40.

———. *Let the Earth Rejoice! A Biblical Theology of Holistic Mission*. Westchester, IL: Crossway, 1983.

Echegaray, Hugo. *The Practice of Jesus*. Maryknoll, NY: Orbis, 1984.

Eliade, Mircea. *The Myth of the Eternal Return*. Princeton, NJ: Princeton University Press, 1974.

Ellul, Jacques. *The Meaning of the City*. Grand Rapids: Eerdmans, 1970.

Flannery, Austin P. *Vatican Council II: The Conciliar and Post Conciliar Documents*. Grand Rapids: Eerdmans, 1981.

"Forging a Fragile Togetherness in the Land of Apartheid Rifts: The South African Christian Leadership Assembly." *CT* (August 17, 1979) 39–40.

Gadamer, Hans. *Truth and Method*. London: Sheed and Ward, 1975.

Galilea, Segundo. *The Beatitudes: To Evangelize as Jesus Did*. Maryknoll, NY: Orbis, 1984.

Geldenhuys, F. E. O'Brien. *In die Stroomversnellings: Vyftig jaar van die NG Kerk*. Cape Town: Tafelberg, 1982.

Gensichen, Hans-Werner. *Glaube für die Welt: Theologische Aspekte der Mission*. Gütersloh, Ger.: Gerd Mohn, 1971.

———. "Mission and Ideology in South Africa." *Miss* 16 (August 1988) 86–97.

Gibbs, Eddie. *I Believe in Church Growth*. London: Hodder & Stoughton, 1982.

Glasser, Arthur. "Church Growth at Fuller." *Missiology* 14 (October 1986) 401–20.

———. "The Evolution of Evangelical Mission Theology since World War II." *IBMR* 9 (January 1985) 9–13.

———, and Donald McGavran. *Contemporary Theologies of Mission*. Grand Rapids: Baker, 1983.

Goodall, Norman. "'Evangelicals' and the WCC-IMC." *IRM* 47 (1958) 210–15.

Gort, Jerald. "Contours of the Reformed Understanding of Christian Mission: An Attempt at Delineation." *OBMR* 4 (October 1980) 156–60.

———. *Your Kingdom Come: World Missionary Conference, Melbourne, May 1980: An Historical and Missiological Interpretation*. Amsterdam: Free University of Amsterdam, 1980.

Goudzwaard, Bob. *Idols of Our Time*. Downers Grove, IL: InterVarsity, 1984.

Green, Michael. *Evangelism in the Early Church*. London: Hodder & Stoughton, 1973.

Bibliography

———. *Evangelism—Now and Then.* Leicester, UK: InterVarsity, 1979.
Guder, Darrell, and Martin Reppenhagen. "The Continuing Transformation of Mission." In *Transforming Mission* (20th edition), edited by David Bosch, 533–55. Maryknoll, NY: Orbis, 1992.
Hahn, Ferdinand. *Mission in the New Testament.* London: SCM, 1965.
Hauerwas, Stanley. *The Peaceable Kingdom.* London: SCM, 1983.
Hauerwas, Stanley, and William Willimon. *Resident Aliens: A Provocative Christian Assessment of Culture and Ministry for People Who Know that Something is Wrong.* Nashville: Abingdon, 1989.
Hedland, Roger. *Roots of the Great Debate in Mission.* Madras, India: Evangelical Literature Service, 1981.
Hering, Wolfgang. *Das Missionsverständnis in der ökumenisch-evangelikalen Auseinandersetzung—ein innerprotestantisches Problem.* St. Augustin. Ger.: Steyler, 1980.
Heron, Alasdair. *A Century of Protestant Theology.* Philadelphia: Westminster, 1980.
Hexham, Irving. *The Irony of Apartheid: The Struggle for National Independence of Afrikaner Calvinism Against British Imperialism.* New York: Edwin Mellin, 1981.
Hinchcliff, Peter. *The Church in South Africa.* London: SPCK, 1968.
Hoekema, A. A. *The Bible and the Future.* Grand Rapids: Eerdmans, 1979.
Hoekendijk, Johannes. *Kirche und Volk in der deutschen Missionswissenschaft.* Munich: Chr. Kaiser, 1967.
Hoekstra, Harvey. *The World Council of Churches and the Demise of Evangelism.* Wheaton, IL: Tyndale, 1979.
Hogg, W. R. *Ecumenical Foundations.* New York: Harper, 1952.
Hollenweger, Walter. *Erfahrungen der Leibhaftigkeit.* Munich: Chr-Kaiser, 1979.
———. *Evangelism Today.* Belfast: Christian Journals, 1976.
Hope, Marjorie, and James Young. *The South African Churches in a Revolutionary Situation.* Maryknoll, NY: Orbis, 1981.
"Hopes for Reconciliation Spurred by South African Church's Change." *Presbyterian Survey* 79 (May 1989) 36.
Horner, Francis E. "Toward a Christian Community." Unpublished PhD disseration, Boston University, 1987.
Horner, Norman, ed. *Protestant Crosscurrents in Mission: The Ecumenical-Conservative Encounter.* Nashville: Abingdon, 1968.
Hubbard, B. J. *The Matthean Redaction of a Primitive Apostolic Commission: An Exegesis of Matthew 28:18–20.* Missoula, MT: Society of Biblical Literature and Scholar's Press Dissertation Series, 1976.
Human Relations and the South African Scene in the Light of Scripture. Cape Town: DRC, 1976.
Hunter, George. *The Contagious Congregation: Frontiers in Evangelism and Church Growth.* Nashville: Abingdon, 1979.
"Initiative for Reconciliation in South Africa." *Trans* 3 (January 1986) 1–8.
International Commission of Jurists, eds. *The Trial of Beyers Naudé: Christian Witness and the Rule of Law.* London: Search, 1975.
International Defence and Aid Fund. *This is Apartheid: A Pictorial Introduction.* London: International Defence and Aid Fund for Southern Africa, 1984.
"Is SACLA Ecumenical or Evangelical?" *Encounter* 4 (June 1979) 1, 4.
Jackson, Herbert. "The Missionary Obligation of Theology." *OBMRL* 15 (January 1964) 1–6.

Jeremias, Joachim. *Jesus' Promise to the Nations*. London: SCM, 1959.

Johanson, Brian. "Race, Mission and Ecumenism: Reflections on the Landman Report." *JTSA* 10 (March 1975) 60–67.

Johnston, Arthur. *The Battle for World Evangelism*. Wheaton, IL: Tyndale, 1978.

———. *World Evangelism and the Word of God*. Minneapolis: Bethany, 1974.

Jonkers, Willie. "Afsonderlike kerke vir afsonderlike bevolkingsgroepe?" *Scriptura* 17 (1986) 12ff.

Jonsson, John. "An Elliptical Understanding of Mission and its Roles." *Miss* 11 (April 1983) 6–7.

Jooste, C. J. *SACLA?* Privately published pamphlet, June 6, 1979.

Journal of Theology for Southern Africa. Special "SACLA" edition. December 29, 1979.

Kähler, Martin. *Schriften zu Christologie und Mission*. Edited by Heinzgünter Frohnes. Munich: Chr. Kaiser, 1971.

The Kairos Document. London: Catholic Institute for International Relations and the British Council of Churches, 1985.

The Kairos Document: Revised Second Edition. Grand Rapids: Eerdmans, 1986.

Kertelge, Karl. *Mission im Neuen Testament*. Freiberg, Ger.: Herder, 1982.

Kirk, Andrew. *A New World Coming*. Basingstoke, UK: Marshalls, 1983.

———. *Theology and the Third World Church*. Downers Grove, IL: InterVarsity, 1983.

Knapp, Stephen. "Mission and Modernization: A Preliminary Critical Analysis of Contemporary Understandings of Mission from a 'Radical Evangelical' Perspective." In *American Missions in Bicentennial Perspective*, edited by R. P. Beaver, 146–209. Pasadena, CA: William Carey, 1977.

"The Koinonia Declaration." *JTSA* 24 (September 1978) 58–64.

König, Adrio. "David J. Bosch: Witness to the World." *TE* 13 (July-September 1980) 11–19.

———. "SACLA: A Rare but True Embodiment of the Church?" *JTSA* 29 (December 1979) 78–81.

Koyama, Kosuke. "The Crucified Christ Challenges Human Power." In *Your Kingdom Come*, 157–70. Geneva: World Council of Churches, 1980.

———. *No Handle on the Cross*. Maryknoll, NY: Orbis, 1977.

Kraemer, Hendrik. *The Christian Message in a Non-Christian World*. London: Edinburgh House, 1938.

Kramm, Thomas. *Analyse und Bewährung theologischer Modelle zur Begründung der Mission*. Aachen, Ger.: Missio Aktuell, 1979.

Krass, Alfred. *Evangelizing Neo-Pagan North America*. Scottdale, PA: Herald, 1982.

Kraus, C. Norman. *Authentic Witness*. Grand Rapids: Eerdmans, 1979.

———. *The Community of the Spirit*. Grand Rapids: Eerdmans, 1974.

———, ed. *Missions, Evangelism, and Church Growth*. Scottdale, PA: Herald, 1980.

Kretzschmar, Louise. *The Voice of Balck Theology in South Africa*. Braamfontein, RSA: Ravan, 1986.

Kritzinger, J. N. J., P. G. J. Meiring, and W. A. Saayman. *You Will Be My Witnesses: An Introduction to Methods of Mission*. Pretoria: N. G. Kerkboekhandel, 1984.

Kritzinger, J. N. J., and W. A. Saayman, eds. *David J. Bosch: Prophetic Integrity, Cruciform Praxis*. Dorpspruit, RSA: Cluster, 2011.

———, eds. *Mission in Creative Tension: A Dialogue with David Bosch*. Pretoria: SAMS, 1990.

Bibliography

Küng, Hans, and David Tracy, eds. *Theologie wohin? Auf dem Weg zu einem neuen Paradigma*. Zurich: Benziger, 1984.

Kuyper, Abraham. *Lectures on Calvinism*. Grand Rapids: Eerdmans, 1931.

Kuzmic, Peter. "History and Eschatology: Evangelical Views." In *In Word and Deed: Evangelism and Social Responsibility*, edited by Bruce Nicholls, 135–63. Exeter, UK: Paternoster, 1985.

Kwak, Sunhee. "Eschatology and Christian Mission." DMiss diss., Fuller Theological Seminary, 1980.

LaGrand, James. "Those Double-Jointed Doppers." *RJ* 36 (February 1986) 3–5.

Latourette, Kenneth S. *A History of the Expansion of Christianity*. Vol. 5, *The Great Century in the Americas, Australasia, and Africa*. London: Eyre and Spottiswoode, 1943.

Leatt, James, Theo Kneifel, and Klaus Nürnberger. *Contending Ideologies in South Africa*. Cape Town: David Philip, 1986.

Lee, Peter. *Guard Her Children: Hope for South Africa Today*. Eastbourne. UK: Kingsway, 1986.

Leeuwen, Arend van. *Christianity in World History*. Translated by H. H. Hoskins. London: Edinburgh, 1964.

Lindsell, Harold. "A Rejoinder." *IRM* 54/216 (October 1965) 439.

Livingston, Kevin. "David Bosch: An Interpretation of Some Main Themes in His Missiological Thought." In *Mission in Creative Tension: A Dialogue with David Bosch*, edited by W. A. Saayman et al., 3–19. Pretoria: Southern African Missiological Society, 1990.

———. "The Legacy of David J. Bosch." *IBMR* 23/1 (January 1999) 26–32.

Lochman, Jan Milic. *Reconciliation and Liberation: Challenging a One-Dimensional View of Salvation*. Philadelphia: Fortress, 1980.

Loff, Chris. "The History of a Heresy." In *Apartheid is a Heresy*, edited by John de Gruchy et al., 10–23. Grand Rapids: Eerdmans, 1983.

Löffler, Paul. "The Confessing Community." *IRM* 264 (October 1977) 341.

Lohfink, Gerhard. *Jesus and Community: The Social Dimension of Christian Faith*. London: SPCK, 1985.

Lohmeyer, Ernst. *Das Evangelium des Matthäus*. Gottingen: Vandenhoeck & Ruprecht, 1956.

Louw-Potgeiter, Joha. "The Social Identity of Dissident Afrikaners." PhD diss., University of Bristol, 1986.

Lückhoff, A. H. *Cottesloe*. Cape Town: Tafelberg, 1978.

McGavran, Donald. "Church Growth Strategy Continued." *IRM* 57 (1968) 339.

———, ed. *The Conciliar-Evangelical Debate: The Crucial Documents 1967–1976*. Pasadena, CA: William Carey, 1977.

———. "A Giant Step in Christian Mission." *Monthly Letter on Evangelism* (August 1985) 1–8.

———. Preface to *A People Reborn*, by Christian Keysser. Pasadena, CA: William Carey, 1980.

———. *Understanding Church Growth*. 2nd ed. Grand Rapids: Eerdmans, 1980.

———, and Arthur Glasser. *Contemporary Theologies of Mission*. Grand Rapids: Baker, 1983.

MacKay, John. *A Preface to Christian Theology*. London: Nisbet, 1942.

Manecke, Dieter. *Mission als Zeugendienst: Karl Barth's Theological Justification of Mission Compared with the Theories of W. Holsten, W. Freytag, and J. C. Hoekendijk*. Wuppertal, Ger.: Brockhaus, 1972.

Manson, William. *Eschatology in the New Testament*. Scottish Journal of Theology Occasional Papers 2. Edinburgh: Oliver and Boyd, 1953.

Margull, Hans J. *Hope in Action: The Church's Task in the World*. Translated by Eugene Peters. Philadelphia: Muhlenberg, 1962.

Marshall, I. Howard. "Slippery Words: Eschatology." *Expository Times* 89 (June 1978) 264–69.

Martin, James. "Towards a Post-Critical Paradigm." *NTS* 33 (July 1987) 370–85.

Martin-Achard, R. *A Light to the Nations*. London: Oliver & Boyd, 1962.

Marty, Martin. "What's Ahead for Evangelism?" In *Mission Trends No. 2: Evangelization*, edited by Gerald Anderson et al., 76–83. Grand Rapids: Eerdmans, 1975.

Matthey, Jacques. "The Great Commission according to Matthew." *IRM* 69 (April 1980) 161–73.

Meiring, P. G. J., and Henry Lederle. *Die Eenheid vand die Kerk*. Cape Town: Tafelberg, 1979.

Metz, Johannes Baptist. *Kirche im Prozess der Aufklärung*. Munich: Kaiser, 1970.

Minear, Paul. "Gratitude and Mission in the Epistle to the Romans." In *Basilea: Walter Freytag zum 60. Geburtstag*, edited by J. Hermelink et al., 42–48. Stuttgart: Evangelische Missionsverlag, 1959.

"Mission and Evangelism: An Ecumenical Affirmation." *IRM* 71 (1982) 427–51.

"Mission and Evangelism: An Historic Congress [SACME '73]" *Pro Veritate* 12 (May 15, 1973) 14–17.

Mission in South Africa. Geneva: World Council of Churches, 1961.

Moltmann, Jürgen. *The Theology of Hope: On the Ground and Implications of a Christian Eschatology*. London: SCM, 1967.

Mosala, Itumeleng. "African Independent Churches: A Study in Socio-Theological Protest." In *Resistance and Hope: South African Essays in Honour of Beyers Naudé*, edited by Charles Villa-Vicencio et al., 103–11. Grand Rapids: Eerdmans, 1985.

———, and Buti Tlhagale, eds. *Hammering Swords into Plowshares. Essays in Honour of Archbishop Desmond Tutu*. Grand Rapids: Eerdmans, 1987.

Mott, John R. *The Decisive Hour of Christian Missions*. London: Young People's Missionary Movement, 1910.

Mott, Stephen C. *Biblical Ethics and Social Change*. New York: Oxford University Press, 1982.

Moule, C. F. D. *Christ's Messengers*. 2nd ed. London: Lutterworth, 1963.

Mphahlele, Es'kia. "South Africa: Two Communities and the Struggle for a Birthright." *JAS* 4 (Spring 1977) 35, 38.

Myklebust, O. G. "Integration or Interdependence." In *Basileia: Walter Freytag zum 60. Geburtstag*, edited by J. Hermelink, 330–40. Stuttgart: Evangelische Missionsverlag, 1959.

Nash, Margaret. *Ecumenical Movement in the 1960s*. Johannesburg: Ravan, 1975.

Neill, Stephen. *Colonialism and Christian Missions*. London: Lutterworth, 1966.

———. *Salvation Tomorrow*. Nashville: Abingdon, 1976.

Neuhaus, Richard. *Dispensations: The Future of South Africa as South Africans See It*. Grand Rapids: Eerdmans, 1986.

Newbigin, Lesslie. "Cross-Currents in Ecumenical and Evangelical Understandings of Mission." *IBMR* 6 (October 1982) 146–51, 154–55.

———. *The Finality of Christ*. London: SCM, 1969.

———. *Foolishness to the Greeks: The Gospel and Western Culture*. London: SPCK, 1986.

———. "The Future of Missions and Missionaries." *RevEx* 74 (Spring 1977) 209–18.

———. *The Good Shepherd*. Grand Rapids: Eerdmans, 1977.

Bibliography

———. *The Gospel in a Pluralist Society*. Grand Rapids: Eerdmans, 1989.

———. *Honest Religion for Secular Man*. London: SCM, 1966.

———. *One Body, One Gospel, One World: The Christian Mission Today*. London: International Missionary Council, 1958.

———. *The Open Secret: Sketches for a Missionary Theology*. Grand Rapids: Eerdmans, 1978.

———. *The Other Side of 1984*. Geneva: World Council of Churches, 1983.

———. "Recent Thinking on Christian Beliefs: VIII. Mission and Missions." *ExpT* 88 (June 1977) 260–64.

———. *The Relevance of Trinitarian Doctrine for Today's Mission*. London: Edinburgh, 1963.

———. *Sign of the Kingdom*. Grand Rapids: Eerdmans, 1981.

Nida, Eugene. *Religion Across Cultures*. New York: Harper and Row, 1968.

Niles, D. T. *Upon the Earth. The Mission of God and the Missionary Enterprise of the Churches*. London: Lutterworth, 1962.

Nolan, Albert. *Jesus Before Christianity: The Gospel of Liberation*. London: Darton, Longman and Todd, 1976.

Nussbaum, Stan. *A Reader's Guide to Transforming Mission*. Maryknoll, NY: Orbis, 2005.

Oestreicher, Paul. "Assessing the Signs." *Trans* 3 (April 1986) 16.

Omond, Roger. *The Apartheid Handbook*. Harmondsworth, UK: Penguin, 1985.

Orchard, R. K. *Out of Every Nation*. London: Lutterworth, 1964.

———, ed. *Witness in Six Continents, Records of the Meeting of the Commission on World Mission and Evangelism of the World Council of Churches held in Mexico City, 8–19 December 1963*. London: Edinburgh, 1964.

Outler, Albert. "Toward a Postliberal Hermeneutic." *TT* 42 (July 1985) 281–91.

Padilla, René. "Evangelism and Social Responsibility: From Wheaton '66 to Wheaton '83." *Trans* 2 (July–September 1985) 27–33.

———. "The Kingdom of God and the Church." *ThFB* 1–2 (1976) 1–25.

———. *Mission Between the Times: Essays on the Kingdom*. Grand Rapids: Eerdmans, 1985.

———, ed. *The New Face of Evangelicalism*. London: Hodder and Stoughton, 1976.

———. "The Unity of the Church and the Homogeneous Unity Principle." *IBMR* 6 (January 1982) 23–30.

———, and Chris Sugden, eds. *Texts on Evangelical Social Ethics*. 2 vols. Bramcote, UK: Grove Books, 1985.

Paton, David, ed. *Breaking Barriers: Nairobi 1975*. London: SPCK, 1976.

Patterson, Sheila. *The Last Trek: A Study of the Boer People and the Afrikaner Nation*. London: Routledge, 1957.

Paul VI (pope). *On Evangelization in the Modern World: Evangelii Nuntiandi*. Washington DC: United States Catholic Conference, 1976.

Peters, George. *A Biblical Theology of Mission*. Chicago: Moody, 1972.

Pham, Paulus. *Towards an Ecumenical Paradigm for Christian Mission: David Bosch's Missionary Vision*. Rome: Gregorian, 2010.

Piet, John. *The Road Ahead: A Theology for the Church in Mission*. Grand Rapids: Eerdmans, 1970.

Pixley, George. *God's Kingdom*. Maryknoll, NY: Orbis, 1981.

Polanyi, Michael. *Personal Knowledge: Toward a Post-Critical Philosophy*. Chicago: University of Chicago, 1958.

Potter, Phillip. "Evangelism and the World Council of Churches." *ER* 20 (April 1968) 171–82.

———. "Evangelization in the Modern World." In *Mission Trends No. 2: Evangelization*, edited by Gerald Anderson and Thomas Stransky, 162-75. New York: Paulist, 1975.
Power, John. *Mission Theology Today*. Maryknoll, NY: Orbis, 1971.
Prior, A., ed. *Catholics in Apartheid Society*. Cape Town: David Philips, 1982.
Randall, Peter, ed. *Apartheid and the Church*. Johannesburg: Spro-Cas, 1972.
Ransford, Oliver. *The Great Trek*. London: Cardinal, 1974.
Ridderbos, Herman. "Church, World, Kingdom." In *Justice in the International Economic Order*, edited by Trustees of Calvin College, 17–33. Grand Rapids: Calvin College, 1980.
Rosin, H. H. *Missio Dei: An Examination of the Origin, Contents and Function of the Term in Protestant Missiological Discussion*. Leiden: Interuniversity Institute for Missiological and Ecumenical Research, 1972.
———, ed. "Worldwide Interest in Evangelism/Evangelization." *Exchange* 10 (1975).
Rottenberg, Isaac. *The Promise and the Presence: Towards a Theology of the Kingdom of God*. Grand Rapids: Eerdmans, 1980.
Russell, David. "A Theological Critique of the Christian Pacifist Perspective, with Special Reference to the Position of John Howard Yoder." PhD thesis, University of Cape Town, 1984.
Rütti, L. *Zur Theologie der Mission*. Munich: Chr. Kaiser, 1972.
Saayman, Willem. "David J. Bosch: A Tribute to the Man." *TE* 13 (July-September 1980) 6–10.
———. "David Bosch—Some Personal Reflections." *Miss Stud* 26 (2009) 214–28.
———. "Eschatological Models in Missionary Thinking." *Miss* 15 (April 1987) 7–13.
———. "Integration, Polarisation and Justification—Another Look at Ecumenicals and Evangelicals." *TE* 17 (March 1984) 78–84.
———. "Rebels and Prophets: Afrikaners Against the System." In *Resistance and Hope*, edited by Charles Villa-Vicencio et al., 52–60. Grand Rapids: Eerdmans, 1985.
———. *Unity and Mission*. Pretoria: University of South Africa, 1984.
———, and J. N. J. Kritzinger, eds. *Mission in Bold Humility: David Bosch's Work Considered*. Maryknoll, NY: Orbis, 1996.
SACLA: Die Verkeerde Weg. Privately published pamphlet. Pretoria, June 1979.
"SACLA Preparations in Top Gear Despite Attacks." *EcuNews* 19 (June 29, 1979) 1–2.
Saunders, Stanley. "Christian Eschatology: The Ground and Impetus for Mission." *Gospel in Context* 2 (October 1979) 3–10.
Scherer, James. *Gospel, Church, and Kingdom: Comparative Studies in World Mission Theology*. Minneapolis: Augsburg, 1987.
———. "Missions in Theological Education." In *The Future of Christian World Mission: Studies in Honor of R. Pierce Beaver*, edited by F. Danker et al., 143–53. Grand Rapids: Eerdmans, 1971.
Schoonhoven, E. Jansen. "Tambaram 1938." *IRM* 67 (July 1978) 299–315.
Schorzmann, Arthur. "Eschatology and Mission." In *Concise Dictionary of the Christian World Mission*, edited by Stephen Neill et al., 191. London: Lutterworth, 1971.
Schreiter, Robert. "The Bible and Mission." *Missiology* 10 (October 1982) 427–34.
———. *Constructing Local Theologies*. Maryknoll, NY: Orbis, 1985.
Schrotenboer, Paul. "Turning the Tide?" *RJ* 37 (January 1987) 10–11, 31–32.
Scott, Waldron. *Bring Forth Justice: A Contemporary Perspective on Mission*. Grand Rapids: Eerdmans, 1980.

Bibliography

———. "The Fullness of Mission." In *Witnessing to the Kingdom: Melbourne and Beyond*, edited by Gerald Anderson, 42–56. Maryknoll, NY: Orbis, 1982.

———. "The Significance of Pattaya." *Missiology* 9 (January 1981) 57–76.

Second Assembly of the World Council of Churches. *The Christian Hope and the Task of the Church: Six Ecumenical Surveys and the Report of the Assembly.* New York: Harper, 1954.

"SEDOS Seminar on the Future of Mission." *East Asian Pastoral Review* 19 (1982) 34–52.

Senior, Donald, and Caroll Stuhlmueller. *The Biblical Foundations of Mission*. Maryknoll, NY: Orbis, 1983.

Serfontein, J. H. P. *Apartheid, Change and the NG Kerk*. Emmarentia, RSA: Taurus, 1982.

———. *The Brotherhood of Power: An Exposé of the Secret Afrikaner Broederbond*. London: Rex Collings, 1978.

Shenk, Wilbert R., ed. *The Challenge of Church Growth*. Elkhart, IN: Institute of Mennonite Studies, 1973.

———, ed. *Exploring Church Growth*. Grand Rapids: Eerdmans, 1983.

Shivute, Tomas. *The Theology of Mission and Evangelism in the International Missionary Council from Edinburgh to New Delhi*. Helsinki: The Finnish Society for Missiology and Ecumenics, 1980.

Sider, Ron. *Christ and Violence*. Scottdale, PA: Herald, 1979.

Smart, Ninian. "Christianity and Nationalism." *SJRS* 5 (1984) 37–50.

Smit, D. "The Symbol of Reconciliation and Ideological Conflict in South Africa." In *Reconciliation and Construction: Creative Options for a Rapidly Changing South Africa*, edited by W. S. Vorster, 79–112. Pretoria: University of South Africa, 1986.

Smith, A. Christopher. "The Eschatological Drive of God's Mission." *RvEx* 82 (Spring 1985) 209–16.

Smith, N. J., F. E. Geldenuys, and P. G. J. Meiring, eds. *Storm-kompas: Opstelle op soek na 'n suiwer koers in die Suid-Afrikaanse konteks van die jare tagtig*. Cape Town: Tafelberg, 1981.

Snook, Steven. "Forgiveness and Justice in South Africa." *RJ* 35 (September 1985) 18–21.

Snyder, Howard. *The Community of the King*. Downers Grove: InterVarsity, 1977.

———. *Liberating the Church: Towards an Ecology of Church and Kingdom*. Downers Grove: InterVarsity, 1983.

———. *Kingdom Lifestyle: Calling the Church to Live Under God's Reign*. Downers Grove: InterVarsity, 1985.

"South African Leadership Assembly Stirs Up Controversy." *RESNE* 16 (August 7, 1979) 1482–83.

Southern Africa: The Continuing Crisis. World Council of Churches Programme to Combat Racism Report 20. Geneva: World Council of Churches, January 1985.

Starling, Allan, ed. *Seeds of Promise: World Consultation on Frontier Missions, Edinburgh '80*. Pasadena, CA: William Carey, 1981.

Stamoolis, Jim. "Church and State in South Africa." *Themelios* 10 (January 1985) 14–24.

"Statement of the Stuttgart Consultation on Evangelism." WCC/CWME's *Monthly Letter on Evangelism* 10/11 (October/November 1987).

Stockwell, Eugene. "What Did I Hear at . . . 'How Shall They Hear?'" Unpublished paper, June 16, 1980.

———. "What Really Did Happen at Melbourne?" *Mid-Stream* 19 (October 1980) 532–37.

Stott, John. *Christian Mission in the Modern World*. Downers Grove: InterVarsity, 1976.

———, ed. *The Pasadena Consultation—Homogeneous Unit*. Lausanne Occasional Papers 1. Wheaton, IL: Lausanne Committee for World Evangelization, 1978.

———. "World Evangelisation: Signs of Convergence and Divergence in Christian Understanding." *Third Way* 1 (December 1, 1977) 3–9.

Stowe, David. *Ecumenicity and Evangelism*. Grand Rapids: Eerdmans, 1970.

Strassberger, Elfriede. *Ecumenism in South Africa 1936–1960*. Johannesberg: South African Council of Churches, 1974.

Strothmann, Maynard. "Eschatology and the Mission of Christianity, with Special Emphasis upon Contemporary Protestant Thought." PhD thesis, Columbia University, 1956.

Stuhlmacher, Peter. *Historical Criticism and the Theological Interpretation of Scripture*. Philadephia: Fortress, 1977.

Sundkler, Bengt. "Jésus et les Païens." *RHP* 16 (1936) 462–99.

———. *The World of Mission*. Grand Rapids: Eerdmans, 1965.

Taylor, John. *The Primal Vision: Christian Presence amid African Religions*. London: SCM, 1963.

Thompson, Leonard. *The Political Mythology of Apartheid*. New Haven, CT: Yale University Press, 1985.

Torrance, James B. "Interpreting the Word by the Light of Christ or the Light of Nature? Calvin, Calvinism and Karl Barth." Unpublished paper, n.d.

———. "The Kairos Debate: Listening to Its Challenge." *JTSA* 55 (1986) 42–45.

Torrance, Thomas F. *Transformation and Convergence in the Frame of Knowledge: Explorations in the Interrelationships of Scientific and Theological Enterprise*. Belfast: Christian Journals, 1984

Turner, Harold. "Afrikaner Church Needs 'Critical Solidarity.'" *CC* 114 (July 29—August 5, 1987) 645–46.

"Transformation: The Church in Response to Human Need." *Trans* 1/1 (January 1984) 23–28.

Trueblood, Elton. *The Validity of the Christian Mission*. New York: Harper & Row, 1972.

University of South Africa 1987 Calendar. Part 7: Faculty of Theology. Pretoria: UNISA, 1987.

Van der Merwe, Willem Jacobus. *The Development of Missionary Attitudes in the Dutch Reformed Church in South Africa*. Cape Town: Nasionale Pers, 1934.

———. *The Road Ahead: Towards the Unity of the D. R. Family*. Cape Town: Lux Verbi, 1985.

Van Engen, Charles. *The Growth of the True Church*. Amsterdam: Rodopi, 1981.

Verkuyl, Johannes. *Contemporary Missiology: An Introduction*. Translated and edited by Dale Cooper. Grand Rapids: Eerdmans, 1978.

Verstraelen, Frans. "Africa in David Bosch's Missiology: Survey and Appraisal." In *Mission in Bold Humility: David Bosch's Work Considered*, edited by Willem Saayman et al., 8–39. Maryknoll, NY: Orbis, 1996.

———. "World and Mission: Towards a Common Missiology." *Miss Stud* 1 (1984) 34–47.

Vicedom, Georg F. *The Mission of God: An Introduction to a Theology of Mission*. Translated by Gilbert Thiele and Dennis Hilgendors. St. Louis: Concordia, 1965.

Villa-Vicencio, Charles. "An All-Pervading Heresy: Racism and the 'English-Speaking Churches.'" In *Apartheid Is a Heresy*, edited by John de W. Gruchy et al., 59–74. Grand Rapids: Eerdmans, 1983.

———. "The Covenant Restructured: A Shift in Afrikaner Ideology." *IBMR* 9 (January 1985) 13–16.

———. "A Life of Resistance and Hope." In *Resistance and Hope*, edited by John W. de Gruchy et al., 3–13. Grand Rapids: Eerdmans, 1985.

———. "Report from a Safe Synod." *RJ* 36 (November 1986) 9–12.

———, ed. *Theology and Violence: The South African Debate*. Grand Rapids: Eerdmans, 1988.

———. *The Theology of Apartheid*. Cape Town: Methodist, n.d.

———. "Where Faith and Ideology Meet: The Political Task of Theology." *JTSA* 41 (December 1982) 78–85.

———, and John W. de Gruchy, eds. *Resistance and Hope: South African Essays in Honour of Beyers Naudé*. Grand Rapids: Eerdmans, 1985.

Visser 't Hooft, Willem A. "The Mandate of the Ecumenical Movement." In *The Uppsala Report 1968*, edited by Norman Goodall, 317–18. Geneva: World Council of Churches, 1968.

———, ed. *The New Delhi Report: The Third Assembly of the World Council of Churches 1961*. London: SCM, 1962.

———. "Pan-Christians Yesterday and Today." *ER* 32 (October 1980) 387–95.

———. "The Word 'Ecumenical'—Its History and Use." In *A History of the Ecumenical Movement: 1517–1948*, edited by Ruth Rouse et al., 735–40. London: SPCK, 1954.

Vogels, W. "Covenant and Universalism: Guide for a Missionary Reading of the Old Testament." *ZMR* 57 (January 1973) 25–32.

Vorster, J. D. *Veelvormigheid en Eenheid* [Pluriformity and Unity]. Cape Town: N. G. Kerk, 1978.

Wagner, Peter. *Church Growth and the Whole Gospel*. New York: Harper & Row, 1981.

———. *The Church Growth Movement: A 30th Anniversary Assessment*. Privately published inaugural lecture at Fuller Theological Seminary, November 6, 1984.

Walls, Andrew F. "The Gospel as the Prisoner and Liberator of Culture." *Faith and Thought* 108 (1982) 39–52. Republished in *Miss* 10 (November 1982) 93–105.

———. "Missiologist of the Road: David Jacobus Bosch (1929–1992)." In *The Cross-Cultural Process in Christian History*, 273–78. Maryknoll, NY: Orbis, 2002.

———. "The Old Age of the Missionary Movement." *IRM* 76 (January 1987) 26–32.

Walsh, John. *Evangelization and Justice*. Maryknoll, NY: Orbis, 1982.

Walshe, Peter. "Mission in a Repressive Society: The Christian Institute of Southern Africa." *IBMR* 5 (October 1981) 146–52.

Warneck, Gustav. *Evangelische Missionslehre*. 2nd ed. 3 vols. Gotha, Ger.: Friedrich Andreas Perthes, 1902.

Warren, Max. *I Believe in the Great Commission*. Grand Rapids, Eerdmans, 1977.

———. *The Truth of Vision: A Study in the Nature of the Christian Hope*. London: Canterbury, 1948.

Weber, Hans-Ruedi. *Empty Hands*. Geneva: World Council of Churches, 1980.

Weiser, Thomas, ed. *Planning for Mission: Working Papers on the New Quest for Missionary Communities*. New York: World Council of Churches, 1966.

Wells, Harold. "Raising Power Against the Power Structures." *JTSA* 30 (March 1980) 63–67.

Wiedenmann, Ludwig. *Mission und Eschatologie. Eine Analyse der neuren deutschen evangelischen Missionstheologie*. Paderborn, Ger.: Bonifacius-Druckerei, 1965.

Wilkins, Ivor, and Hans Strydom. *The Super-Afrikaners*. Johannesburg: Jonathan Ball, 1978.

Willimon, William. "A Crisis of Identity: The Struggle of Modern Mainline Protestantism." *Sojourners* 15 (May 1986) 24–28.

———. *What's Right with the Church*. New York: Harper & Row, 1985.

Wilmore, Gayraud S., and James Cone, eds. *Black Theology: A Documentary History, 1966–1979*. Maryknoll, NY: Orbis, 1979.

Wilson, Monica, and Leonard Thompson, eds. *The Oxford History of South Africa*. 2 vols. London: Oxford University Press, 1969–1971.

Wimber, John. *Power Evangelism*. London: Hodder & Stoughton, 1985.

———. *Power Healing*. London: Hodder & Stoughton, 1986.

Wink, Walter. *Violence and Nonviolence in South Africa: Jesus' Third Way*. Philadelphia: New Society, 1987.

Winter, Gibson. *The New Creation as Metropolis*. New York: Macmillan, 1963.

World Council of Churches. *The Church for Others and the Church for the World: A Quest for Structures for Missionary Congregations. Final Report of the Western European Working Group and North American Working Group of the Department of Studies on Evangelism*. Geneva: World Council of Churches, 1968.

Yates, Timothy. "David Bosch: South African Context, Universal Missiology—Ecclesiology in the Emerging Missionary Paradigm." *IBMR* 33/2 (April 2009) 72–78.

Yoder, John Howard. *The Original Revolution: Essays on Christian Pacifism*. Scottdale, PA: Herald, 1971.

———. *The Politics of Jesus*. Grand Rapids: Eerdmans, 1972.

———. *The Priestly Kingdom: Social Ethics as Gospel*. Notre Dame, IN: University of Notre Dame Press, 1984.

Your Kingdom Come: Mission Perspectives. Report on the World Conference on Mission and Evangelism, Melbourne, Australia, 12–25 May, 1980. Geneva: World Council of Churches, 1980.

Yule, George. *Mission and Unity in Christ*. Edinburgh: Handsel, 1986.

Zwemer, Samuel, *"Into All the World": The Great Commission: A Vindication and an Interpretation*. Grand Rapids: Zondervan, 1943.

Names Index

Aagaard, Johannes, 258n9
Adeyemo, Tokunboh, 129n172
Adonis, Johannes, 40
Ahonen, Tiina, xivn3, xvi, 133n192
Alexander the Great, 309
Allen, Roland, 194n197
Anderson, Gerald, 79
Anderson, Ray, 350n89
Arias, Mortimer, 128, 265
Augustus, 309
Barrett, C. K., 161
Barrett, David, 91n14, 210n3
Barth, Karl, xv, 20n69, 40, 41, 47, 70-71, 73, 107, 108, 192n184, 208, 223n64, 236, 254, 257, 258, 260, 268, 285n126, 286n128, 295, 326, 327, 328
Bavinck, J. H., 82
Beaver, R. Pierce, 82
Bekele, Girma, xivn6
Beker, J. Christiaan, 271n64
Berger, Peter, 6-7, 313
Bergquist, James, 254
Berkhof, Hendrikus, 35, 289, 292, 295, 307, 317, 318, 329
Berkouwer, G. C., 20n69, 47
Beyerhaus, Peter, 263, 264
Biko, Steve, 16-17, 33, 34n147, 55, 142
Blauw, Johannes, 153, 254
Boer, Harry, 246, 247n176, 328n17
Boesak, Allan, 4-5, 36-37, 316, 330-31, 357, 358
Boff, Leonardo, 338
Bonhoeffer, Dietrich, 202, 310
Bonnke, Reinhard, 211
Bortnowska, Halina, 112, 242
Boshoff, Carel, 52, 353
Botha, A. J., 10n22, 22n81
Botha, P. W., 17
Braaten, Carl, 254n7, 257, 269n55
Brueggeman, Walter, 155n11
Brunner, Emil, 234, 254

Bultmann, Rudolf, 257
Burnett, William, 317
Buthelezi, Chief Gatsha, 317
Buthelezi, Manas, 35, 55, 143, 317, 318
Buti, Sam, 316
Calvin, John, 294, 337
Carey, William, 67, 153, 191
Casalis, Georges, 157n19, 159n35
Cassidy, Michael, 35, 38, 316n97, 317
Castro, Emilio, 92, 120n135, 123, 128, 148, 266, 277, 324n141
Celliers, Jan, 43
Chikane, Frank, 39
Comblin, José, 233n114
Cone, James, 55
Cook, Richard, 230
Costas, Orlando, 35, 74, 133-34, 137, 207, 208, 290n145, 317, 318
Cronjé, G., 351
Crumpton, Derek, 125, 317
Cullmann, Oscar, xv, 46, 208, 259, 268, 269-70, 287, 293
Daneel, M. L., 133, 135, 137
Davies, Horton, 161
Descarte, René, 149
Diedrichs, N. D., 351
DuBose, Francis, 156n17, 254n3
Duff, Alexander, 67
Durand, Jaap, 36, 345
Durand, J. J. F., 29n120, 30-31
Echegaray, Hugo, 163n58
Edwards, Jonathan, 67
Eichrodt, Walther, 207
Eliade, Mercia, 166-67
Eliot, John, 67
Ellul, Jacques, 119
Freytag, Walter, 242n154, 259-60, 325
Fung, Raymond, 121
Gadamer, Hans-Georg, 162, 208
Gama, Vasco de, 90
Gatu, John, 134, 138, 317

Names Index

Geldenhuys, F. E. O'B., 26, 320
Gensichen, Hans-Werner, 75, 127, 361
Gibbs, Eddie, 249
Glasser, Arthur, 104, 128
Goba, Bonganjalo, 38
Gort, Jerald, 277–78
Graham, 55n60, 225, 226, 244n161
Green, Michael, 229, 231
Groenewald, E. P., 46, 352
Gruchy, John de, 19, 20n69, 31, 41, 322, 324, 341n62, 363
Guder, Darrell, xiv–xvi
Gutierrez, Gustavo, 149, 257
Gutmann, Bruno, 246–47
Hahn, Ferdinand, 153n7, 154n10, 207
Hanekom, T. M., 352, 353
Harnack, Adolph von, 154n10, 189, 193
Hartenstein, Karl, 259–60, 325, 329n23
Hendricks, Abel, 317
Hengel, Martin, 295, 299
Heurnius, J., 67
Heyns, Johan, 36, 40, 46, 350, 357
Hexham, Irving, 10n22, 11n25
Hirsch, Emmanuel, 288
Hoekendijk, Johannes, 72, 96, 107, 261, 264, 295, 345
Hollenweger, Walter, 225n76, 232n113
Holsten, W., 191
Hunsberger, George, xv
Hunter, George, 224, 227
Hurley, Archbishop Dennis, 38
Illich, Ivan, 81n90
Jackson, Herbert, 61–62
Jansen, G., 50–51
Jeremias, Joachim, 204, 207
John, Apostle, 213
Johnston, Arthur, 104n65, 211n8
Jonkers, Willie, 46, 47, 317, 350, 353, 354, 356
Judson, Adoniram, 67
Jüngel, Eberhard, 80n85
Kagawa, Toyohiko, 361
Kähler, Martin, 63, 71, 85, 158, 246n169, 258, 283n116, 326
Kato, Byang, 134
Keet, B. B., 24n88, 32, 36
Keysser, Christian, 246–47
King, Martin Luther, 146n243, 244n161
Klerk, F. W. de, 40
Klerk, W. A. de, 10n22, 16n54
Knapp, Stephen, 312n79
Koenig, Bob, 321
König, Adrio, 133, 135, 271n65, 319, 362
Koornhof, Piet, 317
Koyama, Kosuke, 93, 121
Kraemer, Hendrik, 52n45, 108, 258

Kramm, Thomas, 267–68
Krass, Alfred, 264n33
Kritzinger, J. J. Klippies, xivn1, 2, 313
Kuhlmann, Kathryn, 224
Küng, Hans, 91, 161
Kuyper, Abraham, 11–14, 71, 82, 325
Las Casas, Bartolomé de, 69
Lash, Nicholas, 161
Latourette, Kenneth S., 67, 82
Lederle, Henry, 345
Lehmann, Paul, 96
Lindsell, Harold, 211–12
Livingston, Kevin, xivn7
Livingstone, David, 67
Lochman, Jan Milic, 364n10
Loff, Chris, 23n84
Lull, Raymond, 67
Löffler, Paul, 216n32
Lohfink, Gerhard, 295n13
Lohmeyer, Ernst, 197
Lückhoff, A. H., 342n66
Luther, Martin, 164, 355
McGavran, Donald, 238–41, 243–45, 247–49, 263
McLuhan, Marshall, 234
MacKay, John, 364
Malan, Daniel F., 15, 19, 27, 351
Mandela, Nelson, 4, 40, 359
Marais, Ben, 28n116, 32, 46
Margull, Hans J., 218
Marshall, I. Howard, 161
Martyn, Henry, 67
Marx, Karl, 287
Mattheos, Juan, 306n50
Matthey, Jacques, 196, 198
Mbiti, John, 134
Metz, J., 121, 268
Meyer, Ben, 161
Meyer, P. J., 27, 351
Milner, Lord Alfred, 12
Minear, Paul, 293
Moffat, Robert, 42n2, 67
Moffett, Samuel, 91n15
Molebatsi, Caesar, 39
Moltmann, Jürgen, 268, 287
Moritzen, N. P., 202
Mott, John R., 68, 257, 361
Mott, Stephen C., 315
Moule, C. F. D., 231
Murray Jr., Andrew, 10
Myklebust, O. G., 83n102
Nacpil, Emerito, 138
Naudé, Beyers, 3, 16, 33–34, 36, 46, 321, 358
Neill, Stephen, 74, 128, 133
Nel, Malan, 36

Names Index

Neuhaus, Richard, 313, 314
Newbigin, Lesslie, xv, 69n33, 75n64, 146, 147n247, 148n254, 162, 168, 228, 232n111, 261, 263, 281, 306n53, 326, 336n43
Nida, Eugene, 89
Niebuhr, H. Richard, 295
Niles, D. T., 72n49, 134, 168n85
Nolan, Albert, 295, 306n51
Noordmans, O., 280
Nussbaum, Stan, xivn4
Oldham, J. H., 361
Origen, 149
Osei-Mensah, Gottfried, 234
Packer, J. I., 225
Padilla, René, 236n128, 272n67, 345n81
Pannenberg, Wolfhart, 257, 268, 287
Paul, Apostle, 62n4, 64, 105, 141, 200, 202, 206, 213, 228, 230, 231, 232, 235, 248, 283n115, 301, 304–6, 309, 335, 344–45, 353, 355, 358
Peter, Apostle, 141, 232, 301, 333, 355
Pham, Paulus, xivn5
Piet, John, 254n7
Piper, Otto, 293
Pixley, George, 212–13
Plessis, J. du, 26, 351
Plutarch, 309
Polanyi, Michael, 162
Postma, W. J., 14
Potgieter, F. J. M., 20n68, 344–45, 354
Potter, Phillip, 98n37, 212n11
Preez, A. B. Du, 353
Prinsterer, Groen van, 13, 15
Rad, Gerhard von, 207
Rahner, Karl, 82, 91
Reppenhagen, Martin, xiv, xvi
Roberts, Oral, 224
Rosin, H. H., 263n32
Roussouw, Pierre, 36
Ruler, A. A. van, 213, 295
Saayman, Willem, xivn1, 2, 10, 54
Samartha, Stanley, 134
Samuel, Vinay, 112
Scherer, James, 80, 83, 128, 215
Schliermacher, F., 82
Schmidlin, Joseph, 153
Schweitzer, Albert, 204, 258
Scott, Waldron, 112, 128, 129, 198
Serfontein, J. H. P., 27–28, 36
Shaull, Richard, 96
Sider, Ron, 35, 214, 310, 317, 318
Sittler, Joseph, 262
Smith, Adam, 287
Smith, John Coventry, 263

Smith, Nico, 36, 46, 358
Smith, William Cantwell, 91
Snyder, Howard, 113, 277
Söderblom, Nathan, 361
Spindler, Marc, 156n16
Stamoolis, Jim, 31
Steenkamp, Anna, 8
Steinmetz, David, 161
Stockwell, Eugene, 118n125
Stott, John, 95, 104, 117, 123, 128, 211n8, 214–17, 225, 266
Strydom, Hans, 351
Stuhlmacher, Peter, 161, 162–63
Sugden, Chris, 133n192
Sundermeier, Theo, 143
Sundkler, Bengt, 72, 175, 186–87, 188, 191, 222, 269n55
Taylor, J. Hudson, 67
Taylor, John, 148, 149, 263
Temple, William, 307
Tertullian, 200n224
Theresa, Mother, 148n252, 224
Thistleton, Anthony, 161
Thomas, M. M., 134, 264
Thompson, Leonard, 7n13, 10n22
Toit, André du, 10n22
Totius (Jakob Daniel du Toit), 12–13, 14, 43, 352
Torrance, James B., xiii, 337n47, 49, 50, 350n89
Tracy, David, 161
Treurnicht, Andreis, 19
Trueblood, Elton, 212
Tutu, Desmond, 4, 38, 148, 311, 317
Trueblood, Elton, 212
Van Engen, Charles, 190n176, 249
Venn, Henry, 67
Verkuyl, Johannes, 73–74, 83n97, 128, 190, 205n251, 213, 277
Verstraelen, Frans, 133n192
Verwoerd, H. F., 20n66
Vicedom, Georg F., 326
Villa-Vicencio, Charles, 3, 20n70
Villiers, Pieter G. R. de
Visser 't Hooft, Willem A, 95, 152, 263, 361
Voetius, Gisbertus, 67
Vorster, J. D., 316n101
Wagner, Peter, 116n119, 244–45, 247
Walls, Andrew F., xiii, xivn8, 151n266
Warneck, Gustav, 25–26, 67, 91, 153, 246, 257, 325
Warren, Max, 91n15, 196n207, 259–60, 326, 327, 328
Weber, Hans-Ruedi, 55n60, 137, 311, 333n36
Webster, Douglas, 216

393

Names Index

Welz, Justinian, 67
Wiedenmann, Ludwig, 46n18
Willimon, William, 313
Wilmore, Gayraud S., 55
Wilson, Monica, 7n13
Wimber, John, 224n72
Winter, Gibson, 212–13
Winter, Ralph, 82
Yates, Timothy, xivn9
Yoder, John Howard, 35, 294, 296n15, 298, 310, 314–15, 317, 318, 323, 324
Yule, George, 340
Zinzendorf, Ludwig von, 25
Zwemer, Samuel, 194

Scripture Index

Genesis
1–11	166, 170
1:2–3	326
10–11	352
11	166n73, 170
12	166, 170
12:1–3	166n73

Exodus
20:2	171

Leviticus
11:44–45	172

Numbers
9:14	172
15:14–16	172

Deuteronomy
4:32, 34–35	171
7:6–8	171

Joshua
20:9	172

Ruth
	173n113

Psalms
22:27	175
22:28	170
24	188
33:5	170
47	188
47:2	170
47:3,8	170
47:9	175
59:14	170
66	170
67	188
68:5–6	171
72:9–11	175
86:9	175
87	175, 188
96:10,13	170
104:27–28	170
117	170
145:15–16	170
147:8–9	170

Isaiah
	178
2:2	177
2:2–4	175, 188
19: 19–24	177
19:23	175
25:6–8	175
29:18–20	181
35:5–6	181
40–55	200, 203
42–43	176
42:1	176
42:6	175, 176
42:18–20	176, 203
43:8–13	176, 203
45:14	175
49:6	175, 176
49:7	200, 201, 177, 201
53	
53:5	334
53:12	176
56:7	175
60–66	177
61	181

Scripture Index

Isaiah (cont.)
61:1–2	181
66:18	175

Jerermiah
3:17	175

Ezekiel
15:5–6	171
38:2	175
38:12	188

Daniel
7:13–14	177

Hosea
2:14	310
12:6	304
12:9	310

Amos
5:12	304

Jonah
	174–75, 182
4:2	174

Micah
4:1	177
4:1–4	175

Zephaniah
2:11	177
3:9	175

Zechariah
8	175, 203
8:7–8	203
9:9–19	203
9:12	332
9:23	203
14:8–11	188
14:16	175

Malachi
1:11	177

Matthew
	62n4, 181, 185, 227
1:2	185
2	188
5:7	306n50
5:20	198, 204n247
5:35	186
5:43	300
5:44	182n146
5:44–45	204n247
5:47	303
6:19–21	306n50
6:24	309
6:33	198, 204n247
7:14	204n247
8	188
8:11–12	185
8:20	304
9:37–38	204n247
10:5–6	185, 187
10:6	204n247
10:16	204n247
11:4–5	216
11:5	302
11:5–6	181
11:6	182
11:11	183n152, 302
12:28–29	302
12:41–42	183n152, 302
13:11	204n247
13:38	204n247
13:52	198
15:24	185, 187
16:19	204n247
16:24	335
17:26	204n247
18:18	204n247
18:21–22	306n50
18:23–27	204n247
19:17	198
19:21	204n247
19:28	187
19:30	306n50
21:43	186, 191
23:15	188
23:23	308
23:37	186, 187
24:14	185, 186, 204, 282
25:31–46	198, 290, 338
26:41	204n247
27:37	186
28:16–20	47, 95, 191–98, 238, 243–46
28:18–20	185, 186n159, 283n115
28:19	245
28:19–20	25, 158

Mark

	181, 185, 199, 227
1:15	110, 184
2:10	183n152, 302
3:31–35	300
7:24–30	185
7:27	185
9:24	336
10:28	204n247
10:37	300
10:42–45	309
10:45	183, 201
11:15–18	187
13:10	186, 199, 204
13:20	282

Luke

	181, 185, 199, 227
2:21–52	185
3:11	120n132
3:38	185
4	296, 300
4:14–30	181
4:16–30	185
4:17–27	189
4:18–19	216
4:21	183n152, 302
4:25	185
6:27–29	182n146
6:28	300
6:41–42	332
7:22–23	181
7:23	182
10:17–18	302
10:17–18,24	183n152
10:24	302
10:25–37	185
11:20	183n152
11:20–22	302
12:32	204n247
13:16	185
13:24	204n247
14:9	204
15	199
17:11–19	185
17:21	183n152, 279, 302
19:9	185
19:41–42	187
19:41–44	186
19:45–48	185
22:16–17	306n50
22:26	303
22:27	183
23:28	186

23:38	187
24:21	300
24:45–49	192
24:46–49	199, 283n115
24:49	187, 328

John

	185, 199, 227
1:11	185
3:3–8	228, 305
3:16	206, 307
3:16–17	204n247
4:19–24	177
4:22	185, 187
6:44	305
8:12–59	185
10:1–16	204n247
11:25–26	204n247
12:19	187
12:19–23	187
12:20–21	188
14:6	168
15:11	306n50
16:24	306n50
20–21	192
20:21	199, 218
20:21–22	328
20:21–23	283n115
20:23	204n247
21:15–17	204n247

Acts

	231
1:3	279
1:6–8	283n119
1:8	192, 283n115, 328
2:42–47	234
4:32	306n50
4:32–35	234
6:5	193n193
10	232
10:34	301
11:3	233
14	235
17	235

Romans

1:5	206, 231
3:21–27	230
5:10	309
9:6	174
10:14	101
12:2	117n123, 303

Scripture Index

Romans *(cont.)*

12:3–8	306n50
12:10	306n50

1 Corinthians

3:9	204n247
4:9–10	334
9:19–23	236
12:4–11	306n50
12:13	306n50
13:12	64
15:10	204n247

2 Corinthians

	200, 202
1:6	202
1:22	303
3:14–16	345, 358
4:10	334
5:5	303
5:14	111n96, 231
5:17	111n93, 119, 272, 304
5:18–20	206, 328n14
5:19	187, 307
6:8–10	334
11:5	202
12:10	334
12:11	202

Galatians

	230n102
1:11	230n102
2	355
2:14	355
2:7	344
3:24	345
3:28	301, 306n50
5:16	305
5:22–23	306n50
6:2	306n50
6:17	334

Ephesians

1:14	303
2:13–16	306n50
2:14–16	301, 345
2:14–17	230, 333
2:14–18	206, 328n14
2:15–16	347
2:22	273, 312
3:6	301, 345
3:18	64n15
3:20	225
4:11–13	
4:24	228, 305

Philippians

2:6–11	197n209, 206, 328n14
2:12–13	204n247
3:3–11	335
3:12–14	308

Colossians

1:13	230
1:24	202
3:11	306n50
3:12–13	306n50
3:13	306n50
3:14	306n50

1 Timothy

3:16	206, 328n14

2 Timothy

1:8	202
1:10	230

Hebrews

4:9	310
11:1	152n3
11:10	310
11:13	310
13:14	310

James

2:19–20	304

1 Peter

1:1	206
2:9	206
2:12	206
2:15	206
3:15	206, 224

Subject Index

African National Congress (ANC) 16–17, 40, 324, 359
African Enterprise 35, 37, 55, 58, 316, 320n126, 363
Afrikaners 7–21
   verligte ("progressive") 26n104, 35–36, 40, 342
   verkrampte ("conservative") 35
Afrikaner sense of providence and "manifest destiny" 9, 13, 18–21, 30n127
Alternative community (AC) 292–324
   AC and a new definition of human community 300–301
   AC and a new eschatological outlook 301–303
   AC and the question of violence 321–24
   AC as model for church's existence in the world 295–96
   Entering the AC: repentance and conversion 303–5
   Functions of the AC concept in Bosch's missiology 311–14
   Jewish models for social existence in 1st century Palestine 296–99
   Life in the AC as compassionate discipleship 306–10
   The priestly, pilgrim existence of the church 310–11
   SACLA as embodiment of AC concept 315–21
   Sources of the AC concept 293–95
Apartheid xiii, 3-41
   and the Broederbond 27–28, 34, 36, 40n173, 52–53
   as a heresy 34, 36–37, 40, 57, 343–46, 357–58
   as an ideology 4–7, 10, 15–18, 20–23, 26–27, 29, 36–37, 247, 339, 345, 351, 357–358
   Bosch's critique of 49–52, 56–58, 314–24, 341–59, 362–64
   Description of 4–7
   DRC and 11, 15, 21–27, 29–41, 49–52, 314–24, 341–59
   Influence of German missiology on 25–27
   Origins of 7–21

Battle of Blood River 9, 20n68
Belhar Confession (1982) 37
Berlin Congress on World Evangelism (1966) 101, 104n64, 113n107, 125n157
Biblical Foundations for Mission
   Bosch's "post-modern" hermeneutical approach 158-165
   Election's purpose and Israel's covenant responsibilities 171–72
   God, Israel and the nations 169–78
   History as the horizon for God's mission 166–69
   Israel's election and the compassion of God 170–71
   Israel and the betrayal of her election 173–74
   Jesus and mission 178–91
   Jesus' ministry: historical particularity and universal significance 184–87
   Jesus' mission to Jews . . . and Gentiles? 187–90
   Jonah as an exceptional example 174
   Missio Dei: God's mission and human responsibility 203–5
   Mission as centrifugal and centripetal 175–76
   Mission as *martyria*, as suffering witness 199–203
   Problems with traditional approaches 154–57
   The eschatological character of the OT 177
   The compassionate ministry of Jesus 180-184
   The "Great Commission" 191–98

Subject Index

The proclamation of Jesus 183–84
The universalist/particularist tension 170
The way of mission as the way of the cross 190–91
The witness of Israel and of the "Servant of the Lord" 176–77
Black Consciousness movement 16–17, 34, 143, 331
Bosch
    Abiding contributions 360–64
    Anabaptist influences on 57, 214, 294–95, 314, 321–23
    Cullmann's influence on 46, 187n163, 208, 259–60, 269–70
    Criticisms of 133–35
    Early life 42–45
    Early theological orientation 45–47
    Interaction with African theology 54, 135–37, 142n228
    Interaction with Black Theology 54–55, 76, 136n203, 141–44
    Interaction with Third World theologies 144–51
    Missionary service 47–52
    Professor at UNISA 52–53
    Remaining in DRC out of prophetic solidarity 358
    Response to apartheid 54–58, 311–24, 329–59, 362–64
    Response to the evangelical/ecumenical impasse 55–56, 93–132, 361–62
    Theological method 61–65

Calvinism 7–15, 26, 35, 37, 67, 294, 337
Christian Institute 16–17, 34, 320
Christendom, see Constantinian era
Church, also see alternative community
    As alternative community 192–324
    As kingdom community 256–91
    As reconciled and reconciling community 325–59
    Kähler, Barth, and new views of church and mission 70–73
    Relationship between older and younger churches 136–41
    Tension between the church and the world 292–93, 295–96
Church Growth 237–49
    Cultural captivity to North American pragmatism 241–43
    Disjunction between "discipling" and "perfecting" 243–44
    Inadequate ecclesiology 247–49
    Misreading of *panta ta ethne* 244–47
    Polemical style 240–41
    Simplistic hermeneutic 243–47
Commission on World Mission and Evangelism of the WCC (CWME) 72, 96, 100, 212n11, 262, 266
    Mexico City 1963 Conference 72, 74n61, 96, 108, 138, 262
    Bangkok 1972 Conference 92n16, 103, 108, 119, 138, 139n217, 264
    Melbourne 1980 Conference 55, 56, 93, 100–129, 215, 242, 267, 277, 285n123
    Stuttgart 1987 Consultation on Evangelism 56, 132, 240n145
Constantinian era 63n88, 89–90, 138, 230n102, 274
Consultation on the Relationship between Evangelism and Social Responsibility (CRESR) 56, 128, 215, 240, 267n47
Contextualization of the gospel 144–51
Cottesloe Consultation 32–33, 341–42, 357

Die Ope Brief (Open Letter, 1982) 36, 57–58, 346–50, 363
"Dopper Kerk" see Gereformeerde Kerk
Dutch Reformed Church (DRC) 21–53, 56–58, 133n187, 137, 314–17, 320, 339, 341–59, 363

Ecumenical mission theology expressed at Melbourne 95–132
    Ecclesiological perspective 107–14
    Eschatological perspective 106–7
    Ethos of 125–26
    Hermeneutical approach and use of Bible 105–6
    Non-Christian religions 124–25
    Salvation and the social dimension of the gospel 115–23
Edinburgh 1910 World Missionary Conference 68, 89, 96, 100, 257, 258n8, 263n31
Eschatology, doctrine of 256–91
    Centrality of the Kingdom/Reign of God 272–82
    Conflicting eschatological models 266–68
    Eschatology and apocalyptic 271–72
    Eschatology and mission in 20th century mission theology 257–66
    Mission as an eschatological event 282–86
    Models of the Kingdom in the history of mission 273–76
    Tensions between eschatology and history in the church's mission 286–91
    The Kingdom of God in contemporary missiology 277–82

Evangelical theology of mission expressed at Pattaya 94–132
  Ecclesiological perspective 107–14
  Eschatological perspective 106–7
  Ethos of 125–26
  Hermeneutical approach and use of Bible 105–6
  Non-Christian religions 124–25
  Salvation and the social dimension of the gospel 115–23
Evangelism
  Aim or goal of 228–29
  As contextual/incarnational 234–36
  As costly call to follow Jesus 236–37
  As invitation 232
  As privilege 231
  As risk 232
  As witness 230–31
  Definition of 103–5, 237
  Essential aspects of 227–37
  God's work 229–30
  Heart of mission 227–28
  Linked to renewal of the church 233–34
  Models of evangelism 224–27

Free University of Amsterdam 12, 13, 18n60, 46n17, 47, 208, 249n186, 277
Fuller Theological Seminary 238–39, 249, 316n97, 350n89

Gereformeerde Kerk, "Dopper Kerk" 10–12, 14–15, 27, 35, 37, 341n63
Great Trek 8–10, 15, 19

Human Relations and the South African Scene in the Light of Scripture 29-32

Ideology 6–7, 10, 10n22, 15–21, 108, 118, 122, 222
International Mission Council (IMC) 26n100, 71, 96, 107, 125, 212, 259–60, 262
  Integration into WCC 96, 107, 212n11, 262
  Jerusalem 1928 IMC Conference 119n128, 125, 133, 137, 138, 212
  Tambaram 1938 IMC Conference 26n100, 96, 108, 110, 258, 259n11, 260
  Whitby 1947 IMC Conference 138, 260, 260n18
  Willingen 1952 IMC Conference 51n42, 103, 107, 108, 110, 110n89, 214n22, 254, 260–61, 279, 326, 327

Jesus, Die Lydende Messias, En Ons Sendingmotief 49–50

Kairos Declaration (1985) 35n149, 38, 39, 322n132, 323, 337, 363
Kerke en Samelewing (1986) 39–40
Koinonia Declaration (1977) 35

Lausanne Congress on World Evangelization (1974) 55, 94–95, 99, 101, 104, 104n64, 104n67, 113, 115, 125n157, 128, 215, 223n66, 226, 228n90, 240n145, 245n162, 264, 266
Lausanne Covenant 104n67, 113n104, 214, 225, 264

Missio Dei 73, 97, 107, 165, 203–5, 220, 253, 260–63, 265n38, 268, 279, 283, 289, 326–29
Missiology
  Benefits of 84–85
  Elements of 76–78
  Functions of 84
  Limitations of 85–86
  Nature and scope of 73–76
  Place in the theological encyclopedia 80–84
  Roots of 66–68
Mission
  Definitions of 65–66, 72–73, 103–5, 253
  Kähler and Barth's new understandings of church and mission 70–73
  Models of mission 219–23
  Motif of mission as evangelical/ecumenical tension 94–132
  Motif of mission as First World/Third World tension 132–51
  Motif of mission in crisis 88–93
  Nature of 217–19
  Motive for 205–7
  Theological framework of 50–52, 78–80
  Traditional understandings as problematic 68–70
Mission and Evangelism: An Ecumenical Affirmation (1982) 98n37, 128, 229, 240n145, 266, 325n2, 341n61
Mutuality in mission 137–41

National Initiative for Reconciliation (NIR) 37–38, 58, 320n126, 321, 330, 363
National Party 5, 14–17, 19–21, 22, 26n104, 27–28, 32, 35, 40n173, 43, 45, 47, 314, 317, 341
Nederduitse Gereformeerde Kerk, see Dutch Reformed Church

Subject Index

Nederduitsch Hervormde Kerk (NHK) 10, 31–33, 37, 341n63, 350, 354

Pan African Christian Leadership Assembly (PACLA) 55, 132, 215, 309–310, 315–316, 333
Pan-Africanist Congress (PAC) 16
Pattaya Consultation on World Evangelization (1980) 55, 94, 100–129, 215, 217n36, 267, 277
Pietism 10–11, 12n31, 15, 22n81, 25–26, 67, 94, 99n47, 142, 153, 179, 273–74, 297, 343, 351
Pretoria Theological Conference (1986) 350–56
Princeton Theological Seminary 58, 67, 161, 194, 271n64, 364
Providence, doctrine of 19, 20, 106, 287, 289

Reconciliation, doctrine of 325–59
   As theological basis for mission 326
   Barth on reconciliation 327
   Bosch's theses on reconciliation 329–39
   Church as a reconciled and reconciling community 340–41
   The triune God's reconciling actions 327–29,
   Unity of DRC family across racial boundaries 341–59
Reformed Ecumenical Synod (RES) 37, 39n170
Relationship of mission and evangelism 210–17
   As distinct terms 213–14
   As synonymous terms 211–13
Response to Lausanne document 228

Salvation, see Reconciliation
Sending in Meervoud 50–52, 214
Sharpeville Massacre 16, 32
Slaves, slavery 5, 7–8, 23, 90, 122, 170, 171n101, 200, 236n128, 237, 278, 301, 309
South African Council of Churches (SACC) 34, 39, 55n60, 211n5, 307, 321n127
South African Christian Leadership Assembly 1979 (SACLA) 35, 37, 40, 55, 57, 132, 145n239, 215, 269, 315–21, 362–63
South African Congress on Mission and Evangelism 1973 (SACME) 55, 143n234, 215, 216, 279, 311, 333n36

Southern African Missiological Society (SAMS) 49, 53, 103n58, 239n138
Soweto uprising 16, 34
Storm-kompas (1981) 36

Theological Reflection and Missionary Praxis 61–65
Third World Christianity
   Communal focus 150
   Holistic, non-dualistic faith 144–46
   Non-intellectualist theological perspectives 148–50
   Vital spiritualties 147–48
Trinity, doctrine of 65, 71, 73, 74, 116n117, 255, 260, 279, 325–29

University of Aberdeen 10, 350n89
University of Edinburgh 67, 77n75
University of South Africa (UNISA) 28n116, 45n12, 52–54, 76, 135, 141, 146n245, 239n138, 313, 362, 363

Wheaton '83 56, 128, 129n73, 240n145, 277n84
Witness of the Eight 35
World Alliance of Reformed Churches (WARC) 36–37, 40, 346, 350, 356–57
World Council of Churches (WCC) 32, 34, 55–56, 71, 82, 94, 96, 98n37, 99–132, 148, 212n11, 229, 240–41, 262–65, 277, 285, 313, 316, 342
   Faith and Order Commission (Lund, 1952) 148, 313
   First Assembly (Amsterdam, 1948) 212n11
   Second Assembly (Evanston, 1954) 152n1, 260n18
   Third Assembly (New Delhi, 1961) 96, 107–8, 124, 212n11, 262, 265n38
   Fourth Assembly (Uppsala, 1968) 74n62, 99, 108, 121, 138, 157, 213, 240, 263, 265
   Fifth Assembly (Nairobi, 1975) 94, 99, 108, 125, 126n162, 128, 223n66, 264–266

Xhosa 8, 47, 53, 131n182

Zulu 9, 18

www.ingramcontent.com/pod-product-compliance
Lightning Source LLC
Chambersburg PA
CBHW081147290426
44108CB00018B/2468